BASIC FEDERAL INCOME TAXATION OF C CORPORATIONS

By

Samuel C. Thompson, Jr.
Dean
University of Miami School of Law

AMERICAN CASEBOOK SERIES®

WEST PUBLISHING CO.
ST. PAUL, MINN., 1995

American Casebook Series and the WP symbol are registered trademarks of West Publishing Co. Registered in the U.S. Patent and Trademark Office.

COPYRIGHT © 1995 By WEST PUBLISHING CO.
610 Opperman Drive
P.O. Box 64526
St. Paul, MN 55164–0526
1–800–328–9352

All rights reserved
Printed in the United States of America

Library of Congress Cataloging-in-Publication Data

Thompson, Samuel C., 1943–
    Basic federal income taxation of C corporations / by Samuel C. Thompson, Jr.
      p.   cm. — (American casebook series)
    Includes index.
    ISBN 0–314–03585–0
    1. Close corporations—Taxation—United States—Cases. I. Title.
II. Series.
KF6484.A7T47   1994
343.7305'267—dc20
[347.3035267]
                                          94–37591
                                              CIP

ISBN 0–314–03585–0

To NF, with love

*

Preface

Purpose and Structure

This book considers the federal income tax aspects of C corporations. The approach focuses on the four principal functional areas: (1) organizations, (2) operations, (3) taxable sales and liquidations, and (4) reorganizations. The final section of many of the chapters focuses on the tax policy aspects of the particular topic.

Chapter 1 is designed to ensure that the student has the proper foundation for studying corporate taxation. Chapter 1 surveys the topics covered in this book, introduces the basic structure for taxing C corporations, partnerships and S corporations, and reviews several fundamental concepts that are of particular importance in dealing with problems in business taxation, such as the *Crane* rule involving transfers of property subject to liabilities, the *General Utilities* doctrine, and the like kind exchange provision. Most of these concepts are covered in the basic course in federal income taxation that virtually every law student takes and that is a prerequisite for all Corporate Taxation courses. Many students who enroll in a Corporate Taxation course have not adequately mastered many of these basic concepts. Chapter 1 is designed to remedy any such deficiency in three to five hours of classroom instruction. Of course, the time the instructor devotes to the basic concepts will be determined by the background of the students.

The first section of each chapter discusses the scope of the chapter. Most major topics are introduced by a textual discussion of the basic tax factors involved. The introductory discussion is generally followed by problems that require the student to read closely the relevant sections of the Internal Revenue Code of 1986 (the Code) and Treasury Regulations (the regulations). Cases, rulings, notes, and problems that deal with more esoteric issues are then presented. The book contains many of the most significant cases and rulings on each major topic. In many instances a summary problem is presented at the end of a topic. This approach is designed first to give the student an understanding of the basic aspects of each topic and then to expose the student to many of the complexities of the topic.

Use of the Book

This book can be covered in a three or four semester hour course. For courses that focus on partnerships and S corporations, *see* Thompson, *Basic Federal Income Taxation of Partnerships and S Corporations* (West, 1995). Both this Corporation Taxation book and the Partnership and S Corporation book are adapted from Thompson, *Taxation of Business Entities: C Corporations, Partnerships and S Corporations*

(West, 1994). The *Business Entities* book takes a comparative approach to the taxation of C corporations, partnerships and S corporations. Also, a separate companion text dealing with mergers and acquisitions is available: Thomp-son, *Federal Income Taxation of Mergers, Acquisitions and LBOs* (West, 1994).

Style

The following is an illustration of the structure of the sections and subsections of the book

    Chapter 6

        Sec. 6.1

            A.

                1.

                    a.

                        i.

Cross references are made to sections and subsections as follows: *See* Sec. 5.3.A.1. The headings to the sections and subsections are designed to help identify the basic issue that the accompanying text, case or ruling addresses. This should be helpful as both a pedagogical tool and as a research tool.

References to the Code and regulations are in most cases merely preceded by a section sign, as follows: *See* § 301 and *see* § 1.301–1(b). The original numbering system for footnotes has been followed, and only the most significant of the original footnotes have been retained. The author's footnotes are numbered consecutively within each section.

Deletions are indicated by three asterisks (***), and some of the citations within cases and rulings have been deleted without asterisks.

Thanks

First, thanks to Dean Susan Prager of the UCLA School of Law who convinced me to leave practice and return to law teaching. If she had not been successful, this book would never have been written.

Second, a special thanks to Professor Bernard Wolfman who first introduced me to this subject in his Corporate Taxation course at the University of Pennsylvania. That course was the most interesting and challenging course of my entire career, and Professor Wolfman ignited my interest in the tax law.

Third, I am particularly indebted to Schiff Hardin & Waite in Chicago, where I practiced for nine years as the head of the firm's Tax Department. My practice there principally focused on the topics covered in this book.

Fourth, I want to thank those law schools at which I have had the opportunity to teach in the areas covered in this book: Northwestern University School of Law, University of Virginia School of Law, ITT Chicago Kent School of Law, and University of Chicago School of Law.

Fifth, my research assistants at UCLA were particularly helpful on this project. Prior to graduating from the UCLA School of Law in 1993, Daniel Bosis and Byron Cooper provided invaluable assistance. Nilofar Niazi, an undergraduate student at UCLA, was particularly helpful in all aspects of this project. I have no doubt that one day she will become an outstanding tax lawyer. Also, Keith Prohaska, a graduate of the Masters in Taxation program at the University of Southern California Graduate Business School read most of the chapters and gave me helpful comments.

Sixth, thanks to my secretary here at the University of Miami, Cynthia Sikorski, who provided me with excellent secretarial service on this project.

Seventh, thanks to the excellent staff at West Publishing for their assistance in the preparation of this book.

Finally, thanks to my mother and father for their encouragement, love, and most of all for just being themselves.

SAMUEL C. THOMPSON, JR.

Coral Gables, Florida
November 1994

Acknowledgements

I thank those who have given permission to reprint excerpts from the following:

Cornell, Guidelines to Tax Practice Second, 43 Tax Lawyer 297 (1990). Reprinted by permission of the American Bar Association. Copyright © 1990, American Bar Association.

Thompson, Impact of the Treasury and ALI Integration Proposals on Mergers, Acquisitions, and LBOs, Tax Notes 923 (August 17, 1992). Reprinted by permission of Tax Notes Magazine. Copyright © 1992, Tax Notes Magazine.

Thompson, Reform of the Taxation of Mergers, Acquisitions, and LBO's, Carolina Academic Press (1993). Reprinted by permission of Carolina Academic Press. Copyright © 1993. Carolina Academic Press.

Thompson, Tax Policy Implications of Contributions of Appreciated and Depreciated Property to Partnerships, Subchapter C Corporations and Subchapter S Corporations in Exchange for Ownership Interests, 31 Tax Law Review 29 (1975). Reprinted by permission of Tax Law Review. Copyright © 1975, Tax Law Review.

Thompson, Wysochi, Pluth, and Jacobson, Federal Taxation of Business Enterprises (1992). Reprinted by permission of Clark Boardman Callaghan. Copyright © 1992, Clark Boardman Callaghan.

*

Summary of Contents

	Page
PREFACE	v
ACKNOWLEDGEMENTS	ix
TABLE OF CASES	xlv
TABLE OF INTERNAL REVENUE CODE SECTIONS	xlvii
TABLE OF REVENUE RULINGS AND PROCEDURES	lxi
TABLE OF TREASURY REGULATIONS	lxiii

Chapter 1. Introduction — 1
Sec.
1.1	Scope of Book	1
1.2	General Descriptions of the Three Basic Forms of Business	2
1.3	Basic Concepts Affecting C Corporations	6
1.4	Selected References	39

Chapter 2. Organization of C Corporations — 40
Sec.
2.1	Scope	40
2.2	Transfers Not Involving Liability Assumptions	40
2.3	Assumption or Transfer of Liabilities in a § 351 Transaction	56
2.4	The Property Transfer Requirement	69
2.5	The Control Requirement	82
2.6	Impact of § 482 in § 351 Context	94
2.7	Impact of Business Purpose and Step Transaction Doctrines in § 351 Transactions	98
2.8	Use of § 351 in Acquisition of Publicly–Held Corporation: Compulsive § 351	105
2.9	Contributions to Capital	106
2.10	Policy Perspective: The Control Requirement	110

Chapter 3. Corporate Capitalization and Related Issues — 113
Sec.
3.1	Scope	113
3.2	Introduction to the Financing Decision	114
3.3	Introduction to Tax Stakes Involved in Debt Equity Issues	114
3.4	Debt–Equity Issues in the Context of § 351	116
3.5	Dividend or Interest	118
3.6	Debt or Preferred Stock	122
3.7	Subordinated Debt Payable in Stock	125
3.8	Outline of Former Proposed Debt–Equity Regulations Under § 385	126

Sec.		Page
3.9	The ARCN Controversy and the Repeal of the § 385 Regulations	130
3.10	Original Issue Discount and Related Rules	133
3.11	Worthlessness of Stock, Securities, and Notes	144
3.12	Ordinary Loss on § 1244 Stock	145

Chapter 4. Cash and Property Distributions by C Corporations ... 147

Sec.		
4.1	Scope	147
4.2	Current Distribution of Cash to Noncorporate Shareholders	148
4.3	Current Distribution of Property to Noncorporate Shareholders	153
4.4	Distributions of Cash and Property to Corporate Shareholders	160
4.5	General Principles Involving Dividend Distributions	162
4.6	Determination of Earnings and Profits	166
4.7	Constructive Dividends	170
4.8	Treatment of Dividend Before Sale	181
4.9	Dividend After Gift of Stock	184
4.10	Policy Perspective: Should the Corporate and Shareholder Taxes be Integrated?	187

Chapter 5. Corporate Redemptions ... 193

Sec.		
5.1	Scope	193
5.2	Introductory Note on § 302 Redemptions and § 318 Attribution	194
5.3	Further Elaboration on § 318 Attribution Rules	196
5.4	Redemption That Terminates a Shareholder's Interest	197
5.5	Redemptions Which Are Substantially Disproportionate Within § 302(b)(2)	201
5.6	Redemptions Not Equivalent to a Dividend Under § 302(b)(1)	206
5.7	Partial Liquidations Under § 302(b)(4)	220
5.8	Suggested Methodology for Determining Redemption Treatment	224
5.9	Summary Problems on § 302 Redemptions and § 318 Attribution	225
5.10	Redemption in Context of Boot–Strap Sales	226
5.11	Redemptions in the Context of Buy–Sell Agreements	233
5.12	Distributions in Redemptions Under § 304	236
5.13	Brief Introduction to Redemptions to Pay Death Taxes	247
5.14	Effect on Corporation	248

SUMMARY OF CONTENTS

		Page
Chapter 6.	**Stock Dividends and § 306 Stock**	**250**

Sec.
6.1	Scope	250
6.2	General Description of the Stock Dividend Provisions	251
6.3	Historical Development of the Stock Dividend Provisions	252
6.4	The Operation of § 305	257
6.5	Operation of § 306	272
6.6	Summary Problems on Stock Dividends	279

| **Chapter 7.** | **Introduction to Accumulated Earnings Tax and Personal Holding Company Tax** | **280** |

Sec.
7.1	Scope	280
7.2	Introductory Note on the Accumulated Earnings Tax and the Personal Holding Company Tax	280
7.3	The Accumulated Earnings Tax	281
7.4	The Personal Holding Company Tax	294

| **Chapter 8.** | **Introduction to Consolidated Returns** | **302** |

Sec.
8.1	Scope	302
8.2	The Historical Perspective	303
8.3	In General	304
8.4	Definition of Affiliated Group	305
8.5	A Quick Walk Through the Regulations	307
8.6	The Steps in Computing Consolidated Tax Liability	309
8.7	Intercompany Transactions Under § 1.1502–13	309
8.8	Intergroup Dividends Under § 1.1502–14	313
8.9	Investment Adjustment System: Stock Basis, Excess Loss Accounts and Earnings and Profits	314
8.10	Summary Problems on Consolidated Returns	329

| **Chapter 9.** | **Liquidation of C Corporations** | **331** |

Sec.
9.1	Scope	331
9.2	General Rule of Shareholder Recognition of Gain or Loss on Complete Liquidation	331
9.3	Non–taxable Liquidations of Subsidiaries Under § 332	341
9.4	Treatment of the Corporation: Repeal of the General Utilities Doctrine	352
9.5	Introduction to § 338	361
9.6	Summary Problems on Liquidations Under §§ 331, 332, 334, 336, and 337	365
9.7	Policy Perspective: Potential Relief From the Repeal of the General Utilities Doctrine	366

		Page
Chapter 10. Reorganizations: Introduction and Historical Perspective		**369**
Sec.		
10.1	Scope	369
10.2	Historical Perspective: The Case Law Under the Pre–1918 Statute	370
10.3	Purpose and Legislative History of the Reorganization Provisions	372
10.4	Introductory Note on the Current Reorganization Provisions	374
10.5	Introductory Problems	383
Chapter 11. Fundamental Reorganization Concepts		**385**
Sec.		
11.1	Scope	385
11.2	The Concept of Continuity of Interest	386
11.3	The Continuity of Business Enterprise Doctrine	434
11.4	The Meaning of Solely for Voting Stock: An Introduction	441
11.5	Definition of Control in § 368(c)	443
11.6	Plan of Reorganization	443
11.7	The Business Purpose Doctrine	444
11.8	Meaning of "Securities Exchanged" Under § 354	446
11.9	Warrants Are Not Stock Within § 354	448
11.10	Substitution of Acquiror's Convertible Securities for Target's Convertible Securities: Treatment Under § 354(a)(2)	450
11.11	Section 358 Substituted Basis for Target Shareholders and Security Holders	452
11.12	Reorganization, A Condition to § 356 Treatment	452
11.13	Determination of Whether a Distribution Has the "Effect" of the Distribution of a Dividend	453
11.14	Treatment of Target Corporation Upon Receipt and Distribution of Stock, Securities, and Boot	462
11.15	Treatment of Liabilities	463
11.16	Increase Basis by Amount of Transferor's Gain Recognized, Not Its Shareholders' Gain Recognized	465
11.17	Impact of § 305 in the Context of Reorganizations	466
11.18	Impact of § 306 in the Context of Reorganizations	468
11.19	Survey of Overlap Issue	472
Chapter 12. Recapitalizations and Mere Changes in Form		**477**
Sec.		
12.1	Scope	477
12.2	Introductory Note on Recapitalizations	477
12.3	Issuance of Preferred in Exchange for Retiring Shareholder's Common	478
12.4	Issuance of Debentures in a Recapitalization	480
12.5	Sale of Stock After a Recapitalization	482
12.6	Exercise of Conversion Privilege	483
12.7	No Continuity of Business Enterprise Requirement	485

Sec.		Page
12.8	Illustration of Impact of § 305 in a Recapitalization: Isolated Transaction That Increases Shareholder's Proportionate Interest	485
12.9	Illustrations of § 306 Stock in a Recapitalization	487
12.10	Summary Problems on Recapitalizations	489
12.11	The (F) Reorganization	490

Chapter 13. The Divisive (D) Reorganization and Section 355 — 493

Sec.		
13.1	Scope	493
13.2	Introduction to § 355 Distributions and (D) Reorganizations	493
13.3	Legislative Background on the (D) Reorganization Under §§ 355 and 354(b)	495
13.4	Introduction to the Regulations, Rulings and Cases	501
13.5	Illustration of § 306 Stock in a (D) Reorganization Under § 355	524
13.6	Determination of Whether Boot Is Treated as a Dividend	525
13.7	Summary Problem on (D) Reorganizations and § 355	527

Chapter 14. Nondivisive (D) Reorganization and the Liquidation Reincorporation Doctrine — 530

Sec.		
14.1	Scope	530
14.2	The § 354(b) Nondivisive (D)	530
14.3	The Liquidation–Reincorporation Doctrine	537
14.4	Liquidation Reincorporation With the Use of a Straw Man: Scope of § 368(a)(1)(D): No Requirement of Issuance of Stock; Possibly Look to Both Corporations in Determining E & P	541

Chapter 15. Acquisitive Reorganizations and Section 382 — 545

Sec.		
15.1	Scope	545
15.2	The Straight (A) Reorganization: Statutory Merger or Consolidation	546
15.3	The Straight (C) Reorganization	551
15.4	The Triangular (C) Reorganization	557
15.5	Forward Subsidiary Merger Under § 368(a)(2)(D)	560
15.6	The § 381 Carryover Rules: Introduction	563
15.7	Summary Problems on Straight and Triangular Acquisitive Asset Reorganizations	564
15.8	The Straight (B) Reorganization	565
15.9	The Triangular (B) Reorganization	575
15.10	Section 368(a)(2)(E) Reverse Subsidiary Mergers	576
15.11	Summary Problems on Straight and Triangular Acquisitive Stock Reorganizations	580

Sec.

15.12 The Impact of § 382 on the Carryover of a Target's Nol After an Acquisition ... 581

Chapter 16. Tax Policy Aspects of Reorganizations ... 586
Sec.
16.1 Scope ... 586
16.2 Proposal for Repeal of Reorganization Provisions ... 586
16.3 Proposal for Rationalization of the Reorganization Provisions ... 592

INDEX ... 595

Table of Contents

	Page
Preface	v
Acknowledgements	ix
Table of Cases	xlv
Table of Internal Revenue Code Sections	xlvii
Table of Revenue Rulings and Procedures	lxi
Table of Treasury Regulations	lxiii

Chapter 1. Introduction 1

Sec.
- 1.1 Scope of Book 1
- 1.2 General Descriptions of the Three Basic Forms of Business ... 2
  - A. The C Corporation 2
  - B. The Partnership 4
  - C. The S Corporation 5
- 1.3 Basic Concepts Affecting C Corporations 6
  - A. Realization and Recognition: The Structure of the Statute ... 6
  - B. Scope of the Realization Concept 7
    - *Cottage Savings Association v. Commissioner* 7
    - Note 11
  - C. Installment Sales Reporting Under § 453 11
    - Problem 12
  - D. Is a Current Distribution of Property by a Corporation a Realization Event? Historical Perspective 13
    - *General Utilities & Operating Co. v. Helvering* 13
    - Note 16
  - E. Treatment of Liabilities 17
    - 1. Introduction 17
    - 2. Bailing Out of Failed Tax Shelters: The Supreme Court Addresses Footnote 37 in Crane 17
      - a. Crane Footnote 37 17
      - b. The Supreme Court's View 17
        - *Commissioner v. Tufts* 17
        - Question 18
  - F. Brief Summary of Principal Capital Gain and Loss Provisions 19
  - G. Substance Over Form Concepts 20
    - 1. Introduction 20
    - 2. The Business Purpose Doctrine 20
      - *Gregory v. Helvering* 20
      - Note 22
    - 3. The Conduit Treatment (or Court Holding) Doctrine ... 23

xvii

Sec.			Page
1.3	Basic Concepts Affecting C Corporations—Continued		
	a. Liquidating Distribution Followed by Sale by Shareholders, Treated as Sale by Corporation		23
	Commissioner v. Court Holding Co.		23
	Questions		24
	b. Liquidating Distribution Followed by Sale by Shareholders Held to Be Bona Fide		25
	United States v. Cumberland Public Service Co.		25
	Questions		27
	4. Step Transaction Doctrine: Purchase of Stock Followed by Liquidation Treated as Purchase of Assets		27
	Kimbell–Diamond Milling Company v. Commissioner		27
	Note		28
	5. Interrelationship Between Conduit Treatment, Step Transaction and Business Purpose Doctrines		29
	Esmark, Inc. v. Commissioner		29
	H. Corporate Entity Doctrine		31
	Commissioner v. Bollinger		31
	I. Introduction to Like Kind Exchanges		33
	1. Introductory Note on § 1031 Like Kind Exchanges		33
	2. Introductory Problems on § 1031		35
	J. Ethical Considerations in Rendering Tax Advice on Business Transactions		36
	Frederic G. Corneel, Guidelines to Tax Practice Second		36
1.4	Selected References		39

Chapter 2. Organization of C Corporations — 40

Sec.		Page
2.1	Scope	40
2.2	Transfers Not Involving Liability Assumptions	40
	A. Introductory NOte on § 351: Federal Income Tax Consequences of the Formation on a Corporation	40
	B. Introductory Problems on § 351(a) and (b)	43
	C. Potential for Assignment of Tax Detriment or Benefit in a § 351 Transaction	44
	Thompson, Tax Policy Implications of Contributions of Appreciated and Depreciated Property to Partnerships, Subchapter C Corporations, and Subchapter S Corporations in Exchange for Ownership Interests	44
	Questions	46
	D. Allocation of Shareholder's Substituted Basis Among Classes of Stock Received and Determination of Holding Period	46
	Revenue Ruling 85–164	46
	E. Treatment of Other Property (Boot) Received by Shareholder	48
	1. Receipt of Account Payable	48
	Revenue Ruling 80–228	48
	2. Installment Sale Treatment for Boot Debt	49
	3. Allocation of Boot Among Assets Transferred	50

Sec.			Page
2.2		Transfers Not Involving Liability Assumptions—Continued	
		Revenue Ruling 68–55	50
		Questions	52
	F.	Allocation of Corporation's § 362(a) Carryover Basis Among Assets Received	52
		P.A. Birren & Son v. Commissioner	52
	G.	Summary Problems on Boot Distributions: Treatment of Shareholders and Corporation	53
	H.	Treatment of a Corporation Upon Issuance of Its Stock	54
		1. Issuance of Stock for Property Not in a § 351 Transaction	54
		2. Issuance of Stock for Services	55
		Revenue Ruling 62–217	55
		Questions and Notes	55
		3. Section 1032 Not Applicable to Sub's Sale of Parent's Stock	55
		Revenue Ruling 70–305	55
		Question	56
2.3		Assumption or Transfer of Liabilities in a § 351 Transaction	56
	A.	The Genesis of the Problem: The Supreme Court Holds That Liabilities Assumed Are Boot in a Reorganization	56
		United States v. Hendler	56
		Questions	57
	B.	Introductory Note on Corporate Assumption of Shareholder's Liabilities	57
	C.	Effect of § 357(a) on Corporation's Assumption of Contributing Shareholder's Expenses	59
		Revenue Ruling 74–477	59
	D.	Applicability of § 357(c) to Transferors	59
		Revenue Ruling 66–142	59
		Question	59
	E.	Effect Under § 357(c) of Issuance by Shareholder-Transferor of His Personal Promissory Note to Corporation	60
		1. The Service's Position	60
		Revenue Ruling 68–629	60
		2. The Second Circuit's View	61
		Lessinger v. Commissioner	61
		Question	63
	F.	Illustration of Current Treatment of Transfers of Accounts Receivable and Accounts Payable of a Cash Basis Taxpayer	64
		Revenue Ruling 80–198	64
		Notes and Questions	66
	G.	Interaction Between the § 357(b) Tax Avoidance Provision and § 357(c) Liabilities in Excess of Basis Provision	66
		Drybrough v. Commissioner	66
		Questions	68

Sec.			Page
2.3	Assumption or Transfer of Liabilities in a § 351 Transaction—Continued		
	H. Summary Problems on Corporate Assumption of Shareholder's Liabilities		69
2.4	The Property Transfer Requirement		69
	A. Scope of the Concept of Services		69
	James v. Commissioner		70
	Notes and Questions		72
	B. Accounts Receivable and Assignment of Income		72
	1. Transfer of Assets and Liabilities of a Going Concern		72
	Hempt Brothers Inc. v. United States		72
	Questions		74
	2. The Limits on Hempt Brothers		75
	Revenue Ruling 80–198		75
	3. Transfer of Selected Assets		76
	Private Letter Ruling 8139073		76
	Question		76
	C. Transfer of Cash		77
	Revenue Ruling 69–357		77
	Questions		77
	D. Transfer of Intangibles		77
	1. Introduction		77
	2. Know How		77
	Revenue Ruling 64–56		77
	3. Meaning of "Perpetuity"		78
	Revenue Ruling 71–564		78
	4. Nonexclusive License: The Service's View		79
	Revenue Ruling 69–156		79
	5. Nonexclusive License: The Court of Claims View		80
	E.I. Du Pont de Nemours & Co. v. United States		80
	Questions		82
2.5	The Control Requirement		82
	A. Introduction		82
	B. Accommodation Transferors		82
	1. The First Circuit's View		82
	Estate of Kamborian v. Commissioner		82
	Questions		84
	2. The Service's Ruling Policy on Accommodation Transferors		84
	Revenue Procedure 77–37, § 3.07		84
	Problem		85
	C. Control Immediately After the Exchange		85
	1. Sale of Stock Pursuant to Best Efforts Underwriting		85
	American Bantam Car Co. v. Commissioner		85
	Questions		87
	2. Sale of Stock Pursuant to Pre-existing Commitment		88
	Intermountain Lumber Co. v. Commissioner		88
	Questions		89
	3. Sale of Stock Pursuant to Best Efforts and Firm Commitment Underwriting		89
	Revenue Ruling 78–294		89

Sec.		Page
2.5	The Control Requirement—Continued	
	4. Issuance of Stock Directly to Donees	91
	D'Angelo Associates, Inc. v. Commissioner	91
	5. Transfer to New Corporation Followed by Sale of Stock to Other Investors	92
	Revenue Ruling 79–194	92
2.6	Impact of § 482 in § 351 Context	94
	Eli Lilly & Co. v. Commissioner	94
	Note and Question	97
2.7	Impact of Business Purpose and Step Transaction Doctrines in § 351 Transactions	98
	A. Incorporation Prior to Reorganization	98
	1. The Commissioner's Position	98
	Revenue Ruling 70–140	98
	Questions	99
	2. The Tax Court's Position	99
	Weikel v. Commissioner	99
	B. Contribution of Stock to New Corporation in Order to Avoid Taxation on Dividends: No Business Purpose	103
	Revenue Ruling 60–331	103
	Questions	104
	C. Successive § 351 Transactions	104
	Revenue Ruling 77–449	104
	Note	104
2.8	Use of § 351 in Acquisition of Publicly–Held Corporation: Compulsive § 351	105
	Revenue Ruling 74–502	105
2.9	Contributions to Capital	106
	1. Shareholder Contributions of Property	106
	2. Nonshareholder Contributions of Property	106
	Revenue Ruling 75–557	106
	3. Shareholder's Prorata Contribution of Stock	107
	Revenue Ruling 70–291	107
	4. Shareholder's Non–Prorata Contribution of Stock	108
	Commissioner v. Fink	108
2.10	Policy Perspective: The Control Requirement	110
	Thompson, Tax Policy Implications of Contributions of Appreciated and Depreciated Property to Partnerships, Subchapter C Corporations and Subchapter S Corporations in Exchange for Ownership Interests	111
	Questions and Note	112

Chapter 3. Corporate Capitalization and Related Issues — 113

Sec.		
3.1	Scope	113
3.2	Introduction to the Financing Decision	114
	Treasury Report, Integration of Individual and Corporate Tax Systems	114
3.3	Introduction to Tax Stakes Involved in Debt Equity Issues	114
3.4	Debt–Equity Issues in the Context of § 351	116
	Piedmont Corp. v. Commissioner	116

Sec.		Page
3.5	Dividend or Interest	118
	Fin Hay Realty Co. v. United States	118
	Question	122
3.6	Debt or Preferred Stock	122
	Ragland Investment Co. v. Commissioner	122
	Notes	124
3.7	Subordinated Debt Payable in Stock	125
	Revenue Ruling 85–119	125
3.8	Outline of Former Proposed Debt–Equity Regulations Under § 385	126
	A. Background	126
	B. Initial Determination	126
	C. Rules for Determining Whether Instruments Are Issued Proportionately	127
	D. Classification of Straight Debt Instruments	128
	E. Classification of Hybrid Instruments	128
	F. Summary	129
3.9	The ARCN Controversy and the Repeal of the § 385 Regulations	130
	A. The ARCN Ruling	130
	Revenue Ruling 83–98, 1983	130
	B. Treasury Department News Release Announcing Repeal of the § 385 Regulations	132
	Treasury Dep't News Release	132
	Question	132
3.10	Original Issue Discount and Related Rules	133
	A. Introduction	133
	B. Guide to the Regulations	133
	Preamble to Proposed Regulations Under OID and Imputed Interest Rules	133
	Questions	140
	C. High Yield Discount Obligations	140
	1. Purpose of Provisions	140
	Senate Finance Committee Report to the Revenue Act of 1989	140
	2. Explanation of Provisions	141
	Conference Report to the Revenue Reconciliation Act of 1989	141
	D. Suggested Methodology for Dealing With OID Provisions	142
	E. Market Discount Bonds	144
	Conference Report to the Revenue Reconciliation Act of 1993	144
3.11	Worthlessness of Stock, Securities, and Notes	144
3.12	Ordinary Loss on § 1244 Stock	145
	The Senate Finance Committee Report on the Revenue Act of 1978	145

Chapter 4. Cash and Property Distributions by C Corporations **147**

Sec.		
4.1	Scope	147

Sec.		Page
4.2	Current Distribution of Cash to Noncorporate Shareholders	148
	A. Introduction	148
	B. Introductory Problem on Current Distribution of Cash	150
	C. Illustration of the Tax Treatment of Distributions to Individual Shareholders	151
	Revenue Ruling 74–164	151
	Question	152
4.3	Current Distribution of Property to Noncorporate Shareholders	153
	A. Treatment of the Shareholder	153
	B. Recognition of Gain or Loss by Corporation: Repeal of the General Utilities Doctrine for Nonliquidating Transactions	153
	1. The General Utilities Doctrine	153
	2. Introductory Note	153
	3. The Repeal of the General Utilities Doctrine by the Tax Reform Act of 1986	154
	General Explanation of Tax Reform Act of 1986	154
	4. Elaboration on § 311 Distribution Rule	157
	C. Impact of Distribution of Appreciated Property on Corporation's Earnings and Profits	158
	D. Problems on Current Distributions of Property	159
4.4	Distributions of Cash and Property to Corporate Shareholders	160
	A. Basic Rules	160
	B. Treatment of Debt Financed Portfolio Stock	160
	General Explanation of Tax Reform Act of 1984	161
	C. Basis Reduction for Nontaxed Portion of Certain Dividends	161
	Senate Finance Committee Report on the Revenue Reconciliation Bill of 1989	161
4.5	General Principles Involving Dividend Distributions	162
	A. Distribution of Life Insurance Proceeds	162
	Revenue Ruling 71–79	162
	B. Dividends Need Not Be Pro Rata	163
	Lincoln National Bank v. Burnet	163
	C. Payments of Accumulated Dividends to Purchaser of Preferred Stock	163
	Revenue Ruling 56–211	163
	Questions	164
	D. Multiple Classes of Stock: Distributions in Excess of E & P	164
	Revenue Ruling 69–440	164
	E. Date of the Dividend	165
	Revenue Ruling 62–131	165
4.6	Determination of Earnings and Profits	166
	A. Introduction	166
	B. The Effect of Taxes Paid or Accrued	166
	William C. Webb v. Commissioner	166

Sec.			Page
4.6	Determination of Earnings and Profits—Continued		
	Note and Question		167
	C. Effect of Net Operating Loss		167
	Revenue Ruling 64–146		167
	D. 1984 Amendments Relating to the Computation of E & P		168
	Senate Finance Committee Report on the Deficit Reduction Tax Bill of 1984		168
	E. Summary Problems on the Computation of E & P		169
4.7	Constructive Dividends		170
	A. Introduction		170
	B. In General		171
	Revenue Ruling 58–1		171
	C. Transfers Between Related Corporations		171
	1. The Tax Court's Position		171
	Rapid Electric Co., Inc. v. Commissioner		171
	Questions		173
	2. The Service's Position		173
	Revenue Ruling 78–83		173
	Questions		175
	D. Shareholder Guarantees of Corporate Loans		175
	Plantation Patterns Inc. v. Commissioner		175
	E. Below Market Loans From Corporation to Shareholder		176
	1. Introduction		176
	Preamble to Proposed Regulations Under § 7872		176
	2. The Proposed Regulations		177
	F. Deny Deduction for Executive Pay Over $1 Million		178
	Senate Report to the Revenue Reconciliation Act of 1993		178
4.8	Treatment of Dividend Before Sale		181
	Litton Industries, Inc. v. Commissioner		181
	Questions and Problems		184
4.9	Dividend After Gift of Stock		184
	Caruth Corporation v. United States		184
4.10	Policy Perspective: Should the Corporate and Shareholder Taxes be Integrated?		187
	A. The Treasury's Reasons for Moving Towards Integration		187
	U.S. Treasury Department Report, Integration of Individual and Corporate Tax Systems		187
	Question		189
	B. Summary of the Treasury and ALI Integration Proposals		189
	Thompson, Impact of the Treasury and ALI Integration Proposals on Mergers, Acquisitions, and LBOS		189
	Questions		192

Chapter 5. Corporate Redemptions 193

Sec.		Page
5.1	Scope	193
5.2	Introductory Note on § 302 Redemptions and § 318 Attribution	194
5.3	Further Elaboration on § 318 Attribution Rules	196
5.4	Redemption That Terminates a Shareholder's Interest	197

Sec.			Page
5.4	Redemption That Terminates a Shareholder's Interest—Continued		
	A. No § 302(c)(2) Waiver Needed Where There Is an Actual Termination		197
	Revenue Ruling 76–524		197
	B. What Constitutes a Prohibited Interest Under § 302(c)(2)(A)(i)		198
	1. Redeemed Shareholder Performs Consulting Services		198
	Revenue Ruling 70–104		198
	2. Redeemed Shareholder Receives a Debt Instrument		199
	Dunn v. Commissioner		199
	C. Intra–Family Transfers Prior to Redemption		200
	Revenue Ruling 77–455		200
	Note and Question		201
5.5	Redemptions Which Are Substantially Disproportionate Within § 302(b)(2)		201
	A. Illustration of Operation of § 302(b)(2)		201
	Revenue Ruling 75–447		201
	Note		203
	B. Redemption of Voting Preferred		203
	Revenue Ruling 81–41		203
	C. Redemption of Both Voting and Nonvoting Common Stock Tested on Overall Basis		204
	Revenue Ruling 87–88		204
	D. Illustration of Series of Redemptions Under § 302(b)(2)		205
	Revenue Ruling 85–14		205
5.6	Redemptions Not Equivalent to a Dividend Under § 302(b)(1)		206
	A. The "Meaningful Reduction" Requirement: The Supreme Court Speaks		206
	United States v. Davis		206
	Questions		211
	B. The Service's Interpretation of the Meaningful Reduction Test		212
	1. Reduction From 27% to 22%		212
	Revenue Ruling 76–364		212
	2. Reduction From 90% to 60%		213
	Revenue Ruling 78–401		213
	3. Public Tender Offer: Redeemed Shareholder Has .2% Both Before and After		214
	Revenue Ruling 81–289		214
	4. Redemption of Nonvoting Preferred From Shareholder Who Owns No Other Stock		215
	Revenue Ruling 77–426		215
	5. Redemption of Nonvoting Preferred Stock from an 18% Common Shareholder		216
	Revenue Ruling 85–106		216
	C. Family Disharmony Rationale: The Service's View		217
	Revenue Ruling 80–26		217
	Note		218

Sec.		Page
5.6	Redemptions Not Equivalent to a Dividend Under § 302(b)(1)—Continued	
	D. Use of Dividend Equivalence for Tax Avoidance Purposes: The IBM Ruling	219
	Revenue Ruling 77–226	219
	Note	220
5.7	Partial Liquidations Under § 302(b)(4)	220
	A. Legislative Background	220
	Senate Finance Committee Report to the Tax Equity and Fiscal Responsibility Act of 1982	220
	B. Treatment of Pro Rata Distributions Under § 302(b)(4)	221
	Revenue Ruling 90–13	221
	C. Genuine Contraction Means Substantial Reduction in Activities	223
	Revenue Ruling 76–526	223
5.8	Suggested Methodology for Determining Redemption Treatment	224
5.9	Summary Problems on § 302 Redemptions and § 318 Attribution	225
5.10	Redemption in Context of Boot–Strap Sales	226
	A. Purchase of Stock From Corporation Followed by Redemption of Old Shareholder: Treatment of Redeemed Shareholder	226
	Zenz v. Quinlivan	226
	Questions and Note	228
	B. Purchase of Stock From Selling Shareholders and Redemption of Other Shareholders: Treatment of Purchasing Shareholder	229
	Adams v. Commissioner	229
	Question	230
	C. Sale of Stock by Shareholder Followed by Redemption of Stock Sold: Treatment of Selling Shareholder	230
	Estate of Schneider v. Commissioner	230
5.11	Redemptions in the Context of Buy–Sell Agreements	233
	A. Introduction	233
	B. Service's Position on Constructive Dividends	234
	Revenue Ruling 69–608	234
5.12	Distributions in Redemptions Under § 304	236
	A. Historical Perspective of the Problem	236
	John Rodman Wanamaker, Trustee v. Commissioner	236
	Question	238
	B. Legislative History of § 304	238
	C. Illustration of Brother–Sister Sale Under § 304(a)(1)	242
	Revenue Ruling 71–563	242
	Questions	243
	D. Subsidiary Acquisitions of Parent's Stock	244
	Caamano v. Commissioner	244
	E. Problems on Section 304 Redemptions	246
5.13	Brief Introduction to Redemptions to Pay Death Taxes	247
	General Explanation of Economic Recovery Act of 1981	247

Sec.		Page
5.13	Brief Introduction to Redemptions to Pay Death Taxes—Continued	
	Note	248
5.14	Effect on Corporation	248
	A. Corporation's Taxable Income, Loss and Deduction on Redemption	248
	B. Effect of Redemption on Earnings and Profits	248
	General Explanation of the Deficit Reduction Act of 1984	248

Chapter 6. Stock Dividends and § 306 Stock — 250

Sec.		
6.1	Scope	250
6.2	General Description of the Stock Dividend Provisions	251
6.3	Historical Development of the Stock Dividend Provisions	252
6.4	The Operation of § 305	257
	A. Scope of § 305(a)	257
	1. In General	257
	2. Distribution by Parent of Subsidiary's Stock Rights	258
	Revenue Ruling 80–292	258
	3. Issuance of Poison Pill	259
	Revenue Ruling 90–11	259
	B. The Exceptions In § 305(b)	261
	1. In General	261
	2. Illustration of Distribution in Lieu of Money Under § 305(b)(1): Immediately Redeemable Preferred	263
	Revenue Ruling 76–258	263
	Note	263
	3. Illustration of Distribution Under § 305(b)(4): Distribution of Common Stock on Convertible Preferred as Anti–Dilution Device	263
	Revenue Ruling 83–42	263
	4. Impact on Earnings and Profit	264
	C. Certain Transactions Treated as Distributions Within § 305(c)	265
	1. Background on the First Sentence of § 305(c)	265
	2. Illustrations of the Operation of the First Sentence of § 305(c)	266
	a. Periodic Redemption Plan Gives Rise to Stock Dividend to Nonredeemed Shareholders	266
	Revenue Ruling 78–60	266
	Questions	268
	b. Isolated Redemptions from Retired–Shareholder Employees	268
	Revenue Ruling 77–19	268
	D. Treatment of Redemption Premiums on Preferred Stock Under Second Sentence of § 305(c)	269
	House Report to the Revenue Reconciliation Act of 1990	269
	E. Stripped Preferred	271
	House Report to the Revenue Reconciliation Act of 1993	271
6.5	Operation of § 306	272
	A. Ordinary Income Under § 306(a)	272

			Page
Sec.			
6.5	Operation of § 306—Continued		
	B. Section 306(b) Exceptions to the Ordinary Income Rules of § 306(a)		274
	1. In General		274
	2. Section 306(b)(4) Transaction Not in Avoidance of Tax		274
	C. Definition of § 306 Stock in § 306(c)		275
	1. In General		275
	2. Section 306 Stock on Formation of Holding Company Under § 351—Application of § 304 Principles		277
	a. The General Principle		277
	Conference Report to Tax Equity and Fiscal Responsibility Act of 1982		277
	b. The Dividend Rule		277
	House Ways and Means Committee Report to the Tax Reform Bill of 1983		277
	3. Determining Whether Stock Is "Other Than Common"		278
6.6	Summary Problems on Stock Dividends		279

Chapter 7. Introduction to Accumulated Earnings Tax and Personal Holding Company Tax — 280

Sec.			
7.1	Scope		280
7.2	Introductory Note on the Accumulated Earnings Tax and the Personal Holding Company Tax		280
7.3	The Accumulated Earnings Tax		281
	A. Imposition of the Tax		281
	1. Corporations Subject to the Tax		281
	2. Evidence of a Purpose to Avoid Tax		281
	3. The Interaction Between §§ 532 and 533: "The Purpose" to Avoid Taxes		282
	a. Introduction		282
	b. Meaning of "The Purpose" to Avoid Income Taxes		283
	United States v. Donruss Co.		283
	Questions		284
	4. Burden of Proof		284
	J.H. Rutter Rex Manufacturing Company v. Commissioner		284
	B. Determination of the Reasonable Needs of the Business		285
	1. In General		285
	2. An Illustration of the Determination of Reasonable Needs of the Business		287
	J.H. Rutter Rex Mfg. Company, Inc. v. Commissioner		287
	C. Computation of Accumulated Taxable Income		290
	D. Interrelationship Between §§ 533 and 535: Impact of Marketable Securities		291
	Ivan Allen Co. v. United States		291
	E. Summary Problems on the Accumulated Earnings Tax		293

Sec.			Page
7.4	The Personal Holding Company Tax		294
	A. Introductory Note on the Personal Holding Company Tax		294
	B. Definition of Personal Holding Company		294
	1. In General		294
	2. The Inadvertent Personal Holding Company		295
	Weiss v. United States		295
	C. Definition of Personal Holding Company Income (PHCI)		297
	D. Definition of AOGI and OGI		297
	E. Significance of OGI and AOGI in Determining Personal Holding Company Status		298
	Pleasant Summit Land Corporation v. Commissioner		298
	F. Undistributed Personal Holding Company Income (UPHCI)		299
	G. Summary Problems on the Personal Holding Company Tax		300

Chapter 8. Introduction to Consolidated Returns — 302

Sec.		Page
8.1	Scope	302
8.2	The Historical Perspective	303
	Charles Ilfeld Co. v. Hernandez	303
	Note and Questions	304
8.3	In General	304
8.4	Definition of Affiliated Group	305
	A. In General	305
	General Explanation of Deficit Reduction Tax Act of 1984	305
	B. The Option Regulations	306
	Preamble to Proposed Regulations Under § 1504	306
8.5	A Quick Walk Through the Regulations	307
8.6	The Steps in Computing Consolidated Tax Liability	309
8.7	Intercompany Transactions Under § 1.1502–13	309
	A. Introduction	309
	B. Excerpt From Deferred Intercompany Transaction Regulations Under § 1.1502–13	311
8.8	Intergroup Dividends Under § 1.1502–14	313
	A. Discussion	313
	B. Excerpts from § 1.1502–14 and –14T Regulations	313
8.9	Investment Adjustment System: Stock Basis, Excess Loss Accounts and Earnings and Profits	314
	A. Introduction	314
	B. The Current Investment Adjustment System	315
	1. In General	315
	Preamble to Proposed Regulations on Investment Adjustments	315
	2. The Woods Investment Problem	316
	3. Section 1503(e)(1)(A) Response to Woods Investment	316

Sec.			Page
8.9	Investment Adjustment System: Stock Basis, Excess Loss Accounts and Earnings and Profits—Continued		
	Preamble to Proposed Regulations on Investment Adjustments	317
	C.	General Approach of Proposed Regulations	317
		Preamble to Proposed Regulations on Investment Adjustments	317
	D.	Basis Adjustment Rules Under Prop.Reg. § 1.1502–32	318
		1. Background	318
		Preamble to Proposed Regulations on Investment Adjustments	318
		2. Stock Basis Under Prop.Reg. § 1.1502–32(b)(2)(i)	319
		3. Amount of the Adjustment Under Prop.Reg. § 1.1502–32(b)(3)	319
		4. Operating Rules Under Prop.Reg. § 1.1502–32(b)(4)(i)	319
		5. Determining the Amount of an Excess Loss Account Under Prop.Reg. § 1.1502–32(b)(2)(ii)	320
		6. Illustration: Taxable Income	320
		7. Illustration: Tax Loss	321
		8. Allocation Among Shares of Stock	321
		Preamble to Proposed Regulations on Investment Adjustments	321
	E.	Earnings and Profits Under Prop.Reg. § 1.1502–33	322
		1. Purpose and Effect of E & P Tiering Rules	322
		Preamble to Proposed Regulations on Investment Adjustments	322
		2. Guiding Principles Under Prop.Reg. § 1.1502–33(a)(1)	323
		3. The Tiering Rules Under Prop.Reg. § 1.1502–33(b)(1)	323
		4. Illustration of Tiering Rules	323
		5. Allocation of Tax Liability in Computing Earnings and Profits	324
		a. Introduction	324
		b. Purpose and Effect of Allocations of Tax Liability Under the Proposed Regulations	324
		Preamble to Proposed Regulations on Investment Adjustments	324
		c. General Rules for Allocating Tax Liability Under Prop.Reg. § 1.1502–33(d)(1)	325
		Preamble to Proposed Regulations on Investment Adjustments	325
		d. The Wait-and-See Method of Prop.Reg. § 1.1502–33(d)(2)	325
		Preamble to Proposed Regulations on Investment Adjustments	325
		e. Illustration of the Wait-and-See Method	326
		Preamble to Proposed Regulations on Investment Adjustments	326
	F.	Excess Loss Accounts Under Prop.Reg. § 1.1502–19	326

		Page
Sec.		
8.9	Investment Adjustment System: Stock Basis, Excess Loss Accounts and Earnings and Profits—Continued	
	1. Purpose and Effect of Excess Loss Accounts	326
	Preamble to Proposed Regulations on Investment Adjustments	327
	2. General Description of the Rules	327
	Preamble to Proposed Regulations on Investment Adjustments	327
	3. Determining the Amount of an Excess Loss Account	328
	4. General Rule of Income Recognition	328
	5. Illustration	328
	6. Modifications of Excess Loss Recapture Rules to Prevent Shifting of ELA to Debt	328
	Senate Finance Committee Report to the Reconciliation Act of 1989	329
	7. The Validity of the § 1.1502–19 Excess Loss Regulations	329
8.10	Summary Problems on Consolidated Returns	329

Chapter 9. Liquidation of C Corporations — 331

Sec.		
9.1	Scope	331
9.2	General Rule of Shareholder Recognition of Gain or Loss on Complete Liquidation	331
	A. Introduction to General Rule of Shareholder Recognition Under § 331 and § 334(a)	331
	B. When Is a Corporation Being Liquidated?	332
	Cleveland v. Commissioner	332
	Questions	333
	C. Series of Liquidating Distributions	333
	Revenue Ruling 85–48	333
	D. Open Transaction Doctrine	334
	1. Recognition of Gain	334
	Commissioner v. Carter	334
	Questions and Problem	336
	2. Recognition of Loss	336
	Revenue Ruling 69–334	336
	E. Installment Sale Treatment Under § 453(h)	336
	F. Corporate Assets Transferred to Partnership	337
	Revenue Ruling 69–534	337
	G. Non–pro Rata Distribution	337
	Revenue Ruling 79–10	337
	Questions	339
	H. Gifts of Stock Before Receipt of Liquidating Proceeds	339
	Jones v. United States	339
9.3	Non–taxable Liquidations of Subsidiaries Under § 332	341
	A. Introduction	341
	B. The Subsidiary Cannot Retain any Assets	342
	Revenue Ruling 76–525	342
	Note	343
	C. Electivity of § 332 Nonrecognition Treatment	343

Sec.		Page
9.3	Non-taxable Liquidations of Subsidiaries Under § 332—Continued	
	George L. Riggs v. Commissioner	343
	Questions	345
	D. Worthless Stock and Securities Under § 165(g)(3) or § 332 Liquidation	345
	1. Is Debt Treated as Debt or as Equity: Is Distribution Within § 332?	345
	Waterman Steamship Corp. v. United States	345
	Question	349
	2. Worthless Common Stock But Not Preferred: Is Distribution Within § 332?	349
	H.K. Porter Company, Inc. v. Commissioner	349
9.4	Treatment of the Corporation: Repeal of the General Utilities Doctrine	352
	A. The General Utilities Doctrine	353
	B. Impact of Repeal of General Utilities on Nonliquidating Distributions	353
	C. The Repeal of the General Utilities Doctrine by the Tax Reform Act of 1986	353
	D. Legislative History of §§ 336 and 337	353
	Excerpts From (1) General Explanation of the Tax Reform Act of 1986, 328–346 (1987), (2) Conference Report to the Revenue Reconciliation Act of 1987, 966–969 (1987), and (3) Senate Finance Committee Report to the Technical and Miscellaneous Revenue Act of 1988, 67–73 (1988) (TAMRA)	353
9.5	Introduction to § 338	361
	1. In General	361
	2. Taxable Reverse Subsidiary Merger Treated as Qualified Stock Acquisition	363
	Revenue Ruling 90–95	363
9.6	Summary Problems on Liquidations Under §§ 331, 332, 334, 336, and 337	365
9.7	Policy Perspective: Potential Relief From the Repeal of the General Utilities Doctrine	366
	General Explanation of the Subchapter C Revision Bill of 1985	366

Chapter 10. Reorganizations: Introduction and Historical Perspective — 369

Sec.		
10.1	Scope	369
10.2	Historical Perspective: The Case Law Under the Pre–1918 Statute	370
	Marr v. United States	370
10.3	Purpose and Legislative History of the Reorganization Provisions	372
	Excerpt from Chapman v. Commissioner	372
10.4	Introductory Note on the Current Reorganization Provisions	374
	A. Introduction	374
	B. In General	375

TABLE OF CONTENTS

Sec.

10.4 Introductory Note on the Current Reorganization Provisions—Continued
    C. Tax Treatment to the Taxpayers Involved in a Reorganization 376
    D. The Acquisitive Reorganizations 378
        1. The (A) Merger 378
        2. The Straight and Triangular (B), Stock for Stock ... 378
        3. The Straight and Triangular (C), Stock for Assets .. 379
        4. The Over and Down (a)(2)(C) 379
        5. Forward Subsidiary Merger Under (a)(2)(D) 380
        6. Reverse Subsidiary Merger Under (a)(2)(E) 380
        7. Summary of Acquisitive Reorganizations 380
    E. The Non–Acquisitive Reorganizations 381
        1. The (D) Reorganization 381
        2. The (E) Recapitalization 382
        3. The (F) Mere Change in Form 382
10.5 Introductory Problems 383

Chapter 11. Fundamental Reorganization Concepts 385

Sec.

11.1 Scope 385

Part A. Concepts Relating to Reorganization Definition: § 368

11.2 The Concept of Continuity of Interest 386
    A. Introduction 386
    B. What Type of Interest Satisfies the Continuity of Interest Requirement 386
        1. Short–Term Notes Do Not Provide Continuity of Interest: The (C) Before the Solely for Voting Stock Requirement 386
        Pinellas Ice & Cold Storage Co. v. Commissioner 386
        Questions 388
        2. Interest Must Be "Definite and Material" and "Substantial Part of Value of the Thing Transferred": Cash and Common Received in a (C) Before the Solely for Voting Stock Requirement 389
        Helvering v. Minnesota Tea Co. 389
        Questions 390
        3. Nonvoting Preferred Carries Continuity of Interest in a (C) Before the Solely for Voting Stock Requirement 391
        John A. Nelson Co. v. Helvering 391
        Questions 392
        4. Receipt of Stock and Bonds in a (B) Before the Solely for Voting Stock Requirement: Bonds Are Securities 392
        Helvering v. Watts 392
        Questions 393

Sec.

11.2 The Concept of Continuity of Interest—Continued
      5. Acquiring Corporation Acquires Stock of Target in Exchange For 25% Stock and 75% Cash Consideration in (B) Reorganization Prior to Enactment of Solely for Voting Stock Requirement 393
         Miller v. Commissioner of Internal Revenue 393
         Questions 395
      6. Receipt of Cash and Bonds in a (C) Before the Solely for Voting Stock Requirement 395
         Le Tulle v. Scofield 395
         Questions 397
      7. Bankrupt Corporation: Noteholders Exchange Notes for Stock 398
         Helvering v. Alabama Asphaltic Limestone Co. 398
         Questions 399
      8. Receipt of Bonds in an (A) 400
         Roebling v. Commissioner 400
         Questions 401
      9. Determination of Whether Stock Represents a Substantial Part of Assets Transferred in an (A) 402
         Southwest Natural Gas Co. v. Commissioner 402
         Questions 403
     10. Receipt of Pass Book Savings Accounts on Merger of Savings and Loan Association 403
         Paulsen v. Commissioner 403
  C. The Service's Ruling Policy Requirement on Continuity of Interest 405
     Revenue Procedure 77–37 405
     Questions 405
  D. An Illustration of the 50% Continuity Requirement 406
     Revenue Ruling 66–224 406
  E. Period for Which Continuity of Interest Must Continue 407
      1. Court Order to Divest Within Seven Years 407
         Revenue Ruling 66–23 407
         Question 407
      2. Redeemable, Preferred Capital Certificates 407
         Revenue Ruling 68–22 407
         Questions 408
      3. Periodic Redemptions and Rescission Rights 408
         Revenue Ruling 78–142 408
         Questions 410
      4. Obligation of Target Shareholders to Sell Back to Acquiror 411
         United States v. Adkins–Phelps, Inc. 411
         Questions 412
      5. Planned Sales at the Time of the Transaction 412
        a. Step Transaction Doctrine Applies: No Reorganization 412
           McDonald's Restaurants of Illinois v. Commissioner 412
        b. Step Transaction Doctrine Not Applicable: Reorganization 417

Sec.		Page
11.2	The Concept of Continuity of Interest—Continued	
	Penrod v. Commissioner	417
	c. Illustration of Differences Between McDonald's and Penrod	419
	Estate of Elizabeth Christian v. Commissioner	419
	F. Impact of Prior Purchase to Target Stock	421
	1. Acquiror Purchases 85% of Target's Stock After Which Target's Assets Acquired by Acquiror's Subsidiary in Exchange for Subsidiary's Stock and Cash	421
	YOC Heating Corp. v. Commissioner	421
	2. Shareholder of Acquiror Purchases Target's Stock Followed by Merger of Target Into Acquiror	423
	Superior Coach of Florida, Inc. v. Commissioner	423
	G. Remote Continuity	425
	1. Party to the Reorganization; Remote Continuity; The Groman and Bashford Doctrines	425
	2. The Early Anti–Triangular Reorganization Cases	425
	a. Acquisition of Stock of Target in Exchange for (1) Stock of Acquiring Parent, (2) Stock of Acquiring Sub, and (3) Cash	425
	Groman v. Commissioner	425
	b. Acquisition of Three Targets by Consolidation with Target's Shareholders Receiving (1) Stock of Acquiring Parent, (2) Stock of Acquiring Sub, and (3) Cash	427
	Helvering v. Bashford	427
	Questions	428
	3. Distribution of Acquiring Corporation's Stock to Target's Parent Corporation	428
	Revenue Ruling 84–30	428
	4. Drop Down of Acquiring Stock to Partnership	429
	General Counsel Memorandum	429
	H. Use of Contingent or Escrow Stock in a Reorganization	431
	1. General Principles	431
	Revenue Ruling 84–42	431
	2. Applicability of Imputed Interest Rules to Contingent Payouts	433
	Solomon v. Commissioner	433
11.3	The Continuity of Business Enterprise Doctrine	434
	A. Introduction to the Current Regulations	434
	Preamble Regulations Under § 1.368–1(d)	434
	B. Sale of Assets in Anticipation of Reorganization	435
	1. Sale by Target Before a (C) Reorganization	435
	Revenue Ruling 79–434	435
	2. Sale by Target Before a (B) Reorganization	436
	Revenue Ruling 81–92	436
	3. Acquisition of Investment Company in a (C) Reorganization	437

Sec.		Page
11.3	The Continuity of Business Enterprise Doctrine—Continued	
	Revenue Ruling 87–76	437
	C. Continuity of Business Enterprise in an Over and Down Triangular Reorganization	439
	Revenue Ruling 81–247	439
	D. No Continuity of Business Enterprise Requirements in a Recapitalization	441
	Revenue Ruling 82–34	441
11.4	The Meaning of Solely for Voting Stock: An Introduction	441
	Helvering v. Southwest Consolidated Corporation	441
	Questions and Notes	442
11.5	Definition of Control in § 368(c)	443
	Revenue Ruling 76–223	443
11.6	Plan of Reorganization	443
11.7	The Business Purpose Doctrine	444
	A. In General	444
	B. Business Purpose in the (D) Before § 355	444
	C. Business Purpose in a Recapitalization	444
	Bazley v. Commissioner	444
	Questions	446

Part B. Concepts Relating to Exchanging Stockholders and Security Holders Under §§ 354 and 358

Sec.		Page
11.8	Meaning of "Securities Exchanged" Under § 354	446
	A. Exchange of Short–Term Notes for Debentures	446
	Neville Coke & Chemical Co. v. Commissioner	446
	Questions	447
	B. Exchange of Bonds for Stock: Are Bonds Securities?	447
	Revenue Ruling 59–98	447
	Note	448
11.9	Warrants Are Not Stock Within § 354	448
	William H. Bateman v. Commissioner	448
	Questions	449
11.10	Substitution of Acquiror's Convertible Securities for Target's Convertible Securities: Treatment Under § 354(a)(2)	450
	Revenue Ruling 79–155	450
11.11	Section 358 Substituted Basis for Target Shareholders and Security Holders	452

Part C. Concepts Relating to Treatment of Boot Under § 356

Sec.		Page
11.12	Reorganization, A Condition to § 356 Treatment	452
	Turnbow v. Commissioner	452
	Questions	453
11.13	Determination of Whether a Distribution Has the "Effect" of the Distribution of a Dividend	453
	A. The Supreme Court Decision	453
	Commissioner v. Clark	453
	Note and Questions	458
	B. The Service's Position	459

Sec.

11.13 Determination of Whether a Distribution Has the "Effect" of the Distribution of a Dividend—Continued
    Revenue Ruling 93–61, IRB 1993–36 459
    C. Application of § 318 Attribution Rules Under § 356(a)(2) 460
        House Conference Report, to the Tax Equity and Fiscal Responsibility Act of 1982 460
    D. Cash for Fractional Shares 460
        Revenue Procedure 77–41 460
    E. No Dividend Where Boot Paid in Respect of Securities .. 461
        Revenue Ruling 71–427 461
    F. Determination of E & P Under § 356(a)(2) 462

Part D. Concepts Relating to Treatment of Target Under §§ 361 and 357

11.14 Treatment of Target Corporation Upon Receipt and Distribution of Stock, Securities, and Boot 462
    Technical Corrections Provisions of House Miscellaneous Revenue Bill of 1988 462

11.15 Treatment of Liabilities 463
    A. Introduction 463
    B. Discharge of Intercorporate Debt in an (A) Reorganization 464
        Revenue Ruling 72–464 464

Part E. Concepts Relating to Treatment of Acquiror

11.16 Increase Basis by Amount of Transferor's Gain Recognized, Not Its Shareholders' Gain Recognized 465
    Schweitzer & Conrad, Inc. v. Commissioner 465
    Problems 466

Part F. Concepts Relating to Impact of Stock Dividends and § 306 Preferred Stock in Reorganizations

11.17 Impact of § 305 in the Context of Reorganizations 466
    A. In General 466
    B. Illustration of Impact of § 305 in Acquisitive Reorganizations 466
        1. Is Issuance of Acquiring Corporation Preferred: A § 305 Distribution? 466
            Revenue Ruling 82–158 466
        2. Redeemable Preferred Issued in a (B) Reorganization 467
            Revenue Ruling 81–190 467

11.18 Impact of § 306 in the Context of Reorganizations 468
    A. In General 468
    B. Introduction to § 306(c)(1)(B) 468

	Page
Sec.	
11.18 Impact of § 306 in the Context of Reorganizations—Continued	
C. Illustration of Impact of § 306(c)(1)(B) in an Acquisitive Reorganization	469
1. Issuance of Acquiring Corporation's Preferred for Substantially Similar Target Preferred	469
Revenue Ruling 88–100	469
2. Impact of § 306(b)(4) on § 306(c)(1)(B) Determination: Widely Held Target	471
Revenue Ruling 89–63	471
Part G. Concepts Relating to Overlap Between § 351 and Reorganizational Provisions	
11.19 Survey of Overlap Issue	472
A. Incorporation in Anticipation of Reorganization	472
B. Impact of §§ 357(c) and 381(a) in a Transaction Qualifying as Both a § 351 Exchange and a (C) Reorganization	472
Revenue Ruling 76–188	472
C. Combination Triangular Reorganization and Purported § 351. Determination of Control	474
Revenue Ruling 84–44	474
D. Use of § 351 to Avoid Continuity of Interest Requirement	475
Revenue Ruling 84–71	475
Chapter 12. Recapitalizations and Mere Changes in Form	**477**
Sec.	
12.1 Scope	477
12.2 Introductory Note on Recapitalizations	477
12.3 Issuance of Preferred in Exchange for Retiring Shareholder's Common	478
Revenue Ruling 74–269	478
Note and Questions	479
12.4 Issuance of Debentures in a Recapitalization	480
A. Debenture Distribution Equals Dividend	480
Review Bazley v. Commissioner	480
B. No Requirement of Continuity of Interest in a Recapitalization	480
Revenue Ruling 77–415	480
12.5 Sale of Stock After a Recapitalization	482
Revenue Ruling 77–479	482
12.6 Exercise of Conversion Privilege	483
A. Conversion of Debentures into Stock	483
Revenue Ruling 72–265	483
B. Conversion of Common into Preferred and Conversion of Preferred into Common: Requirement of Business Purpose	484
Revenue Ruling 77–238	484
Note and Question	485

		Page
Sec.		
12.7	No Continuity of Business Enterprise Requirement	485
12.8	Illustration of Impact of § 305 in a Recapitalization: Isolated Transaction That Increases Shareholder's Proportionate Interest	485
	Revenue Ruling 75-93	485
12.9	Illustrations of § 306 Stock in a Recapitalization	487
	Revenue Ruling 82-191	487
12.10	Summary Problems on Recapitalizations	489
12.11	The (F) Reorganization	490
	A. The Current Statute	490
	Conference Committee Report to Tax Equity and Fiscal Responsibility Act	490
	Note	490
	B. Illustration of § 306 Issue in an (F) Reorganization	491
	Revenue Ruling 79-287	491

Chapter 13. The Divisive (D) Reorganization and Section 355 493

Sec.		
13.1	Scope	493
13.2	Introduction to § 355 Distributions and (D) Reorganizations	493
13.3	Legislative Background on the (D) Reorganization Under §§ 355 and 354(b)	495
	A. Legislative Developments Through 1954	495
	B. Legislative Developments Since 1954	497
	1. Prevention of Use of § 355 as Surrogate for a Mirror Transaction	497
	House Report to the Revenue Act of 1987	497
	2. Amendment to § 355(c) Relating to Treatment of Distributing Corporation	498
	House Report to Miscellaneous Revenue Act of 1988	498
	3. Potential Recognition of Gain in Certain Disqualified Distributions	499
	Conference Report to Revenue Reconciliation Act of 1990	499
13.4	Introduction to the Regulations, Rulings and Cases	501
	A. Introduction to the Regulations	501
	Preamble to the § 355 Regulations	501
	B. The Business Purpose Requirement	501
	1. The Regulations	501
	Preamble to the § 355 Regulations	502
	2. Illustration: Combination of Business Purpose and Estate Planning Purpose	504
	Revenue Ruling 75-337	504
	C. Device for Distribution of Earnings and Profits	506
	1. The Regulations	506
	Preamble to the § 355 Regulations	506
	2. Illustration: Non-pro Rata Split Off	510
	Revenue Ruling 71-383	510
	D. Subsequent Sale or Exchange of Stock: Impact on the Device Clause	512

Sec.		Page
13.4	Introduction to the Regulations, Rulings and Cases—Continued	
	1. Background	512
	a. Spin–Off of Controlled Corporation Followed by Sale of Distributing Corporation	512
	Revenue Ruling 55–103	512
	b. Spin–Off of Controlled Corporation Followed by Merger of Distributing Corporation into Acquiring Corporation	513
	Commissioner v. Morris Trust	513
	c. The Service Accepts Morris Trust	516
	Revenue Ruling 68–603	516
	2. The Regulations	516
	Preamble to the § 355 Regulations	516
	E. Continuity of Interest Requirement: The Regulations	517
	Preamble to the § 355 Regulations	518
	F. Active Conduct of a Trade or Business	518
	1. The Regulations	518
	Preamble to the § 355 Regulations	518
	2. Illustration: Non-operator Owner of Working Interest in Oil and Gas Property	521
	Revenue Ruling 89–27	521
	G. Is Retention by Distributing Corporation of Stock or Securities of Controlled Corporation Not for Tax Avoidance Within § 355(a)(1)(D)(ii)?	523
	Revenue Ruling 75–321	523
	Note	523
	H. Carryover of Tax Attributes in a Divisive § 355	524
13.5	Illustration of § 306 Stock in a (D) Reorganization Under § 355	524
	Revenue Ruling 77–335	524
13.6	Determination of Whether Boot Is Treated as a Dividend	525
	Revenue Ruling 93–62, IRB 1993–30	525
13.7	Summary Problem on (D) Reorganizations and § 355	527

Chapter 14. Nondivisive (D) Reorganization and the Liquidation Reincorporation Doctrine 530

Sec.		
14.1	Scope	530
14.2	The § 354(b) Nondivisive (D)	530
	A. In General	530
	B. 1984 Amendment to the Control Requirement in the Nondivisive (D)	531
	The Senate Finance Committee's Report on the Deficit Reduction Tax Bill of 1984	531
	C. Transfer of "Substantially All" the Assets	534
	1. Illustration	534
	Moffatt v. Commissioner	534
	2. Service's Position on Determining Whether "Substantially All" the Distributing Corporation's Assets Are Contributed to the Controlled Corporation	536

Sec.		Page
14.2	The § 354(b) Nondivisive (D)—Continued	
	D. Carryover of Tax Attributes	536
14.3	The Liquidation–Reincorporation Doctrine	537
	A. An Illustration	537
	Revenue Ruling 61–156	537
	B. Continuing the Business of a Subsidiary After the Liquidation	539
	Telephone Answering Service Co. v. Commissioner	539
	Questions	540
14.4	Liquidation Reincorporation With the Use of a Straw Man: Scope of § 368(a)(1)(D): No Requirement of Issuance of Stock; Possibly Look to Both Corporations in Determining E & P	541
	Davant v. Commissioner	541
	Questions	544

Chapter 15. Acquisitive Reorganizations and Section 382 — 545

Sec.		
15.1	Scope	545
15.2	The Straight (A) Reorganization: Statutory Merger or Consolidation	546
	A. Introduction	546
	B. The Continuity of Interest Requirement	547
	C. Purchase of a Portion of Target's Stock Followed by Upstream Merger With Minority Shareholders Receiving Parent's Stock	547
	Kass v. Commissioner	547
	Questions	550
15.3	The Straight (C) Reorganization	551
	A. Introductory Note	551
	B. What Constitutes Substantially All?	554
	Excerpt From Revenue Procedure 77–37	554
	Problems	554
	C. The Creeping (C)	555
	Bausch & Lomb Optical Co. v. Commissioner	555
15.4	The Triangular (C) Reorganization	557
	A. Legislative History of the Triangular (C) and § 368(a)(2)(C)	557
	B. Introduction	558
	C. Use of Acquiring Subsidiary to Avoid Bausch & Lomb Problem	558
	Revenue Ruling 57–278	558
	Question	560
	D. Dealing With the Zero Basis Problem	560
15.5	Forward Subsidiary Merger Under § 368(a)(2)(D)	560
	A. Legislative History of the Forward Subsidiary Merger	560
	B. Introductory Note	561
	C. Creation of Holding Company	562
	Revenue Ruling 77–428	562
	D. Dealing With the Zero Basis Problem	563

TABLE OF CONTENTS

Sec.		Page
15.6	The § 381 Carryover Rules: Introduction	563
15.7	Summary Problems on Straight and Triangular Acquisitive Asset Reorganizations	564
15.8	The Straight (B) Reorganization	565
	A. Introduction	565
	B. Can There Be Boot in a (B)? The First Circuit's View of ITT–Hartford	567
	Chapman v. Commissioner	567
	Notes	571
	C. Boot Flowing Directly From Acquiror to Target's Shareholders	572
	1. Purchase of Fractional Shares	572
	Revenue Ruling 66–365	572
	2. Stock for Services	573
	Revenue Ruling 77–271	573
	D. Reverse Subsidiary Merger May Constitute a (B)	573
	Revenue Ruling 67–448	573
	Questions	574
15.9	The Triangular (B) Reorganization	575
	A. Legislative History of the Triangular B	575
	B. Introductory Note	575
	C. Zero Basis Problem	576
15.10	Section 368(a)(2)(E) Reverse Subsidiary Mergers	576
	A. Legislative History of the Reverse Subsidiary Merger	576
	B. Introductory Note	577
	C. Excerpt From Preamble to Final Regulations (T.D. 8059)	578
	Preamble to Final Regulations Under § 368(a)(2)(E)	578
	D. Creation of a Holding Company	580
	E. Zero Basis Problem	580
15.11	Summary Problems on Straight and Triangular Acquisitive Stock Reorganizations	580
15.12	The Impact of § 382 on the Carryover of a Target's Nol After an Acquisition	581
	A. Introduction to the Scope and Purpose of § 382	581
	The General Explanation of the Tax Reform Act of 1986	581
	B. Outline of Section 382 and the Regulations	583
	Preamble to Temporary Regulations Under § 382	583
	C. Example of Ownership Change in a Stock Acquisition	584
	D. Example of Ownership Change in an Equity Structure Shift	584
	E. Illustration of Computation of Section 382 Limitation	585

Chapter 16. Tax Policy Aspects of Reorganizations — **586**

Sec.		
16.1	Scope	586
16.2	Proposal for Repeal of Reorganization Provisions	586
	Report of Staff of Senate Finance Committee on Subchapter C Revision Bill of 1985	586

Sec.		Page
16.3	Proposal for Rationalization of the Reorganization Provisions	592
	Samuel C. Thompson, Jr., Reform of The Taxation of Mergers, Acquisitions and LBOs	592
INDEX		595

Table of Cases

The principal cases are in bold type. Cases cited or discussed in the text are roman type. References are to pages. Cases cited in principal cases and within other quoted materials are not included.

Adams v. Commissioner of Internal Revenue, 229, 230
Adkins–Phelps, Inc., United States v., 411
Alabama Asphaltic Limestone Co., Helvering v., 398, 399
Albers v. Commissioner, 212
American Bantam Car Co. v. Commissioner, 85, 87, 89
American Manufacturing Co., Inc. v. Commissioner, 462, 544
Atlas Tool Co., Inc. v. Commissioner, 462, 544

Bashford, Helvering v., 425, 427, 428, 555
Bateman, William H. v. Commissioner, 448
Bausch & Lomb Optical Co. v. C.I.R., 555, 558
Bazley v. Commissioner, 444, 446, 478, 480
Bollinger, Commissioner v., 31
Brown v. Commissioner, 75
Burnet v. Logan, 12, 336

Caamano v. Commissioner, 244
Caruth Corp. v. United States, 184
Carter, Commissioner v., 334, 336
Central Cuba Sugar Co. v. Commissioner, 98
Chamberlin v. Commissioner, 251
Chapman v. Commissioner, 372, 567
Charles Ilfeld Co. v. Hernandez, 303, 304, 314
Christian, Estate of v. Commissioner, 419
Clark, Commissioner v., 453, 458, 469, 547
Cleveland v. Commissioner, 332
Carter, Commissioner v., 334, 336

Cottage Sav. Ass'n v. Commissioner, 7, 11
Court Holding Co., Commissioner v., 20, 23, 24, 27, 251, 353
Covil Insulation Co., 329
Coyle v. United States, 243
Crane v. Commissioner, 17, 57, 58
C.T. Inv. Co. v. Commissioner, 444
Cumberland Public Service Co., United States v., 25, 27, 353

D'Angelo Associates, Inc. v. Commissioner of Internal Revenue, 91
Davant v. Commissioner, 462, 541
David Metzger Trust v. C.I.R., 218
Davis, United States v., 195, **206,** 213
Donruss Co., United States v., **282,** 283
Drybrough v. Commissioner, 66
Dunn v. Commissioner, 199

E. I. Du Pont de Nemours & Co. v. United States, 80
Eisner v. Macomber, 251, 253, 254
Eli Lilly and Company and Subsidiaries v. Commissioner of Internal Revenue, 94
Esmark, Inc. v. Commissioner, 29
Estate of (see name of party)

Fin Hay Realty Co. v. United States, 118, 120
Fink, Commissioner v., 108

General Utilities & Operating Co. v. Helvering, 13, 16, 24, 27, 29, 46, 147, 248, 319, 331, 353, 366
George L. Riggs, Inc. v. Commissioner of Internal Revenue, 343
Generes, United States v., 145
Gowran, Helvering v., 255
Gregory v. Helvering, 20, 22, 104, 444, 496
Griffiths, Helvering v., 255
Groman v. Commissioner, 425, 428, 557

xlv

TABLE OF CASES

Helvering v. _____ (see opposing party)
Hempt Bros., Inc. v. United States, 66, **72**, 76
Hendler, United States v., **56**, 57, 58, 463, 551
H.K. Porter Co., Inc. and Subsidiaries v. Commissioner, 349

Intermountain Lumber Co. and Subsidiaries v. Commissioner of Internal Revenue, **85**, 89
International Freighting Corp. Inc. v. Commissioner, 55
Ivan Allen Co. v. United States, 291

James v. Commissioner, **70**, 72, 85
J.H. Rutter Rex Mfg. Co., Inc. v. Commissioner, **284**, 287
John A. Nelson Co. v. Helvering, **391**, 392, 397, 580
John B. Lambert & Associates v. United States, 285
Jones v. United States, 339

Kamborian, Estate of v. Commissioner, **82**, 84
Kass v. Commissioner of Internal Revenue, 547
Kimbell–Diamond Mill. Co. v. Commissioner, **27**, 28
Koshland v. Helvering, 254, 255

Lessinger v. Commissioner, **61**, 63
Le Tulle v. Scofield, **395**, 397, 401
Lincoln Nat Bank v. Burnet, 163
Litton Industries, Inc. v. Commissioner of Internal Revenue, **181**, 184

Marr v. United States, **370**, 384
McDonald's Restaurants of Illinois, Inc. v. Commissioner, **412**, 594
Miller v. Commissioner of Internal Revenue, **393**, 395
Minnesota Tea Co., Helvering v., **389**, 390, 463, 588
Moffatt v. Commissioner, 534
Morris Trust, Commissioner v., 513

Neville Coke & Chemical Co. v. Commissioner, **446**, 447

P.A. Birren & Son v. Commissioner, 52
Paulsen v. Commissioner, 403
Penrod v. Commissioner, 417

Piedmont Corp. v. Commissioner, 116
Pinellas Ice & Cold Storage Co. v. Com'r of Int. Rev., **386**, 388, 390, 392, 546
Plantation Patterns, Inc. v. Commissioner, 175
Pleasant Summit Land Corp. v. Commissioner, 298

Ragland Investment Co. v. Commissioner, 122
Rapid Electric Co., Inc. v. Commissioner, **171**, 175
Roebling v. Commissioner, 400
Rooney v. United States, 98
Rosenberg, Estate of v. Commissioner, 251

Schneider, Estate of v. Commissioner, 230
Schweitzer & Conrad, Inc. v. Commissioner, **465**, 553
Solomon v. Commissioner, 433
Southwest Consol. Corp., Helvering v., **441**, 442, 567
Southwest Natural Gas Co. v. Commissioner, **402**, 403
Sprouse, Helvering v., 255
Strassburger v. Commissioner, 255
Superior Coach of Florida, Inc. v. Commissioner, 423

Telephone Answering Service Co., Inc. v. Commissioner, **539**, 540
Towne v. Eisner, 252, 253
Tufts, Commissioner v., 17
Turnbow v. Commissioner, 452

United States v. _____ (see opposing party)

Wanamaker's Trust v. Commissioner, **236**, 238
Waterman S. S. Corp. v. United States, 184, **345**, 349
Watts, Helvering v., 392
Webb, William C. v. Commissioner, 166
Weikel v. Commissioner, 99
Weiss v. United States, 295
Woods Investment Co. v. Commissioner, 316
Wortham Machinery Co. v. United States, 464

Yoc Heating Corp. v. Commissioner, **421**, 551

Zenz v. Quinlivan, 220, **226**, 228, 230

Table of Internal Revenue Code Sections

UNITED STATES

UNITED STATES CODE ANNOTATED

26 U.S.C.A.—Internal Revenue Code

Sec.	This Work Page
1	3
	280
1(a)	19
1(h)	3
	19
	281
2(a)	252
11	2
	3
	4
	280
	307
	309
11(b)	3
55	4
61(a)(7)	3
61(a)(12)	106
83(h)	72
112(b)(11)	496
112(g)(1)(A)	556
112(g)(1)(B)	441
112(g)(1)(C)	441
113(a)(19)	255
115	254
118	40
	41
	43
	106
162	170
162(k)	248
162(m)	178
162(m)(1)	178
162(m)(3)	179
162(m)(4)(A)	179
162(m)(4)(B)	180
162(m)(4)(C)	180
163	114
163(e)	134
163(e)(5)	115
	140
	141
	144
163(e)(5)(B)	141
163(e)(5)(B)(i)	141
163(e)(5)(C)	141

UNITED STATES CODE ANNOTATED

26 U.S.C.A.—Internal Revenue Code

Sec.	This Work Page
163(e)(5)(C) (Cont'd)	142
163(f)	115
163(i)	115
	140
	141
	144
165	115
165(g)	144
165(g)(1)	144
	145
165(g)(2)	144
	145
165(g)(3)	144
	145
	345
	348
166	115
	145
166(a)	144
	145
	347
166(d)	144
	145
166(e)	145
172	170
174	97
201(d)	253
203(h)(1)(A)	390
243	3
	103
	115
	308
	313
243 et seq.	290
243(a)	160
243(c)	160
246A	160
267(a)(1)	44
269	581
279	115
301	54
	129
	148
	160
	170
	193
	194
	225
	228
	239

xlvii

UNITED STATES CODE ANNOTATED
26 U.S.C.A.—Internal Revenue Code

Sec.	This Work Page
301 (Cont'd)	248
	251
	261
	265
	268
	272
	332
	445
	446
	495
301—307	157
301(a)	68
	148
301(b)	158
301(b)(1)	148
	153
	259
301(b)(2)	153
301(b)(3)	153
301(c)	68
	159
	194
301(c)(1)	150
	153
	166
	194
	313
301(c)(2)	150
	166
	194
301(c)(3)	150
	166
	194
301(d)	68
	153
	159
	313
302	115
	129
	193
	194
	195
	203
	225
	233
	236
	237
	238
	239
	248
	408
	455
	458
302(a)	194
	225
	251
	268
302(b)	194
	195
	196
	224

UNITED STATES CODE ANNOTATED
26 U.S.C.A.—Internal Revenue Code

Sec.	This Work Page
302(b) (Cont'd)	225
	226
	239
	494
302(b)(1)	193
	195
	206
	212
	225
	227
	239
302(b)(2)	193
	194
	195
	201
	205
	212
	225
	226
	239
	455
302(b)(3)	193
	194
	195
	196
	225
	226
	227
	228
	239
	272
	274
302(b)(4)	193
	195
	220
	221
	225
	239
302(c)	195
	460
302(c)(1)	195
	196
	226
302(c)(2)	196
	197
302(c)(2)(A)	196
	225
302(c)(2)(A)(i)	198
302(c)(2)(B)	196
	200
	201
	225
302(c)(2)(C)	196
302(d)	194
	225
	241
	251
302(e)	195
	221
	223
	224

TABLE OF INTERNAL REVENUE CODE SECTIONS

UNITED STATES CODE ANNOTATED
26 U.S.C.A.—Internal Revenue Code

Sec.	This Work Page
303	193
	233
	247
	248
	285
304	193
	236
	238
	240
	241
	246
	248
	277
	278
304(a)(1)	238
	239
	241
	242
304(a)(2)	239
304(b)	239
304(b)(2)	239
	241
304(b)(3)	240
	241
	277
304(b)(3)(A)	240
	241
304(b)(3)(B)	241
304(b)(3)(B)(iii)	241
304(b)(3)(C)	242
304(b)(4)	242
304(b)(4)(B)	275
304(c)	240
304(c)(1)	240
304(c)(2)	240
304(c)(3)	240
304(c)(3)(B)	240
305	250
	251
	255
	256
	257
	385
	466
	468
	477
	485
305(a)	251
	257
	261
	272
	275
	384
305(a)(1)(C)	272
305(b)	251
	257
	261
	264
	272
305(b)(1)	254
	261

UNITED STATES CODE ANNOTATED
26 U.S.C.A.—Internal Revenue Code

Sec.	This Work Page
305(b)(2)	261
305(b)(3)	261
305(b)(4)	261
	263
305(b)(5)	261
305(c)	251
	257
	264
	265
	266
	269
	272
	467
305(c)(1)	467
305(d)	257
305(e)	271
	272
306	250
	251
	256
	272
	274
	275
	277
	278
	384
	385
	466
	468
	469
	477
	487
	489
	491
	493
	524
306(a)	272
	274
306(a)(1)	272
306(a)(1)(A)	272
306(a)(1)(B)	273
306(a)(1)(C)	273
306(a)(2)	272
	273
306(b)	272
	274
306(b)(1)	274
306(b)(2)	274
306(b)(3)	274
306(b)(4)	274
	471
306(b)(4)(A)	274
306(b)(4)(B)	274
306(c)	272
	275
	276
	384
	468
306(c)(1)(A)	275
	276
306(c)(1)(B)	275

TABLE OF INTERNAL REVENUE CODE SECTIONS

UNITED STATES CODE ANNOTATED
26 U.S.C.A.—Internal Revenue Code

Sec.	This Work Page
306(c)(1)(B) (Cont'd)	276
	279
	468
	469
	471
306(c)(1)(C)	275
	276
306(c)(2)	275
	276
306(c)(3)	275
	277
	278
306(c)(4)	275
	468
307	250
	251
	252
	254
	255
	256
	257
307(b)	257
311	16
	24
	27
	42
	44
	153
	157
	160
	353
311(a)	16
	157
	159
311(b)	44
	157
	158
	159
	248
311(b)(1)	157
	158
311(b)(2)	158
311(b)(3)	158
312	148
	150
	166
312(a)	148
	158
	159
	160
	166
312(a)(3)	159
312(b)	158
	166
312(b)(1)	158
	159
312(b)(2)	158
	159
312(c)	159
	166
312(k)	149

UNITED STATES CODE ANNOTATED
26 U.S.C.A.—Internal Revenue Code

Sec.	This Work Page
312(k) (Cont'd)	166
	316
312(n)(1)	168
312(n)(2)	168
312(n)(3)	169
312(n)(4)	169
312(n)(5)	169
312(n)(7)	248
316	54
	68
	148
	152
	170
	194
316(a)	160
316(a)(2)	148
316(b)	150
316(b)(2)(B)	332
317	478
317(a)	148
	449
317(b)	194
318	127
	193
	194
	195
	196
	218
	225
	275
	294
	460
	468
318(a)	224
318(a)(1)	195
	196
	224
	225
	294
318(a)(2)	195
	196
	197
	224
	225
	295
318(a)(2)(A)	196
318(a)(2)(C)	195
	196
	226
318(a)(3)	195
	196
	197
	224
	225
318(a)(3)(A)	197
318(a)(3)(C)	197
	226
	239
	240
318(a)(4)	195
	196

TABLE OF INTERNAL REVENUE CODE SECTIONS

UNITED STATES CODE ANNOTATED
26 U.S.C.A.—Internal Revenue Code

Sec.	This Work Page
318(a)(4) (Cont'd)	197
	224
	225
318(a)(5)	195
	196
	197
	224
	225
	226
318(a)(5)(A)	197
	225
	226
318(a)(5)(B)	197
	225
318(a)(5)(C)	226
318(a)(5)(D)	197
318(a)(5)(E)	197
331	304
	314
	331
	332
	335
	341
	342
	365
	494
	531
331(b)	332
332	27
	28
	331
	341
	342
	343
	345
	348
	349
	353
	359
	360
	365
	377
	379
	564
332(a)	341
332(b)	341
	342
	550
332(b)(1)	341
	342
332(b)(2)	342
332(b)(3)	342
334	365
334(a)	331
	332
	342
334(b)	27
	28
	342
334(b)(1)	342
	360

UNITED STATES CODE ANNOTATED
26 U.S.C.A.—Internal Revenue Code

Sec.	This Work Page
334(b)(1) (Cont'd)	377
	379
	564
335(d)(2)	501
335(d)(3)	501
336	16
	24
	27
	153
	331
	352
	353
	356
	357
	365
	531
336(a)	46
	357
336(b)	158
	357
336(c)	357
336(d)	357
336(d)(1)	357
336(d)(2)(B)(ii)	358
336(d)(2)(B)(iii)	358
336(d)(3)	358
336(e)	359
	366
337	331
	342
	352
	353
	357
	359
	360
	363
	365
337 (former)	336
337(a)	497
337(c)	360
337(d)	361
338	28
	331
	361
	362
	363
	366
	549
338(a)	361
338(a)(1)	362
338(a)(2)	362
338(b)	362
338(d)(1)	361
	362
338(d)(2)	361
	362
338(d)(3)	361
	362
338(g)	362
338(h)(1)	362
338(h)(2)	362

TABLE OF INTERNAL REVENUE CODE SECTIONS

UNITED STATES CODE ANNOTATED
26 U.S.C.A.—Internal Revenue Code

Sec.	This Work Page
338(h)(8)	362
338(h)(10)	363
341	355
346 (former)	220
	221
351	33
	40
	41
	42
	43
	44
	46
	49
	50
	52
	54
	55
	56
	57
	58
	69
	72
	74
	77
	82
	85
	87
	88
	89
	94
	98
	99
	103
	104
	110
	112
	113
	114
	116
	240
	241
	256
	275
	277
	365
	379
	381
	383
	385
	462
	472
	474
	475
	531
351(a)	40
	41
	42
	43
	48
	58

UNITED STATES CODE ANNOTATED
26 U.S.C.A.—Internal Revenue Code

Sec.	This Work Page
351(a) (Cont'd)	241
351(b)	43
	50
	54
	58
	241
351(b)(1)	42
351(b)(2)	42
351(d)	69
351(d)(1)	69
	70
351(f)	42
	44
354	33
	98
	99
	375
	376
	378
	379
	381
	382
	383
	384
	392
	394
	446
	448
	449
	453
	478
	495
	544
	547
	554
354—362	375
354—368	157
354(a)	84
	425
	443
	447
	531
	566
	592
354(a)(1)	376
	446
	495
354(a)(2)	376
	446
	450
	478
	547
	554
	592
354(b)	2
	381
	495
	530
	531
	536
	546

TABLE OF INTERNAL REVENUE CODE SECTIONS

UNITED STATES CODE ANNOTATED
26 U.S.C.A.—Internal Revenue Code

Sec.	This Work Page
354(b) (Cont'd)	564
354(b)(1)	585
355	2
	23
	275
	369
	381
	382
	383
	444
	468
	493
	494
	495
	496
	497
	501
	502
	506
	516
	518
	524
	527
	536
	544
355(a)	382
	494
	495
355(a)(1)	494
355(a)(1)(A)	382
	494
355(a)(1)(B)	23
	382
	494
355(a)(1)(C)	382
	494
355(a)(1)(D)	382
	494
355(a)(1)(D)(ii)	523
355(a)(2)	382
	494
355(a)(3)	494
	495
355(b)	382
	494
355(b)(2)(D)	497
	498
	499
355(c)	494
	498
	499
355(d)	494
	499
355(d)(1)	499
355(d)(2)	499
	500
355(d)(4)	500
355(d)(5)	500
355(d)(9)	501
356	376
	381

UNITED STATES CODE ANNOTATED
26 U.S.C.A.—Internal Revenue Code

Sec.	This Work Page
356 (Cont'd)	382
	383
	385
	446
	449
	452
	478
	494
	495
	544
	547
	554
	566
356(a)	50
	382
	494
	495
356(a)(1)	376
	382
	452
	453
356(a)(2)	376
	382
	458
	460
	462
	478
	547
	554
	592
356(b)	382
	494
	495
356(c)	376
356(d)	547
356(d)(1)	376
356(d)(2)(A)	376
356(d)(2)(B)	376
	446
	478
356(f)	479
357	56
	57
	383
	384
	462
357(a)	58
	59
	377
	463
	464
	547
	551
	554
357(b)	66
	377
	464
357(b)(1)	58
357(c)	59
	60
	63

liii

TABLE OF INTERNAL REVENUE CODE SECTIONS

UNITED STATES CODE ANNOTATED
26 U.S.C.A.—Internal Revenue Code

Sec.	This Work Page
357(c) (Cont'd)	66
	377
	472
357(c)(1)	58
357(c)(1)(B)	464
357(c)(3)	58
358	40
	50
	98
	106
	241
	372
	375
	376
	377
	379
	381
	382
	383
	384
	446
	452
	478
	494
	531
	547
	554
	566
358(a)	42
	43
	56
	57
	58
	376
358(a)(1)	41
358(a)(1)(A)	42
358(a)(1)(A)(ii)	58
358(a)(1)(B)	42
358(a)(2)	42
	376
358(b)	56
358(d)	58
358(d)(2)	58
358(f)	463
361	56
	57
	377
	378
	381
	383
	384
	462
	463
	464
	466
	494
	531
	547
	554
361(a)	377
	379

UNITED STATES CODE ANNOTATED
26 U.S.C.A.—Internal Revenue Code

Sec.	This Work Page
361(a) (Cont'd)	425
	443
	462
	553
361(b)	377
	463
	531
	554
361(b)(2)	387
	391
361(b)(3)	463
361(c)	377
	463
	554
361(c)(2)(B)	463
361(c)(3)	463
361(c)(4)	357
362	40
	50
	54
	379
	381
	383
	384
	494
	531
362(a)	41
	42
	43
	44
	52
	53
	241
	531
362(a)(1)	393
362(b)	375
	377
	378
	379
	465
	531
	547
	553
	566
362(c)	379
367(d)	77
368	33
	54
	55
	375
	377
	385
	386
	444
	446
	453
	546
	584
368(a)	376
	469
	497

TABLE OF INTERNAL REVENUE CODE SECTIONS

UNITED STATES CODE ANNOTATED
26 U.S.C.A.—Internal Revenue Code

Sec.	This Work Page
368(a)(1)	375
	388
	389
	391
	394
	396
	398
	400
	401
	402
	496
368(a)(1)(A)	375
	376
	380
	383
	402
	411
	545
	546
	564
368(a)(1)(B)	84
	98
	99
	375
	380
	383
	452
	545
	565
	575
368(a)(1)(C)	375
	380
	383
	545
	555
	557
	564
	594
368(a)(1)(D)	2
	23
	375
	383
	495
	530
	541
	564
	584
	594
368(a)(1)(E)	2
	375
	384
	469
	477
	594
368(a)(1)(F)	2
	375
	384
	477
	564
	585
368(a)(1)(G)	585

UNITED STATES CODE ANNOTATED
26 U.S.C.A.—Internal Revenue Code

Sec.	This Work Page
368(a)(2)	375
	453
368(a)(2)(A)	552
368(a)(2)(B)	379
	383
	551
	555
368(a)(2)(C)	374
	379
	383
	557
	575
368(a)(2)(D)	374
	380
	381
	383
	388
	390
	392
	395
	405
	545
	546
	560
	562
	564
	576
368(a)(2)(E)	374
	380
	381
	383
	386
	388
	390
	392
	395
	405
	545
	574
	576
	578
368(a)(2)(G)	379
	551
	553
368(a)(2)(H)	530
	531
	534
368(b)	376
	383
	384
	425
	426
	557
	575
368(c)	41
	43
	82
	86
	87
	110
	378

TABLE OF INTERNAL REVENUE CODE SECTIONS

UNITED STATES CODE ANNOTATED
26 U.S.C.A.—Internal Revenue Code

Sec.	This Work Page
368(c) (Cont'd)	383
	443
	566
381	377
	378
	379
	524
	536
	545
	547
	563
	564
	581
381 to 383	375
381(a)	423
	472
	563
	564
381(a)(1)	564
381(a)(2)	564
381(b)	490
	564
381(b)(1)	490
381(b)(3)	382
	490
381(c)	411
	564
382	2
	363
	377
	546
	547
	564
	581
	583
	585
382 (former)	581
	582
382(g)(3)(A)	585
382(g)(3)(B)	585
382(h)(1)(C)	363
383	547
385	113
	116
	124
	126
	130
	132
385(b)	116
386(a)(1)(G)	375
386(a)(2)(F)	375
446	308
453	11
	12
	13
	50
	140
	357
	365
	408
453(a)	11

UNITED STATES CODE ANNOTATED
26 U.S.C.A.—Internal Revenue Code

Sec.	This Work Page
453(a) (Cont'd)	13
453(b)	13
453(b)(1)	11
453(c)	11
453(d)	12
	13
453(f)(3)	12
453(f)(6)	50
453(h)	12
	336
453(h)(1)(A)	336
453(h)(1)(B)	336
453(h)(1)(C)	336
453(k)(2)	12
453A	12
453B(a)	357
453B(d)	360
482	40
	94
483	11
	133
	142
	143
	144
531	4
	281
	290
	293
531 et seq.	281
532	282
532(a)	281
	282
	288
532(b)	281
532(c)	281
533	282
	291
533(a)	281
	282
533(b)	282
534	284
535	291
	293
	294
	300
535(a)	290
535(b)	290
	299
535(c)	291
535(c)(1)	288
	291
535(c)(2)	291
537	285
	286
	288
537(a)	285
537(b)(1)	285
537(b)(3)	285
537(b)(4)	285
537(b)(5)	285
541	4

TABLE OF INTERNAL REVENUE CODE SECTIONS

lvii

UNITED STATES CODE ANNOTATED 26 U.S.C.A.—Internal Revenue Code	
Sec.	This Work Page
541 (Cont'd)	294
	299
	300
	301
541 et seq.	281
542	301
542(a)	294
542(a)(1)	294
542(a)(2)	294
	300
542(b)	295
542(c)	295
543(a)	294
	297
543(a)(1)	297
	301
543(a)(2)	297
	301
543(a)(3)	297
543(a)(4)	297
543(a)(5)	297
543(a)(6)	297
543(a)(7)	297
543(a)(8)	297
543(b)(1)	297
	301
543(b)(2)	294
	297
	301
543(b)(3)	297
544	294
	300
544(a)(1)	295
544(a)(2)	294
545	300
	301
545(a)	299
	301
545(b)	299
545(b)(1)	301
545(b)(5)	301
545(c)	299
545(d)	299
547	300
	301
561	290
	299
	300
561—565	291
562	290
562(b)	290
562(c)	290
	293
562(e)	293
563	290
563(a)	290
	294
563(b)	300
563(c)	294
564	300
565	290

UNITED STATES CODE ANNOTATED 26 U.S.C.A.—Internal Revenue Code	
Sec.	This Work Page
565 (Cont'd)	294
	300
701	4
702	4
704(a)	5
704(b)	5
704(d)	4
705	5
721	110
1001	6
	16
	21
	40
	332
	335
	375
	394
	549
1001(a)	6
1001(b)	7
1001(c)	7
	372
1001(d)	11
1011	6
	7
1012	6
	7
	55
	375
1014	281
1015(a)	6
1016	6
	7
1016(a)(1)	109
1031	7
	33
	34
	35
	44
	50
1031(a)(3)	34
1031(d)	34
	35
1031(e)	34
1031(f)	34
1032	40
	41
	43
	44
	54
	55
	72
	106
	375
	377
	378
	379
	381
	382
	383
	384

TABLE OF INTERNAL REVENUE CODE SECTIONS

UNITED STATES CODE ANNOTATED
26 U.S.C.A.—Internal Revenue Code

Sec.	This Work Page
1032 (Cont'd)	478
	494
	531
	547
	553
	566
1032(a)	54
1036	485
1044	20
1059	161
	164
	184
1201	19
1201(a)	19
1202	20
1211	19
1211(a)	19
	290
1211(b)	19
1212	19
	290
1212(a)	19
1212(b)	19
1221	19
	54
1221(1)	19
1221(1)—(5)	19
1221(2)	19
1222	19
	54
1222(3)	19
1222(10)	19
1222(11)	19
1223	19
1223(1)	42
	43
	44
1223(2)	42
	43
	44
1231	35
	42
	54
	308
1231(b)	297
1239	54
1244	113
	115
	145
1245	35
	54
1271	115
	142
1271—1275	133
1271 et seq.	11
	115
	142
1271(a)	196
1272	136
	143
1272(a)	134
	136

UNITED STATES CODE ANNOTATED
26 U.S.C.A.—Internal Revenue Code

Sec.	This Work Page
1272(a) (Cont'd)	138
1272(a)(3)	136
	138
1272(a)(3)(A)(ii)	138
1272(a)(4)	136
	138
1272(a)(5)	136
	138
1272(a)(7)	138
	139
1272(b)	134
1272(c)(3)	138
1273	136
	137
	143
1273(a)	134
1273(a)(1)	136
1273(a)(2)	136
	137
1273(a)(3)	137
	138
	467
1273(a)(5)	136
1273(b)	137
1273(b)(1)	137
1273(b)(2)	137
1273(b)(3)	137
1273(b)(4)	137
1274	134
	137
	143
	433
1274(a)	135
1274(a)(2)	137
1274(a)(3)	136
1274(b)(1)	135
1274(b)(2)	135
1274(b)(3)	135
1274(c)(1)	134
	135
	137
1274(c)(1)(A)(ii)	135
1274(c)(2)	134
	135
1274(c)(3)	134
1274(c)(4)	134
	135
1274(d)(1)	135
1274A	143
1274A(a)	135
1274A(b)	135
1275	139
	433
1275(d)	139
1278	144
1361(a)	5
1362	5
1363(a)	281
1371(a)	6
1374	6
1375	6
1501	304
1502	304
1503	304

TABLE OF INTERNAL REVENUE CODE SECTIONS

UNITED STATES CODE ANNOTATED 26 U.S.C.A.—Internal Revenue Code		UNITED STATES CODE ANNOTATED 26 U.S.C.A.—Internal Revenue Code	
Sec.	This Work Page	Sec.	This Work Page
1503(e)(1)(A)	316	6042(b)(3)	166
1503(e)(4)	328	7701(a)(42)	7
	329		42
1504	304		375
	306	7701(a)(43)	7
1504(a)(1)	305		42
1504(a)(2)	305	7701(a)(44)	7
	341		41
	342	7701(g)	357
1504(a)(4)	305	7872	115
1504(a)(5)	305		143
1552	324		176

Table of Revenue Rulings and Procedures

REVENUE RULINGS		REVENUE RULINGS	
Rev.Rul.	This Work Page	Rev.Rul.	This Work Page
55–103	512	70–305	55
55–745	228	70–609	167
56–179	485	71–79	162
56–211	163	71–350	257
	164	71–383	510
56–220	469	71–427	461
56–556	201	71–563	242
56–584	201	71–564	78
56–653	257	72–265	483
57–132	278	72–354	572
57–278	558	72–464	464
	560	73–54	442
58–1	171	74–164	151
59–98	447	74–269	478
59–259	82	74–477	59
60–331	103	74–501	257
	105	74–502	105
61–156	537	74–515	458
62–131	165	74–544	540
62–217	55	75–93	485
64–56	77	75–321	523
	79	75–337	504
64–146	167	75–447	201
66–23	407		228
	408	75–469	523
66–142	59	75–502	214
66–224	406	75–557	106
66–365	442	75–561	490
	572	76–188	472
67–326	546	76–223	443
67–448	573	76–258	263
	574	76–364	212
	577	76–386	278
68–22	407	76–387	278
68–55	50	76–524	197
68–603	516	76–525	342
68–629	60	76–526	223
	63	77–19	268
69–156	79	77–206	478
69–334	336	77–226	219
69–357	77		228
69–440	164	77–237	203
69–534	337	77–238	484
69–608	233	77–271	573
	234	77–293	201
70–104	198	77–297	34
70–140	98	77–335	524
	99	77–415	478
	472		480
		77–426	215
70–291	107	77–428	562

lxi

TABLE OF REVENUE RULINGS AND PROCEDURES

REVENUE RULINGS

Rev.Rul.	This Work Page
77–428 (Cont'd)	580
77–449	104
77–455	200
77–479	482
78–60	266
	268
78–83	173
78–142	406
	408
78–294	89
78–375	263
78–401	213
79–10	337
79–69	167
79–155	450
79–194	92
79–273	228
79–287	491
79–434	435
80–26	217
80–198	64
	75
80–228	48
80–292	258
81–41	203
81–70	566
81–92	436
81–186	228
81–190	467
81–247	439
81–289	214
82–34	441
	485
82–158	466
82–191	487
83–34	104
83–42	263
83–98	130
83–156	105
84–2	343
84–30	428
84–42	431

REVENUE RULINGS

Rev.Rul.	This Work Page
84–44	474
84–71	475
	590
85–14	205
85–48	333
85–106	216
85–119	125
85–164	46
	452
87–76	437
87–88	204
88–100	469
89–27	521
89–63	471
90–11	259
90–13	221
90–16	19
90–95	363
90–98	263
93–61	459
93–62	525

REVENUE PROCEDURES

Rev.Proc.	This Work Page
77–37	85
	405
	408
	431
	554
77–37, § 3.01	536
77–37, § 3.02	547
77–37, § 3.07	72
	84
77–41	460

PRIVATE LETTER RULINGS

No.	This Work Page
8139073	76

Table of Treasury Regulations

PROPOSED TREASURY REGULATIONS

Reg.	This Work Page
1.338–1(e)(1)	362
1.358–6	560
	580
1.358–6(a)	563
1.358–6(b)	576
1.385–10(a)	124
1.453–1(c)	12
1.453–1(f)(3)	50
1.1032–2	560
	563
	576
	580
1.1502–19	326
1.1502–19(b)(1)	328
1.1502–19(c)	328
1.1502–19(e), Ex. (1)	328
1.1502–32	318
1.1502–32(b)(2)(i)	319
1.1502–32(b)(2)(ii)	320
1.1502–32(b)(3)	319
1.1502–32(b)(4)(i)	319
1.1502–32(b)(5), Ex. (1)	320
1.1502–32(b)(5), Ex. (2)	321
1.1502–32(o)	321
1.1502–33	322
	323
1.1502–33(a)(1)	323
1.1502–33(b)(1)	323
1.1502–33(b)(3), Ex. (1)	323
1.1502–33(d)(1)	325
1.1502–33(d)(2)	325
1.1502–33(d)(3)	325
1.1502–33(d)(4)	325
1.1502–33(d)(6), Ex. (1)	326
1.7872–4(d)	177
1.7872–14(b), Ex. (1)	178

TEMPORARY TREASURY REGULATIONS

Reg.	This Work Page
1.1502–13T	308
	311
1.1502–14T	308
	313
1.1502–14T(a)	313
1.1502–14T(c)(1)	313
1.1502–31T	308
1.1502–32T	308
1.1502–33T	308

TEMPORARY TREASURY REGULATIONS

Reg.	This Work Page
1.1502–75T	308
15A.453–1(b)(2)(ii)	11
15A.453–1(b)(2)(iii)	11
15A.453–1(b)(2)(v)	11

TREASURY REGULATIONS

Reg.	This Work Page
1.61–12	547
1.61–12(a)	106
	109
1.61–12(c)	478
	494
	531
	553
1.61–12(c)(1)	377
1.118–1	106
1.166–5(b)	145
1.263(a)–2(f)	109
1.301–1(g)	153
1.301–1(j)	170
1.301–1(*l*)	446
	478
	480
1.302–1(a)	195
1.302–2(a)	212
1.302–2(c), Ex. (2)	243
1.305–3	261
1.305–3(e), Ex. (8)	268
1.305–6	261
1.305–7	265
1.306–2(b)(3)	274
1.306–3	275
1.306–3(d)	468
1.312–1(d)	264
	279
1.312–3	159
1.312–6(b)	149
1.312–10	524
1.318–1(b)	197
1.331–1(b)	332
1.331–1(e)	332
1.332–2(d)	342
	550
1.332–2(e)	342
	550
1.351–1(a)(1)(ii)	72
	85
1.351–1(a)(2), Ex. (3)	72
1.351–2(d)	54

lxiii

TABLE OF TREASURY REGULATIONS

TREASURY REGULATIONS

Reg.	This Work Page
1.354–1(a)	531
1.355–2(b)	501
	506
1.355–2(c)	517
1.355–2(d)(2)(iii)	516
1.355–3	518
1.358–3	56
1.368–1	386
1.368–1(b)	444
1.368–1(c)	444
1.368–1(d)	434
1.368–1(g)	444
1.368–2	386
1.368–2(b)(1)	378
1.368–2(b)(2)	561
	562
1.368–2(c)	566
1.368–2(d)	551
	558
1.368–2(d)(1)	464
1.368–2(e)	478
1.368–2(e)(1)	478
1.368–2(e)(2)	478
1.368–2(e)(3)	478
1.368–2(e)(4)	478
1.368–2(e)(5)	478
1.368–2(g)	443
1.368–3	444
1.368–3(a)	376
1.382–2(b)(2)	560
1.385–3(b)	126
1.385–3(c)	127
1.385–3(d)	127
1.385–3(e)	127
1.385–4(c)	129
1.385–5(a)	129
1.385–5(c)(2)	129
1.385–5(c)(3)	129
1.385–5(d)	129
1.385–5(d)(2)	129
1.385–5(f), Ex. (1)	129
1.385–6	127
1.385–6(a)(1)	127
1.385–6(a)(2)	127
	128
1.385–6(a)(2)(ii)	127
1.385–6(a)(2)(vi)	128
1.385–6(b)	128
1.385–6(d)(1)	128
1.385–6(d)(2)	128
1.385–6(g)(1)	128
1.385–6(g)(2)	128
1.385–6(g)(3)	128
1.385–6(g)(4)	128
1.385–6(h)(1)	128
1.385–6(h)(2)	128
1.502–34	360
1.532–1(a)(1)	281
1.532–1(a)(2)	281
1.533–1(a)(2)	282
1.533–1(b)	282
1.537–1(a)	286
1.537–1(b)(1)	286

TREASURY REGULATIONS

Reg.	This Work Page
1.537–1(b)(2)	286
1.537–2(b)	286
1.537–2(c)	287
1.537–3	282
1.537–3(a)	287
1.537–3(b)	287
1.562–2	293
1.562–2(a)	290
1.1001–2(a)	19
1.1001–3	11
1.1031(d)–2	35
1.1272–1(b)	137
1.1272–1(f)	138
1.1274–4(c)	144
1.1274–4(d)	144
1.1502–1	307
1.1502–1 to 1.1502–4	306
1.1502–1(a)	307
1.1502–1(b)	307
1.1502–1(c)	307
1.1502–2	307
	309
	329
1.1502–2—1.1502–7	307
1.1502–3	307
1.1502–4	307
	309
1.1502–5	307
	309
1.1502–6(a)	307
1.1502–6(b)	307
1.1502–6(c)	307
1.1502–11	307
	309
	329
1.1502–11(b)	307
1.1502–12	307
	309
	329
1.1502–12—1.1502–19	307
1.1502–12(o)	309
1.1502–13	307
	308
	309
	311
	313
1.1502–13(a)(1)(i)	310
1.1502–13(a)(2)	310
1.1502–13(c)	310
1.1502–13(c)(3)	311
1.1502–13(c)(4)	311
1.1502–13(d)	310
1.1502–13(d)(1)(i)	310
1.1502–13(d)(1)(ii)	310
1.1502–13(d)(3)	310
1.1502–13(e)	310
1.1502–13(f)	310
	311
1.1502–14	313
1.1502–14(a)	307
	308
	313
1.1502–14(a)(1)	313
1.1502–14(a)(2)	313
1.1502–14(b)	307

TABLE OF TREASURY REGULATIONS

TREASURY REGULATIONS

Reg.	This Work Page
1.1502–15	308
1.1502–16	308
1.1502–17	308
1.1502–18	308
1.1502–19	308
	320
	329
1.1502–20	315
1.1502–21	308
1.1502–21—1.1502–27	308
1.1502–22	308
1.1502–23	308
1.1502–24	308
1.1502–31	307
1.1502–31—1.1502–34	308

TREASURY REGULATIONS

Reg.	This Work Page
1.1502–32	307
1.1502–33	307
1.1502–41—1.1502–47	308
1.1502–75	308
1.1502–75—1.1502–79	308
1.1502–75(c)	308
1.1502–76	308
1.1502–76(a)	308
1.1502–76(b)	308
1.1502–77	308
1.1502–78	308
1.1502–79	308
1.1504–4(g)	306
1.1504–4(g)(3)	306
1.1552–1(b)	324

*

BASIC FEDERAL INCOME TAXATION OF C CORPORATIONS

*

Chapter 1

INTRODUCTION

§ 1.1 SCOPE OF BOOK

This book, which is adapted from a companion volume, *Taxation of Business Entities: C Corporations, Partnerships and S Corporations,* presents an analysis of the Federal income tax treatment of the C corporation[1]. A life cycle approach is followed, first looking at organizations, then operations, and finally, sales, liquidations, and reorganizations.

These materials focus on the statutory, regulatory, and judicial doctrines affecting C corporations. Also, the policy aspects of these concepts are examined. Chapter 1 contains this introduction, a general description of the manner in which the C corporation, the partnership, and the S corporation are taxed (Sec. 1.2), a review of several basic concepts of Federal income taxation that are of particular importance in dealing with C corporations (Sec. 1.3), and selected references dealing with C corporations (Sec. 1.4).

Chapter 2 deals with the organization of C corporations, which involves an examination of the tax-free treatment that is available upon the transfer of property to a corporation in exchange for stock. Chapter 3 examines various issues concerning the debt and equity capitalization of C corporations.

Chapter 4 deals principally with the treatment of dividend and non-dividend distributions by C corporations, and Chapter 5 addresses corporate redemption transactions, which involve the repurchase by a corporation of its outstanding stock. Chapter 6 examines the treatment of stock dividends, which are dividends paid in stock of the corporation. Chapter 7 contains a brief introduction to the accumulated earnings tax and

---

1. For a textual treatment of the C corporation, the partnership, and the S corporation, see Samuel C. Thompson Jr., Paul R. Wysocki, Robert R. Pluth and Catherine A. Jacobson, *Federal Taxation of Business Enterprises* (supplemented quarterly 1989) [hereinafter cited as "*Federal Taxation of Business Enterprises*"], published by Clark Boardman Callaghan, 155 Pfingsters Road, Deerfield, IL, 60015. This casebook contains several modifications of sections of *Federal Taxation of Business Enterprises,* published with permission.

personal holding company tax. These are two penalty taxes that can apply to C corporations that do not distribute sufficient income to their shareholders. Chapter 8 introduces the rules governing the filing of consolidated returns, which affect certain commonly controlled C corporations. Chapter 9 examines the tax consequences to both the shareholders and the corporation on the liquidation of a C corporation.

Corporate reorganizations are examined in Chapters 10 through 16. Chapter 10 introduces the reorganization provisions and gives a historical perspective of the legislative background of these provisions. Chapter 11 deals with fundamental reorganization concepts, such as the continuity of interest requirement and the continuity of business enterprise doctrine. Chapter 12 examines the recapitalization reorganization under § 368(a)(1)(E) and the mere change in form reorganization under § 368(a)(1)(F). Both of these reorganizations involve the restructuring of a single corporation.

Chapter 13 discusses the divisive (D) reorganization under §§ 368(a)(1)(D) and 355. This type of transaction involves the tax-free breakup of a single corporation into two or more corporations. Chapter 14 considers the non-divisive (D) reorganization under §§ 368(a)(1)(D) and 354(b) and the liquidation reincorporation doctrine. These transactions involve the transfer of the property of one commonly controlled corporation to another.

Chapter 15 addresses all forms of direct and triangular acquisitive reorganizations and briefly introduces § 382, which limits losses after an acquisition. Finally, Chapter 16 addresses policy issues arising in reorganizations.

Each chapter begins with a brief discussion of the scope of the chapter. Many topics are introduced by a textual discussion of the relevant provisions of the Code and regulations. This introductory material is followed by cases, rulings, notes, and problems that deal with more esoteric issues in the particular area. Most of the topics covered are addressed in greater detail in *Federal Taxation of Business Enterprises.*[2] A companion volume, *Taxable and Tax-Free Mergers, Acquisitions, and LBOs*, considers in detail all forms of acquisition transactions. Another companion volume, *Basic Federal Income Taxation of Partnerships and S Corporations,* examines those entities.

§ 1.2 GENERAL DESCRIPTIONS OF THE THREE BASIC FORMS OF BUSINESS[3]

A. THE C CORPORATION

A subchapter C corporation is a separate taxable entity that is distinct from its shareholders. Section 11 imposes a tax on the taxable income of a subchapter C corporation. Any dividends distributed from a

---

2. See *Federal Taxation of Business Enterprises, supra* note 1.

3. See *Federal Taxation of Business Enterprises, supra* Chapter 1 note 1, at § 2:02.

§ 1.2   THREE BASIC FORMS OF BUSINESS   3

subchapter C corporation to its shareholders are included in the gross income of the shareholders. *See* § 61(a)(7). Dividends received by shareholders are subject to a separate tax imposed under § 1 in the case of noncorporate shareholders and under § 11 in the case of corporate shareholders. Thus, earnings of a business operated as a subchapter C corporation are subject to a corporate level tax and a shareholder level tax.

The corporate tax imposed by § 11 is equal to 15% of the first $50,000 of taxable income, 25% of the next $25,000 of taxable income, 34% of taxable income in excess of $75,000 but not in excess of $10 million, and 35% of taxable income in excess of $10 million. Section 11(b). The Revenue Reconciliation Act of 1993 (the 1993 Act) added the 35% bracket.

The lower 15% and 25% rates are phased out for corporations that have taxable income in excess of $100,000 for any taxable year. *See* § 11(b). This phase out is implemented by imposing an additional tax on income in excess of $100,000 equal to the lesser of (1) 5% of the excess, or (2) $11,750. This $11,750 is the difference between the tax at the 15%, 25% and 34% graduated rates on the first $100,000 of taxable income and the tax on such income at 34%. This means that the benefit of the 15% and 25% rates is completely phased out at $335,000 of taxable income. Thus, any corporation with taxable income between $335,000 and $10 million is subject to a 34% effective rate of tax.

The 34% rate is phased out for corporations with taxable income in excess of $15 million. In such cases, taxable income is increased by an additional amount equal to the lesser of (1) 3% of such excess or (2) $100,000. *See* § 11(b). Thus, the benefit of the 34% rate is completely recaptured when a corporation's taxable income reaches $18,333,333 (3% of $3,333,333 is $100,000).

As indicated, shareholders are subject to a tax on the receipt of dividends, which are current distributions of cash or property from a corporation. As a result of the 1993 Act, dividends received by individual shareholders are subject to a maximum tax rate of 39.6% under § 1. The maximum tax on the long term capital gains of shareholders is 28%. *See* § 1(h).

Corporate shareholders receive the benefit of a dividends received deduction in the amount of 70%, 80% or 100% of the dividends received. *See* § 243 and Chapter 4.

The combined corporate and individual rates can result in an aggregate tax rate of approximately 61% on the earnings of a Subchapter C corporation. This double tax is illustrated as follows:

> Individuals A and B form a corporation (C) as equal shareholders. C earns $1 million of taxable income for the taxable year and pays a corporate tax of $340,000. C then distributes the $660,000 after tax earnings to A and B as a dividend. A and B are taxed at a 39.6% rate, say 40%, on the dividend, resulting in a total sharehold-

er level tax of $264,000. Thus, the combined corporate and shareholder tax on C's $1 million of taxable income is $604,000 or 60.4%.

In addition to being subject to the basic corporate tax under § 11, a corporation may be subject to the alternative minimum tax under § 55. This tax is not examined here.

A subchapter C corporation may be subject to the personal holding company tax under § 541. This tax applies to certain closely held corporations that have a substantial amount of undistributed passive income. The accumulated earnings tax under § 531 may apply to a subchapter C corporation that is not a personal holding company and that accumulates earnings for the purpose of avoiding the shareholder tax on dividend distributions. These two penalty taxes are examined in Chapter 7.

In view of the fact that as a result of the 1993 Act, the maximum individual rate of 39.6% exceeds the maximum corporate rate of 35%, there may be a greater tax incentive for corporations to retain earnings. This could put more pressure on the personal holding company tax and the accumulated earnings tax.

Thus, there are several taxes that must be considered when operating a C corporation: the regular tax under § 11, the alternative minimum tax under § 55, the personal holding company tax under § 541, and the accumulated earnings tax under § 531.

The tax treatment of the current operations of a C corporation, which encompass such matters as distributions of cash and property, redemptions, stock dividends, consolidated returns, and the penalty taxes, is examined in Chapters 4 through 8. The formation of a subchapter C corporation can be accomplished in a tax-free exchange in which the shareholders contribute property to the corporation in exchange for stock. These organization transactions are examined in Chapter 2. A liquidation of a C corporation, however, is generally a taxable transaction at both the corporate and shareholder levels. *See* Chapter 9. A C corporation may participate in either a taxable or tax-free acquisition. Tax-free acquisitions are known as reorganizations. Also, the reorganization concept includes certain restructuring transactions in which the debt or equity capital of a single corporation is restructured. Corporate reorganizations and related concepts are examined in Chapters 10 through 16.

B. THE PARTNERSHIP

Partnerships, unlike C corporations, are not subject to federal income tax. *See* § 701. Each partner includes in gross income her share of the partnership's gross income, without regard to the distribution of partnership property. *See* § 702. Also, a partner deducts from gross income her share of partnership losses to the extent of the partner's basis for her partnership interest. *See* §§ 702 and 704(d).

A partner's basis for her partnership interest is increased by her allocable share of partnership income and decreased by her allocable share of partnership losses. *See* § 705. Distributions of cash or other property from a partnership to a partner are generally tax-free to the partner and result in a reduction in the basis of the partner's partnership interest.

Thus, the fundamental differences between the taxation of partnerships and C corporations are that (1) C corporations are subject to tax but partnerships are not, and (2) partners are taxed on the partnership's income even though the income may not be distributed, but shareholders are taxed only upon the receipt of a distribution from the C corporation.

The following example illustrates the tax treatment of partnerships:

> A and B form a partnership (P) as equal partners. P earns income of $1 million for the taxable year and distributes $500K (K = $1000) of cash to each of A and B. A and B each (1) report $500K of gross income from the partnership, (2) increase the basis of their individual partnership interest by the $500K of allocated income, (3) receive the $500K of cash tax-free, and (4) reduce the basis of their individual partnership interest by $500K. Thus, the $1 million is subject to a maximum 39.6% rate, or approximately $400K, as compared with the approximately 61% combined rate that obtained in the case of the operation of the Subchapter C corporation in the example above. On the other hand, if the business was formed as a C corporation and the after tax income was retained by the corporation, the immediate corporate tax would be only $340K.

The Code permits flexibility in allocating income, gain, loss deductions, and credits among the partners. *See* § 704(a). This flexibility is much greater than that which is available with C or S corporations. This flexibility is illustrated as follows:

> A and B form partnership P as equal partners. In the fifth year of operation, A and B agree that A has contributed more to the success of the partnership operations than B. As a consequence, A is allocated 75% of the partnership's income for the year, with only 25% going to B. This type of allocation is respected for tax purposes, provided it has substantial economic effect under § 704(b).

Contributions of property to a partnership in an initial organization transaction generally are tax-free. The liquidation of a partnership also is generally tax-free, but the disposition of either partnership assets or an interest in a partnership is generally taxable.

C. THE S CORPORATION

Only certain corporations qualify to be treated as S corporations. For example, an S corporation may issue only one class of stock, and it can have no more than 35 shareholders. *See* § 1361(a). An election for subchapter S treatment must be made by the shareholders and the corporation. *See* § 1362. If a business can be operated in the form of an S corporation, the tax consequences from regular operations are similar to those of a partnership. Thus, the S corporation is generally not subject to tax, and a shareholder (1) reports her allocable share of the corporation's income or loss, (2) increases the basis for her stock by her allocable share of income, and (3) decreases the basis by her allocable share of any loss. Distributions from S corporations are generally tax-free to the shareholder and result in a reduction in the basis of the shareholder's shares. The operation of an S corporation is illustrated as follows:

> A and B form an S corporation (S) as equal shareholders. S earns taxable income for its first taxable year of $1 million and distributes $500K to each of A and B. S is not subject to tax. As in the case of a partnership, A and B each (1) report $500K of income from S, (2) increase the basis of their shares by $500K, (3) receive a tax-free distribution of the $500K of cash, and (4) reduce the basis of their stock by $500K. S's $1 million of income is subject to a maximum 39.6% rate, or approximately $400,000. Thus, by operating as an S corporation, the combined approximately 61% rate of corporate and shareholder taxes on C corporations is avoided. On the other hand, if the business was operated as a C corporation and the corporation retained its after tax income, the immediate tax would be only $340,000.

An S corporation is subject to tax in two circumstances. First, if an S corporation was previously a C corporation, did not distribute all of its C period earnings and profits, and earns a substantial amount of passive income, a tax may be imposed on the passive income. See § 1375. Further, if an S corporation was formerly a C corporation, a tax may be imposed on the disposition by the S corporation of appreciated property held by the C corporation at the time of the conversion from C to S. See § 1374.

The provisions of Subchapter C apply to S corporations, except where explicitly made inapplicable or where such rules are inconsistent with the rules of subchapter S. See § 1371(a). Consequently, the rules governing the transfer of property to C corporations and sales and liquidations of C corporations also generally apply to S corporations.

§ 1.3 BASIC CONCEPTS AFFECTING C CORPORATIONS

A. REALIZATION AND RECOGNITION: THE STRUCTURE OF THE STATUTE

See §§ 1001, 1011, 1012, 1015(a) and 1016.

The tax consequences of many business transactions revolve around the concepts of realization and recognition and the breadth of certain exceptions to the recognition rule. The starting point for determining the tax consequences upon the disposition of property is § 1001(a) of the Code, which provides that gain or loss on a sale or other disposition of property shall be the difference between the amount realized and the adjusted basis of the property transferred. The "amount realized" on a sale or other disposition of property is defined in § 1001(b) as "the sum of money received plus the fair market value of property (other than money) received." Under § 1011, the "adjusted basis" of property for purposes of determining gain or loss is, in general, the taxpayer's cost of the property as provided in § 1012, less depreciation, if any, and plus or minus certain other adjustments, all as provided in § 1016.

Pursuant to § 1001(c), realized gain or loss is "recognized" (*i.e.*, taken into account for tax purposes), except as otherwise provided in the income tax provisions of the Code. The corporate and partnership provisions of the Code contain several exceptions to the general rule of recognition. Many of these nonrecognition provisions are analogous to the nonrecognition rule of § 1031 for like kind exchanges of property. For this reason, this introductory chapter contains an examination of § 1031.

In order to preserve (defer) the gain or loss that is not recognized in a transaction governed by an exception to the rule of recognition, the basis of the property received is, generally, the basis of the property exchanged. This is known, in tax parlance, as a *substituted basis* and is an exception to the cost basis rule of § 1012.[1] Thus, if a particular transaction is excepted from the rule of recognition, there will also be an exception to the cost basis rule for the property received in the transaction. In describing the relationship between the like kind exchange exception to the recognition rule and the correlative exception to the cost basis rule, the House Report to the 1924 Revenue Act said: "[T]hese provisions result not in an exemption from tax but in a postponement of tax until the gain is realized by a pure sale or by such an exchange as amounts to a pure sale." H.R.Rep. No. 179, 68th Cong., 1st Sess. (1924) 1939–1 C.B. (Part 2) at 253.

B. SCOPE OF THE REALIZATION CONCEPT

COTTAGE SAVINGS ASSOCIATION v. COMMISSIONER

United States Supreme Court, 1991.
499 U.S. 554, 111 S.Ct. 1503, 113 L.Ed.2d 589.

JUSTICE MARSHALL delivered the opinion of the Court.

The issue in this case is whether a financial institution realizes tax-deductible losses when it exchanges its interests in one group of residential mortgage loans for another lender's interests in a different group of

---

1. The property received in such an exchange is defined in § 7701(a)(44) as "exchanged basis property." In certain situations a transferee takes the transferor's basis for property. This is referred to in tax parlance as a carryover basis. Under § 7701(a)(43) such property falls under the definition of "transferred basis property." Section 7701(a)(42) defines "substituted basis property" as property that is either transferred basis property or exchanged basis property.

residential mortgage loans. We hold that such a transaction does give rise to realized losses.

I

Petitioner Cottage Savings Association (Cottage Savings) is a savings and loan association (S & L). * * *

On December 31, 1980, Cottage Savings sold "90% participation" in 252 mortgages to four S & L's. It simultaneously purchased "90% participation interests" in 305 mortgages held by these S & L's. All of the loans involved in the transaction were secured by single-family homes, most in the Cincinnati area. The fair market value of the package of participation interests exchanged by each side was approximately $4.5 million. The face value of the participation interests Cottage Savings relinquished in the transaction was approximately $6.9 million.

On its 1980 federal income tax return, Cottage Savings claimed a deduction for $2,447,091, which represented the adjusted difference between the face value of the participation interests that it traded and the fair market value of the participation interests that it received. * * * [The Service disallowed the deduction.]

II

Rather than assessing tax liability on the basis of annual fluctuations in the value of a taxpayer's property, the Internal Revenue Code defers the tax consequences of a gain or loss in property value until the taxpayer "realizes" the gain or loss. The realization requirement is implicit in § 1001(a) of the Code, which defines "[t]he gain [or loss] from the sale or other disposition of property" as the difference between "the amount realized" from the sale or disposition of the property and its "adjusted basis." As this Court has recognized, the concept of realization is "founded on administrative convenience." * * *

Section 1001(a)'s language provides a straightforward test for realization: to realize a gain or loss in the value of property, the taxpayer must engage in a "sale or other disposition of [the] property." The parties agree that the exchange of participation interests in this case cannot be characterized as a "sale" under § 1001(a); the issue before us is whether the transaction constitutes a "disposition of property." The Commissioner argues that an exchange of property can be treated as a "disposition" under § 1001(a) only if the properties exchanged are materially different. The Commissioner further submits that, because the underlying mortgages were essentially economic substitutes, the participation interests exchanged by Cottage Savings were not materially different from those received from the other S & L's. Cottage Savings, on the other hand, maintains that *any* exchange of property is a "disposition of property" under § 1001(a), regardless of whether the property exchanged is materially different. Alternatively, Cottage Savings contends that the participation interests exchanged were materially different because the underlying loans were secured by different properties.

We must therefore determine whether the realization principle in § 1001(a) incorporates a "material difference" requirement. If it does, we must further decide what that requirement amounts to and how it applies in this case. We consider these questions in turn.

A

Neither the language nor the history of the Code indicates whether and to what extent property exchanged must differ to count as a "disposition of property" under § 1001(a). Nonetheless, we readily agree with the Commissioner that an exchange of property gives rise to a realization event under § 1001(a) only if the properties exchanged are "materially different." The Commissioner himself has by regulation construed § 1001(a) to embody a material difference requirement:

> "Except as otherwise provided ... the gain or loss realized from the conversion of property into cash, *or from the exchange of property for other property differing materially either in kind or in extent*, is treated as income or as loss sustained." Treas.Reg. § 1.1001-1, 26 CFR § 1.1001-1 (1990) (emphasis added).

* * *

Treasury Regulation § 1.1001-1 is also consistent with our landmark precedents on realization. In a series of early decisions involving the tax effects of property exchanges, this Court made clear that a taxpayer realizes taxable income only if the properties exchanged are "materially" or "essentially" different. *See United States v. Phellis,* 257 U.S. 156, 173, 42 S.Ct. 63, 67, 66 L.Ed. 180 (1921); *Weiss v. Stearn,* 265 U.S. 242, 253–254, 44 S.Ct. 490, 491–492, 68 L.Ed. 1001 (1924); *Marr v. United States,* 268 U.S. 536, 540–542, 45 S.Ct. 575, 576–577, 69 L.Ed. 1079 (1925); [*see* Sec. 10.2]; *see also Eisner v. Macomber,* 252 U.S. 189, 207–212, 40 S.Ct. 189, 193–195, 64 L.Ed. 521 (1920) (recognizing realization requirement). * * *

B

Precisely what constitutes a "material difference" for purposes of § 1001(a) of the Code is a more complicated question. The Commissioner argues that properties are "materially different" only if they differ in economic substance. * * * We conclude that § 1001(a) embodies a much less demanding and less complex test.

* * *

We start with the classic treatment of realization in *Eisner v. Macomber, supra.* In *Macomber,* a taxpayer who owned 2,200 shares of stock in a company received another 1,100 shares from the company as part of a pro rata stock dividend meant to reflect the company's growth in value. At issue was whether the stock dividend constituted taxable income. We held that it did not, because no gain was realized. We reasoned that the stock dividend merely reflected the increased worth of the taxpayer's stock, and that a taxpayer realizes increased worth of property only by receiving "something of exchangeable value *proceeding from* the property".

In three subsequent decisions—*United States v. Phellis, supra; Weiss v. Stearn, supra;* and *Marr v. United States, supra*—we refined *Macomber*'s conception of realization in the context of property exchanges. In each case, the taxpayer owned stock that had appreciated in value since its acquisition. And in each case, the corporation in which the taxpayer held stock had reorganized into a new corporation, with the new corporation assuming the business of the old corporation. While the corporations in *Phellis* and *Marr* both changed from New Jersey to Delaware corporations, the original and successor corporations in *Weiss* both were incorporated in Ohio. In each case, following the reorganization, the stockholders of the old corporation received shares in the new corporation equal to their proportional interest in the old corporation.

The question in these cases was whether the taxpayers realized the accumulated gain in their shares in the old corporation when they received in return for those shares stock representing an equivalent proportional interest in the new corporations. In *Phellis* and *Marr*, we held that the transactions were realization events. We reasoned that because a company incorporated in one State has "different rights and powers" from one incorporated in a different State, the taxpayers in *Phellis* and *Marr* acquired through the transactions property that was "materially different" from what they previously had. In contrast, we held that no realization occurred in *Weiss*. By exchanging stock in the predecessor corporation for stock in the newly reorganized corporation, the taxpayer did not receive "a thing really different from what he theretofore had." As we explained in *Marr,* our determination that the reorganized company in *Weiss* was not "really different" from its predecessor turned on the fact that both companies were incorporated in the same State.

Obviously, the distinction in *Phellis* and *Marr* that made the stock in the successor corporations materially different from the stock in the predecessors was minimal. Taken together, *Phellis, Marr,* and *Weiss* stand for the principle that properties are "different" in the sense that is "material" to the Internal Revenue Code so long as their respective possessors enjoy legal entitlements that are different in kind or extent. Thus, separate groups of stock are not materially different if they confer "the same proportional interest of the same character in the same corporation." However, they *are* materially different if they are issued by different corporations, or if they confer "differen[t] rights and powers" in the same corporation. No more demanding a standard than this is necessary in order to satisfy the administrative purposes underlying the realization requirement in § 1001(a). * * *

C

Under our interpretation of § 1001(a), an exchange of property gives rise to a realization event so long as the exchanged properties are "materially different"—that is, so long as they embody legally distinct entitlements. Cottage Savings' transactions at issue here easily satisfy this test. * * *

Note

The Treasury has issued proposed regulations under § 1.1001–3 dealing with the impact of *Cottage Savings* on the determination of whether a modification of a debt instrument constitutes an exchange of debt instruments.

C. INSTALLMENT SALES REPORTING UNDER § 453 *

Skim § 453

The following is a brief summary of the basic elements of the installment sales provision.

Section 1001(d) allows recognized gain to be reported on the installment method under § 453. This method permits a taxpayer to pay the federal income tax over the periods during which payments of the sales price are received, thus relieving the taxpayer of the burden of paying taxes on income not yet received.

Section 453(a) provides that income from an installment sale is to be reported on the installment method except as otherwise provided in § 453. Section 453(b)(1) defines an installment sale as a "disposition of property where at least 1 payment is to be received after the close of the taxable year in which the disposition occurs."

The installment method is defined in § 453(c) as a "method under which the income recognized for any taxable year from a disposition is that proportion of the payments received in that year which the gross profit * * * bears to the total contract price." The "gross profit" is equal to the selling price less the adjusted basis of the property sold.[2]

The "selling price" means the gross selling price without any reductions for any mortgage on the property,[3] and the "total contract price" generally equals the selling price.[4] These concepts are illustrated in the following example:

Individual *A* sells unencumbered property for $10,000 in cash and a note with a face of $90,000, which has adequate stated interest.[5] The note is to be paid in the amount of $10,000 per year during the next nine years. Both the selling price and the total contract price are $100,000.

---

* Based on §§ 2:19 to 2:20 of *Federal Taxation of Business Enterprises, supra* Chapter 1 note 1, with permission.

2. Temp.Reg. § 15A.453–1(b)(2)(v).
3. Temp.Reg. § 15A.453–1(b)(2)(ii).
4. Temp.Reg. § 15A.453–1(b)(2)(iii).
5. The rules regarding original issue discount (OID) under § 1271 et seq. and imputed interest under § 483 apply to installment sales. As a consequence, if the instrument fails to provide for the payment of interest at an adequate rate of interest, a portion of the principal payments due under the instrument are recharacterized as interest. This recharacterization reduces the principal amount of the note and the gross profit realized on the sale. This issue is discussed further when considering the OID provisions in Chapter 3.

If *A*'s basis for the property is $40,000, then *A*'s gross profit is $60,000. Consequently, the portion of each $10,000 payment which the gross profit ($60,000) bears to the total contract price ($100,000) is gain to *A* in each year. *A* will, therefore, have $6,000 of gain and will recover $4,000 of her $40,000 basis in each of the ten years during which payments are received.

Under § 453(f)(3), installment sale treatment is not available if the evidence of indebtedness is either payable on demand or issued by a corporation (or government) in a readily tradeable form. Also, under § 453(k)(2), a sale of stock or securities that are traded on an established securities market does not qualify for installment sale treatment.

Under § 453(d), installment reporting is automatic for a qualified sale unless the taxpayer elects to apply the general recognition rule. An election out of installment treatment must be made on or before the due date for filing the taxpayer's return for the taxable year in which the installment sale occurs.

Prior to the Installment Sale Revision Act of 1980, installment reporting was not available unless the selling price was fixed and determinable. An installment sale subject to a price contingency thus was not eligible for installment treatment and the taxpayer was required to recognize the total gain in the year of sale. In cases where the payments were determined to have no readily ascertainable fair market value, however, a taxpayer could treat the transaction as open and use the cost recovery method adopted by the Supreme Court in *Burnet v. Logan,* which is set out below. Section 453 now applies to contingent payment sales. *See* Prop.Reg. § 1.453–1(c).

Finally, if the sales price of property exceeds $150,000, § 453A imposes an interest charge on the deferred tax liability inherent in installment obligations arising from such sales, provided that the taxpayer holds at the end of the year installment obligations from such sales arising during the year with a principal amount in excess of $5 million. Also, § 453A treats the pledging of any installment obligations arising from a sale of property for a price in excess of $150,000 as a sale of the obligation. Section 453(h), which provides for installment sale treatment for the shareholders of certain liquidating corporations, is addressed in Sec. 9.2.E.

Problem

The following problem is designed to illustrate the basic operation of § 453 as it relates to the sale of real property and casual sales of personal property, such as stock of a closely held corporation.

Individual *A*, a cash basis taxpayer, owns a parcel of real property that has a value of $125K and an adjusted basis of $50K. Corporation Y has offered to purchase the parcel for $25K down and $10K a year for each of the succeeding ten years, plus interest on the unpaid balance at 10 percent. There is no OID. The deferred payment obligations are to be evidenced by an unsecured note.

(a) What result if A elects out of § 453? *See* § 453(d).

(b) What result if A does not elect out of § 453 treatment? *See* § 453(a) and (b). What is the "selling price" the "gross profit," and the "total contract price"?

D. IS A CURRENT DISTRIBUTION OF PROPERTY BY A CORPORATION A REALIZATION EVENT? HISTORICAL PERSPECTIVE

GENERAL UTILITIES & OPERATING CO. v. HELVERING

Supreme Court of the United States, 1935.
296 U.S. 200, 56 S.Ct. 185, 80 L.Ed. 154.

Mr. Justice McReynolds delivered the opinion of the Court.

January 1, 1927, petitioner, General Utilities, a Delaware corporation, acquired 20,000 shares (one-half of total outstanding) common stock of Islands Edison Company, for which it paid $2,000. Gillet & Company owned the remainder.

During January, 1928, Whetstone, president of Southern Cities Utilities Company, contemplated acquisition by his company of all Islands Edison common stock. He discussed the matter with Lucas, petitioner's president, also with Gillet & Company. The latter concern agreed to sell its holdings upon terms acceptable to all. But Lucas pointed out that the shares which his company held could only be purchased after distribution of them among stockholders, since a sale by it would subject the realized profit to taxation, and when the proceeds passed to the stockholders there would be further exaction. Lucas had no power to sell, but he, Gillet, and Whetstone were in accord concerning the terms and conditions under which purchase of all the stock might become possible—"it being understood and agreed between them that petitioner would make distribution of the stock of the Islands Edison Company to its stockholders and that counsel would prepare a written agreement embodying the terms and conditions of the said sale, agreement to be submitted for approval to the stockholders of the Islands Edison Company after the distribution of said stock by the petitioner."

Petitioner's directors, March 22, 1928, considered the disposition of the Islands Edison shares. Officers reported they were worth $1,122,500, and recommended an appreciation on the books to that figure. Thereupon a resolution directed this change; also "that a dividend in the amount of $1,071,426.25 be and it is hereby declared on the Common Stock of this Company payable in Common Stock to The Islands Edison Company at a valuation of $56.12½ a share, out of the surplus of the Company arising from the appreciation in the value of the Common Stock of The Islands Edison Company held by this Company, viz., $1,120,500.00, the payment of the dividend to be made by the delivery to the stockholders of this Company, pro rata, of certificates for the Common Stock of The Islands Edison Company held by this Company at the rate of two shares of such stock for each share of Company Stock of this Corporation."

Accordingly, 19,090 shares were distributed amongst petitioner's thirty-three stockholders and proper transfers to them were made upon the issuing corporation's books. It retained 910 shares.

After this transfer, all holders of Islands Edison stock sold to Southern Cities Utilities Company at $56.12½ per share. Petitioner realized $46,346.30 net profit on 910 shares and this was duly returned for taxation. There was no report of gain upon the 19,090 shares distributed to stockholders.

The Commissioner of Internal Revenue declared a taxable gain upon distribution of the stock in payment of the dividend declared March 22d, and made the questioned deficiency assessment. Seeking redetermination by the Board of Tax Appeals, petitioner alleged: "The Commissioner of Internal Revenue has erroneously held that the petitioner corporation made a profit of $1,069,517.25 by distributing to its own stockholders certain capital stock of another corporation which it had theretofore owned." And it asked a ruling that no taxable gain resulted from the appreciation upon its books and subsequent distribution of the shares. Answering, the Commissioner denied that his action was erroneous, but advanced no new basis of support. A stipulation concerning the facts followed; and upon this and the pleadings, the Board heard the cause.

It found: "The respondent has determined a deficiency in income tax in the amount of $128,342.07 for the calendar year 1928. The only question presented in this proceeding for redetermination is whether petitioner realized taxable gain in declaring a dividend and paying it in the stock of another company at an agreed value per share, which value was in excess of the cost of the stock to petitioner." Also: "On March 26, 1928, the stockholders of the Islands Edison Company (one of which was petitioner, owning 910 shares) and the Southern Cities Utilities Company, entered into a written contract of sale of the Islands Edison Company stock. At no time did petitioner agree with Whetstone or the Southern Cities Utilities Company, verbally or in writing, to make sale to him or to the Southern Cities Utilities Company of any of said stock except the aforesaid 910 shares of the Islands Edison Company."

The opinion recites: The Commissioner's "theory is that upon the declaration of the dividend on March 22, 1928, petitioner became indebted to its stockholders in the amount of $1,071,426.25, and that the discharge of that liability by the delivery of property costing less than the amount of the debt constituted income, citing *United States v. Kirby Lumber Co.*, 284 U.S. 1, 52 S.Ct. 4, 76 L.Ed. 131." "The intent of the directors of petitioner was to declare a dividend payable in Islands Edison stock; their intent was expressed in that way in the resolution formally adopted; and the dividend was paid in the way intended and declared. We so construe the transaction, and on authority of *First Savings Bank v. Burnet, supra* [60 App.D.C. 307, 53 F.(2d) 919, 82

A.L.R. 549], we hold that the declaration and payment of the dividend resulted in no taxable income."

The Commissioner asked the Circuit Court of Appeals, Fourth Circuit, to review the Board's determination. He alleged: "The only question to be decided is whether the petitioner [taxpayer] realized taxable income in declaring a dividend and paying it in stock of another company at an agreed value per share, which value was in excess of the cost of the stock."

The court stated: "There are two grounds upon which the petitioner urges that the action of the Board of Tax Appeals was wrong: First, that the dividend declared was in effect a *cash* dividend and that the respondent realized a taxable income by the distribution of the Islands Edison Company stock to its stockholders equal to the difference between the amount of the dividend declared and the cost of the stock. Second, that the sale made of the Islands Edison Company stock was in reality a sale by the respondent (with all the terms agreed upon before the declaration of the dividend), through its stockholders who were virtually acting as agents of the respondent, the real vendor."

Upon the first ground, it sustained the Board. Concerning the second, it held that, although not raised before the Board, the point should be ruled upon.

"When we come to consider the sale of the stock of the Islands Edison Company we cannot escape the conclusion that the transaction was deliberately planned and carried out for the sole purpose of escaping taxation. The purchaser was found by the officers of the respondent; the exact terms of the sale as finally consummated were agreed to by the same officers; the purchaser of the stock stated that the delivery of all stock was essential and that the delivery of a part thereof would not suffice; the details were worked out for the express and admitted purpose of avoiding the payment of the tax and for the reason that the attorneys for the respondent had advised that unless some such plan was adopted the tax would have to be paid; and a written agreement was to be prepared by counsel for the respondent which was to be submitted to the stockholders; all this without the stockholders, or any of them, who were ostensibly making the sale, being informed, advised or consulted. Such admitted facts plainly constituted a plan, not to use the harsher terms of scheme, artifice or conspiracy, to evade the payment of the tax. For the purposes of this decision it is not necessary to consider whether such a course as is here shown constituted a fraud, it is sufficient if we conclude that the object was to evade the payment of a tax justly due the government.

"The sale of the stock in question was, in substance, made by the respondent company, through the stockholders as agents or conduits through whom the transfer of the title was effected. The stockholders, even in their character as agents, had little or no option in the matter and in no sense exercised any independent judgment. They automatically ratified the agreement prepared and submitted to them."

A judgment of reversal followed.

Both tribunals below rightly decided that petitioner derived no taxable gain from the distribution among its stockholders of the Islands Edison shares as a dividend. This was no sale; assets were not used to discharge indebtedness.

The second ground of objection, although sustained by the court, was not presented to or ruled upon by the Board.

* * *

Here the court undertook to decide a question not properly raised. Also it made an inference of fact directly in conflict with the stipulation of the parties and the findings, for which we think the record affords no support whatever. To remand the cause for further findings would be futile. The Board could not properly find anything which would assist the Commissioner's cause.

The judgment of the court below must be reversed. The action of the Board of Tax Appeals is approved.

Reversed.

Note

The Commissioner advanced two theories here: First, that the taxpayer, General Utilities, realized income on the distribution of the Islands Edison shares because the distribution discharged General Utilities' obligation to its shareholders; and Second, that General Utilities in fact made the sale. Why did the Commissioner not argue that as a general principle a corporation has a realized and recognized gain or loss whenever it distributes appreciated or depreciated property to its shareholders? Is such a rule consistent with the general realization and recognition rule of § 1001? Would such a rule be wise from a policy standpoint? Is it consistent with the treatment of the corporation as a separate taxable entity?

In its brief, the Government in fact argued that the distribution was a realization event. The Court did not discuss the point, however, apparently because it had not been raised in the lower courts.

The implicit holding in *General Utilities,* that a current distribution is not a realization event, was codified in 1954 as § 311(a). Also, § 336, which was initially added in 1954, provided that a liquidating distribution by a corporation was not a realization event.

In the Tax Reform Act of 1986, Congress substantially repealed the *General Utilities* doctrine by amending §§ 311 and 336. Section 311, which deals with the impact of current distributions of property, is considered in Chapter 4, which addresses operations by C corporations, and § 336 which deals with liquidating distributions, is examined in Chapter 9, which examines liquidating distributions. As a consequence of the substantial repeal of the *General Utilities* doctrine, a distribution by corporations of appreciated property generally is treated as a sale or exchange by the corporation of such property. Thus, the distribution is a constructive realization and recognition event to the distributing corporation.

E. TREATMENT OF LIABILITIES

1. *Introduction*

Liabilities are present in many, if not most, business transactions. For example, property subject to a mortgage may be transferred to a newly-formed corporation. Or, such property may be sold or distributed by a corporation.

The proper treatment of liabilities can present significant issues in business taxation, and the following materials are designed to lay the proper foundation for addressing these issues.

2. *Bailing Out of Failed Tax Shelters: The Supreme Court Addresses Footnote 37 in Crane*

a. **Crane** *Footnote 37*

In footnote 37 of *Crane v. Commissioner*, 331 U.S. 1, 67 S.Ct. 1047, 91 L.Ed. 1301 (1947), the Supreme Court said:

> Obviously, if the value of the property is less than the amount of the mortgage, [on the sale of the property] a mortgagor who is not personally liable cannot realize a benefit equal to the mortgage. Consequently, a different problem might be encountered where a mortgagor abandoned the property or transferred it subject to the mortgage without receiving boot. That is not this case.

The following case addresses the issue in footnote 37. The situation involves a failed tax shelter, which in this situation is an investment in which the value of the property is less than the amount of the outstanding mortgage.

b. The Supreme Court's View

COMMISSIONER v. TUFTS

Supreme Court of the United States, 1983.
461 U.S. 300, 103 S.Ct. 1826, 75 L.Ed.2d 863.

JUSTICE BLACKMUN delivered the opinion of the Court.

Over 35 years ago, in *Crane v. Commissioner,* this Court ruled that a taxpayer, who sold property encumbered by a nonrecourse mortgage (the amount of the mortgage being less than the property's value), must include the unpaid balance of the mortgage in the computation of the amount the taxpayer realized on the sale. The case now before us presents the question whether the same rule applies when the unpaid amount of the nonrecourse mortgage exceeds the fair market value of the property sold.

* * *

We are disinclined to overrule *Crane,* and we conclude that the same rule applies when the unpaid amount of the nonrecourse mortgage exceeds the value of the property transferred. *Crane* ultimately does not rest on its limited theory of economic benefit; instead, we read *Crane* to have approved the Commissioner's decision to treat a nonrecourse mortgage in this context as a true loan. This approval underlies *Crane's* holdings that the amount of the nonrecourse liability is to be included in calculating both the basis and the amount realized on disposition. That the amount of the loan exceeds the fair market value of the property thus becomes irrelevant.

* * *

When encumbered property is sold or otherwise disposed of and the purchaser assumes the mortgage, the associated extinguishment of the mortgagor's obligation to repay is accounted for in the computation of the amount realized. * * * Because no difference between recourse and nonrecourse obligations is recognized in calculating basis, *Crane* teaches that the Commissioner may ignore the nonrecourse nature of the obligation in determining the amount realized upon disposition of the encumbered property. He thus may include in the amount realized the amount of the nonrecourse mortgage assumed by the purchaser. The rationale for this treatment is that the original inclusion of the amount of the mortgage in basis rested on the assumption that the mortgagor incurred an obligation to repay. Moreover, this treatment balances the fact that the mortgagor originally received the proceeds of the nonrecourse loan tax-free on the same assumption. Unless the outstanding amount of the mortgage is deemed to be realized, the mortgagor effectively will have received untaxed income at the time the loan was extended and will have received an unwarranted increase in the basis of his property. The Commissioner's interpretation of § 1001(b) in this fashion cannot be said to be unreasonable.

* * *

In the specific circumstances of *Crane,* the economic benefit theory did support the Commissioner's treatment of the nonrecourse mortgage as a personal obligation. The footnote in *Crane* acknowledged the limitations of that theory when applied to a different set of facts. *Crane* also stands for the broader proposition, however, that a nonrecourse loan should be treated as a true loan. We therefore hold that a taxpayer must account for the proceeds of obligations he has received tax-free and included in basis. Nothing in either § 1001(b) or in the Court's prior decisions requires the Commissioner to permit a taxpayer to treat a sale of encumbered property asymmetrically, by including the proceeds of the nonrecourse obligation in basis but not accounting for the proceeds upon transfer of the encumbered property.

* * *

Question

Individual *A* owns property with a basis of $50K and a fair market value of $70K. The property is subject to a nonrecourse debt of $100K. *A* transfers the property to the mortgagee in discharge of the debt. What result to *A*? What result if *A*, who is insolvent, was personally obligated on the $100K debt, and *A* transferred the property to the mortgagee in discharge of the debt. *See* § 1.1001–2(a), and Rev.Rul. 90–16, 1990–1 C.B. 12.

F. BRIEF SUMMARY OF PRINCIPAL CAPITAL GAIN AND LOSS PROVISIONS

See §§ 1221, 1222, 1223, 1(h), 1201, 1211 and 1212.

The starting point for determining whether a recognized gain or loss is a capital gain or loss is § 1221 which defines capital asset as property held by a taxpayer (whether or not connected with his trade or business), but not including the property specified in § 1221(1) through (5). Under § 1221(1), a capital asset does not include, for example, inventory and under § 1221(2), a capital asset does not include business property subject to an allowance for depreciation. The classic example of a capital asset is stock purchased for investment. Another is the taxpayer's personal residence.

Section 1222 sets out certain netting rules under which capital gains and losses are first segregated between short and long term gains and losses and then netted to come up with either a net capital loss (*see* § 1222(10)) or a net capital gain (*see* § 1222(11)). Capital gain or loss is long term if the asset has been held for more than 1 year. *See* § 1222(3). Section 1223 sets out certain holding period rules relating to such things as when the holding period of one asset will be tacked to another. This section will be examined later.

If an individual has a net capital gain for the year under § 1222(11) (that is, an excess of net long term capital gain over net short term capital loss), then under § 1(h) the maximum tax on the net capital gain is 28%. Thus, the maximum tax on an individual's net capital gain is approximately 12 percentage points less than the 39.6% maximum tax on ordinary income. *See* § 1(a).

Under § 1201(a), corporations are subject to a maximum 35% tax on net capital gain. Thus, a corporation is subject to a maximum 35% tax on both ordinary income and capital gains.

The deduction for net capital losses is severely restricted both for corporations and individuals.

For corporations, capital losses are allowed only to the extent of capital gains. *See* § 1211(a). For taxpayers other than corporations, capital losses are allowed only to the extent of gains from such transactions plus $3,000 for each year. *See* § 1211(b).

Section 1212(a) provides that corporations can generally carry a net capital loss for a year back 3 years and forward 5 years, and § 1212(b) provides that individuals can generally carry net capital losses forward indefinitely.

The Revenue Reconciliation Act of 1993 amended § 1202 to provide for a 50% exclusion for gain from certain small business stock and added § 1044 which provides for the rollover of gains from the sale of publicly traded securities into specialized small business investment companies.

G. SUBSTANCE OVER FORM CONCEPTS

1. Introduction

In *Gregory v. Helvering,* which is set out below, the Supreme Court said:

> The legal right of a taxpayer to decrease the amount of what would otherwise be his taxes, or altogether avoid them, by means which the law permits, cannot be doubted.

Thus, taxpayers may search for legal ways to reduce or eliminate their tax burdens. In doing so, taxpayers may structure a transaction so that it literally falls within a particular section of the Code although Congress may not have contemplated the transaction at the time of enactment of the provision. This could lead to a dispute between the taxpayer and the Commissioner concerning the scope of the particular provision.

In dealing with this type of issue, courts have developed several substance over form doctrines to assist in determining the proper tax treatment of a transaction.

The substance over form doctrines most applicable to business transactions are:

1. The business purpose doctrine,
2. The conduit treatment (or *Court Holding*) doctrine, and
3. The step transaction doctrine.

The following cases illustrate the application of these doctrines. Although all of these cases deal with a section of the law that has been repealed, the principles discussed still have vitality in a variety of contexts.

2. *The Business Purpose Doctrine*

GREGORY v. HELVERING

Supreme Court of the United States, 1935.
293 U.S. 465, 55 S.Ct. 266, 79 L.Ed. 596.

MR. JUSTICE SUTHERLAND delivered the opinion of the Court.

Petitioner in 1928 was the owner of all the stock of United Mortgage Corporation. That corporation held among its assets 1,000 shares of the Monitor Securities Corporation. For the sole purpose of procuring a transfer of these shares to herself in order to sell them for her individual profit, and, at the same time, diminish the amount of income tax which would result from a direct transfer by way of dividend, she sought to bring about a "reorganization" under section 112(g) of the Revenue Act of 1928, c. 852, 45 Stat. 791, 816, 818, 26 USCA § 2112(g), set forth later in this opinion. To that end, she caused the Averill Corporation to be organized under the laws of Delaware on September 18, 1928. Three days later, the United Mortgage Corporation transferred to the Averill Corporation the 1,000 shares of Monitor stock, for which all the shares of the Averill Corporation were issued to the petitioner. On September 24, the Averill Corporation was dissolved, and liquidated by distributing all its assets, namely, the Monitor shares, to the petitioner. No other business was ever transacted, or intended to be transacted, by that company. Petitioner immediately sold the Monitor shares for $133,-333.33. She returned for taxation, as capital net gain, the sum of $76,007.88, based upon an apportioned cost of $57,325.45. Further details are unnecessary. It is not disputed that if the interposition of the so-called reorganization was ineffective, petitioner became liable for a much larger tax as a result of the transaction.

The Commissioner of Internal Revenue, being of opinion that the reorganization attempted was without substance and must be disregarded, held that petitioner was liable for a tax as though the United corporation had paid her a dividend consisting of the amount realized from the sale of the Monitor shares. In a proceeding before the Board of Tax Appeals, that body rejected the commissioner's view and upheld that of petitioner. 27 B.T.A. 223. Upon a review of the latter decision, the Circuit Court of Appeals sustained the commissioner and reversed the board, holding that there had been no "reorganization" within the meaning of the statute. 69 F.(2d) 809. Petitioner applied to this court for a writ of certiorari, which the government, considering the question one of importance, did not oppose. We granted the writ.

Section 112 of the Revenue Act of 1928 [now § 1001] deals with the subject of gain or loss resulting from the sale or exchange of property. Such gain or loss is to be recognized in computing the tax, except as provided in that section. The provisions of the section, so far as they are pertinent to the question here presented, follow:

"Sec. 112 * * * (g) *Distribution of Stock on Reorganization.* If there is distributed, in pursuance of a plan of reorganization, to a shareholder in a corporation a party to the reorganization, stock or securities in such corporation or in another corporation a party to the reorganization, without the surrender by such shareholder of stock or securities in such a corporation, no gain to the distributee from the receipt of such stock or securities shall be recognized. * * *

"(i) *Definition of Reorganization.* As used in this section * * *

"(1) The term 'reorganization' means * * * (B) a transfer by a corporation of all or a part of its assets to another corporation if immediately after the transfer the transferor or its stockholders or both are in control of the corporation to which the assets are transferred. * * *" 26 USCA § 2112(g), (i)(1).

It is earnestly contended on behalf of the taxpayer that since every element required by the foregoing subdivision (B) is to be found in what was done, a statutory reorganization was effected; and that the motive of the taxpayer thereby to escape payment of a tax will not alter the result or make unlawful what the statute allows. It is quite true that if a reorganization in reality was effected within the meaning of subdivision (B), the ulterior purpose mentioned will be disregarded. The legal right of a taxpayer to decrease the amount of what otherwise would be his taxes, or altogether avoid them, by means which the law permits, cannot be doubted. * * * But the question for determination is whether what was done, apart from the tax motive, was the thing which the statute intended. The reasoning of the court below in justification of a negative answer leaves little to be said.

When subdivision (B) speaks of a transfer of assets by one corporation to another, it means a transfer made "in pursuance of a plan of reorganization" (section 112(g)) of corporate business; and not a transfer of assets by one corporation to another in pursuance of a plan having no relation to the business of either, as plainly is the case here. Putting aside, then, the question of motive in respect of taxation altogether, and fixing the character of the proceeding by what actually occurred, what do we find? Simply an operation having no business or corporate purpose—a mere device which put on the form of a corporate reorganization as a disguise for concealing its real character, and the sole object and accomplishment of which was the consummation of a preconceived plan, not to reorganize a business or any part of a business, but to transfer a parcel of corporate shares to the petitioner. No doubt, a new and valid corporation was created. But that corporation was nothing more than a contrivance to the end last described. It was brought into existence for no other purpose; it performed, as it was intended from the beginning it should perform, no other function. When that limited function had been exercised, it immediately was put to death.

In these circumstances, the facts speak for themselves and are susceptible of but one interpretation. The whole undertaking, though conducted according to the terms of subdivision (B), was in fact an elaborate and devious form of conveyance masquerading as a corporate reorganization, and nothing else. The rule which excludes from consideration the motive of tax avoidance is not pertinent to the situation, because the transaction upon its face lies outside the plain intent of the statute. To hold otherwise would be to exalt artifice above reality and to deprive the statutory provision in question of all serious purpose.

Judgment affirmed.

Note

The type of transaction in *Gregory* is known generally as a spin-off, that is, a corporation puts part of its assets into a new corporation and then spins off the new corporation to its shareholders. Mrs. Gregory was hoping for tax-free treatment for her spin-off so that she could get capital gain on the subsequent liquidation and sale of the spun-off assets (the Monitor shares).

The Court held that although she had literally complied with the statute, she had received a mere dividend taxable as ordinary income rather than a tax-free spin-off.

A spin-off can be done on a tax-free basis under the current statute provided all of the conditions of §§ 368(a)(1)(D) and 355 are satisfied. (*See* Chapter 24.) One of the conditions in § 355 is that the transaction "not be used principally as a device for the distribution of earnings and profits * * *." *See* § 355(a)(1)(B).

3. *The Conduit Treatment (or Court Holding) Doctrine*

a. *Liquidating Distribution Followed by Sale by Shareholders, Treated as Sale by Corporation*

COMMISSIONER v. COURT HOLDING CO.

Supreme Court of the United States, 1945.
324 U.S. 331, 65 S.Ct. 707, 89 L.Ed. 981.

Mr. Justice Black delivered the opinion of the Court.

An apartment house, which was the sole asset of the respondent corporation, was transferred in the form of a liquidating dividend to the corporation's two shareholders. They in turn formally conveyed it to a purchaser who had originally negotiated for the purchase from the corporation. The question is whether the Circuit Court of Appeals properly reversed the Tax Court's conclusion that the corporation was taxable under Section 22 of the Internal Revenue Code for the gain which accrued from the sale. The answer depends upon whether the findings of the Tax Court that the whole transaction showed a sale by the corporation rather than by the stockholders were final and binding upon the Circuit Court of Appeals.

It is unnecessary to set out in detail the evidence introduced before the Tax Court or its findings. Despite conflicting evidence, the following findings of the Tax Court are supported by the record:

The respondent corporation was organized in 1934 solely to buy and hold the apartment building which was the only property ever owned by it. All of its outstanding stock was owned by Minnie Miller and her husband. Between October 1, 1939 and February, 1940, while the corporation still had legal title to the property, negotiations for its sale took place. These negotiations were between the corporation and the lessees of the property, together with a sister and brother-in-law. An oral agreement was reached as to the terms and conditions of sale, and on February 22, 1940, the parties met to reduce the agreement to writing. The purchaser was then advised by the corporation's attorney that the sale could not be consummated because it would result in the imposition of a large income tax on the corporation. The next day the corporation declared a "liquidating dividend," which involved complete liquidation of its assets, and surrender of all outstanding stock. Mrs. Miller and her husband surrendered their stock, and the building was deeded to them. A sale contract was then drawn, naming the Millers individually as vendors, and the lessees' sister as vendee, which embodied substantially the same terms and conditions previously agreed upon. One thousand dollars, which a month and a half earlier had been paid to the corporation by the lessees, was applied in part payment of the purchase price. Three days later, the property was conveyed to the lessees' sister.

The Tax Court concluded from these facts that, despite the declaration of a "liquidating dividend" followed by the transfers of legal title, the corporation had not abandoned the sales negotiations; that these were mere formalities designed "to make the transaction appear to be other than what it was", in order to avoid tax liability. The Circuit Court of Appeals drawing different inferences from the record, held that the corporation had "called off" the sale, and treated the stockholders' sale as unrelated to the prior negotiations.

There was evidence to support the findings of the Tax Court, and its findings must therefore be accepted by the courts. * * * On the basis of these findings, the Tax Court was justified in attributing the gain from the sale to respondent corporation. The incidence of taxation depends upon the substance of a transaction. The tax consequences which arise from gains from a sale of property are not finally to be determined solely by the means employed to transfer legal title. Rather, the transaction must be viewed as a whole, and each step, from the commencement of negotiations to the consummation of the sale, is relevant. A sale by one person cannot be transformed for tax purposes into a sale by another by using the latter as a conduit through which to pass title. To permit the true nature of a transaction to be disguised by mere formalisms, which exist solely to alter tax liabilities, would seriously impair the effective administration of the tax policies of Congress.

It is urged that respondent corporation never executed a written agreement, and that an oral agreement to sell land cannot be enforced in Florida because of the Statute of Frauds, Comp.Gen.Laws of Florida, 1927, vol. 3, Sec. 5779, F.S.A. § 725.01. But the fact that respondent corporation itself never executed a written contract is unimportant, since the Tax Court found from the facts of the entire transaction that the executed sale was in substance the sale of the corporation. The decision of the Circuit Court of Appeals is reversed, and that of the Tax Court affirmed.

It is so ordered.

Reversed.

Questions

What are the tax stakes in *Court Holding*? What are the controlling facts? Would the transaction in *Court Holding* have taken place if the Supreme Court had found in *General Utilities* (*see* Sec. 1.3.D.) that a distribution of property is a realization event? The *General Utilities* doctrine was repealed by the Tax Reform Act of 1986. *See* §§ 311 and 336 and Chapters 4 and 9. What result in *Court Holding* under the law today?

b. *Liquidating Distribution Followed by Sale by Shareholders Held to Be Bona Fide*

UNITED STATES v. CUMBERLAND PUBLIC SERVICE CO.

Supreme Court of the United States, 1950.
338 U.S. 451, 70 S.Ct. 280, 94 L.Ed. 251.

MR. JUSTICE BLACK delivered the opinion of the Court.

A corporation selling its physical properties is taxed on capital gains resulting from the sale. There is no corporate tax, however, on distribution of assets in kind to shareholders as part of a genuine liquidation. The respondent corporation transferred property to its shareholders as a liquidating dividend in kind. The shareholders transferred it to a purchaser. The question is whether, despite contrary findings by the Court of Claims, this record requires a holding that the transaction was in fact a sale by the corporation subjecting the corporation to a capital gains tax.

Details of the transaction are as follows. The respondent, a closely held corporation, was long engaged in the business of generating and distributing electric power in three Kentucky counties. In 1936 a local cooperative began to distribute Tennessee Valley Authority power in the area served by respondent. It soon became obvious that respondent's Diesel-generated power could not compete with TVA power, which respondent had been unable to obtain. Respondent's shareholders, realizing that the corporation must get out of the power business unless it obtained TVA power, accordingly offered to sell all the corporate stock to the cooperative, which was receiving such power. The cooperative refused to buy the stock, but countered with an offer to buy from the corporation its transmission and distribution equipment. The corporation rejected the offer because it would have been compelled to pay a heavy capital gains tax. At the same time the shareholders, desiring to save payment of the corporate capital gains tax, offered to acquire the transmission and distribution equipment and then sell to the cooperative. The cooperative accepted. The corporation transferred the transmission and distribution systems to its shareholders in partial liquidation. The remaining assets were sold and the corporation dissolved. The shareholders then executed the previously contemplated sale to the cooperative.

Upon this sale by the shareholders, the Commissioner assessed and collected a $17,000 tax from the corporation on the theory that the shareholders had been used as a mere conduit for effectuating what was really a corporate sale. Respondent corporation brought this action to recover the amount of the tax. The Court of Claims found that the method by which the stockholders disposed of the property was avowedly chosen in order to reduce taxes, but that the liquidation and dissolution genuinely ended the corporation's activities and existence. The court also found that at no time did the corporation plan to make the sale itself. Accordingly it found as a fact that the sale was made by the shareholders rather than the corporation, and entered judgment for respondent. One judge dissented, believing that our opinion in *Comm'r v. Court Holding Co.*, 324 U.S. 331, 65 S.Ct. 707, 708, 89 L.Ed. 567, required a finding that the sale had been made by the corporation. Certiorari was granted, 338 U.S. 846, 70 S.Ct. 88, to clear up doubts arising out of the *Court Holding Co.* case.

Our *Court Holding Co.* decision rested on findings of fact by the Tax Court that a sale had been made and gains realized by the taxpayer corporation. * * * The Tax Court found that the corporation never really abandoned its sales negotiations, that it never did dissolve, and that the sole purpose of the so-called liquidation was to disguise a corporate sale through use of mere formalisms in order to avoid tax liability. The Circuit Court of Appeals took a different view of the evidence. In this Court the Government contended that whether a liquidation distribution was genuine or merely a sham was traditionally a question of fact. We agreed with this contention, and reinstated the Tax Court's findings and judgment. Discussing the evidence which supported the findings of fact, we went on to say that "the incidence of taxation depends upon the substance of a transaction" regardless of "mere formalisms," and that taxes on a corporate sale cannot be avoided by using the shareholders as a "conduit through which to pass title."

This language does not mean that a corporation can be taxed even when the sale has been made by its stockholders following a genuine liquidation and dissolution. While the distinction between sales by a corporation as compared with distribution in kind followed by shareholder sales may be particularly shadowy and artificial when the corporation is closely held, Congress has chosen to recognize such a distinction for tax purposes. The corporate tax is thus aimed primarily at the profits of a going concern. This is true despite the fact that gains realized from corporate sales are taxed, perhaps to prevent tax evasions, even where the cash proceeds are at once distributed in liquidation. But Congress has imposed no tax on liquidating distributions in kind or on dissolution, whatever may be the motive for such liquidation. Consequently, a corporation may liquidate or dissolve without subjecting itself to the corporate gains tax, even though a primary motive is to avoid the burden of corporate taxation.

Here, on the basis of adequate subsidiary findings, the Court of Claims has found that the sale in question was made by the stockholders rather than the corporation. The Government's argument that the shareholders acted as a mere "conduit" for a sale by respondent corporation must fall before this finding. The subsidiary finding that a major motive of the shareholders was to reduce taxes does not bar this conclusion. Whatever the motive and however relevant it may be in determining whether the transaction was real or a sham, sales of physical properties by shareholders following a genuine liquidation distribution cannot be attributed to the corporation for tax purposes.

The oddities in tax consequences that emerge from the tax provisions here controlling appear to be inherent in the present tax pattern. For a corporation is taxed if it sells all its physical properties and distributes the cash proceeds as liquidating dividends, yet is not taxed if that property is distributed in kind and is then sold by the shareholders. In both instances the interest of the shareholders in the business has been transferred to the purchaser. Again, if these stockholders had succeeded in their original effort to sell all their stock, their interest would have been transferred to the purchasers just as effectively. Yet on such a transaction the corporation would have realized no taxable gain.

Congress having determined that different tax consequences shall flow from different methods by which the shareholders of a closely held corporation may dispose of corporate property, we accept its mandate. It is for the trial court, upon consideration of an entire transaction, to determine the factual category in which a particular transaction belongs. Here as in the *Court Holding Co.* case we accept the ultimate findings of fact of the trial tribunal. Accordingly the judgment of the Court of Claims is affirmed.

Affirmed.

Questions

What are the important factual differences between *Court Holding* and *Cumberland Service?* What result in *Cumberland Service* if the Supreme Court had found in *General Utilities* that a distribution is a realization event? The *General Utilities* doctrine was repealed by the Tax Reform Act of 1986. See §§ 311 and 336 and Chapters 4 and 9. What result in *Cumberland Service* under the law today?

4. Step Transaction Doctrine: Purchase of Stock Followed by Liquidation Treated as Purchase of Assets

KIMBELL–DIAMOND MILLING COMPANY v. COMMISSIONER

Tax Court of the United States, 1950.
14 T.C. 74, *affirmed* 187 F.2d 718 (5th Cir.1951), *cert. denied*
342 U.S. 827, 72 S.Ct. 50, 96 L.Ed. 626 (1951).

[Kimbell–Diamond Milling Company, the petitioner, purchased all the stock of Whaley Mill J. Elevator Co. and then immediately liquidated Whaley. Thus, after the stock acquisition and liquidation, Kimbell–Diamond held Whaley's assets. Kimbell–Diamond's position was that the two steps were separate and that, therefore, the liquidation of Whaley was governed by the predecessor of § 332, which applies to a liquidation of subsidiary corporation into parent corporation. If the transaction were governed by the predecessor of § 332, Kimbell–Diamond would take as its basis for the Whaley assets, Whaley's basis for those assets. *See* predecessor of § 334(b). The Commissioner argued that the two steps should be treated as an acquisition of assets and that Kimbell–Diamond's basis should be its cost of the stock.]

Petitioner argues that the acquisition of Whaley's assets and the subsequent liquidation of Whaley brings petitioner within the provisions of section 112(b)(6) [now § 332] and, therefore, by reason of section 113(a)(15) [now § 334(b)] petitioner's basis in these assets is the same as the basis in Whaley's hands. In so contending, petitioner asks that we treat the acquisition of Whaley's stock and the subsequent liquidation of Whaley as separate transactions. It is well settled that the incidence of taxation depends upon the substance of a transaction. *Commissioner v. Court Holding Co.*, 324 U.S. 331. It is inescapable from petitioner's minutes set out above and from the "Agreement and Program of Complete Liquidation" entered into between petitioner and Whaley, that the only intention petitioner ever had was to acquire Whaley's assets.

We think that this proceeding is governed by the principles of *Commissioner v. Ashland Oil & Refining Co.*, 99 Fed. (2d) 588, certiorari denied, 306 U.S. 661. In that case the stock was retained for almost a year before liquidation. Ruling on the question of whether the stock or the assets of the corporation were purchased, the court stated:

> The question remains, however, whether if the entire transaction, whatever its form, was essentially in intent, purpose and result, a purchase by Swiss of property, its several steps may be treated separately and each be given an effect for tax purposes as though each constituted a distinct transaction. * * * And without regard to whether the result is imposition or relief from taxation, the courts have recognized that where the essential nature of a transaction is the acquisition of property, it will be viewed as a whole, and closely related steps will not be separated either at the instance of the taxpayer or the taxing authority. * * *

* * *

We hold that the purchase of Whaley's stock and its subsequent liquidation must be considered as one transaction, namely, the purchase of Whaley's assets which was petitioner's sole intention. This was not a reorganization within section 112(b)(6), and petitioner's basis in these assets, both depreciable and nondepreciable, is, therefore, its cost, or $110,721.74 * * *

Note

Although the *Kimbell–Diamond* doctrine has been overridden by § 338 (*see* Sec. 9.5.), the principle enunciated in the case may apply in similar circumstances.

5. *Interrelationship Between Conduit Treatment, Step Transaction and Business Purpose Doctrines*

ESMARK, INC. v. COMMISSIONER

Tax Court of the United States, 1988.
90 T.C. 171, *affirmed* 886 F.2d 1318 (7th Cir.1989).

[Mobil arranged with Esmark to purchase the stock of Vickers, a subsidiary of Esmark pursuant to the following arrangement. First, Mobil made a tender offer for part of the stock of Esmark, a publicly-held corporation. Second, Mobil then transferred to Esmark the stock of Esmark it had purchased in the tender offer in exchange for the stock of Vickers. Thus, Esmark redeemed its stock held by Mobil in exchange for the Vickers stock. If the transaction was taxed in accordance with its form (*i.e.*, a tender offer followed by a redemption), then Esmark would not be taxed on the distribution of the stock of Vickers in the redemption from Mobil. As a result of the repeal of the *General Utilities* doctrine by the Tax Reform Act of 1986, this type of distribution now would be subject to tax. The Service challenged the transaction on a variety of grounds, including the following:]

* * *

Mobil as a Conduit

Respondent's fourth ground for disregarding Mobil's ownership of petitioner's shares is that Mobil was a mere "conduit." The issue raised by respondent is essentially the same as that raised in *Commissioner v. Court Holding Co.,* 324 U.S. 331 (1945), and *Cumberland Public Service Co. v. United States,* 338 U.S. 451 (1950).

* * * The existence of a prearrangement does not necessarily signify the presence of a conduit that is to be disregarded. In order to disregard an entity as a conduit, the entity must be a mere intermediary in a transaction where the true "obligation," legal or otherwise, runs between other parties.

* * *

The Step–Transaction Doctrine

Finally, respondent maintains that Mobil's ownership of the Esmark shares must be disregarded under the step-transaction doctrine. We recently described the step-transaction doctrine as another rule of substance over form that "treats a series of formally separate 'steps' as a single transaction if such steps are in substance integrated, interdependent, and focused toward a particular result." *Penrod v. Commissioner,* 88 T.C. 1415, 1428 (1987). Respondent contends that Mobil's acquisition and subsequent disposition of petitioner's shares were simply steps in an integrated transaction designed to result in Mobil's acquisition of Vickers and petitioner's redemption of its stock.

That Mobil's tender offer was but part of an overall plan is not in dispute. The existence of an overall plan does not alone, however, justify application of the step-transaction doctrine. Whether invoked as a result of the "binding commitment," "interdependence," or "end result" tests, the doctrine combines a series of individually meaningless steps into a single transaction. In this case, respondent has pointed to no meaningless or unnecessary steps that should be ignored.

Petitioner had two objectives: a disposition of its energy business and a redemption of a substantial portion of its stock. Three direct routes to these objectives were available:

First, petitioner could have distributed the Vickers stock to its shareholders in exchange for their shares. The shareholders could then have sold the Vickers stock for cash to interested buyers. See *Commissioner v. Court Holding Co.* and *Cumberland Public Service Co. v. United States, supra.*

Second, petitioner could have sold the Vickers stock for cash and then distributed the cash to its shareholders in exchange for their stock. As appears from our findings (pp. 176–177), however, Mobil might not have been the successful bidder.

Third, the parties could have proceeded as they did, with Mobil purchasing petitioner's stock in a tender offer and exchanging such stock for the Vickers stock. No route was more "direct" than the others. Each route required two steps, and each step involved two of three interested parties. Each route left petitioner, petitioner's shareholders, and the purchaser in the same relative positions. Faced with this choice, petitioner chose the path expected to result in the least tax.

Respondent proposes to recharacterize the tender offer/redemption as a sale of the Vickers shares to Mobil followed by a self-tender. This recharacterization does not simply combine steps; it invents new ones. Courts have refused to apply the step-transaction doctrine in this manner. * * *

* * *

III. Conclusion

Although much more might be written about each of respondent's attacks on the form of petitioner's transaction, we have refrained from doing so. Stripped to its essentials, this case is a rematch of the principles expressed in *Gregory v. Helvering,* 293 U.S. 465 (1935), the source of most "substance over form" arguments.

* * *

In *Gregory,* the taxpayer's transaction was not "the thing that the statute intended" because a reorganization, as that term was defined in the statute, did not in fact take place.

* * *

In this case, in contrast, there were no steps without independent function. Each of the steps—the purchase of petitioner's stock by Mobil and the redemption of that stock by petitioner—had permanent economic consequences. Mobil's tender offer was not a "mere device" having no business purpose; the tender offer was an essential element of petitioner's plan to redeem over 50 percent of its stock. Mobil's ownership, however transitory, must thus be respected, and if Mobil's ownership of petitioner's shares is respected, a "distribution with respect to * * * stock" in fact occurred.

* * *

H. CORPORATE ENTITY DOCTRINE

COMMISSIONER v. BOLLINGER

Supreme Court of the United States, 1988.
485 U.S. 340, 108 S.Ct. 1173, 99 L.Ed.2d 357.

JUSTICE SCALIA delivered the opinion of the Court.

Petitioner, the Commissioner of Internal Revenue, challenges a decision by the United States Court of Appeals for the Sixth Circuit holding that a corporation which held record title to real property as agent for the corporation's shareholders was not the owner of the property for purposes of federal income taxation. 807 F.2d 65 (1986). We granted certiorari, * * *.

I

Respondent Jesse C. Bollinger, Jr., developed, either individually or in partnership with some or all of the other respondents, eight apartment complexes in Lexington, Kentucky. [In order to obtain financing for the projects without violating the state usury laws, Bollinger formed a separate corporation for each project. A written agreement provided that the corporation would hold title to the project as the agent for Bollinger or the partnership that Bollinger formed to own and operate the project.]

The Commissioner of Internal Revenue disallowed the losses reported by respondents, on the ground that the standards set out in *National Carbide Corp. v. Commissioner,* 336 U.S. 422, 69 S.Ct. 726, 93 L.Ed. 779 (1949), were not met. The Commissioner contended that *National Carbide* required a corporation to have an arm's-length relationship with its shareholders before it could be recognized as their agent. Although not all respondents were shareholders of the corporation, the Commissioner took the position that the funds the partnerships disbursed to pay expenses should be deemed contributions to the corporation's capital, thereby making all respondents constructive stockholders. Since, in the Commissioner's view, the corporation rather than its shareholders owned the real estate, any losses sustained by the ventures were attributable to the corporation and not respondents. Respondents sought a redetermination in the United States Tax Court. The Tax Court held that the corporation was the agent of the partnerships and should be disregarded for tax purposes. On appeal, the United States Court of Appeals for the Sixth Circuit affirmed. We granted the Commissioner's petition for certiorari.

II

For federal income tax purposes, gain or loss from the sale or use of property is attributable to the owner of the property. * * *

The Commissioner contends, * * * that the normal indicia of agency cannot suffice for tax purposes when, as here, the alleged principals are the controlling shareholders of the alleged agent corporation. That, it asserts, would undermine the principle of *Moline Properties v. Commissioner,* 319 U.S. 436, 63 S.Ct. 1132, 87 L.Ed. 1499 (1943), which held that a corporation is a separate taxable entity even if it has only one shareholder who exercises total control over its affairs. * * *

* * * The parties have debated at length the significance of our opinion in *National Carbide Corp. v. Commissioner, supra.* In that case, three corporations that were wholly owned subsidiaries of another corporation agreed to operate their production plants as "agents" for the parent, transferring to it all profits except for a nominal sum. The subsidiaries reported as gross income only this sum, but the Commissioner concluded that they should be taxed on the entirety of the profits because they were not really agents. We agreed, reasoning first, that the mere fact of the parent's control over the subsidiaries did not establish the existence of an agency, since such control is typical of all shareholder-corporation relationships, and second, that the agreements to pay the parent all profits above a nominal amount were not determinative since income must be taxed to those who actually earn it without regard to anticipatory assignment. We acknowledged, however, that there was such a thing as "a true corporate agent ... of [an] owner-principal," and proceeded to set forth four indicia and two requirements of such status, the sum of which has become known in the lore of federal income tax law as the "six *National Carbide* factors":

> "[1] Whether the corporation operates in the name and for the account of the principal, [2] binds the principal by its actions, [3] transmits money received to the principal, and [4] whether receipt of income is attributable to the services of employees of the principal and to assets belonging to the principal are some of the relevant considerations in determining whether a true agency exists. [5] If the corporation is a true agent, its relations with its principal must not be dependent upon the fact that it is owned by the principal, if such is the case. [6] Its business purpose must be the carrying on of the normal duties of an agent."

Ibid. (footnotes omitted).

* * *

The Commissioner contends that the last two *National Carbide* factors are not satisfied in the present case. To take the last first: The

Commissioner argues that here the corporation's business purpose with respect to the property at issue was not "the carrying on of the normal duties of an agent," since it was acting not as the agent but rather as the owner of the property for purposes of Kentucky's usury law. We do not agree. It assuredly was not acting as the owner in fact, since respondents represented themselves as the principals to all parties concerned with the loans. Indeed, it was the lenders themselves who required the use of a corporate nominee. * * * In sum, we see no basis in either fact or policy for holding that the corporation was the principal because of the nature of its participation in the loans.

Of more general importance is the Commissioner's contention that the arrangements here violate the fifth *National Carbide* factor—that the corporate agent's "relations with its principal must not be dependent upon the fact that it is owned by the principal." The Commissioner asserts that this cannot be satisfied unless the corporate agent and its shareholder principal have an "arm's-length relationship" that includes the payment of a fee for agency services. The meaning of *National Carbide*'s fifth factor is, at the risk of understatement, not entirely clear. * * * We think the fifth *National Carbide* factor—so much more abstract than the others—was no more and no less than a generalized statement of the concern, expressed earlier in our own discussion, that the separate-entity doctrine of *Moline* not be subverted.

In any case, we decline to parse the text of *National Carbide* as though that were itself the governing statute. * * * It seems to us that the genuineness of the agency relationship is adequately assured, and tax-avoiding manipulation adequately avoided, when the fact that the corporation is acting as agent for its shareholders with respect to a particular asset is set forth in a written agreement at the time the asset is acquired, the corporation functions as agent and not principal with respect to the asset for all purposes, and the corporation is held out as the agent and not principal in all dealings with third parties relating to the asset. Since these requirements were met here, the judgment of the Court of Appeals is

Affirmed.

JUSTICE KENNEDY took no part in the consideration or decision of this case.

I. INTRODUCTION TO LIKE KIND EXCHANGES

1. *Introductory Note on § 1031 Like Kind Exchanges*

See § 1031.

Section 1031, the like kind exchange provision, had its genesis at the same time as the nonrecognition provision for transfers of property to controlled corporations, § 351, and the provisions governing corporate reorganizations, §§ 354 and 368. It is structured similarly to the corporate organization and reorganization provisions, and consequently, is an appropriate point of departure for the study of many corporate tax concepts.

The basic outline of § 1031 is described in part in Rev.Rul. 77-297, 1977-2 C.B. 304:

> Section 1031(a) of the Code provides that no gain or loss shall be recognized if property held for productive use in trade or business or for investment (not including stock in trade or other property held primarily for sale, nor stocks, bonds, notes, choses in action, certificates of trust or beneficial interest, [interest in partnerships], or other securities or evidence of indebtedness or interest) is exchanged solely for property of a like kind to be held either for productive use in trade or business or for investment.
>
> Section 1031(b) of the Code states that if an exchange would be within the provisions of subsection (a) if it were not for the fact that the property received in exchange consists not only of property permitted by such provisions to be received without the recognition of gain, but also of other property or money, then the gain, if any, to the recipient shall be recognized, but in an amount not in excess of the sum of such money and the fair market value of such other property.
>
> Section 1.1031(b)-1(c) of the Income Tax Regulations states that consideration received in the form of an assumption of liabilities is to be treated as "other property or money" for the purpose of section 1031(b) of the Code. However, if, on an exchange described in section 1031(b), each party to the exchange assumes a liability of the other party, then, in determining the amount of "other property or money" for purposes of section 1031(b), consideration given in the form of an assumption of liabilities shall be offset against consideration received in the form of an assumption of liabilities.
>
> The last sentence of § 1031(d) provides that any liability transferred is treated as money received by the taxpayer. The above cited regulations implement this provision.
>
> Under § 1031(e), no loss is recognized on a like kind exchange, and under § 1031(d), the basis of the property received is a substituted basis (*i.e.,* the basis of the property exchanged) decreased by the amount of any money received and increased by the amount of any gain or decreased by the amount of any loss recognized. The basis so determined is allocated among the properties received in accordance with their relative fair market values. The initial substituted basis will include any money paid.
>
> Section 1031(a)(3) provides rules for deferred like kind exchanges, and § 1031(f) deals with exchanges between related persons. These provisions are not addressed here.

2. *Introductory Problems on § 1031*

The following problems are designed to illustrate the basic elements of § 1031.

1. Corporation X owns a crane, which it purchased nine years ago for $100K in cash. X has taken $50K of depreciation on the crane, and the crane, therefore, has an adjusted basis of $50K. The current fair market value is $80K. X trades in the old crane for a new crane with a fair market value of $80K.

   (a) What is X's gain or loss realized?

   (b) What is X's gain or loss recognized, if any?

   (c) What is X's adjusted basis for the new crane?

2. Same as 1, except X trades the old crane for a new crane costing $200K, paying $120K in cash and receiving credit for the $80K fair market value of the old crane.

   (a) What is X's gain or loss realized?

   (b) What is X's gain or loss recognized, if any?

   (c) What is X's adjusted basis for the new crane?

3. Same as 1, except X trades the old crane valued at $80K for a new crane with a fair market value of $60K. X also receives $20K in cash.

   (a) What is X's gain or loss realized?

   (b) What is X's gain or loss recognized, if any?

   (c) What is X's adjusted basis for the new crane?

   (d) What is the character of the gain or loss recognized by X, if any? *See* §§ 1245 and 1231.

4. Same as 1, except the old crane with a fair market value of $80K and subject to a liability of $20K is exchanged in a one for one trade for a new crane with a fair market value of $60K.

   (a) What is X's gain or loss realized? *See* § 1031(d) (last sentence) and § 1.1031(d)-2.

   (b) What is X's gain or loss recognized, if any?

   (c) What is X's adjusted basis for the new crane?

   (d) What is the character of the gain or loss recognized by X, if any?

5. Same as 4, except the new crane received by X has a fair market value of $80K and is subject to a liability of $20K.

   (a) What is X's gain or loss realized? *See* § 1031(d) (last sentence) and § 1.1031(d)-2.

   (b) What is X's gain or loss recognized, if any?

   (c) What is X's adjusted basis for the new crane?

(d) What is the character of the gain or loss recognized by X, if any?

6. In general, what is the treatment to the crane dealer that swapped cranes with X?

J. ETHICAL CONSIDERATIONS IN RENDERING TAX ADVICE ON BUSINESS TRANSACTIONS

FREDERIC G. CORNEEL, GUIDELINES TO TAX PRACTICE SECOND

43 Tax Lawyer 297, 311–314 (1990).*

[Set out below are suggested guidelines to be followed in providing tax advice on business transactions.]

VI. Tax Planning

A. Complexities of Tax Law

Tax law has grown to the point where no one can possibly know all of the rules and approaches to various business and personal planning problems. Research, continuing education, the use of checklists, and consultation with others are all essential to prevent harm to our clients and malpractice exposure to the firm. We should not hesitate to suggest to the client consultation with experts outside our office whenever that appears in the client's best interest.

B. The Interest of Clients and Others

In tax planning we seek to assist our clients, within the limits of the law, to achieve their personal and economic objectives at the least tax cost.

1. We are likely to do our best planning if before turning to the legal technicalities, we seek to obtain a clear understanding of the "big picture"—for example, the overall strategic planning goals of the client—with which the tax plan should be consistent.

2. Frequently a form of transaction chosen by our client will have tax consequences for those with whom he is transacting business. Examples are situations where our client is borrowing or lending money, buying or selling a business, acting as franchisor or franchisee, etc. While as a matter of professional ethics our responsibility to non-clients may be limited to recommending representation by counsel, we should generally consider the tax consequences for all concerned, so that the client can make an informed choice that takes into account the resulting tax benefits and burdens of all.

3. We must remember that in addition to the client who pays us, others may rely on our advice. Examples are investors in a partnership promoted by our client; both husband and wife for whom we are preparing estate plans, even though only one will pay for our services;

---

* Copyright © 1990 American Bar Association. Reprinted by permission of the American Bar Association.

employees of a corporate client who rely on our advice as to the tax consequences of a compensation plan; and many more. In appropriate cases, we should recommend that they consult with another counsel or adviser. In all events, any written advice to clients should be worded so that it will not confuse or mislead non-clients who are likely to rely on it.

C. Plans Must Be Conditioned on Compliance with Tax Law

A tax plan should not be suggested without taking into consideration how the transaction should be reported and what the consequences of an audit of the return are likely to be. We will not suggest and we should counsel against plans that are bound to fail if all of the facts become known to the Service. We will not participate in transactions entirely lacking in economic substance and intended solely to conceal or mislead.

1. It is unethical to assist the client in the preparation of evidence designed to mislead the Service, such as a bill to a corporate client that includes, without disclosing, the cost of personal services to the owner of the corporation.[48] On the other hand, it is entirely proper to advise clients on the best ways of documenting legitimate positions.

2. At times the client in ignorance of the tax law has taken steps resulting in adverse tax consequences or has failed to take steps to prevent such consequences. It is not unethical to make every effort to correct this result, provided that this can be done without destruction of existing documents, backdating of new documents or other steps intended to mislead the Service as to what in fact happened.

D. Borderline Plans

We should remember that our objective in tax planning is to produce a good tax plan, a plan that works. A plan that is not sustained on audit or by litigation was not a good plan, no matter how brilliantly conceived, unless the client desired to consummate the transaction despite the possibility or probability of adverse tax consequences. The decision whether to risk the adverse consequences of borderline plans should be the client's, based upon our advice.

Clients are less well-informed than we are as to whether a proposed plan involves ethical but risky "skating on thin ice" or whether it involves "walking on water," that is, a breach of law. We must make the difference clear to them, and explain that being on the right side of this line is vital to our working with them on their tax plans. Lawyers' lectures to clients on morality are likely to be resented and useless, but clients can understand that we do not want to jeopardize continuing to make our living in our accustomed way. Further, it is often helpful to tell clients that if they do something clearly wrong, they can never

---

48. ABA Comm. on Ethics and Professional Responsibility, Informal Op. 1517 (1988), superseding Informal Op. 1494 (1982), requires disclosure on the corporate bill both of the personal services (without necessarily disclosing their nature) and the amount of the bill applicable to them.

thereafter be comfortable, that they will always be hostage to all who know or may come to know of their breach of law.

1. It would be unusual for us to suggest or recommend a plan which in our view would more likely than not result in negligence or similar penalties to the client if all the facts became known to the Service. Indeed, in planning, our standards are likely to be higher than in planning returns, since there will usually be opportunities in planning to reduce the risk of challenge.

2. Clients contemplating proceeding with a highly aggressive tax plan should make certain in advance that their tax return preparer will be willing to sign the return.

3. Sometimes we are blinded by our own brightness. If we have devised what we consider to be a particularly clever tax plan, we should remember the maxim, "If it is too good to be true, it isn't," and view each aspect and the overall plan through the eyes of an ambitious Service agent, determined to collect as much as possible. Finally, we should ask another experienced tax practitioner to review our plan and opinion carefully, both as to the technical details and as to the overall concept.

E. Tax Shelter Plans

We will not assist in the offering of a tax shelter program in which the tax benefits are important to the success of the investment unless it is substantially more likely than not that the material tax benefits will, in fact, be available to the investors. The degree of assurance we require as to the availability of the tax benefits depends upon the importance of the tax benefits to the success of the investment.[50]

1. We should decline to participate in a tax opinion on a shelter program unless this firm also handles the balance of the legal work or has confidence in the other counsel involved and has adequate opportunity to explore any matters considered potentially troublesome. Familiarity with all of the facts is vital to such an opinion.

F. Following Up

A perfectly good tax plan may be spoiled in its implementation: there may be a failure to execute the proper documents, to make a timely filing of notices or elections, or to pay the amount necessary to avoid a gift or a dividend. We should make every effort to have our engagement in a tax planning matter also cover the implementation.

The desirability of assuring proper implementation of a plan that we helped create is very different from assuming any obligation to advise with respect to future changes in the law that may have a bearing on plans we have devised or on the repetition in future years of acts that we have previously approved. Most clients understand that nothing is less

---

50. ABA Comm. on Ethics and Professional Responsibility, Formal Op. 346 (rev. 1982), and 31 C.F.R. § 10.33 (1988), set forth ethical guidance for tax shelter opinions. Although they authorize "negative opinions," this firm will not undertake representation in such offerings.

constant than the tax law and that what is right today may be wrong tomorrow. But it is a truth worth repeating both to our clients and ourselves.

§ 1.4 SELECTED REFERENCES

A companion volume Samuel C. Thompson, Jr., *Taxable and Tax-Free Mergers, Acquisitions, and LBOs* (West Publishing 1994), addresses in greater detail the various forms of acquisitions.

For a discussion of the taxation of corporations, partnerships and S corporations, see *Federal Taxation of Business Enterprises, supra* note 1, and Bureau of National Affairs, Inc. (BNA), *Tax Management Portfolio Series: U.S. Income Series*. The BNA service contains separate books (portfolios) dealing with many of the topics addressed here, such as Portfolio 343–2d, *Corporate Stock Redemptions*. See also Commerce Clearing House, *Tax Transactions Library*.

For a comprehensive treatment of the taxation of corporations and shareholders see Boris I. Bittker and James S. Eustice, *Federal Income Taxation of Corporations and Shareholders* (5th Ed.1987) [hereinafter "Bittker and Eustice, *Corporations* "].

For a comprehensive treatment of corporate acquisitions and related transactions see Martin D. Ginsburg and Jack S. Levin, *Mergers, Acquisitions and Leveraged Buyouts,* (CCH, Tax Transactions Library, 1992) [hereinafter "Ginsburg and Levin, *Mergers* "], and Practicing Law Institute, *Tax Strategies for Corporate Acquisitions, Dispositions, Financings, Joint Ventures, Reorganizations and Restructurings* (1992) [hereinafter "PLI, *Tax Strategies* "]. *Tax Strategies* is published annually, and is a good source for current developments.

For a comprehensive treatment of consolidated returns, see Fred W. Peel, *Consolidated Tax Returns* (3rd Ed.1990) [hereinafter "Peel, *Consolidated Returns* "].

For a discussion of many of the policy aspects of corporate taxation see The American Law Institute, *Federal Income Tax Project Subchapter C* (1980) [hereinafter "*ALI 1980 Subchapter C Study*"]; The American Law Institute, *Federal Income Tax Project, Reporter's Study Draft* (1989) [hereinafter "*ALI 1989 Subchapter C Study*"]; The American Law Institute, *Federal Income Tax Project, Integration of Individual and Corporate Income Taxes* (Reporter's Study) (1993) [hereinafter "*ALI 1993 Integration Study*"]; and U.S. Treasury Department Report, *Integration of Individual and Corporate Tax Systems,* (1992) [hereinafter "*Treasury Integration Study*"]. See also Samuel C. Thompson, Jr., *Reform of the Taxation of Mergers, Acquisitions and LBOs* (Carolina Academic Press, 1993) [hereinafter "Thompson, *Reform of The Taxation of Mergers, Acquisitions and LBOs*"]. Chapter 1 of this last referred to book cites much of the literature dealing with the taxation of corporate mergers and acquisitions.

Chapter 2

ORGANIZATION OF C CORPORATIONS

§ 2.1 SCOPE

This chapter focuses on various issues that can arise upon the formation of a C corporation. Most of the issues covered here also apply upon the organization of an S corporation. Sec. 2.2 examines incorporation transactions that do not involve the transfer to the corporation of liabilities, and Sec. 2.3 examines such transactions in which liabilities are transferred to the corporation. Sec. 2.4 explores the scope of the requirement under § 351 that "property" be contributed to the corporation, and Sec. 2.5 explores the requirement under § 351 that the transferors be in "control" of the corporation.

Sec. 2.6 considers the impact of § 482 (the arm's length standard) on incorporation transactions, and Sec. 2.7 examines the impact of the business purpose and step transaction doctrines. Sec. 2.8 illustrates the use of § 351 in the context of an acquisition of a publicly-held firm. Sec. 2.9 looks at various issues that arise with contributions to the capital of a corporation. Finally, Sec. 2.10 considers the policy implications of the control requirement in § 351.

These issues are also addressed in Chapter 3 of *Federal Taxation of Business Enterprises, supra* Chapter 1, note 1 and in Chapter 3 of Bittker and Eustice, *Corporations, supra* Sec. 1.4.

§ 2.2 TRANSFERS NOT INVOLVING LIABILITY ASSUMPTIONS

A. INTRODUCTORY NOTE ON § 351: FEDERAL INCOME TAX CONSEQUENCES ON THE FORMATION OF A CORPORATION

See §§ 351, 358, 362, 1032 and 118.

Section 351(a), the provision governing contributions to both subchapter C and S corporations, provides an exception to the general rule of recognition in § 1001:

> No gain or loss shall be recognized if property is transferred to a corporation by one or more persons solely in exchange for stock in such corporation and immediately after the exchange such person or persons are in control (as defined in section 368(c)) of the corporation.

The price of nonrecognition treatment is the requirement in § 358(a)(1) that the shareholder substitute as her basis for the stock received the adjusted basis of the property contributed (*i.e.*, a substituted basis).

The term "property" is not defined for purposes of § 351. The scope of the concept is determined by the case law and IRS pronouncements, which are examined in Section 2.4 below. The phrase "stock" is not defined in the Code. In general, the term refers to common or preferred stock without regard to particular characteristics.

Under § 351(a), only transferors in control singly or as a group can qualify for nonrecognition treatment on the receipt of stock. Control is defined in § 368(c) as ownership of "at least 80 percent of the total combined voting power of all classes of stock entitled to vote and at least 80 percent of the total number of shares of all other classes of stock of the corporation." The control must exist "immediately after" the exchange, and multiple transferors are counted together for purposes of determining whether the requisite control exists. Furthermore, if one person has control of a corporation she can make a contribution of property at any time and receive nonrecognition treatment. This control concept is explored further below in § 2.5.

From the corporation's side of the transaction, § 1032 provides that a corporation receives nonrecognition treatment on the issuance of stock in exchange for property, and § 118 provides that a corporation does not have income on the receipt of a contribution to capital. Contributions to capital are explored below in § 2.9. A corporation's basis for property received in a § 351(a) transaction is a carryover basis pursuant to § 362(a).

The general results on a contribution of property by control persons to a corporation in exchange solely for stock can be summarized as follows:

(1) The contributing shareholder does not recognize her potential gain or loss because § 351(a) provides an exception to the general rule of recognition.

(2) Pursuant to § 358(a)(1), the contributing shareholder substitutes as her basis in the stock received the adjusted basis of the property contributed, thus deferring any potential gain or loss. The stock received is "exchanged basis" property under § 7701(a)(44) because the basis of the stock is determined by reference to the basis of property contributed by the shareholder.

(3) Pursuant to § 1032, the corporation does not recognize gain or loss on the exchange of its stock for property.

(4) Pursuant to § 362(a), the corporation carries over as its basis in the contributed property the basis of the shareholders in such property. The property received is "transferred basis property" within § 7701(a)(43) because the corporation's basis for the property is determined by reference to the shareholder's basis for such property.[1]

In addition to the receipt of stock on the formation of a corporation, a shareholder may receive a distribution of cash or other property from the corporation. This could happen, for instance, if a 50–50 owned corporation is being formed and one shareholder is contributing cash and the other is contributing property that has a fair market value in excess of the cash. In such case, the shareholder who contributes the property may receive a concurrent distribution of cash ("boot") in order to equalize the contributions.

If boot is distributed in § 351 transactions, § 351(b)(1) carves out an exception to the nonrecognition rule. Section 351(b)(1) requires that the gain realized in the transaction be recognized to the extent of the boot received. Section 351(b)(2), however, provides that no loss is recognized. The distributing corporation recognizes gain on the distribution of any boot that is appreciated property. *See* §§ 351(f) and 311. The treatment of distributing corporations is addressed in Chapter 4.

A distribution of boot and any gain recognition to the shareholders modifies the general substituted basis rule under § 358(a) by giving the shareholder a basis for the stock equal to her substituted basis, minus the boot distributed, plus the gain recognized. *See* § 358(a)(1)(A) and (B). Under § 358(a)(2), the basis of any boot received is the fair market value of such property. Since cash has a basis equal to its face, no basis is allocated to cash. Also, under § 362(a), the corporation has a basis in the property received equal to the normal carryover basis plus any gain recognized. The boot gain rules are explored further in Sec. 2.2.E., F., and G.

If a corporation issues a debt instrument in the context of a § 351 transaction, the instrument is considered "other property" and is, therefore, subject to the boot rules. Prior to the Revenue Reconciliation Act of 1989 (RRA 1989), if a corporation issued securities (*i.e.*, long term debt instruments) in the context of a § 351 transaction, the securities qualified for nonrecognition treatment under § 351(a). After the RRA 1989, securities, like all other debt instruments, are treated as boot. The use of debt in capitalizing a corporation is examined in Chapter 3.

Under § 1223(1), the shareholder tacks to the stock received the holding period of any capital assets or § 1231 assets transferred to the corporation. Under § 1223(2), the corporation takes the shareholder's holding period for the property contributed.

---

1. Section 7701(a)(42) defines the term "substituted basis property" to mean property that is transferred basis property or exchanged basis property.

The operation of § 351 is illustrated in the following example: *A* owns equipment with a fair market value of $25K and a basis of $10K. *B* owns a manufacturing plant with a fair market value of $75K and a basis of $100K. *A* and *B* organize *C* Corporation, with *A* transferring to *C* the equipment for 25% of the *C* stock and *B* transferring to *C* the manufacturing plant for 75% of the stock. This transaction qualifies as a transfer of property in exchange for stock of a controlled corporation under § 351(a). Therefore, *A* does not recognize gain, and *B* does not recognize loss on the exchange of property for *C* stock. Under § 358(a), *A* takes a $10K substituted basis for her stock and *B* takes a $100K basis for her stock. Under § 362(a), *C* takes a $10K basis for the equipment and a $100K basis for the plant.

B. INTRODUCTORY PROBLEMS ON § 351(a) AND (b)

See §§ 358(a), 1032, 362(a), 368(c) and 1223(1) and (2).

1. Individuals *A* and *B*, both cash basis, calendar year taxpayers are planning to organize a C corporation, *X*, to engage in the operation of a resort on Virginia Beach. *A* will be contributing to *X* a tract of beach front and *B* will be contributing $200K of cash to be used in the construction of a hotel. The land has a current fair market value of $200K and *A*'s adjusted basis is $100K. *A* acquired the land several years ago. *X* will issue to each of *A* and *B* 100 shares of no par voting common stock in exchange for the property contributed. Consequently, there will be 200 common shares outstanding with a total initial value of $400K.

(a) What result to *A* and *B* under the general rules of § 1001?

(b) What result to *A* and *B* under § 351(a)? What are the basic elements of a § 351(a) transaction?

(c) What are *A*'s and *B*'s bases under § 358(a) for the stock received?

(d) What result to *X* from the receipt of the property and the issuance of the stock? *See* § 1032; *see also* § 118.

(e) What is *X*'s basis under § 362(a) for the property received?

(f) What are *A*'s and *B*'s holding periods for the stock received and *X*'s holding period for property received? *See* § 1223(1) and (2).

(g) In general, what result if *X* sells the land? Suppose *A* and *B* sell their stock?

2. The facts are the same as in 1., except the value of *A*'s tract of land is $210K, and in order to equalize the contributions of the two shareholders, *X*, as part of the transaction, distributes to *A* $10K ("boot") of the $200K of cash contributed by *B*.

(a) What result to *A* and *B* under § 351(a) and (b)?

(b) What are *A*'s and *B*'s bases under § 358(a) for the stock received?

(c) What result to X from the issuance of the stock and the distribution of the money? *See* §§ 1032 and 311.

(d) What is X's basis under § 362(a) for the property received?

(e) What are A's and B's holding periods for the stock received and X's holding period for the property received? *See* § 1223(1) and (2).

(f) What has happened here from an economic standpoint?

(g) How might this transaction be recharacterized?

3. The facts are the same as in 2. except A's adjusted basis for the tract is $220K.

Same questions as in 2.(a)–(g). *See also* § 267(a)(1).

4. The facts are the same as in 2. except (i) instead of contributing $200K of cash, B contributed a $190K of cash and 100 shares of IBM stock which had a value of $10K, an adjusted basis of $5K, and a holding period of ten years, and (ii) in order to equalize the contributions of the shareholders, X distributed the IBM stock as boot to A.

(a) Same questions as in 2.(a)–(g). *See* §§ 351(f) and 311(b).

5. What are the similarities between § 1031, the like kind exchange provision, and § 351 with respect to nonrecognition treatment, boot gain and basis?

C. POTENTIAL FOR ASSIGNMENT OF TAX DETRIMENT OR BENEFIT IN A § 351 TRANSACTION

THOMPSON, TAX POLICY IMPLICATIONS OF CONTRIBUTIONS OF APPRECIATED AND DEPRECIATED PROPERTY TO PARTNERSHIPS, SUBCHAPTER C CORPORATIONS, AND SUBCHAPTER S CORPORATIONS IN EXCHANGE FOR OWNERSHIP INTERESTS

31 Tax L.Rev. 29, at 60–87 (1975), with permission.

INTRODUCTION

* * *

An investor who contributes [to a corporation in a § 351 transaction] property with a fair market value in excess of the adjusted basis will be shifting (assigning) to the other investors part of the tax liability in respect of the gain when the asset is disposed of. Also, if the asset is depreciable, the depreciation deduction will be lower than it otherwise would be. Both the potential tax liability and the reduced depreciation are referred to here as tax detriments to the other investors. On the other hand, an investor who contributes property with an adjusted basis in excess of fair market value will be shifting (assigning) to the other investors part of the benefit of the loss deduction to be realized on the disposition of the property. Further, if the asset is depreciable, the depreciation will be higher than it otherwise would be. Both the potential loss deduction and the higher depreciation charge are tax benefits to the other investors. The discussion here relates only to cases involving the assignment of tax detriment; that is, cases where the fair market value of the property contributed is higher than the adjusted basis. In general, the results in the case of the assignment of tax benefit are the opposite of those which obtain in case of the assignment of tax detriment.

Traditional assignments of income similar to those in *Lucas v. Earl* and *Helvering v. Horst* may occur on the formation of an enterprise. However, in all cases where the fair market value of the property contributed exceeds the adjusted basis there is a potential for an assignment of tax detriment without respect to whether the contribution is within the traditional assignment of income doctrine.

The problem with assignments of tax detriment can be particularly acute where there is a "midstream" contribution of assets of a going concern, such as a sole proprietorship. This could happen if, for instance, *A* and *B* formed the *AB* equal enterprise, and *A* contributed $50K in cash and *B* contributed accounts receivable earned by him as a sole proprietor with a $50K fair market value and a zero adjusted basis.

* * *

PREVENTION OF ASSIGNMENT OF TAX DETRIMENT AND BENEFIT

Subchapter C ... Provisions.

Section 351 in providing for nonrecognition and sections 358 and 362 in providing for a substituted and carryover basis, statutorily mandate assignments of tax detriment and benefit. * * *

In attacking the use of section 351 as a device for assignments of income, the Commissioner might attempt to circumscribe the breadth of the term "property" in section 351(a). If he is successful in asserting that the unripe income transferred is not property, then the transferor would receive immediate recognition in the amount of the stock received in exchange therefor. Also, the Commissioner might attempt to use the clear reflection of income provision of section 446(b) to tax income collected by the corporation to the transferor shareholder. Section 482 might be used to reallocate items between the corporation and shareholders. As an alternative to these statutory provisions, the Commissioner might attempt to use the judicial doctrines of assignment of income, tax benefit, business purpose or step transaction in order to reallocate items between shareholders and corporations. * * *

Adjustments in Business Bargain as a Way of Compensating for the Assignment of Tax Detriment. The assignment of tax detriment can be mitigated * * * by adjusting the business bargain. An estimate of the tax cost in respect of contributed property can be taken into account in valuing the property for purposes of determining the amount of each investor's capital contribution. For instance, the contributing investor's property might be valued at less than its actual fair market value for purposes of determining the amount of ownership interest he will receive in exchange for this property. The discount from the actual fair market value should equal the present value of the expected tax detriment the noncontributing investor will suffer in respect of such property. Alternatively, a compensating security interest or other ownership interest, such as preferred stock * * *, could be given to the noncontributing investors to compensate them for the expected tax detriment. * * *

Another option is to have the owner of the property with a disparate fair market value and adjusted basis sell it to the enterprise. * * *

* * *

Questions

1. In the *Introductory Problems on Section 351*, A contributed to X a beach property worth $200K with a basis of $100K, and B contributed cash of $200K. Each received one half of the X stock, which had a total value of $400K. Is it likely that the stock would have a value equal to the aggregate fair market values of the properties contributed? Assume that X abandoned the plan to develop a hotel and sold the beach front property for $200K. What would be the approximate tax liability resulting from the sale? How much cash would X have after paying the tax? What would the value of A's and B's stock be after the payment of the tax? Who would bear the ultimate burden of the tax? What concerns would you have if you were representing B, and how would you propose to solve them?

2. Assume that A formed X by himself, contributing the $200K beach front property. After the transfer, what is the potential gain in respect of (i) the property at the corporate level, and (ii) the stock held by A?

3. Does the lawyer have any particular ethical concerns in representing several prospective investors who are planning to organize a corporation?

4. After contributing the property to the corporation, A and B decide that the formation of the corporation was a bad idea. They, therefore, decide to liquidate the corporation and have the corporation distribute the beach front property to A and the cash to B. In general, what result to the corporation on the distribution? *See* § 336(a). What does the repeal of the *General Utilities* doctrine have to do with the distribution?

D. ALLOCATION OF SHAREHOLDER'S SUBSTITUTED BASIS AMONG CLASSES OF STOCK RECEIVED AND DETERMINATION OF HOLDING PERIOD

REVENUE RULING 85–164
1985–2 C.B. 117.

Issue

May a transferor determine the bases and holding periods of stock * * * received in a transfer under section 351 of the Internal Revenue Code by designating the specific property to be exchanged for particular stock * * *?

* * *

Law and Analysis

* * *

Section 358(a)(1) of the Code and section 1.358–1 of the Income Tax Regulations provide that in the case of an exchange to which section 351 applies in which only non-recognition property is received, the basis of all of the stock * * * received in the exchange shall be the same as the basis of all property exchanged therefor. Section 358(b)(1) directs that, under regulations prescribed by the Secretary, the basis determined under subsection (a)(1) shall be allocated among the properties permitted to be received without the recognition of gain or loss.

Section 1.358–2(a) of the regulations prescribes rules for the allocation of basis among nonrecognition property received in corporate reorganization exchanges governed by sections 354, 355, 356 and 371(b). In general, these rules allow limited tracing of the basis of old stock * * * into new only with respect to (i) persons who owned stock * * * of more than one class * * * before the exchange and (ii) corporate recapitalizations under section 368(a)(1)(E). In all other cases, including exchanges under section 351, section 1.358–2(b)(2) provides that the basis of property transferred shall be allocated among all the stock * * * received in proportion to the fair market values of the stock of each class. * * *

Section 1223(1) and section 1.1223–1(a) of the regulations require that, in determining the period for which a taxpayer has held property received in an exchange, there shall be included the period for which he held the property exchanged if (i) in the taxpayer's hands the property received has the same basis in whole or in part as the property exchanged and (ii) for exchanges after March 1, 1954, the property exchanged was at the time of exchange a capital asset as defined in section 1221 or property used in a trade or business as described in section 1231.

Rev.Rul. 62–140, 1962–2 C.B. 181, holds that a share of stock received in exchange for a debenture and a cash payment had a split holding period. The portion of each share received attributable to ownership of the debenture was treated as including the period for which the taxpayer held the debenture and the portion of each share received attributable to the cash payment was treated as held beginning with the data following the date of acquisition.

Rev.Rul. 68–55, 1968–1 C.B. 140, holds that when property is transferred to a corporation under section 351(a) of the Code each asset must be considered transferred separately in exchange for a proportionate share of each of the various categories of the total consideration received.

In the instant case, A formed Y by transferring all of the business assets of the sole proprietorship to Y in exchange solely for all of Y's stock * * * Y will continue to carry on the business that A conducted, and A will remain in control of Y. The transfer, therefore, is subject to section 351 of the Code, with the bases and holding periods of the Y stock * * * in the hands of A determined under sections 358 and 1223 of the Code respectively.

Holding

A may not determine the bases and holding periods of the Y stock * * * received by designating specific property to be exchanged for particular stock * * * Under sections 1.358–1 and 1.358–2(b)(2) of the regulations, the aggregate basis of the property transferred is allocated among the stock * * * received in proportion to the fair market values of each class. The holding period of the Y stock * * * received by A is determined by referring to the assets deemed exchanged for each portion of the stock * * *

* * *

E. TREATMENT OF OTHER PROPERTY (BOOT) RECEIVED BY SHAREHOLDER

1. *Receipt of Account Payable*

REVENUE RULING 80–228
1980–2 C.B. 115.

In the facts described below, did X corporation receive "other property" from Y corporation within the meaning of section 351(b) of the Internal Revenue Code?

Facts

X corporation operated its business in two entirely separate divisions ("Division 1" and "Division 2"), keeping a separate bank account and a separate set of books for each division. Each division also maintained an intracompany account in their respective books of account and transactions between the two divisions were recorded therein. For valid business reasons X organized a new corporation, Y. All of the assets of Division 2 were transferred by X to Y at net book value in exchange for all of the stock of Y. At the time of the transfer, the intracompany account payable due to Division 1 from Division 2 was 100x dollars. On its opening balance sheet Y listed an account payable to X of 100x dollars and X, conversely, listed an account receivable from Y of 100x dollars. Within one year after the transfer the account payable of Y was paid in full to X.

* * *

It is a well established principle of tax law that short-term notes and other evidences of indebtedness received in a reorganization constitute "other property." See *Cortland Specialty Co. v. Commissioner,* 60 F.2d 937 (2nd Cir.1932), XXII–1 C.B. 164 and *Pinellas Ice & Cold Storage Co. v. Commissioner,* 287 U.S. 462 (1933), XII–1 C.B. 161. [As a result of the deletion of securities from tax free treatment under § 351(a), long term debt instruments (*i.e.* securities) are now also treated as boot under § 351.]

When *Y* was organized as a separate corporation, and an account payable from *Y* to *X* was established (and, correlatively, an account receivable was reflected by *X* on its books), a real liability on the part of *Y* (and a real asset on the part of *X*) came into being. The intracompany account payable (and the intracompany account receivable) did not simply "carry over" to the books of *Y*. Instead, *X* received something other than merely the stock of *Y*.

In the instant case the account receivable to *X* from *Y* was a note or other evidence of indebtedness received by *X* in a section 351 transaction and it constituted "other property" for purposes of section 351(b) of the Code. This is due to the fact that the preincorporation intracompany accounts could not have given rise to a debtor-creditor relationship between *X* and *Y* because *X* could not, prior to incorporation of *Y*, have been liable for a debt to itself. The intracompany accounts were mere bookkeeping entries by *X*, a single corporation, to show the activities of separate divisions for internal accounting purposes.

In *Wham Construction Company, Inc. v. United States,* Civil No. 72–689 (D.S.C., Feb. 16, 1976), *aff'd* Civil No. 76–2047 (4th Cir.1979), on facts similar to those set forth above, the District Court, in holding for the taxpayer, determined that the account receivable represented a mere loan to the new subsidiary from the transferor for which the transferor received only a return of capital. In its affirmance of the District Court's decision in *Wham,* the Court of Appeals reasoned that where there was but one transferor and where the transferee corporation had no assets other than those derived from the transferor, it found it difficult to conceive of a concept wherein the transferor, as a result of the transaction, received anything which it did not have prior to the incorporation. However, the facts indicate that there was indisputably no borrowing from a bank by the new subsidiary, nor was there any loan from the transferor to the new subsidiary subsequent to the incorporation of the new subsidiary. The Court of Appeals also ignored the fact that prior to the incorporation of the new subsidiary there was no debt owned by it to the transferor.

Consequently, the Internal Revenue Service will not follow the decision of the United States Court of Appeals for the Fourth Circuit in *Wham.*

HOLDING

X did receive "other property" in the form of the 100*x* dollar account receivable and, pursuant to section 351(b) of the Code, must recognize gain in that amount.

2. *Installment Sale Treatment for Boot Debt*

If, in connection with a § 351 transaction, the corporation issues a debt instrument to a contributing shareholder, the instrument is treated as boot under § 351(b). Prior to the Revenue Reconciliation Act of 1989 (RRA 1989) corporate securities (*i.e.,* long term debt instruments) issued by a corporation in a § 351 transaction qualified for nonrecognition treatment. After the RRA 1989, securities, like all other debt instruments, issued in a § 351 transaction are treated as other property and are subject to the boot distribution rules of § 351(b).

Although debt instruments are treated as boot, such instruments may qualify for installment sale treatment under § 453. *See* Prop.Reg. § 1.453–1(f)(3). The statutory basis for this exception is found in § 453(f)(6), which specifically provides for § 453 treatment in § 1031 like kind exchanges and in § 356(a) reorganization transactions. The Treasury apparently feels that since § 351 is similar to these provisions, § 453 installment sale treatment should also be available in § 351(b) transactions.

The preamble to the Proposed Regulations gives the following explanation of this provision:

> These regulations also permit installment method reporting in certain nonrecognition exchanges (for example, section 351(b) exchanges) which are not explicitly dealt with in the Act. For these nonrecognition exchanges, the same basic rules apply: basis in the transferred property is first allocated to the nonrecognition property received, but not in excess of the fair market value of that property. Any excess basis is allocated to the installment note and any nonqualifying property. *See* Notice of Proposed Regulations, LR–186–80, (May 3, 1984).

This position is implemented in Prop.Reg. § 1.453–1(f)(3), which can be illustrated by the following example. Individual S transfers property with a fair market value of $100K to corporation C in exchange for $75K of C stock and a note from C that has both a face and a fair market value of $25K. The note has adequate stated interest and, therefore, no OID. The property contributed has a basis of $20K, and, therefore, S has an $80K realized gain. The transaction is within § 351(b) and, consequently, S recognizes $25K of her $80K gain, which is the portion of the gain represented by the note. However, under § 453, the $25K gain is only recognized as the payments are actually received on the note. S has a zero basis for the note and under § 358, S has a $20K basis for the C stock. As S recognizes gain on the receipt of payments on the note, C increases the basis of the note by the amount of the gain recognized. *See* § 362.

3. Allocation of Boot Among Assets Transferred

REVENUE RULING 68–55
1968–1 C.B. 140.

Advice has been requested as to the correct method of determining the amount and character of the gain to be recognized by Corporation X

under section 351(b) of the Internal Revenue Code of 1954 under the circumstances described below.

Corporation Y was organized by X and A, an individual who owned no stock in X. A transferred $20x$ dollars to Y in exchange for stock of Y having a fair market value of $20x$ dollars and X transferred to Y three separate assets and received in exchange stock of Y having a fair market value of $100x$ dollars plus cash of $10x$ dollars.

In accordance with the facts set forth in the table below if X had sold at fair market value each of the three assets it transferred to Y, the result would have been as follows:

	Asset I	*Asset II*	*Asset III*
Character of asset	Capital asset held more than 6 months.	Capital asset held not more than 6 months.	Section 1245 property.
Fair market value	$22x$	$33x$	$55x$
Adjusted basis	$40x$	$20x$	$25x$
Gain (loss)	($18x$)	$13x$	$30x$
Character of gain or loss	Long-term capital loss.	Short-term capital gain.	Ordinary income.

The facts in the instant case disclose that with respect to the section 1245 property the depreciation subject to recapture exceeds the amount of gain that would be recognized on a sale at fair market value. Therefore, all of such gain would be treated as ordinary income under section 1245(a)(1) of the Code.

* * *

The first question presented is how to determine the amount of gain to be recognized under section 351(b) of the Code. The general rule is that each asset transferred must be considered to have been separately exchanged. See the authorities cited in Revenue Ruling 67–192, C.B. 1967–2, 140, and in Revenue Ruling 68–23, page 144, this Bulletin, which hold that there is no netting of gains and losses for purposes of applying sections 367 and 356(c) of the Code. Thus, for purposes of making computations under section 351(b) of the Code, it is not proper to total the bases of the various assets transferred and to subtract this total from the fair market value of the total consideration received in the exchange. Moreover, any treatment other than an asset-by-asset approach would have the effect of allowing losses that are specifically disallowed by section 351(b)(2) of the Code.

The second question presented is how, for purposes of making computations under section 351(b) of the Code, to allocate the cash and stock received to the amount realized as to each asset transferred in the exchange. The asset-by-asset approach for computing the amount of gain realized in the exchange requires that for this purpose the fair market value of each category of consideration received must be separately allocated to the transferred assets in proportion to the relative fair market values of the transferred assets. See section 1.1245–4(c)(1) of the Income Tax Regulations which, for the same reasons, requires that for purposes of computing the amount of gain to which section 1245 of the Code applies each category of consideration received must be allocated to the properties transferred in proportion to their relative fair market values.

Accordingly, the amount and character of the gain recognized in the exchange should be computed as follows:

	Total	Asset I	Asset II	Asset III
Fair market value of asset transferred	$110x$	$22x$	$33x$	$55x$
Percent of total fair market value		20%	30%	50%
Fair market value of Y stock received in exchange	$100x$	$20x$	$30x$	$50x$
Cash received in exchange	$10x$	$2x$	$3x$	$5x$
Amount realized	$110x$	$22x$	$33x$	$55x$
Adjusted basis		$40x$	$20x$	$25x$
Gain (loss) realized		($18x$)	$13x$	$30x$

Under section 351(b)(2) of the Code the loss of $18x$ dollars realized on the exchange of Asset Number I is not recognized. Such loss may not be used to offset the gains realized on the exchanges of the other assets. Under section 351(b)(1) of the Code, the gain of $13x$ dollars realized on the exchange of Asset Number II will be recognized as short-term capital gain in the amount of $3x$ dollars, the amount of cash received. Under sections 351(b)(1) and 1245(b)(3) of the Code, the gain of $30x$ dollars realized on the exchange of Asset Number III will be recognized as ordinary income in the amount of $5x$ dollars, the amount of cash received.

Questions

What is X's basis for the Y stock received in the above ruling?

F. ALLOCATION OF CORPORATION'S § 362(a) CARRYOVER BASIS AMONG ASSETS RECEIVED

P.A. BIRREN & SON v. COMMISSIONER

United States Circuit Court of Appeals, Seventh Circuit, 1940.
116 F.2d 718.

[An undertaking business that operated as a sole proprietorship was transferred to the petitioner corporation in a § 351 transaction. The assets transferred included accounts receivable that had a zero basis to the transferor. The issue was whether the petitioner had income on collection of the receivables.]

The crux of the controversy is whether collections made during a taxable year by a taxpayer on the accrual basis, on accounts receivable taken from a predecessor's individual business, represents taxable income.

In this case the Board of Tax Appeals sustained the Commissioner in his contention that the $6,953.67 collected on the accounts receivable during the taxable period constituted income, found as a fact that Birren, the transferor, had the benefit of deductions for the cost of his sales in his tax returns filed for previous years, and that under this method the full amount collected on the accounts receivable would have been income taxable as such to the transferor when received.

Now, petitioner contends that the collections made during the taxable year should not be included in its income for the reason that all sales by the transferor were includable in his, Birren's taxable income in the year in which the sales occurred, and all accounts thus created have a basis of 100% of the amount thereof for the purpose of computing income upon any future collection thereof.

With this contention we cannot agree. It is clear that the petitioner acquired Birren's undertaking business, including accounts receivable, in exchange for 98% of the stock of P.A. Birren and Son, Inc., immediately upon the organization of the corporation.... Therefore, under the statute, no gain was recognized to Birren upon the transfer of his undertaking business to the corporation.

The answer to our problem has been suggested in *Portland Oil Co. v. Commissioner,* 1 Cir., 109 F.2d 479. In that case the Revenue Act of 1928 was under discussion, but what was said there applies as well to the 1932 Act. The court said (109 F.2d at page 487): "If a gain ... is not recognized in a transfer under Section 112(b)(5), the basis of the property to the transferee, by force of Section 113(a)(8) [now § 362(a)] becomes the same as it would be in the hands of the transferor," and in 109 F.2d at page 486, "the transferee steps into the shoes of the transferor so far as the tax basis for the property is concerned."

* * * [I]n the instant case the transferor's basis for the accounts receivable taken over by the petitioner was zero, and not 100%; consequently, the petitioner, standing in the shoes of the transferor, using the same basis, realized a gain upon the collection of the accounts receivable during the taxable year.

It follows that the decision of the Board of Tax Appeals must be affirmed.

G. SUMMARY PROBLEMS ON BOOT DISTRIBUTIONS: TREATMENT OF SHAREHOLDERS AND CORPORATION

1. Individual *A* is the sole shareholder of corporation *X*, the stock of which has a current fair market value of $20K. It is proposed that individual *B* become an 80 percent shareholder of *X* by contributing the following properties to *X*:

	Fair Market Value	Adjusted Basis	Original Cost
Equipment	$21K	$10K	$10.5K
IBM Stock	$21K	$10K	$10K
Building	$21K	$25K	$30K
Accounts receivable	$21K	–0–	–0–
Total	$84K	$45K	$50.5K

In order to make B's contributions equal the value of 80 percent of the outstanding stock of X after the contribution, X will distribute $4K of cash to B as part of the transaction.

(a) What is B's gain or loss realized and recognized?

(b) What is the character of B's gain or loss? See §§ 1221, 1222, 1231, 1239 and 1245.

(c) What is the basis and holding period of B's stock?

(d) What is X's basis and holding period for the assets?

2. Same as 1, except instead of distributing cash, X distributes to B its note with a fair market value and face amount of $4K. The note has adequate stated interest.

(a) Same as 1(a) to (c).

(b) What is B's basis and holding period for the note?

3. A is the sole shareholder of corporation X, an operating corporation that has a large amount of earnings and profits. A contributes to X IBM stock with a value of $10K and a basis of $1K and receives in exchange cash of $5K and X stock of $5K. What result to A under § 351? Is the cash properly treated as boot under § 351(b)? Should it be treated as a dividend under §§ 301 and 316? See § 1.351–2(d).

4. What result if, in a § 351 transaction, a shareholder receives a boot distribution consisting of contract rights, the value of which cannot be ascertained?

H. TREATMENT OF A CORPORATION UPON ISSUANCE OF ITS STOCK

See § 1032.

1. *Issuance of Stock for Property Not in a § 351 Transaction*

Section 1032(a) provides that a corporation does not recognize gain or loss on the issuance of stock for money or other property. This nonrecognition rule applies to all types of stock issuances, not just those within § 351. Also, it applies to the issuance of treasury stock (that is, stock that was repurchased from shareholders).

The regulations under § 1032 make it clear that the carryover basis rule of § 362 applies only to transactions coming within §§ 351 and 368 (the reorganization provision). If stock is issued for property in a transaction which is not within § 351 or § 368, the corporation takes a cost basis for the property under § 1012.

2. Issuance of Stock for Services

REVENUE RULING 62–217
1962–2 C.B. 59.

A corporation distributed shares of its treasury stock to its employees as compensation for services rendered. The cost basis of the treasury stock to the corporation was less than its fair market value on the date of the distribution to the employees. In filing its Federal income tax return for the taxable year, the corporation deducted the fair market value of the stock on the date of the distribution as a business expense.

In accordance with the nonrecognition of gain or loss provisions of section 1032(a) of the Internal Revenue Code of 1954 and section 1.1032–1(a) of the Income Tax Regulations, relating to the receipt by a corporation of money or other property in exchange for its own stock (including a transfer of shares as compensation for services), the corporation did not report gain upon the distribution of treasury stock.

Held, the fair market value of the treasury stock on the date of the distribution is deductible as a business expense in accordance with the provisions of section 162(a) of the Code. The nonrecognition of gain or loss provisions of section 1032(a) of the Code have no effect upon a business expense deduction that is otherwise allowable under section 162(a) of the Code.

Questions and Notes

1. Is this ruling sound? Is it a license for tax avoidance, or is it no different economically from an issuance by a corporation of its stock for cash, followed by the payment of the employees' salaries with the cash? What result if a corporation pays its employees with appreciated IBM stock? *See International Freighting Corp. v. Commissioner,* 135 F.2d 310 (2d Cir.1943).

2. The treatment of the shareholder upon the receipt of stock for services is considered in Sec. 2.4.

3. Section 1032 Not Applicable to Sub's Sale of Parent's Stock

REVENUE RULING 70–305
1970–1 C.B. 169.

S, a wholly owned domestic subsidiary of domestic corporation *P,* purchased shares of *P*'s stock on the open market and sold the stock to outside interests at a gain. *S* received dividends from *P* prior to the sale of the stock.

Held, the stock of *P* held by *S* is not treasury stock and the sale of such stock is not to be treated as a sale by the corporation of its own capital stock pursuant to the provisions of section 1032 of the Internal Revenue Code of 1954. The sale of such stock to outside interests is a transaction resulting in a gain or loss.

The dividends, however, will be treated as prescribed by section 243 of the Code, pertaining to dividends received by corporations.

* * *

Question

What result if in connection with the receipt of property in a § 351 transaction, the corporation issues in exchange for the property the following: (1) its common stock, (2) its preferred stock, (3) the common stock of its subsidiary, and (4) an inventory of widgets?

§ 2.3 ASSUMPTION OR TRANSFER OF LIABILITIES IN A § 351 TRANSACTION

See § 357 and Regulation and § 358(a) and (b) and § 1.358–3.

A. THE GENESIS OF THE PROBLEM: THE SUPREME COURT HOLDS THAT LIABILITIES ASSUMED ARE BOOT IN A REORGANIZATION

UNITED STATES v. HENDLER

Supreme Court of the United States, 1938.
303 U.S. 564, 58 S.Ct. 655, 82 L.Ed. 1018.

Under [the predecessor of § 361], gains are not taxed if one corporation, pursuant to a "plan of reorganization" exchanges its property "solely for *stock* or *securities,* in another corporation a party to the reorganization." But, when a corporation not only receives "stock or securities" in exchange for its property, but also receives "other property or money" in carrying out a "plan of reorganization,"

(1) If the corporation receiving such other property or money *distributes* it in pursuance of the plan of reorganization, no gain to the corporation shall be recognized from the exchange, but

(2) If the corporation receiving such other property or money *does not distribute* it in pursuance of the plan of reorganization, the gain, if any, to the corporation shall be recognized [taxed]. * * *

In this case, there was a merger or "reorganization" of the Borden Company and the Hendler Creamery Company, Inc., resulting in gains of more than six million dollars to the Hendler Company, Inc., a corporation of which respondent is transferee. The Court of Appeals, believing there was an exemption under [the predecessor of § 361], affirmed the judgment of the District Court holding all Hendler gains non-taxable.

This controversy between the government and respondent involves the assumption and payment—pursuant to the plan of reorganization—by the Borden Company of $534,297.40 bonded indebtedness of the Hendler Creamery Co., Inc. We are unable to agree with the conclusion reached by the courts below that the gain to the Hendler Company, realized by the Borden Company's payment, was exempt from taxation under [the predecessor of § 361].

It was contended below and it is urged here that since the Hendler Company did not actually receive the money with which the Borden Company discharged the former's indebtedness, the Hendler Company's gain of $534,297.40 is not taxable. The transaction, however, under which the Borden Company assumed and paid the debt and obligation of the Hendler Company is to be regarded in substance as though the $534,297.40 had been paid directly to the Hendler Company. The Hendler Company was the beneficiary of the discharge of its indebtedness. Its gain was as real and substantial as if the money had been paid it and then paid over by it to its creditors. The discharge of liability by the payment of the Hendler Company's indebtedness constituted income to the Hendler Company and is to be treated as such.[6]

[The predecessor of § 361] provides no exemption for gains—resulting from corporate "reorganization"—neither received as "stocks or securities," nor received as "money or other property" and distributed to stockholders under the plan of reorganization. In *Minnesota Tea Co. v. Helvering,* 302 U.S. 609, 58 S.Ct. 393, 394, 82 L.Ed. 474, it was said that this exemption "contemplates a distribution to stockholders, and not payment to creditors." The very statute upon which the taxpayer relies provides that "If the corporation receiving such other property or money does not distribute it in pursuance of the plan of reorganization, the gain, if any, to the corporation shall be recognized [taxed]. * * *"

Since this gain or income of $534,297.40 of the Hendler Company was neither received as "stock or securities" nor distributed to its stockholders "in pursuance of the plan of reorganization" it was not exempt and is taxable gain as defined in the 1928 Act. This $534,297.40 gain to the taxpayer does not fall within the exemptions of § 112, and the judgment of the court below is

Reversed.

Questions

What is the relationship between *Hendler* and *Crane*? What would be the result under the *Hendler* principle when a shareholder transfers property subject to a liability to a corporation in a § 351 transaction?

B. INTRODUCTORY NOTE ON CORPORATE ASSUMPTION OF SHAREHOLDER'S LIABILITIES

See §§ 357 and 358(d).

In § 351 transactions, a shareholder may transfer to the corporation property subject to a liability. Alternatively, the corporation may as-

---

6. *Old Colony Trust Co. v. Commissioner, 279 U.S. 716, 729.*

sume a shareholder's liability. In such cases, § 357(a) (which overrides *Hendler*) provides that the release of the liability is not a boot distribution to the shareholder. Therefore, the transaction is within § 351(a), rather than the boot gain rule of § 351(b).

Section 358(d) provides that, for purposes of determining the shareholder's basis in her stock, the amount of the liability is treated as "money received." Thus, the assumption of a liability by a corporation generates a downward basis adjustment under § 358(a)(1)(A)(ii).

The operation of these provisions is illustrated as follows. Individual S transfers a building to newly formed corporation C in exchange for all of the stock of C. The building has a fair market value of $100K and a basis of $50K. Also, the building is subject to a $20K nonrecourse mortgage. The mortgage has been on the property since it was acquired 10 years ago. Under the principles of *Crane*, S is deemed to receive a $20K cash amount realized as a result of the transfer of the property subject to the $20K mortgage to C, and under the principle in *Hendler* this cash would be recognized under the boot gain rule of § 351(b). However, § 357(a) provides that the transfer of the property subject to the liability is not treated as the receipt by S of money or other property. Consequently, S has no gain under § 351(b). Under § 358(a) and (d), S's basis for her shares is $30K, which is $50K minus the $20K liability.

Section 357(c)(1) provides an exception to the general rule of § 357(a) when the amount of the liability is greater than the basis of the property transferred. The excess of the aggregate liabilities assumed over the adjusted basis of the assets transferred is treated as gain recognized to the transferor. The character of the gain is dependent upon the character of the assets transferred. Thus, in the above example if the liability was for $80K, S would have a $30K gain under § 357(c)(1).

Section 357(c)(3) provides an exception to the liabilities in excess of basis rule in the case of the transfer of accounts payable by a cash basis taxpayer. A conforming change is also made to § 358(d)(2). Thus, if a cash basis taxpayer transfers to a corporation accounts receivables with a fair market value of $100K and an adjusted basis of zero and accounts payables of $80K, the liability in excess of basis gain rule does not apply. *See* § 357(c)(3). This exception is discussed in detail below. *See* Sec. 2.3.F.

Section 357(b)(1) provides an exception to § 357(a) in cases where the transfer of the liabilities to the corporation is for tax avoidance purposes. In such cases, the full amount of the liabilities assumed or transferred is treated as boot distributed. This provision is examined further in Sec. 2.3.G.

C. EFFECT OF § 357(a) ON CORPORATION'S ASSUMPTION OF CONTRIBUTING SHAREHOLDER'S EXPENSES

REVENUE RULING 74–477
1974–2 C.B. 116.

A, an individual, proposes to transfer property to *X* corporation solely in exchange for all of the outstanding voting common stock of *X*. Pursuant to the agreement between *A* and *X*, appraisal fees, legal fees, and shipping and packaging expenses, incurred by *A* in connection with the transfer will be paid or assumed by *X*. These expenses are bona fide expenses directly relating to the transfer by *A* of property to *X*.

Held, under section 357(a) of the Code, *X* may assume such liabilities that arise out of the transfer of the property.

Such expenses paid or assumed by *X* will not be considered as "boot" received by *A* under section 351(b) of the Code. However, any bona fide expenses of *X* paid by *A* will be treated as a contribution by *A* to the capital of *X*.

Compare Rev.Rul. 73–54, 1973–1 C.B. 187, which holds that an acquiring corporation's payment of, or assumption of, bona fide reorganization expenses attributable to the acquired corporation or its shareholders will not violate the solely for voting stock requirement of section 368(a)(1)(B) or (C) of the Code. Rev.Rul. 73–54 further holds that expenses not solely and directly related to the transaction are other property if paid or assumed by the acquiring corporation and will violate the solely for voting stock requirement of section 368(a)(1)(B) or (C).

D. APPLICABILITY OF § 357(c) TO TRANSFERORS

REVENUE RULING 66–142
1966–1 C.B. 66.

In an exchange to which section 351 of the Internal Revenue Code of 1954 is applicable, the provisions of section 357(c) of the Code apply separately to each transferor so that the gain to each transferor is the excess of the sum of the amount of his liabilities assumed over the adjusted basis of all property transferred by him pursuant to the exchange determined without regard to the adjusted basis and liabilities of any other transferors.

Question

Does § 357(c) apply separately to each asset contributed by a transferor, or does it apply on an aggregate basis?

E. EFFECT UNDER § 357(c) OF ISSUANCE BY SHAREHOLDER-TRANSFEROR OF HIS PERSONAL PROMISSORY NOTE TO CORPORATION

1. *The Service's Position*

REVENUE RULING 68–629
1968–2 C.B. 154.

Advice has been requested whether section 357(c) of the Internal Revenue Code of 1954 applies when property is transferred under section 351(a) of the Code and the transferor issues a note equal to the amount by which the liabilities assumed by the transferee exceed the adjusted basis of the assets transferred.

The taxpayer, an individual, was engaged in a business that he operated as a sole proprietorship. He had no income that has been earned but not reported. He transferred all of the assets of the sole proprietorship to a newly organized corporation in exchange solely for all of the outstanding stock of the corporation and the assumption by it of all of the liabilities pertaining to the sole proprietorship. At the time of transfer, the liabilities of the business assumed exceeded the adjusted basis of the assets transferred. In order that the assets shown on the balance sheet of the corporation would equal the liabilities assumed, the taxpayer agreed to make up this difference through a capital contribution to the corporation. This agreement was evidenced by his personal promissory note in an amount equal to the difference between the assets transferred and the liabilities assumed.

* * *

Section 1012 of the Code provides that the basis of property is its cost except as otherwise provided in the Code. Since the taxpayer incurred no cost in making the note, its basis to him was zero. Therefore, the transfer of the note to the corporation did not increase the basis of the assets transferred and the liabilities assumed by the corporation exceeded the taxpayer's basis in the assets transferred.

Accordingly, section 357(c) of the Code applies to the transaction and gain is recognized to the taxpayer on the transfer of the assets of the sole proprietorship and the promissory note in exchange solely for stock of the corporation plus the assumption of the liabilities of the proprietorship in the amount by which the liabilities assumed exceeds the basis of the assets transferred.

2. The Second Circuit's View

LESSINGER v. COMMISSIONER
United States Court of Appeals, Second Circuit, 1989.
872 F.2d 519.

OAKES, CHIEF JUDGE:

* * *

The Tax Court found, and the parties seem to agree, that section 351 of the Internal Revenue Code governs the transaction at issue here. Section 351 provides for the nonrecognition of income when a controlling shareholder transfers property to a corporation. The taxpayer here transferred the assets and liabilities of a proprietorship he operated to a corporation he owned for reasons entirely unrelated to tax planning. It is clear that he was oblivious to the ramifications of his actions in terms of his tax liability. Prior to the consolidation, the proprietorship had a negative net worth. Nevertheless the Tax Court found that the taxpayer had to recognize a gain because he transferred liabilities to the corporation which exceeded his adjusted basis in the assets of the proprietorship. The Tax Court applied section 357(c) of the Code, which is an exception to the general rule of nonrecognition in section 351 transactions. Under section 357(c), gain is recognized to the extent that a transferor-shareholder disposes of liabilities exceeding the total adjusted basis of the assets transferred.

The taxpayer attacks the Tax Court's decision from two directions. First, he argues that the Tax Court overstated the amount of liabilities transferred, because, he claims, he did not actually transfer short-term accounts payable to the corporation. His second argument is that the Tax Court understated the amount of assets transferred. The Tax Court decided to ignore a $255,500 accounting entry which, the taxpayer argues, represented his personal debt to the corporation and should be counted as a transferred asset.

* * *

DISCUSSION

The first question is whether section 351 applies when no new shares are issued to the shareholder, having in mind the statutory language that a transfer must be made "solely in exchange for stock * * *.

* * * We agree * * * with the Tax Court's ultimate conclusion that the exchange requirements of section 351 are met where a sole stockholder transfers property to a wholly-owned corporation even though no stock [is] issued therefor. Issuance of new stock in this situation would be a meaningless gesture.

* * *

The taxpayer's principal argument, broadly stated, is that section 357 is inapplicable to him because in neither an accounting nor an economic sense did he realize a gain. He "merely exchanged creditors" from trade creditors to Universal, and his gain, therefore, was a "phantom" which Congress did not intend to tax.

Narrowly stated, the taxpayer's argument takes two different forms, each of which complements the other.

First, the corporation did not take the affirmative action necessary to assume the trade accounts payable of the taxpayer's proprietorship, in contrast to its affirmative action to assume the notes payable. * * *

Second, even if the corporation did "assume" the taxpayer's trade accounts payable, there was no taxable gain since he contributed "property," that is, the account receivable from him in the approximate amount of $250,000, which, contrary to Alderman v. Commissioner, 55 T.C. 662 (1971), should be deemed to have a basis equal to its face value.

* * *

We now turn to the Tax Court's second reason for ignoring the debt. The Tax Court quoted *Alderman, supra,* which, like our case, involved the incorporation of an accrual basis proprietorship with a negative net worth. In *Alderman*, the Tax Court disregarded the taxpayers' personal promissory note to their corporation because

> [t]he Aldermans incurred no cost in making the note, so its basis to them was zero. The basis to the corporation was the same as in the hands of the transferor, i.e., zero. Consequently, the application of section 357(c) is undisturbed by the creation and transfer of the personal note to the corporation.

Alderman purported to follow the literal language of the Tax Code. Section 357(c) does support the *Alderman* court's reliance on the concept of basis, but the statutory language is not addressed to a transaction such as Lessinger's, where the transferor's obligation has a value to the transferee corporation. The *Alderman* court did not consider the value of the obligation to the transferee.

* * *

"Basis," as used in tax law, refers to assets, not liabilities. Section 1012 provides that "[t]he basis of property shall be the cost of such property, except as otherwise provided." Liabilities by definition have no "basis" in tax law generally or in section 1012 terms specifically. The concept of "basis" prevents double taxation of income by identifying amounts that have already been taxed or are exempt from tax. The taxpayer could, of course, have no "basis" in his own promise to pay the corporation $255,000, because that item is a liability for him. We would add parenthetically that to this extent *Alderman* was correct in describing the taxpayers' note there. But the corporation should have a basis in its obligation from Lessinger, because it incurred a cost in the transaction involving the transfer of the obligation by taking on the liabilities of the proprietorship that exceeded its assets, and because it would have to recognize income upon Lessinger's payment of the debt if it had no basis in the obligation. Assets transferred under section 351 are taken by the corporation at the transferor's basis, to which is added any gain recognized in the transfer. § 362(a). Consideration of "adjusted basis" in section 357(c) therefore normally does not require determining whether the section refers to the "adjusted basis" in the hands of the transferor-shareholder or the transferee-corporation, because the basis does not change. But here, the "basis" in the hands of the corporation should be the face amount of the taxpayer's obligation. We now hold that in the situation presented here, where the transferor undertakes genuine personal liability to the transferee, "adjusted basis" in section 357(c) refers to the transferee's basis in the obligation, which is its face amount.

Yet the Commissioner says that to reverse the Tax Court would, as *Alderman* suggested, "effectively eliminate section 357(c) from the Internal Revenue Code." Would it? * * *

* * *

We conclude that our holding will not "effectively eliminate section 357(c)." Lessinger experienced no enrichment and had no unrecognized gains whose recognition was appropriate at the time of the consolidation. Any logic that would tax him would certainly represent a "trap for the unwary." Lessinger could have achieved incorporation without taxation under the Commissioner's theory by borrowing $260,000 cash, transferring the cash to the corporation (or paying some of the trade accounts payable personally); and later causing the corporation to buy his promissory note from the lender (or pay it off in consideration of his new promise to pay the corporation). If taxpayers who transfer liabilities exceeding assets to controlled corporations are willing to undertake genuine personal liability for the excess, we see no reason to require recognition of a gain, and we do not believe that Congress intended for any gain to be recognized.

Question

In Rev.Rul. 68–629, 1968–2 C.B. 154, the Service holds that the contribution by a shareholder of a promissory note does not shield the shareholder from gain under the liabilities in excess of basis rule of § 357(c). The Service holds that the shareholder has no basis in the note. The court in *Lessinger* agrees that the contributing shareholder has no basis in the note, but then says that in the situation presented in the case the " 'adjusted basis' in section 357 refers to the transferee's [*i.e.*, the corporation's] basis in the obligation which is its face amount." Is the court correct in its analysis? What planning opportunity is presented by the court's decision?

F. ILLUSTRATION OF CURRENT TREATMENT OF TRANSFERS OF ACCOUNTS RECEIVABLE AND ACCOUNTS PAYABLE OF A CASH BASIS TAXPAYER

REVENUE RULING 80–198
1980–2 C.B. 113.

Issue

Under the circumstances described below, do the nonrecognition of gain or loss provisions of section 351 of the Internal Revenue Code apply to a transfer of the operating assets of an ongoing sole proprietorship (including unrealized accounts receivable) to a corporation in exchange solely for the common stock of a corporation and the assumption by the corporation of the proprietorship liabilities?

Facts

Individual A conducted a medical practice as a sole proprietorship, the income of which was reported on the cash receipts and disbursements method of accounting. A transferred to a newly organized corporation all of the operating assets of the sole proprietorship in exchange for all of the stock of the corporation, plus the assumption by the corporation of all of the liabilities of the sole proprietorship. The purpose of the incorporation was to provide a form of business organization that would be more conducive to the planned expansion of the medical services to be made available by the business enterprise.

The assets transferred were tangible assets having a fair market value of $40,000 and an adjusted basis of $30,000 and unrealized trade accounts receivable having a face amount of $20,000 and an adjusted basis of zero. The liabilities assumed by the corporation consisted of trade accounts payable in the face amount of $10,000. The liabilities assumed by the corporation also included a mortgage liability, related to the tangible property transferred, of $10,000. A had neither accumulated the accounts receivable nor prepaid any of the liabilities of the sole proprietorship in a manner inconsistent with normal business practices in anticipation of the incorporation. If A had paid the trade accounts payable liabilities, the amounts paid would have been deductible by A as ordinary and necessary business expenses under section 162 of the Code. The new corporation continued to utilize the cash receipts and disbursements method of accounting.

Law and Analysis

The applicable section of the Code is section 351(a), which provides that no gain or loss shall be recognized when property is transferred to a corporation in exchange solely for stock and securities and the transferor is in control (as defined by section 368(c)) of the transferee corporation immediately after the transfer.

In *Hempt Bros., Inc. v. United States,* 490 F.2d 1172 (3rd Cir.1974), *cert. denied,* 419 U.S. 826 (1974), the United States Court of Appeals for the Third Circuit held, as the Internal Revenue Service contended, that a cash basis transferee corporation was taxable on the monies it collected on accounts receivable that had been transferred to it by a cash basis partnership in a transaction described in section 351(a) of the Code. The corporate taxpayer contended that it was not obligated to include the accounts receivable in income; rather the transferor partnership should have been taxed on the stock the partnership received under the assignment of income doctrine which is predicated on the well established general principle that income be taxed to the party that earned it.

The court in *Hempt Bros.* solved the conflict between the assignment of income doctrine and the statutory nonrecognition provisions of section 351 of the Code by reasoning that if the cash basis transferor were taxed on the transfer of the accounts receivable, the specific congressional intent reflected in section 351(a) that the incorporation of an ongoing business should be facilitated by making the incorporation tax free would be frustrated.

The facts of the instant case are similar to those in *Hempt Bros.* in that there was a valid business purpose for the transfer of the accounts receivable along with all of the assets and liabilities of A's proprietorship to a corporate transferee that would continue the business of the transferor. Further, A had neither accumulated the accounts receivable nor prepaid any of the account payable liabilities of the sole proprietorship in anticipation of the incorporation, which is an indication that, under the facts and circumstances of the case, the transaction was not designed for tax avoidance.

Holding

The transfer by A of the operating assets of the sole proprietorship (including unrealized accounts receivable) to the corporation in exchange solely for the common stock of the corporation and the assumption by the corporation of the proprietorship liabilities (including accounts payable) is an exchange within the meaning of section 351(a) of the Code. Therefore, no gain or loss is recognized to A with respect to the property transferred, including the accounts receivable. For transfers occurring on or after November 6, 1978 (the effective date of the Revenue Act of 1978, Pub.L. 95–600, 1978–3 C.B. (Vol. 1) 1, 88, with respect to sections 357(c)(3) and 358(d)(2) of the Code) the assumption of the trade accounts payable that would give rise to a deduction if A had paid them is not, pursuant to section 357(c)(3), considered as an assumption of a liability for purposes of sections 357(c)(1) and 358(d). See Rev.Rul. 80–199, this page, this Bulletin, for transfers occurring before November 6, 1978, which holds that trade accounts payable transferred to a corporation in a transaction to which section 351(a) applies are not liabilities for the purposes of sections 357(c) and 358(d) if the transferor of the accounts payable could have deducted the amounts paid in satisfaction thereof under section 162 if the transferor had paid these amounts in satisfaction of the payables prior to the exchange. The corporation, under the cash receipts and disbursements method of accounting, will report in its income the account receivables as collected, and will be allowed deductions under section 162 for the payments it makes to satisfy the assumed trade accounts payable when such payments are made.

A's basis in the stock received in the exchange of property for stock under section 358(a)(1) of the Code is $20,000 which is calculated by decreasing A's $30,000 basis in the assets transferred by the $10,000 mortgage liability under sections 358(a)(1)(A)(ii) and 358(d)(1). No adjustment to such basis is made under section 358(a)(1)(A)(ii) because of the assumption by the corporation of the $10,000 in accounts payable inasmuch as the general rule of section 358(d)(1), which requires the basis in the stock received to be decreased by the liabilities assumed, does not apply by reason of section 358(d)(2), which provides that section 358(d)(1) does not apply to the amount of any liabilities defined in section 357(c)(3) such as accounts payable that would have been deductible by A as ordinary and necessary business expenses under section 162 in the taxable year paid if A had paid these liabilities prior to the exchange.

* * *

Notes and Questions

1. The *Hempt Brothers* decision, which is discussed above, is examined more completely below.

2. Individual A is planning to incorporate her consulting firm, which is a sole proprietorship. The business, which is on the cash basis of accounting, leases all of its office space and equipment. The only assets and liabilities are $10K of cash, $90K of accounts receivables, and $50K of accounts payables. What result on the transfer by A of all of the assets and liabilities to a new corporation in exchange solely for stock? What is A's basis for her shares? What is the corporation's basis for the assets? What result to the corporation when it collects the receivables and pays the payables?

G. INTERACTION BETWEEN THE § 357(b) TAX AVOIDANCE PROVISION AND § 357(c) LIABILITIES IN EXCESS OF BASIS PROVISION

DRYBROUGH v. COMMISSIONER

United States Court of Appeals, Sixth Circuit, 1967.
376 F.2d 350.

LISTER, SENIOR CIRCUIT JUDGE.

[In 1957, the taxpayer, Drybrough, formed several corporations to which he transferred real property subject to mortgages. In all but one case the mortgages were placed on the property in 1953. Drybrough mortgaged one property just prior to the incorporation and used the proceeds for nonbusiness purposes.]

To guard against abuse of the privilege granted, Congress attached an exception which now as part of § 357 provides in subsection (b) * * * that if in making the exchange, the principal purpose of the taxpayer with respect to the assumption or acquisition was a purpose to avoid federal income tax *"on the exchange,"* or if not such purpose, was not a bona fide business purpose, then the assumption or acquisition should in the total amount thereof be considered "as money received by the taxpayer on the exchange." This section also provides that in determining the principal purpose of the taxpayer there should be taken "into consideration the nature of the liability and the circumstances in the light of which the arrangement for the assumption or acquisition was made." Notwithstanding this broad contextual area to be considered, we emphasize that the purpose to avoid income tax is precisely narrowed to a purpose *"with respect to the assumption"* and to a purpose to avoid income tax *"on the exchange."*

We read this language as excluding from identification as a purpose to avoid tax *on the exchange,* the original and unrelated motivation for borrowing the money which created the assumed obligation. In this case, Drybrough in 1953 borrowed $700,000; substantially one-half of this sum was used to pay off existing mortgage indebtedness and expenses connected with the borrowing, and the other half was deposited in Drybrough's bank account. Of this latter amount, Drybrough used $203,602 to pay accrued interest and principal on a note allegedly owing to his wife; he also paid some $90,493.00 to his collection agency and $5,000 to his wife to reimburse advances which had admittedly been made to him to purchase further real estate. We may accept the Tax Court's unclear assertion that the note to Drybrough's wife was a sham, and that of the money allegedly paid thereon, $200,000 had been in truth borrowed and used to purchase tax exempt securities. We cannot find or infer, however, that the purposes thus served revealed as a matter of fact or law a purpose to avoid income tax "on the exchange" made *four years later* when in 1957 Drybrough's business as an investor in real estate was converted from a proprietorship to corporate enterprises. Assuming an intent by Drybrough to save or avoid income tax by the 1953 purchase of tax exempt securities, such purpose cannot be said to be a part of "the principal purpose of the taxpayer (Drybrough) with respect to the assumption" of the balance of the 1953 loan by the corporations which came into existence in 1957.

It is clear that the Tax Court was of the view that under the facts of this case a purpose to avoid income tax "on the exchange" could be found by inquiry into the reasons for, and the use of the proceeds of, the 1953 borrowing.

* * *

Under the statute's language, it was proper to consider "the nature of the liability assumed" but under the facts of this case we do not consider that the use that Drybrough made of the 1953 borrowing was of controlling importance here.

* * *

2) Corporate assumption of the 1957 $150,000.00 mortgage.

We sustain the Tax Court's holding that the assumption by 620 South Fifth Street, Inc., on June 28, 1957, of the $150,000 mortgage which had been placed on the assets transferred to that corporation on March 15, 1957, had not been proven by Drybrough to be otherwise than for a principal purpose "to avoid income tax on the exchange." In late 1956 Drybrough had, with reference to the 620 South Fifth Street property, written to National Life "620 South Fifth and the Mexican Village property are both clear and I am eager to mortgage them to the limit before combining these two properties in a corporation." This was a clear expression that the creation of the debt was directly in anticipation of, and connected in purpose with, having the corporation assume the debt, thus releasing to Drybrough $150,000 of the value of this asset without a present realization of taxable gain on the exchange. The borrowed money was used to purchase tax-exempt securities; it was not used to carry on the purposes of the business enterprise of 620 South Fifth Street, Inc., nor in furtherance of Drybrough's general real estate investments, justifying also a finding that the assumption could not be accommodated under the "bona fide business purpose" requirement of § 357(b)(1)(B). We think it was a fair inference too that Drybrough's conduct was equivalent to a pro tanto liquidation of the involved asset, and that his purpose "with respect to the assumption" disclosed a plan to avoid realization of gain on this liquidation by selling the mortgaged asset to his controlled corporation. It was permissible for the Tax Court to find in this transaction "a purpose to avoid Federal income tax on the exchange," § 357(b)(1)(A).

We find no fault with the legal standard employed to reach the above conclusions; and cannot hold as clearly erroneous the factual findings involved.

Questions

Individual S is planning to transfer a building to a newly formed corporation in exchange for all of the stock. The building has a value of $100K and a basis of $50K. The building is not subject to a liability. What result if prior to the transfer S takes out a $40K loan and gives a $40K nonrecourse mortgage on the property. S then transfers the building to the corporation and retains the $40K of cash? What if the cash is transferred to the corporation as working capital? In general, what result if S transfers the building free and clear and the corporation then takes out the mortgage and distributes the $40K of cash to S? *See* §§ 301(a), (c) and (d) and § 316.

H. SUMMARY PROBLEMS ON CORPORATE ASSUMPTION OF SHAREHOLDER'S LIABILITIES

1. A and B form the X corporation as equal shareholders, with A contributing property with a fair market value of $100K and an adjusted basis of $50K. The property is subject to a nonrecourse liability of $50K. B contributes cash of $50K. Assume that the stock each receives has a fair market value of $50K because X has a net worth of $100K (*i.e.*, $150K of assets and a $50K liability).

    (a) What result to A, B and X?

    (b) What are A's and B's bases for the stock?

    (c) What is X's basis for the property contributed by A?

2. Same as 1, except the building has a basis to A of $30K.

3. Same as 1, except A is a cash basis taxpayer who contributed accounts receivable with a fair market value of $100K and an adjusted basis of zero, and the corporation assumed A's accounts payable in the amount of $50K.

    (a) Same questions as 1(a)–(c).

4. Same as 1, except one month prior to the contribution A held the property free and clear of all liabilities and at that time A borrowed $50K from a bank giving a nonrecourse mortgage on the property.

    (a) Same questions as in 1(a)–(c).

    (b) What if A contributed the property free and clear, and X mortgaged the property and distributed the $50K?

5. Individual A owns property with an adjusted basis of $10K and a fair market value of $50K. The property is subject to a liability of $75K. A transfers the property to X in a § 351 transaction. What result to A?

§ 2.4 THE PROPERTY TRANSFER REQUIREMENT

One of the elements of a § 351 transaction is that "property" be transferred. The following materials illustrate various aspects of this requirement. This issue also arises on the organization of a partnership.

Section 351(d) provides that stock issued for (1) services, (2) indebtedness of the transferee corporation that is not evidenced by a security (*i.e.*, a long term debt instrument), or (3) certain accrued but unpaid interest, is not considered as issued for property.

A. SCOPE OF THE CONCEPT OF SERVICES

See § 351(d)(1).

JAMES v. COMMISSIONER
Tax Court of the United States, 1969.
53 T.C. 63.

SIMPSON, JUDGE: [Mr. James and Mr. and Mrs. Talbot entered into an agreement to build an FHA housing project. The project was to be owned by a corporation which was to be formed later. James in his individual capacity arranged for the financing commitments for the project from a mortgage company (United Mortgagee) and FHA. James also performed certain other pre-incorporation services. James assigned the commitments plus certain agreements to the corporation (Chicora) in exchange for one half of the stock. Talbot contributed real property with a value of $44K in exchange for the other half.]

OPINION

The first, and critical, issue for our determination is whether Mr. James received his Chicora stock in exchange for the transfer of property or as compensation for services. The petitioners argue that he received such stock in consideration of his transfer to Chicora of the FHA and United Mortgagee commitments and that such commitments constituted "property" within the meaning of section 351. The respondent does not appear to challenge the petitioners' implicit assertion that Mr. James was not expected to render future services to the corporation in exchange for the issuance of stock to him. Although the accuracy of this assertion is subject to some question, the state of the record is such that we must decide the issues as the parties have presented them. Thus, the sole question on this issue is whether Mr. James' personal services, which the petitioners freely admit were rendered, resulted in the development of a property right which was transferred to Chicora, within the meaning of section 351.

Section 351(a) provides, in pertinent part:

> (a) General Rule.—No gain or loss shall be recognized if property is transferred to a corporation * * * by one or more persons solely in exchange for stock or securities in such corporation and immediately after the exchange such person or persons are in control (as defined in section 368(c)) of the corporation. For purposes of this section, stock or securities issued for services shall not be considered as issued in return for property.

The second sentence of this subsection [which is now contained in § 351(d)(1)] was first included in the statute as a part of the 1954 Code, although it is said merely to restate the case law. See Bittker & Eustice, Federal Income Taxation of Corporations and Shareholders 70 (2d ed. 1966). In explaining the second sentence, the House Ways and Means Committee stated:

> In accordance with this provision, such stock or securities received by a person who has rendered or will render services to the transferee corporation would be fully taxable as compensation upon receipt.

Your committee does not intend, however, to vitiate the remaining portion of the transaction, through application of this provision. [H.Rept. No. 1337, to accompany H.R. 8300 (Pub.L. 591), 83d Cong., 2d Sess., p. A117 (1954).]

According to the petitioners' argument, Mr. James, as a result of the services performed by him, acquired certain contract rights which constituted property and which he transferred to Chicora. The fact that such rights resulted from the performance of personal services does not, in their view, disqualify them from being treated as property for purposes of section 351. * * *

It is altogether clear that for purposes of section 351, not every right is to be treated as property. The second sentence of such section indicates that, whatever may be considered as property for purposes of local law, the performance of services, or the agreement to perform services, is not to be treated as a transfer of property for purposes of section 351. Thus, if in this case we have merely an agreement to perform services in exchange for stock of the corporation to be created, the performance of such services does not constitute the transfer of property within the meaning of section 351.

Although patents and secret processes—the product of services—are treated as property for purposes of section 351, we have carefully analyzed the arrangement in this case and have concluded that Mr. James did not transfer any property essentially like a patent or secret process; he merely performed services for Chicora. In January of 1963, he entered into an agreement to perform services for the corporation to be created. He was to secure the necessary legal and architectural work and to arrange for the financing of the project, and these were the services performed by him. Although he secured the services of the lawyer and the architect, they were paid for by the corporation. He put in motion the wheels that led to the FHA commitment, but it was not a commitment to him—it was a commitment to United Mortgagee to insure a loan to Chicora, a project sponsored by Mr. James. It was stipulated that under the FHA regulations, a commitment would not be issued to an individual, but only to a corporation. Throughout these arrangements, it was contemplated that a corporation would be created and that the commitment would run to the corporation. * * * In these circumstances, it seems clear that Mr. James received his share of the stock in the corporation in return for the services performed by him and that he did not transfer any property, within the meaning of section 351, to the corporation. * * *

The next question is whether the Talbots are taxable on the gain realized from the exchange of their land for Chicora stock. Section 351(a) applies only if immediately after the transfer those who transferred property in exchange for stock owned at least 80 percent of Chicora's stock. Sec. 368(c). Since Mr. James is not to be treated as a transferor of property, he cannot be included among those in control for purposes of this test. * * * The transferors of property, the Talbots, did not have the required 80–percent control of Chicora immediately after the transfer, and therefore, their gain must be recognized. This result is inconsistent with the apparent meaning of the second sentence from the committee report, but the statutory scheme does not permit any other conclusion.

In their petition, the Jameses alleged that the respondent erred in valuing the 10 shares Mr. James received at $22,000. However, they have failed to offer any evidence to establish a different value, and they appear to have dropped this allegation. Accordingly, we sustain the respondent's determination of value.

Decisions will be entered for the respondent.

* * *

Notes and Questions

1. What result if James had received the loan commitments prior to entering into the arrangement with the Talbots? Would the commitments have then constituted property?

2. As indicated in *James,* the House Report states that the fact that services are not property should not "vitiate the remaining portion of the transaction. * * *" See § 1.351–1(a)(2) (Example 3). Suppose James had contributed real property to the corporation in exchange for one half of the stock he received with the other half being received in exchange for the commitments? See § 1.351–1(a)(1)(ii) and Rev.Proc. 77–37, § 3.07, 1977–2 C.B. 568, 570, *infra.*

3. The Talbots received recognition treatment for the gain they realized on the transaction. Such gain was measured by the difference between the adjusted basis of the property contributed and $22K, which was the fair market value of the stock received. Since the property they contributed had a value of $44K, why did they receive only $22K in stock? Do they have a loss deduction of $22K? Note that James was taxed on $22K of income. Does the corporation get a deduction? See §§ 1032 and 83(h).

4. James argued that the loan commitments were property. Presumably the commitments had value. Why then did the court find that the value of the stock James and the Talbots received was only $44,000, the value of the property the Talbots contributed? Should the value of the commitments have been reflected in the value of the stock?

B. ACCOUNTS RECEIVABLE AND ASSIGNMENT OF INCOME

1. *Transfer of Assets and Liabilities of a Going Concern*

HEMPT BROTHERS INC. v. UNITED STATES

United States Court of Appeals, Third Circuit, 1974.
490 F.2d 1172, *cert. denied* 419 U.S. 826, 95 S.Ct. 44, 42 L.Ed.2d 50 (1974).

[The Hempt Bros. partnership, which was on cash basis, was incorporated in a § 351 transaction. Accounts receivable in excess of $600K were transferred to the corporation (Taxpayer). The Taxpayer also filed on the cash basis. After audit, the Commissioner and the Taxpayer agreed that the Taxpayer was required to be on the accrual method because it had inventories. As a result, the Commissioner required the Taxpayer to include the full amount of the accounts receivable in its income. The Taxpayer argued that it had a basis for the receivables equal to their value because the receivables were not "property" within the meaning of § 351. Alternatively, the Taxpayer argued that the assignment of income doctrine was applicable and that the shareholders should have been taxed on the transfer to the corporation.]

I. Taxpayer argues here, as it did in the district court, that because the term "property" as used in Section 351 does not embrace accounts receivable, the Commissioner lacked statutory authority to apply principles associated with Section 351. The district court properly rejected the legal interpretation urged by the taxpayer.

* * *

We fail to perceive any special reason why a restrictive meaning should be applied to accounts receivables so as to exclude them from the general meaning of "property." Receivables possess the usual capabilities and attributes associated with jurisprudential concepts of property law. They may be identified, valued, and transferred. Moreover, their role in an ongoing business must be viewed in the context of Section 351 application. The presence of accounts receivable is a normal, rather than an exceptional accoutrement of the type of business included by Congress in the transfer to a corporate form. * * *

The taxpayer next makes a strenuous argument that "[t]he government is seeking to tax the wrong person." It contends that the assignment of income doctrine as developed by the Supreme Court applies to a Section 351 transfer of accounts receivable so that the transferor, not the transferee-corporation, bears the corresponding tax liability. It argues that the assignment of income doctrine dictates that where the right to receive income is transferred to another person in a transaction not giving rise to tax at the time of transfer, the transferor is taxed on the income when it is collected by the transferee; that the only requirement for its application is a transfer of a right to receive ordinary income; and that since the transferred accounts receivable are a present right to future income, the sole requirement for the application of the doctrine is squarely met. In essence, this is a contention that the nonrecognition provision of Section 351 is in conflict with the assignment of income doctrine and that Section 351 should be subordinated thereto. Taxpayer relies on the seminal case of *Lucas v. Earl,* 281 U.S. 111, 50 S.Ct. 241, 74 L.Ed. 731 (1930), and its progeny for support of its proposition that the application of the doctrine is mandated whenever one transfers a right to receive ordinary income.

* * *

* * * By its explicit terms Section 351 expresses the Congressional intent that transfers of property for stock or securities will not result in

recognition. It therefore becomes apparent that this case vividly illustrates how Section 351 sometimes comes into conflict with another provision of the Internal Revenue Code or a judicial doctrine, and requires a determination of which of two conflicting doctrines will control.

As we must, when we try to reconcile conflicting doctrines in the revenue law, we endeavor to ascertain a controlling Congressional mandate. Section 351 has been described as a deliberate attempt by Congress to facilitate the incorporation of ongoing business and to eliminate any technical constructions which are economically unsound.

* * *

While we cannot fault the general principle "that income be taxed to him who earns it," to adopt taxpayer's argument would be to hamper the incorporation of ongoing businesses; additionally it would impose technical constructions which are economically and practically unsound. None of the cases cited by taxpayer, including *Lake* itself, persuades us otherwise. * * *

We are persuaded that, on balance, the teachings of Lake must give way in this case to the broad Congressional interest in facilitating the incorporation of ongoing businesses. * * * Here we are influenced by the fact that the subject of the assignment was accounts receivable for partnership's goods and services sold in the regular course of business, that the change of business form from partnership to corporation had a basic business purpose and was not designed for the purpose of deliberate tax avoidance, and by the conviction that the totality of circumstances here presented fit the mold of the Congressional intent to give nonrecognition to a transfer of a total business from a non-corporate to a corporate form.

But this too must be said. Even though Section 351(a) immunizes the transferor from immediate tax consequences, Section 358 retains for the transferors a potential income tax liability to be realized and recognized upon a subsequent sale or exchange of the stock certificates received. As to the transferee-corporation, the tax basis of the receivables will be governed by Section 362.

Questions

1. Why was the taxpayer arguing that the accounts receivable were not property within § 351?

2. Why was the taxpayer arguing that the assignment of income doctrine applied to override the nonrecognition rule of § 351 and the Commissioner arguing to the contrary? Can you posit a case where the positions of the parties would be reversed? What do you make of the Court's statement in the latter part of the opinion that it was "influenced by the fact that the subject of the assignment was accounts receivable for the partnership's goods and services sold in the regular course of the business * * *"?

2. The Limits on Hempt Brothers

REVENUE RULING 80–198
1980–2 C.B. 113.

* * *

LIMITATIONS

Section 351 of the Code does not apply to a transfer of accounts receivable which constitute an assignment of an income right in a case such as *Brown v. Commissioner,* 40 B.T.A. 565 (1939), *aff'd* 115 F.2d 337 (2d Cir.1940). In *Brown,* an attorney transferred to a corporation, in which he was the sole owner, a one-half interest in a claim for legal services performed by the attorney and his law partner. In exchange, the attorney received additional stock of the corporation. The claim represented the corporation's only asset. Subsequent to the receipt by the corporation of the proceeds of the claim, the attorney gave all of the stock of the corporation to his wife. The United States Court of Appeals for the Second Circuit found that the transfer of the claim for the fee to the corporation had no purpose other than to avoid taxes and held that in such a case the intervention of the corporation would not prevent the attorney from being liable for the tax on the income which resulted from services under the assignment of income rule of *Lucas v. Earl,* 281 U.S. 111 (1930). Accordingly, in a case of a transfer to a controlled corporation of an account receivable in respect of services rendered where there is a tax avoidance purpose for the transaction (which might be evidenced by the corporation not conducting an ongoing business), the Internal Revenue Service will continue to apply assignment of income principles and require that the transferor of such a receivable include it in income when received by the transferee corporation.

Likewise, it may be appropriate in certain situations to allocate income, deductions, credits, or allowances to the transferor or transferee under section 482 of the Code when the timing of the incorporation improperly separates income from related expenses. See *Rooney v. United States,* 305 F.2d 681 (9th Cir.1962), where a farming operation was incorporated in a transaction described in section 351(a) after the expenses of the crop had been incurred but before the crop had been sold and income realized. The transferor's tax return contained all of the expenses but none of the farming income to which the expenses related. The United States Court of Appeals for the Ninth Circuit held that the expenses could be allocated under section 482 to the corporation, to be matched with the income to which the expenses related. Similar adjustments may be appropriate where some assets, liabilities, or both, are retained by the transferor and such retention results in the income of the transferor, transferee, or both, not being clearly reflected.

3. *Transfer of Selected Assets*

PRIVATE LETTER RULING 8139073
(June 30, 1981).

P, a cash-basis medical partnership, proposes to incorporate its business in a transaction intended to qualify under section 351 of the Internal Revenue Code. The incorporation of the business will be accomplished in a two-step transaction involving a pro rata distribution, on the same basis as the partners' share profits, of all the *P* liabilities and a portion of *P*'s assets to the partners, and a subsequent transfer of such assets and liabilities to Corporation, a cash-basis transferee, by the partners in exchange for all the Corporation stock. *P* will distribute the unrealized accounts receivable, miscellaneous supplies and accounts payable to the partners. However, *P* will retain the land and building where the partners practice medicine, and the medical and office equipment which it will lease to the Corporation. [The ruling here discusses *Hempt Brothers* and *Brown.*]

Based on the information submitted and the cases cited above, we conclude that the pro rata share of unrealized accounts receivable transferred by each partner to Corporation are includable in the income of such partner when payment is received by the Corporation. In this case, the assignment of income doctrine of *Lucas v. Earl* applies to the transfer of the unrealized accounts receivable. The facts discussed in the Revenue Ruling and case law which have held that the assignment of income doctrine does not apply to the incorporation of an ongoing business (and the transfer of the unrealized accounts receivable by a cash transferor) are not similar to those of the proposed transaction in this case. The proposed transaction involves more than a mere change in form of an ongoing business from a partnership to a corporation since only a portion of the *P* assets will be transferred to Corporation (mainly the unrealized accounts receivable) and *P* will continue in existence following the incorporation for the purpose of leasing preincorporation *P* assets to Corporation.

* * *

Question

In *Hempt Bros.,* the Service's position was that the assignment of income doctrine did not apply, and in the above ruling the Service applied the doctrine. Do you agree with the Service's position?

C. TRANSFER OF CASH

REVENUE RULING 69–357
1969–1 C.B. 101.

The word "property" as used in section 351 of the Internal Revenue Code of 1954 and corresponding provisions of prior Revenue Acts (relating to a transfer of property to a corporation controlled by the transferor) includes money.

* * *

Questions

Is it significant that cash is property for purposes of § 351? Since cash has a basis equal to its value, is not the nonrecognition treatment of § 351 completely irrelevant? Suppose there is a contribution of foreign currency?

D. TRANSFER OF INTANGIBLES

1. Introduction

The materials below deal with the issue of whether intangibles, such as know how, are "property" within the meaning of § 351. Although the issue arose principally in the context of transfers to foreign subsidiaries, the principles are equally applicable to transfers to domestic corporations. The Tax Reform Act of 1986 essentially eliminated this issue in the context of transfers to foreign subsidiaries by deeming the transfer of an intangible as a deemed sale for a contingent payment. *See* § 367(d).

2. Know How

REVENUE RULING 64–56
1964–1 C.B. 133.

The Internal Revenue Service has received inquiries whether technical "know-how" constitutes property which can be transferred, without recognition of gain or loss, in exchange for stock * * * under section 351 of the Internal Revenue Code of 1954.

The issue has been drawn to the attention of the Service, particularly in cases in which a manufacturer agrees to assist a newly organized foreign corporation to enter upon a business abroad of making and selling the same kind of product as it makes. The transferor typically grants to the transferee rights to use manufacturing processes in which the transferor has exclusive rights by virtue of process patents or the protection otherwise extended by law to the owner of a process. The transferor also often agrees to furnish technical assistance in the construction and operation of the plant and to provide on a continuing basis technical information as to new developments in the field.

Some of this consideration is commonly called "know-how." In exchange, the transferee typically issues to the transferor all or part of its stock.

* * *

The transfer of all substantial rights in [know-how] will be treated as a transfer of property for purposes of section 351 of the Code. The transfer will also qualify under section 351 of the Code if the transferred rights extend to all of the territory of one or more countries and consist of all substantial rights therein, the transfer being clearly limited to such territory, notwithstanding that rights are retained as to some other country's territory.

* * *

The unqualified transfer in perpetuity of the exclusive right to use a secret process or other similar secret information qualifying as property within all the territory of a country, or the unqualified transfer in perpetuity of the exclusive right to make, use and sell an unpatented but secret product within all the territory of a country, will be treated as the transfer of all substantial rights in the property in that country.

* * *

3. Meaning of "Perpetuity"

REVENUE RULING 71–564
1971–2 C.B. 179.

The Internal Revenue Service has been asked to explain the phrase "in perpetuity" as used in Revenue Ruling 64–56, C.B. 1964–1 (Part 1), 133.

Revenue Ruling 64–56 discusses whether technical "know-how" (trade secrets) constitutes property that can be transferred, without recognition of gain or loss, in exchange for stock or securities under section 351 of the Internal Revenue Code of 1954.

* * *

Secret information is sufficiently akin to patents to warrant the application, by analogy, of some of the principles of law relating to the transfer of patent rights. * * *

In order for a grant of patent rights to constitute a sale or exchange, the grant must consist of all substantial rights to the patent. One substantial right which must be transferred is the right of the transferee to use the patent for its full life, i.e., the remaining statutory length of the patent. * * *

Trade secrets, however, have useful periods which may last for an indefinite period of time, that is until they become public knowledge. Once a trade secret becomes public knowledge it is no longer protectible under the applicable law of the country in which the rights have been granted to the transferee. At this point, the property interest in the trade secret ceases.

Accordingly, it is held that an unqualified transfer of the exclusive right to use a trade secret until it becomes public knowledge and no longer protectible under the applicable law of the country where the transferee is to operate is a transfer of property for purposes of Revenue Ruling 64–56.

Revenue Ruling 64–56 is amplified.

4. *Nonexclusive License: The Service's View*

REVENUE RULING 69–156
1969–1 C.B. 101.

Advice has been requested whether the transaction described below is a transfer of property within the meaning of section 351 of the Internal Revenue Code of 1954.

X, a domestic corporation, proposes to grant certain patent rights in a chemical compound to Y, its foreign subsidiary, in exchange for Y's stock. The patent rights to be granted are the exclusive rights to import, make, use, sell, and to sublicense others under patents owned and registered by X in the country in which Y is organized and operated, covering the manufacture of the chemical compound. However, Y will agree not to assert these rights to prevent X and its subsidiaries from importing, using, and selling the chemical compound in Y's country of operation. The rights to import, use, and sell the chemical compound in Y's country of operation are substantial rights.

* * *

The grant of patent rights to a corporation will constitute a transfer of property within the meaning of section 351 of the Code only if the grant of these rights in a transaction which would ordinarily be taxable, would constitute a sale or exchange of property rather than a license for purposes of determining gain or loss. In order for such a grant of patent rights to Y to constitute a sale or exchange, the grant must consist of all substantial rights to the patent [citing, *inter alia,* Rev.Rul. 64–56, *supra*].

* * *

In the present case, the overall effect of the transaction is that X will retain for itself and its subsidiaries the substantial rights to import, use, and sell the chemical compound in the country in which Y is operated.

Accordingly, since Y will not have all substantial rights in the patent, the grant of the patent rights will not constitute a transfer of property within the meaning of section 351 of the Code, and the receipt of stock of Y by X will result in ordinary income to X.

* * *

5. *Nonexclusive License: The Court of Claims View*

E.I. DU PONT de NEMOURS & CO. v. UNITED STATES

United States Court of Claims, 1973.
471 F.2d 1211.

DAVIS, JUDGE.

* * *

In 1959, Du Pont was engaged in the domestic sale and exportation (to France, among other places) of urea herbicides. Although doing the manufacturing in this country, the company owned French patents for the product. French law provided that French-patented items must be manufactured in France within three years of the issuance of the patent. If this were not done, the owner had to grant, upon request, a license to a French producer. In order to forestall that result, with its potential loss of income, Du Pont organized (in October 1959) a wholly-owned French subsidiary, Du Pont de Nemours (France) S.A., to manufacture the herbicide in France. By agreement in December 1959 plaintiff granted to the subsidiary a royalty-free, non-exclusive license to make, use and sell urea herbicides under the French patents. Du Pont thereby gave up its right to assert patent infringement against the subsidiary's products for the duration of the license, which was for the remaining life of the patents. The subsidiary had the right to sublicense manufacturing for its own needs, but any other sublicensing could only be done with the parent's consent. In exchange for this grant, and in lieu of royalties, Du Pont received stock in the subsidiary valued at $411,500. After the award of the license, the subsidiary proceeded to arrange for manufacture of the herbicides for its own account by an unrelated French firm.

Before undertaking this arrangement, taxpayer requested rulings from the Commissioner of Internal Revenue as to whether the proposed transaction would comply with the requirements of sections 351 and 367 of the Code.

* * *

There is no question, of course, that plaintiff meets the condition of section 351 that it must be in control of the subsidiary after the transaction. The controversy implicates the other prime elements of the provision: "property", "transfer", "exchange." The Government has vacillated somewhat in tying the articulation of its position to one or another of those statutory terms. The 1959 ruling given to taxpayer deemed the patent rights transferred to the subsidiary not to be "property". Conceding that this "did not adequately express the basis for the Government's action," the defendant now stresses the reasoning of Rev.Rul. 69–156, 1969–1 Cum.Bull. 101:

> The grant of patent rights to a corporation will constitute a transfer of property within the meaning of section 351 of the Code

only if the grant of these rights in a transaction which would ordinarily be taxable, would constitute a sale or exchange of property rather than a license for purposes of determining gain or loss. In order for such a grant of patent rights to * * * constitute a sale or exchange, the grant must consist of all substantial rights to the patent.

The present emphasis is thus on the "exchange" requirement, with that factor being equated with the concept of "sale or exchange" under the capital gains provisions of the Code. If a transaction does not qualify as a "sale or exchange" for those purposes, it cannot (according to the defendant) be a "transfer" of "property" "in exchange" under section 351. On that view, the Government would be entitled to its offset since it is settled that the proceeds of a grant of a simple nonexclusive patent license are not eligible for capital gains treatment. To attain that status there must normally be a transfer of an interest in all substantial rights to the patent, or of exclusive rights in a defined area.

* * *

Having rejected defendant's chief point that "transfer * * * in exchange" under section 351 is tied to and has the same scope as "sale or exchange" under the capital gains sections, we still have to determine whether 351, as an autonomous provision, covers plaintiff's transaction.
* * *

Once the capital gains concepts are seen as irrelevant, it is not difficult to find that the non-exclusive license handed over to the subsidiary was "property". Both patents themselves and the exclusive licensing of patents have long been considered "property" under 351. It is not a far step to include a non-exclusive license of substantial value—commonly thought of in the commercial world as a positive business asset. Unless there is some special reason intrinsic to the particular provision (as there is with respect to capital assets), the general word "property" has a broad reach in tax law.

* * *

Finally, the Government suggests, quite generally, that applying section 351 to this type of transaction can open up the gate to improper tax avoidance by allowing the conversion of ordinary income into capital gain. The Revenue Service has, however, officially determined under [the predecessor of] section 367 that that is not so in this case, and that provision of the Code is adequate protection where the transfer is to a foreign corporation. If the transaction is wholly domestic, there are other principles, such as those relating to the assignment of income, step transactions, and the Commissioner's power to allocate income, which have been (and no doubt will continue to be) utilized by the Service and the courts if an attempt is made to employ section 351 for an improper end outside of the congressional purpose to postpone imposition of the tax until disposition to an outsider.

In this instance, we see no such possibility of tax avoidance. Du Pont's subsidiary has a zero basis in the license, under section 362(a), and its gain from use of the patent would be ordinary income, just as it would have been if Du Pont had not formed the subsidiary but had exploited the patent itself. There is no adequate reason here to refuse to apply section 351 according to its terms. Nor have we been shown any real need to adopt a wholesale prophylactic rule, rigidly excluding all transactions of this type from section 351, in order to forestall possible tax avoidance in other circumstances not before us and not even known to exist.

For these reasons, we hold that section 351 applies to taxpayer's transaction, and defendant is not entitled to the offset it claims.

Questions

1. Do you agree with the court's holding that a nonexclusive patent is property for purposes of § 351?

2. Individual S transferred a nonexclusive patent right to Y, a newly formed domestic corporation, in exchange for Y stock. S's basis for the patent was zero. After holding the Y stock for two years, S sold the stock for $100K. What result to S? Has S converted ordinary income into capital gain? If so, is this type of transaction any more abusive than a situation in which S transfers an inventory of widgets to Y and then sells the Y stock after holding it for the long-term holding period?

§ 2.5 THE CONTROL REQUIREMENT

A. INTRODUCTION

In order to qualify under § 351, the transferors must be in "control" of the corporation "immediately after" the exchange. The term "control" is defined in § 368(c) as "the ownership of stock possessing at least 80 percent of the total combined voting power of all classes of stock entitled to vote and at least 80 percent of the total number shares of all other classes of stock of the corporation." The Service has ruled that the second prong of this test requires the ownership of 80 percent of the total number of shares of "each" class of non-voting stock. *See* Rev.Rul. 59–259, 1959–2 C.B. 115. The following materials explore both the "control" requirement and the "immediately after" requirement.

B. ACCOMMODATION TRANSFERORS

1. *The First Circuit's View*

ESTATE OF KAMBORIAN v. COMMISSIONER
United States Court of Appeals, First Circuit, 1972.
469 F.2d 219.

ALDRICH, SENIOR CIRCUIT JUDGE.

Four individuals, hereinafter taxpayers, owned some 76% of the stock of X corporation, and two of them, as trustees for the wife of

§ 2.5 THE CONTROL REQUIREMENT

another, held 50,000 additional shares, or slightly in excess of 13%. Taxpayers individually owned all of the stock of Y corporation. For bona fide business reasons X corporation decided to acquire the Y stock in exchange for 22,871 X shares. The exchange was perfected pursuant to a formal agreement which included, with the wife's consent, the purchase of 418 X shares by the trust. This resulted in increasing taxpayers' combined holdings in X to 77.3%; the trust's interest was reduced to just under 13%, notwithstanding its purchase. However, the combined holdings of taxpayers and the trust remained in excess of 80%, and taxpayers took the position that the transaction was, accordingly, to be viewed as a tax-free exchange. 1954 Int.Rev.Code, §§ 351, 368(c). The Commissioner disagreed, claiming that the "control" group, or the transaction, see post, was to be limited to taxpayers as the former owners of the Y stock. In refusing to include the trust's purchase the Commissioner relied, in part, upon Regulation 1.351–1(a)(1)(ii).

The Tax Court ruled in favor of the Commissioner, 56 T.C. No. 66 (1971), and taxpayers seek review. Basically, they make a frontal attack on the regulation, urging us to hold it invalid as going beyond what they claim is a plain and positive statute.

Taxpayers' brief contains a wistful aside that there is involved a large tax and only a small discrepancy. We are not moved, legally or emotionally, by this fact. But in order to avoid any overfall therefrom, we will imagine another case that would have to be decided against the government if taxpayers are correct and all arranged transactions, regardless of their purpose or their connection with one another, are to be viewed as a single exchange. Let us suppose that P owns 10% and S 90% of the stock of W, and P owns all of the stock of Z. If P transfers his Z stock to W for further W shares, ending up with a 30% interest, it is obviously not a tax-free exchange. But if P induces S to buy, contemporaneously, one share of W stock for cash the present petitioners would say that P and S are to be considered jointly as exchanging property, and since together they owned over 80% of the transferee corporation, P may claim the statutory exception.

Our analysis does not lead to such a result. By the term "property [that] is transferred," the statute contemplates a single transaction, even though, as it goes on to recognize, there may be a number of transferors or participants. What is a transaction must be determined in the light of the statutory purpose, lest taxpayers be allowed to frustrate that purpose by manipulation of clearly taxable exchanges.

* * * [I]n our hypothetical, considering P alone, there was not a "mere change in the form of ownership." Before the transaction P "owned" Z corporation, since he owned 100% of its stock. After the transaction his ownership of Z was reduced to 30% because he held only a 30% interest in W, the transferee corporation. In keeping with "economic sense" a taxpayer may be allowed a certain amount of slack. This has been ruled to be 20%; and had P ended with an 80% interest in W, and thus of Z, his ownership of the latter would not be thought to be materially changed. 1954 Int.Rev.Code § 368(c). But where P does not own that 80% it can be permissible to consider transfers by other owners only if those transfers were, in economic terms, sufficiently related to P's to make all of the transfers parts of a single transaction.

* * * The four shareholders of Y decided it would be advantageous to merge Y with X. Finding themselves short of the requirements for tax-free treatment, they persuaded a shareholder of X, who was a complete stranger to Y, to make a token purchase of X shares. Other than the fact that the trust's participation was incorporated into the acquisition agreement, there was no relation between the exchange of Y shares and this very minor purchase. The trust transferred no Y shares. The cash it contributed to X—$5,000 for 418 shares of a corporation with nearly 400,000 shares outstanding—could have had no significant impact on X's ability to conduct its business. The trustees' desire to help the Y stockholders avoid taxes, warrantably found by the Tax Court to have been the primary motive for the trust's purchase, cannot be used to make a single transaction out of otherwise unrelated transfers.

Without going into every ramification of the Regulation, in this case it appropriately and fairly fits our interpretation of the statute.

* * *

Affirmed.

Questions

In his opinion, Judge Aldrich poses a hypothetical in which *P*, a 10 percent shareholder of *W*, transfers 100 percent of the stock of *Z* to *W* for additional *W* shares, thereby ending up with 30 percent of *W*'s stock. The Judge concludes that this transaction is "obviously not a tax free exchange." Is the judge correct? *See* §§ 368(a)(1)(B) and 354(a). How could the transaction in *Kamborian* have been restructured so that the taxpayers would have received the desired nonrecognition treatment?

2. *The Service's Ruling Policy on Accommodation Transferors*

REVENUE PROCEDURE 77–37, § 3.07

1977–2 C.B. 568 at 570.

When a person transfers property to a corporation in exchange for stock or securities of such corporation and the primary purpose of the transfer is to qualify under section 351 of the Code the exchanges of property by other persons transferring property, the property transferred will not be considered to be of relatively small value, within the meaning of section 1.351–1(a)(1)(ii) of the regulations, if the fair market value of the property transferred is equal to, or in excess of, 10 percent of the fair market value of the stock and securities already owned (or to be received for services) by such person.

§ 2.5   THE CONTROL REQUIREMENT   85

Problem

Recall that in the *James* case, *supra,* James contributed to the newly formed corporation the loan commitments, and the Talbots contributed $44K in real property. The stock which was valued at $44K was distributed 50–50. The court held that since the loan commitments were not property, the transaction did not qualify for non-recognition treatment. How much cash or property would James have had to contribute in order to qualify the transaction under § 351? *See* § 1.351–1(a)(1)(ii). Does Rev.Proc. 77–37 apply to this case?

C. CONTROL IMMEDIATELY AFTER THE EXCHANGE

1. *Sale of Stock Pursuant to Best Efforts Underwriting*

AMERICAN BANTAM CAR CO. v. COMMISSIONER

Tax Court of the United States, 1948.
11 T.C. 397.

[Four individuals (the "associates") purchased the assets of Austin, a bankrupt corporation, for $5,000. The assets were subject to liabilities of approximately $219,000. The associates conceived a plan to organize the petitioner corporation, American Bantam Car, to take over the Austin assets.

The plan provided that in exchange for the assets, the associates would receive 300,000 shares of common stock of American Bantam Car and that 90,000 shares of preferred would be offered to the public in a "best efforts" underwriting. The underwriters would receive a portion of the associates' common stock as a partial commission.

Five days after the incorporation and transfer of the Austin assets, American Bantam Car entered into a best efforts contract with the underwriters. About two months later, the associates placed their 300,000 shares of common stock in escrow at Butler County National Bank & Trust, subject to an agreement that the bank would hold the stock until the completion of the sale of the publicly offered preferred. The sale by the underwriters was completed about 15 months later, and at that time 87,900 of the 300,000 common shares were transferred to the underwriters by the escrow agent.

American Bantam Car argued that because the associates did not have control "immediately after" the initial exchange, the corporation took a cost basis for the Austin assets.]

HILL, JUDGE:

The first major test of a tax-free exchange under section 112(b)(5) [now § 351] is whether the transferors have "control" of the corporation immediately after the exchange. * * *

The first question, then, is whether the associates had such "control" over the petitioner immediately after the exchange on June 3, 1936. Prima facie, when the various steps taken to organize the new corporation and transfer assets to it are considered separately, the associates did have "control" of the petitioner immediately after the exchange within the statutory definition of the word. We think that from June 3 to June 8, 1936, they owned 100 per cent of all the issued stock, and from June 8, 1936, until October 1937 they owned stock possessing at least 80 per cent of the total combined voting power of all classes of stock. On June 3, 1936, the associates were issued absolutely and unconditionally 300,000 shares of no par common stock. The resolution of the board of directors of petitioner accepting the associates' offer of the Austin assets attached no strings whatsoever to the issuance of the stock to them. It is true that on June 2, 1936, petitioner had an authorized capital stock of 700,000 shares, 600,000 common shares and 100,000 preferred shares, but in determining control only stock actually issued is considered. * * *

On June 8, no other common stock had been issued, and a contract regarding possible future assignment of those 300,000 shares already issued was not entered into before that date. No preferred stock had been issued on June 3, nor was a contract for its sale provided until June 8. The statutory words "immediately after the exchange" require control for no longer period; in fact, momentary control is sufficient. * * * Certainly, therefore, the associates had absolute control over the corporation from June 3 to June 8, 1936, due to their complete ownership of all outstanding stock.

It is true that, by virtue of their agreement with the associates on June 8, 1936, the underwriters did at that time acquire the right to earn shares of the common stock issued to the associates by the sale of certain percentages of preferred stock, but the ownership of the 300,000 shares remained in the associates until such sales were completed. It is significant to note that this agreement stated that the associates were the owners of the 300,000 shares. On August 16, 1936, the associates deposited all their shares in escrow with the Butler County National Bank & Trust Co., but they only surrendered possession by the terms of their agreement with the bank and retained all other attributes of ownership.

During all of 1936 the associates retained ownership over the 300,000 shares of common stock and during that interval the underwriters sold only 14,757 shares of preferred stock, which did not entitle them to any common stock under the agreement of June 8, 1936. * * * It was not until October 1937 when the underwriter Grant received 87,900 shares of the associates' common stock in fulfillment of the underwriting agreement, that the associates lost "control" of petitioner within the statutory definition of the word. Retention of "control" for such a duration of time satisfies the governing provision of section 112(b)(5) [now § 368(c)].

Petitioner, however, contends that the series of steps organizing the new corporation, transferring assets to it, and arranging for the sale of its preference stock must be considered as parts of the integrated plan formulated in May 1936, and, therefore, considered as parts of a single transaction. * * *

In determining whether a series of steps are to be treated as a single indivisible transaction or should retain their separate entity, the courts use a variety of tests. Among the factors considered are the intent of the parties, the time element, and the pragmatic test of the ultimate result. An important test is that of mutual interdependence. Were the steps so interdependent that the legal relations created by one transaction would have been fruitless without a completion of the series?

* * *

A close examination of the facts surrounding the exchange in the present case makes it clear that the exchange of assets for stock and the subsequent transfer of a portion of that stock to Grant * * * should not be considered part of the same transaction so as to deprive the associates of "control" immediately after the exchange. * * * First, there was no written contract prior to the exchange binding the associates to transfer stock to the underwriters. * * * Secondly, when the transfer of shares to the underwriters was embodied specifically in a formal contract, the underwriters received no absolute right to ownership of the common stock, but only when, as, and if, certain percentages of preferred stock were sold. How clearly contingent was the nature of their rights is illustrated by the fact that only one underwriter, Grant, met the terms of the agreement and became entitled to any shares. Thirdly, the necessity of placing the 300,000 shares in escrow with a bank is indicative of complete ownership of such stock by the associates following the exchange.

The standard[s] required by the courts to enable them to say that a series of steps are interdependent and thus should be viewed as a single transaction do not exist here. * * *

* * *

Thus we conclude that in the present case the exchange of assets for stock between the associates and petitioner on June 3, 1936, was a separate completed transaction, distinct from the subsequent transfer of common stock to Grant, so that the associates were in control of petitioner immediately after the exchange within the provisions of section 112(b)(5) [now § 368(c)].

Reviewed by the court.

Questions

What element of a § 351 transaction is at issue in *American Bantam Car*? Why is the taxpayer arguing against nonrecognition? Does the court take an overly mechanical approach in determining whether the associates had control "immediately after"? Would the result have been the same if it were the Commissioner arguing that the associates did not have control immediately after? How do you evaluate the court's step transaction analysis?

2. Sale of Stock Pursuant to Pre-existing Commitment

INTERMOUNTAIN LUMBER CO. v. COMMISSIONER

Tax Court of the United States, 1976.
65 T.C. 1025.

[Shook organized S & W corporation, transferring to it property in exchange for stock. Shook and S & W treated the organization as a § 351 transaction. One half of the S & W stock received by Shook was subject to a purchase agreement with Wilson, and shortly after the organization, Wilson purchased the stock. The taxpayer, Intermountain Lumber Co., later purchased the S & W stock from Shook and Wilson, and Intermountain and S & W filed a consolidated return. In order to increase S & W's depreciation deduction, Intermountain took the position that the organization of S & W was not a § 351 transaction and that, therefore, S & W had a cost basis for the assets received from Shook.]

Opinion

* * * [I]f section 351 was applicable to the incorporators when S & W was formed, S & W and Intermountain must depreciate the assets of S & W on their consolidated returns on the incorporators' basis. Sec. 362(a). If section 351 was inapplicable, and the transfer of assets to S & W was accordingly to be treated as a sale, S & W and Intermountain could base depreciation on those returns on the fair market value of those assets at the time of incorporation, which was higher than the incorporators' cost and which would accordingly provide larger depreciation deductions. Secs. 167(g), 1011, and 1012.

Petitioner thus maintains that the transfer to S & W of all of S & W's property at the time of incorporation by the primary incorporator, one Dee Shook, was a taxable sale. It asserts that section 351 was inapplicable because an agreement for sale required Shook, as part of the incorporation transaction, to sell almost half of the S & W shares outstanding to one Milo Wilson over a period of time, thereby depriving Shook of the requisite percentage of stock necessary for "control" of S & W immediately after the exchange.

Respondent, on the other hand, maintains that the agreement between Shook and Wilson did not deprive Shook of ownership of the shares immediately after the exchange, as the stock purchase agreement merely gave Wilson an option to purchase the shares. Shook accordingly was in "control" of the corporation and the exchange was thus nontaxable under section 351.

* * *

After considering the entire record, we have concluded that Shook and Wilson intended to consummate a sale of the S & W stock, that they never doubted that the sale would be completed, that the sale was an integral part of the incorporation transaction, and that they considered

§ 2.5   **THE CONTROL REQUIREMENT**   89

themselves to be coowners of S & W upon execution of the stock purchase agreement in 1964. * * *

We accordingly cannot accept respondent's contention that the substance varied from the form of this transaction, which was, of course, labeled a "sale." The parties executed an "option" agreement on the same day that the "agreement for sale" was executed, and we have no doubt that they could and indeed did correctly distinguish between a sale and an option.

* * *

We thus believe that Shook, as part of the same transaction by which the shares were acquired (indeed, the agreement for sale was executed before the sawmill was deeded to S & W), had relinquished when he acquired those shares the legal right to determine whether to keep them. Shook was under an obligation, upon receipt of the shares, to transfer the stock as he received Wilson's principal payments. * * * We note also that the agreement for sale gave Wilson the right to prepay principal and receive all 182 shares at any time in advance. Shook therefore did not own, within the meaning of section 368(c), the requisite percentage of stock immediately after the exchange to control the corporation as required for nontaxable treatment under section 351.

* * *

Questions

1. Could the transaction in *Intermountain Lumber* have been modified to ensure § 351 treatment?

2. If you had represented Shook on the sale of the S & W stock to Intermountain would you have requested any type of representation from Intermountain relating to its future treatment of the contribution transaction?

3. In both *Intermountain* and *American Bantam Car,* the Commissioner argued that § 351 was applicable. Why? The Commissioner prevailed in *American Bantam Car* and the taxpayer prevailed in *Intermountain.* What is the reason for the different results? Is the reason a sound justification for determining whether a transaction is within or without § 351?

3. *Sale of Stock Pursuant to Best Efforts and Firm Commitment Underwriting*

REVENUE RULING 78–294
1978–2 C.B. 141.

Advice has been requested regarding the effect of a sale of stock by an underwriter to the general public on the control requirement of section 351 of the Internal Revenue Code of 1954 in the situations described below.

A is a person who conducted business in a noncorporate form. The business needed additional capital. *A* decided to incorporate the business to increase its capital through a public offering of stock. Therefore, A sought the assistance of U, an underwriter of corporate stock, in order to engage in the transactions described below. In accordance with the plan, A organized a new corporation, Z. Z had capital stock of 1,000 authorized but unissued shares upon its formation.

Situation 1

Pursuant to an agreement among A, U, and Z, A transferred all of A's business property to Z in exchange for 500 shares of Z stock. U agreed to use its best efforts as Z's agent to sell the 500 unissued shares of Z stock to the general public at $200 per share. U succeeded in selling the 500 shares within two weeks of the initial offering with no change in the terms of the offering. This transaction is considered to fall within the general definition of a "best efforts" underwriting.

Situation 2

Pursuant to an agreement among A, U, and Z, A transferred all of A's business property to Z in exchange for 500 shares of Z stock, and U transferred $100,000 in cash to Z in exchange for the remaining 500 shares. At the time of U's purchase of 500 Z shares U had not entered into a binding contract to dispose of the Z shares. However, U intended to sell its 500 shares of Z stock, but, if unsuccessful, was required to retain them. Following the A–Z and U–Z exchanges, U sold its 500 shares of Z stock to the general public within two weeks of the initial offering. A retained A's 500 shares of Z stock. This transaction is considered to fall within the general definition of a "firm commitment" underwriting.

In a public offering of stock, the function of a best-efforts underwriter is solely to bring the parties together as agent of the corporation. The best-efforts underwriter transfers no property to the corporation and should not be considered a transferor for purposes of section 351 of the Code under these circumstances. On the other hand, in a best-efforts underwriting the movement of property from the public investors to the corporation is direct and uninterrupted so that in appropriate cases the public investors should be deemed to be transferors in testing whether the requirements of section 351 have been met.

Situation 1—Analysis and Holding

In *Situation 1* the business needed additional capital so that the public stock offering was integral to A's plan to incorporate the going business. In such circumstances it is appropriate to treat the incorporation and subsequent public offering as elements in a single transaction that may be tested for qualification under section 351 of the Code.

* * *

Furthermore, the charter and bylaws of the issuing corporation as well as various public documents required to be filed with governmental agencies in connection with a public offering of stock set forth the rights of the parties to the offering. Thus, the rights of the parties in *Situation*

1 are previously defined as required by section 1.351–1(a)(1) of the regulations.

Finally, the sale of stock to the public in *Situation 1* took place in a short period of time with no change in the terms of the offering. These facts indicate that the transfers in *Situation 1* occurred with an expedition consistent with orderly procedure within the meaning of section 1.351–1(a)(1) of the regulations.

Therefore, the public investors in *Situation 1* should be treated, along with A, as transferors for purposes of section 351 of the Code.

Accordingly, in *Situation 1* the transferors are in control of Z immediately after the exchange within the meaning of section 1.351–1(a)(1) of the regulations. The overall transaction qualifies under section 351 of the Code since the other requirements of that section are also met in *Situation 1*. * * *

SITUATION 2—ANALYSIS AND HOLDING

In a firm-commitment underwriting, the underwriter transfers its own property to the issuing corporation in exchange for stock of that corporation. Therefore, such underwriter should be considered a transferor for purposes of section 351 of the Code.

Furthermore, the firm-commitment underwriter in the instant case assumes the risk of reselling the acquired stock to the general public and in so doing recognizes that it may be forced to retain a portion of that stock for an extended period. Consequently, since the transaction is completed for section 351 purposes with the underwriter's exchange of property for the stock, its subsequent resale of that stock will not violate the control "immediately after" requirement of that Code section. See *American Bantam Car Co.* * * *

Accordingly, under *Situation 2,* since A and the firm-commitment underwriter hold 100 percent of the Z stock at culmination of the incorporation transaction, the transferor group is in control of Z immediately after the exchange. Furthermore, as the other requirements of section 351 of the Code are also satisfied, the transaction is entitled to treatment thereunder.

4. *Issuance of Stock Directly to Donees*

D'ANGELO ASSOCIATES, INC. v. COMMISSIONER

Tax Court of the United States, 1978.
70 T.C. 121.

[Dr. D'Angelo and his wife transferred $15,000 to a newly formed corporation and caused the 60 shares to be issued 10 each to Mrs. D'Angelo and the couple's five children. Shortly after the transfer Dr. and Mrs. D'Angelo purportedly sold certain assets to the corporation for cash and notes. One of the issues was whether Dr. and Mrs. D'Angelo had control of the corporation (taxpayer). On this issue, the court reasoned:]

Control: We view the events before us as equivalent to the formation and capitalization of the corporation, followed by a gift to the D'Angelo children of the controlling interest when Dr. and Mrs. D'Angelo caused petitioner to directly issue the 50 shares to the children. At the end of the series of transactions on June 30, 1960, all of the assets remaining in the corporation were contributed by Dr. and Mrs. D'Angelo, including the $15,000 in cash. This cash was in the possession of Dr. and Mrs. D'Angelo both before and after the transfers with the petitioner merely issuing stock directly to Mrs. D'Angelo and in the names of the children. The D'Angelo children did not purchase the stock issued in their names, but were simply the beneficiaries of a gift from their parents.

The loss of control of petitioner resulting from the gift of stock does not preclude the application of section 351(a), which requires that the transferors be in control of the transferee corporation "immediately after the exchange." This requirement is satisfied where, as here, the transferors transfer by gift the stock they were entitled to receive in exchange for the property they transferred to the corporation, regardless of whether such disposition was planned before or after acquiring control. See *Wilgard Realty Co.*

* * *

The issuance of the stock by petitioner to the D'Angelo children is the direct consequence of "the absolute right" of Dr. and Mrs. D'Angelo to designate who would receive all of the stock. * * * Since it is possession of this power which is essential under section 351 for control, it follows that the transferors herein, Dr. and Mrs. D'Angelo, were in control of petitioner immediately after the exchange. See *American Bantam Car Co.* * * *.

* * *

5. Transfer to New Corporation Followed by Sale of Stock to Other Investors

REVENUE RULING 79–194
1979–1 C.B. 145.

Issue

Is the control requirement of section 351(a) of the Internal Revenue Code of 1954, which provides for non-recognition of gain or loss on transfers of property to a controlled corporation, satisfied where part of the stock of the controlled corporation received by a transferor in exchange for property is sold to other persons who also transferred property to the corporation in exchange for stock?

Facts
Situation (1)

Corporation Z and a group of investors, pursuant to a binding agreement between them, transferred property to a newly organized corporation, Newco, in exchange for all of Newco's stock (a single class of voting common stock). Z and the investors received 80 percent and 20 percent, respectively, of Newco's stock. Pursuant to the agreement Z sold an amount of its Newco stock for its fair market value to the investors to bring its ownership down to 49 percent. Newco would not have been formed if the investors had not agreed to transfer property to it and their agreement to do so was conditioned on the sale by Z to them of part of Z's Newco stock.

Situation (2)

X, a domestic corporation, operates a branch in a foreign country. The foreign country enacted a nationalization law that required that the business that X's branch was engaged in be incorporated in the foreign country and that its citizens be the majority owners of such corporation. A governmental agency in the foreign country directed X to transfer all of the assets of its branch to a newly formed foreign country corporation that is, or will be, at least 51 percent owned by its citizens. Accordingly, X and a group of investors, who were citizens of the foreign country, pursuant to a binding agreement between them, transferred property to Newco, a corporation newly organized in the foreign country, in exchange for all of Newco's stock (a single class of voting common stock). X and the investors received 99 percent and one percent, respectively, of Newco's stock. Pursuant to the agreement, X sold an amount of its Newco stock for its fair market value to the investors to bring its ownership down to 49 percent; the investors would pay X in a series of yearly installments. Newco would not have been formed if the investors had not agreed to transfer property to it and their agreement to do so was conditioned on the sale by X to them of part of X's Newco stock. Further, the investors transferred property to Newco in order to become co-transferors with X, and they purchased X's Newco stock in lieu of the assets of X's branch because of the foreign governmental agency's directive. * * *

LAW AND ANALYSIS

* * *

Since the sales of Newco stock by Z to the investors, and of Newco stock by X to the investors, were integral parts of the incorporations and pursuant to binding agreements entered into prior to the exchanges, the control requirement of section 351(a) of the Code is determined after the respective sales.

In Situation (1), after the sales were completed, 49 percent of the Newco stock was owned by Z and 51 percent of the stock was owned by the investors. Therefore, the persons transferring property to Newco in exchange for Newco stock owned 100 percent of the Newco stock "immediately after the exchange" within the meaning of section 351(a). The fact that there was a shift in ownership of stock among the transferors after their exchanges with Newco does not affect the application of section 351(a). See example (1) under section 1.351–1(b). * * *

In Situation (2), after the sales were completed, 49 percent of the Newco stock was owned by X and 51 percent of the Newco stock was owned by the investors. Because the amount of stock issued directly to the investors for property is of relatively small value in comparison to the value of all the stock received by them in the transaction, the stock received by the investors is not taken into account in considering whether the transaction qualifies under section 351(a) of the Code. Compare section 1.351–1(a)(1)(ii) of the regulations. Thus, for purposes of determining control under section 351, the investors were not transferors. Therefore, since the person (X) transferring property to Newco in exchange for Newco stock owned only 49 percent of the Newco stock "immediately after the exchange", the control requirement of section 351(a) is not satisfied. * * *

* * *

§ 2.6 IMPACT OF § 482 IN § 351 CONTEXT

See § 482.

ELI LILLY & CO. v. COMMISSIONER

Tax Court of the United States, 1985.
84 T.C. 996, *affirmed this issue* 856 F.2d 855 (7th Cir.1988).

[*Eli Lilly & Co.*, a domestic corporation, (Lilly) transferred certain patent rights to pharmaceuticals to Lilly P.R., a wholly owned subsidiary incorporated in Puerto Rico. Lilly P.R. manufactured the pharmaceutical (DARVON) in Puerto Rico and then sold the product to Lilly. Lilly P.R.'s income was exempt from tax under a special provision under the Code. In this case, the Service is attempting to use § 482 to tax Lilly on all of Lilly P.R.'s income. The Service first argued that § 482 overrides § 351.]

* * *

The issue now before us is whether Lilly P.R. should be considered the owner of the propoxyphene and napsylate patents and manufacturing know-how for purposes of determining arm's-length prices to petitioner for Lilly P.R.'s Darvon and Darvon–N products. Respondent concedes the validity of petitioner's section 351 transfer of the manufacturing intangibles to Lilly P.R. and that Lilly P.R. is the legal owner of the intangibles. Respondent alleges, however, that he has the authority under section 482 to disregard the legal ownership of the intangibles and to reallocate the income attributable to the intangibles from Lilly P.R. back to petitioner in order to prevent the evasion of taxes or clearly to reflect petitioner's income.

* * *

As we stated earlier, section 482 provides that respondent may make allocations between related parties when necessary either to prevent the evasion of taxes, or in order clearly to reflect their incomes. Moreover, section 1.482–1(d)(5), Income Tax Regs., specifically provides:

> Section 482 may, when necessary to prevent the avoidance of taxes or to clearly reflect income, be applied in circumstances described in sections of the Code (such as section 351) providing for nonrecognition of gain or loss.

National Securities Corp. v. Commissioner, 137 F.2d 600 (3d Cir. 1943), affg. 46 B.T.A. 562 (1942), and its progeny delineate the situations in which courts have upheld section 482 allocations that, in effect, ignored nonrecognition transfers. Those situations can be separated into two narrowly defined categories: (1) Cases in which property was transferred in a nonrecognition transaction and subsequently disposed of by the transferee, and in which the sole purpose of the transfer was to achieve tax consequences on the disposition of the property by the transferee that were more favorable than the tax consequences of a disposition by the transferor (see, e.g., *National Securities Corp. v. Commissioner, supra* * * * and (2) cases in which the nonrecognition transfer of property resulted in an artificial separation of income from the expenses of earning the income. See, e.g., *Rooney v. United States,* 305 F.2d 681 (9th Cir.1962); *Central Cuba Sugar Co. v. Commissioner,* 198 F.2d 214 (2d Cir.1952). * * *

I. NATIONAL SECURITIES CORP. AND AVOIDANCE OF TAXES

The leading case in the first category is *National Securities Corp. v. Commissioner, supra.* In that case, a parent corporation transferred shares of stock in an unrelated corporation, Standard Gas & Electric Co. (Standard), to the taxpayer, its wholly owned subsidiary, in exchange for additional shares of the taxpayer's stock. The transaction qualified as a nonrecognition exchange under the predecessor of section 351. The parent's basis in the Standard stock was approximately $140,000, but the stock had only a market value of approximately $8,500 at the time of the transfer. At the end of the transfer year, the taxpayer sold the stock for $7,175 and reported on its return a loss of $133,202, the difference between the parent's basis in the stock (the taxpayer's carryover basis under section 362) and the amount realized by the taxpayer. The parent, having already realized a net capital loss for that year in excess of the amount deductible under the relevant revenue provision, could not have derived any tax benefit from the loss on the sale if it had retained and then sold the Standard stock itself.

Acting pursuant to section 482, the Commissioner disregarded the nonrecognition transfer of stock and allocated the entire loss on the sale from the taxpayer to the parent. The taxpayer contended that the nonrecognition and basis provisions of sections 351 and 362, respectively, precluded the application of section 482 to the taxpayer. The Court of Appeals for the Third Circuit upheld the Commissioner's allocation from the taxpayer to the parent under section 482 of the deduction for the portion of the loss sustained before the transfer.

The Court of Appeals based its holding in *National Securities Corp.* upon the clear reflection of income standard rather than the tax avoidance test of section 482. Factually, however, the case involved a tax avoidance situation in which a nonrecognition transaction was used solely to shift to the taxpayer the tax consequences of a preconceived disposition of stock in order to obtain a tax benefit that could not be obtained by the parent. Because there was no valid business purpose for the transfer, we view *National Securities Corp.* and all members of the first category primarily as tax avoidance cases.

The facts of the case before us are readily distinguishable from those discussed above. Petitioner's transfer of the patents and manufacturing know-how to Lilly P.R. was motivated by bona fide business reasons, and Lilly P.R. did not thereafter dispose of the transferred assets. * * *

* * * Accordingly, *National Securities Corp. v. Commissioner, supra,* and the tax avoidance standard of section 482 are inapplicable.

II. CENTRAL CUBA SUGAR, ROONEY, AND CLEAR REFLECTION OF INCOME

Central Cuba Sugar Co. v. Commissioner, 198 F.2d 214 (2d Cir. 1952), and *Rooney v. United States,* 305 F.2d 681 (9th Cir.1962), are typical of the second category of cases noted earlier, i.e., cases in which nonrecognition transfers or property resulted in artificial separations of income from the expenses of earning that income. In each of those cases, the taxpayer transferred a planted crop, together with other assets, to a newly formed corporation in exchange for all the stock of the corporation. The crop was harvested and the profit from the sale of the crop was reported as income by the new corporation. The taxpayer deducted the expenses incurred in growing the crop prior to its transfer and as a result, sustained a net operating loss which it sought to carry back to prior years. In each case, the Court of Appeals upheld the Commissioner's allocation of all the expenses of raising the crop from the taxpayer to the transferee corporation.

* * *

Both *Central Cuba Sugar* and *Rooney* dealt with bifurcations of a single taxable year. Both cases involved nonrecognition transfers of unharvested crops to new corporations, with the transferee corporations reporting the crop income and the transferors deducting the crop growing expenses and, consequently, suffering net operating losses. Both cases also involved transfers which the Courts acknowledged were motivated by valid business reasons. * * *

Several of the factors mentioned above distinguish those cases from the one before us. In our case, petitioner's transfer of the intangibles in 1966 effected a change of ownership of those intangibles to Lilly P.R. Lilly P.R. did not sell or otherwise dispose of the intangibles in the year of the transfer, or in any other year, but held them and used them in the active conduct of its business of manufacturing and selling Darvon and Darvon–N products. It is the income from the conduct of that business in 1971, 1972, and 1973, *not* the income (or loss) realized upon the disposition of the transferred assets, that respondent is attempting to allocate from Lilly P.R. to petitioner.

* * *

Therefore, the income produced by Lilly P.R. attributable to its use of the transferred property cannot be allocated to petitioner under § 482 because it is income *earned* by Lilly P.R. from the use of *its* property in *its* business. * * *

Finally, *Central Cuba Sugar* and *Rooney* each involved the mismatching of income and expenses occurring within a single taxable year. * * * Respondent argues that petitioner's transfer of the intangibles to Lilly P.R. under section 351 without reimbursement for the expenses incurred in connection with the research and development of Darvon and Darvon–N created a distortion of income. However, no mismatching of income and expenses, as occurred in *Central Cuba Sugar* and *Rooney,* resulted from petitioner's 1966 transfer of patents and know-how to Lilly P.R. The income in question was income earned by Lilly P.R., using the patents and know-how in its business during 1971, 1972, and 1973. * * *

In any event, we believe the expenses giving rise to the development of the patents and know-how simply are too remote in time to be matched with the income earned by Lilly P.R. during the years in issue. * * *

III. Substance Over Form

* * * Respondent argues that, although he is not attacking the validity of the section 351 transfer, he is authorized by section 482 to allocate the income from the transferred property back to petitioner. In essence, respondent is making the ubiquitous "substance over form" argument: he acknowledges the valid "form" of the transaction but challenges the "substance" thereof because of the alleged income distortion resulting from the transfer. Quoting extensively from *Gregory v. Helvering,* 293 U.S. 465 (1935), and its progeny, respondent contends that the technical form of a transaction cannot control its true nature where that form does not accord with economic reality.

We find that both the form and the substance of petitioner's transfer of assets to Lilly P.R. comported with economic reality. * * *

Note and Question

In this case, Lilly conducted research and development that led to the DARVON patents. Lilly properly deducted those expenditures under § 174. Rather than using the patents to manufacture DARVON in the U.S., Lilly transferred the patents to its wholly owned subsidiary, Lilly P.R., which was not subject to U.S. tax. Lilly P.R. then used the patents in manufacturing DARVON in Puerto Rico for sale back to Lilly. Thus, the economic effect of this transaction is that the expenses of creating the patent are deductible from U.S. gross income; however, the income from using the patents is not included in U.S. gross income. Can this case be properly distinguished from *Central Cuba* and *Rooney,* which are discussed by the court?

§ 2.7 IMPACT OF BUSINESS PURPOSE AND STEP TRANSACTION DOCTRINES IN § 351 TRANSACTIONS

A. INCORPORATION PRIOR TO REORGANIZATION

The following materials present issues involving the stock for stock (B) reorganization, which is defined in § 368(a)(1)(B). In this type of reorganization, an acquiring corporation issues its voting stock to the target corporation's shareholders in exchange for at least 80 percent of the outstanding voting stock of a target corporation. In such cases, the target shareholders receive nonrecognition treatment under § 354 and take a substituted basis under § 358 for the acquiring corporation's stock. (B) reorganizations are considered in detail in Chapter 15.

1. *The Commissioner's Position*

REVENUE RULING 70–140
1970–1 C.B. 73.

Advice has been requested whether the provisions of section 351 of the Internal Revenue Code of 1954 apply to the transfer of property under the circumstances described below.

All the outstanding stock of X corporation was owned by A, an individual. A also operated a similar business in the form of a sole proprietorship on the accrual basis of reporting income. Pursuant to an agreement between A and Y, an unrelated corporation, A transferred all the assets of the sole proprietorship to X in exchange for additional shares of X stock. A then transferred all his X stock to Y solely in exchange for voting common stock of Y, which was widely held.

* * *

Section 368(a)(1)(B) of the Code provides, in part, that the term reorganization includes the acquisition by one corporation, in exchange solely for all or a part of its voting stock, of stock of another corporation if, immediately after the acquisition, the acquiring corporation has control of such other corporation.

The two steps of the transaction described above were part of a prearranged integrated plan and may not be considered independently of each other for Federal income tax purposes. The receipt by A of the additional stock of X in exchange for the sole proprietorship assets is transitory and without substance for tax purposes since it is apparent that the assets of the sole proprietorship were transferred to X for the purpose of enabling Y to acquire such assets without the recognition of gain to A.

Section 351 of the Code is not applicable to the transfer of the sole proprietorship assets to Y inasmuch as A was not in control of Y immediately after the transfer. The sole proprietorship cannot be a party to a reorganization within the meaning of section 368(b) of the Code. Thus, the transfer of the sole proprietorship assets to X is treated as a sale by A of the assets to Y followed by a transfer of these assets by Y to the capital of X.

Accordingly, that portion of the stock of Y received by A equal to the fair market value of the sole proprietorship assets is treated as an amount received from the sale of those assets. Gain or loss is recognized to A as provided in sections 1001 and 1002 of the Code. The exchange by A of all the outstanding stock of X, solely for voting common stock of Y, other than the Y stock received in payment for the sole proprietorship assets, is a reorganization within the meaning of section 368(a)(1)(B) of the Code.

Questions

Rev.Rul. 70–140 above holds that the purported § 351 transaction is a taxable exchange. How does the ruling treat the purported stock for stock (B) reorganization (§§ 368(a)(1)(B) and 354)? Is the treatment of the (B) any different from a swap of assets of the sole proprietorship for Y stock and a separate swap of the X stock for Y stock?

2. *The Tax Court's Position*

WEIKEL v. COMMISSIONER

Tax Court of the United States, 1986.
51 T.C.M. 432.

[The taxpayer transferred property to Dispersalloy, Inc. in a § 351 transaction. Shortly thereafter, Dispersalloy was acquired by J & J Inc. in a transaction that was intended to qualify as a stock for stock reorganization under § 368(a)(1)(B).]

OPINION

The issue in this case is whether petitioners' exchange of stock of Dispersalloy, Inc., for stock of J & J was a non-taxable transaction under sections 354 and 368(a)(1)(B), or whether the exchange should be "stepped together" with the incorporation of Dispersalloy and characterized as a taxable sale of Dispersalloy assets by petitioner for J & J stock pursuant to the step-transaction doctrine.

Section 354 provides as a general rule that no gain or loss is to be recognized if stock or securities in a corporation which is a party to a reorganization are exchanged pursuant to a plan of reorganization for stock or securities in another corporation also a party to the reorganization. A reorganization is defined in section 368(a)(1)(B) as:

the acquisition by one corporation, in exchange solely for all or a part of its voting stock (or in exchange solely for all or a part of the voting stock of a corporation which is in control of the acquiring corporation), of stock of another corporation if, immediately after the acquisition, the acquiring corporation has control of such other corporation (whether or not such acquiring corporation had control immediately before the acquisition).

What constitutes control for purposes of section 368(a)(1)(B) is defined in section 368(c) as:

the ownership of stock possessing at least 80 percent of the total combined voting power of all classes of stock entitled to vote and at least 80 percent of the total number of shares of all other classes of stock of the corporation.

On the surface this transaction qualified as a reorganization; J & J acquired all of the stock of Dispersalloy, Inc. in exchange solely for a part of its voting stock. But, stock for stock exchanges between corporations have been subjected to additional scrutiny pursuant to a judicially created doctrine called the step-transaction doctrine. Under the step-transaction doctrine an analysis is made of the separate steps of a transaction to determine whether each step should be accorded independent legal significance or whether the steps should be treated as related steps in one unified transaction, and "stepped together" to produce the actual result.

* * *

[The court here briefly outlines the three-step transaction tests: (1) the end result test, (2) the interdependence test, and (3) the binding committment test. *See* Sec. 1.3.G.5.]

* * *

Petitioners contend that their incorporation of Dispersalloy followed by an exchange of all of the stock of Dispersalloy, Inc. for an amount of J & J stock was a tax-free "B" reorganization under sections 354 and 368(a)(1)(B). Petitioners argue that the step-transaction doctrine is inapplicable to their transaction because Dispersalloy, Inc. was not a sham corporation; it was in operation conducting business for almost three years after the exchange of stock occurred. In addition, petitioners contend that the incorporation of Dispersalloy and the exchange of stock were two separate transactions since petitioners did not execute a definitive agreement for the exchange of stock until several months after the incorporation of Dispersalloy, and the incorporation would not have been fruitless if the exchange of stock had not occurred. Moreover, petitioners contend that they had formulated the intent to incorporate Dispersalloy regardless of their negotiations with J & J since Dispersalloy had begun to produce a profit. * * *

Respondent contends that petitioners' transfer of his sole proprietorship assets to Dispersalloy, Inc., was one step in a prearranged integrated plan to transfer his assets to J & J in exchange for stock. Therefore respondent contends the incorporation of Dispersalloy and the exchange of stock should be stepped together to demonstrate that the transaction was in essence a purchase of petitioners' assets by J & J, not a tax-free reorganization.

The question presented is a factual one; therefore a careful examination must be made of the transaction at hand. After making such an examination, we agree with petitioners.

We must first determine whether the incorporation of Dispersalloy was an event with independent economic substance. Respondent does not contend that the incorporation of Dispersalloy was a sham; rather, respondent argues that the incorporation lacked economic substance independent from the later exchange of stock. Respondent urges us to find that the incorporation of Dispersalloy was simply one link in a chain of steps to transfer the assets of petitioners' sole proprietorship to J & J for stock. Respondent cites *West Coast Marketing Corp. v. Commissioner,* 46 T.C. 32 (1966), and Rev.Rul. 70–140, 1970–1 C.B. 73, as support for his contentions.

In *West Coast Marketing Corp.,* this Court held that the taxpayer formed a corporation called Manatee solely for the purpose of transferring to it the title to certain properties in exchange for Manatee's stock. An agreement for the sale of the properties to an unrelated corporation, Universal, had been detailed in a letter dated April 16, 1959. Thereafter, on April 30, 1959, Manatee was formed and received title to the properties noted. All of Manatee's stock was then transferred to Universal. Universal liquidated Manatee on December 18, 1959.

While the transaction in *West Coast Marketing Corp.* and the transaction herein do contain similarities, there are several crucial distinctions that demonstrate why the step-transaction doctrine is not applicable in petitioners' situation. In *West Coast Marketing Corp.* when Manatee was formed the sale of the taxpayer's properties to Universal was imminent and was in fact prearranged. Universal had made a formal offer to the taxpayer. The sale had been approved by Universal's Board of Directors. All that remained was for the taxpayer to obtain a release of the mineral rights on the properties.

In contrast, in the instant case petitioners never arranged a sale of their sole proprietorship assets to J & J. The transaction was from the beginning a stock for stock exchange. * * *

Petitioners also differ from the taxpayer in *West Coast Marketing Corp.* in the purpose behind their incorporation. In *West Coast Marketing Corp.,* Manatee was not formed for a business purpose but was instead formed when the sale of land to Universal was imminent to serve as a conduit for passing title to Universal. Manatee did not engage in any business activities and was dissolved shortly thereafter.

In contrast, petitioner formulated the intent to manufacture Dispersalloy in corporate form as early as 1970 when he first filed the articles of incorporation for ASMP. * * * After Dispersalloy was incorporated and its stock exchanged for stock of J & J it continued in operation for almost three years. Based upon the above discussion, we do not find *West Coast Marketing Corp.* to be controlling as regards the characterization of petitioners' transaction.

Rev.Rul. 70–140, 1970–1 C.B. 73, is also distinguishable from petitioners' situation. In Rev.Rul. 70–140, A, an individual owned all of the outstanding stock of X corporation. A also operated a sole proprietorship. Y, an unrelated corporation, made an agreement with A that A would transfer the assets of his sole proprietorship to X for X stock. A then transferred all of his X stock to Y for Y voting stock. The ruling holds that the two steps of the transaction were part of a prearranged integrated plan and were thus "stepped together" to reflect the true nature of the transaction which was a sale by A of his assets to Y followed by a transfer of these assets by Y to the capital of X.

This ruling is similar to the facts of *West Coast Marketing Corp.* and is thus distinguishable from petitioners' transaction for some of the same reasons. The facts of the ruling illustrate a transaction that was conducted pursuant to a prearranged plan with X serving as a mere conduit for the transfer of A's assets from X to Y in order to attempt a tax-free transaction. As noted previously, petitioners did not incorporate and then conduct an exchange of stock with J & J pursuant to a prearranged plan. Petitioners had independent valid business purposes for incorporating. Moreover, Dispersalloy, Inc. was not a mere conduit. Dispersalloy, Inc. operated for almost three years after the agreement with J & J was finalized.

* * *

Viewing the facts of the instant case in light of the step-transaction doctrine we are not persuaded that the doctrine is applicable under any of its various tests. Under the "end result" test, for reasons previously discussed, we are not convinced that when petitioners incorporated Dispersalloy they intended for the end result of their transaction to be a sale of their assets to J & J for stock. * * *

Under the interdependence test it is clear that petitioners intended to incorporate whether or not they finalized an agreement with J & J for an exchange of stock. The incorporation of Dispersalloy would therefore not have been fruitless without the exchange of stock. Accordingly, petitioners' transaction does not run afoul of the interdependence test.

Moreover, petitioners did not have a binding commitment with J & J to exchange the stock of Dispersalloy for the stock of J & J prior to the incorporation of Dispersalloy. The incorporation of Dispersalloy was a separate transaction. It was not until sometime after the incorporation of Dispersalloy that petitioners reached a definitive agreement with J & J to exchange stock. Therefore, once they had incorporated Dispersalloy petitioners were free to carry on the manufacture of Dispersalloy.

After a consideration of the relevant authorities we have determined that the transaction in the instant case is controlled by our decision in

Vest v. Commissioner, 57 T.C. 128 (1971), affd. in part, revd. on another issue 481 F.2d 238 (5th Cir.1973), cert. denied 414 U.S. 1092 (1973).

In *Vest,* the taxpayers organized a corporation, V Bar, for the purpose of correcting certain title problems in some land interests and to develop the mineral interests in the land. At the time the corporation was formed the taxpayers were unaware that an exchange of stock was being contemplated between V Bar, and Standard, an unrelated corporation that was interested in a lease of the oil and gas rights on taxpayers' land. The taxpayers' attorney had discussed the possibility of an exchange of stock with a representative from Standard but had not informed the taxpayers of this possibility. V Bar was incorporated on July 21, 1965. On August 25, 1965 a plan of reorganization was signed by Standard and V Bar that provided for an exchange of stock. V Bar did not engage in any business operations and was dissolved shortly after the reorganization occurred. Despite the close proximity of the incorporation of V Bar, to the exchange of V Bar stock for Standard stock, we held that the step-transaction doctrine was inapplicable. We held thusly because there was a business purpose for the formation of V Bar, *i.e.,* to develop the mineral rights of the taxpayers' properties and to resolve the title problems inherent in those properties. *Vest v. Commissioner, supra* at 143–146.

It is equally true in the instant case that petitioners had a business purpose for incorporating Dispersalloy—a purpose that was formulated as early as 1970. * * *

We therefore conclude that Dispersalloy, Inc. was organized for substantial business purposes. Hence, we agree with petitioner that the transaction herein was effective as a tax-free reorganization.

* * *

B. CONTRIBUTION OF STOCK TO NEW CORPORATION IN ORDER TO AVOID TAXATION ON DIVIDENDS: NO BUSINESS PURPOSE

REVENUE RULING 60–331
1960–2 C.B. 189.

[Corporation *M* was required by the personal holding company provisions of the Code to distribute a dividend to its sole shareholder, *A*. In order to avoid direct taxation on the dividend, *A* transferred the stock of *M* to corporation *N*, a wholly owned corporation, in a § 351 transaction. Corporation *N* collected the dividend and claimed the 85 percent [now 80%] dividends received deduction under § 243.]

The question in this case then is whether, under the facts as disclosed, the distribution to the corporate entity may be disregarded and the deficiency dividend, distributed by the personal holding company to avoid imposition of personal holding company tax, considered constructively received by the individual shareholders for Federal income tax purposes.

* * *

Throughout the above-cited cases [including *Gregory v. Helvering*, Sec. 1.3.G.2.] is an underlying theme that only bona fide business transactions having a legitimate business purpose in addition to the minimization of taxes will be recognized for tax purposes, and then only if the characterization the taxpayer places on the transactions is in reality what it purports to be in form. A transaction which has no purpose other than the avoidance or reduction of taxes, will be ignored for tax purposes.

In the instant case the motive for the transfer by the individual shareholders of their stock of corporation M in exchange for stock of corporation N was that of minimizing Federal income taxes. Accordingly, it is held that the deficiency dividend distributed by the personal holding company is to be treated as having been constructively received by A and his wife, rather than by corporation N, and is includible in their gross incomes under section 61 of the Code.

Questions

What is the precise holding of Rev.Rul. 60–331? Is A taxed on the gain inherent in the M stock? That is, is the transfer completely outside of § 351? Should it be?

C. SUCCESSIVE § 351 TRANSACTIONS

REVENUE RULING 77–449
1977–2 C.B. 110.

Corporation P has a wholly owned subsidiary, $S1$, which has a wholly owned subsidiary, $S2$. All of the corporations are domestic corporations. P transferred machinery used in its trade or business to $S1$, solely in exchange for additional shares of $S1$ stock. As part of the same plan, $S1$ transferred the same machinery to $S2$ solely in exchange for additional shares of $S2$ stock, $S2$ retained the machinery for use in its business and P and $S1$ retained the stock received by them in the exchanges.

* * *

Under the circumstances described above, the transfers are viewed separately for purposes of section 351 of the Code.

* * *

Accordingly, since each transfer satisfies the requirements of section 351 of the Code, no gain or loss is recognized by the transferors.

Note

The principles of Rev.Rul. 77–449 were also applied to a transfer by a subsidiary (1) to an 80% owned second-tier subsidiary (*see* Rev.Rul. 83–34,

1983–1 C.B. 79) and (2) to a partnership in which the subsidiary became a partner (*see* Rev.Rul. 83–156 1983–2 C.B. 66).

§ 2.8   USE OF § 351 IN ACQUISITION OF PUBLICLY–HELD CORPORATION: COMPULSIVE § 351

Normally § 351 is utilized in the formation of small closely-held corporations. As the following ruling illustrates, § 351 also may be used in the acquisition of a publicly-held target firm.

REVENUE RULING 74–502
1974–2 C.B. 116.

Corporation Y wanted to acquire 100–percent control of corporation X, which stock is widely held, in a stock-for-stock exchange intended to be nontaxable to the exchanging shareholders under section 351 of the Internal Revenue Code of 1954. Under the laws of the state involved, subject to approval of the board of directors of each corporation and of the proper State authority, and subject to a favorable vote of at least two-thirds of the outstanding stock of the acquired corporation, the acquiring corporation, by operation of law, becomes the owner of all of the outstanding stock of the acquired corporation, except for stock owned by dissenters, on the effective date of the transaction. At such time, those shareholders of the acquired corporation who do not dissent are entitled to receive shares of stock of the acquiring corporation in exchange for their shares of stock of the acquired corporation. Any shareholder of the acquired corporation who dissents is entitled to receive in cash the appraised value of his shares from the acquired corporation.

At a meeting of the shareholders of X (after prior approval of the plan by the X board of directors and the State authority), 70 percent of the outstanding X stock was voted in favor of a plan of acquisition of the X stock by newly formed corporation Y, and two percent was voted against. The remaining 28 percent of the X stock was not voted. On the effective date of the transaction, Y became the owner of all the outstanding X stock by operation of State law except for two percent of such stock which was owned by those X shareholders who exercised their appraisal rights and who received cash from X for their X stock. In exchange for their X stock, the X shareholders, including those who did not vote on the plan but who participated in the exchange because they did not dissent received voting common stock and nonvoting preferred stock of Y which represented all of the Y stock outstanding after the transaction.

Held, inasmuch as the identity and rights of all the transferors (the nondissenting X shareholders) were defined by state law and the exchange of their X stock for Y stock was by operation of law simultaneous on the effective date of the transaction, the nondissenting X shareholders were in control of Y immediately after the exchange within the meaning of section 351 of the Code. Therefore, under section 351 no gain or loss is recognized to the former X shareholders who exchanged their X stock for Y stock. Those X shareholders who received cash for their X stock are treated as having had such stock redeemed by X with the redemption being subject to the provisions of section 302.

§ 2.9 CONTRIBUTIONS TO CAPITAL

1. *Shareholder Contributions of Property*

Shareholder contributions to capital are transactions in which the shareholders do not receive additional stock. The corporation receives nonrecognition treatment under § 118 rather than under § 1032.

Regulation § 1.118–1 says that pro rata shareholder contributions "represent an additional price paid for the shares of stock held by the individual shareholders * * *." Thus, it seems clear that in a pro rata shareholder contribution, the shareholders will, under § 358, increase the basis of their outstanding stock by the basis of the property contributed.

Section 61(a)(12) of the Code includes in gross income, the income from the discharge of indebtedness. This general rule of inclusion is qualified in § 1.61–12(a), however, when a shareholder forgives an indebtedness owed to him by his corporation. This regulation provides:

In general, if a shareholder in a corporation which is indebted to him gratuitously forgives the debt, the transaction amounts to a contribution to the capital of the corporation to the extent of the principal of the debt.

2. *Nonshareholder Contributions of Property*

REVENUE RULING 75–557
1975–2 C.B. 33.

Advice has been requested whether, under the circumstances described below, amounts received by the taxpayer for connection fees are includible in its gross income under section 61 of the Internal Revenue Code of 1954 or are excludable as contributions to its capital under section 118.

The taxpayer, a domestic corporation, is engaged in furnishing water through its facilities. It is regulated by the state in which it is incorporated as a public utility subject to a continuing duty to provide services to its customers.

The purchaser of a home in a new subdivision is charged a connection fee to obtain water service. The fee includes a construction charge for furnishing and installing a service line and water meter to the water line running to the purchaser's lot.

Section 1.61–1(a) of the Income Tax Regulations provides, in part, that gross income means all income from whatever source derived, unless excluded by law.

Section 118 of the Code provides that in the case of a corporation, gross income does not include any contribution to the capital of the taxpayer. Section 1.118–1 of the regulations recognizes that the exclusion from gross income extends to non-shareholder contributions to capital. However, the regulation further provides that the exclusion does not apply to money or property transferred in exchange for goods or services to be supplied by the taxpayer.

The Internal Revenue Service has acquiesced in a series of cases in which the United States Board of Tax Appeals held that contributions in aid of the construction of facilities by a public utility or railroad do not result in taxable income to the recipient if the facilities are used to provide services to the contributor at rates subject to regulation by a regulatory body. [Citations omitted.]

* * *

The Service has decided that a change in the position represented by the cited acquiescences in the public utility decisions is warranted in light of the decision of the Supreme Court of the United States in *United States v. Chicago, Burlington and Quincy Railroad Co.*, 412 U.S. 401 (1973), where the taxpayer was a railroad whose rates were subject to regulatory supervision. The Court held that government payments received for improvements at grade-crossings and intersections were not contributions to capital under the Internal Revenue Code of 1939. The Court set forth five characteristics of a nonshareholder contribution to capital for purposes of both the 1939 and 1954 Internal Revenue Code, including that the amounts received must not constitute payments for specific, quantifiable services. * * *

Accordingly, in the instant case, since the connection fees charged to a new lot owner are necessary to obtain water services, the amounts will constitute gross income to the taxpayer under section 61 of the Code.

* * *

3. *Shareholder's Prorata Contribution of Stock*

REVENUE RULING 70–291
1970–1 C.B. 168.

All of the stockholders of a company surrendered to the company, pro rata, fifty percent of the company's outstanding capital stock in order to eliminate a deficit appearing on the books of the company.

Held, the effect of the transaction was to decrease by one-half the number of shares of stock attributable to each stockholder. Upon the surrender of fifty percent of the company's stock to the company the cost or other basis of the stock surrendered by each stockholder is added to the basis of the shares retained by him as provided by section 1016 of the Internal Revenue Code of 1954. No gain or loss is recognized to the stockholders on the transaction.

* * *

4. Shareholder's Non–Prorata Contribution of Stock

COMMISSIONER v. FINK

Supreme Court of the United States, 1987.
483 U.S. 89, 107 S.Ct. 2729, 97 L.Ed.2d 74.

JUSTICE POWELL delivered the opinion of the Court.

The question in this case is whether a dominant shareholder who voluntarily surrenders a portion of his shares to the corporation, but retains control, may immediately deduct from taxable income his basis in the surrendered shares.

I

Respondents Peter and Karla Fink were the principal shareholders of Travco Corporation, a Michigan manufacturer of motor homes. Travco had one class of common stock outstanding and no preferred stock. Mr. Fink owned 52.2 percent, and Mrs. Fink 20.3 percent, of the outstanding shares. Travco urgently needed new capital as a result of financial difficulties it encountered in the mid–1970s. The Finks voluntarily surrendered some of their shares to Travco in an effort to "increase the attractiveness of the corporation to outside investors." * * * As a result, the Finks' combined percentage ownership of Travco was reduced from 72.5 percent to 68.5 percent. The Finks received no consideration for the surrendered shares, and no other shareholder surrendered any stock. The effort to attract new investors was unsuccessful, and the corporation eventually was liquidated.

On their 1976 and 1977 joint federal income tax returns, the Finks claimed ordinary loss deductions totaling $389,040, the full amount of their adjusted basis in the surrendered shares. The Commissioner of Internal Revenue disallowed the deductions. He concluded that the stock surrendered was a contribution to the corporation's capital. Accordingly, the Commissioner determined that the surrender resulted in no immediate tax consequences, and that the Finks' basis in the surrendered shares should be added to the basis of their remaining shares of Travco stock.

In an unpublished opinion, the Tax Court sustained the Commissioner's determination for the reasons stated in *Frantz v. Commissioner*, 83 T.C. 162, 174–182 (1984), aff'd, 784 F.2d 119 (CA2 1986), cert. pending, No. 86–11. In *Frantz* the Tax Court held that a stockholder's non pro rata surrender of shares to the corporation does not produce an immediate loss. The court reasoned that "[t]his conclusion * * * necessarily follows from a recognition of the purpose of the transfer, that is, to bolster the financial position of [the corporation] and, hence, to protect and make more valuable [the stockholder's] retained shares." 83 T.C., at 181. Because the purpose of the shareholder's surrender is "to decrease or avoid a loss on his overall investment," the Tax Court in *Frantz* was "unable to conclude that [he] sustained a loss at the time of the transaction." "Whether [the shareholder] would sustain a loss, and if so, the amount thereof, could only be determined when he subsequently disposed of the stock that the surrender was intended to protect and make more valuable." *Ibid.* * * *

In this case, a divided panel of the Court of Appeals for the Sixth Circuit reversed the Tax Court. 789 F.2d 427 (1986). The court concluded that the proper tax treatment of this type of stock surrender turns on the choice between "unitary" and "fragmented" views of stock ownership. Under the "'fragmented view,'" "each share of stock is considered a separate investment," and gain or loss is computed separately on the sale or other disposition of each share. According to the "'unitary view,'" "the 'stockholder's entire investment is viewed as a single indivisible property unit,'" and a sale or disposition of some of the stockholder's shares only produces "an ascertainable gain or loss when the stockholder has disposed of his remaining shares." * * *

We granted certiorari to resolve a conflict among the circuits, * * * and now reverse.

II

A

It is settled that a shareholder's voluntary contribution to the capital of the corporation has no immediate tax consequences. [*See* § 1.263(a)–2(f).] Instead, the shareholder is entitled to increase the basis of his shares by the amount of his basis in the property transferred to the corporation. [*See* § 1016(a)(1).] When the shareholder later disposes of his shares, his contribution is reflected as a smaller taxable gain or a larger deductible loss. This rule applies not only to transfers of cash or tangible property, but also to a shareholder's forgiveness of a debt owed to him by the corporation. [*See* § 1.61–12(a).] Such transfers are treated as contributions to capital even if the other shareholders make proportionately smaller contributions, or no contribution at all. * * *

III

A shareholder who surrenders a portion of his shares to the corporation has parted with an asset, but that alone does not entitle him to an immediate deduction. Indeed, if the shareholder owns less than 100 percent of the corporation's shares, any non pro rata contribution to the corporation's capital will reduce the net worth of the contributing shareholder. A shareholder who surrenders stock thus is similar to one who forgives or surrenders a debt owed to him by the corporation; the latter gives up interest, principal, and also potential voting power in the event of insolvency or bankruptcy. But, as stated above, such forgiveness of corporate debt is treated as a contribution to capital rather than a current deduction. The Finks' voluntary surrender of shares, like a shareholder's voluntary forgiveness of debt owed by the corporation, closely resembles an investment or contribution to capital. * * *

* * *

In this case, as in many cases involving closely-held corporations whose shares are not traded on an open market, there is no reliable method of determining whether the surrender will result in a loss until the shareholder disposes of his remaining shares. Thus, the Finks' stock surrender does not meet the requirement that an immediately deductible loss must be "actually sustained during the taxable year." § 1.165–1(b) (1986).

Finally, treating stock surrenders as ordinary losses might encourage shareholders in failing corporations to convert potential capital losses to ordinary losses by voluntarily surrendering their shares before the corporation fails. In this way shareholders might avoid the consequences of § 165(g)(1), that provides for capital loss treatment of stock that becomes worthless. Similarly, shareholders may be encouraged to transfer corporate stock rather than other property to the corporation in order to realize a current loss.

We therefore hold that a dominant shareholder who voluntarily surrenders a portion of his shares to the corporation, but retains control, does not sustain an immediate loss deductible from taxable income. Rather, the surrendering shareholder must reallocate his basis in the surrendered shares to the shares he retains. The shareholder's loss, if any, will be recognized when he disposes of his remaining shares. * * *

* * *

§ 2.10 POLICY PERSPECTIVE: THE CONTROL REQUIREMENT

The nonrecognition treatment under § 351 is available only if the contributing shareholder or shareholders have control of the corporation immediately after the exchange. Control is defined in § 368(c) as the ownership of at least 80% of the total combined voting power of the corporation and at least 80% of each nonvoting class of stock. There is no control requirement under § 721, which provides nonrecognition treatment on the transfer of property to a partnership. The following excerpt proposes a modification in the control test under § 351 and the addition of a control test under § 721.

THOMPSON, TAX POLICY IMPLICATIONS OF CONTRIBUTIONS OF APPRECIATED AND DEPRECIATED PROPERTY TO PARTNERSHIPS, SUBCHAPTER C CORPORATIONS AND SUBCHAPTER S CORPORATIONS IN EXCHANGE FOR OWNERSHIP INTERESTS

31 Tax L.Rev. 29, 51–60 (1975), with permission.

SEARCH FOR A RATIONAL POLICY—POLICY IMPLICATIONS OF CONTROL REQUIREMENT

It is unsound from a tax policy standpoint for all contributions to partnerships in exchange for partnership interests to be given nonrecognition treatment while only a limited number of contributions to corporations in exchange for stock are given nonrecognition treatment. There is no economic difference between contributions to the two types of enterprises; therefore, contribution transactions should be treated the same without respect to the nature of the enterprise. Since the investor group on an initial organization exchange ends up with 100 percent of the ownership interests, there is no difference in the treatment with respect to an initial organization exchange, because section 351 with its 80 percent control group test is analogous to the treatment under section 721. Different treatment can occur, however, in the case of contributions to operating enterprises. A transfer to an operating partnership in exchange for a partnership interest will not give rise to recognition, whereas a transfer to an operating corporation in exchange for stock may give rise to recognition.

The strongest policy reason for giving either transaction nonrecognition treatment would seem to be the facilitation of business development through the attraction of additional capital. A second reason is that, in general, there could be no sound policy justification for taxing exchanges which are mere changes in form of ownership. Set off against these rationales is the desirability of treating exchanges which resemble pure sales as taxable. In the partnership area, the legislative judgment appears to have been that no contribution of property in exchange for a partnership interest resembles a pure sale. In the corporate area, the tension between the two policies is resolved by the legislative judgment that contributions in which less than 80 percent control is received more nearly resemble pure sales than mere changes in form of ownership. Such transactions will, therefore, be treated as taxable. The 80 percent control test for corporations and the complete absence of a control test for partnerships can produce illogical results. A contribution of property to an operating partnership in exchange for a 1 percent partnership interest will not produce recognition, but a contribution of property to an operating corporation in exchange for 79 percent of the stock in the case of gain property or 50 percent of the stock in the case of loss property will produce recognition. A contribution to a partnership in exchange for a 1 percent partnership interest obviously resembles a pure sale, and, more importantly, a contribution to a corporation in exchange for 79 percent of the stock is clearly the type of transaction which both (1) will facilitate business development and (2) resembles an exchange which is a mere change in form of ownership.

Since the 80 percent control requirement can lead to absurd results but at the same time may be easily circumvented with creative tax planning, what meaningful purpose does it serve? Is it not just a trap for the uninformed? On the other hand, cannot the blanket nonrecognition treatment for any and all contributions to partnerships operate to treat transactions which are in economic substance sales as nonrecognition events? There is, however, logic and illogic in both rules. The problem from a tax policy standpoint is to attempt to eliminate the absurdities which are alien to both common sense and economic reality and to design a simple and logical scheme that would be equally applicable to partnerships and corporations. * * *

* * *

[T]he following rules of nonrecognition for contributors to partnerships and corporations are proposed:

(1) Nonrecognition treatment should continue to apply to contributions to newly organized enterprises.

(2) Nonrecognition should apply to contributions of property to operating enterprises by a group of investors in exchange for at least 50 percent of the value of the outstanding ownership interests determined as of immediately after the contribution, and only the ownership interests received for the property contributed should be considered in determining whether the 50 percent test is met.

(3) Nonrecognition treatment should be accorded to contributions of property to an operating enterprise by a single investor in exchange for at least 25 percent of the value of the outstanding ownership interests determined as of immediately after the contribution, and only the ownership interests received for the property contributed should be considered in determining whether the 25 percent test is met.

Questions and Note

1. Is there a sound basis for the absence of a control test for partnership contributions? Is the corporate control test sound? Is the suggested approach sound? Can you suggest any alternatives to or modifications of the suggested approach?

2. The American Law Institute has proposed that § 351 nonrecognition treatment be available to transfers by 20% shareholders. *See* American Law Institute, *Federal Income Tax Project, Subchapter C,* 188–192 (June 13, 1980).

Chapter 3

CORPORATE CAPITALIZATION AND RELATED ISSUES

§ 3.1 SCOPE

This chapter focuses on issues that can arise in structuring the capitalization of a corporation. Sec. 3.2 provides general background information on corporate capital structures, and Sec. 3.3 introduces many of the tax considerations involved in structuring the debt and equity capital of a corporation. Sec. 3.4 explores the debt/equity issue in the context of a § 351 transaction, and Sec. 3.5 explores this issue in the context of the characterization of the payment made on a corporate instrument as either interest or a dividend. Sec. 3.6 considers the distinction between debt and preferred stock, and Sec. 3.7 examines the treatment of subordinated debt that is payable in stock of the issuer.

Sec. 3.8 presents an outline of the former proposed debt/equity regulations under § 385. Although these regulations have been withdrawn, they can be of assistance in analyzing debt/equity issues. Sec. 3.9 discusses the ARCN controversy which lead to the withdrawal of the § 385 regulations. Sec. 3.10 introduces the basic rules governing the issuance of debt instruments with original issue discount. This section also takes a brief look at the treatment of applicable high yield discount obligations. Sec. 3.11 examines the treatment of worthless stock and debt, and Sec. 3.12 discusses the treatment of losses on Section 1244 stock.

The issues covered here are explored in greater detail in Chapter 4 of *Federal Taxation of Business Enterprises, supra,* Chapter 1, note 1 and in Chapter 4 of Bittker and Eustice, *Corporations, supra* Sec. 1.4.

§ 3.2 INTRODUCTION TO THE FINANCING DECISION

TREASURY REPORT, INTEGRATION OF INDIVIDUAL AND CORPORATE TAX SYSTEMS

5–6, (January 6, 1992).

CORPORATE CAPITAL STRUCTURE

Corporations have three alternatives for financing new investments: (1) issuing new equity, (2) using retained earnings, or (3) issuing debt. There can be important nontax benefits and costs of alternative corporate financing arrangements, and the tax system should avoid prejudicing financial decisions.

The current classical corporate tax system discriminates against equity financing of new corporate investment. Because of the two levels of taxation of corporate profits, the cost of equity capital generally exceeds the cost of debt capital. The Congressional Research Service estimates, under realistic assumptions, the total effective Federal income tax rate on corporate debt to be 20 percent, compared with 48 percent for corporate equity. Moreover, the total effective tax rate on debt can be negative. The lower effective tax rate for debt financed corporate investment than for equity financed corporate investment encourages the use of debt by corporations, assuming nontax factors that affect financing decisions do not change.

If a corporation borrows from an individual to finance an investment, the corporation deducts the interest payments from its taxable income and is therefore not taxed on the investment's pre-tax return to the extent of interest payments, although the lender is taxable on the interest at the individual tax rate. * * *

§ 3.3 INTRODUCTION TO TAX STAKES INVOLVED IN DEBT EQUITY ISSUES*

This section introduces the various tax issues presented when structuring the capital of a corporation. Capitalization issues arise throughout the life cycle of a corporation, from the initial incorporation transaction under § 351 to the liquidation, sale or reorganization of the corporation. Some of the more important considerations include:

(1) Under § 351, the contributing shareholders receive nonrecognition treatment on the receipt of stock in exchange for property but not on receipt of debt instruments.

(2) Interest paid on debt is generally deductible by a corporation in computing its taxable income. See § 163. Dividend payments

---

* Based on § 4.02 of *Federal Taxation of Business Enterprises, supra* Chapter 1 note 1, with permission.

by a corporation with respect to its stock are not deductible. Therefore, capitalizing a corporation with debt is generally favored over equity. If the corporation is too heavily financed with debt, the debt may be recharacterized as equity. This is one of the major tax issues in leverage buyouts (LBOs).

(3) In general, a corporate shareholder receives a dividend received deduction with respect to dividends received from domestic corporations. *See* § 243 and Sec. 4.4. The deduction can be either 70%, 80%, or 100% of the dividend. Therefore, a corporate holder may prefer to have the instrument treated as preferred stock rather than debt, whereas a corporate issuer may prefer a debt classification. *See* Sec. 3.6.

(4) The redemption by a corporation of its stock may be treated as either (a) a dividend taxable as ordinary income, or (b) a sale or exchange that produces return of capital treatment and a capital gain. *See* § 302 and Chapter 5. On the other hand, the redemption of a debt instrument generally gives rise to a return of capital and capital gain. *See* § 1271. Although the rate distinction between capital gain and ordinary income has been narrowed, holders generally prefer sale or exchange treatment on a redemption in order to recover basis.

(5) On the issuance of a debt instrument for cash or property, consideration must be given to the original issue discount provisions. *See* § 1271 et seq. and Sec. 3.10. The interest on debt instruments with excessive amounts of OID (*i.e.*, applicable high yield discount obligations) may be either disallowed or deferred. *See* § 163(i) and (e)(5) and Sec. 3.10.C Also, in any lending transaction between a corporation and either a shareholder or an employee, consideration must be given to the below market loan provisions. *See* § 7872 and Sec. 4.7.E.

(6) When stock or debt becomes worthless or is disposed of at a loss, the issue is presented as to whether the loss is characterized as a capital or ordinary loss under the rules of §§ 165, 166 or 1244. *See* Secs. 3.11 and 3.12. The impact of §§ 165 and 166 in a liquidation context is examined in Sec. 9.3.D. Section 1244 provides for ordinary loss treatment, rather than capital loss treatment, for small business corporation stock. *See* Sec. 3.12.

(7) Even if debt is treated as debt for federal income tax purposes, if the debt is used in the acquisition of stock or assets (*i.e.*, corporate acquisition indebtedness), the interest deduction may be disallowed. *See* § 279.

(8) The interest deduction with respect to publicly offered debt instruments is generally disallowed if the instruments are not in registered form. *See* § 163(f).

In resolving the issue of whether an interest in a corporation is, for example, (1) debt or equity, (2) stock or a security, (3) preferred stock or debt, or (4) preferred stock or common stock, it is necessary to look principally at court decisions, and in some cases the regulations and rulings. The Code does not define these terms.

In order to promote greater certainty in resolving debt equity classification issues, Congress enacted § 385 in 1969. Under this section, the Treasury is authorized to promulgate regulations that determine "whether an interest in a corporation is to be treated for purposes of * * * [the Code] as stock or indebtedness (or as in part stock and in part indebtedness." Section 385(b) enumerates the following factors the Treasury may take into account in determining whether an interest in a corporation is stock or indebtedness:

(1) whether there is a written unconditional promise to pay on demand or on a specified date a sum certain in money in return for an adequate consideration in money or money's worth, and to pay a fixed rate of interest,

(2) whether there is subordination to or preference over any indebtedness of the corporation,

(3) the ratio of debt to equity of the corporation,

(4) whether there is convertibility into the stock of the corporation, and

(5) the relationship between holdings of stock in the corporation and holdings of the interest in question.

Although § 385 was enacted in 1969, the Treasury did not promulgate proposed regulations until March 24, 1980. These regulations were amended several times and then withdrawn. Notwithstanding the absence of regulations under § 385, an analysis of these former regulations can assist in resolving debt equity issues. For that reason Sec. 3.8 outlines the last set of § 385 regulations.

§ 3.4 DEBT–EQUITY ISSUES IN THE CONTEXT OF § 351

PIEDMONT CORP. v. COMMISSIONER

United States Court of Appeals, Fourth Circuit, 1968.
388 F.2d 886.

WINTER, CIRCUIT JUDGE: The essential question we must decide is whether the assignment to the taxpayer of certain option rights held by its sole stockholders in return for $10,000 cash and $160,000 in unsecured promissory notes constituted a *bona fide* sale or a contribution to capital. The Tax Court concluded that the successive transfers of the option were in effect a contribution of capital and that the promissory notes must be regarded as evidencing an equity investment, with the interest paid thereon regarded as a non-deductible dividend on preferred stock. * * * Finding no evidentiary basis on which to conclude that the transaction should be treated other than a sale, we reverse.

* * *

§ 3.4 DEBT–EQUITY ISSUES

As the Tax Court observed, the essential question we must decide arises because of § 351 of the Internal Revenue Code, 26 U.S.C.A. § 351. Our problem is whether the successive transfers of the option were *bona fide* sales, paid for by promissory notes, or whether Burnett and Loewenstein transferred their option rights to taxpayer at the risk of taxpayer's business as a contribution to capital. The Tax Court correctly noted that the essential nature of the transaction is to be determined from a consideration of all of the surrounding circumstances.

As factors indicating that the transactions were sales, the Tax Court, correctly we think, pointed out that the notes were unconditional promises to pay, with fixed and not unreasonably prolonged maturity dates, that they bore reasonable interest and that they conferred no voting rights on the holders. Moreover, the notes were not subordinated to the debts due other creditors and until the *bona fides* of the transactions were questioned, the interest and installments of principal were paid when due. An additional factor establishing the validity of the transactions as sales was the reasonableness of the price paid for assignments of portions of the option when compared to their actual value, because any evidence that the value was inflated would support the inference that the notes were pretextuous devices to channel income to Burnett and Loewenstein taxable solely as capital gains.

The Tax Court did find significant the fact that Burnett and Loewenstein received notes in equal principal amounts, since they each owned an equal amount of taxpayer's capital stock. It noticed this fact as "consistent with a conclusion that the notes represent an equity interest in the corporation." While a disproportion between stock ownership and note ownership [is] evidence of bona fide indebtedness since the advance made by a stockholder in greater proportion than his stock may be treated as some evidence of what an outside lender would advance, * * * the converse is not necessarily true. * * *

The Tax Court also concluded that since Burnett and Loewenstein had identical interests in the notes and in taxpayer's capital stock, it was reasonable to infer that if taxpayer had not been financially successful, the notes would have been subordinated to the taxpayer's debts to other creditors. Our review of the record discloses no evidentiary basis from which this inference can properly be drawn. Mere equality of position as creditors and owners of capital stock gives no basis for determining what might have happened if taxpayer had gone bankrupt. In that event, Burnett and Loewenstein, as creditors, could share in *pari passu* with other unsecured creditors; their ownership of equity would provide no compulsion, or indeed, incentive to subordinate their claims.

As the Tax Court ultimately recognized, the only substantial factor supporting a determination that the transfers were not sales is the factor of taxpayer's undercapitalization, at the time of the first transfer of a portion of the option. The Tax Court rested its conclusion on *Burr Oaks Corporation v. C.I.R.*, 365 F.2d 24 (7 Cir.1966), and *Aqualane Shores, Inc. v. C.I.R.*, 269 F.2d 116 (5 Cir.1959), both of which upheld the treatment of a purported sale as a contribution to capital. The Tax Court distinguished the instant case from *Sun Properties v. United States,* 220 F.2d 171 (5 Cir.1955), in which, notwithstanding a "thin" capitalization, the transfer of an income-producing warehouse in exchange for an unsecured promise to pay was deemed a sale and not a contribution to capital. Our analysis of these decisions leads us to conclude that *Burr Oaks* and *Aqualane* are clearly distinguishable from the instant case, and that we should follow the *Sun Properties* decision. Stated otherwise, we can find no basis to ignore the form of the transaction into which the parties cast their dealings. In arriving at this result, we are mindful that each case must be decided on its own facts.

[The court pointed out that the venture here was much less speculative than the venture in *Burr Oaks* and *Aqualane*.]

In the *Sun Properties* case, a warehouse building, which was rented, and which produced substantial revenues, was transferred for a consideration of $125,000, payable at the rate of $4,000 semi-annually, without interest. Sun Properties had only nominal equity capital but, notwithstanding, the transaction was treated as a sale and not a contribution to capital. The mere fact that Sun Properties was a "thin corporation" was held by the Court not enough, standing alone, to require that the transaction be treated as a contribution of capital, rather than a sale.

Admittedly, in the case at bar the success of the venture was not as sure as the venture in the *Sun Properties* case, because, in the *Sun Properties* case, the ability of the warehouse to produce revenue had been demonstrated, and the warehouse was under lease when the transfer was made. But in the instant case, the risk of the noteholders was far less than the noteholders in *Burr Oaks* or *Aqualane*. We are thus persuaded that *Sun Properties*, rather than the *Burr Oaks* or *Aqualane* cases, is controlling. See also, *Murphy Logging Co. v. United States,* 378 F.2d 222 (9 Cir.1967), in which probable success of the future enterprise was considered along with nominal capitalization in determining that a transfer was a *bona fide* sale. We conclude that an evidentiary basis to disregard the purported sales as *bona fide* sales is lacking, and the decision of the Tax Court was in error.

Reversed.

§ 3.5 DIVIDEND OR INTEREST

FIN HAY REALTY CO. v. UNITED STATES

United States Court of Appeals, Third Circuit, 1968.
398 F.2d 694.

FREEDMAN, CIRCUIT JUDGE: We are presented in this case with the recurrent problem whether funds paid to a close corporation by its shareholders were additional contributions to capital or loans on which the corporation's payment of interest was deductible under § 163 of the Internal Revenue Code of 1954.

The problem necessarily calls for an evaluation of the facts, which we therefore detail.

Fin Hay Realty Co., the taxpayer, was organized on February 14, 1934, by Frank L. Finlaw and J. Louis Hay. Each of them contributed $10,000 for which he received one-half of the corporation's stock and at the same time each advanced an additional $15,000 for which the corporation issued to him its unsecured promissory note payable on demand and bearing interest at the rate of six per cent per annum. The corporation immediately purchased an apartment house in Newark, New Jersey, for $39,000 in cash. About a month later the two shareholders each advanced an additional $35,000 to the corporation in return for six per cent demand promissory notes and the next day the corporation purchased two apartment buildings in East Orange, New Jersey, for which it paid $75,000 in cash and gave the seller a six per cent, five year purchase money mortgage for the balance of $100,000.

Three years later, in October, 1937, the corporation created a new mortgage on all three properties and from the proceeds paid off the old mortgage on the East Orange property, which had been partially amortized. The new mortgage was for a five year term in the amount of $82,000 with interest at four and one-half per cent. In the following three years each of the shareholders advanced an additional $3,000 to the corporation, bringing the total advanced by each shareholder to $53,000, in addition to their acknowledged stock subscriptions of $10,000 each.

Finlaw died in 1941 and his stock and notes passed to his two daughters in equal shares. A year later the mortgage, which was about to fall due, was extended for a further period of five years with interest at four per cent. From the record it appears that it was subsequently extended until 1951. In 1949 Hay died and in 1951 his executor requested the retirement of his stock and the payment of his notes. The corporation thereupon refinanced its real estate for $125,000 and sold one of the buildings. With the net proceeds it paid Hay's estate $24,000 in redemption of his stock and $53,000 in retirement of his notes. Finlaw's daughters then became and still remain the sole shareholders of the corporation.

Thereafter the corporation continued to pay and deduct interest on Finlaw's notes, now held by his two daughters. In 1962 the Internal Revenue Service for the first time declared the payments on the notes not allowable as interest deductions and disallowed them for the tax years 1959 and 1960. The corporation thereupon repaid a total of $6,000 on account of the outstanding notes and in the following year after refinancing the mortgage on its real estate repaid the balance of $47,000. A short time later the Internal Revenue Service disallowed the interest deductions for the years 1961 and 1962. When the corporation failed to obtain refunds it brought this refund action in the district court. After a nonjury trial the court denied the claims and entered judgment for the United States. From this judgment the corporation appeals.

This case arose in a factual setting where it is the corporation which is the party concerned that its obligations be deemed to represent a debt and not a stock interest. In the long run in cases of this kind it is also important to the shareholder that his advance be deemed a loan rather than a capital contribution, for in such a case his receipt of repayment may be treated as the retirement of a loan rather than a taxable dividend. There are other instances in which it is in the shareholder's interest that his advance to the corporation be considered a debt rather than an increase in his equity. A loss resulting from the worthlessness of stock is a capital loss under § 165(g), whereas a bad debt may be treated as an ordinary loss if it qualifies as a business bad debt under § 166. * * * These advantages in having the funds entrusted to a corporation treated as corporate obligations instead of contributions to capital have required the courts to look beyond the literal terms in which the parties have cast the transaction in order to determine its substantive nature.

In attempting to deal with this problem courts and commentators have isolated a number of criteria by which to judge the true nature of an investment which is in form a debt: (1) the intent of the parties; (2) the identity between creditors and shareholders; (3) the extent of participation in management by the holder of the instrument; (4) the ability of the corporation to obtain funds from outside sources; (5) the "thinness" of the capital structure in relation to debt; (6) the risk involved; (7) the formal indicia of the arrangement; (8) the relative position of the obligees as to other creditors regarding the payment of interest and principal; (9) the voting power of the holder of the instrument; (10) the provision of a fixed rate of interest; (11) a contingency on the obligation to repay; (12) the source of the interest payments; (13) the presence or absence of a fixed maturity date; (14) a provision for redemption by the corporation; (15) a provision for redemption at the option of the holder; and (16) the timing of the advance with reference to the organization of the corporation.

While the Internal Revenue Code of 1954 was under consideration, and after its adoption, Congress sought to identify the criteria which would determine whether an investment represents a debt or equity, but these and similar efforts have not found acceptance. It still remains true that neither any single criterion nor any series of criteria can provide a conclusive answer in the kaleidoscopic circumstances which individual cases present. See *John Kelley Co. v. Commissioner,* 326 U.S. 521, 530, 66 S.Ct. 299, 90 L.Ed. 278 (1946).

The various factors which have been identified in the cases are only aids in answering the ultimate question whether the investment, analyzed in terms of its economic reality, constitutes risk capital entirely subject to the fortunes of the corporate venture or represents a strict debtor-creditor relationship. Since there is often an element of risk in a loan, just as there is an element of risk in an equity interest, the conflicting elements do not end at a clear line in all cases.

In a corporation which has numerous shareholders with varying interests, the arm's-length relationship between the corporation and a shareholder who supplies funds to it inevitably results in a transaction whose form mirrors its substance. Where the corporation is closely held, however, and the same persons occupy both sides of the bargaining table, form does not necessarily correspond to the intrinsic economic nature of the transaction, for the parties may mold it at their will with no countervailing pull. This is particularly so where a shareholder can have the funds he advances to a corporation treated as corporate obligations instead of contributions to capital without affecting his proportionate equity interest. Labels, which are perhaps the best expression of the subjective intention of parties to a transaction, thus lose their meaningfulness.

To seek economic reality in objective terms of course disregards the personal interest which a shareholder may have in the welfare of the corporation in which he is a dominant force. But an objective standard is one imposed by the very fact of his dominant position and is much fairer than one which would presumptively construe all such transactions against the shareholder's interest. Under an objective test of economic reality it is useful to compare the form which a similar transaction would have taken had it been between the corporation and an outside lender, and if the shareholder's advance is far more speculative than what an outsider would make, it is obviously a loan in name only.

In the present case all the formal indicia of an obligation were meticulously made to appear. The corporation, however, was the complete creature of the two shareholders who had the power to create whatever appearance would be of tax benefit to them despite the economic reality of the transaction. Each shareholder owned an equal proportion of stock and was making an equal additional contribution, so that whether Finlaw and Hay designated any part of their additional contributions as debt or as stock would not dilute their proportionate equity interests. There was no restriction because of the possible excessive debt structure, for the corporation had been created to acquire real estate and had no outside creditors except mortgagees who, of course, would have no concern for general creditors because they had priority in the security of the real estate. The position of the mortgagees also rendered of no significance the possible subordination of the notes to other debts of the corporation, a matter which in some cases this Court has deemed significant.

The shareholders here, moreover, lacked one of the principal advantages of creditors. Although the corporation issued demand notes for the advances, nevertheless, * * * it could not have repaid them for a number of years. * * *

The burden was on the taxpayer to prove that the determination by the Internal Revenue Service that the advances represented capital contributions was incorrect. The district court was justified in holding that the taxpayer had not met this burden.

The judgment of the district court will be affirmed.

[Dissenting opinion deleted.]

Question

What test does the court in *Fin Hay* apply in determining whether the instrument is debt or equity?

§ 3.6 DEBT OR PREFERRED STOCK

RAGLAND INVESTMENT CO. v. COMMISSIONER

Tax Court of the United States, 1969.
52 T.C. 867.

OPINION

This case offers for our determination the familiar issue of whether ostensible dividend payments on preferred stock are, in reality, interest on indebtedness. We are, however, presented with a slightly different twist to the usual factual pattern in that the petitioners here are contending for an equity rather than a debt classification in order to qualify for the 85–percent [now 80%] dividends-received deduction prescribed in section 243(a)(1), I.R.C. 1954. Of course this twist in no way alters the applicable legal principles.

* * *

The intent of the parties in creating the relationship with the corporation is a highly significant factor in deciding these questions.

* * *

The facts herein reveal that Malone & Hyde amended its corporate charter to authorize the issuance of the preferred stock and pursuant thereto issued preferred stock certificates to Ragland Investment and Dixie Investment. The latter two companies demanded and obtained the written opinion of counsel for Malone & Hyde that the preferred stock was validly issued. On their own behalf the two companies executed investment intent letters stating that the preferred stock was being acquired by them for investment purposes. The preferred stock dividend payments were periodically authorized by action of Malone & Hyde's board of directors, were charged to surplus on its books, and were reported under the heading of "Dividends and other distributions" on Form 1099 information returns filed by Malone & Hyde with the Internal Revenue Service.

During the years in issue, the parties consistently, and without exception, referred in a multiplicity of documents [treated the preferred as stock.] * * * Malone & Hyde[, however] decided to claim a deduction for interest and to file the requisite refund claims. * * *

A second important indicium of preferred stock is the provision in the charter amendment that dividends on the preferred stock are "payable quarterly out of the *earnings* of the corporation."

* * *

A requirement that corporate distributions be made only out of earnings is a traditional requirement for dividend payments. In contrast, a bondholder or other creditor normally has a legally enforceable right to the payment of interest irrespective of the availability of current or accumulated earnings.

Thirdly, the charter amendment provides that in the event of the liquidation or dissolution of Malone & Hyde, the preferred shareholders take priority only over the holders of the common stock, and it follows that they are *not* entitled to share in the assets on a parity with secured and general creditors. * * *

* * *

If we include the letter agreements between the majority stockholders of Malone & Hyde and the sellers as part of the controlling documents, the stock in issue does assume some of the characteristics of a "hybrid" security. These agreements provide that the majority shareholders agree to "take all actions within their power and authority" to cause Malone & Hyde to redeem the preferred stock within 4 years from issuance. Respondent urges that this, together with the other protective provisions contained in the letter agreements, amounts to a guarantee of redemption at a fixed maturity date. A fixed maturity date is, of course, a usual provision in a debt instrument.

However, we note that redemption of the preferred stock is contingent upon, among other things, the availability of corporate funds for this purpose, the retention of majority control, and continued willingness to redeem on the part of the signing shareholders. The fact that the parties saw fit to include in the charter amendment a provision for the creation of a sinking fund at the beginning of the fifth year after issuance would seem to indicate tacit recognition on their part that some contingency may well prevent redemption within the initial 4–year period.

Moreover, we deem it significant that the corporation, as distinguished from some of its shareholders in their individual capacities, is *not* obligated to redeem the preferred stock. * * * Clearly the failure to redeem here would not result in a cause of action against Malone & Hyde. In contrast, the holder of a debt instrument normally has prescribed remedies available to him upon an act of default by the debtor.

* * *

In any event, even assuming *arguendo* the existence of a fixed maturity date, that factor alone, while relevant, is not conclusive.

* * *

One final consideration influences our decision. Prior to engaging in this transaction, the parties entered into protracted arm's-length bargaining concerning the form the transaction should take with full awareness that a tax advantage to one would result in a concomitant tax disadvantage to the other. * * * It is our view that, given a transaction where the contract is negotiated between parties with conflicting tax interests and where the resultant document sets forth duties and obligations which conform to the business or economic realities of the situation, this Court should not take upon itself the task of recasting the agreement. Rather, under such circumstances, we are inclined to leave the parties to live up to their own agreement.

Therefore, having carefully weighed the foregoing factors, we conclude that the indicia of the preferred stock clearly predominate. Consequently, we hold that the petitioners are entitled to the 85–percent dividends-received deduction claimed by them for the taxable years in issue.

Reviewed by the Court.

Notes

1. The initial set of proposed regulations under § 385 contained a rule of convenience that provided that an interest in a corporation would be treated as preferred stock and not as an instrument, if the interest satisfied each of the following conditions:

   (1) The interest was denominated preferred stock and treated as preferred stock under applicable nontax law;

   (2) The excess (if any) of the preferred stock's redemption price over its issue price was a reasonable redemption premium;

   (3) Current dividends on the preferred stock were payable out of earnings or only at the discretion of the board of directors;

   (4) The right to receive dividends and redemption payments was not enforceable if any of those payments would render the corporation insolvent or impair its capital;

   (5) A default in any payment would not accelerate the rights to any redemption payments; and

   (6) The preferred stock had a term of at least 10 years during which the holder could not compel redemption. *See* Prior Prop.Reg. § 1.385–10(a).

2. The use of preferred stock can be particularly important in structuring a LBO. If the proposed capital structure is too heavily loaded with debt, some of the debt can be converted to preferred stock. This will reduce the debt to equity ratio, provided the preferred stock is in fact treated as preferred stock for federal income tax purposes.

§ 3.7 SUBORDINATED DEBT PAYABLE IN STOCK

REVENUE RULING 85-119

1985-2 C.B. 60.

Issue

For federal income tax purposes, should the instruments described below be treated as debt, so that amounts to be paid periodically with respect thereto will be treated as interest for purposes of section 163 of the Internal Revenue Code, or should they be treated as equity?

Facts

[Corporation (HC), a publicly traded bank holding company, issued unsecured and subordinated notes for cash. At maturity, the notes are payable either in stock of HC with an appraised value equal to the principal amount of notes or in cash from the sale of such stock by HC. The notes otherwise have conventional terms.]

Law and Analysis

* * *

An analysis of all the terms and conditions of the instruments and all the facts and circumstances surrounding the issuance of the instruments indicates that HC and the purchasers of the instruments intend to create a debtor-creditor relationship, and that as a legal matter a debtor-creditor relationship will be created. Notes also contain many other attributes that are commonly treated as supporting debt characterization for federal income tax purposes. They are issued for cash at 100 percent of their face amount in a public offering, are widely held, are not held proportionately to HC's stock, and have been designated by the parties as debt. Amounts designated as interest are payable quarterly, irrespective of earnings, at a floating rate comparable to the market rate of interest on similar debt instruments payable in money. Any default on the payment of such amount or amounts results in a legally enforceable right in the Noteholders against HC for payment of the amount or amounts in default. The Notes remain outstanding for a limited 12-year term and do not contain any restrictions on transferability. In addition, HC is not thinly capitalized and its debt-to-equity ratio is within the industry norm. Noteholders are not entitled to vote or to participate in management. Finally, because the number of shares of stock to be issued at maturity in exchange for Notes is not fixed but is based on the face amount of Notes, Noteholders, during the term of the Notes, do not share in the increase or decrease in the market value of such HC stock.

On the other hand, the subordination of the rights of Noteholders to the rights of general creditors as well as the provision for the issuance of stock in exchange for Notes at maturity are features indicating that

Notes may constitute equity. Although Noteholders are subordinated to the rights of general creditors, on insolvency or bankruptcy Noteholders have the status of creditors and are entitled to priority, in payment of amounts denominated as principal and accrued but unpaid interest, over the claims of all shareholders. In form, Notes are payable at maturity in stock; however, for any Noteholder who does not elect to receive stock, HC is unconditionally obligated to effect a secondary offering of this stock and to deliver, at maturity, cash equal to the principal amount of Notes. Failure by HC to perform on its obligation to effect a secondary offering and to deliver cash equal to the principal amount of the Notes would constitute a breach of HC's obligation and would provide the Noteholders with a cause of action for money damages under state law. Accordingly, in substance, Notes are payable at the Noteholder's option in a fixed amount of cash or in stock of equivalent value.

HOLDING

Notes represent debt of HC for federal income tax purposes. Periodic payments with respect to Notes constitute interest deductible by HC under section 163 of the Code (provided the requirements contained therein are satisfied) and includible by Noteholders in income under Section 61.

* * *

§ 3.8 OUTLINE OF FORMER PROPOSED DEBT–EQUITY REGULATIONS UNDER § 385

A. BACKGROUND

Although § 385 was added to the Code in 1969, the Treasury did not promulgate proposed regulations until March 24, 1980, and final regulations were issued on December 29, 1980. These final regulations were initially scheduled to become effective on April 30, 1981, but the effective date was delayed until January 1, 1982. The final regulations were amended by proposed regulations issued on December 30, 1981.

These regulations were suspended in June, 1983, and were later withdrawn, as noted below. However, they provide important guidance for analyzing debt equity issues. The following is an outline of some of the major features of these regulations.

B. INITIAL DETERMINATION

The initial issue is the determination of what section of the regulations is applicable. The following methodology is suggested:

1. *First. Instruments.* Determine whether an "instrument" is being issued. An instrument is defined as any "bond, note, debenture, or similar written evidence of an *obligation.*" *See* § 1.385–3(b). (The

term *"obligation"* is defined as an "interest in a corporation that is treated as indebtedness under applicable nontax law." *See* § 1.385-3(c).)

2. *Second. Hybrid Instruments.* Determine whether the instrument is a "hybrid instrument." A hybrid instrument is defined as an "instrument that is convertible into stock or one (such as an income bond or a participating bond) that provides for any contingent payment to the holder (other than a call premium)." *See* § 1.385-3(d). Thus, for example, a convertible debenture would be a hybrid instrument. Also, a participating debenture would be a hybrid instrument. The basic rules for determining whether a hybrid instrument is treated as stock or indebtedness are covered under Sec. 3.8.E.

3. *Third. Straight Debt Instruments.* Determine whether the instrument is a "straight debt instrument." A straight debt instrument is defined as "any instrument other than a hybrid instrument." *See* § 1.385-3(e). Thus, for example, a bond that is neither convertible nor participating would be a straight debt instrument. The basic rules for determining whether a straight debt instrument is stock or indebtedness are covered under Sec. 3.8.D.

4. *Fourth. Proportionality.* If straight debt or hybrid instruments are issued, it is necessary to determine whether the instruments are issued proportionately to the issuing corporation's shareholders. *See* § 1.385-6. The basic rules for determining whether instruments are issued proportionately are covered in Sec. 3.8.C.

C. RULES FOR DETERMINING WHETHER INSTRUMENTS ARE ISSUED PROPORTIONATELY

1. *General Rule.* Instruments are held proportionately if the holdings of the stock and the class of instruments are "substantially proportionate." *See* § 1.385-6(a)(1).

2. *Substantial Proportionality.* If the total overlap of ownership ("total overlap factor") with respect to stock and a class of instruments is greater than 50 percent, there is substantial proportionality. The "total overlap factor" is the sum of the overlap factors of each person. The overlap factor of a person is the lesser of the percentage of stock or instrument owned (constructively or actually). The stock attribution rules of § 318 apply, as substantially modified by § 1.385-6(a)(2)(ii). *See* § 1.385-6(a)(2).

3. *Examples.* The following example from the regulations shows a case in which the holdings are not substantially proportionate.

Example The only class of stock of corporation X and a class of its instruments are owned as follows by unrelated individuals A, B, C, and I:

	A	*B*	*C*	*I*
Stock	40%	10%	50%	0
Instruments	20%	60%	10%	10%

The "total overlap factor" with respect to the class of instruments is 20% + 10% + 10%, or 40%, and, accordingly, holdings of the X stock and the class of instruments are not substantially proportionate. See § 1.385–6(a)(2).

D. CLASSIFICATION OF STRAIGHT DEBT INSTRUMENTS

1. *Held Non–Proportionately.* If straight debt instruments are not issued proportionately, then such instruments are ordinarily treated as indebtedness. See § 1.385–6(b). However, if a straight debt instrument is issued to a 25 percent or more shareholder and the corporation's debt-to-equity ratio exceeds 10:1, then the instrument is treated as if it were issued proportionately. See § 1.385–6(a)(2)(vi).

2. *Held Proportionately.* If straight debt instruments are issued proportionately, they are treated as *indebtedness* unless the debt is excessive.

3. *Excessive Debt.*

a. *General Rule.* If the corporation's debt is "excessive" at the time of issuance of the instrument, the instrument is treated as stock. See § 1.385–6(g)(1).

b. *Definition of Excessive Debt.* A corporation's debt is excessive if all of the instrument's terms and conditions (including the stated interest rate) and the corporation's financial structure, taken together, would not be satisfactory to an independent creditor. See § 1.385–6(g)(2).

c. *Safe Harbor.* A corporation's debt is not excessive, if corporation's "outside" debt-to-equity ratio is less than or equal to 10:1 and the corporation's "inside" debt-to-equity ratio is less than or equal to 3:1. See § 1.385–6(g)(3).

The "outside" debt-to-equity ratio is the ratio that the corporation's liabilities (excluding trade accounts payable, accrued operating expenses and taxes, and other similar items) bears to the stockholders' equity. See § 1.385–6(h)(1). The "inside" ratio is computed in the same manner except liabilities to independent creditors are not included (except in computing stockholders' equity). See § 1.385–6(g)(4). Stockholders' equity in the corporation is the excess of the adjusted basis in its assets over all its liabilities. See § 1.385–6(h)(2).

E. CLASSIFICATION OF HYBRID INSTRUMENTS

1. *Held Proportionately.*

a. *General Rule.* Hybrid instruments are treated as stock if they are issued proportionately. See § 1.385–6(d)(1).

b. *Exception.* The general rule does not apply where independent creditors own at least 20 percent of the class of hybrid instruments. See § 1.385–6(d)(2).

2. *Held Non–Proportionately.*

a. *General Rule.* A hybrid instrument that is not held proportionately is treated as stock, if on the day of issuance the present value of the straight debt payments (as defined in § 1.385–5(d)(2)) with respect to the instrument is less than 50 percent of the fair market value of the instrument. *See* § 1.385–5(a) and (d).

b. *Straight Debt Payments.* Straight debt payments with respect to the right to fixed payments of principal or interest (as defined in § 1.385–5(c)(2) and (3)) are the fixed payments themselves. With respect to the right to contingent payments, the straight debt payments are the payments that must be made on the occurrence of the contingencies resulting in the lowest possible fair market value of payments under the instruments.

c. *Example.* Example 1 of § 1.385–5(f) illustrates the basic principle. There, on July 1, 1987, corporation L issues subordinated income debenture bonds in the principal amount of $1,000 each. The bonds are due on December 31, 2006 and pay interest at 8 percent, but the interest is payable only if earned (*i.e.*, contingent interest). Thus, each bond provides for a fixed payment of principal and a contingent payment of interest. The fair market value of each bond is assumed to be $1,000 at time of issuance and the straight debt payment is a $1,000 subordinated payment of principal due on December 31, 2006. The present value of the straight debt payment on July 1, 1987 is assumed to be $261. Therefore, under the rule set out above, the bonds are treated as stock, because the fair market value of the straight debt payment (*i.e.*, $261) is less than 50 percent of the fair market value of the instruments (*i.e.*, $1,000/2 = $500). Since the instrument is treated as stock, it is considered preferred stock. *See* § 1.385–4(c). Consequently, payments of "interest" are treated as distributions under § 301 (*i.e.*, dividends) and payments of "principal" are treated as redemptions of stock under § 302 and thereby may be treated as dividends.

F. SUMMARY

These regulations can be outlined as follows:

First Level: Determine if an instrument is issued.

Second Level: Determine whether the instrument is:
1. A straight debt instrument, or
2. A hybrid instrument.

Third Level: Determine whether the instrument is held proportionately.

Fourth Level:
1. Straight debt instruments held nonproportionately are treated as debt.
2. Straight debt instruments held proportionately are treated as debt, unless the debt is excessive.

Fifth Level:
1. Hybrid instruments held proportionately are treated as equity.

2. Hybrid instruments held nonproportionately are treated as equity if the present value of the straight debt payments is less than 50% of the value of the instrument.

§ 3.9 THE ARCN CONTROVERSY AND THE REPEAL OF THE § 385 REGULATIONS

A. THE ARCN RULING

REVENUE RULING 83–98
1983–2 C.B. 40.

For federal income tax purposes, should the adjustable rate convertible notes (ARCNs) described below be treated as debt, so that amounts paid periodically with respect thereto are deductible as interest under section 163 of the Internal Revenue Code, or should they be treated as equity?

FACTS

X corporation has outstanding one class of common stock that is traded on a national securities exchange. This stock has traded recently at about $20 per share; its current dividend rate is $.78 per share, or about 3.9 percent, annually.

X proposes to issue $10 million worth of ARCNs. An ARCN will be offered at a price of $1000 cash or fifty shares of X common stock (worth $1000). The terms of the ARCNs will be as follows. They will mature in 20 years, and on maturity the holder will be entitled to elect to receive either $600 cash or 50 shares of X common stock. Each ARCN will be convertible at any time into 50 shares of X common stock. X will have no right to compel redemption of ("call") an ARCN until two years after issuance, after which it will have the right to call any ARCN at a price of $600 cash. Upon call, the holder may exercise his conversion right.

An amount designated as interest will be paid on the ARCNs quarterly at a rate based upon dividends paid on X common stock. More specifically, the annual amount payable with respect to an ARCN will be equal to the dividends paid on 50 shares of X common stock, plus an amount ($20) equal to two percent of the issue price ($1,000) of the note. However, such payments may not be less than $60, or more than $175, per ARCN. The current yield for non-convertible, non-contingent debt instruments of corporations similar to X is 12 percent.

The ARCNs will be subordinated to all present and future senior and general creditors of X. In the event of bankruptcy, the holder of an ARCN will be treated as a creditor in the amount of $600.

LAW AND ANALYSIS

Whether an instrument represents indebtedness or an equity investment for federal income tax purposes depends on the facts and circumstances of each case. * * *

The ARCNs in this case are structured so that under most likely eventualities they will be converted into X common stock. At maturity the holder of an ARCN will convert the ARCN to stock rather than take cash if the stock can be sold for more than $600 in the aggregate. Because the X stock is worth $1,000 when the ARCNs are issued, redemption for cash at maturity will occur only if the stock drops in price by more than 40 percent. Further, as long as the 50 shares of X common stock are trading at more than $600 in the aggregate (*i.e.,* for more than $12 per share), it would be economically disadvantageous for the holder of an ARCN to permit X to redeem it for $600. Thus, in such a situation, X may in effect force conversion at any time beginning two years after issuance by calling the ARCN.

Moreover, in many circumstances it will be to X's advantage to force conversion because by doing so it would avoid having to pay out cash. * * *

Because of the very high probability that all of the ARCNs issued will be converted into stock, the ARCNs do not in reality represent a promise to pay a sum certain. * * *

Other factors in this case that support a conclusion that the ARCNs constitute equity rather than debt include (i) the guaranteed annual return of $60 with respect to the $1,000 investment is unreasonably low in comparison to the annual return on comparable non-convertible, non-contingent instruments at the time the ARCNs are issued, (ii) under the terms of the ARCNs, more than 65 percent of the future annual yield may be discretionary based on the level of discretionary dividends paid on X common stock, and (iii) the ARCNs are subordinated to X's general creditors.

The fixed principal and fixed minimum interest payable on the ARCNs are insufficient factors to support their classification as debt. It is apparent that neither X nor the purchasers of ARCNs ascribe any economic value or practical significance to the fixed debt features of the ARCNs since the ARCNs will be sold for a price approximately equal to the value of the common stock into which the ARCNs can be converted, rather than at a substantial premium.

* * *

HOLDING

The ARCNs constitute an equity interest in X and will be treated as stock for Federal income tax purposes. Accordingly, the periodic distributions with respect to the ARCNs, although denominated as interest, are distributions subject to section 301 of the Code, and are not deductible by X.

* * *

B. TREASURY DEPARTMENT NEWS RELEASE ANNOUNCING REPEAL OF THE § 385 REGULATIONS

TREASURY DEP'T NEWS RELEASE
June 24, 1983.

We appreciate your interest in the question of whether "adjustable rate convertible notes" ("ARCNs") will be classified as debt or equity for Federal income tax purposes.

As you know, the IRS announced that it was studying the proper classification of ARCNs on March 30, 1983. The IRS study has been completed, and a revenue ruling in the form enclosed has been announced today. The revenue ruling concludes that, under current law, a typical ARCN is equity for tax purposes. The IRS must rule unfavorably with respect to ARCNs because to allow instruments that are in economic terms substantially the equivalent of equity to be treated as debt would mean that taxpayers would have little reason to issue equity. Payments to holders of the "debt" instruments would be deductible as interest, even though they represent dividends on equity investments.

The sole remaining question, therefore, is whether some reliance on the regulations that were promulgated under section 385 requires "grandfather" protection for specific transactions. * * *

* * * We believe that the taxpayers had no right to rely on the section 385 regulations until they became effective.

Furthermore, we believe that allowing interest deductions for payments made with respect to ARCNs and similar arrangements has serious implications, and that ARCNs were not contemplated by Congress or by the draftsmen of the section 385 regulations. * * *

We also have decided to take administrative steps to revoke the outstanding section 385 regulations in order to remove any possible uncertainty whether they are fully reflective of our views on debt-equity matters. * * *

We are continuing to study the general question of the appropriate Treasury response to section 385 and expect to complete our examination in the near future.

Question

Which provision of the proposed regulations under § 385 did taxpayers rely on in concluding that ARCNs were debt? Should ARCNs be treated as debt?

§ 3.10 ORIGINAL ISSUE DISCOUNT AND RELATED RULES

A. INTRODUCTION

This section examines briefly the original issue discount (OID) provisions in §§ 1271 through 1275. This section also examines the related imputed interest rules under § 483 and the treatment of applicable high yield discount obligations (HYDOs). The OID provisions are based on the principle of economic accrual of interest, that is the compounding of interest. Although these provisions are filled with complexity, they are particularly important in structuring the capital of a corporation. For that reason, they are examined here. For a more detailed discussion of these provisions, see *Federal Taxation of Business Enterprises, supra* Chapter 1 note, 1 at Sec. 3:27 et seq.

B. GUIDE TO THE REGULATIONS

PREAMBLE TO PROPOSED REGULATIONS UNDER OID AND IMPUTED INTEREST RULES

LR-189-84 (April 8, 1986).

II. INTRODUCTION

The regulations under sections 163(e), 483, and 1271 through 1275 provide two principal sets of rules: The imputed interest rules and the original issue discount rules. The imputed interest rules are prescribed by sections 1274 and 483, and the original issue discount rules by sections 163(e), 1271, 1272, 1273 and 1275.

The imputed interest rules of sections 1274 and 483 relate to the measurement of interest and principal for tax purposes in a sale or exchange of property (other than publicly traded property) involving deferred payments. For transactions subject to the imputed interest rules, interest will be imputed to the transaction if a minimum amount of interest is not stated. If a transaction states at least the minimum amount of interest, it is said to provide for adequate stated interest. When interest is imputed to a transaction, a portion of the stated principal amount of the debt instrument is recharacterized as interest for tax purposes. The imputed interest rules do not require an increase in the total amount of payments agreed to by the parties to a transaction. These rules merely recharacterize as interest for Federal tax purposes a portion of the payments denominated as principal by the parties. In the case of transactions to which section 1274 applies, imputed interest is treated as original issue discount and is accounted for under those rules. In the case of transactions subject to section 483, imputed interest (and any stated interest) is subject to a new set of rules provided under section 446 and is accounted for under those rules.

In general, under the original issue discount rules, a portion of the original issue discount on a debt instrument is required to be included in income by the holder and deducted from income by the issuer annually without regard to their regular accounting methods. [*See* §§ 1272(a) and 163(e).] The total amount of original issue discount is defined as the difference between the debt instrument's stated redemption price at maturity and its issue price [*See* § 1273(a)] and arises in one of three ways. First, in the case of a debt instrument subject to section 1274 that does not provide for adequate stated interest, [*See* § 1274(c)(1) & (2)] interest is imputed and is treated as original issue discount. [*See* § 1274.] Second, in the case of a debt instrument issued for cash or publicly traded property, original issue discount arises if the debt instrument is issued for less than its face amount. [*See* § 1272(a) & (b).] Third, in the case of all debt instruments, original issue discount arises if the debt instrument does not call for interest that is payable currently at a single constant rate over its entire term.

III. THE IMPUTED INTEREST RULES

A. *Applicability*

1. Section 1274

Section 1274 applies to any debt instrument issued in exchange for property if neither the debt instrument nor the property is publicly traded and if one or more of the payments under the debt instrument are due more than 6 months after the date of the sale or exchange. [*See* § 1274(c)(1).] Section 1274, however, does not apply to the [situations specified in § 1274(c)(3) and (4).]

2. Section 483

Section 483 applies to sales or exchanges of non-publicly traded property excepted from the provisions of section 1274. Thus, section 483 applies to: the sale or exchange of a farm if the sales price does not exceed $1,000,000, sales involving total payments of $250,000 or less, sales of principal residences, qualified sales of land, and cash method debt instruments. Unlike section 1274, however, section 483 applies only if the contract for the sale or exchange calls for payments due more than one year from the date of the sale or exchange. * * *

* * *

B. *Stating Adequate Interest To Avoid the Imputation of Interest*

1. In General [See § 1274.]

To prevent the imputation of interest, a debt instrument must provide for adequate stated interest. For this purpose, a debt instrument generally provides for adequate stated interest if it calls for interest over its entire term at a rate no lower than the test rate of interest applicable to the debt instrument. If a debt instrument does not provide for a fixed rate of interest at least equal to the test rate of interest, the adequacy of interest is determined by comparing the stated principal amount involved in the transaction with the sum of present values of all payments due under the debt instrument, determined by discounting the payments at a rate equal to the test rate of interest.

[*See* § 1274(c)(1) and (4).] A debt instrument generally has adequate stated interest if the stated principal amount of debt instrument is less than or equal to the sum of these present values. [*See* § 1274(c)(2).] However, in the case of a potentially abusive situation as discussed below, the debt instrument does not have adequate stated interest unless the stated principal amount is less than or equal to the fair market value of the property sold or exchanged. [*See* § 1274(b)(3).]

The test rate of interest applicable to a debt instrument generally depends on the amount of seller financing (based on stated principal) involved in the transaction. For sales or exchanges of property (other than new section 38 property) involving seller financing of $2,800,000 [adjusted for inflation] or less, the test rate of interest is the lower of the applicable Federal rate or 9 percent, compounded semiannually (or an equivalent rate based on an appropriate compounding period). If the sales price is contingent, the 9 percent rate is not available unless the sales price cannot exceed $2,800,000. [*See* § 1274A(a) and (b).] For sales or exchanges of property with seller financing in excess of $2,800,-000, and all sales or exchanges of new section 38 property, the test rate of interest is 100 percent of the applicable Federal rate. * * *

The applicable Federal rate is either the Federal short-term rate (for debt instruments with terms not over 3 years), the Federal mid-term rate (for debt instruments, with terms over 3 years but not over 9 years), or the Federal long-term rate (for debt instruments with terms over 9 years). [*See* § 1274(d)(1).] The Federal rates are annual stated rates of interest based on semiannual compounding. The Federal rates are published monthly by the Commissioner in Revenue Rulings along with equivalent annual, quarterly and monthly rates. In general, the appropriate compounding period depends on the intervals between payments.
* * *

* * *

C. *Imputation of Interest*

Under section 1274, if a debt instrument does not provide for adequate stated interest, the issue price of the debt instrument is its imputed principal amount. [*See* § 1274(c)(1) and (2).] Except in the case of potentially abusive situations, the imputed principal amount of a debt instrument is the sum of the present values of all the payments due under the instrument determined by discounting the payments at the imputed rate of interest. [*See* § 1274(b)(1) and (2).] Generally, for purposes of imputing interest, the imputed rate of interest is the same as the test rate of interest. * * *

When interest is imputed, the imputed principal amount becomes the issue price. [*See* § 1274(a) and (c)(1)(A)(ii).] This issue price is lower than the stated principal amount of the debt instrument, since it reflects the fact that a portion of the stated principal is recharacterized as interest. Thus, the imputed interest is treated as original issue discount. In potentially abusive situations, the imputed principal amount of the debt instrument is the fair market value of the property sold or exchanged.

Under section 483, imputed interest is referred to as unstated interest. Unstated interest is defined as the excess of the deferred payments (all payments of the sales price due more than 6 months after the date of the sale or exchange) over the sum of the present values of the deferred payments and any stated interest. For this purpose, the present values are determined by discounting the payments at the imputed rate of interest. * * *

IV. Accounting for Original Issue Discount
A. *In General [See §§ 1272 and 1273.]*

Original issue discount is defined as the excess of a debt instrument's stated redemption price at maturity over its issue price. [*See* § 1273(a)(1) and (2).] A portion of the original issue discount on a debt instrument is accounted for on a current basis by both the issuer and the holder. The amount of original issue discount that is accounted for on a current basis is the amount that accrues on a constant interest or economic accrual basis, regardless of whether the issuer or holder is an accrual basis taxpayer. [*See* § 1272(a).]

For purposes of determining the accrual of original issue discount, the term of a debt instrument generally is divided into accrual periods of equal length as discussed in greater detail below. [*See* § 1273(a)(5).] Original issue discount is allocated to each accrual period according to a formula based upon the adjusted issue price of the debt instrument at the beginning of the accrual period, the yield of the debt instrument, and the actual interest payments (if any) for that period. [*See* § 1272(a)(3), (4) and (5).] To determine the holder's annual inclusion under section 1272, the original issue discount allocated to each accrual period is then apportioned ratably among the days within the accrual period to produce the daily portion of original issue discount for each day during that accrual period. [*See* § 1272(a)(3).] The total amount of original issue discount includible for any taxable year is the sum of the daily portions of original issue discount for each day during the taxable year that the taxpayer held the debt instrument. [*See* § 1274(a)(3).] * * *

In general, the amount of original issue discount deductible by an issuer under section 163(e) is determined in the same manner as the amount includible by the holder under section 1272. The regulations contain several exceptions to this general rule.

B. *Paying Interest Currently at Constant Rate to Avoid the Original Issue Discount Rules*

In the case of any debt instrument subject to section 1274 that provides for adequate stated interest, or in the case of any debt instrument issued at par for cash or publicly traded property, the original issue discount rules do not apply if all interest is payable currently at a constant rate over the entire term of the debt instrument. For this purpose, interest is considered payable currently if the interest is payable unconditionally and at regular intervals of one year or less. Interest is not considered payable at a constant rate if the debt instrument involves deferred interest (if the debt instrument has a lower initial rate of interest or an interest holiday for an initial period) or prepaid interest (if it has a higher initial rate of interest).

C. Determining the Total Amount of Original Issue Discount [See 1273.]

1. Stated Redemption Price at Maturity [See 1273(a)(2).]

Except in the case of installment obligations, the stated redemption price at maturity of a debt instrument is defined as the amount fixed by the last modification of the purchase agreement including interest and other amounts payable at that time. [See § 1274(a)(2).] The stated redemption price at maturity does not include any interest based on a fixed or variable rate that is actually and unconditionally payable at intervals of one year or less over the entire term of the debt instrument. These amounts are referred to as qualified periodic interest payments. In the case of an installment obligation, the stated redemption price at maturity equals the sum of all payments under the debt instrument less any qualified periodic interest payments. [See § 1.1272-1(b).]

2. Determination of Issue Price [See §§ 1274 and 1273(b).]

If a debt instrument subject to section 1274 states adequate interest, the issue price is the stated principal amount of the debt instrument. If the debt instrument does not state adequate interest as discussed above, the issue price is the imputed principal amount determined according to the provisions of section 1274. [See § 1274(c)(1).]

The issue price of a debt instrument not subject to section 1274 is determined as follows [See § 1273(b)]:

(a) A debt instrument that is part of an issue of debt instruments publicly offered and issued for cash—the initial price at which a substantial portion of the issue is sold to the public; [See § 1273(b)(1).]

(b) A debt instrument that is part of an issue of debt instruments not publicly offered and issued for cash—the price paid by the first buyer; [See § 1273(b)(2).]

(c) A debt instrument that is issued for property and is part of an issue of debt instruments a portion of which is traded on an established securities market—the fair market value of that debt instrument determined as of the first trading date after the date of issue of the debt instrument; [See § 1273(b)(3).]

(d) A nonpublicly traded debt instrument issued in exchange for publicly traded property—the fair market value of the property; [See § 1273(b)(3).] and

(e) A debt instrument that does not fall within the first four categories set forth above and that is not governed by section 1274—its stated redemption price at maturity. [See § 1273(b)(4).]

3. De Minimis Rules [See § 1273(a)(3).]

In the case of the holder, a debt instrument having a *de minimis* amount of original issue discount is treated as if the original issue discount were zero. [*See* § 1273(a)(3).] Except in the case of an installment obligation, discount is considered *de minimis* if it is less than one-quarter of one percent of the stated redemption price at maturity multiplied by the number of complete years to maturity.

* * *

D. Allocation of Original Issue Discount to an Accrual Period [*See* § 1272(a).]

1. In General

The amount of original issue discount allocable to an accrual period generally is equal to the product of the adjusted issue price at the beginning of the accrual period and the yield of the debt instrument, less amounts of stated interest payable during the accrual period. [*See* § 1272(c)(3).] Each of the terms used in this calculation is defined under section 1272 and the proposed regulations as described in the succeeding discussion.

2. Accrual Period [*See* § 1272(a)(5).]

Generally, for debt instruments issued after December 31, 1984, the accrual period is the interval between payment or compounding dates provided by the debt instrument (but in no event longer than one year), with the final accrual period ending on the maturity date of the debt instrument. [*See* § 1272(a)(5).] Rules are provided for debt instruments with irregular payment or compounding intervals. For debt instruments that provide for a single payment at maturity and that have no other payment or compounding dates, the accrual period is the six-month period ending on the date in each calendar year that corresponds to the maturity date of the debt instrument or the date that is six months prior to that date. * * *

3. Adjusted Issue Price [*See* § 1272(a)(4).]

The adjusted issue price at the beginning of the first accrual period is the issue price. The adjusted issue price at the beginning of each succeeding accrual period is equal to the adjusted issue price at the beginning of the immediately preceding accrual period increased by the amount of original issue discount accrued during that period [*See* § 1272(a)(4).] * * *

4. Yield [*See* § 1272(a)(3).]

The yield of a debt instrument is that rate of interest that, when used to determine the present value of all payments of principal and interest to be made under the debt instrument, provides an amount equal to the issue price of the debt instrument. [*See* §§ 1272(a)(3)(A)(ii) and 1.1272–1(f).] Yield is expressed as an annual interest rate and is determined by compounding at the end of the accrual period. * * *

5. Acquisition Premium [*See* § 1272(a)(7).]

In determining the amount a holder must include in income, the daily portion of original issue discount is reduced by an appropriate share of any acquisition premium paid by that holder. [*See* § 1272(a)(7).] Acquisition premium arises when a person purchases a debt instrument at a price which is in excess of the revised issue price on the date of purchase, but which is less than the stated redemption price at maturity. * * *

E. Special Rules

1. Serial Maturity and Installment Obligations

* * *

3. Contingent Payments [*See* § 1275(d).]

Under the proposed regulations, contingent payments are generally not taken into account in applying the original issue discount and imputed interest rules. Instead, contingent payments are segregated from noncontingent payments and are accounted for separately. [*See* § 1275.] In determining whether a payment is contingent, the Commissioner may disregard remote and incidental contingencies. The parties to a transaction are, however, bound by its form and must treat a payment subject to a stated contingency as contingent. The contingent payment rules do not affect whether rights to receive contingent payments constitute debt or equity for Federal tax purposes or whether an instrument evidences a valid indebtedness.

Under the separate accounting rules for contingent payments, contingent payments may be recharacterized in certain situations. First, any payment of principal made on account of a sale or exchange of nonpublicly traded property that is not accompanied by a payment of adequate stated interest will be recharacterized in part as interest. Second, in the case of a debt instrument that does not provide for adequate stated interest and that accordingly has imputed interest, certain contingent interest payments may be recharacterized in part as principal to restore to basis amounts previously recharacterized as imputed interest. In these cases, a payment subject to recharacterization is treated as a payment of principal in an amount equal to the present value of the payment and as a payment of interest to the extent of the difference between the amount of the payment and the present value of the payment. The amount of all payments characterized as principal, however, cannot exceed the amount of the fixed or maximum stated principal amount under a debt instrument.

* * *

V. Accounting for Interest

Under the revised section 483, unstated interest is required to be accounted for on an economic accrual basis consistent with the allocation of original issue discount under section 1272(a) and Rev.Rul. 83-84, 1983-1 C.B. 97. Unlike original issue discount, however, unstated interest is not subject to annual periodic inclusion or deduction. The proposed regulations prescribe rules under section 446 governing the method of accounting for interest in lending and deferred payment transactions outside the scope of the original issue discount rules. Thus, these rules apply to the accounting for unstated interest (and any stated interest) in transactions to which section 483 applies. Under the proposed section 446 regulations, interest accrues in generally the same manner as original issue discount. * * *

Questions

1. A corporation issues for $30K in cash a note with a principal amount of $100K. The note is payable in full 10 years from the date of issuance. In general, what is the treatment to the issuer and holder of the note?

2. A corporation (X) issues its note with a face amount of $100K to individual (A) in exchange for stock of a closely held corporation. The note provides for interest at less than the AFR so that the imputed principal amount of the instrument is $90K. What is the issue price and stated redemption price at maturity of the note? How much OID is there, if any? Can the note qualify for installment sale treatment under § 453?

C. HIGH YIELD DISCOUNT OBLIGATIONS

See §§ 163(i) and (e)(5).

1. *Purpose of Provisions*

SENATE FINANCE COMMITTEE REPORT TO THE REVENUE ACT OF 1989
70 (1989).

* * *

REASONS FOR CHANGE

The committee is concerned about the frequent use of high-yield, long-term OID instruments and instruments that make payments in instruments of the issuer (*e.g.,* so-called "payment-in-kind" (PIK) bonds) and the effect these instruments may have on the amount of debt in the corporate sector of economy. The committee believes that the interest deduction permitted for these instruments, even though no cash is paid, encourages their use in highly-leveraged financial structures. The committee believes that the tax benefit from the deduction prior to payment is particularly strong when the issuer is subject to the corporate income tax.

The committee believes that the amount of long-term high-yield OID and PIK instruments issued by corporations will be reduced if the interest deduction on such instruments is postponed until the interest is paid.

* * *

2. Explanation of Provisions

CONFERENCE REPORT TO THE REVENUE RECONCILIATION ACT OF 1989
45–47 (1989).

* * *

HOUSE BILL

Certain obligations issued by corporations are treated as preferred stock. Issuers and holders alike are subject to this treatment. * * *

The provision applies to any debt instrument that has a term of more than five years, significant OID, and a yield that equals or exceeds the sum of 5 percentage points plus the applicable Federal rate (applicable instruments). [See § 163(i).]

* * *

SENATE AMENDMENT

The interest deduction of corporations for OID with respect to certain instruments is deferred until actually paid. The holder, however, continues to include such discount, as interest, in income as it accrues.

* * *

CONFERENCE AGREEMENT

The conference agreement generally follows the Senate amendment, with modifications that incorporate aspects of the House bill. This combined approach is adopted because the conferees believe that a portion of the return on certain high-yield OID obligations is similar to a distribution of corporate earnings with respect to equity. [See § 163(e)(5).] Thus, the conference agreement bifurcates the yield on applicable instruments, creating an interest element that is deductible when paid and a return on equity element for which no deduction is granted and for which the dividends received deduction may be allowed.

The provision applies to any applicable high-yield obligation issued by a corporation, but not for any period during which the corporation is an S corporation. [See § 163(i).] * * *

A portion of the OID ("the disqualified portion") on an applicable instrument is afforded special treatment. [See § 163(e)(5)(B) and (C).] The issuer is allowed no deduction with respect to the disqualified portion. The holder, however, is allowed a dividends received deduction for that part of the disqualified portion that would have been treated as a dividend had it been distributed by the issuing corporation with respect to stock. [See § 163(e)(5)(B)(i).]

In general, the disqualified portion of OID is the portion of the total return on the obligation that bears the same ratio to the total return as the disqualified yield bears to the total yield to maturity on the instrument. [*See* § 163(e)(5)(C).] The term "disqualified yield" means that portion of the yield that exceeds the applicable Federal rate for the month in which the obligation is issued (the "AFR") plus six percentage points. If the yield to maturity on the obligation determined by disregarding the OID exceeds the AFR plus six percentage points, then the disqualified portion is the entire amount of the OID. * * * The remainder of the OID on the instrument (the portion other than the disqualified portion) is not deductible until paid in property other than stock or obligations of the issuer.

Example 1.—Assume a corporation issues an applicable instrument at the beginning of the year with an issue price of $100 and a yield to maturity of 20 percent in a month when the AFR is 9 percent. The AFR plus 6 percentage points is 15 percent. The return on the instrument in the first year is $20 ($100 issue price times the 20 percent yield to maturity) and the adjusted issue price is $120 at the end of the year. The return on the instrument in the second year is $24 ($120 adjusted issue price times the 20 percent yield to maturity). The ratio of the disallowed portion of the yield to the yield is 25 percent ((20 percent yield to maturity minus 15 percent) divided by 20 percent yield to maturity). The amount of the disqualified portion in the first year is $5 ($20 return for the year times 25 percent). The ratio of the disallowed portion of the yield to the yield is constant throughout the term of the instrument (in this case, 25 percent). Thus, the disallowed portion in the second year is $6 ($24 return for the year times 25 percent).

* * *

D. SUGGESTED METHODOLOGY FOR DEALING WITH OID PROVISIONS *

The following methodology is suggested for approaching issues under these provisions:

(1) *Do Sections 1271 etc. or Section 483 Apply?* Determine whether the debt instrument is an obligation subject to the provisions of § 1271 et seq. and if so determine whether the instrument is issued for (a) cash, (b) traded property, or (c) nontraded property. If the rules of § 1271 et seq. do not apply determine whether § 483 applies.

(2) *Instruments Issued for Cash.* If the instrument is issued for cash, determine whether the amount of cash paid for the instrument is equal to the instrument's stated redemption price at maturity.

   (i) If the cash paid is equal to the stated redemption price, there is no OID with respect to the instrument.

---

* Based on § 4.27 of *Federal Taxation of Business Enterprises, supra* Chapter 1, note 1, with permission.

(ii) If the instrument is not issued with OID, determine whether such a loan is a gift loan or a loan between a corporation and a shareholder or between an employer and an employee. If so, interest is imputed if the loan does not provide for the payment of an arms-length interest rate. See § 7872.

(iii) If the stated redemption price at maturity exceeds the issue price, there is OID unless a de minimis exception applies. Any OID is included in the income of the holder and deducted by the issuer on a yield to maturity basis. See §§ 1272 and 1273.

(3) *Instruments Issued for Publicly Traded Property.* If the instrument is issued for property that is publicly traded (e.g., marketable stock), the fair market value of the publicly traded property is the issue price of the instrument. If the stated redemption price of the instrument exceeds the issue price, there is OID. See § 1273.

(4) *Instruments Issued for Nonpublicly Traded Property.* If the instrument is issued for property that is not publicly traded and the stated principal amount of the instrument exceeds $2.8 million (adjusted for inflation) (*see* § 1274A), the issue price is computed by discounting all of the payments due under the instrument at the applicable federal rate (APR) to determine the imputed principal amount. See § 1274. If the stated principal amount of the instrument is less than or equal to the imputed principal amount, the issue price is the stated principal amount; otherwise, the issue price is the imputed principal amount. If the issue price so determined is less than the stated redemption price at maturity, there is OID. This is illustrated in the following example.

If an instrument provides for interest at less than the AFR so that the imputed principal amount of the instrument is $90,000 although the stated principal amount is $100,000, the issue price of the instrument is $90,000. Assuming the stated redemption price at maturity is $100,000, there is $10,000 of OID. On the other hand, if the instrument provides for interest at a rate greater than the AFR, so that the imputed principal amount is $100,000 and the stated principal amount is $90,000, the issue price is the stated principal amount. Assuming the stated redemption price at maturity is $90,000, there is no OID.

If the stated principal amount of the obligation is less than $2.8 million (adjusted for inflation) the AFR cannot exceed 9% and if the stated principal amount of the obligation does not exceed $2 million, a special cash basis election can be made. See § 1274A.

(5) *Applicability of Section 483.* If the OID provisions do not apply, determine whether § 483 applies. Under this provi-

sion, the total amount to be treated as interest in a deferred payment transaction is determined on a yield to maturity basis. Any imputed interest is allocated over the actual payments made. Amounts characterized as interest pursuant to § 483 are accordingly included in income and deducted only in those years in which actual interest payments are made.

(6) *Treatment of Contingent Payments.* In general, contingent payments are treated similarly to payments under § 483. See § 1.1274–4(c) and (d).

(7) *High Yield Discount Obligations.* Determine whether the instrument is an applicable high yield discount obligation, the interest on which is disallowed and delayed. See §§ 163(i) and (e)(5).

E. MARKET DISCOUNT BONDS

See § 1278

CONFERENCE REPORT TO THE REVENUE RECONCILIATION ACT OF 1993

80 (1993).

Generally, a market discount bond is a bond that is acquired for a price that is less than the principal amount of the bond.[2] Market discount generally arises when the value of a debt obligation declines after issuance (typically, because of an increase in prevailing interest rates or a decline in the credit-worthiness of the borrower).

Gain on the disposition of a market discount bond generally must be recognized as ordinary income to the extent of the market discount that has accrued. * * *

§ 3.11 WORTHLESSNESS OF STOCK, SECURITIES, AND NOTES

See §§ 165(g), and 166(a), and (d).

Under § 165(g)(1), if a security of a nonaffiliated corporation becomes worthless, the loss is treated as a loss from the sale or exchange of a capital asset. The holding period of the security determines whether the loss is long or short term. The term "security" is defined in § 165(g)(2) as a share of stock, etc., and as a bond, etc., with coupons attached or in registered form. Affiliated corporations are defined in § 165(g)(3) as 80 percent owned, active subsidiaries of domestic parents. Under § 165(g)(3), a domestic parent is allowed an ordinary loss with

---

2. Or, in the case of a bond issued with original issue discount (OID), a price that is less than the amount of the issue price plus accrued OID.

respect to the worthlessness of stock and securities of an 80%, owned active subsidiary. Section 165(g)(3) is examined further in Sec. 17.3.D.

Under the above rules, stock held by individuals and stock held by corporations in non–80% subsidiaries gives rise to capital loss on worthlessness. See § 165(g)(1) and (2). However, under § 1244 (see Sec. 3.12), individual shareholders may qualify for ordinary loss treatment on the sale or worthlessness of certain small business stock. As a result of the Supreme Court's decision in *Arkansas Best Corp. v. Commissioner,* 485 U.S. 212 (1988), corporate shareholders of non–80% subsidiaries are unlikely to prevail in arguing that the loss from the sale or worthlessness of such stock is a business loss within the *Corn Products* doctrine and, therefore, ordinary.

Section 166(a) allows an ordinary loss deduction for any debt that becomes worthless or partially worthless. Section 166(d) treats a loss from the worthlessness of a "nonbusiness bad debt" held by noncorporate taxpayers as a short-term capital loss rather than an ordinary loss under § 166(a). Section 166 is not applicable to bonds, etc., which are within the definition of the term security in § 165(g)(2). See § 166(e).

The leading case dealing with the question of whether a debt is a business or nonbusiness debt is *United States v. Generes,* 405 U.S. 93, 92 S.Ct. 827, 31 L.Ed.2d 62 (1972). There the Court said that for a debt to be "proximately" related to the taxpayer's trade or business as required by § 1.166–5(b), the trade or business motivation must be "dominant." In applying this "dominant motivation" test, the Court there held that the taxpayer-creditor, a part-time employee and shareholder of a corporation, did not and could not prove that his status as a creditor was predominantly associated with his trade or business as a part-time employee.

§ 3.12 ORDINARY LOSS ON § 1244 STOCK

See § 1244.

THE SENATE FINANCE COMMITTEE REPORT ON THE REVENUE ACT OF 1978

S.Rep. No. 95–1263, 95th Cong., 2d Sess., 158–60 (1976).

Present law

Ordinary loss treatment, rather than capital loss treatment, is provided in certain cases for small business corporation stock (section 1244 stock) which is disposed of at a loss. This special treatment is accorded only to individual shareholders (not trusts or estates) to whom the stock was originally issued.

* * *

For stock to qualify as section 1244 stock, * * * (3) the corporation issuing the stock must be a domestic corporation; * * * (6) the stock must be issued for money or other property, subject to certain exceptions; (7) more than 50 percent of the gross receipts of the corporation must be derived from the active conduct of a trade or business during the corporation's existence or for its five most recent taxable years prior to the taxable year during which the loss is incurred, whichever period is less; * * *

REASONS FOR CHANGE

* * *

EXPLANATION OF PROVISION

* * *

The bill increases the amount of section 1244 stock that a qualified small business corporation may issue from $500,000 to $1,000,000. * * *

If a qualified corporation issues common stock the aggregate value of which exceeds $1,000,000, the committee intends that the issuing corporation must designate which of the shares of stock issued are to be treated as section 1244 stock. The designation must be made in accordance with regulations to be issued by the Treasury Department. * * * [See § 1.1244(c)–2(b).] The bill repeals the equity capital limitation. Thus, after the date of enactment of this bill, a corporation, assuming other requirements are met, may issue additional common stock under the provisions of section 1244 without regard to the amount of its equity capital to the extent that the amount received for the common stock to be issued does not exceed $1,000,000 reduced by the amount received for the common stock already issued.

* * * Under the provisions of the bill, the maximum amount that may be treated as an ordinary loss is increased to $50,000; in the case of a husband and wife filing a joint return for the taxable year in which the loss is incurred, the maximum amount that may be treated as an ordinary loss is increased to $100,000.

The bill repeals the present law requirement that a written plan to issue section 1244 stock must be adopted by the issuing corporation. Additionally, the bill repeals the present law requirement that provides that no prior offering of stock of the corporation or any portion of a prior offering of stock may be outstanding at the time a written plan is adopted.

The bill provides that a corporation may issue common stock under the provisions of section 1244 without adopting a written plan, but that only the first $1,000,000 worth of common stock may qualify as section 1244 stock. If the $1,000,000 common stock limitation is exceeded, the regulations are to provide which portion of the aggregate amount of issued common stock is qualified stock and how such shares of stock are to be distinguished as qualifying stock by both the issuing corporation and its shareholders.

* * *

Chapter 4

CASH AND PROPERTY DISTRIBUTIONS BY C CORPORATIONS

§ 4.1 SCOPE

This chapter examines various aspects involving the treatment of distributions of cash or property by a C corporation to its shareholders. Sec. 4.2 looks at the treatment of distributions of cash to noncorporate shareholders, and Sec. 4.3 considers the distributions of property to noncorporate shareholders. This section examines the repeal, by the Tax Reform Act of 1986, of the *General Utilities* doctrine in the context of nonliquidating distributions. Sec. 4.4 examines the treatment of the distribution of cash and property to corporate shareholders. Sec. 4.5 examines certain principles governing dividend distributions, such as the non-pass through of tax exempt income. Sec. 4.6 looks at the earnings and profit concepts, which is at the heart of the dividend provisions. Sec. 4.7 considers constructive dividends, which arise in various situations in which a transaction may not appear to be a dividend but is treated as a dividend as a matter of substance.

Sec. 4.8 examines the treatment of dividends paid by a subsidiary to its parent prior to the sale by the parent of the stock of the subsidiary. Sec. 4.9 examines the treatment of dividends paid after a gift of stock. Finally, Sec. 4.10 examines the policy issue of whether the corporate tax should be eliminated, thereby effectively integrating the corporate and shareholder income taxes.

This topic is explored in greater detail in Chapter 9 of *Federal Taxation of Business Enterprises, supra* Chapter 1, note 1 and in Chapter 7 of Bittker and Eustice, *Corporations, supra* Sec. 1.4.

§ 4.2 CURRENT DISTRIBUTION OF CASH TO NONCORPORATE SHAREHOLDERS

A. INTRODUCTION

Section 301 governs the tax treatment to both noncorporate and corporate shareholders on the receipt of a distribution of property from a subchapter C corporation. Section 301(a) provides that "a distribution of property (as defined in § 317(a)) made by a corporation to a shareholder with respect to its stock shall be treated in the manner provided in subsection (c)." The term property is defined in § 317(a) as "money, securities and any other property; except that such term does not include stock in the corporation making the distribution (or rights to acquire such stock)." Securities for this purpose are long term debt obligations of the distributing corporation. Under § 301(b)(1), the amount of the distribution is the amount of the cash.

The term dividend is defined in § 316 as any distribution of property (1) out of the earnings and profits of a corporation accumulated after February 28, 1913 (accumulated earnings and profits), or (2) out of the earnings and profits of the corporation for the current taxable year (current earnings and profits). Under § 316(a)(2), current earnings and profits are calculated "as of the close of the taxable year without diminution by reason of distributions made during the taxable year * * *, [and] without regard to the amount of earnings and profits at the time of the distribution ...". Distributions are considered as first made out of the most recently accumulated earnings and profits. A distribution of property is treated as a dividend to the extent of the earnings and profits of the corporation for the year of the distribution and then to the extent of accumulated earnings and profits.

Thus, for a distribution to be a dividend, the distribution must come from the corporation's earnings and profits. The term "earnings and profits," although not defined in the Code, refers to the earnings of a corporation after operational expenses and taxes, not to the liquid funds in a corporation. Earnings and profits are positive if the corporation operates at a profit and negative if it operates at a loss, the latter being commonly referred to as a deficit in earnings and profits. Section 312 specifies the effect certain transactions have on earnings and profits. Pursuant to § 312(a), earnings and profits are, in general, reduced (but not to a deficit) by the following amounts:

(1) the amount of money distributed,

(2) the principal amount of obligations of the corporation distributed, and

(3) the adjusted basis of property distributed.

The operation of § 312 is examined in Sec. 4.6.

Current earnings and profits are the earnings and profits of the current tax year of the corporation. Accumulated earnings and profits are the undistributed earnings and profits of prior tax years. This concept is similar to the financial accounting concept of retained earnings. Unless distributed, current earnings and profits become accumulated earnings and profits at the end of a tax year. Under these rules, accumulated earnings and profits may be positive while current earnings and profits are negative or vice versa. This is illustrated by the following example.

Corporation C has (1) a deficit in its accumulated earnings and profits account of $100K, and (2) current earnings and profits of $10K. C distributes $10K during the current year. The distribution is treated as a dividend because the amount of the distribution does not exceed the current earnings and profits of the distributing corporation. On the other hand, if C distributes the $10K in the following year (at which time the $10K of current earnings has reduced the deficit to $90K), the distribution is not a dividend unless the corporation has current earnings and profits in the year of the distribution.

Tax exempt income increases earnings and profits because it is money that the corporation has available for distribution to its shareholders. *See* § 1.312-6(b). Although tax exempt interest is not subject to tax on receipt by the corporation, the tax exempt character does not pass through on distribution. Tax exempt interest is an example of an item excluded from taxable income but included in earnings and profits. Certain items, such as the excess of accelerated depreciation over straight line depreciation, reduce taxable income but not earnings and profits. *See* § 312(k).

The computation of earnings and profits is illustrated in the following example. Assume that an accrual basis, calendar year corporation has gross income during calendar year 1992 of $1,000,000, tax exempt income of $10K, operating expenses of $500K (with depreciation computed on a straight line basis), and a tax liability of $250K. The corporation's current earnings and profits are $260K, calculated as follows:

Gross Income	$1,000,000
Less: Operating Expenses	500,000
Taxable Income	$ 500,000
Less: Taxes	250,000
Tentative Earnings and Profits	250,000
Add: Tax Exempt Interest	10,000
Current Earnings and Profits	$ 260,000

If the corporation distributes cash of $260K during calendar year 1992, the shareholders have a dividend in the amount of $260K.

Any distribution in excess of current earnings and profits is deemed to come out of accumulated earnings and profits as demonstrated by the following example.

C corporation has $260K of current earnings and profits and $400 of accumulated earnings and profits. On the last day of the taxable year, C distributes $500K of cash. Under § 316(b), all of the $500K distribution is treated as a dividend; $260K comes out of current earnings and profits and $240K comes out of accumulated earnings and profits. Under § 312, C's total earnings and profits of $660K are reduced by $500K to $160K all of which is accumulated earnings and profits.

Under § 301(c)(2), any distribution in excess of both current and accumulated earnings and profits is treated as a return of capital to the extent of the shareholder's adjusted basis for her stock. Under § 301(c)(3), any distribution in excess of the adjusted basis is treated as gain from the sale of the stock. This is illustrated as follows: Assume that C corporation has $260K in current earnings and profits, and $400K in accumulated earnings and profits. C distributes $800K to its sole shareholder who has a basis in her stock of $100K. The following results obtain. $260K of the $800K distribution is a dividend from current earnings and profits. The $540K portion of the distribution in excess of current earnings and profits is deemed to be out of accumulated earnings and profits to the extent of $400K. The $140K portion of the distribution in excess of such accumulated earnings and profits is a nontaxable return of capital to the extent of the shareholder's adjusted basis for her stock, which is $100K. The $40K portion in excess of the adjusted basis of the shareholder's stock is treated as gain from the sale of such stock.

These results can be summarized by reference to the four levels of distribution in subchapter C:

First Level: A distribution is first deemed to be out of current earnings and profits. *See* § 301(c)(1).

Second Level: A distribution in excess of current earnings and profits is deemed to be out of accumulated earnings and profits. *See* § 301(c)(1).

Third Level: A distribution in excess of both current and accumulated earnings and profits is deemed to be a nontaxable return of capital to the extent of the adjusted basis of the shareholder's stock. *See* § 301(c)(2).

Fourth Level: A distribution in excess of current and accumulated earnings and profits and the adjusted basis of the shareholder's stock normally produces a capital gain. *See* § 301(c)(3).

B. INTRODUCTORY PROBLEM ON CURRENT DISTRIBUTION OF CASH

Corporation X is wholly owned by individual A. X has $100K of current earnings and profits and $200K of accumulated earnings and profits. A has a basis of $50K for his stock. X distributes to A a cash dividend of $400K. Specify the results to A by reference to the four levels of distribution discussed above. Also, what result to X upon distribution of the cash?

C. ILLUSTRATION OF THE TAX TREATMENT OF DISTRIBUTIONS TO INDIVIDUAL SHAREHOLDERS

REVENUE RULING 74-164
1974-1 C.B. 74.

Advice has been requested concerning the taxable status of corporate distributions under the circumstances described below.

X corporation and Y corporation each using the calendar year for Federal income tax purposes made distributions of $15,000 to their respective shareholders on July 1, 1971, and made no other distributions to their shareholders during the taxable year. The distributions were taxable as provided by section 301(c) of the Internal Revenue Code of 1954.

SITUATION 1.

At the beginning of its taxable year 1971, X corporation had earnings and profits accumulated after February 28, 1913, of $40,000. It had an operating loss for the period January 1, 1971 through June 30, 1971, of $50,000 but had earnings and profits for the entire year 1971 of $5,000.

SITUATION 2.

At the beginning of its taxable year 1971, Y corporation had a deficit in earnings and profits accumulated after February 28, 1913, of $60,000. Its net profits for the period January 1, 1971 through June 30, 1971, were $75,000 but its earnings and profits for the entire taxable year 1971 were only $5,000.

SITUATION 3.

Assume the same facts as in *Situation* 1 except that X had a deficit in earnings and profits of $5,000 for the entire taxable year 1971.

SITUATION 4.

Assume the same facts as in *Situation* 1 except that X had a deficit in earnings and profits of $55,000 for the entire taxable year 1971.

* * *

[I]n *Situation* 1, the earnings and profits of X corporation for the taxable year 1971 of $5,000 and the earnings and profits accumulated since February 28, 1913, and prior to the taxable year 1971, of $40,000 were applicable to the distribution paid by it on July 1, 1971. Thus, $5,000 of the distribution of $15,000 was paid from the earnings and profits of the taxable year 1971 and the balance of $10,000 was paid from the earnings and profits accumulated since February 28, 1913. Therefore, the entire distribution of $15,000 was a dividend within the meaning of section 316 of the Code.

In *Situation* 2 the earnings and profits of Y corporation for the taxable year 1971 of $5,000 were applicable to the distribution paid by Y corporation on July 1, 1971. Y corporation had no earnings and profits accumulated after February 28, 1913, available at the time of the distribution. Thus, only $5,000 of the distribution by Y corporation of $15,000 was a dividend within the meaning of section 316 of the Code. The balance of such distribution, $10,000 which was not a dividend, applied against and reduced the adjusted basis of the stock in the hands of the shareholders, and to the extent that it exceeded the adjusted basis of the stock was gain from the sale or exchange of property.

In the case of a deficit in earnings and profits for the taxable year in which distributions are made, the taxable status of distributions is dependent upon the amount of earnings and profits accumulated since February 28, 1913, and available at the dates of distribution. In determining the amount of such earnings and profits, section 1.316–2(b) of the regulations provides, in effect, that the deficit in earnings and profits of the taxable year will be prorated to the dates of distribution.

Applying the foregoing to Situations 3 and 4 the distribution paid by X corporation on July 1, 1971, in each situation was a dividend within the meaning of section 316 of the Code to the extent indicated as follows:

Situation # 3

Accumulated Earnings and Profits (E & P) 1/1	$40,000
E & P deficit for entire taxable year ($5,000) Prorate to date of distribution 7/1 (½ of $5,000)	(2,500)
E & P available 7/1	$37,500
Distribution 7/1 ($15,000)	(15,000) taxable as a dividend
E & P deficit from 7/1–12/31	(2,500)
Accumulated E & P balance 12/31	$20,000

Situation # 4

Accumulated E & P 1/1	$40,000
E & P deficit for entire taxable year ($55,000) Prorate to date of distribution 7/1 (½ of $55,000)	(27,500)
E & P available 7/1	$12,500
Distribution 7/1 ($15,000)	(12,500) taxable as a dividend
E & P deficit from 7/1–12/31	(27,500)
Accumulated E & P balance 12/31	$(27,500)

Question

Is this a correct interpretation of § 316? State precisely the controlling principle in each of the four situations in the ruling.

§ 4.3 CURRENT DISTRIBUTION OF PROPERTY TO NONCORPORATE SHAREHOLDERS

A. TREATMENT OF THE SHAREHOLDER

The treatment of the distributee shareholder on receipt of a distribution of property is essentially the same as the treatment on the receipt of cash with the following additional rules. First, under § 301(b)(1) the amount of the distribution is the fair market value of the property received. The fair market value is determined as of the date of the distribution. *See* § 301(b)(3).

Under § 301(d), the basis of the property distributed is the fair market value of the property. Second, if the property is subject to a liability or in connection with the distribution the shareholder assumes a liability of the corporation, then the amount of the distribution is reduced by the amount of the liability. *See* § 1.301–1(g). This rule is illustrated as follows. Corporation C distributes property to shareholder S. The property has a fair market value of $100K and is subject to a nonrecourse liability of $60K. Under § 301(b)(2), the amount of the distribution is $40K, which is the fair market value of the property ($100K) less the liability ($60K). If the corporation has sufficient E & P, S has a dividend of $40K under § 301(c)(1). Under § 301(d) S's basis for the property is $100K, the fair market value of the property.

B. RECOGNITION OF GAIN OR LOSS BY CORPORATION: REPEAL OF THE GENERAL UTILITIES DOCTRINE FOR NONLIQUIDATING TRANSACTIONS

1. *The General Utilities Doctrine*

Review the *General Utilities* case, Sec. 1.3.D.

2. *Introductory Note*

The General Utilities doctrine was essentially repealed both for liquidating and nonliquidating corporate distributions by the Tax Reform Act of 1986. Section 311 embodies the repeal for current distributions, and § 336 does the same for liquidating distributions. The materials in this section deal with the repeal of the doctrine under § 311 for current distributions of property.

3. The Repeal of the General Utilities Doctrine by the Tax Reform Act of 1986

GENERAL EXPLANATION OF TAX REFORM ACT OF 1986
328–346, (1986).

PRIOR LAW

Overview

As a general rule, under prior law (as under present law) corporate earnings from sales of appreciated property were taxed twice, first to the corporation when the sale occurred, and again to the shareholders when the net proceeds were distributed as dividends. At the corporate level, the income was taxed at ordinary rates if it resulted from the sale of inventory or other ordinary income assets, or at capital gains rates if it resulted from the sale of a capital asset held for more than six months. With certain exceptions, shareholders were taxed at ordinary income rates to the extent of their pro rata share of the distributing corporation's current and accumulated earnings and profits.

An important exception to this two-level taxation of corporate earnings was the so-called *General Utilities* rule. The *General Utilities* rule permitted nonrecognition of gain by corporations on certain distributions of appreciated property to their shareholders and on certain liquidating sales of property. Thus, its effect was to allow appreciation in property accruing during the period it was held by a corporation to escape tax at the corporate level. At the same time, the transferee (the shareholder or third-party purchaser) obtained a stepped-up, fair market value basis under other provisions of the Code, with associated additional depreciation, depletion, or amortization deductions. Accordingly, the "price" of a step up in the basis of property subject to the *General Utilities* rule was typically a single capital gains tax paid by the shareholder on receipt of a liquidating distribution from the corporation.

* * *

Case law and statutory background

Genesis of the General Utilities rule

The precise meaning of *General Utilities* was a matter of considerable debate in the years following the 1935 decision. The essential facts were as follows. General Utilities had purchased 50 percent of the stock of Islands Edison Co. in 1927 for $2,000. In 1928, a prospective buyer offered to buy all of General Utilities' shares in Islands Edison, which apparently had a fair market value at that time of more than $1 million. Seeking to avoid the large corporate-level tax that would be imposed if it sold the stock itself, General Utilities offered to distribute the Islands Edison stock to its shareholders with the understanding that they would then sell the stock to the buyer. The company's officers and the buyer negotiated the terms of the sale but did not sign a contract. The shareholders of General Utilities had no binding commitment upon receipt of the Islands Edison shares to sell them to the buyer on these terms.

General Utilities declared a dividend in an amount equal to the value of the Islands Edison stock, payable in shares of that stock. The corporation distributed the Islands Edison shares and, four days later, the shareholders sold the shares to the buyer on the terms previously negotiated by the company's officers.

The Internal Revenue Service took the position that the distribution of the Islands Edison shares was a taxable transaction to General Utilities. Before the Supreme Court, the Commissioner argued that the company had created an indebtedness to its shareholders in declaring a dividend, and that the discharge of this indebtedness using appreciated property produced taxable income to the company under the holding in *Kirby Lumber Co. v. United States*. Alternatively, he argued, the sale of the Islands Edison stock was in reality made by General Utilities rather than by its shareholders following distribution of the stock. Finally, the Commissioner contended that a distribution of appreciated property by a corporation in and of itself constitutes a realization event. All dividends are distributed in satisfaction of the corporation's general obligation to pay out earnings to shareholders, he argued, and the satisfaction of that obligation with appreciated property causes a realization of the gain.

The Supreme Court held that the distribution did not give rise to taxable income under a discharge of indebtedness rationale. The Court did not directly address the Commissioner's third argument, that the company realized income simply by distributing appreciated property as a dividend. There is disagreement over whether the Court rejected this argument on substantive grounds or merely on the ground it was not timely made. Despite the ambiguity of the Supreme Court's decision, however, subsequent cases interpreted the decision as rejecting the Commissioner's third argument and as holding that no gain is realized on corporate distributions of appreciated property to its shareholders.

* * *

Nonliquidating distributions: section 311

Congress subsequently enacted a number of statutory exceptions to the *General Utilities* rule. Under prior law (as under present law), the presumption under *General Utilities* was reversed for nonliquidating distributions: the general rule was that a corporation recognized gain (but not loss) on a distribution of property as a dividend or in redemption of stock. The distributing corporation is treated as if it sold the property for its fair market value on the date of the distribution. A number of exceptions to the general rule were provided. [These exceptions to recognition applied to distributions of appreciated property in the following circumstances:

(1) Distributions to long term noncorporate shareholders who owned at least 10% of the stock;

(2) Distributions of the assets of a trade or business that had been conducted by the corporation for at least five years;

(3) Distributions of the stock of certain subsidiaries; and

(4) Certain distributions to pay death taxes.]

* * *

Section 311 also provided under separate rules that a corporation recognized gain on the distribution of encumbered property to the extent the liabilities assumed or to which the property was subject exceeded the distributing corporation's adjusted basis; on the distribution of LIFO inventory, to the extent the basis of the inventory determined under a FIFO method exceeded its LIFO value; and on the distribution of an installment obligation, to the extent of the excess of the face value of the obligation over the distributing corporation's adjusted basis in the obligation.

* * *

Reasons for Change

In general

Congress believed that the *General Utilities* rule, even in its more limited form, produced many incongruities and inequities in the tax system. First, the rule could create significant distortions in business behavior.

* * *

Second, the *General Utilities* rule tended to undermine the corporate income tax. Under normally applicable tax principles, nonrecognition of gain is available only if the transferee takes a carryover basis in the transferred property, thus assuring that a tax will eventually be collected on the appreciation. Where the *General Utilities* rule applied, assets generally were permitted to leave corporate solution and to take a stepped-up basis in the hands of the transferee without the imposition of a corporate-level tax.[72] Thus, the effect of the rule was to grant a permanent exemption from the corporate income tax.

* * *

Conforming changes to provisions relating to nonliquidating distributions

The tax treatment of corporations with respect to nonliquidating distributions of appreciated property historically has been the same as liquidating distributions. In recent years, however, nonliquidating dis-

---

72. The price of this basis step up was, at most, a single, shareholder-level capital gains tax (and perhaps recapture, tax benefit, and other similar amounts). In some cases, moreover, payment of the capital gains tax was deferred because the shareholder's gain was reported under the installment method.

tributions have been subjected to stricter rules than liquidating distributions, and corporations have generally been required to recognize gain as a result of nonliquidating distributions of appreciated property. Consistent with this relationship, the Act generally conforms the treatment of nonliquidating distributions with liquidating distributions.

* * *

Explanation of Provisions
Overview

The Act provides that gain or loss generally is recognized by a corporation on liquidating distributions of its property as if the property had been sold at fair market value to the distributee.

* * *

The Act also makes certain conforming changes in the provisions relating to nonliquidating distributions of property to shareholders.

* * *

Nonliquidating distributions [See § 311(a) and (b).]

The Act makes certain conforming changes to the provisions relating to nonliquidating distributions of property. For purposes of determining the amount realized on a distribution of property, the fair market value of the property is treated as being no less than the amount of any liability to which it is subject or which is assumed by the shareholder under the principles applicable to liquidating distributions. The prior-law exceptions to recognition that were provided for nonliquidating distributions to ten percent, long-term noncorporate shareholders, and for certain distributions of property in connection with the payment of estate taxes or in connection with certain redemptions of private foundation stock, are repealed. As under prior law, no loss is recognized to a distributing corporation on a nonliquidating distribution of property to its shareholders.

* * *

4. *Elaboration on § 311 Distribution Rule*

Section 311(a) provides that "[e]xcept as provided in subsection (b), no gain or loss [is] recognized to a corporation on the distribution (not in complete liquidation) with respect to its stock, of—(1) its stock (or rights to acquire its stock), or (2) property." Section 311(b)(1) overpowers this general nonrecognition rule by providing that "[i]f—(A) a corporation distributes property (other than an obligation of such corporation) to a shareholder in a distribution to which subpart A applies, and (B) the fair market value of such property exceeds its adjusted basis (in the hands of the distributing corporation), then gain [is] recognized to the distributing corporation as if such property were sold by the distributee at its fair market value."

The gain recognition rule of § 311(b) applies only to distributions to which subpart A applies. Subpart A encompasses §§ 301 through 307, which deal with current distributions of property and stock. Therefore, the gain recognition rule does not apply to distributions of stock and securities pursuant to reorganizations which are governed by §§ 354 through 368.

Under § 311(b)(2), rules similar to the rules of § 336(b) apply for the purposes of determining the effect of a distribution of property accompanied by distributions of liabilities. Under § 336(b), the fair market value of property distributed in a liquidating distribution is not treated as less than the amount of the distributed liability. Thus, if a corporation distributes property encumbered by a liability in excess of the basis of the property, gain is recognized in the amount of the excess even though the fair market value of the property is less than the amount of the liability.

Section 311(b)(3) authorizes the Treasury to promulgate regulations that apply to distributions of an interest in a partnership or trust where loss property is contributed to the partnership or trust for the principal purpose of recognizing the loss on the distribution. The regulations may provide that the amount of the gain recognized under Section 311(b)(1) is computed without regard to the loss property contributed.

C. IMPACT OF DISTRIBUTION OF APPRECIATED PROPERTY ON CORPORATION'S EARNINGS AND PROFITS

Section 312(a) provides that on a distribution of property by a corporation with respect to its stock the earnings and profits to the extent thereof are reduced by the sum of the following distributed amounts:

(1) the amount of money;

(2) the principal amount of obligations; or

(3) the adjusted basis of property.

Thus, it would appear that on the distribution of appreciated property, the corporation's earnings and profits would be reduced by the adjusted basis of the property even though the amount of the distribution to the shareholders, as determined under § 301(b), is the fair market value of the property.

Section 312(b) eliminates this potential asymmetry by requiring two adjustments on the distribution of appreciated property. First, under § 312(b)(1), earnings and profits are increased by the excess of the fair market value over the adjusted basis. Thus, the earnings and profits are increased by the gain that is realized by the corporation under § 311(b). This increase in earnings and profits is, however, reduced under general principles by the corporate tax liability generated by the distribution.

The second adjustment, which is in § 312(b)(2), provides that the earnings and profits (after the net increase from the gain and the associated tax liability) are reduced under § 312(a)(3) by the fair market value of the property rather than by the adjusted basis.

These principles are illustrated as follows. Corporation C has earnings and profits of $100K. C distributes to shareholder S property with a value of $20K and a basis of $10K. As a result of the distribution C has a $10K gain under § 311(b), and C incurs a $3.4K tax on the gain. Under § 301(c), S has a $20K dividend, and under § 301(d), S takes a $20K basis for the property. Under § 312(b)(1), C's earnings and profits are increased by the gain of $10K, and under general principles C's earnings and profits are reduced by the $3.4K tax. Thus, before reducing earnings and profits for the distribution, C's earnings and profits are $106.6K, that is, the starting earnings and profits of $100K plus the net increase of $6.6K from the distribution. Under §§ 312(b)(2) and 312(a)(3), C reduces its earnings and profits by the $20K fair market value of the property. Thus, after the distribution C has earnings and profits of $86.6K.

If a corporation distributes depreciated property, that is property with an adjusted basis in excess of fair market value, the following rules apply:

(1) Under § 311(a), no loss is recognized; and

(2) Under § 312(a), the earnings and profits are reduced by the adjusted basis of the property.

If in connection with a distribution, the property distributed is subject to a liability or the shareholder assumes a liability of the corporation, then under § 312(c) "proper adjustments" are to be made in computing earnings and profits. Under § 1.312–3, the decrease in earnings and profits is reduced by the amount of any such liability.

D. PROBLEMS ON CURRENT DISTRIBUTIONS OF PROPERTY

1. Corporation X, an accrual basis taxpayer, is wholly owned by individual A. At a time when X has no earnings and profits or deficit in earnings and profits, X distributes to A property with a fair market value of $20K and an adjusted basis of $5K. The tax rate applicable to X is 33.33%. What impact on X and A?

2. Same as question 1, except the property is subject to a liability of $15K.

3. Corporation X, which has substantial earnings and profits, distributes to its sole shareholder, A, property with an adjusted basis of $20K and a fair market value of $5K. What result to X and A?

§ 4.4 DISTRIBUTIONS OF CASH AND PROPERTY TO CORPORATE SHAREHOLDERS

A. BASIC RULES

The rules of §§ 301, 316(a), 311 and 312(a) that govern cash and property distributions to noncorporate distributees (*see* Sec. 4.2 and 4.3) also generally apply to distributions to corporate distributees. Such distributees are, however, subject to a variety of other rules some of which are discussed below. Also, the special rules that apply to corporations that file consolidated returns are examined in Chapter 8.

If a corporation pays dividends to an individual, the dividends are subject to two levels of tax. If dividends are paid to another corporation there is a potential for more than two levels of tax. To mitigate the effect of these multiple levels of tax, corporations are given a dividends received deduction.

Under § 243(a), a domestic corporate shareholder that owns less than 20% of the stock of a distributing corporation that is a domestic corporation is allowed a deduction in an amount equal to 70% of the amount of the dividends received. Under § 243(c), a domestic corporate shareholder that owns at least 20% of the stock of the distributing corporation is allowed either an 80% or 100% dividends received deduction. In general, the 80% dividends received deduction applies if the corporations are not members of a consolidated group, and the 100% deduction applies if the corporations are members of such a group. To qualify as a consolidated group, the parent distributee corporation must own at least 80% of the stock of the distributing subsidiary and an election to file consolidated returns must be made. *See* Chapter 8.

These basic rules may be summarized as follows:

% of Stock of Distributing Corporation Held by Corporate Distributee	Corporate Distributee's Dividends Received Deduction
1. Less than 20%	70%
2. More than 20% but less than 80%	80%
3. More than 80% and consolidated returns filed	100%

B. TREATMENT OF DEBT FINANCED PORTFOLIO STOCK

See § 246A.

GENERAL EXPLANATION OF TAX REFORM ACT OF 1984
128–131 (December 31, 1984).

* * *

REASONS FOR CHANGE

The purpose of the dividends received deduction is to reduce multiple corporate-level taxation of income as it flows from the corporation that earns it to the ultimate noncorporate shareholder. However, under prior law, when dividends were paid on debt-financed portfolio stock, the conjunction of the dividends received deduction and the interest deduction enabled corporate taxpayers to shelter unrelated income. The Congress believed that these two deductions were not intended to provide such shelter.

Specifically, under prior law, corporate taxpayers were borrowing money and using the proceeds to acquire dividend-paying portfolio stock. On the receipt of dividends paid with respect to such stock, such corporate taxpayers generally qualified for dividends received deductions, which reduced the amount of tax paid on the dividends. Further, the fact that the loan proceeds were used to generate tax-favored dividend income did not limit the deduction for interest paid or accrued on the indebtedness. * * *

EXPLANATION OF PROVISION

In general

The provision generally reduces the deduction for dividends received on debt-financed portfolio stock so that the deduction is available, in effect, only with respect to dividends attributable to that portion of the stock which is not debt financed. Generally, this is accomplished by determining the percentage of the cost of an investment in stock which is debt financed and by reducing the otherwise allowable dividends received deduction with respect to any dividends received on that stock by that percentage. * * *

C. BASIS REDUCTION FOR NONTAXED PORTION OF CERTAIN DIVIDENDS

See § 1059.

SENATE FINANCE COMMITTEE REPORT ON THE REVENUE RECONCILIATION BILL OF 1989
86–87 (October 10, 1989).

PRESENT LAW

* * *

A corporate shareholder's basis in stock is reduced by the portion of a dividend eligible for the dividends received deduction if the dividend is "extraordinary." In general, a dividend is extraordinary if the amount of the dividend equals or exceeds 10 percent (5 percent in the case of preferred stock) of the shareholder's adjusted basis in the stock and the shareholder has not held the stock, subject to a risk of loss, for at least 2 years prior to the date the amount or payment of the dividend is declared, announced, or agreed to, whichever is the earliest (sec. 1059).

REASONS FOR CHANGE

Corporate stockholders may receive dividends eligible for the dividends received deduction in circumstances where the dividends more appropriately should be characterized as a return of capital. In many of these cases, the dividends are not subject to the "extraordinary dividend" rules of present law, so the holder's basis in the stock is not reduced as it should be economically. Thus, the holder can sell the stock and create an artificial capital loss in an amount approximately equal to the return-of-capital dividends. The committee believes that basis reduction in such cases is appropriate to accurately reflect the true economic effect of these types of transactions.

EXPLANATION OF PROVISION

The provision treats dividends with respect to certain preferred stock as extraordinary dividends under section 1059 (regardless of holding period), thus requiring reduction in stock basis. The provision applies to dividends with respect to preferred stock if (1) when issued, such stock has a dividend rate which declines (or reasonably can be expected to decline) in the future, (2) the issue price of such stock exceeds its liquidation rights or its stated redemption price, or (3) such stock is otherwise structured to enable corporate shareholders to reduce tax through a combination of dividend received deductions and loss on [disposition].

* * *

§ 4.5 GENERAL PRINCIPLES INVOLVING DIVIDEND DISTRIBUTIONS

A. DISTRIBUTION OF LIFE INSURANCE PROCEEDS

REVENUE RULING 71-79
1971-1 C.B. 112.

* * *

The question presented is whether corporate distributions to stockholders of the proceeds of a life insurance policy received by the corporation as beneficiary upon the death of the insured are dividends to the stockholders.

Upon the death of the insured, the proceeds of a life insurance contract were received by the corporation as the beneficiary of the policy. The proceeds were not includible in the gross income of the corporation as provided by section 101(a) of the Internal Revenue Code of 1954. The corporation distributed the proceeds to its stockholders.

There is no provision in the Code exempting life insurance proceeds from tax except in the hands of the beneficiaries. Where the proceeds of a life insurance policy are paid to the corporation as a beneficiary, the proceeds lose their identity after such payment.

Accordingly, in the instant case the distributions of the insurance proceeds to the stockholders are dividends to the extent of the earnings and profits available for the payment of dividends as provided by section 316 of the Code.

* * *

B. DIVIDENDS NEED NOT BE PRO RATA

LINCOLN NATIONAL BANK v. BURNET

United States Court of Appeals, District of Columbia Circuit, 1933.
63 F.2d 131.

* * * [Neither] the fact that the distribution was to some of the shareholders only and not to others, nor that it was divided among the stockholders in proportions other than their respective holdings of stock in the corporation [affects the dividend status of the payments as dividends]. The other shareholders have not complained of this inequality, and must therefore in this proceeding be deemed to have ratified the distribution. The character of the distribution as a division of profits was not changed by the manner in which it was accomplished, nor by the personal motives which induced the respective stockholders or directors to approve of such action, for it nevertheless remained in contemplation of law a distribution of dividends. It was made from the earnings or profits of the distributing corporation, and was divided among the stockholders of the distributing company in such proportion as was satisfactory to its directors and stockholders.

* * *

C. PAYMENTS OF ACCUMULATED DIVIDENDS TO PURCHASER OF PREFERRED STOCK

REVENUE RULING 56-211
1956–1 C.B. 155.

Advice has been requested as to the proper method of reporting, for Federal income tax purposes, payments received during a taxable year and applied against accumulated dividends on preferred stock.

In 1950 the taxpayer purchased a certain number of shares of cumulative preferred stock of a corporation at 170x dollars per share. At that time the accumulated dividends on the preferred stock were 150x dollars per share. In the taxable year 1954 the corporation paid the current dividend of 8x dollars per share on the preferred stock and 12x dollars on account of the accumulated dividends.

* * *

The Internal Revenue Service has consistently held that dividends on stock do not accrue as interest accrues, but represent ordinary income to the stockholder of record when actually or constructively received by him, regardless of the period for which the dividends are paid. * * *

Accordingly, it is held that the entire 20x dollars per share shall be treated as dividend income in the year received, to the extent it was paid out of the corporation's earnings and profits as defined in section 316(a) of the Code.

Questions

As illustrated in Rev.Rul. 56–211, although the purchase price of stock may reflect a corporation's accumulated earnings, the purchaser is nevertheless taxed on the earnings when distributed. Thus, the earnings are taxed three times: first, at the corporate level; second, at the selling shareholder level as a capital gain; and third, at the purchasing shareholder level when distributed. Should a purchaser take into account the potential tax liability on the distribution of accumulated earnings in determining his offering price? In general, should the offering price for the purchase of a corporation's assets be higher than the offering price for the purchase of stock? What is the impact of § 1059 if the purchaser of the stock is a corporation?

D. MULTIPLE CLASSES OF STOCK: DISTRIBUTIONS IN EXCESS OF E & P

REVENUE RULING 69–440

1969–2 C.B. 46.

The question presented concerns the source of distributions under section 316 of the Internal Revenue Code of 1954 and section 1.316–2 of the Income Tax Regulations when such distributions are made with respect to classes of stock having priority over other classes of stock and the sum of the payments on all classes for the year is in excess of the earnings and profits.

* * *

There is nothing in section 316 of the Code which impairs the contractual right of the stockholders.

* * *

[I]t appears that Congress intended that a corporation should compute its net earnings and profits as of the end of the year, and that if dividend distributions had been made in excess of that amount, the amount of each distribution that was paid out of earnings and profits would be determined on the pro rata basis rather than looking to the actual earnings on hand at the time of each distribution. However, it does not follow that where dividends are paid to different classes of stockholders the priorities as between stockholders must be disregarded. If, for example, a corporation earns only an amount sufficient to meet its preferred stock requirements and pays the required dividends on its preferred stock and also makes distributions on its common stock, the preferred stockholders should, nevertheless, report as dividends the entire amount distributed to them even though the corporation also made distributions to its common stockholders which, when added to the preferred stock dividends, were in excess of the corporate earnings and profits for that year. In such a case, if the preferred stockholders are entitled to payment of their dividends before any distribution can be made to common stockholders, it is apparent that the earnings and profits are used first for the preferred stockholders, and if the earnings and profits are thereby exhausted, the payments to the common stockholders merely reduce their equity and constitute in effect a return of capital.

* * *

Accordingly, in the present case, the earnings and profits must be regarded as having been first used for the payment of the dividends on the prior preferred stock as required by the charter of the corporation and the contract with the prior preferred stockholders, and only the earnings and profits remaining after such dividend requirements have been met should be regarded as having been paid to the junior stockholders.

* * *

E. DATE OF THE DIVIDEND

REVENUE RULING 62–131

1962–2 C.B. 94.

The date of payment, rather than the date of declaration, constitutes the date of distribution of a dividend. Accordingly, the taxable status of a distribution and its effect on the earnings and profits of the declaring corporation will be determined by reference to the earnings and profits of the corporation for the corporation's taxable year of payment, if the distribution is out of current earnings and profits, or on the date of payment, if the distribution is out of accumulated earnings and profits. For sources of distributions in general, see section 1.316–2 of the Income Tax Regulations.

§ 4.6 DETERMINATION OF EARNINGS AND PROFITS

A. INTRODUCTION

The term earnings and profits ("E & P") is not defined in the Code. Section 312 does, however, specify the effect various transactions have on the computation of earnings and profits.

As outlined above, § 312(a), (b) and (c) specify the effect distributions of cash and property have on E & P. Other subsections of § 312 deal with the impact of various types of transactions. For example, § 312(k) requires that the straight line method of depreciation be used in computing E & P. The treatment of transactions not specifically addressed in § 312 is governed by the case law, regulations, and ruling. The guiding principle is that E & P is a measure of a corporation's after-tax economic income.

Any distributions made out of E & P are treated as dividends under § 316 and are required to be included in gross income under § 301(c)(1). A distribution in excess of E & P is treated first as a return of capital to the extent of the shareholder's basis under § 301(c)(2) and then as a capital gain under § 301(c)(3).

A distribution is treated as a return of capital or capital gain under § 301(c)(2) or (3), only if the corporation establishes that it has no E & P. Under § 6042(b)(3), if a corporation is unable to determine whether a distribution or portion thereof is a dividend, then "the entire amount" of the distribution is treated as a dividend.

In computing the precise amount of E & P it is necessary to consider each year of the corporation's operations.

The following materials examine some of the factors that go into the computation of E & P.

B. THE EFFECT OF TAXES PAID OR ACCRUED

WILLIAM C. WEBB v. COMMISSIONER

Tax Court of the United States, 1977.
67 T.C. 1008.

* * *

The last issue for decision is whether Continental, a cash method corporation, may deduct from its earnings and profits taxes which accrue during a taxable year but which are not paid until a subsequent year. The relevant Treasury regulations have long provided that a corporation in computing its earnings and profits for a taxable year must follow the same accounting method it uses for computing its taxable income. Sec. 1.312–6(a), Income Tax Regs. Consequently, under the regulations, it is clear that Continental may deduct its taxes only in the year of payment and not in the year of accrual.

There exists a conflict among the circuits on this issue—three of them allow a cash method taxpayer to reduce its earnings and profits by the amount of accrued but unpaid taxes * * * and one of them allows taxes to reduce the earnings and profits of a cash method taxpayer only in the year of payment. * * * In *M.H. Alworth Trust,* 46 B.T.A. 1045 (1942), we held that a cash method taxpayer could reduce its earnings and profits by accruable taxes, but subsequent to the Eighth Circuit's reversal of our opinion in that case, we have consistently followed that reversal and have not allowed cash method taxpayers to reduce their earnings and profits on account of accrued but unpaid taxes. * * * All accrued but unpaid expenses represents a realistic and economic cost to a cash method corporation, but no reason has been advanced in any of the cases for treating accrued taxes differently from other accrued but unpaid expenses. The decisions that have treated taxes differently are not persuasive because they were either decided under a statutory and regulatory scheme different from that now in existence, or their rationale was based upon certain fallacies.

* * *

[The court went on to hold that the corporation could not deduct the unpaid taxes in computing its E & P.]

Note and Question

1. The Service's position is set out in Rev.Rul. 70–609, 1970–2 C.B. 78. In Rev.Rul. 79–69, 1979–1 CB 134, the Service says that in computing E & P, estimated tax payments of a cash basis taxpayer are deducted in the year paid and refunds are included in the year received.

2. What is the potential impact on the shareholders of an accrual basis corporation that pays dividends in one year and after audit in a subsequent year acknowledges a higher tax liability for the year in which the dividends were paid?

C. EFFECT OF NET OPERATING LOSS

REVENUE RULING 64–146
1964–1 (1 Part I) C.B. 129.

Advice has been requested as to the year in which earnings and profits should be adjusted because of a right accruing to a corporation for refund of Federal income taxes paid in prior years, resulting from a carryback of a net operating loss sustained in a current year.

A corporation, using the accrual method of accounting, sustained a net operating loss for the year 1960. The corporation filed a timely claim for refund of its Federal income taxes paid for the years 1958 and 1959, based on the carryback of the loss it sustained for the year 1960.

* * *

In this case, the event which fixed the corporation's right to a refund of income taxes paid for 1958 and 1959 occurred at the close of the year 1960, when the amount of the net operating loss for that year became definite and certain. The corporation could not have foreseen with certainty that a net operating loss for the year 1960 would become the basis of a claim for refund of taxes paid for the years 1958 and 1959, prior to the end of the year in which the loss occurred.

In the instant case, it is held that, in the computation of earnings and profits for dividend purposes under section 312 of the Code, the amount of the claim for refund of taxes paid for the years 1958 and 1959 is reflected in the current year earnings and profits for the year 1960.

D. 1984 AMENDMENTS RELATING TO THE COMPUTATION OF E & P

SENATE FINANCE COMMITTEE REPORT ON THE DEFICIT REDUCTION TAX BILL OF 1984
198–202 (1984).

REASONS FOR CHANGE

The committee is aware that, under present law, a corporation's earnings and profits may not reflect its economic income.

* * *

Accordingly, the committee bill contains a number of provisions designed to ensure that a corporation's earnings and profits more closely conform to its economic income. * * *

EXPLANATION OF PROVISION

The committee bill requires that a number of changes be made in the way in which a corporation's earnings and profits are calculated. However, no change is intended in the calculation of accumulated earnings and profits (except as they are affected by current earnings and profits). Except as otherwise provided, the committee intends that these changes apply for all purposes of the Internal Revenue Code * * *

The committee anticipates that regulations will provide such adjustments as may be necessary to prevent amounts from being duplicated or omitted. For example, deferred gain on an installment sale included in earnings and profits under this provision is not to be included in earnings and profits a second time, i.e., when recognized.

Construction period interest, taxes, and carrying charges [See § 312(n)(1).]

Construction period interest, taxes, and carrying charges are required to be capitalized as a part of the asset to which they relate for purposes of computing a corporation's earnings and profits. This rule applies to all corporations. Further, it applies with respect to both residential and nonresidential real property, and to personal property. That capitalized amount is to be written off for earnings and profits purpose as is the asset itself.

* * *

§ 4.6 DETERMINATION OF EARNINGS AND PROFITS

Intangible drilling costs and mine development costs [See § 312(n)(2).]

Intangible drilling costs allowable as a deduction for any taxable year under section 263(c), and mineral exploration and development costs allowable as a deduction under sections 616(a) or 617, are required to be capitalized for purposes of computing earnings and profits, but only if the expenditures give rise to the creation of an asset having an anticipated economic life of more than one year. Intangible drilling costs capitalized under the provision are to be amortized on a straight-line basis over 5 years. The amortization period for mineral exploration and development expenses is 10 years. No amortization is to occur, however, prior to the date the asset is placed in service.

* * *

Certain trademark, trade name, and other expenditures [See § 312(n)(3).]

Amounts amortized under sections 173 (relating to circulation expenditures), 177 (relating to trademark and trade name expenditures), and 248 (relating to organizational expenditures) are to be capitalized and treated as part of the basis of the asset to which they relate. Expenditures made in connection with property having a reasonably determinable useful life are to be recovered for earnings and profits purposes over such useful life.

* * *

Changes in LIFO reserves [See § 312(n)(4).]

A corporation's earnings and profits are to be increased by the amount of any increase in the corporation's LIFO reserve for a taxable year. In addition, any decrease in the amount of a corporation's LIFO reserve will generally decrease and profits. However, decreases in reserve amounts below the LIFO reserve as of the beginning of the taxable year beginning after the date of enactment will not, except as provided by regulations, reduce earnings and profits.

* * *

Deferred gain from installment sales [See § 312(n)(5).]

A corporation's earnings and profits for a year in which the corporation sells property on the installment basis are to be increased by the amount of any deferred gain on the installment sale. This is accomplished by treating all principal payments as having been received in the year of the sale.

* * *

E. SUMMARY PROBLEMS ON THE COMPUTATION OF E & P

1. Individual A forms a new wholly owned corporation, X, and transfers to X cash of $50K, IBM stock with a value of $50K and a basis

of $25K, and operating assets with a value of $100K and a basis of $50K. X computes depreciation on the straight line basis.

(a) During its first year of operation, X breaks even, except for a $25K capital gain on the sale of the IBM stock. X pays a $7K tax on the capital gain. What is X's E & P for the year? Suppose, instead, that X has a net operating loss of $25K, which is available to be carried forward?

(b) During its second year, S has $25K of taxable income before taking account of its net operating loss carryover of $25K. What is its E & P for the second year:

(c) In its third year, X collects $10K of tax exempt interest, has $100K of taxable income and pays $35K in taxes. What is its E & P for the third year?

(d) In its fourth year, X breaks even, except for a capital loss of $10K which is available to be carried forward. What is X's E & P for the fourth year?

2. During its first year of operation, corporation Y has a $50K net operating loss. During its second year of operation, Y has taxable income of $50K, but incurs no tax liability because of the $50K net operating loss carryover from its first year (see § 172). On December 31, Y distributes a cash dividend of $10K to its shareholder B. What result to Y and B? Assume that the dividend is paid on January 1 of Y's third year. What result to Y and B if Y breaks even during the third year? What result if it has a $50K net operating loss? What result if it has $50K of after-tax income?

§ 4.7 CONSTRUCTIVE DIVIDENDS

See §§ 316 and 301.

A. INTRODUCTION

Constructive dividends are transactions in which a shareholder, by reason of this status, extracts an economic benefit from his corporation in a form other than a straight dividend distribution. See, e.g., § 1.301–1(j). For instance, a shareholder-employee may receive an unreasonably large salary from his corporation. The portion of the salary held to be nondeductible under § 162 is treated as a constructive dividend. Another example of a constructive dividend is the payment by a corporation of its shareholder's liability. There are a myriad of other situations in which constructive dividends may arise. The following materials illustrate just a few of these situations.

B. IN GENERAL

REVENUE RULING 58-1
1958-1 C.B. 173.

Where a corporation is formed to own and operate an apartment project for profit and its stockholders are allowed by the corporation to rent an apartment in the project at a lower rental than is charged the general public, the excess of the fair rental value of the apartment over the amount of rent paid by each stockholder as a tenant is treated, for Federal income tax purposes, as a distribution by the corporation under the provisions of section 301 of the Internal Revenue Code of 1954. The amount of such excess is includible in the gross income of each stockholder to the extent that it constitutes a dividend. The amount of the excess which constitutes a dividend is that part of such excess which is considered to have been derived from the corporation's earnings and profits to the extent provided by section 316 of the Code.

C. TRANSFERS BETWEEN RELATED CORPORATIONS

1. *The Tax Court's Position*

RAPID ELECTRIC CO., INC. v. COMMISSIONER
Tax Court of the United States, 1973.
61 T.C. 232.

OPINION

The first question for our decision is whether the extension of credit on its books by Rapid Puerto Rico to its sister corporation, Rapid New York, in the course of their business dealings in 1964, 1965, and 1966, constitutes a constructive dividend in each of such years to their common sole shareholder [Viola].

During the years in question, Rapid New York was in the business of manufacturing and selling rectifiers, which are electrical apparatus used to convert alternating electrical current into direct electrical current. Its brother corporation, Rapid Puerto Rico, was responsible for supplying all its requirements for metal containers which were used to house the rectifiers. In accordance with a procedure agreed to by both sides, Rapid Puerto Rico set up an accounts receivable on its books for all sales of metal containers it made to Rapid New York during each of the years 1964 through 1966, against which it would credit any cash payments made by Rapid New York and any amounts expended by Rapid New York to purchase raw materials on its behalf. A corresponding accounts payable was set up on the books of Rapid New York. In each of the years in question, there was a net balance in the accounts receivable. Rapid Puerto Rico decided not to force collection on any of such balances owing since Rapid New York was under serious financial pressures throughout this period and was already making whatever cash payments it could spare without jeopardizing its business. Instead, it extended a line of credit on all such amounts.

Respondent contends that the net increases in the accounts receivable of Rapid Puerto Rico in each of the years in question constitute a constructive dividend to Viola. Although respondent does not question the bona fide nature of the obligation when initially reflected on Rapid Puerto Rico's books, he argues that the net increases in the accounts receivable became the equivalent of equity advances over the passage of time as a result of Rapid Puerto Rico's failure to collect thereon. Respondent contends that Viola, as sole shareholder of both corporations, had unfettered control over both the timing and the amount of these so-called equity advances. As respondent views this arrangement, Viola's control over the net increases in the accounts receivable is substantially equivalent to having received a dividend from Rapid Puerto Rico to the extent of such increases and a capital reinvestment by him of such amounts in Rapid New York.

Respondent has not raised the issue of thin capitalization. Moreover, he also concedes that there is no basis for the application of section 482 since the sales prices of the containers sold by Rapid Puerto Rico to Rapid New York were reasonable in amount.

It is well established that distribution by a corporation can be treated as a dividend to its shareholder if it is made for his personal benefit or in discharge of his personal obligations. This is so in spite of the fact that the funds are not distributed directly to him. * * *

The transfer of funds between related corporations will also constitute a dividend to the sole shareholder if it was made primarily for his benefit and if he received a direct or tangible benefit therefrom. * * * The mere fact, however, that an individual as sole shareholder might derive some indirect or incidental benefit from the transfer will not be sufficient to give rise to a constructive dividend. *W.B. Rushing, supra.*

Although no cash was ever transferred between Rapid Puerto Rico and Rapid New York, the extension of credit may be treated as the equivalent thereof since its effect, which was to give Rapid New York increased working capital, is similar in substance to a cash advance.

Looking to the facts in our case, we find that the advances of credit in each of the years in question were neither made primarily for the benefit of Viola nor resulted in his receiving any direct benefit therefrom.

Rapid New York was the dominant and principal customer of Rapid Puerto Rico as reflected by the fact that its purchases of metal containers accounted for 64 percent, 92 percent, and 90 percent, respectively, of Rapid Puerto Rico's total sales during the years 1964 through 1966. Rapid Puerto Rico was thus almost wholly dependent on Rapid New York for the sales of its metal containers. Either Rapid Puerto Rico or Rapid New York had to carry the surplus inventory of containers which were manufactured in order that Rapid Puerto Rico might meet its employment commitment to the Puerto Rican Government. For all practical purposes, because of the common ownership of both corporations, it was immaterial which carried the surplus.

Throughout this time, Rapid New York was experiencing financial difficulties as a result of increased competition in its sale of low-voltage rectifiers and its attempted expansion of its product line to include high-voltage rectifiers. Rapid New York made payments on the balances owing to Rapid Puerto Rico both in cash and in the form of raw materials purchased for the account of Rapid Puerto Rico to the fullest extent possible. Rapid New York was also faced with the necessity of carrying increased accounts receivable and inventories if the business of both corporations was to survive. The circumstances which necessitated the extension of credit by Rapid Puerto Rico to Rapid New York clearly negates any inference that such action was taken for the benefit of Viola. * * * Any benefit which may have accrued to Viola as a result of the extension of credit was merely derivative in nature and insufficient to justify the inference of a taxable dividend. *W.B. Rushing, supra.*

Whether we classify the extension of credit as debt or as some other kind of investment, the working capital which was provided to Rapid New York by Rapid Puerto Rico remained in the corporate solution throughout the years in question. There is no indication that any of it was siphoned off to or for the benefit of Viola. * * * Moreover, we find no basis for disregarding Rapid New York as a viable taxable entity separate and apart from its sole shareholder, Viola. What we have here is merely the reverse of the more commonplace situation where the manufacturer "carries" its supplier through financial difficulties with no direct benefit accruing to the supplier's shareholders. * * * In accordance with the above, we find no basis for concluding that a taxable dividend is chargeable to Viola on account of the intercorporate advances.

Questions

What result if there were no dealings between Rapid Puerto Rico and Rapid New York other than interest free loans made by Rapid Puerto Rico to Rapid New York?

2. *The Service's Position*

REVENUE RULING 78–83
1978–1 C.B. 79.

Advice has been requested whether income of X corporation diverted to Y corporation will be treated as a distribution taxable as a dividend to P corporation to the extent of the earnings and profits of X and a capital contribution by P to Y, under the circumstances described below.

The taxpayer, P, a domestic corporation, owned all of the stock of X, a foreign corporation incorporated in country M. X produces and exports fiber for sale on the world market, but due to monetary restrictions, X has had difficulty in securing dollars needed to pay refunds to foreign customers and to pay travel expenses of its employees outside country M. P, therefore, formed Y, a wholly owned foreign corporation incorporated in country T to act on behalf of X to receive part of the sales price charged by X. Thereafter, some of these dollars accumulated by Y were used to pay the above-mentioned refunds and expenses, as well as certain promotion expenses in connection with the fiber sales. P provided incidental services for X in connection with these disbursements, but performed no services in connection with the fiber sales. The funds diverted from X to Y were in excess of the amounts necessary to provide Y with reasonable compensation for its services to X and to reimburse Y for the expenses it incurred on behalf of X.

* * *

Where an allocation is made under section 482 as a result of an excessive charge for services rendered between brother-sister corporations, the amount of the allocation will be treated as a distribution to the controlling shareholder with respect to the stock of the entity whose income is increased and as a capital contribution by the controlling shareholder to the other entity involved in the transaction. See Rev.Rul. 69–630, 1969–2 C.B. 112, relating to a bargain sale between brother-sister controlled corporations.

A constructive dividend is paid when a corporation diverts property, directly or indirectly, to the use of a shareholder without expectation of repayment, even though no formal dividend has been declared.

Generally, in those cases involving corporations controlled by the same persons, the courts have found a constructive dividend to have been distributed to the common shareholders where one of the corporations was used as a device for siphoning off the earnings and profits.

However, a constructive dividend is a diversion of the property, not of the income. Income is a characterization which tax law attributes to certain receipts of property, whereas a constructive distribution is that of property itself. Thus, where property is transferred from one affiliate to a sister corporation without adequate consideration therefor, there is a constructive distribution to the common parent whether or not the motive for the transfer was an attempt improperly to allocate income or deductions between the corporations.

However, any amount diverted to Y for disbursements on behalf of X, or as reasonable compensation for services rendered to X, would not be considered as constructive dividend income to P.

Accordingly, the income of X diverted to Y in excess of the disbursements on behalf of X and reasonable compensation for services of Y will be treated as a distribution taxable as a dividend to P to the extent of the earnings and profits of X, and a capital contribution by P to Y.

Questions

Is the Service correct in saying that a constructive dividend is a "diversion of property, not of income"? Is this position consistent with the Service's position in *Rapid Electric, supra?* What property had been diverted in *Rapid Electric?*

D. SHAREHOLDER GUARANTEES OF CORPORATE LOANS

PLANTATION PATTERNS INC. v. COMMISSIONER

United States Court of Appeals, Fifth Circuit, 1972
462 F.2d 712.

[A shareholder, Jemison, guaranteed the debt of a corporation, New Plantation, New Plantation later repaid the debt.]

The issues presented for our consideration are these:

2. Whether $509,878.33 of guaranteed 5½% notes issued by New Plantation to the sellers of Old Plantation are to be treated as debt for income tax purposes where the notes were subordinated to general creditors but were senior to $150,000 of other debentures which the Tax Court did treat as debt for income tax purposes? * * *

The Commissioner continues that the guarantee was in reality a contribution of capital and that in substance the payments on the notes were dividends on the Jemison capital investment taxable to them as income.

More specifically the Commissioner places primary emphasis on the Tax Court's findings that the assets of the new corporation vis a vis its debts were insufficient to give New Plantation viable independence as a corporation. The Tax Court found that the corporate assets of New Plantation were "wholly inadequate to sustain a debt of $609,878.33". The Commissioner suggests that *Murphy Logging,* supra, the keystone in appellants' argument, is distinguishable. The Commissioner argues that in *Murphy Logging,* the guarantee of a guarantor-stockholder was held not significant because the corporation had substantial ability to meet its debts without the aid of a guarantor, a factor absent in this case. Further distinction is noted in that in *Murphy Logging* the Ninth Circuit was not dealing with a thinly capitalized corporation, as is the case here. The commissioner discounts the fact that New Plantation was in actuality able to pay its obligations without resort to its guarantors, pointing out that we must view the transaction on the basis of the economic realities as they existed at New Plantation's inception, and not in the light of later developments. As matters stood September 28, 1962, asserts the Commissioner, the deal had not set up a bona fide corporation reasonably to be expected to manage to go it alone, and later developments do not alter the nature of the transaction for tax purposes. * * *

After the dissolution of Old Plantation the new corporation had tangible assets, at fair market value, of approximately $1,064,000 securing debts of approximately $1,078,000. We regard this as thin capitalization, as did the Tax Court.

The guarantee enabled Mr. Jemison to put a minimum amount of cash into New Plantation immediately, and to avoid any further cash investment in the corporation unless and until it should fall on hard times. At the same time he exercised total control over its management. Adding together the personal guarantee of Mr. Jemison to the guarantee of Jemison Investment Company, which was wholly owned by him and Mr. Jemison's control of New Plantation, we think that the result is that Mr. Jemison's guarantee simply amounted to a covert way of putting his money "at the risk of the business". Stated differently the guarantee enabled Mr. Jemison to create borrowing power for the corporation which normally would have existed only through the presence of more adequate capitalization of New Plantation.

[The court went on to hold that the guaranteed debt was the debt of the shareholder Jemison and not the corporation. Consequently, upon repayment of the debt by the corporation, Jemison received a dividend to the extent of the corporation's E & P.]

E. BELOW MARKET LOANS FROM CORPORATION TO SHAREHOLDER

1. *Introduction*

PREAMBLE TO PROPOSED REGULATIONS UNDER § 7872

L.R. 165–84 (August 30, 1985).

IN GENERAL

Prior to the enactment of section 7872, some taxpayers used interest-free loans or loans with an interest rate below the current market rate (in each case, "below-market loans") which purported to circumvent well-established rules of taxation.

* * *

Corporations have made below-market loans to shareholders with the effect of avoiding taxation of income at the corporate level which is the economic equivalent of receiving a deduction for dividends paid to those shareholders.

* * *

Section 7872 addresses these and similar practices, generally, by treating certain below-market loans described in one of the categories specified in section 7872(c) as economically equivalent to loans bearing interest at the applicable Federal rate coupled with a payment by the lender to the borrower sufficient to fund the payment of interest by the borrower. Thus, the lender is treated as making (i) a loan to the borrower in exchange for a note requiring the payment of interest at the applicable Federal rate, and (ii) a transfer of funds to the borrower in an amount generally equal to the amount of interest imputed under section 7872.

* * *

Character and Timing of Transfers

The character of the imputed transfer by the lender to the borrower is determined in accordance with the substance of the transaction.

* * *

The timing and amount of the imputed interest payments by the borrower to the lender depend on the character of the amount transferred by the lender to the borrower and on whether the loan is a term loan or a demand loan.

* * *

The imputed interest payment in the case of term loans other than gift loans is computed on the date the loan is made and is subject to the original issue discount rules of section 1272.

Definition of Loan

Because the purpose of section 7872 is to eliminate the use of below-market loans as a vehicle for tax avoidance, the term "loan" is interpreted broadly in the regulations. Accordingly, any extension of credit or any transaction under which the owner of money permits another person to use the money for * * * a period of time after which the money is to be transferred back to the owner or applied according to an agreement with the owner, such as a refundable deposit, is a loan for purposes of section 7872. However, only those below-market loans that are gift loans, compensation-related loans, corporation-shareholder loans, tax avoidance loans or loans to be specified as significant-effect loans (see below), are subject to the provisions of section 7872.

* * *

2. The Proposed Regulations

§ 1.7872–4(d)

(d) *Corporation-shareholder loans*—(1) *In general.* A below-market loan is a corporation-shareholder loan if the loan is made directly or indirectly between a corporation and any shareholder of the corporation. The amount of money treated as transferred by the lender to the borrower is a distribution of money (characterized according to section 301 or, in the case of an S corporation, section 1368) if the corporation is the lender, or a contribution to capital if the shareholder is the lender.

* * *

§ 1.7872–14(b), Example (1)

Example (1). (i) On July 1, 1984, corporation A makes a $200,000 interest-free three-year term loan to shareholder B. The applicable Federal rate is 10-percent, compounded semiannually.

(ii) The present value of this payment is $149,243.08, determined as follows:

$$\$149{,}243.08 = \frac{\$200{,}000}{[1+(.1\tfrac{1}{2})]^6}$$

(iii) The excess of the amount loaned over the present value of all payments on the loan ($200,000 − $149,243.08), or $50,756.92, is treated as a distribution of property (characterized according to section 301) paid to B on July 1, 1984. The same amount, $50,756.92, is treated as original issue discount under sections 1272 and 163(e).

F. DENIAL OF DEDUCTION FOR EXECUTIVE PAY OVER $1 MILLION

See § 162(m)

SENATE REPORT TO THE REVENUE RECONCILIATION ACT OF 1993
69–74 (1993).

Present Law

The gross income of an employee includes any compensation received for services rendered. An employer is allowed a corresponding deduction for reasonable salaries and other compensation. Whether compensation is reasonable is determined on a case-by-case basis. However, the reasonableness standard has been used primarily to limit payments by closely-held companies where nondeductible dividends may be disguised as deductible compensation.

Reasons for Change

Recently, the amount of compensation received by corporate executives has been the subject of scrutiny and criticism. The committee believes it is appropriate to place an upper limit on the deductibility of such compensation to the extent it is not explicitly based on objective performance standards.

Explanation of Provision

In general [See § 162(m)(1).]

Under the bill, for purposes of the regular income tax and the alternative minimum tax, the otherwise allowable deduction for compensation paid or accrued with respect to a covered employee of a publicly held corporation is be limited to no more than $1 million per year.[1]

Definition of publicly held corporation

For this purpose, a corporation is treated as publicly held if the corporation has a class of common equity securities that is required to be registered under section 12 of the Securities Exchange Act of 1934. In general, the Securities Exchange Act requires a corporation to register its common equity securities under section 12 if (1) the securities are listed on a national securities exchange or (2) the corporation has $5 million or more of assets and 500 or more holders of such securities.

Covered employees [See § 162(m)(3).]

Covered employees are defined by reference to the Securities and Exchange Commission (SEC) rules governing disclosure of executive compensation. Thus, with respect to a taxable year, a person is a covered employee if (1) the employee is the chief executive officer of the corporation (or an individual acting in such capacity) as of the close of the taxable year or (2) the employee's total compensation is required to be reported for the taxable year under the Securities Exchange Act of 1934 because the employee is one of the four highest compensated officers for the taxable year (other than the chief executive officer). If disclosure is required with respect to fewer than four executives (other than the chief executive officer) under the SEC rules, then only those for whom disclosure is required are covered employees.

Compensation subject to the deduction limitation
In general [See § 162(m)(4)(A).]

Unless specifically excluded, the deduction limitation applies to all remuneration for services, including cash and the cash value of all remuneration (including benefits) paid in a medium other than cash. If an individual is a covered employee for a taxable year, the deduction limitation applies to all compensation not explicitly excluded from the deduction limitation, regardless of whether the compensation is for services as a covered employee and regardless of when the compensation was earned. The $1 million cap is reduced by excess parachute payments (as defined in sec. 280G) that are not deductible by the corporation.

The deduction limitation applies when the deduction would otherwise be taken. Thus, for example, in the case of a nonqualified stock option, the deduction is normally taken in the year the option is exercised, even though the option was granted with respect to services performed in a prior year.[2]

---

1. The provision does not modify the present-law requirement that, in order to be deductible, compensation must be reasonable. Thus, as under present law, in certain circumstances compensation less than $1 million may not be deductible.

2. Of course, if the executive is no longer a covered employee at the time the options are exercised, then the deduction limitation would not apply.

Certain types of compensation are not subject to the deduction limit and are not taken into account in determining whether other compensation exceeds $1 million. The following types of compensation are not taken into account: (1) remuneration payable on a commission basis; (2) remuneration payable solely on account of the attainment of one or more performance goals if certain outside director and shareholder approval requirements are met; (3) payments to a tax-qualified retirement plan (including salary reduction contributions); (4) amounts that are excludable from the executive's gross income (such as employer-provided health benefits and miscellaneous fringe benefits (sec. 132)); and (5) any remuneration payable under a written binding contract which was in effect on February 17, 1993, and all times thereafter before such remuneration was paid and which was not modified thereafter in any material respect before such remuneration was paid.

Commissions [See § 162(m)(4)(B).]

In order to qualify for the exception for compensation paid in the form of commissions, the commission must be payable solely on account of income generated directly by the individual performance of the executive receiving such compensation. Thus, for example, compensation that equals a percentage of sales made by the executive qualifies for the exception. Remuneration does not fail to be attributable directly to the executive merely because the executive utilizes support services, such as secretarial or research services, in generating the income. However, if compensation is paid on account of broader performance standards, such as income produced by a business unit of the corporation, the compensation would not qualify for the exception because it is not paid with regard to income that is directly attributable to the individual executive.

Other performance-based compensation [See § 162(m)(4)(C).]

Compensation qualifies for the exception for performance-based compensation only if (1) it is paid solely on account of the attainment of one or more performance goals, (2) the performance goals are established by a compensation committee consisting solely of two or more outside directors, (3) the material terms under which the compensation is to be paid, including the performance goals, are disclosed to and approved by the shareholders in a separate vote prior to payment, and (4) prior to payment, the compensation committee certifies that the performance goals and any other material terms were in fact satisfied.

* * *

In the case of compensation paid pursuant to a plan (including a stock option plan), the shareholder approval requirement generally is satisfied if the shareholders approve the specific terms of the plan and the class of executives to which it applies and the amount of compensation payable under the plan is not subject to discretion. Further shareholder approval of payments under the plan is not required after the plan has been approved. Of course, if there are material changes to the plan, shareholder approval would have to be obtained again in order for the exception to apply to payments under the modified plan.

Under present law, in the case of a privately held company that becomes publicly held, the prospectus is subject to the rules similar to those applicable to publicly held companies. Thus, if there has been disclosure that would satisfy the rules described above, persons who buy stock in the publicly held company will be aware of existing compensation arrangements. No further shareholder approval is required of compensation arrangements existing prior to the time the company became public unless there is a material modification of such arrangements.

* * *

§ 4.8 TREATMENT OF DIVIDEND BEFORE SALE

LITTON INDUSTRIES, INC. v. COMMISSIONER

Tax Court of the United States, 1987.
89 T.C. 1086.

CLAPP, JUDGE:

After concessions, the issue for decision is whether Litton Industries received a $30,000,000 dividend from Stouffer Corporation, its wholly owned subsidiary, or whether that sum represented proceeds from the sale of Stouffer stock to Nestle Corporation.

OPINION

The issue for decision is whether the $30,000,000 dividend declared by Stouffer on August 23, 1972, and paid to its parent, Litton by means of a negotiable promissory note was truly a dividend for tax purposes or whether it should be considered part of the proceeds received by Litton from the sale of all of Stouffer's stock on March 1, 1973. If, as petitioner contends, the $30,000,000 constitutes a dividend, petitioner may deduct 85 percent of that amount as a dividend received credit pursuant to section 243(a), as that section read during the year at issue. However, if the $30,000,000 represents part of the selling price of the Stouffer stock, as contended by respondent, the entire amount will be added to the proceeds of the sale and taxed to Litton as additional capital gain. Respondent's approach, of course produces the larger amount of tax dollars.

The instant case is substantially governed by Waterman Steamship Corp. v. Commissioner, 50 T.C. 650 (1968), revd. 430 F.2d 1185 (5th Cir.1970), cert. denied 401 U.S. 939 (1971). Respondent urges us to follow the opinion of the Fifth Circuit, which in substance adopted the position of Judge Tannenwald's dissent (concurred in by three other judges) from our Court-reviewed opinion. If we hold for respondent, we must overrule our majority opinion in Waterman Steamship. Petitioner contends that the reasoning of the Fifth Circuit in Waterman Steamship should not apply since the facts here are more favorable to petitioner. Additionally, petitioner points out that several business purposes were served by the distribution here which provide additional support for recognition of the distribution as a dividend. For the reasons set forth below, we conclude that the $30,000,000 distribution constituted a dividend which should be recognized as such for tax purposes. We believe that the facts in the instant case lead even more strongly than did the facts in Waterman Steamship to the conclusion that the $30,000,000 was a dividend. Accordingly, we hold that the Stouffer distribution to Litton was a dividend within the meaning of section 243(a).

In many respects, the facts of this case and those of Waterman Steamship are parallel. The principal difference, and the one which we find to be most significant, is the timing of the dividend action. In Waterman Steamship, the taxpayer corporation received an offer to purchase the stock of two of its wholly-owned subsidiary corporations, Pan–Atlantic and Gulf Florida, for $3,500,000 cash. The board of directors of Waterman Steamship rejected that offer but countered with an offer to sell the two subsidiaries for $700,000 after the subsidiaries declared and arranged for payments of dividends to Waterman Steamship amounting in the aggregate to $2,800,000. Negotiations between the parties ensued, and the agreements which resulted therefrom included, in specific detail, provisions for the declaration of a dividend by Pan–Atlantic to Waterman Steamship prior to the signing of the sales agreement and the closing of that transaction. Furthermore, the agreements called for the purchaser to loan or otherwise advance funds to Pan–Atlantic promptly in order to pay off the promissory note by which the dividend had been paid. Once the agreement was reached, the entire transaction was carried out by a series of meetings commencing at 12 noon on January 21, 1955, and ending at 1:30 p.m. the same day. At the first meeting the board of directors of Pan–Atlantic met and declared a dividend in the form of a promissory note in the amount of $2,799,820. The dividend was paid by execution and delivery of the promissory note. At 12:30 p.m., the board of directors of the purchaser's nominee corporation ('Securities') met and authorized the purchase and financing of Pan–Atlantic and Gulf Florida. At 1 p.m., the directors of Waterman authorized the sale of all outstanding stock of Pan–Atlantic and Gulf Florida to Securities. Immediately following that meeting, the sales agreement was executed by the parties. The agreement provided that the purchaser guaranteed prompt payment of the liabilities of Pan–Atlantic and Gulf Florida including payment of any notes given by either corporation as a dividend.

Finally at 1:30 p.m., the new board of directors of Pan–Atlantic authorized the borrowing of sufficient funds from the purchaser personally and from his nominee corporation to pay off the promissory note to Waterman Steamship, which was done forthwith. As the Fifth Circuit pointed out, "By the end of the day and within a ninety minute period, the financial cycle had been completed. Waterman had $3,500,000, hopefully tax-free, all of which came from Securities and McLean, the buyers of the stock." This Court concluded that the distribution from Pan-Atlantic to Waterman was a dividend. The Fifth Circuit reversed, concluding that the dividend and sale were one transaction.

The timing in the instant case was markedly different. The dividend was declared by Stouffer on August 23, 1972, at which time the promissory note in payment of the dividend was issued to Litton. There had been some general preliminary discussions about the sale of Stouffer, and it was expected that Stouffer would be a very marketable company which would sell quickly. However, at the time the dividend was declared, no formal action had been taken to initiate the sale of Stouffer. It was not until 2 weeks later that Litton publicly announced that Stouffer was for sale. There ensued over the next 6 months many discussions with various corporations, investment banking houses, business brokers, and underwriters regarding Litton's disposition of Stouffer through sale of all or part of the business to a particular buyer, or through full or partial public offerings of the Stouffer stock. All of this culminated on March 1, 1973, over 6 months after the dividend was declared, with the purchase by Nestle of all of Stouffer's stock. Nestle also purchased the outstanding promissory note for $30,000,000 in cash.

In the instant case, the declaration of the dividend and the sale of the stock were substantially separated in time in contrast to Waterman Steamship where the different transactions occurred essentially simultaneously. In Waterman Steamship, it seems quite clear that no dividend would have been declared if all of the remaining steps in the transaction had not been lined up in order on the closing table and did not in fact take place. Here, however, Stouffer declared the dividend, issued the promissory note and definitely committed itself to the dividend before even making a public announcement that Stouffer was for sale. * * *

Since the facts here are distinguishable in important respects and are so much stronger in petitioner's favor, we do not consider it necessary to consider further the opinion of the Fifth Circuit in Waterman Steamship.

The term "dividend" is defined in section 316(a) as a distribution by a corporation to its shareholders out of earnings and profits. The parties have stipulated that Stouffer had earnings and profits exceeding $30,000,000 at the time the dividend was declared. This Court has recognized that a dividend may be paid by a note. Based on these criteria, the $30,000,000 distribution by Stouffer would clearly constitute a dividend if the sale of Stouffer had not occurred. We are not persuaded that the subsequent sale of Stouffer to Nestle changes that result merely because it was more advantageous to Litton from a tax perspective.

* * *

Under these facts, where the dividend was declared 6 months prior to the sale of Stouffer, where the sale was not prearranged, and since Stouffer had earnings and profits exceeding $30,000,000 at the time the dividend was declared, we cannot conclude that the distribution was merely a device designed to give the appearance of a dividend to a part of the sales proceeds. In this case the form and substance of the transaction coincide; it was not a transaction entered into solely for tax reasons, and it should be recognized as structured by petitioner.

On this record, we hold that for Federal tax purposes Stouffer declared a dividend to petitioner on August 23, 1972, and, subsequently, petitioner sold all of its stock in Stouffer to Nestle for $75,000,000.

Decision will be entered under Rule 155.

Questions and Problems

1. Compare and contrast *Litton,* and *Waterman Steamship.*

2. Parent corporation (PC) owns all the stock of target corporation (TC), with a basis of $100K. TC has operating assets with a value of $600K and cash of $500K. TC has $500K of E & P. The value of TC's stock is $1.1 million. Acquiring corporation (AC) has offered to purchase the stock of TC for $1.1 million. PC and TC do not file consolidated returns.

(a) What would be the tax impact on PC if it sold the TC stock to AC for $1.1 million, assuming a 34% tax rate?

(b) Suppose instead that PC countered with an offer to sell a stripped-down TC, with operating assets only, for $600K. AC accepted the offer, and PC caused TC to distribute to it the $500K of cash as a dividend prior to the sale of the TC stock to AC. What is the tax impact on PC upon receipt of the dividend and the sale of the stock.

(c) How can PC ensure that the transaction in (b) will be taxed in accordance with its form?

(d) What is the impact of § 1059 on the above transaction?

§ 4.9 DIVIDEND AFTER GIFT OF STOCK
CARUTH CORPORATION v. UNITED STATES

United States Court of Appeals, Fifth Circuit, 1989.
865 F.2d 644.

PATRICK E. HIGGINBOTHAM, CIRCUIT JUDGE:

A taxpayer owns an appreciated asset. The asset's value is attributable largely to an imminent and inevitable payment of earnings. A few days before the payment is due, the taxpayer donates to charity the entire asset, with the right to any income upon it. We must decide if the inevitable payment is taxable as income to the donor. The IRS says that it is; the taxpayer says that it is not. The district court agreed with the taxpayer, reasoning that the taxpayer gave away an appreciated asset without ever himself realizing the appreciation upon it. We affirm on the same grounds.

I

This case is complicated, but its basic contours are easily described. The case involves the interaction between a peculiar rule and a peculiar asset. The peculiar rule is this: as the tax code stood in 1978, a taxpayer could donate an appreciated asset to charity and obtain a deduction for the full, appreciated value of the asset while never taking the appreciation into his income stream. * * * Thus a donor who owns appreciated stock would do much better to give the stock to charity than he would to sell the stock and donate the proceeds. * * *

[T]he taxpayer in this case, soon after a dividend had been declared but a few days before the dividend record date, donated the preferred stock to charity. The charity held the stock on the record date, and so collected the dividend. The taxpayer claimed a charitable deduction for the enhanced value of the stock, "pregnant" with dividend. The IRS concedes the legitimacy of this deduction. But the taxpayer contends that the "pregnant" stock is an appreciated asset, and that because he gave away the appreciated value without first realizing it, he need not include the appreciation in his income stream. The IRS disagrees, contending that to the extent the asset's value is attributable to the imminent income payment, the increase in value is income chargeable to the taxpayer. The district court agreed with the taxpayer.

We, too, agree with the taxpayer. The details of our reasoning are presented below, but, again, it is possible to summarize the gist of our answer. The taxpayer has given away an appreciated asset, because he has parted with the asset as well as any income derivable from it. He has surrendered not just the golden egg but also the goose. It does not matter that the taxpayer may cause the corporation to redeem the surrendered stock—to, in effect, kill the goose—or that the taxpayer will himself determine when, if ever, the asset becomes "pregnant" with value again. That the goose's original owner may kill the goose or keep it from laying golden eggs certainly reduces the value of the goose to its new owner, but neither of these powers entitle the original owner to more golden eggs. If the taxpayer's corporation redeems the preferred shares, the taxpayer does not himself get the shares. If, after such a redemption, the taxpayer's corporation issues another dividend, his proportionate share will be less than it would have been were the preferred shares still outstanding and in his possession. So there is nothing fictitious about the taxpayer's claim to have parted with an income-producing asset, rather than merely an asset plus income produced.

* * *

A. *Assignment of Income*

The assignment of income doctrine holds that one who earns income cannot escape tax upon the income by assigning it to another. * * *

* * *

* * * When stock is sold after the declaration of a dividend and after the date as of which the seller becomes entitled to the dividend, the dividend ordinarily is income to the seller. When stock is sold between the time of declaration and the time of payment of the dividend, and the

sale takes place at such time that the purchaser becomes entitled to the dividend, the dividend ordinarily is income to him. Treas.Reg. s 1.61–9(c). When we apply this distinction between declaration and entitlement to this case, we notice that Caruth never enjoyed any legal right to the dividend from the preferred shares. * * *

* * *

* * * Caruth gave away the goose that laid the golden eggs, and so lost his entitlement to any later eggs the goose might lay. At the risk of mixing metaphors, the preferred stock was the tree that grew the fruit, rather than merely a crate for conveying the fruit.

The assignment of income doctrine does not apply.

B. Sham Transaction Doctrine

The IRS also contends that the distinction between declaration date and record date is without a business purpose, and that we should therefore disregard the distinction as a sham. See, e.g., Gregory v. Helvering. Caruth contends that the distinction between the two dates was designed to encourage his nephews, who owned the remaining 25% of North Park Incorporated's common stock, to sell their shares to him. Caruth and his nephews had not been getting along well. * * *

* * * With these factual findings in place, we believe it obvious that the distinction between declaration and record date did, as Caruth contends, serve a legitimate business purpose.

* * *

* * * The shares of preferred stock donated by Caruth were appreciated income-producing assets, rather than assets accompanied by income earned through other means. The dividend did not vest until the record date, which was after the donation. Moreover, Caruth donated the entire asset, rather than merely a partial interest in it. The assignment of income doctrine is therefore inapplicable. The dividend was not taxable to Caruth.

The judgment of the district court is therefore in all respects AFFIRMED.

§ 4.10 POLICY PERSPECTIVE: SHOULD THE CORPORATE AND SHAREHOLDER TAXES BE INTEGRATED?

A. THE TREASURY'S REASONS FOR MOVING TOWARDS INTEGRATION

U.S. TREASURY DEPARTMENT REPORT,
INTEGRATION OF INDIVIDUAL AND
CORPORATE TAX SYSTEMS

Chapter 1 (January 9, 1992)

* * *

Issues

Current U.S. tax law treats corporations and their investors as separate taxable entities. Under this classical system of corporate income taxation, two levels of income tax are generally imposed on earnings from investments in corporate equity. First, corporate earnings are taxed at the corporate level. Second, if the corporation distributes earnings to shareholders, the earnings are taxed again at the shareholder level. In contrast, investors in business activities conducted in noncorporate form, such as sole proprietorships or partnerships, are generally taxed only once on the earnings, and this tax is imposed at the individual level. Corporate earnings distributed as interest to suppliers of debt capital also are taxed only once because interest is deductible by the corporation and generally taxed to lenders as ordinary income.

Despite its long history, considerable debate surrounds the role of the corporate income tax in the Federal tax structure. The central issue is whether corporate earnings should be taxed once rather than taxed both when earned and when distributed to shareholders. Integration of the individual and corporate income tax refers to the taxation of corporate income once. * * *

Despite their differences, the methods of integration studied in this Report reflect a common goal: where practical, fundamental economic considerations, rather than tax considerations, should guide business investment, organization, and financial decisions. The Tax Reform Act of 1986 (the 1986 Act) made the tax system significantly more neutral in its impact on business decisions about capital investment by reducing tax rates and tax preferences. The 1986 Act, however, did not address tax-related distortions of business organizational and financing decisions. In fact, the 1986 reforms may have increased the pressure to select noncorporate organizational forms by imposing a higher marginal rate on corporations than on individuals and by repealing the *General Utilities* doctrine, which had protected corporations from corporate level tax on liquidating dispositions of corporate assets. Corporate integration can thus be regarded as a second phase of tax reform in the United

States, extending the goal of neutral taxation to the choice of business organization and financial policy.

The current two-tier system of corporate taxation discourages the use of the corporate form even when incorporation would provide nontax benefits, such as limited liability for the owners, centralized management, free transferability of interests, and continuity of life. The two-tier tax also discourages new equity financing of corporate investment, encourages debt financing of such investment, distorts decisions with respect to the payment of dividends, and encourages corporations to distribute earnings in a manner designed to avoid the double-level tax.

These distortions have economic costs. The classical corporate tax system reduces the level of investment and interferes with the efficient allocation of resources. In addition, the tax bias against corporate equity can encourage corporations to increase debt financing beyond levels supported by nontax considerations, thereby increasing risks of financial distress and bankruptcy.

Historically, the corporation has been an important vehicle for economic growth in the United States, but the classical corporate tax system often perversely penalizes the corporate form of organization. With the increasing integration of international markets for products and capital, one must consider effects of the corporate tax system on the competitiveness of U.S. firms. Most of the major trading partners of the United States have revised their tax systems to provide for some integration of the corporate and individual tax systems.

This Report provides a comprehensive study of integration, including both the legal and economic foundations for implementing integration in the United States. We present three prototypes representing a range of integration systems. * * *

The Report also documents the substantial economic benefits of integration. We estimate that any of the three prototypes would increase the capital stock in the corporate sector by $125 to $500 billion and would decrease the debt to asset ratio in the corporate sector from 1 to 7 percentage points. Further, efficiency gains from integration would be equivalent to annual welfare gain for the U.S. economy as a whole of 0.07 to 0.7 percent of annual consumption (or $2.5 to $25 billion in 1991 dollars). * * *

1.B The Corporate Tax and Economic Distortions

The classical corporate income tax system distorts three economic and financial decisions: (1) whether to invest in noncorporate rather than corporate form, (2) whether to finance investments with debt rather than equity, and (3) whether to retain rather than distribute earnings. Apart from corporate and investor level tax considerations, nontax benefits and costs also influence these decisions. To the extent that the classical tax system distorts the choice of organizational form, financial structure, and dividend policy, economic resources can be misallocated.

* * *

Question

What are the strongest reasons for moving to an integrated system? What are the reasons for staying with the current classical system?

B. SUMMARY OF THE TREASURY AND ALI INTEGRATION PROPOSALS

THOMPSON, IMPACT OF THE TREASURY AND ALI INTEGRATION PROPOSALS ON MERGERS, ACQUISITIONS, AND LBOS

Tax Notes 923, 924–927 (August 17, 1992), with permission.

The issuance [on January 6, 1992] of the Treasury 1992 Integration Study was followed on March 2, 1992, with the release of an [American Law Institute (ALI)] Reporter's Study on Integration (ALI Reporter's 1992 Integration Draft). * * *

B. THE CLASSICAL SYSTEM AND THE INTEGRATION PROTOTYPES

* * *

The Treasury 1992 Integration Study "presents three prototypes representing a range of integration systems":

(1) The dividend exclusion prototype;

(2) The shareholder allocation prototype; and

(3) The comprehensive business income tax prototype (CBIT).

Treasury indicates that it currently prefers the dividend exclusion prototype, but that the "CBIT prototype represents a very long term, comprehensive option for equalizing the tax treatment of debt and equity." Treasury recommends further study of the dividend exclusion and CBIT prototypes.

Although the Treasury 1992 Integration Study discusses under the heading "The Roads Not Taken" a shareholder credit prototype, the ALI Reporter's 1992 Integration Draft recommends that such a prototype be adopted. The three principal Treasury and the one ALI prototype are explored here.

C. BASIC DESCRIPTION OF EACH PROTOTYPE

* * *

2. Treasury's dividend exclusion prototype.

Under Treasury's dividend exclusion prototype, a corporation's taxable income, which is determined under current law, is subject to a 34-percent tax. The after-tax income is added to an excludable distributions account (EDA), and dividends paid out of the EDA are not subject to shareholder level tax. Thus, dividends are subject to a single corporate level tax. A corporation's tax preference income is not added to the EDA, therefore, dividends paid out of preference income are taxable to shareholders. Dividends are considered as first being paid out of the EDA and then, only after the EDA has been reduced to zero, from preference income.

An indirect, second-level shareholder tax on retained earnings can arise upon the sale of stock by a shareholder. This second-level tax can be avoided, however, if the corporation elects a dividend reinvestment plan (DRIP), which treats the shareholders as if they receive a distribution of the retained earnings as an excludable cash dividend and then reinvest the cash in the corporation. The DRIP is limited to the balance in the EDA. The reinvestment results in an increase in the basis of the shareholders' shares, and therefore, upon sale of the stock, the shareholder is not subject to a second level tax on the retained earnings. Subsequent distributions of income deemed distributed and reinvested pursuant to a DRIP election are tax-free, and the shareholder reduces the basis of shares by the amount of a tax-free distribution.

The dividend exclusion prototype eliminates the shareholder level tax on dividends out of nonpreference income, thereby imposing only a 34-percent tax on corporate income. Since this prototype provides an exclusion from gross income, tax-exempt shareholders and foreigners (i.e., the tax-exempt sector), which in 1990 owned in the aggregate 43 percent of corporate equity, do not benefit from this prototype. The principal beneficiaries of the tax cut associated with the dividend exclusion prototype are individual holders of corporate equity.

3. Treasury's shareholder allocation prototype.

Under Treasury's shareholder allocation prototype, corporations are subject to a 34-percent tax rate on taxable income, determined under current law. The corporation's taxable income is allocated to the shareholders and included in their income. The shareholders compute a tax on this income at their personal rate. The shareholders credit the corporate tax against their tax liability. If the corporate tax rate is 34 percent and the maximum individual rate is 31 percent, an adjustment would be made to the "amount of tax passed through to shareholders to allow shareholders a tax credit no greater than the maximum 31-percent individual rate." If, except for the adjustment just described, the corporate tax exceeds the shareholder's tax on the allocated income, the excess can be used to offset the shareholder's tax liability on other income. Excess credits cannot, however, be utilized to generate a refund (i.e., the credit is nonrefundable). Corporate level preferences are generally extended to shareholders under this prototype.

The shareholder's basis for shares is increased by the amount of the allocated after-tax income, that is, the basis increases in an amount equal to the allocated taxable income minus the allocated taxes paid by the corporation. Also, if the corporation has preference income, such as tax-exempt interest, the shareholder's basis is increased by an allocable share of the preference income. The shareholder does not have income upon the distribution by the corporation of the after-tax or preference income, and the basis of the shareholder's shares is reduced by the amount of the distribution. Any distribution in excess of basis would produce gain. Corporate tax credits are passed through to shareholders, however, corporate losses do not pass through.

This system is similar to the current treatment of S corporations, except the tax is paid at the corporate level and the character of the various items of corporate income and deduction generally do not pass through to the shareholders.

Treasury does not recommend adoption of the shareholder allocation prototype because of the "policy results and administrative complexities it produces." For example, various administrative problems would result from any attempted allocation of the income by corporations with complex capital structures. Allocations by S corporations are rather simple because S corporations can have only one class of stock.

4. *Treasury's comprehensive business income tax (CBIT) prototype.*

Under Treasury's CBIT prototype, all businesses, including corporations, partnerships, and sole proprietorships, would be subject to a single level of tax. An exception would apply, however, for small businesses with gross receipts of less than $100,000. In computing taxable income, no deduction is allowed for interest on funded indebtedness, like bonds. CBIT entities would be subject to tax on taxable income at a 31-percent rate. Dividends and interest would be excluded from income of shareholders and debtholders, and under certain circumstances, investors would not be taxed on capital gains on the equity and debt of CBIT entities.

This exclusion applies both to taxable and tax-exempt holders of debt and equity. The effect of the corporate-level tax on the interest is to impose a tax on the interest received by tax-exempt entities. These entities currently bear the burden of the corporate level tax on dividends, but bear no tax on interest income. The beneficiaries of a pension plan, IRA, or Keogh, each of which is tax-exempt, exclude from income distributions by such entities of CBIT interest and dividends.

Losses do not pass through to shareholders. A CBIT entity adds its after-tax income to an EDA. The EDA is reduced by all dividend and interest payments. A CBIT entity could make a DRIP election to treat all undistributed equity income as distributed and then recontributed by the shareholders. The deemed distribution is limited to the amount of the EDA and is excluded from the shareholder's income. The shareholder increases the basis of shares by the amount of the deemed distribution.

To prevent the passthrough of tax preferences, a flat nonrefundable tax of 31 percent could be imposed at the entity level on dividends and interest paid out of preference income. This tax is referred to as a "compensatory tax." Alternatively, the recipients of preference income could be required to include such dividends and interest in income.

Treasury concludes that the "CBIT prototype represents a very long-term, comprehensive option for equalizing the tax treatment of debt and equity."

5. The ALI's shareholder credit prototype.

Under the ALI's shareholder credit prototype, a withholding tax is levied on dividend distributions. This is referred to as the dividend withholding tax (DWT). The DWT is imposed at the highest individual shareholder rate, which is currently 31 percent. Shareholders are required to include in income both the actual dividend and the associated DWT, and receive a refundable tax credit for the DWT.

Corporations are, however, still subject to the corporate tax, which is fully creditable against the DWT. The corporate tax rate is the highest individual tax rate. The corporation maintains a taxes paid account (TPA) that is increased by corporate taxes paid and decreased in the amount of the DWT due on payment of dividends. As a practical matter, if a corporation does not have any preference income, the amount in the TPA will equal the DWT, and no additional DWT would be due upon payment of dividends.

* * *

A withholding tax is also levied on payments of corporate interest. This is referred to as the interest withholding tax (IWT), and this tax is fully creditable and refundable by the recipient of the interest. The IWT applies to interest paid to both taxable and tax-exempt debtholders. A new tax is to be levied on the investment income (including interest, dividends, and capital gains) of tax-exempt investors such as pension funds. The DWT and IWT are fully creditable against the tax on tax-exempts (TTE). The TTE on foreign investors is referred to as the foreign investors tax (FIT).

The ALI Reporter's 1992 Integration Draft does not make a recommendation for the rate of the TTE. Thus, the ALI draft says that the rate of TTE could be set at different levels for different categories of tax-exempt entities. Thus, for example, the TTE on charities might be higher or lower than the TTE on retirement plans. The stated purpose of the TTE is to eliminate the distortion in the treatment of debt and equity held by tax-exempts.

Corporations could make credits available to shareholders by declaring constructive dividends and reinvestments. This procedure, which prevents the double taxation of retained earnings, is similar to the DRIP election that applies under Treasury's proposals. Distributions of previously taxed retained earnings would be tax-free to the shareholders and would reduce the basis of the shareholder's shares.

* * *

Questions

Which of the four integration prototypes would provide the most complete form of integration? Which is administratively least burdensome?

Chapter 5

CORPORATE REDEMPTIONS

§ 5.1 SCOPE

This chapter deals with corporate redemption transactions, which involve the repurchase by a corporation of its stock. Such transactions, which are governed by §§ 302, 303, and 304, can be treated either as a distribution under § 301 or a sale or exchange by the shareholder of her stock to the redeeming corporation.

Sec. 5.2 introduces redemptions under § 302 and the related attributions rules under § 318, which treat a redeemed shareholder as owning stock held by certain related parties. Sec. 5.3 provides a further elaboration on the § 318 attribution rules. Sec. 5.4 examines the treatment under § 302(b)(3) of redemptions that terminate a shareholder's interest; Sec. 5.5 examines substantially disproportionate redemptions under § 302(b)(2); Sec. 5.6 considers redemptions that are not equivalent to a dividend under § 302(b)(1); and Sec. 5.7 looks at redemptions that are partial liquidations under § 302(b)(4). Sec. 5.8 sets out a methodology for examining redemptions under § 302 and Sec. 5.9 contains summary problems on § 302 redemptions.

Sec. 5.10 examines redemptions in the context of boot-strap sales, which are transactions in which a target corporation's assets are used to pay part of the purchase price in the acquisition of a target's stock. Sec. 5.11 examines related issues in the context of buy-sale agreements.

Sec. 5.12 considers the treatment under § 304 of constructive redemptions by related corporations, such as the purchase by one commonly controlled corporation of the stock of another commonly controlled corporation from a controlling shareholder. Sec. 5.13 contains a brief introduction to the treatment of § 303 redemptions to pay death taxes. Finally Sec. 5.14 considers the effect of a redemption on the redeeming corporation.

These issues are explored in greater detail in Chapter 4 of *Federal Taxation of Business Enterprises, supra* Chapter 1, note 1, and in Chapter 9 of Bittker and Eustice, *Corporations, supra* Sec. 1.4.

§ 5.2 INTRODUCTORY NOTE ON § 302 REDEMPTIONS AND § 318 ATTRIBUTION

Section 302 governs the treatment of stock redemptions. Section 317(b) says "stock shall be treated as redeemed by a corporation if the corporation acquires its stock from a shareholder in exchange for property, whether or not the stock so acquired is cancelled, retired, or held as treasury stock." Thus, stock redemptions are transactions in which a corporation purchases its outstanding stock in exchange for cash or property.

Under § 302(a), a redemption of stock is treated as a sale or exchange only if the redemption satisfies one of the four tests in § 302(b). Section 302(d) provides that a redemption that is not treated as a sale or exchange under § 302(a) is "treated as a distribution of property to which § 301 applies." As explained in Chapter 4, § 301(c) provides four levels of treatment of distributions:

First Level: A distribution is first deemed to be out of current earnings and profits. See §§ 301(c)(1) and 316.

Second Level: A distribution in excess of current earnings and profits is deemed to be out of accumulated earnings and profits. See §§ 301(c)(1) and 316.

Third Level: A distribution in excess of both current and accumulated earnings and profits is deemed to be a nontaxable return of capital to the extent of the adjusted basis of the shareholder's stock. See § 301(c)(2).

Fourth Level: A distribution in excess of current and accumulated earnings and profits and the adjusted basis of the shareholder's stock normally produces a capital gain. See § 301(c)(3).

A redemption that does not alter the redeemed shareholder's control of the corporation is functionally equivalent to a dividend. For instance, if a sole shareholder has 50 percent of her stock redeemed, the shareholder remains the sole shareholder after the transaction. Consequently, in economic terms the redemption is the same as a dividend. Such a transaction does not satisfy the requirements of any of the paragraphs in § 302(b) and, therefore, is treated under § 302(d) as a distribution under § 301.

Section 302(b) covers four types of redemptions. First, § 302(b)(3) treats a redemption that terminates the stock interest of a shareholder as a sale or exchange of the stock. See Sec. 5.4.

Second, § 302(b)(2) treats as a sale or exchange a redemption after which a shareholder's ownership of the outstanding voting stock is less than 80 percent of her ownership before the redemption. Also, the shareholder must own less than 50 percent of the stock after the redemption. This is known as the "substantially disproportionate" redemption test. *See* Sec. 5.5.

Third, § 302(b)(1) provides that any redemption that is "not essentially equivalent to a dividend" is given sale or exchange treatment. This is a general test as contrasted with the specific tests of § 302(b)(3) and (b)(2). This test has spawned quite a bit of case law on the question of what kinds of redemptions are not essentially equivalent to a dividend. The Supreme Court spoke on the question in *United States v. Davis,* which is set out below. There the Court held that in order for § 302(b)(1) to apply, a redemption must result in a "meaningful reduction" of the shareholder's proportionate interest in the corporation. *See* Sec. 5.6.

Fourth, under § 302(b)(4), any redemption of stock of a noncorporate shareholder in a partial liquidation, as defined in § 302(e), of the distributing corporation is given sale or exchange treatment.

Redemptions of the stock of closely held corporations present many possibilities for tax avoidance. For instance, shareholder A could transfer 50 percent of the stock of one wholly owned corporation (X) to a second wholly owned corporation (Y) and then cause X to redeem his remaining 50 percent interest. The redemption on its face would satisfy the termination of interest test of § 302(b)(3). A would have received sale or exchange treatment rather than a dividend, although he continued to control, through his exclusive ownership of Y, all of the stock of X.

The attribution rules of § 318, which, by reason of § 302(c), apply for purposes of § 302, prevent these types of avoidance schemes. Section 318 attributes to certain persons the ownership of stock owned by certain related parties. If, under § 318, a person is the constructive owner of stock held by a related person, the constructively owned stock is taken into consideration in determining whether a redemption satisfies any of the tests in § 302(b). *See* § 302(c)(1) and § 1.302–1(a).

In the above hypothetical situation, A is treated under § 318(a)(2)(C) as the constructive owner of the X stock he transferred to Y. Consequently, the redemption of his 50 percent direct stock interest in X constitutes a dividend to him because he owns 100 percent of X both before and after the redemption.

Section 318 attributes stock ownership (1) from one family member to another, *i.e.,* the family attribution rules, (*see* § 318(a)(1)); (2) from partnerships, corporations, estates and trusts, to the partners, shareholders and beneficiaries, *i.e.,* the attribution-out rules, (*see* § 318(a)(2)); and (3) from partners, shareholders and beneficiaries, to partnerships, corporations, estates and trusts, *i.e.,* the attribution-in rules. *See* § 318(a)(3). The operational rules, set out in § 318(a)(5), provide for multiple attribution in certain cases. Section 318(a)(4) provides that the holder of an option to acquire stock is deemed to own the underlying stock. The rules in § 318 must be studied closely. *See* Sec. 5.3.

Section 318 applies only to those provisions of the Code to which it is expressly made applicable. Section 302(c)(1) provides: "Except as provided in paragraph (2) of this subsection, section 318(a) shall apply in determining the ownership of stock for purposes of this section." Section 302(c)(2) provides an exception to the family attribution rules of § 318(a)(1) (but not to the entity attribution rules of §§ 318(a)(2) and (3)) for determining whether a redemption is a termination of interest under § 302(b)(3). Study closely the requirements of § 302(c)(2)(A). What is the purpose of § 302(c)(2)(B)? Section 302(c)(2)(C) provides for the waiver of the attribution rules by entities in certain limited circumstances.

A stock redemption must "run the gauntlet" of § 302(b) in order to be treated as a sale or exchange. Section 302(b) does not, however, apply to the redemption of debt instruments. Under § 1271(a), redemptions of corporate debt receive sale or exchange treatment. Recall, however, that purported debt may be reclassified as equity in which case § 302(b) applies to the redemption.

§ 5.3 FURTHER ELABORATION ON § 318 ATTRIBUTION RULES

Section 318 can be divided broadly into five sets of rules:

(1) The family attribution rules of § 318(a)(1);

(2) The attribution-out rules of § 318(a)(2);

(3) The attribution-in rules of § 318(a)(3);

(4) The option attribution rule of § 318(a)(4); and

(5) The operating rules of § 318(a)(5).

Under the family attribution rules of § 318(a)(1), an individual is considered as owning the stock owned directly or indirectly, by or for the following family members:

(1) her nonseparated spouse;

(2) her children;

(3) her grandchildren; and

(4) her parents.

Under the attribution-out rules of § 318(a)(2), stock owned by partnerships, estates, certain trusts, and corporations is considered as owned by the partners, beneficiaries and shareholders. Partners are considered to own proportionately stock held by the partnership (*see* § 318(a)(2)(A)), and if a shareholder owns, directly or indirectly, at least 50% in value of the stock of a corporation, such shareholder is deemed to own a proportionate share of any stock in another corporation held by that corporation. *See* § 318(a)(2)(C).

Under the attribution-in rules of § 318(a)(3), partnerships, estates, certain trusts, and corporations are deemed to own stock held by the partners, beneficiaries and shareholders. A partnership is deemed to own any stock held by a partner (*see* § 318(a)(3)(A)), and if a shareholder owns at least 50% in value of the stock of a corporation, the corporation is considered as owning the stock of any other corporation held by such shareholder. *See* § 318(a)(3)(C) and § 1.318–1(b).

Under the option attribution rule of § 318(a)(4), if a person owns an option to acquire stock, the person is considered as owning the stock.

There are several operating rules under § 318(a)(5). First, under § 318(a)(5)(A) stock constructively owned by reason of the application of any of the above four attribution rules is considered as actually owned by such person for purposes of again applying such attribution rules, subject to the following exceptions. The first exception to this general multiple attribution principle is that there is no multiple attribution among family members. *See* § 318(a)(5)(B). The second exception is that stock constructively owned by reason of the attribution-in rule of § 318(a)(3) is not considered as owned for purposes of applying the attribution-out rule of § 318(a)(2). Under this anti-sidewise attribution rule, stock is not, for example, attributed from one partner into a partnership and then out to another partner.

Under § 318(a)(5)(D) of the operating rules, the option attribution rule takes precedence over the family attribution rule. Finally, under § 318(a)(5)(E), an S corporation is treated as a partnership and any shareholder of an S corporation is treated as a partner of such partnership. These rules do not apply, however, for purposes of determining whether stock in an S corporation is constructively owned by any person.

§ 5.4 REDEMPTION THAT TERMINATES A SHAREHOLDER'S INTEREST

A. NO § 302(c)(2) WAIVER NEEDED WHERE THERE IS AN ACTUAL TERMINATION

REVENUE RULING 76–524
1976–2 C.B. 94.

Corporation *X* had outstanding one class of stock consisting of 100 shares of common stock. *A*, an individual, owned 30 shares of *X* common stock and held positions as president and chairman of the board of directors of *X*. *A*'s spouse, *B*, and their son, *C*, each owned 30 shares of *X* common stock. No other *X* shareholder (all of whom were individuals) was related to *A*, *B*, or *C* within the meaning of section 318(a)(1) of the Code.

X redeemed for cash all of its common stock held by *A*, *B*, and *C*. After the redemption, *A* remained as president and director of *X*.

In the instant case, if either *B* or *C* had not redeemed their stock in the same transaction, or if other *X* shareholders were related to *A*, within the meaning of section 318(a)(1) of the Code, the constructive ownership rules would be applicable to A's redemption through section 302(c)(1), and the waiver of attribution provided for by section 302(c)(2) would not be available to A if A retained the positions of officer and director. A redeeming shareholder, who must waive family attribution so that that shareholder's redemption will qualify as a complete termination of interest under section 302(b)(3), may not retain any interest in the corporation, other than an interest as a creditor.

However, where there is no stock outstanding after the redemption the ownership of which would be attributed to the redeeming shareholder, the waiver rule of section 302(c)(2) of the Code, and the conditions under which waiver can occur, are not applicable. Section 302(b)(3), by itself, places no restriction on the retention of interests in the corporation after the redemption, as long as the entire stock interest is terminated. Thus, if a shareholder's direct stock interest is completely terminated in a redemption, and that shareholder has no indirect ownership of stock after the redemption through application of the constructive ownership rules of section 318(a)(1), the redemption qualifies under section 302(b)(3) regardless of whether the shareholder retains positions as officer and director.

Accordingly, since A's actual stock ownership was completely terminated in the redemption, and since, after the redemption, A had no constructive ownership of stock, the redemption was a termination of a shareholder's interest within the meaning of section 302(b)(3) of the Code, and therefore, qualified as an exchange under section 302(a).

B. WHAT CONSTITUTES A PROHIBITED INTEREST UNDER § 302(c)(2)(A)(i)

1. Redeemed Shareholder Performs Consulting Services

REVENUE RULING 70–104
1970–1 C.B. 66.

A corporation engaged in the retail jewelry business was owned by a father and his children. The corporation redeemed all the stock owned by the father in exchange for cash, and the redeeming shareholder timely filed the agreement described in section 302(c)(2)(A)(iii) of the Internal Revenue Code of 1954. The corporation and the redeeming shareholder entered into a five-year consulting agreement that provided that the individual would perform services as a consultant and advisor to the corporation in exchange for compensation of 10x dollars per year.

Held, the performance by the father of services pursuant to the consulting agreement is an "interest in the corporation" within the meaning of section 302(c)(2)(A)(i) of the Code. Therefore, the filing of the agreement provided by section 302(c)(2)(A)(iii) of the Code does not terminate the attribution to him under section 318(a)(1) of the Code of stock owned by his children. The redemption is, therefore, not a termination of the shareholder's interest within the meaning of section 302(b)(3) of the Code.

2. Redeemed Shareholder Receives a Debt Instrument

DUNN v. COMMISSIONER
United States Court of Appeals, Second Circuit, 1980.
615 F.2d 578.

DOOLING, DISTRICT JUDGE: The Commissioner appeals from a decision of the Tax Court (Theodore Tannenwald, Jr., Judge) holding that amounts received by appellee taxpayer, Georgia Dunn, in 1970 and 1971 from Bresee Chevrolet Co., Inc. ("Bresee") were received in complete redemption of all her stock in Bresee, and that immediately after the distribution she had no interest in Bresee as an officer, director, employee or otherwise, other than an interest as a creditor. In consequence, the Tax Court held, the amounts the taxpayer received were capital gains and not dividends, as the Commissioner contended.

When the redemption transaction was entered into the taxpayer owned 249 of the 500 shares of Bresee, her son William Dunn owned 149 shares and each of her married daughters owned 51 shares. In May 1970 taxpayer contracted to "sell or redeem from" Bresee her 249 shares of the company's stock for $335,154 payable $100,000 on June 1, 1970, and the balance with 5% interest over a period of ten years. Bresee redeemed the taxpayer's stock on the June 1, 1970, closing date; she was then paid the $100,000, and in 1971 was paid $45,260.34.

* * *

Judge Tannenwald found on the evidence that the taxpayer was not an officer, director or employee of Bresee after the redemption, that up to the date of trial she had not acquired any stock in Bresee and that she had filed with the tax return the required agreement to notify the Secretary of the Treasury of any acquisition of interest in the company. Hence the sole question is whether immediately after the distribution the taxpayer was anything more than a creditor of Bresee.

The Commissioner argues that the Treasury regulation, 26 C.F.R. § 1.302–4(d), defining the term creditor in the context of § 302(b)(3) stock redemptions, is decisive of the case when it is applied to the postponement of payment provision of the Agreement. The regulation reads (as it has read since 1955):

> For the purpose of Section 302(c)(2)(A)(i), a person will be considered to be a creditor only if the rights of such person with respect to the corporation are not greater or broader in scope than necessary for the enforcement of his claim. Such claim must not in any sense be proprietary and must not be subordinate to the claims of general creditors. An obligation in the form of a debt may thus constitute a proprietary interest. For example, if under the terms of the instrument the corporation may discharge the principal amount of its obligation to a person by payments, the amount or certainty of which are dependent upon the earnings of the corporation, such a

person is not a creditor of the corporation. Furthermore, if under the terms of the instrument the rate of purported interest is dependent upon earnings, the holder of such instrument may not, in some cases, be a creditor.

The Commissioner's contentions rest upon the fact that under the Stock Purchase Agreement if the making of any of the installment payments to the taxpayer would result in Bresee's failing to meet the net owned working capital requirement and the 50% of net profit retention clause, then payment of all or part of the installment is postponed until the payment can be made in whole or part without transgressing the GM agreement.

* * *

The regulation, then, does not support the Commissioner's position, for the instrument under review does not exhibit a single one of the characteristics given significance by the regulation. What is more important, the obligation here, to the extent that it differs from the classic debt of fixed amount and inexorable due date, does not differ in the direction of being a proprietary or equity type of interest, but differs simply in being unmistakably debt, but of a seemingly somewhat inferior quality because of the postponement clause.

C. INTRA-FAMILY TRANSFERS PRIOR TO REDEMPTION

See § 302(c)(2)(B).

REVENUE RULING 77-455
1977-2 C.B. 93.

Advice has been requested whether a proposed redemption of common and preferred stock, in connection with sales of the remaining common and preferred stock of the distributing corporation owned by the shareholder whose stock will be redeemed, will qualify as a complete termination of interest under section 302(b)(3) of the Internal Revenue Code of 1954. * * *

Corporation X has outstanding $115x$ shares of voting common stock and $300x$ shares of voting preferred stock. Individual A owns $69x$ shares of the common stock and all of the preferred stock. B, who is A's son, owns $22x$ shares of X common stock. The remaining $24x$ shares of X common stock are owned by 10 employees of X, none of whom is related to either A or B under section 318 of the Code.

* * *

A desires to retire from the business and to terminate all stock and other interests in X. To accomplish this objective A proposes to sell $10x$ shares of common stock and $18x$ shares of preferred stock to B, sell $25x$ shares of common stock to a key employee of X who is not related to A or B, and have the remaining common and preferred stock redeemed by X.

A's reasons for selling some of the preferred stock to B rather than having all of the preferred stock redeemed are to leave B with voting control of X for a smaller investment than would otherwise be necessary while giving the key employees other than B a greater participation in the growth of X than they would have if B owned more than half of the common stock. These goals will be accomplished because the preferred stock is worth only one-tenth as much per share as the common stock but entitles its holder to one vote per share, the same as the common stock.

* * *

In this case, the avoidance of Federal income tax within the meaning of section 302(c)(2)(B) of the Code will not be considered to be one of the principal purposes of A's sale of X stock to B. The purposes of the sale are to enable A to retire from the business and to give B, who is active and knowledgeable in the affairs of the business, control of X. See Rev.Rul. 77–293, 1977–34 I.R.B. 9, which holds that a gift of stock, under circumstances similar to the sale of stock in this case, did not have Federal income tax avoidance as a principal purpose.

Accordingly, if A satisfies all of the requirements of section 302(c)(2)(A) of the Code, A may waive constructive ownership of B's stock, and the redemption of part of A's stock, combined with the sales of A's remaining stock, will qualify as a complete termination of interest under section 302(b)(3).

Note and Question

See also Rev.Rul. 56–556, 1956–2 C.B. 177 (gift and sale of stock to son prior to redemption of parent's stock; held: no tax avoidance purposes); Rev.Rul. 56–584, 1956–2 C.B. 179 (redemption of son's stock received by gift from father; held: no tax avoidance purpose for gift); Rev.Rul. 77–293, 1977–2 C.B. 91 (redemption of father's stock after gift of stock to son; held: no tax avoidance purpose for gift). What would constitute a tax avoidance purpose under § 302(c)(2)(B)?

§ 5.5 REDEMPTIONS WHICH ARE SUBSTANTIALLY DISPROPORTIONATE WITHIN § 302(b)(2)

A. ILLUSTRATION OF OPERATION OF § 302(b)(2)

REVENUE RULING 75–447
1975–2 C.B. 113.

Advice has been requested as to the Federal income tax consequences, in the situations described below, of the redemption by a corporation of part of its stock.

SITUATION 1

Corporation X had outstanding 100 shares of voting common stock of which A and B each owned 50 shares. In order to bring C into the business with an equal stock interest, and pursuant to an integrated plan, A and B caused X to issue, at fair market value, 25 new shares of voting common stock to C. Immediately thereafter, as part of the same plan, A and B caused X to redeem 25 shares of X voting common stock from each of them. Neither A, B, nor C owned any stock in X indirectly under section 318 of the Internal Revenue Code of 1954.

SITUATION 2

Corporation X had outstanding 100 shares of voting common stock of which A and B each owned 50 shares. In order to bring C into the business with an equal stock interest, and pursuant to an integrated plan, A and B each sold 15 shares of X voting common stock to C at fair market value and then caused X to redeem five shares from both A and B. Neither A, B, nor C owned any stock of X indirectly under section 318 of the Code.

In determining whether the "substantially disproportionate" provisions of section 302(b)(2) of the Code have been satisfied in *Situation 1* and in *Situation 2*, it is proper to rely upon the holding in *Zenz* [discussed in Sec. 5.10.A.] that the sequence in which the events (that is, the redemption and sale) occur is irrelevant as long as both events are clearly part of an overall plan. Therefore, in situations where the redemption is accompanied by an issuance of new stock (as in *Situation 1*), or a sale of stock (as in *Situation 2*), and both steps (the sale, or issuance of stock, as the case may be, and the redemption) are clearly part of an integrated plan to reduce a shareholder's interest, effect will be given only to the overall result for purposes of section 302(b)(2) and the sequence in which the events occur will be disregarded.

Since the *Zenz* holding requires that effect be given only to the overall result and proscribes the fragmenting of the whole transaction into its component parts, the computation of the voting stock of the corporation owned by the shareholder *immediately before* the redemption for purposes of section 302(b)(2)(C)(ii) of the Code should be made before any part of the transaction occurs. Likewise, the computation of the voting stock of the corporation owned by the shareholder *immediately after* the redemption for purposes of section 302(b)(2)(C)(i) should be made after the whole transaction is consummated. Making the immediately before and the immediately after computations in this manner properly reflect the extent to which the shareholder involved in each situation actually reduces his stock holdings as a result of the whole transaction.

Therefore, for purposes of the computations required by section 302(b)(2)(C) of the Code, A and B, in *Situation 1*, will each be viewed as having owned 50 percent (50/100 shares) of X before the transaction and 33⅓ percent (25/75 shares) immediately thereafter. In *Situation 2*, A and B will each be viewed as having owned 50 percent (50/100 shares) of X before the transaction and 33⅓ percent (30/90 shares) immediately thereafter. Furthermore, in each situation, the result would be the same if the redemption had preceded the issuance, or sale, of stock.

Accordingly, in both *Situations 1* and *2*, the requirements of section 302(b)(2) of the Code are satisfied. Therefore, the amounts distributed to A and B in both situations are distributions in full payment in exchange for the stock redeemed pursuant to section 302(a).

Note

Section 302(b)(2) does not on its face apply to redemptions of nonvoting stock. However, in Rev.Rul. 77-237, 1977-2 C.B. 88, the Service ruled that if § 302(b)(2) applies to a redemption of common, it also applies to a concurrent redemption of nonvoting preferred.

B. REDEMPTION OF VOTING PREFERRED

REVENUE RULING 81-41

1981-1 C.B. 121.

Can a redemption of voting preferred stock qualify as a substantially disproportionate redemption under section 302(b)(2) of the Internal Revenue Code, even though the redeeming shareholder, as a result of not owning any common stock either directly or constructively, is unable to have a reduction in common stock ownership?

* * *

The Senate Finance Committee Report accompanying the enactment of section 302 states:

> Paragraph (2) of subsection (b) sets forth a general rule that if the redemption is substantially disproportionate, it will be treated as a sale under subsection (a), if the other conditions described in the paragraph are met. *It is intended that the general rule shall apply with respect to a redemption of preferred stock (other than section 306 stock) as well as common stock.*

Moreover, section 1.302-3 of the Income Tax Regulations states that section 302(b)(2) of the Code only applies to a redemption of voting stock or to a redemption of both voting stock and other stock, but does not apply to the redemption solely of nonvoting stock. Therefore, both the legislative history and the regulations accompanying section 302(b)(2) indicate that the provision should apply to the redemption of voting preferred stock.

In the same report, the Senate Finance Committee does make two statements that a substantially disproportionate redemption requires a reduction in the redeemed shareholder's ownership of common stock in the redeeming corporation. However, the context of the first of these statements indicates that this requirement is a safeguard against abuse where the redeeming shareholder holds common stock.

* * *

In the present case, A owns no common stock either directly or constructively. Therefore, the additional "safeguard" provided by the second "80 percent test" of section 302(b)(2)(C) is inapplicable to A.

Holding

A redemption of voting preferred stock can qualify as a substantially disproportionate redemption under section 302(b)(2) even though the redeeming shareholder does not experience a reduction in common stock ownership, if the shareholder owns no common stock either directly or constructively.

* * *

C. REDEMPTION OF BOTH VOTING AND NONVOTING COMMON STOCK TESTED ON OVERALL BASIS

REVENUE RULING 87-88
1987-2 C.B. 81.

Issue

If shares of both voting and nonvoting common stock are redeemed from a shareholder in one transaction, are the two classes aggregated for purposes of applying the substantially disproportionate requirement in section 302(b)(2)(C) of the Internal Revenue Code?

Facts

X corporation had outstanding 10 shares of voting common stock and 30 shares of nonvoting common stock. The fair market values of a share of voting common stock and a share of nonvoting common stock are approximately equal. A owned 6 shares of X voting common stock and all the nonvoting common stock. The remaining 4 shares of the X voting common stock were held by persons unrelated to A within the meaning of section 318(a) of the Code.

X redeemed 3 shares of voting common stock and 27 shares of nonvoting common stock from A in a single transaction. Thereafter, A owned 3 shares of X voting common stock and 3 shares of nonvoting common stock. The ownership of the remaining 4 shares of X voting common stock was unchanged.

Law and Analysis

* * *

[S]ection 302(b)(2)(C) of the Code provides that, if there is more than one class of common stock outstanding, the fair market value of all of the common stock (voting and nonvoting) will govern the determination of whether there has been the requisite reduction in common stock ownership. * * *

* * *

Holding

If more than one class of common stock is outstanding, the provisions of section 302(b)(2)(C) of the Code are applied in an aggregate and not a class-by-class manner. Accordingly, the redemption by X of 3 shares of voting common stock and 27 shares of nonvoting common stock qualifies as substantially disproportionate within the meaning of section 302(b)(2), even though A continues to own 100 percent of the outstanding nonvoting common stock.

D. ILLUSTRATION OF SERIES OF REDEMPTIONS UNDER § 302(b)(2)

REVENUE RULING 85–14
1985–1 C.B. 93.

ISSUE

Should qualification under section 302(b)(2) of the Internal Revenue Code of a redemption of one shareholder be measured immediately after that redemption, or after a second redemption of another shareholder that followed soon after the first redemption, under the following acts?

FACTS

X, a corporation founded by A, is engaged in an ongoing business. As of January 1, 1983, X's sole class of stock, voting common stock, was held by A, B, C, and D, who are unrelated to each other. A owned 1,466 shares, B owned 210 shares, C owned 200 shares, and D owned 155 shares of X stock. A was president and B was vice-president of X.

X has a repurchase agreement with all X shareholders, except A. This agreement provides that if any such shareholder ceases to be actively connected with the business operations of X, such shareholder must promptly tender to X the then-held X shares for an amount equal to the book value of such stock. X has a reciprocal obligation to purchase such shares at book value within 6 months of such shareholder's ceasing to be actively connected with X's business operations.

On January 1, 1983, B informed A of B's intention to resign as of March 22, 1983. Based on this information, A caused X to adopt a plan of redemption and to redeem 902 shares of A's X stock, on March 15, 1983, for which A received $700x$ dollars. Thus, A then held 564 shares of the 1129 shares (49.96 percent) of the X stock still outstanding, temporarily yielding majority control over the affairs of X until B ceased to be a shareholder. On March 22, 1983, B resigned from X and, in accordance with the X stock purchase agreement, X redeemed for cash all of B's shares within the next 6 months, thus leaving 919 shares of X stock outstanding, restoring majority control to A.

LAW AND ANALYSIS

* * *

Section 302(b)(2)(D) of the Code, in dealing with a series of redemptions, provides that section 302(b)(2) is not applicable to any redemption made pursuant to a plan the purpose or effect of which is a series of redemptions resulting in a distribution which (in the aggregate) is not substantially disproportionate with respect to the shareholder.

* * *

Under the facts and circumstances here, section 302(b)(2)(D) of the Code requires that the redemptions of A and B be considered in the aggregate. Accordingly, A's redemption meets neither the 50 percent limitation of section 302(b)(2)(B) nor the 80 percent test of section 302(b)(2)(C). Thus, the redemption of A's shares was not substantially disproportionate within the meaning of section 302(b)(2).

HOLDING

Under the facts of this ruling, qualification under section 302(b)(2) of the Code of A's redemption should not be measured immediately after that redemption, but, instead, should be measured after B's redemption that followed soon after A's redemption.

§ 5.6 REDEMPTIONS NOT EQUIVALENT TO A DIVIDEND UNDER § 302(b)(1)

A. THE "MEANINGFUL REDUCTION" REQUIREMENT: THE SUPREME COURT SPEAKS

UNITED STATES v. DAVIS

United States Supreme Court, 1970.
397 U.S. 301, 90 S.Ct. 1041, 25 L.Ed.2d 323.

MR. JUSTICE MARSHALL delivered the opinion of the Court.

In 1945, taxpayer and E.B. Bradley organized a corporation. In exchange for property transferred to the new company, Bradley received 500 shares of common stock, and taxpayer and his wife similarly each received 250 such shares. Shortly thereafter, taxpayer made an additional contribution to the corporation, purchasing 1,000 shares of preferred stock at a par value of $25 per share.

The purpose of this latter transaction was to increase the company's working capital and thereby to qualify for a loan previously negotiated through the Reconstruction Finance Corporation. It was understood that the corporation would redeem the preferred stock when the RFC loan had been repaid. Although in the interim taxpayer bought Bradley's 500 shares and divided them between his son and daughter, the total capitalization of the company remained the same until 1963. That year, after the loan was fully repaid and in accordance with the original understanding, the company redeemed taxpayer's preferred stock.

In his 1963 personal income tax return taxpayer did not report the $25,000 received by him upon the redemption of his preferred stock as income. Rather, taxpayer considered the redemption as a sale of his preferred stock to the company—a capital gains transaction under § 302 of the Internal Revenue Code of 1954 resulting in no tax since taxpayer's basis in the stock equaled the amount he received for it. The Commissioner of Internal Revenue, however, did not approve this tax treatment. According to the Commissioner, the redemption of taxpayer's stock was essentially equivalent to a dividend and was thus taxable as ordinary income under §§ 301 and 316 of the Code. Taxpayer paid the resulting deficiency and brought this suit for a refund. * * *

The Court of Appeals held that the $25,000 received by taxpayer was "not essentially equivalent to a dividend" within the meaning of that phrase in § 302(b)(1) of the Code because the redemption was the final step in a course of action that had a legitimate business (as opposed to a tax avoidance) purpose. That holding represents only one of a variety of treatments accorded similar transactions under § 302(b)(1) in the circuit courts of appeals. We granted certiorari, in order to resolve this recurring tax question involving stock redemptions by closely held corporations. We reverse.

I

The Internal Revenue Code of 1954 provides generally in §§ 301 and 316 for the tax treatment of distributions by a corporation to its shareholders; under those provisions, a distribution is includable in a taxpayer's gross income as a dividend out of earnings and profits to the extent such earnings exist. There are exceptions to the application of these general provisions, however, and among them are those found in § 302 involving certain distributions for redeemed stock. The basic question in this case is whether the $25,000 distribution by the corporation to taxpayer falls under that section—more specifically, whether its legitimate business motivation qualifies the distribution under § 302(b)(1) of the Code. Preliminarily, however, we must consider the relationship between § 302(b)(1) and the rules regarding the attribution of stock ownership found in § 318(a) of the Code.

Under subsection (a) of § 302, a distribution is treated as "payment in exchange for the stock," thus qualifying for capital gains rather than ordinary income treatment, if the conditions contained in any one of the four paragraphs of subsection (b) are met. In addition to paragraph (1)'s "not essentially equivalent to a dividend" test, capital gains treatment is available where (2) the taxpayer's voting strength is substantially diminished, (3) his interest in the company is completely terminated, or (4) certain railroad stock is redeemed. Paragraph (4) is not involved here, and taxpayer admits that paragraphs (2) and (3) do not apply. Moreover, taxpayer agrees that for the purposes of §§ 302(b)(2) and (3) the attribution rules of § 318(a) apply and he is considered to own the 750 outstanding shares of common stock held by his wife and children in addition to the 250 shares in his own name.

Taxpayer, however, argues that the attribution rules do not apply in considering whether a distribution is essentially equivalent to a dividend under § 302(b)(1). According to taxpayer, he should thus be considered to own only 25 percent of the corporation's common stock, and the distribution would then qualify under § 302(b)(1) since it was not pro rata or proportionate to his stock interest, the fundamental test of dividend equivalency. See Treas.Reg. 1.302–2(b). However, the plain language of the statute compels rejection of the argument. In subsection (c) of § 302, the attribution rules are made specifically applicable "in determining the ownership of stock for purposes of this section." Applying this language, both courts below held that § 318(a) applies to all of § 302, including § 302(b)(1)—a view in accord with the decisions of the other courts of appeals, a longstanding treasury regulation, and the opinion of the leading commentators.

Against this weight of authority, taxpayer argues that the result under paragraph (1) should be different because there is no explicit reference to stock ownership as there is in paragraphs (2) and (3). Neither that fact, however, nor the purpose and history of § 302(b)(1) support taxpayer's argument. The attribution rules—designed to provide a clear answer to what would otherwise be a difficult tax question—formed part of the tax bill that was subsequently enacted as the 1954 Code. As is discussed further, *infra,* the bill as passed by the House of Representatives contained no provision comparable to § 302(b)(1). When that provision was added in the Senate, no purpose was evidenced to restrict the applicability of § 318(a). Rather, the attribution rules continued to be made specifically applicable to the entire section, and we believe that Congress intended that they be taken into account wherever ownership of stock was relevant.

Indeed, it was necessary that the attribution rules apply to § 302(b)(1) unless they were to be effectively eliminated from consideration with regard to §§ 302(b)(2) and (3) also. For if a transaction failed to qualify under one of those sections solely because of the attribution rules, it would according to taxpayer's argument nonetheless qualify under § 302(b)(1). We cannot agree that Congress intended so to nullify its explicit directive. We conclude, therefore, that the attribution rules of § 318(a) do apply; and, for the purposes of deciding whether a distribution is "not essentially equivalent to a dividend" under § 302(b)(1), taxpayer must be deemed the owner of all 1,000 shares of the company's common stock.

II

After application of the stock ownership attribution rules, this case viewed most simply involves a sole stockholder who causes part of his shares to be redeemed by the corporation. We conclude that such a redemption is always "essentially equivalent to a dividend" within the meaning of that phrase in § 302(b)(1) and therefore do not reach the Government's alternative argument that in any event the distribution should not on the facts of this case qualify for capital gains treatment.

The predecessor of § 302(b)(1) came into the tax law as § 201(d) of the Revenue Act of 1921, 42 Stat. 228:

"A stock dividend shall not be subject to tax but if after the distribution of any such dividend the corporation proceeds to cancel or redeem its stock at such time and in such manner as to make the distribution and cancellation or redemption essentially equivalent to the distribution of a taxable dividend, the amount received in redemption or cancellation of the stock shall be treated as a taxable dividend. * * *"

Enacted in response to this Court's decision that pro rata stock dividends do not constitute taxable income, *Eisner v. Macomber,* 252 U.S. 189, 40 S.Ct. 189, 64 L.Ed. 521 (1920), the provision had the obvious purpose of preventing a corporation from avoiding dividend tax treatment by distributing earnings to its shareholders in two transactions—a pro rata stock dividend followed by a pro rata redemption—that would have the same economic consequences as a simple dividend. Congress, however, soon recognized that even without a prior stock dividend essentially the same result could be effected whereby any corporation, "especially one which has only a few stockholders, might be able to make a distribution to its stockholders which would have the same effect as a taxable dividend." H.R.Rep. No. 1, 69th Cong., 1st Sess., 5. In order to cover this situation, the law was amended to apply "(whether or not such stock was issued as a stock dividend)" whenever a distribution in redemption of stock was made "at such time and in such manner" that it was essentially equivalent to a taxable dividend. Revenue Act of 1926, § 201(g), 44 Stat. 11.

This provision of the 1926 Act was carried forward in each subsequent revenue act and finally became § 115(g)(1) of the Internal Revenue Code of 1939. Unfortunately, however, the policies encompassed within the general language of § 115(g)(1) and its predecessors were not clear, and there resulted much confusion in the tax law. At first, courts assumed that the provision was aimed at tax avoidance schemes and sought only to determine whether such a scheme existed. Although later the emphasis changed and the focus was more on the effect of the distribution, many courts continued to find that distributions otherwise like a dividend were not "essentially equivalent" if, for example, they were motivated by a sufficiently strong nontax business purpose. See cases cited n. 2, *supra.* There was general disagreement, however, about what would qualify as such a purpose, and the result was a case-by-case determination with each case decided "on the basis of the particular facts of the transaction in question."

By the time of the general revision resulting in the Internal Revenue Code of 1954, the draftsmen were faced with what has aptly been described as "the morass created by the decisions." In an effort to eliminate "the considerable confusion which exists in this area" and thereby to facilitate tax planning, the authors of the new Code sought to provide objective tests to govern the tax consequences of stock redemptions. Thus, the tax bill passed by the House of Representatives contained no "essentially equivalent" language. Rather, it provided for "safe harbors" where capital gains treatment would be accorded to corporate redemptions that met the conditions now found in §§ 302(b)(2) and (3) of the Code.

It was in the Senate Finance Committee's consideration of the tax bill that § 302(b)(1) was added, and Congress thereby provided that capital gains treatment should be available "if the redemption is not essentially equivalent to a dividend." Taxpayer argues that the purpose was to continue "existing law," and there is support in the legislative history that § 302(b)(1) reverted "in part" or "in general" to the "essentially equivalent" provision of § 115(g)(1) of the 1939 Code. According to the Government, even under the old law it would have been improper for the Court of Appeals to rely on "a business purpose for the redemption" and "an absence of the proscribed tax avoidance purpose to bail out dividends at favorable tax rates." ... However, we need not decide that question, for we find from the history of the 1954 revisions and the purpose of § 302(b)(1) that Congress intended more than merely to re-enact the prior law.

In explaining the reason for adding the "essentially equivalent" test, the Senate Committee stated that the House provisions "appeared unnecessarily restrictive, particularly, in the case of redemptions of preferred stock which might be called by the corporation without the shareholder having any control over when the redemption may take place." This explanation gives no indication that the purpose behind the redemption should affect the result. Rather, in its more detailed technical evaluation of § 302(b)(1), the Senate Committee reported as follows:

> "The test intended to be incorporated in the interpretation of paragraph (1) is in general that currently employed under section 115(g)(1) of the 1939 Code. Your committee further intends that in applying this test for the future * * * the inquiry will be devoted solely to the question of whether or not the transaction by its nature may properly be characterized as a sale of stock by the redeeming shareholder to the corporation. For this purpose the presence or absence of earnings and profits of the corporation is not material. Example: X, the sole shareholder of a corporation having no earnings or profits causes the corporation to redeem half of its stock. Paragraph (1) does not apply to such redemption notwithstanding the absence of earnings and profits." S.Rep. No. 1622, *supra*, at 234, U.S.Code Cong. & Admin.News 1954, p. 4870.

The intended scope of § 302(b)(1) as revealed by this legislative history is certainly not free from doubt. However, we agree with the Government that by making the sole inquiry relevant for the future the narrow one whether the redemption could be characterized as a sale, Congress was apparently rejecting past court decisions that had also considered factors indicating the presence or absence of a tax-avoidance motive. At least that is the implication of the example given. Congress clearly mandated that pro rata distributions be treated under the general rules laid down in §§ 301 and 316 rather than under § 302 and nothing suggests that there should be a different result if there were a "business purpose" for the redemption. Indeed, just the opposite inference must be drawn since there would not likely be a tax-avoidance purpose in a situation where there were no earnings or profits. We conclude that the Court of Appeals was therefore wrong in looking for a business purpose and considering it in deciding whether the redemption was equivalent to a dividend. Rather, we agree with the Court of Appeals for the Second Circuit that "the business purpose of a transaction is irrelevant in determining dividend equivalence" under § 302(b)(1).

Taxpayer strongly argues that to treat the redemption involved here as essentially equivalent to a dividend is to elevate form over substance. Thus, taxpayer argues, had he not bought Bradley's shares or had he made a subordinated loan to the company instead of buying preferred stock, he could have gotten back his $25,000 with favorable tax treatment. However, the difference between form and substance in the tax law is largely problematical, and taxpayer's complaints have little to do with whether a business purpose is relevant under § 302(b)(1). It was clearly proper for Congress to treat distributions generally as taxable dividends when made out of earnings and profits and then to prevent avoidance of that result without regard to motivation where the distribution is in exchange for redeemed stock.

We conclude that that is what Congress did when enacting § 302(b)(1). If a corporation distributes property as a simple dividend, the effect is to transfer the property from the company to its shareholders without a change in the relative economic interests or rights of the stockholders. Where a redemption has that same effect, it cannot be said to have satisfied the "not essentially equivalent to a dividend" requirement of § 302(b)(1). Rather, to qualify for preferred treatment under that section, a redemption must result in a meaningful reduction of the shareholder's proportionate interest in the corporation. Clearly, taxpayer here, who (after application of the attribution rules) was the sole shareholder of the corporation both before and after the redemption, did not qualify under this test. The decision of the Court of Appeals must therefore be reversed and the case remanded to the District Court for dismissal of the complaint.

It is so ordered.

Reversed and remanded.

MR. JUSTICE DOUGLAS, with whom MR. JUSTICE BRENNAN concurs, dissenting.

* * *

When the Court holds it was a dividend, it effectively cancels § 302(b)(1) from the Code. This result is not a matter of conjecture, for the Court says that in the case of closely held or one-man corporations a redemption of stock is "always" equivalent to a dividend. I would leave such revision to the Congress.

Questions

Would it be reasonable to base the characterization of a redemption on the purpose for the redemption? Is the Supreme Court's "meaningful reduction" test sensible? What is the relationship between the "meaningful reduction" test and the "substantially disproportionate" test of § 302(b)(2)? Is Justice Douglas correct in saying that the decision "cancels § 302(b)(1) from the Code"? Would a redemption of preferred fit within § 302(b)(1)? If so, under what circumstances? See § 1.302–2(a). For a suggestion that the meaningful reduction test be replaced by a business purpose test, see Justice Powell's dissenting opinion on the denial of certiorari in *Albers v. Commissioner,* 414 U.S. 982, 94 S.Ct. 279, 38 L.Ed.2d 225 (1973).

B. THE SERVICE'S INTERPRETATION OF THE MEANINGFUL REDUCTION TEST

The following rulings set out the Service's current view on what constitutes a meaningful reduction. Are these rulings consistent? Is there a common thread running through them? If so, what is it?

1. *Reduction from 27% to 22%*

REVENUE RULING 76–364
1976–2 C.B. 91.

Corporation X had outstanding one class of stock consisting of 200,000 shares of common stock each of which was entitled to one vote. A, an individual, owned 54,000 shares of X common stock (27 percent), each of which was entitled to one vote. Because A was retired from business, A took no active part in the management of X. The remaining 146,000 shares of outstanding X common stock (73 percent) were held in equal portions by individuals B, C, and D. None of the X shareholders were related within the meaning of section 318(a)(1) of the Code.

X redeemed for cash 12,160 shares of its stock held by A. After the redemption, A owned 41,840 shares of the outstanding stock of X which represented 22.27 percent of the 187,840 shares then outstanding. The redemption reduced A's percentage of ownership and voting rights in X from 27 percent to 22.27 percent. This reduction in A's percentage ownership in X failed to meet the percentage requirement of section 302(b)(2)(C) of the Code.

* * *

Rev.Rul. 75–502, 1975–2 C.B. 111, indicates factors to be considered in determining whether a reduction in a shareholder's proportionate interest in a corporation results in a meaningful reduction within the meaning of *Davis.* The factors considered relate to a shareholder's right to vote and exercise control, a shareholder's right to participate in current earnings and accumulated surplus, and a shareholder's right to share in net assets on liquidation.

In the instant case, the fact that A failed to meet the requirements of section 302(b)(2) of the Code is not to be taken into consideration in determining whether the redemption meets the requirements of section

302(b)(1) as provided in section 302(b)(5). In determining whether the redemption meets the requirements of section 302(b)(1), it is significant that the redemption, in reducing A's interest from 27 percent to 22.27 percent, correspondingly reduced A's right to vote, A's right to earnings, and A's right to share in net assets on liquidation. Moreover, the reduction of A's voting rights from 27 percent to 22.27 percent is meaningful in itself in that it caused A to go from a position of holding a block of X stock that afforded A control of X if A acted in concert with only one other stockholder, to a position where such action was not possible. Thus, under the facts and circumstances of the instant case, the reduction constitutes a meaningful reduction of A's interest in X within the meaning of *Davis*.

Accordingly, the redemption was not essentially equivalent to a dividend within the meaning of section 302(b)(1) of the Code and, therefore, qualified as an exchange under section 302(a).

2. *Reduction from 90% to 60%*

REVENUE RULING 78–401
1978–2 C.B. 127.

Issue

Does the redemption of stock described below qualify as a distribution not essentially equivalent to a dividend within the meaning of section 302(b)(1) of the Internal Revenue Code of 1954?

Facts

X corporation, incorporated under the laws of state D, had outstanding one class of stock consisting of 1,000 shares of voting common stock. A, an individual, owned 900 shares (90 percent of the total voting rights) and B, an individual unrelated to A within the meaning of section 318 of the Code, owned the remaining 100 shares (10 percent of the total voting rights). A and B were both active in the management of X.

X redeemed 750 shares of its stock held by A. After the redemption, the common stock held by A (150 shares) represented 60 percent of the total voting rights of the then 250 outstanding shares of X stock. Thus, the redemption reduced A's voting rights in X from 90 percent to 60 percent. A and B both continued to be active in the management of X after the redemption.

Pursuant to the articles of incorporation of X and the laws of state D, a holder of over 50 percent of the X stock controlled X's day to day affairs through the board of directors, and a holder of 66.67 percent of the X stock controlled broader corporate decisions such as those regarding corporate liquidation, merger, or disposition of substantial amounts of operating assets.

Law and Analysis

* * *

In applying the [factors of Rev.Rul. 75–502] to the instant case, it is most significant that the redemption did not reduce A's voting rights in X to 50 percent or less, even though there was a reduction in A's right to participate in current earnings and accumulated surplus and A's right to share in net assets in liquidation. Although A has surrendered the ability to individually control those corporate decisions requiring a 66.67 percent vote, A has retained control of the day to day affairs of X. Since A is in control of the day to day affairs of X and because there is no indication that the type of corporate action requiring a 66.67 percent shareholder vote is imminent, the retention by A of 60 percent of the voting rights in X becomes a predominant factor in determining whether the redemption results in a meaningful reduction of A's interest in X.

In Rev.Rul. 75–502 the reduction in a shareholder's interest from 57 percent to 50 percent indirectly (with the remaining 50 percent held by a single unrelated individual) was regarded to be meaningful within the meaning of *Davis*. However, that Rev.Rul. points out that if the redeeming shareholder had retained more than 50 percent of the voting rights the redemption would not qualify under section 302(b)(1) of the Code because the redeeming shareholder would continue to have dominant voting rights in the corporation.

* * *

Holding

Under the facts and circumstances, the redemption by X of A's stock did not constitute a meaningful reduction in A's interest in X within the meaning of *Davis* despite the fact that A's voting rights were reduced below 66.67 percent. Accordingly, the redemption does not qualify as a distribution not essentially equivalent to a dividend under section 302(b)(1) of the Code and, therefore, is not a distribution in part or full payment in exchange for the X stock under section 302(a). Thus, under section 302(d), the redemption is a distribution of property to which section 301 applies.

3. Public Tender Offer: Redeemed Shareholder Has .2% Both Before and After

REVENUE RULING 81–289
1981–2 C.B. 82.

Issue

Whether a redemption of stock pursuant to an isolated tender offer is taxable as an exchange under section 302(a) and (b)(1) of the Internal Revenue Code.

Facts

X corporation has outstanding $1,000,000x$ shares of voting common stock which are widely held and publicly traded. X has approximately $1,000x$ shareholders, none of whom owns a significant amount of the X

common stock. In an isolated transaction and not as part of a periodic redemption plan, X offered to purchase from its shareholders $25,000x$ shares of its common stock at the rate of $\$20x$ per share. Approximately 10 percent of X's shareholders tendered stock for redemption. X redeemed a total of 20,000x shares of its stock pursuant to the tender offer. Individual A, who owned $2,000x$ shares of X stock at the time of the tender offer, surrendered $40x$ shares for redemption. Accordingly, A's proportionate interest in X was .2 percent ($2,000x$ shares divided by $1,000,000x$ shares) before the tender offer and remained .2 percent ($1,960x$ shares divided by $980,000x$ shares) after the tender offer. A was not related to any other shareholder of X within the meaning of section 318.

LAW AND ANALYSIS

* * *

[T]he meaningful reduction standard was applied to a redemption by a publicly traded corporation in Rev.Rul. 76–385, 1976–2 C.B. 92. In that revenue ruling, the Internal Revenue Service took the position that a redemption that resulted in a reduction of a minority shareholder's proportionate interest from .0001118 percent to .0001081 percent was not essentially equivalent to a dividend, since the minority shareholder experienced a reduction of its voting rights, its right to participate in current earnings and accumulated surplus, and its right to share in net assets on liquidation.

HOLDING

In the present situation the redemption did not result in any reduction of A's right to vote, to participate in current earnings and accumulated surplus, or to share in the corporation's net assets on liquidation. Thus, this redemption with regard to A does not satisfy the meaningful reduction standard and does not qualify as an exchange within the meaning of section 302(a) and (b)(1) of the Code.

4. *Redemption of Nonvoting Preferred From Shareholder Who Owns No Other Stock*

REVENUE RULING 77–426

1977–2 C.B. 87.

A corporation had voting common stock and nonvoting preferred stock outstanding. The preferred stock is not convertible into common stock. The preferred stock is limited and preferred as to dividends and in liquidation and has a stated redemption price. The preferred stock * * * is all owned by one shareholder who owns no common stock of the corporation either directly or by application of the constructive ownership of stock rules of section 318 of the Code. * * * The corporation redeemed 5 percent of the preferred stock.

* * *

Here, the preferred stock was nonvoting, nonconvertible, and limited and preferred as to dividends and in liquidation. The taxpayer did not own any of the common stock of the corporation. Under these circumstances, the rights represented by the redeemed shares were yielded to the common shareholders of the corporation and could not be recovered through the taxpayer's continued stock ownership. Thus, the redemption here is properly characterized as a sale rather than as a dividend. See *S.Rep. No. 1622*, 83d Cong., 2d Sess. 234 (1954), wherein the Senate Committee on Finance said that the section 302(b)(1) inquiry is to be devoted solely to the question of whether or not the transaction by its nature may properly be characterized as a sale of stock.

Accordingly, the redemption of any amount of stock that is nonvoting, nonconvertible, and limited and preferred as to dividends and in liquidation represents a meaningful reduction of the shareholder's proportionate interest in the corporation if the shareholder does not own stock of any other class, either directly or indirectly. Therefore, the redemption in this case qualifies as not essentially equivalent to a dividend under section 302(b)(1) of the Code.

5. *Redemption of Nonvoting Preferred Stock from an 18% Common Shareholder*

REVENUE RULING 85–106
1985–2 C.B. 116.

Issue

Is a redemption of nonvoting preferred stock not essentially equivalent to a dividend within the meaning of section 302(b)(1) of the Internal Revenue Code when there is no reduction in the percentage of voting and nonvoting common stock owned by the redeemed shareholder [i.e. 18%] and when the redeemed shareholder continues to have an undiminished opportunity to act in concert with other shareholders as a control group, under the circumstances described below?

* * *

Holding

The redemption of nonvoting preferred stock held by *T* does not qualify as a redemption under section 302(b)(1) of the Code, under the facts of this ruling when there is no reduction in the percentage of voting and nonvoting common stock owned by *T*, and when *T* continues to have an undiminished opportunity to act in concert with other shareholders as a control group. Since the redemption does not otherwise qualify under section 302(b), it is not a distribution in part or full payment for the stock under section 302(a). Consequently, under section 302(d), the redemption will be treated as a distribution of property to which section 301 applies.

C. FAMILY DISHARMONY RATIONALE: THE SERVICE'S VIEW

REVENUE RULING 80-26
1980-1 C.B. 67.

ISSUE

Are the rules of attribution under section 318 of the Internal Revenue Code applicable under the facts described below in determining whether a distribution in redemption of stock qualifies under section 302(a) of the Code?

FACTS

X corporation had outstanding one class of voting common stock. The stock was owned by 8 shareholders: A; B (A's brother); C (A's brother-in-law); TA, a trust for the benefit of A, B, and D (A's sister); $T1$, $T2$, $T3$, and $T4$, 4 separate trusts for the benefit of A's children created by a parent of A's spouse. A's interest in the shares of TA was one-third. B, C, and D are individuals unrelated to the other shareholders within the meaning of section 318 of the Code. As a result of a bitter divorce and acrimonious property settlement between A and A's spouse, all the stock owned by $T1$, $T2$, $T3$, and $T4$ was redeemed by X. Due to the family hostility these 4 trusts were prevented from exercising actual control over the X stock attributed to them. Before the redemption $T1$, $T2$, $T3$, and $T4$ each owned, actually and constructively, 31 percent of the X stock and after the redemption each owned, solely by attribution under sections 318(a)(1)(A)(ii) and 318(a)(3)(B)(i), 33 percent of the X stock.

LAW AND ANALYSIS

Pursuant to section 302(c) of the Code section 318(a) applies in determining the ownership of stock for purposes of determining whether a redemption qualifies under section 302(a).

In *United States v. Davis,* 397 U.S. 301 (1970), *rehearing denied,* 397 U.S. 1071 (1970), Ct.D.1937, 1970-1 C.B. 62, the Supreme Court of the United States, in considering whether a distribution was a redemption under section 302(b)(1) of the Code, held that the attribution rules were "specifically applicable to the entire section, and * * * that Congress intended that they be taken into account. * * *"

Furthermore, the legislative history of section 318 of the Code indicates that before the enactment of the 1954 Code there was "no specific statutory guidance * * * for stock ownership in the area of corporate distributions. * * *" In order to remove the uncertainties Congress provided, through section 318, "precise standards whereby under specific circumstances, a shareholder may be considered as owning stock held by members of his family (* * * or trusts which he controls)." H.R.Rep. No. 1337, 83rd Cong., 2d Sess. A96 and 36 (1954).

In *Robin Haft Trust, et al. v. Commissioner*, 510 F.2d 43 (1st Cir.1975), *rev'g and remanding*, 61 T.C. 398 (1973), *supplemented*, 62 T.C. 145 (1974), on facts similar to those set forth above, the court viewed the attribution rules as a presumption of continuing influence over corporate affairs and, therefore, because of the family hostility disregarded the attribution rules in testing the redemption of the taxpayers' stock for dividend equivalency. Such an interpretation is, however, inconsistent with both the legislative history of section 318 of the Code and the language and the rationale of *Davis*. The purpose of the attribution rules under section 318 was to replace the confusion of prior law with clear and objective standards for attribution of stock ownership among related shareholders. The facts and circumstances of a particular case cannot contradict the mechanical determination under section 318 of how much stock a shareholder owns.

Consequently, the Internal Revenue Service will not follow the decision of the United States Court of Appeals for the First Circuit in *Haft*. Also, the acquiescence in the decision in *Estate of Squier v. Commissioner*, 35 T.C. 950 (1961), *acq.*, 1961–2 C.B. 5, upon which the decision in *Haft* relies, has been withdrawn and nonacquiescence substituted therefor. See 1978–2 C.B. 4.

Holding

The rules of attribution under section 318 of the Code are applicable in determining whether a distribution in redemption of stock qualifies under section 302(a). Therefore, in the instant case, pursuant to section 318, *T1, T2, T3*, and *T4* each was the owner of 33 percent of the *X* stock after the redemption and, consequently, the redemption of the stock owned by *T1, T2, T3*, and *T4* is not (i) a complete termination of interest in *X* within the meaning of section 302(b)(3); (ii) a substantially disproportionate redemption of stock within the meaning of section 302(b)(2); or (iii) a redemption not essentially equivalent to a dividend within the meaning of section 302(b)(1). Accordingly, the redemption is not a distribution in part or full payment in exchange for the *X* stock under section 302(a). Thus, under section 302(d), the redemption by *X* of the stock held by *T1, T2, T3*, and *T4* is a distribution of property to which section 301 applies.

* * *

Note

The Second Circuit in *David Metzger Trust v. Commissioner*, 693 F.2d 459 (5th Cir.1982), *cert. denied* 463 U.S. 1207, 103 S.Ct. 3537, 77 L.Ed.2d 1388 (1983), adopted the Service's position and held that family discord should not be taken into account in applying the § 318 attribution rules.

D. USE OF DIVIDEND EQUIVALENCE FOR TAX AVOIDANCE PURPOSES: THE IBM RULING

REVENUE RULING 77-226
1977-2 C.B. 90.

X corporation has outstanding approximately 200,000x shares of voting common stock, which is widely held and publicly traded. On April 4, 1976, X offered to purchase shares of its common stock at the rate of $250 per share. On April 5, 1976, Y corporation, which owned no X common stock either actually or constructively under section 318 of the Internal Revenue Code of 1954 prior to the tender offer, purchased 4,000 shares of X stock on the market for a total price of $1,000,000, and immediately tendered 800 shares to X for redemption. On April 21, 1976, Y sold the remaining 3,200 shares of X stock on the market for $800,000.

On its Federal income tax return for its fiscal year ended September 30, 1976, Y reported the $200,000 redemption proceeds as a dividend, claimed the 85 percent dividends received deduction of section 243 of the Code and paid a tax of $14,400. Y claimed a $200,000 short-term capital loss on the sale of the 3,200 shares of X stock and applied this loss against short-term capital gains of $200,000 from other sources, realizing a tax savings of $96,000. The net effect of the entire transaction, as reported by Y, was a tax saving of $81,600.

* * *

In *Zenz v. Quinlivan,* 213 F.2d 914 (6th Cir.1954), the sole shareholder of a corporation, desiring to dispose of her entire interest therein, sold part of her stock to a competitor and shortly thereafter sold the remainder of her stock to the corporation. The Government contended the redemption was a dividend because the result was the same as if the steps had been reversed, that is, as if the stock had been redeemed first and the sale of stock to the competitor had followed. The court rejected the Government's contention and held that the redemption of the stock was not a dividend to the shareholder because the redemption, coupled with the earlier sale, extinguished the shareholder's interest in the corporation.

In Rev.Rul. 55-745, 1955-2 C.B. 223, the Internal Revenue Service agreed to follow *Zenz* in cases that present similar facts and circumstances. In Rev.Rul. 75-447, 1975-2 C.B. 113, the Service held that if the sale and the redemption are undertaken pursuant to an integrated plan, then the two steps will be treated as a unit for the purpose of making the computations under section 302(b)(2) of the Code, regardless of whether the redemption or sale occurs first.

Section 1.302-2(c) of the Income Tax Regulations provides that if the redemption of part of a shareholder's stock of a corporation is treated as a distribution of a dividend, the shareholder's basis in its remaining stock of the corporation will be increased by the basis of the stock redeemed.

In this case, the redemption and the sale were undertaken pursuant to an integrated plan. Therefore, even assuming the redemption distribution, standing by itself, would have been essentially equivalent to a dividend, the redemption and sale combined completely terminated Y's interest in X within the meaning of section 302(b)(3) of the Code. That the redemption occurred before the sale is irrelevant.

Accordingly, the redemption by X of the 800 shares of X stock held by Y should have been treated as an exchange under section 302(a) of the Code rather than as the distribution of a dividend. Y was not entitled to a deduction for dividends received. Y's basis in the 3,200 shares of X stock sold should not have been increased by the basis of the 800 shares of X stock redeemed. Y recognized no loss on the later sale of the remaining 3,200 shares of X stock because the amount realized ($800,000) was equal to the adjusted basis of the stock sold.

Note

The *Zenz* case, discussed in the ruling, is examined in Sec. 10.10.A. when considering bootstrap acquisitions (*i.e.*, a combination purchase and redemption of stock).

§ 5.7 PARTIAL LIQUIDATIONS UNDER § 302(b)(4)

A. LEGISLATIVE BACKGROUND

SENATE FINANCE COMMITTEE REPORT TO THE
TAX EQUITY AND FISCAL RESPONSIBILITY
ACT OF 1982

186–187 (July 12, 1982).

PRESENT LAW

A distribution in redemption of a corporation's stock pursuant to a plan is a partial liquidation if it is one of a series of distributions in redemption of all the stock or it is not essentially equivalent to a dividend and occurs within the taxable year in which the plan is adopted or the succeeding year [former § 346]. * * *

* * *

Shareholders receiving a distribution in partial liquidation are treated as receiving the amount distributed in exchange for their stock and, if the stock redeemed in the transaction is a capital asset to the shareholder, capital gain or loss results from the transaction. The basis of any assets received in a partial liquidation is their fair market value at the time of the distribution.

REASONS FOR CHANGE

The current treatment of partial liquidations affords the possibility of capital gain treatment to shareholders and a stepped-up basis for distributed assets in transactions that, in some cases, are not readily distinguishable from dividends. A distribution, even though it accomplishes a corporate contraction, resembles a dividend and should be classified as a dividend if there are sufficient earnings and profits, the distribution is pro rata among the shareholders, and the corporation continues to carry on a trade or business.

* * *

Under the present rules, a partial liquidation may consist of the distribution of a trade or business to noncorporate shareholders who wish to conduct it as an individual enterprise or as a partnership while retaining a separate trade or business in corporate form. The committee believes that the retention of a rule permitting capital gain treatment at the shareholder level in this limited class of cases will preserve this option.

* * *

Explanation of Provision

The bill repeals the provisions of existing law defining partial liquidations [former § 346] and the rules governing the treatment of both shareholders and the distributing corporation on such transactions. The treatment of such distributions will be determined by the provisions of present law as amended by the bill governing nonliquidating distributions by corporations. [*See* §§ 302(b)(4) and (e).]

Distributions consisting of the assets of, or attributable to the corporation's ceasing to conduct, a trade or business and constituting a partial liquidation under section 346(b) of present law will qualify as distributions not essentially equivalent to a dividend when made to noncorporate shareholders, resulting in sale or exchange treatment under section 302(a) even though the distribution is made pro rata to the shareholders. Distributions qualifying under this provision would be the only transactions where the effect on the distributing corporation is relevant in determining that a stock redemption is not essentially equivalent to a dividend.

* * *

B. TREATMENT OF PRO RATA DISTRIBUTIONS UNDER § 302(b)(4)

REVENUE RULING 90–13
1990–1 C.B. 65.

Issue

Must shareholders surrender stock in the distributing corporation to qualify for partial liquidation treatment under section 302(b)(4) and (e) of the Internal Revenue Code, if the distribution is pro rata?

Facts

Corporation X operated two divisions of equal size and had one class of stock outstanding, which was owned by individuals A and B. There were no outstanding rights, such as warrants, options, convertible securities, shareholder agreements or rights of first refusal, affecting the stock of X.

Pursuant to a plan of partial liquidation, X sold one of its divisions to an unrelated party for cash and distributed the cash proceeds of the sale to A and B pro rata. A and B did not surrender any stock in exchange for the cash distributed by X.

Except for the question as to whether there must be a surrender of stock by the shareholders, the transaction qualifies as a partial liquidation under section 302(b)(4) and (e) of the Code.

Law and Analysis

* * *

Section 302(b)(4) of the Code provides that section 302(a) applies to a distribution if the distribution is both (A) in redemption of stock held by a shareholder who is not a corporation, and (B) in partial liquidation of the distributing corporation.

Section 302(e)(1) of the Code provides that, for purposes of section 302(b)(4), a distribution is treated as in partial liquidation of a corporation if it is not "essentially equivalent to a dividend" (determined at the corporate level rather than at the shareholder level), is pursuant to a plan, and occurs within the tax year in which the plan is adopted or within the succeeding tax year. Section 302(e)(2) and (3) provides a safe-harbor rule similar to the safe-harbor rule in former section 346(b).

Under section 302(b)(4)(A) and (B) of the Code, respectively, two requirements for partial liquidation treatment are that (1) stock be redeemed and (2) the redemption be in partial liquidation within the meaning of section 302(e). The second requirement can be satisfied (as the facts here indicate it has been satisfied) irrespective of an actual stock surrender because under section 302(b)(4)(B) and (e) this requirement is tested at the corporate level, not the shareholder level, and is not concerned with stock ownership.

However, the first requirement—that stock be redeemed—is tested at the shareholder level. Moreover, the reference to section 317(b) of the Code in section 302(a) raises the question whether an actual surrender of stock is required for a transaction to be treated as a partial liquidation under section 302(b)(4).

* * *

The TEFRA conference report, in explaining the treatment of partial liquidations, states:

> Under present law, a distribution in partial liquidation may take place without an actual surrender of stock by the shareholders

(*Fowler Hosiery Co. v. Commissioner*), 301 F.2d 394 (7th Cir.1962). A constructive redemption of stock is deemed to occur in such transactions (Rev.Rul. 81–3, 1981–1 C.B. 125). The conferees intend that the treatment of partial liquidations under present law section 346(a)(2) and (b) is to continue for such transactions under new section 302(e).

* * *

Holding

The pro rata distribution by X to its shareholders, individuals A and B, qualifies as a distribution in redemption of stock held by A and B in partial liquidation of X under section 302(b)(4) and (e) of the Code, even though the shareholders did not surrender any of their stock.

See Rev.Rul. 77–245, 1977–2 C.B. 105, for computation of the tax consequences to A and B resulting from the partial liquidation.

* * *

C. GENUINE CONTRACTION MEANS SUBSTANTIAL REDUCTION IN ACTIVITIES

REVENUE RULING 76–526
1976–2 C.B. 101.

Advice has been requested whether, under the circumstances described below, a distribution qualifies as a partial liquidation within the meaning of section 346(a)(2) [now § 302(e)] of the Internal Revenue Code of 1954.

X corporation owned two parcels of real property (parcel A and parcel B), each consisting of land and a building thereon. X has only one class of stock outstanding. Both parcel A and parcel B are leased. Under both leases, the lessee is required to pay all real estate taxes and similar assessments and is responsible for all interior maintenance and the operation of the building's equipment.

Both parcel A and parcel B are the subject of a management agreement whereby another corporation, wholly owned by one of X's shareholders, provides renting, leasing, operating, and managing services. These services include advertising, billing, paying bills (including mortgages), taking care of all phases of repairs and alterations (such as hiring employees and purchasing supplies), obtaining insurance, and enforcing the terms of all contracts.

X distributed parcel A pro rata to its shareholders in redemption of a part of their stock. X had accumulated earnings and profits in excess of the fair market value of parcel A.

At issue in the instant case is whether a genuine contraction of X's business results since X itself engaged in no substantial activities with respect to parcel A, or with respect to parcel B, which is retained by X.

* * *

[F]or purposes of finding that a genuine contraction of a business has occurred for purposes of section 346(a)(2) [now § 302(e)] of the Code, there must be a substantial reduction of activities performed by the corporation making the distribution. In the instant case, there was no substantial reduction in activities because X under its lease and its management contract has no substantial activities to perform. Thus, the distribution does not constitute a genuine contraction of X's business within the meaning of section 346(a)(2) [now § 302(e)].

Accordingly, the distribution by X does not qualify as a partial liquidation under section 346(a)(2) [now § 302(e)] of the Code. Therefore, section 346(a) [now § 302(e)] is inapplicable. Since the distribution, because it was pro rata, does not qualify under section 302(a) as payment in exchange for the stock redeemed, the distribution by virtue of section 302(d) is treated as a distribution of property to which section 301 applies. Furthermore, since X had accumulated earnings and profits in excess of the amount distributed, the entire amount of the distribution to each shareholder is taxable as a dividend under the provisions of section 301.

§ 5.8 SUGGESTED METHODOLOGY FOR DETERMINING REDEMPTION TREATMENT *

The following methodology is a suggested procedure to determine whether a redemption qualifies under § 302(b).

First, a determination must be made of the stock ownership immediately before and immediately after the redemption. This includes examining both actual ownership and constructive ownership under the attribution rules of § 318(a) as follows:

(a) Before redemption
    (1) Actual   _____
    (2) Constructive
        Section 318(a)(1)   _____
        Section 318(a)(2)   _____
        Section 318(a)(3)   _____
        Section 318(a)(4)   _____
        Section 318(a)(5)   _____
        Total   _____
    (3) TOTAL   _____
(b) After redemption
    (1) Actual   _____
    (2) Constructive
        Section 318(a)(1)   _____

---

* This section is reprinted from *Federal Taxation of Business Enterprises, supra* Chapter 1, note 1, with permission.

Section 318(a)(2) _____
Section 318(a)(3) _____
Section 318(a)(4) _____
Section 318(a)(5) _____
Total _____
(3) TOTAL _____

Secondly, a determination must be made of whether the redemption qualifies under § 302(b), resulting in capital gain to the distributee under § 302(a) or whether it is a distribution controlled by § 301 by reason of § 302(d). Each redemption must be examined to determine if one of the tests in § 302(b) is satisfied:

(a) Section 302(b)(3) inquiry: Has the shareholder completely terminated ownership of the corporation?

(b) Section 302(b)(2) inquiry: Is the redemption substantially disproportionate with respect to the shareholder?

(c) Section 302(b)(1) inquiry: Is the redemption not essentially equivalent to a dividend?

(d) Section 302(b)(4) inquiry: Does the redemption qualify as a partial liquidation?

§ 5.9 SUMMARY PROBLEMS ON § 302 REDEMPTIONS AND § 318 ATTRIBUTION

The following problems are designed to highlight the major elements in §§ 302 and 318. In approaching these problems, the reader should determine, both before and after the redemption, the number of shares the redeemed shareholder owns *actually* and *constructively*.

1. The 100 shares of stock of *X* are held 50–50 (50 shares each) by *A* and *B*, two unrelated individuals. What result to *B* if *X* redeems 10 of his shares? *See* § 302(b)(1) and (2). What result to *B* if *X* redeems 20 of his shares?

2. Each of *A*, *B*, *C* and *D* owns 25 of *X*'s 100 outstanding shares. *X* redeems all of *D*'s 25 shares. What result to *D*? *See* § 302(b)(3). Is additional information required? If so, what? Suppose *D* is *C*'s grandchild? *See* § 318(a)(1). Suppose *C* and *D* are father and son? *See* §§ 318(a)(1) and 302(c)(2)(A). Suppose *D* owned 50 shares and made a gift of 25 shares to his father, *C*, one year before the redemption of the remaining 25 shares? *See* § 302(c)(2)(B). Suppose *C*'s rather than *D*'s shares are redeemed? Suppose *E*, a nonshareholder, is *D*'s wife and *B*'s daughter? *See* § 318(a)(5)(A) and (B).

3. Individual *A* owns 80 of the 100 outstanding shares of corporation *X*, and the balance of *X*'s shares are owned by the public. Corporation *X* in turn owns 50 of the 100 outstanding shares of corporation *Y*. *A* owns 10 shares of corporation *Y* and the balance (40) of the *Y* shares is

owned by the public. What result to A if Y redeems his 10 shares? *See* §§ 302(b)(2), (3); 302(c)(1) and 318(a)(2)(C). What result if, instead of redeeming the 10 shares owned by A, Y redeems 20 of its shares owned by X? *See* §§ 302(b)(2) and 318(a)(3)(C).

4. A and B each own 50 of the 100 outstanding shares of X corporation and 50 of the 100 outstanding shares of Y corporation. A and B are unrelated individuals. What result to B if Y corporation redeems all of his 50 shares? *See* § 318(a)(5)(A) and (C). Do the operating rules of § 318(a)(5) permit attribution from one shareholder to his corporation and out to another shareholder?

5. Individual A has a 75 percent interest in the ABCD partnership. The partners are unrelated. A also owns 50 percent of the stock of X corporation. X and ABCD each own 50 percent of Y corporation. What result if Y redeems all of its stock held by X? *See* § 318(a)(5)(A) and (C). Would X want the transaction to come within § 302(b)? What result if, instead of redeeming the stock held by X, Y redeems all of its stock held by ABCD? Do the operating rules of § 318(a)(5) permit attribution from a corporation to a shareholder and from the shareholder to another corporation?

6. Individual A owns all of the stock of corporation X. X is engaged in two lines of business, manufacturing widgets and manufacturing wodgets. X sells its widget business and distributes the proceeds to A. X continues to operate its wodget business. What result to A? What result to A and X if X distributes the widget business to A?

§ 5.10 REDEMPTION IN CONTEXT OF BOOT-STRAP SALES

A. PURCHASE OF STOCK FROM CORPORATION FOLLOWED BY REDEMPTION OF OLD SHAREHOLDER: TREATMENT OF REDEEMED SHAREHOLDER

ZENZ v. QUINLIVAN
United States Court of Appeals, Sixth Circuit, 1954.
213 F.2d 914.

GOURLEY, DISTRICT JUDGE.

The appeal relates to the interpretation of Section 115(g) [now § 302(b)] of the Internal Revenue Code and poses the question—Is a distribution of substantially all of the accumulated earnings and surplus of a corporation, which are not necessary to the conduct of the business of the corporation, in redemption of all outstanding shares of stock of said corporation owned by one person *essentially equivalent to the distribution of a taxable dividend under the Internal Revenue Code?*

The District Court answered in the affirmative and sustained a deficiency assessment by the Commissioner of Internal Revenue.

After consideration of the records, briefs and arguments of counsel for the parties, we believe the judgment should be reversed.

* * * Whether a distribution in connection with a cancellation or redemption of stock is essentially equivalent to the distribution of a taxable dividend depends upon the facts and circumstances of each case.

The question stems from the following circumstances:

Appellant is the widow of the person who was the motivating spirit behind the closed corporation which engaged in the business of excavating and laying of sewers. Through death of her husband she became the owner of all shares of stock issued by the corporation. She operated the business until remarriage, when her second husband assumed the management. As a result of a marital rift, separation, and final divorce, taxpayer sought to dispose of her company to a competitor who was anxious to eliminate competition.

Prospective buyer did not want to assume the tax liabilities which it was believed were inherent in the accumulated earnings and profits of the corporation. To avoid said profits and earnings as a source of future taxable dividends, buyer purchased part of taxpayer's stock for cash. Three weeks later, after corporate reorganization and corporate action, the corporation redeemed the balance of taxpayer's stock, purchasing the same as treasury stock which absorbed substantially all of the accumulated earnings and surplus of the corporation.

Taxpayer, in her tax return, invoked [the predecessor of § 302(b)(3)] as constituting a cancellation or redemption by a corporation of all the stock of a particular shareholder, and therefore was not subject to being treated as a distribution of a taxable dividend.

The District Court sustained the deficiency assessment of the Commissioner that the amount received from accumulated earnings and profits was ordinary income since the stock redeemed by the corporation was "at such time and in such manner as to make the redemption thereof essentially equivalent to the distribution of a taxable dividend" under [the predecessor of § 302(b)(1)].

The District Court's findings were premised upon the view that taxpayer employed a circuitous approach in an attempt to avoid the tax consequences which would have attended the outright distribution of the surplus to the taxpayer by the declaration of a taxable dividend.

The rationale of the District Court is dedicated to piercing the external manifestations of the taxpayer's transactions in order to establish a subterfuge or sham.

Nevertheless, the general principle is well settled that a taxpayer has the legal right to decrease the amount of what otherwise would be his taxes or altogether avoid them, by means which the law permits. *Gregory v. Helvering.* * * * The taxpayer's motive to avoid taxation will not establish liability if the transaction does not do so without it. * * *

The question accordingly presented is not whether the overall transaction, admittedly carried out for the purpose of avoiding taxes, actually avoided taxes which would have been incurred if the transaction had taken a different form, but whether the sale constituted a taxable dividend or the sale of a capital asset. *Chamberlain v. Commissioner of Internal Revenue,* supra.

It is a salutary fact that Section 115(c) [now § 302(b)(3)] is an exception to Section 115(a) [now § 301] that all distributions of earning and profits are taxable as a dividend.

The basic precept underlying the capital gains theory of taxation as distinguished from ordinary income tax is the concept that a person who has developed an enterprise in which earnings have been accumulated over a period of years should not be required to expend the ordinary income tax rate in the one year when he withdraws from his enterprise and realizes his gain.

Common logic dictates that a fair basis of measuring income is not determined upon the profits on hand in the year of liquidation but is properly attributable to each year in which the profits were gained.

We cannot concur with the legal proposition enunciated by the District Court that a corporate distribution can be essentially equivalent to a taxable dividend even though that distribution extinguishes the shareholder's interest in the corporation. To the contrary, we are satisfied that where the taxpayer effects a redemption which completely extinguishes the taxpayer's interest in the corporation, and does not retain any beneficial interest whatever, that such transaction is not the equivalent of the distribution of a taxable dividend as to him.

* * *

Since the intent of the taxpayer was to bring about a complete liquidation of her holdings and to become separated from all interest in the corporation, the conclusion is inevitable that the distribution of the earnings and profits by the corporation in payment for said stock was not made at such time and in such manner as to make the distribution and cancellation or redemption thereof essentially equivalent to the distribution of a taxable dividend.

* * *

Questions and Note

1. What planning opportunities does *Zenz* give rise to? Suppose individual *A* owns all the stock of corporation *X*, which has a value of $1 million, $500K of which is attributable to operating assets and $500K of which is attributable to IBM stock for which *X* has a basis of $400K. *X* has no liabilities. Individual *B* would like to buy *X*'s operating assets but not the IBM stock. *B* is willing to pay $500K. What result if *X* sells its operating assets to *B* and then liquidates? What if *A* insists upon a sale of the stock?

2. In Rev.Rul. 55–745, 1955–2 C.B. the Service agreed to follow Zenz. For other illustrations of the Zenz principle, see Rev.Rul. 77–226 at Sec. 10.6.D., Rev.Rul. 75–447 at Sec. 10.5.A. (which holds that the sequence of the purchase and redemption is irrelevant), Rev.Rul. 79–273, 1979–2 C.B. 125, and Rev.Rul. 81–186, 1981–2 C.B. 85.

B. PURCHASE OF STOCK FROM SELLING SHAREHOLDERS AND REDEMPTION OF OTHER SHAREHOLDERS: TREATMENT OF PURCHASING SHAREHOLDER

ADAMS v. COMMISSIONER
Tax Court of the United States, 1978.
69 T.C. 1040.

OPINION

Petitioner set about to acquire, on behalf of himself and certain members of the Adams family, the stock of First Security Bank of Sutherland, Nebr. First Security had outstanding 500 shares of stock, of which 335 shares were held in the Whitlake estates and 165 shares were held by the directors and officers of the bank. In the course of negotiations, petitioner was the successful bidder for the estates' stock at a price of $1,350 per share, or $452,250, and by agreement with the minority shareholders had the right to purchase their stock for $820 per share, or a total of $135,300. In such negotiations, petitioner purported to act as "Mel Adams, Agent."

From the outset, petitioner had disclosed to the sellers that he proposed to obtain a part of the funds for the purchase of the First Security stock by having the bank redeem an undetermined number of shares of that stock. He had obtained approval of the Nebraska banking authorities for the redemption on the condition that immediately thereafter the equivalent number of shares be issued as a stock dividend, thereby maintaining intact the capital and paid-in surplus of the bank.

In order to consummate the transaction, petitioner opened an account in the name of "Mel Adams, Agent," with a bank of which he was then president. Pending approval of the sale by the County Court of Lincoln County, he proceeded to issue checks in payment both for the stock held by the estates and the stock held by the minority shareholders. At that time, there were no funds in the account. Once court approval was obtained, petitioner completed the transaction by having First Security redeem 217 shares of its stock for a total of $206,850 and by obtaining the balance of the purchase price through a series of loans from the Omaha National Bank. Simultaneously, First Security reissued 217 shares of its stock to the petitioner as a stock dividend. The respondent determined that the redemption of the stock discharged an obligation for which the petitioners were personally liable, and is taxable as a dividend to the extent of the earnings and profits of First Security. Such earnings and profits exceeded the redemption price.

Petitioner contends that in the negotiations and the agreements resulting therefrom, which were conducted by "Mel Adams, Agent," petitioner acted on behalf of First Security Bank. * * *

* * *

Whether the transaction in question resulted in the payment of a taxable dividend depends on the facts. * * *

Applying the guidelines set forth by the Eighth Circuit in *Sullivan v. United States, supra,* it is clear that petitioner, constructively if not directly, received a taxable dividend. Any business purpose for the redemption by First Security of 217 shares of its stock was wholly lacking. When coupled with the simultaneous reissuance of the 217 shares as a stock dividend, there was no change in the capital and paid-in surplus of First Security. The only result was the distribution of $206,850 out of its earnings and profits.

From the standpoint of the petitioner, whether his obligation to purchase the stock was conditional or otherwise is immaterial. In accordance with a prearranged plan, he caused First Security to redeem 217 shares of its stock for $206,850 in order to meet that obligation. * * *

* * *

Question

Compare the transaction in *Adams* with that in *Zenz*. Which party was the Service asserting a liability against in each case, the seller of the stock or the purchaser? How can the type of transaction in *Zenz* and *Adams* be structured to ensure that neither the purchaser nor seller gets hit with dividend treatment?

C. SALE OF STOCK BY SHAREHOLDER FOLLOWED BY REDEMPTION OF STOCK SOLD: TREATMENT OF SELLING SHAREHOLDER

ESTATE OF SCHNEIDER v. COMMISSIONER

United States Court of Appeals, Seventh Circuit, 1988.
855 F.2d 435.

FLAUM, CIRCUIT JUDGE.

Al J. Schneider ("Schneider") was the principal shareholder of American National Corporation ("ANC"), a holding company, which in turn owned 100% of the stock of Schneider Transport, Inc. ("Transport"). In 1974, 1975 and 1976 Schneider sold portions of his ANC stock to certain Transport employees who were participating in an employee stock ownership plan. [The employees, pursuant to an elective stock bonus plan, received bonus checks from Transport and immediately endorsed the checks to Schneider as payment for stock transferred to them by Schneider.] Schneider reported these transactions on the 1974–76 federal income tax returns he filed jointly with his wife, Agnes Schneider, characterizing them as sales of capital assets which generated long-term capital gains. The Internal Revenue Service (the "IRS") alleged that these sales actually constituted a redemption of Schneider's stock by ANC followed by a distribution of this stock pursuant to the

§ 5.10　REDEMPTION IN CONTEXT OF BOOT–STRAP SALES　231

employee stock ownership plan. The IRS asserted that Schneider should have reported the entire amounts he received from these alleged sales as dividend distributions. The IRS therefore issued deficiency notices for 1975 and 1976. The matter proceeded to trial and the Tax Court entered judgment against Schneider and his wife for $17,046 and $20,716 for the tax years of 1975 and 1976 respectively. We affirm.

* * *

On appeal, the issue is how Schneider's sales of his ANC class B nonvoting stock to Transport's employees should be characterized for tax purposes. It is Schneider's position that the transactions which occurred should be respected. He contends that Transport paid cash bonuses to a select number of its employees and these employees decided to purchase the ANC stock from Schneider. Because the shares were capital assets in Schneider's hands and were sold in bona fide sales to Transport's employees, in Schneider's view, he correctly reported as a capital gain each year the sum of the differences between the selling prices and his tax basis in the shares he sold.

The Tax Court rejected this view. The court held that the transactions involving the payment of the 1975 and 1976 bonuses and stock sales should be characterized as stock redemptions followed by distributions of the redeemed shares as compensation to the electing bonus recipients. The Tax Court specifically found that the intended employee compensation was the stock, not the preendorsed checks.[4]

Once the transactions are characterized in this manner, the appropriate tax treatment for Schneider's exchange of his stock for cash is determined by the rules governing stock redemptions. Schneider concedes on appeal that if it is determined that his stock was redeemed by ANC, the sum he received is properly taxed as ordinary income to him.

* * *

* * *

[W]e affirm the Tax Court's characterization of Schneider's stock sales as constructive redemptions. As the Tax Court observed, "[a]t the start of each year's stock bonus process, [Schneider] had stock and the corporations had funds. At the end of each year's stock bonus process, [Schneider] had funds that came from the corporations, and the corporations' employees had stock that came from [Schneider]." Our specific focus is on how ANC class B stock which Schneider initially held subject to the restrictions imposed by the Buy–Sell Agreement ended up in the hands of Transport employees subject to the limitations of the ANC

---

4. The Tax Court employed the step-transaction doctrine, ruling in part that the employees were mere conduits for the "second check" and therefore the cash flowed directly from Transport to Schneider. We approach the other half of the transaction, focusing on how the stock got from Schneider to the Transport employees. Because we hold that there were more steps— the stock was transferred to ANC, Transport and then to the employees—than Schneider would wish to recognize, we do not speak in terms of the step-transaction doctrine.

Plan. We agree with the explanation arrived at by the Tax Court: a redemption followed by a stock distribution.

Schneider attempts to avoid this characterization by emphasizing that the Tax Court specifically found that he was not in need of cash at the time of the alleged stock sales. In Schneider's view this indicates that the arrangement was not an effort to "bail" money out of the corporation at capital gain rates, but rather was motivated by legitimate business purposes. * * *

* * *

The fact that Schneider did not need cash and therefore allegedly did not have a tax motive for participating in this particular arrangement is not dispositive. * * *

Schneider claims that the cash payment and stock sales must be viewed as independent steps for tax purposes. He asserts that the bonus recipients constructively received their bonus entirely in cash at the time they were required to elect the form their bonus would take. In Schneider's view, cash is the standard form of compensation and the election itself constituted an independent step under which an employee who received cash chose to use a portion of it to purchase stock.

Even if we assume that this characterization of the specific operation of the election feature is correct, it does not indicate whether Transport or Schneider was the direct source of the stock that the electing bonus recipients received. * * *

* * *

The stock received by the employees was subject to the restrictions imposed by the ANC Plan, including the vesting provisions. In contrast, this same stock in Schneider's hands, which the electing bonus recipients allegedly purchased directly from him, was subject to the Buy–Sell Agreement, not the ANC Plan. Paragraph 2 of the Buy–Sell Agreement set forth ANC's right of first refusal and provided that "[i]f stock of [ANC] is sold under the terms of [paragraph 2] to a person other than [ANC], such shares shall be free of all further restrictions hereunder." Because ANC had waived its right of first refusal with respect to the stock Schneider sold to the employees, absent other agreements, the employees' stock should not have been subject to any restrictions.

* * *

Once it is determined that the bonus recipients received their stock from Transport, the rest of the pieces fall into place. In order to administer the ANC Plan, Transport needed to acquire the necessary ANC stock. ANC was the most obvious source, but it was reluctant to issue new stock because of the dilution and cash build-up effects. Both problems were solved by having ANC obtain the stock from Schneider. There was no dilution because the stock was previously outstanding. In addition, ANC suffered no cash build-up because the funds Transport paid to it were used to satisfy the obligations to Schneider it incurred to acquire his stock. ANC's acquisition of Schneider's stock, however, is a redemption under § 317 of the Internal Revenue Code. The decision of the Tax Court is AFFIRMED.

§ 5.11 REDEMPTIONS IN THE CONTEXT OF BUY–SELL AGREEMENTS

A. INTRODUCTION

In order to provide for the disposition of the shares of a closely held corporation upon the death or retirement of a shareholder, the shareholders may enter into a buy-sell agreement. Such an agreement can serve many purposes:

(1) Provide a market for the shares;

(2) Maintain control of the corporation in the hands of the active shareholders, thus eliminating the possibility of contentious outside shareholders, such as the spouse of a deceased shareholder;

(3) Provide certainty in valuing the shares for estate tax purposes and also provide the funds to pay estate taxes;

(4) Provide a method of withdrawing earnings from the corporation as capital gains and return of capital; and

(5) Ensure the continued existence of a subchapter S election.

There are two basic forms of buy-sell agreements: entity plans and cross purchase plans. In an entity plan the corporation purchases the stock of the deceased or retiring shareholder. These plans, commonly referred to as stock redemption plans, may be set out in a separate agreement or made part of the bylaws or the articles.

The rules of § 302 or § 303 apply for purposes of determining the tax treatment of the redeemed shareholder; that is, dividend or capital gain. Section 302 is covered in Sec. 5.2–5.7, and Section 303 is briefly introduced in Sec. 5.13.

Care must be taken in structuring an entity plan to ensure that the continuing shareholders do not have a constructive dividend. This problem is addressed below in Rev.Rul. 69–608 below.

In a cross purchase plan, the continuing shareholders purchase the stock of the deceased or retiring shareholder. A cross purchase plan is reflected in a separate shareholder agreement. The selling shareholder has a capital gain or loss, and the purchasing shareholder takes a cost basis for the purchased shares.

A major problem in structuring buy-sell agreements is the determination of the price at which the stock will be sold at an uncertain point in the future. The price might be specifically stated and periodically reviewed, determined by appraisal at the time of a required purchase, determined by formula, such as a multiple of earnings, or determined by the book value of the corporation.

If properly structured, a price set in a buy-sell agreement may be accepted as the value of the stock for estate tax purposes. Thus, in structuring a buy-sell agreement it is important to have the document reviewed by an attorney knowledgeable in estate tax matters.

Another major problem with buy-sell agreements is ensuring that either the corporation or the shareholders have sufficient funds to make the purchase. In addition to a sufficiency of funds, the corporation must also be authorized under the relevant business corporation law to make the redemption. If the corporation accumulates funds to make a purchase, it may run afoul of the accumulated earnings tax. *See* chapter 6.

Life insurance on the lives of the shareholders may be utilized to fund, partially or wholly, the purchase of the shares. The use of life insurance can present significant issues that are not addressed here.

B. SERVICE'S POSITION ON CONSTRUCTIVE DIVIDENDS

REVENUE RULING 69–608
1969–2 C.B. 43.

Advice has been requested as to the treatment for Federal income tax purposes of the redemption by a corporation of a retiring shareholder's stock where the remaining shareholder of the corporation has entered into a contract to purchase such stock.

Where the stock of a corporation is held by a small group of people, it is often considered necessary to the continuity of the corporation to have the individuals enter into agreements among themselves to provide for the disposition of the stock of the corporation in the event of the resignation, death, or incapacity of one of them. Such agreements are generally reciprocal among the shareholders and usually provide that on the resignation, death, or incapacity of one of the principal shareholders, the remaining shareholders will purchase his stock. Frequently such agreements are assigned to the corporation by the remaining shareholder and the corporation actually redeems its stock from the retiring shareholder.

Where a corporation redeems stock from a retiring shareholder, the fact that the corporation in purchasing the shares satisfies the continuing shareholder's executory contractual obligation to purchase the redeemed shares does not result in a distribution to the continuing shareholder provided that the continuing shareholder is not subject to an existing primary and unconditional obligation to perform the contract and that the corporation pays no more than fair market value for the stock redeemed.

On the other hand, if the continuing shareholder, at the time of the assignment to the corporation of his contract to purchase the retiring shareholder's stock, is subject to an unconditional obligation to purchase the retiring shareholder's stock, the satisfaction by the corporation of his obligation results in a constructive distribution to him. The constructive distribution is taxable as a distribution under section 301 of the Internal Revenue Code of 1954.

If the continuing shareholder assigns his stock purchase contract to the redeeming corporation prior to the time when he incurs a primary and unconditional obligation to pay for the shares of stock, no distribution to him will result. If, on the other hand, the assignment takes place after the time when the continuing shareholder is so obligated, a distribution to him will result. While a pre-existing obligation to perform in the future is a necessary element in establishing a distribution in this type of case, it is not until the obligor's duty to perform becomes unconditional that it can be said a primary and unconditional obligation arises.

The application of the above principles may be illustrated by the situations described below.

SITUATION 1

A and *B* are unrelated individuals who own all of the outstanding stock of corporation *X*. *A* and *B* enter into an agreement that provides in the event *B* leaves the employ of *X*, he will sell his *X* stock to *A* at a price fixed by the agreement. The agreement provides that within a specified number of days of *B*'s offer to sell, *A* will purchase at the price fixed by the agreement all of the *X* stock owned by *B*. *B* terminates his employment and tenders the *X* stock to *A*. Instead of purchasing the stock himself in accordance with the terms of the agreement, *A* causes *X* to assume the contract and to redeem its stock held by *B*. In this case, *A* had a primary and unconditional obligation to perform his contract with *B* at the time the contract was assigned to *X*. Therefore, the redemption by *X* of its stock held by *B* will result in a constructive distribution to *A*. * * *

* * *

SITUATION 4

A and *B* owned all of the outstanding stock of *X* corporation. *A* and *B* entered into a contract under which, if *B* desired to sell his *X* stock, *A* agreed to purchase the stock or to cause such stock to be purchased. If *B* chose to sell his *X* stock to any person other than *A*, he could do so at any time. In accordance with the terms of the contract, *A* caused *X* to redeem all of *B*'s stock in *X*.

At the time of the redemption, *B* was free to sell his stock to *A* or to any other person, and *A* had no unconditional obligation to purchase the stock and no fixed liability to pay for the stock. Accordingly, the redemption by *X* did not result in a constructive distribution to *A*. See *S.K. Ames, Inc., v. Commissioner,* 46 B.T.A. 1020 (1942), acquiescence, C.B. 1942–1, 1.

SITUATION 5

A and *B* owned all of the outstanding stock of *X* corporation. An agreement between *A* and *B* provided that upon the death of either, *X* will redeem all of the *X* stock owned by the decedent at the time of his death. In the event that *X* does not redeem the shares from the estate, the agreement provided that the surviving shareholder would purchase the unredeemed shares from the decedent's estate. *B* died and, in accordance with the agreement, *X* redeemed all of the shares owned by his estate.

In this case *A* was only secondarily liable under the agreement between *A* and *B*. Since *A* was not primarily obligated to purchase the *X* stock from the estate of *B*, he received no constructive distribution when *X* redeemed the stock.

* * *

§ 5.12 DISTRIBUTIONS IN REDEMPTIONS UNDER § 304

A. HISTORICAL PERSPECTIVE OF THE PROBLEM

JOHN RODMAN WANAMAKER, TRUSTEE v. COMMISSIONER

Tax Court of the United States, 1948.
11 T.C. 365, *affirmed per curiam* 178 F.2d 10 (3d Cir.1949).

* * *

The questions presented are whether cash receipts by petitioners resulting from transactions between wholly owned corporations constituted distributions taxable as dividends under Internal Revenue Code, section 115(g) [predecessor of § 302]; * * *

FINDINGS OF FACT

The facts so stipulated are hereby found accordingly.

Petitioners are the surviving and succeeding trustees of a testamentary trust created by the will of Rodman Wanamaker, who died March 9, 1928.

* * *

John Wanamaker Philadelphia at all times held all of the capital stock of John Wanamaker New York. * * *

In each of the years 1942, 1943, and 1944 the minutes of petitioners recite their obligation under the will to provide funds for the monthly payments to Violet; the nonavailability of funds for this purpose; the offer of John Wanamaker New York to purchase 100 shares of John Wanamaker Philadelphia at $495 a share, stated to be its approximate book value as of February 1, 1942 and 1943, and $505 a share, stated to be its approximate book value as of February 1, 1944; and the acceptance of the offers by petitioners and the authorization for the transactions.

The minutes of meetings of the board of directors of John Wanamaker New York evidence corporate authorizations for the transactions. John Wanamaker New York, by check dated December 29, 1943, paid petitioners $49,500.

* * *

In petitioners' fiduciary income tax returns for the three years here involved they reported the above transactions as sales of stock to John Wanamaker New York, and deducted the resulting capital loss to the extent of $1,000.

In his notice of deficiency respondent stated:

The proceeds from the alleged sales of 100 shares of common stock of John Wanamaker Philadelphia in each of the taxable years 1942, 1943 and 1944 to John Wanamaker New York are determined to have been taxable dividends within the meaning of section 115(g) [predecessor of § 302] of the Internal Revenue Code.

OPINION

OPPER, JUDGE: The first issue turns on whether section 115(g) [predecessor of § 302] fits the transaction here involved. The provision is:

> (g) Redemption of Stock.—If a corporation cancels or redeems its stock (whether or not such stock was issued as a stock dividend) at such time and in such manner as to make the distribution and cancellation or redemption in whole or in part essentially equivalent to the distribution of a taxable dividend, the amount so distributed in redemption or cancellation of the stock, to the extent that it represents a distribution of earnings or profits accumulated after February 28, 1913, shall be treated as a taxable dividend.

Petitioners insist that when John Wanamaker New York bought the stock of its parent, John Wanamaker Philadelphia, it did not deal in "its stock" at all, much less cancel or redeem it. The contention is virtually identical with that upheld in *Mead Corporation v. Commissioner* upon which petitioner relies, and in which it was held that section 104 of the 1928 Act, penalizing the accumulation of a corporation's earnings for the purpose of avoiding surtax upon "its" shareholders, did not apply to the accumulations of a subsidiary, even though for the purpose of avoiding surtax upon the shareholders of the parent.

In reversing our decision, the Circuit Court said in words equally applicable here: "To say that the term 'its shareholders' means not only the corporation's actual shareholders but also the shareholders of its shareholders would be to add to the statute something that is not there and to give it an effect which its plain words do not compel."

If application of the word "its" to a subsidiary was unauthorized in the *Mead* case, it must be even more so here. There we were able to gather from the legislative history of the section involved a congressional purpose calling for the broader interpretation. Here no assistance can be drawn from that quarter, the committee reports and other usual sources of information being completely silent on the point of the present controversy. Following *Mead Corporation v. Commissioner, supra,* we conclude that the New York subsidiary did not cancel or redeem its stock when it bought the stock of its Philadelphia parent, and hence that section 115(g) [predecessor of § 302] is inapplicable to the present facts.

* * *

Question

What abuse was the Commissioner concerned with in *Wanamaker?*

B. LEGISLATIVE HISTORY OF § 304

THIS SECTION CONTAINS EXCERPTS FROM THE FOLLOWING COMMITTEE REPORTS: SENATE FINANCE COMMITTEE REPORT TO THE 1954 CODE; HOUSE CONFERENCE REPORT TO THE TAX EQUITY AND FISCAL RESPONSIBILITY ACT OF 1982 (TEFRA); HOUSE WAYS AND MEANS COMMITTEE REPORT TO THE DEFICIT REDUCTION TAX ACT OF 1984 (DEFRA); AND HOUSE CONFERENCE REPORT ON THE REVENUE ACT OF 1987 (1987 ACT).

[*General Rule*] Section 304 corresponds to § 304 of the House bill and incorporates the substance of § 115(g)(2) of existing law, [which overruled the result in the *Wanamaker* case above for acquisitions by a subsidiary of a parent's stock from a shareholder of the parent.] As in the House bill, the principle of § 115(g)(2), [relating to parent-sub corporations], is expanded to include cases of so-called "brother-sister corporations." The effect of the operation of § 304 is to characterize as redemptions distributions which are cast in the form of sales. The distributions in redemption shall be examined for taxability subject to the rules of §§ 302 (relating to distributions in redemption of stock) [*see* Secs. 5.2—5.9] and 303 (relating to distributions in redemption of stock to pay death taxes). [*See* Sec. 5.13.]

[*Brother–Sister Redemptions.*] [Section 304(a)(1)] sets forth the new general rule added by this section by providing * * * that in any case in which 1 or more persons who are in control of each of 2 corporations (brother-sister corporations) sell the stock of one of the corporations to another of such corporations the proceeds of such sale shall be considered to be an amount distributed in redemption of the stock of the corporation which purchased the stock. [To the extent the distribution is treated as a § 301 distribution, the] stock thus acquired will be treated as a contribution to the capital of the acquiring corporation made by such shareholder, and accordingly will take as its basis the basis in the hands of the shareholder. [*See* § 304(a)(1).]

[This rule can be illustrated as follows. Individual A, who owns all the stock of corporations X and Y, sells 25% of his stock in X to Y for $100K. The transaction is described in § 304(a)(1) and is treated as a redemption of Y's stock. As set forth below, A is treated as receiving a distribution under § 301 because the transaction does not fall within § 302(b)(1), (2), (3), or (4).]

[*Parent–Subsidiary Redemptions.*] The general rule of present law, preserved in the parent-subsidiary area, is set forth in [§ 304(a)(2).] Under this rule, * * * if a subsidiary corporation purchases outstanding stock of its parent the proceeds of such sale shall be considered to be [a distribution in redemption of the parent's stock].

[This rule can be illustrated as follows. Individual A owns all of the stock of corporation P, which owns all of the stock of corporation S. A sells to S 25% of his P stock for $100K. The transaction is described in § 304(a)(2) and is treated as a redemption of P's stock. As set forth below, A is treated as receiving a distribution under § 301 because the deemed redemption does not fall within §§ 302(b)(1), (2), (3), or (4).]

[*Application of § 302.*] [Section 304(b)] contains special rules for the purpose of applying § 302(b) (relating to redemptions of stock treated as exchanges). In the case of any acquisition of stock to which § 304(a) applies, determinations as to whether the acquisition is, by virtue of § 302(b), to be treated as a distribution in part or full payment in exchange for such stock because such redemption is: (1) not equivalent to a dividend, (2) substantially disproportionate, (3) in complete termination of an interest, [or (4) in partial liquidation] shall be made by reference to the stock of the corporation issuing the stock purchased. [Thus, in an acquisition by a sister corporation of the stock of a brother corporation under § 304(a)(1), the § 302(b) determination is made with reference to the stock of the brother corporation that is sold. In the acquisition by a subsidiary of stock of a parent, the § 302(b) determination is made by reference to the stock of the parent.] In applying § 318(a) (relating to constructive ownership of stock) with respect to § 302(b) for purposes of this paragraph, § 318(a)(2)(C) [and § 318(a)(3)(C)] shall be applied without regard to the 50 percent limitation contained therein.

[*Determination of E & P.*] DEFRA provides that [under § 304(b)(2)] the amount which is a dividend shall be determined as if the property were distributed by the acquiring corporation to the extent of its earnings and profits and then by the corporation whose stock is acquired (the issuing corporation). The transaction would have no effect on the issuing corporation if earnings and profits of the acquiring corporation equal or exceed the amount treated as a distribution in the hands of the shareholders. If the distribution is in excess of the acquiring corporation's earnings and profits, the amount treated as distributed by the issuing corporation will not exceed the earnings and profits of such corporation.

[*Determination of Control.*] [Section 304(c)] provides that control, for purposes of this section, means the ownership of stock possessing at least 50 percent of the total combined voting power of all classes of stock entitled to vote, or at least 50 percent of the total value of shares of all classes of stock. It is possible under this definition for 4 unrelated shareholders to be in control of a corporation, *i.e.,* 2 shareholders may own 50 percent of the total combined voting power and 2 shareholders own 50 percent of the total value of the shares. [*See* § 304(c)(1).]

If a person is in control (within the meaning of the preceding sentence) of a corporation which in turn owns at least 50 percent of the total combined voting power of all stock entitled to vote of another corporation, or owns at least 50 percent of the total value of the shares of stock of another corporation, such person will be deemed to be in control of such other corporation. For example, if individual *X* owns 50 percent of the total combined voting power of corporation *A,* which in turn owns 50 percent of total combined voting power of corporation *B, X* will be deemed to be in control of corporation *B.* [*See* § 304(c)(1).] TEFRA provides that [under § 304(c)(2)], in determining whether corporations are commonly controlled for purposes of § 304, all shareholders transferring stock to a holding company would be counted even though some of them do not receive property other than stock.

[Section 304(c)(3)] provides that the rules of section 318(a) (relating to constructive ownership of stock) shall be applicable for purposes of determining control under [§ 304(c)(1)]. For purposes of the preceding sentence § 318(a)(2)(C) [and § 318(a)(3)(C)] shall be applied without regard to the 50 percent limitation contained therein.

[However, § 304(c)(3)(B), which was amended by DEFRA,] provides a de minimis rule [under which] constructive ownership [does] not apply to and from a corporation and a shareholder owning less than 5 percent in value of the stock of the corporation, for purposes of determining whether or not control exists under § 304. Further, under the bill, where the stock owned by or for a shareholder is less than 50 percent in value of the corporation's stock, attribution of ownership from the shareholder to the corporation is limited to the proportion of the value of the corporation's outstanding stock owned by the shareholder.

[*Section 351/304 Overlap*] The conference agreement [to TEFRA] extends the anti-bailout rules of § 304 * * * of present law to the use of corporations, including holding companies, formed or availed of to avoid such rules. Such rules are made applicable to a transaction that, under present law, otherwise qualifies as a tax-free incorporation under § 351.

[Under § 304(b)(3),] section 351 generally will not apply to transactions described in § 304. Thus, § 351, if otherwise applicable, will generally apply only to the extent such transaction consists of an exchange of stock for stock in the acquiring corporation. [*See* § 304(b)(3)(A).]

[This provision can be illustrated as follows. Individual *A* owns all of the stock of corporation *X.* The *X* stock has a fair market value of

§ 5.12   DISTRIBUTIONS IN REDEMPTIONS UNDER § 304   241

$100K, and A's adjusted basis for the stock is $10K. A transfers all of the stock of X to newly formed corporation Y in exchange for all of Y's stock, which has a value of $75K, plus $25 of cash. In the absence of § 304(b)(3), this transaction would qualify under § 351; A would have a $25K capital gain under § 351(b); the $65K balance of A's gain would be nonrecognized under § 351(a); A's basis for his Y shares would be $10K under § 358; and Y's basis for the X shares would be $35K under § 362(a). As a result of § 304(b)(3)(A), the receipt by A of the $25K cash is treated as a distribution governed by the brother-sister rules of § 304(a)(1), and therefore A has a distribution under § 302(d). The distribution is a dividend to the extent of the earning and profits of Y and X. See § 304(b)(2). Otherwise the results are the same.]

* * * [Under the §§ 351/304 overlap rules of § 304(b)(3),] 304 will not apply to debt incurred to acquire the stock of an operating company and assumed by a controlled corporation acquiring the stock since assumption of such debt is an alternative to a debt-financed direct acquisition by the acquiring company. [See § 304(b)(3)(B).] This exception for acquisition indebtedness applies to an extension, renewal, or refinancing of such indebtedness. The provisions of § 357 (other than § 357(b)) and § 358 apply to such acquisition indebtedness provided they would be applicable to such transaction without regard to § 304. In applying these rules, indebtedness includes debt to which the stock is subject as well as debt assumed by the acquiring company.

* * *

[DEFRA] clarifies that only the nonrecognition provision governing transfers to a corporation in which the shareholders have 80 percent control (§ 351) would be made inapplicable to exchanges involving controlled corporations treated as redemptions. [See § 304(b)(3)(A).] Thus, where the reorganization provisions apply, including those governing the treatment of exchanges by shareholders pursuant to a plan of reorganization, the rules of § 304(a) providing treatment as a stock redemption would not apply.

In order to prevent the "bail out" of earnings by purchasing stock from a related party with borrowed funds and later transferring the stock to a related corporation with the acquisition debt assumed, the bill restricts the exclusion from the rules providing stock redemption treatment for acquisition indebtedness to cases in which the indebtedness is incurred to purchase stock from a person whose stock ownership is not attributable, under § 318(a), to the person transferring the stock to the acquiring corporation. [See § 304(b)(3)(B)(iii).] Attribution resulting from ownership of an option is to be ignored in applying this rule. Finally, the bill provides that where the shareholders receive property consisting of the assumption of acquisition indebtedness in a corporation in which their control is between 50 and 80 percent, the transaction would be subject to redemption and possible dividend treatment under § 304(a).

[Under § 304(b)(3)(C), which was added by TEFRA,] an exception [applies] to the receipt of [stock] in a bank holding company by certain minority shareholders. * * *

[*Treatment of Certain Intra-group Transactions. See § 304(b)(4).*] [Prior to the 1987 Act, a] sale of stock of a subsidiary to a related corporation is generally "deemed" to be a dividend to the extent of earnings and profits of the two corporations, and the statute provides specific rules for the movement of earnings and profits and other aspects related to such a dividend (sec. 304). In determining whether two corporations are related for purposes of this rule, certain "back attribution" rules apply with the result that a corporation can be deemed to receive a dividend or other distribution from another corporation in which it owns no stock (sec. 318). In some instances the deemed dividend rules may produce tax results more favorable than an actual sale or an actual dividend.

* * *

Under the conference agreement [to the 1987 Act], if stock of a member of an affiliated group is transferred to another member of such group in a transaction described in section 304(a) of the Code, proper adjustments must be made in the bases of intragroup stock and in the earnings and profits of each member of the group to the extent necessary to carry out the purposes of this provision. [See § 304(b)(4).]

As one example, if one subsidiary ("X") in a group sells the stock of its appreciated subsidiary ("Y") to a sister corporation ("Z") in an affiliated group, in a transaction that is treated as a dividend of accumulated earnings and profits of the sister corporation Z to the selling corporation X and a contribution of the transferred corporation Y to the capital of sister corporation Z, adjustments must be made to the stock bases of members of the group so that neither X, Z, nor any other corporation that is part of the same chain of includible corporations (excluding the common parent) may thereafter be sold without recognition of the built-in appreciation in the Y stock at the time of the section 304 transaction.

C. ILLUSTRATION OF BROTHER–SISTER SALE UNDER § 304(a)(1)

REVENUE RULING 71–563
1971–2 C.B. 175.

A, an individual, owns 100 shares of corporation X which is all the outstanding stock of X. B, the son of A, owns all the outstanding stock of Corporation Y. A sold 25 shares of stock of X to Y for cash. The purchase price of the X stock was its fair market value. The earnings and profits of Y exceeded the amount of cash paid by Y to A for the X stock.

* * *

§ 5.12   DISTRIBUTIONS IN REDEMPTIONS UNDER § 304   243

A actually owned 100 percent of the stock of *X* before the transaction and by the application of section 318(a)(1)(A) of the Code *A* is considered to have owned all of the stock of *Y* before the transaction. Accordingly, since *Y* acquired the stock of *X* for cash from a person (*A*) in control of both the issuing corporation (*X*) and the acquiring corporation (*Y*), the transaction is considered to be an acquisition of stock by a related corporation within the meaning of section 304(a)(1) of the Code and thus a redemption of the stock of *Y,* the acquiring corporation. See, in this connection, *George L. Coyle, Jr., et al. v. United States,* 415 F.2d 488 (1968), reversing 268 F.Supp. 233 (1967).

* * *

Through the application of section 318(a)(2)(C) of the Code, *B* owns the 25 shares of the stock of *X* held by *Y*. The ownership by *B* of the 25 shares of the stock of *X* is attributed to *A* by reason of application of section 318(a)(1)(A) of the Code. Therefore, after the transaction *A* still owns 100 percent of *X* and there is no complete termination of *A*'s interest in the stock of *X* within the meaning of section 302(b)(3) of the Code nor is there a substantially disproportionate redemption within the meaning of section 302(b)(2) of the Code.

The "not essentially equivalent to a dividend" test of section 302(b)(1) of the Code cannot be met since there has been no meaningful reduction in *A*'s proportionate interest in the stock of *X* as a result of the transaction. * * *

The inapplicability of section 303 and section 302(a) of the Code results in the amount received by *A* being treated, pursuant to section 302(d) of the Code, as a distribution to which section 301 of the Code applies. Accordingly, the distribution is treated as a dividend to *A* from *Y* under section 301(c)(1) and section 316 of the Code.

Section 1.304–2(a) of the regulations provides that with respect to transactions to which section 304(a)(1) of the Code applies, the stock received by the acquiring corporation shall be treated as a contribution to the capital of such corporation and that section 362(a) of the Code is applicable in determining the basis of such stock. Section 1.304–2(a) of the regulations further provides that the transferor's basis for his stock in the acquiring corporation shall be increased by the basis of the stock surrendered by him.

Accordingly, the basis of the *X* stock in the hands of *Y* is the same as the basis of the *X* stock in the hands of *A*. Furthermore, since *A* owns no stock in *Y* directly after the transaction, the basis of the *X* stock surrendered is added to the basis of the 75 shares of *X* stock which *A* owns after the transaction.

Questions

What result if in the above ruling *A* sold all of his *X* stock to *Y*? What would happen to *A*'s basis for his shares? *See Coyle* cited in the ruling. *Cf.* § 1.302–2(c) (Exp. 2).

D. SUBSIDIARY'S ACQUISITION OF PARENT'S STOCK

CAAMANO v. COMMISSIONER
United States Court of Appeals, Fifth Circuit, 1989.
879 F.2d 156.

GEE, CIRCUIT JUDGE:

FACTS

Taxpayers Edward and Janice Caamano, the appellees, were shareholders of McDermott, Inc. McDermott was a Delaware corporation and the parent of McDermott International, its Panamanian, wholly-owned subsidiary. The Board of Directors decided to change the corporate structure to make McDermott, Inc. the subsidiary of McDermott International. The Tax Court stated the motivation for the change was to reduce corporate taxes.

To make the structural change, McDermott International gave 30 million shares of its own common stock and 35 cents per share to the shareholders of McDermott, Inc. in return for 30 million shares of common stock of McDermott, Inc. Since the taxpayers in the today's case were shareholders, they were affected by the transaction. The taxpayers exchanged 50 shares of stock of McDermott, Inc. for $17.50 and 50 shares of McDermott International.

Following the exchange, McDermott International held 68% of the voting power of McDermott, Inc., whose former shareholders then held 90% of the voting power in McDermott International. The Tax Court held that this exchange was not one taxable as a distribution under I.R.C. section 304(a)(2)(A).

ANALYSIS

The Tax Court was faced with deciding whether the McDermott International common stock fell within the meaning of "property" under section 304(a)(2)(A).

As is mentioned above, the primary purpose for the McDermott restructuring was to lower corporate taxes. The prospectus issued by McDermott International stated in relevant part:

> The principal purpose of the reorganization is to enable the McDermott Group to retain * * * earnings from operations outside the United States without subjecting such earnings to United States income tax. This will enable the McDermott Group to compete more effectively with foreign companies by taking advantage of additional opportunities for expansion which require long-term commitments, the redeployment of assets and the reinvestment of earnings.

According to the offer, McDermott International was to exchange one share and 35 cents for each McDermott share. In December 1982,

§ 5.12 DISTRIBUTIONS IN REDEMPTIONS UNDER § 304 245

McDermott International accepted all tenders of individual shareholders owning 99 or fewer shares, and some of the shares tendered by shareholders owning more than 100 shares. The Tax Court found that the taxpayers tendered 50 shares and received 50 shares of McDermott International and $17.50.

Tax treatment of the exchange turns on interpretation of I.R.C. section 304(a)(2). * * *

* * *

The term "control" in this statute requires "ownership of stock possessing at least 50% of the total combined voting power of all classes of stock entitled to vote, or at least 50% of the total value of shares of all classes of stock." I.R.C. section 304(c).

The Tax Court noted that if section 304(a)(2) applied to the taxpayers exchange, then the stock and cash received would have to be treated as a distribution in redemption of the McDermott stock. Section 302 would then be applied to determine the character of the receipts. The parties already agreed that the cash constituted "property" under section 304(a)(2). They also agreed that if section 304 were not to apply to the stock of McDermott International, the receipt of it would be taxed under section 1001.

The term "property" as used in section 304(a)(2)(A) is defined in another section of the Code, namely 317(a), which provides:

> For purposes of this part, the term "property" means money, securities, and any other property; except that such term does not include stock in the corporation making the distribution (or rights to acquire such stock).

Commentators are split on the issue of whether the stock received in a section 304(a)(2) transaction is properly termed "property". The Tax Court, hearing this issue for the first time, held that such stock did not constitute property. * * *

* * *

The Tax Court concluded that McDermott International distributed its own stock to the taxpayers in the December 1982 exchange and that the stock is not properly characterized "property" for the purposes of I.R.C. section 304. The result of the decision is that the property received is taxed under more favorable capital gains rates rather than as dividends. The issue under appeal is controlled by the tax code of 1954, rather than today's code.

The Tax Court noted too that the Conference Report makes it clear that the Congress was concerned with characterization of property subject to both sections 304 and 351. Since the distribution of stock in the instant case was the corporation's own stock, section 304 does not apply. The court's reasoning is persuasive and is reinforced by other courts' interpretations of the purpose of section 304. * * *

* * *

The Commissioner argues, however, that Congress sought to change section 115(g)(2), from which section 304 was derived, after the decision in *Rodman Wanamaker Trust v. Commissioner,* 11 T.C. 365 (1948), affirmed, 178 F.2d 10 (3d Cir.1949). *Wanamaker* treated cash received by the taxpayer from a subsidiary in return for shares of stock in the parent corporation as sale proceeds rather than dividends.

The Tax Court found that while section 304 applied to the cash, the taxpayers did not withdraw assets from either McDermott, Inc. or McDermott International; and the transaction resulted in a change of the ownership structure of the two corporations, which Congress did not intend to prevent under section 304. In addition, the court noted an important change in the language of section 304(a)(2) from that in 115(g)(2): the receipt of property was required for the statute to apply. The court's view of the "property" term is sound in light of the legislative history and purpose for the provision.

* * *

AFFIRMED.

E. PROBLEMS ON SECTION 304 REDEMPTIONS

1. Father, F, and son, S, each own 50 of the 100 outstanding shares of common stock of X corporation. F and S each have an adjusted basis of $50K for the stock. F also owns all of the 100 outstanding shares of common stock of Y corporation, and his basis for the stock is $100K. X has substantial accumulated earnings and profits, but Y has a deficit in earnings and profits. What result if F sells 50 of his 100 shares of Y stock to X for $100K in cash? What result if F sells all of his Y shares to X for $200K in cash? What result if F sells all of his X shares to Y for $100K? What result if S sells all of his X shares to Y for $100K?

2. A owns all of the outstanding shares of P corporation, which in turn owns all of the outstanding shares of S corporation. A's basis for his P shares is $100K and P's basis for S's shares is $50K. S has $25K of accumulated earnings and profits and P has a $10K deficit in earnings and profits. What result if A sells to S 10% of his shares of P for $25K?

3. A owns all the outstanding shares of C corporation. C has substantial earnings and profits. The C shares have a value of $100K, and A's basis for his shares is $25K. A transfers all of his C shares to newly formed corporation X in exchange for all of X shares, which have a value of $60K, plus cash of $40K. X borrowed the cash from a bank. What result to A, C, and X? What result if instead of issuing cash, X distributed its note with an issue price of $40K?

§ 5.13 BRIEF INTRODUCTION TO REDEMPTIONS TO PAY DEATH TAXES

See § 303.

GENERAL EXPLANATION OF ECONOMIC RECOVERY ACT OF 1981
255–257 (1982).

PRIOR LAW

Under section 303, if more than 50 percent of the gross estate (reduced by allowable expenses, losses, and indebtedness) consisted of stock in a single corporation, redemption of all or a portion of that stock to pay estate taxes, funeral expenses, and administration expenses was treated as a sale or exchange subject to capital gains treatment instead of a dividend which would be taxed as ordinary income.

* * *

REASONS FOR CHANGE

* * *

The redemption of stock in certain closely held businesses to pay estate taxes, funeral expenses, and administration expenses is treated as a sale or exchange (eligible for capital gains treatment) instead of a dividend (treated as ordinary income) (sec. 303). However, under prior law, the definition of an interest in a closely held business and the rules for aggregating multiple interests in closely held businesses provided by section 303 were different from the definitions contained in either of the provisions which permitted installment payment of the estate taxes attributable to an interest in a closely held business. The Congress believed that a single definition of a closely held business and a single set of aggregation rules should apply to govern redemptions of closely held business stock to pay estate taxes, funeral expenses, and administration expenses and the installment payment of estate taxes attributable to an interest in a closely held business.

EXPLANATION OF PROVISION

* * *

The Act also makes conforming changes to section 303, which provides special treatment for the redemption of stock in a closely held business to pay estate taxes, funeral expenses, and administration expenses. Under the Act, redemptions will be treated as a sale or exchange eligible for capital gains treatment if the decedent's interest in a closely held corporation comprises at least 35 percent of the decedent's adjusted gross estate. In addition, the section 303 rules regarding the aggregation of interests in two or more corporations are conformed to those in section 6166.

Note

In planning for a redemption under § 303, it is important to coordinate closely with an attorney knowledgeable in estate tax matters.

§ 5.14 EFFECT ON CORPORATION

A. CORPORATION'S TAXABLE INCOME, LOSS AND DEDUCTION ON REDEMPTION

As a result of the repeal of the *General Utilities* doctrine by the Tax Reform Act of 1986, § 311(b) provides that a corporation recognizes gain, but not loss, on the distribution of property with respect to its stock. This rule applies both to dividend distributions under § 301 and to redemption distributions under §§ 302, 303 and 304.

Under § 162(k), a corporation is not allowed a deduction for amounts paid in redemption of stock.

B. EFFECT OF REDEMPTION ON EARNINGS AND PROFITS

See § 312(n)(7)

GENERAL EXPLANATION OF THE DEFICIT REDUCTION ACT OF 1984
181 (1984).

REDEMPTIONS

In the case of a distribution by a corporation in redemption of its own stock, earnings and profits are to be reduced in proportion to the amount of the corporation's outstanding stock that is redeemed. However, it is not intended that earnings and profits be reduced by more than the amount of the redemption.

For example, assume that X corporation has 1,000 shares of $10 par value stock outstanding and that A and B each acquired 500 of original issue shares at a price of $20 per share. Assume further that X corporation, which has operated a profitable services-oriented business since its inception, holds net assets worth $100,000 consisting of cash ($50,000) and appreciated improved real property ($50,000), and has current and accumulated earnings and profits of $50,000. If X corporation distributes $50,000 in cash to A in redemption of A's shares in X corporation, earnings and profits and capital account would each be reduced by $25,000. After the transaction, X corporation would have $25,000 of earnings and profits.

If a corporation has more than one class of stock outstanding, its earnings and profits generally should be allocated among the different classes in determining the amount by which a redemption of all or a part of one class of stock reduces earnings and profits. However, earnings and profits generally should not be allocated to preferred stock which is not convertible and which does not participate to any significant extent in corporate growth. Therefore, a redemption of such preferred stock should result in a reduction of the capital account only, unless the distribution includes dividend arrearages, which will reduce earnings and profits.

Similarly, priorities legally required as between different classes of stock should be taken into account in allocating earnings and profits between classes. For example, assume that corporation X has 1,000 shares of class A common stock and 1,000 shares of class B common stock. Both classes are $10 par value stock and were issued at the same time at a price of $20. The class A common stock has a preference as to dividends and liquidating distributions in a 2:1 ratio to the class B common stock, and only the class B common stock has voting rights. Assume further that corporation X holds net assets worth $210,000 and has current and accumulated earnings and profits of $120,000. If X distributes $140,000 in cash in redemption of all of the class A common stock, earnings and profits should be reduced by $80,000 and capital account by $60,000.

Chapter 6

STOCK DIVIDENDS AND § 306 STOCK

§ 6.1 SCOPE

Stock dividends are distributions by a corporation of its stock as a dividend on its outstanding stock. "Section 306 stock" is certain preferred stock that is distributed as a stock dividend. A holder of Section 306 stock may have ordinary income upon its disposition. Stock dividends and Section 306 stock can arise in reorganizations, which are examined in Parts V and VI. For example, stock dividends are similar to the recapitalization reorganization in which only stock is issued. (*See* Chapter 12.) In both cases, the capital structure of the corporation is modified. In a stock dividend, there is a mere issuance of stock; in a stock recapitalization, there is an exchange of old stock for new stock. Moreover, stock dividend problems can arise in acquisitive reorganizations and in divisive and nondivisive (D) reorganizations. (*See* Chapters 11, 13, and 15.) The purpose of this chapter is to explore the fundamental concepts involving stock dividends; these provisions will also be examined later in the context of various forms of reorganizations.

Sec. 6.2 contains a general description of the stock dividend provisions, and Sec. 6.3 presents a historical sketch of the development of these provisions from the 1913 Act through the Revenue Reconciliation Act of 1990. An understanding of the historical development is crucial in comprehending the operation of these provisions. Sec. 6.4 explores the operation of § 305, which provides for non-taxable treatment for some stock dividends and taxable treatment for others. Sec. 6.4 also covers § 307, which provides certain rules requiring allocation of basis in stock dividends. Sec. 6.5 explores the operation of § 306, which provides that certain preferred stock dividends that are tax-free on receipt under § 305 give rise to ordinary income on disposition. Finally, Sec. 6.6 presents a set of summary problems dealing with stock dividends and § 306.

These issues are explored in greater detail in Chapter 10 of *Federal Taxation of Business Enterprises, supra* Chapter 1, note 1 and in Chapters 7 and 10 of Bittker and Eustice, *Corporations, supra* Sec. 1.4.

§ 6.2 GENERAL DESCRIPTION OF THE STOCK DIVIDEND PROVISIONS

The stock dividend rules are set out in §§ 305, 306, and 307. These provisions are in Part I of subchapter C, dealing with the taxation of distributions by corporations. Section 305(a) sets out the general rule that stock dividends are not included in gross income of the distributee shareholder except as otherwise provided in that section. The general rule of § 305(a) codifies the principles of *Eisner v. Macomber,* 252 U.S. 189, 40 S.Ct. 189, 64 L.Ed. 521 (1920), which held that a common stock dividend on common stock where the common was the only class outstanding could not be taxed under the 16th Amendment. *Eisner v. Macomber* is discussed below in Sec. 6.3, which deals with the historical development of the stock dividend provisions. Section 305(b) and (c) set forth certain exceptions to the general rule of nontaxability in § 305(a). Stock dividends covered by §§ 305(b) and (c) are treated as regular distributions under § 301.

Section 306 is aimed at an abuse known as a preferred stock bail out. In its simplest form, the bail out can occur, absent § 306, by the shareholders' causing a corporation to declare a preferred stock dividend on its outstanding common. The preferred is treated as nontaxable under § 305(a) since it is distributed on common. After receipt of the preferred dividend, the stockholders sell it to a third party, possibly an insurance company, claiming a capital gain on the sale. The corporation then exercises a redemption right and redeems the preferred. The end result is that the shareholders get money out of the corporation in the form of capital gains on the sale of the stock, rather than as ordinary dividends. If the preferred had been redeemed directly from the shareholders, they probably would have had a dividend under § 302(d), but a redemption from the purchasing shareholder is treated as a sale or exchange under § 302(a). *Compare Chamberlin v. Commissioner,* 207 F.2d 462 (6th Cir.1953), *cert. denied* 347 U.S. 918, 74 S.Ct. 516, 98 L.Ed. 1073 (1954), *with Rosenberg v. Commissioner,* 36 T.C. 716 (1961).

Both cases, decided under the law prior to § 306, involved a preferred stock dividend followed by sale and redemption. In *Chamberlin* the Sixth Circuit, reversing the Tax Court, held that (1) the transaction was not taxable under the proportionate interest test then applicable to stock dividends, and (2) since the redemption feature was reasonable, the transaction would be taxed in accordance with its form. On the other hand, in *Rosenberg,* the Tax Court held that the shareholders had a dividend because under *Court Holding* principles the sale was made pursuant to a prearranged plan the "net effect [of which] was the realization of a dividend by the shareholders. * * *"

Under § 306, the recipient of such a preferred stock dividend ("§ 306 stock") is, in general, taxed at ordinary income rates on the disposition of the § 306 stock, to the extent the recipient would have had a dividend if cash had been distributed in place of the preferred.

Under § 307, a portion of the basis of stock on which a nontaxable stock dividend is paid is allocated to the dividend stock.

§ 6.3 HISTORICAL DEVELOPMENT OF THE STOCK DIVIDEND PROVISIONS

Stock dividends were first made specifically taxable by § 2(a) of the 1916 Act, which provided that the amount of the cash value of stock dividends was taxable to shareholders to the extent of a corporation's post–1913 E & P. The Internal Revenue Service, however, had taken the position that stock dividends were taxable under the 1913 Act, which provided that dividends were to be included in gross income.

The Service's position under the 1913 Act was rejected in 1918 by the Supreme Court in *Towne v. Eisner*.[1] In *Towne* a corporation declared a stock dividend on December 17, 1913, transferred a portion of its pre–1913 retained earnings to its capital account, and issued 15,000 shares as a stock dividend representing the capitalized retained earnings. The Service took the position that the distribution of the shares had to be included in the shareholder's gross income by the 1913 Act. The District Court, agreed, holding that the 1913 Act, as construed by the Service, was constitutional. In reversing, the Supreme Court, through Justice Holmes, analogized the question of whether a stock dividend was income or capital to the trust law question of whether stock dividends should be allocated to the income beneficiary or to the remainderman. On this point, the Court said:

> What was said by this court upon the [trust law] question is equally true for the [income tax question]. "A stock dividend really takes nothing from the property of the corporation, and adds nothing to the interests of the shareholders. Its property is not diminished, and their interests are not increased. * * * The proportional interest of each shareholder remains the same. The only change is in the evidence which represents that interest, the new shares and the original shares together representing the same proportional interest that the original shares represented before the issue of the new ones."[2]

Justice Holmes then proceeded to sum up this reasoning. "In short, the corporation is no poorer and the stockholder is no richer than they were before."[3]

The emphasis on the continued proportionality of interest both before and after the stock dividend, which was imported into the income tax law from the trust law by Justice Holmes, has developed as the principal determinant of whether stock dividends are income or capital.

After *Towne*, litigation continued on the question of whether stock dividends were taxable under the 1916 Act, which, unlike the 1913 Act,

---

1. 245 U.S. 418, 38 S.Ct. 158, 62 L.Ed. 372 (1918).
2. *Id.* at 426, 38 S.Ct. at 159.
3. *Id.* at 426, 38 S.Ct. at 159.

specifically provided that stock dividends were taxable out of post–1913 E & P. The litigation under the 1916 Act culminated in 1920 with the Supreme Court decision in *Eisner v. Macomber*.[4] There the court held that the provision in the 1916 Act that specifically provided for the taxation of stock dividends was unconstitutional.

After discussing *Towne* and setting out Justice Holmes' reasoning there, the court proceeded to reexamine the constitutional question of whether a stock dividend fits within the rubric of "income from whatever source derived" as provided in the Sixteenth Amendment. In defining income the Court said:

> Income may be defined as the gain derived from capital, from labor, or from both combined, provided it be understood to include profits gained through a sale or conversion of capital assets.[5]

Emphasizing that under this definition the *gain* must be *derived* from *capital,* the Court went on to say:

> Here we have the essential matter: not a gain accruing to capital, not a growth or increment of value in the investment; but a gain, a profit, something of exchangeable value proceeding from the property, served from the capital however, invested or employed, and coming in, being "derived," that is, received or drawn by the recipient (the taxpayer) for his separate use, benefit and disposal;— that is income derived from property. Nothing else answers the description.[6]

The Court then held that the stock dividend did not constitute income within the Sixteenth Amendment, saying:

> The essential and controlling fact is that the stockholder has received nothing out of the company's assets for his separate use and benefit. * * * Having regard to the very truth of the matter, to substance and not to form, he has received nothing that answers the definition of income within the meaning of the Sixteenth Amendment. * * *[7]

Congress' response to *Eisner v. Macomber* was § 201(d) of the 1921 Act, which read as follows:

> A stock dividend shall not be subject to tax but if after the distribution of any such dividend the corporation proceeds to cancel or redeem its stock at such time and in such manner as to make the distribution and cancellation or redemption essentially equivalent to the distribution of a taxable dividend, the amount received in redemption or cancellation of the stock shall be treated as a taxable dividend to the extent of the earnings or profits accumulated by such corporation after February 28, 1913.

4. 252 U.S. 189, 40 S.Ct. 189, 64 L.Ed. 521 (1920).

5. *Id.* at 207, 40 S.Ct. at 193.

6. *Id.* at 207, 40 S.Ct. at 193.

7. *Id.* at 211, 40 S.Ct. at 194.

The stock dividend provision was amended by the 1924 Act to prohibit certain redemptions before the issuance of stock dividends.

The next congressional action in the stock dividend area came in the 1936 Act and was a response to the Supreme Court's decision in *Koshland v. Helvering*.[8] The taxpayer in *Koshland* held both preferred and common stock in a corporation that paid a common stock dividend on the preferred. Subsequently, the preferred was redeemed at a price that did not exceed the taxpayer's original basis. The Commissioner, relying on his regulations, which were similar to the present § 307, argued that a portion of the taxpayer's original basis of the preferred had to be allocated to the common stock dividend. As a consequence of this allocation, the redemption price exceeded the taxpayer's basis for the preferred, thus giving the taxpayer income on the redemption.

The taxpayer prevailed in her argument that the basis of her preferred should not be allocated to the common stock dividend. The Court's theory was that since the common stock dividend was paid in respect of preferred stock, it was income, not capital, as in *Eisner v. Macomber*, and, therefore, was constitutionally taxable. The Court reasoned that a stock dividend that gives the shareholder an interest different from that which his former stockholding represented is income within the meaning of the constitution. Notwithstanding the Court's decision, stock dividends were not taxable because of Congress' specific exclusion, which originated with the 1921 Act as a response to *Eisner v. Macomber*.

The reasoning in *Koshland* seems to depart from that in *Eisner v. Macomber*, where the court emphasized the lack of separability of corporate assets. In *Koshland*, there was also a lack of separability, but the thrust of the court's reasoning switched to the question of whether the shareholder's interest had changed as a result of the stock dividend. Throughout the *Koshland* litigation, the Commissioner apparently was operating under the assumption that no stock dividend was constitutionally taxable. Thus, *Koshland* was a judicial windfall for the Commissioner, albeit a victory for Mrs. Koshland.

As a result of the *Koshland* decision, the 1936 Act repealed the old stock dividend rule and replaced it with the following provision:

> A distribution made by a corporation to its shareholders in its stock or in rights to acquire its stock shall not be treated as a dividend to the extent that it does not constitute income to the shareholder within the meaning of the Sixteenth Amendment to the Constitution.[9]

This provision opened the door for the courts to draw the line between taxable and non-taxable stock dividends. In the 1936 Act, Congress also added the predecessor of § 305(b)(1), which specifically provided that if shareholders had the election of receiving a stock dividend or other

8. 298 U.S. 441, 56 S.Ct. 767, 80 L.Ed. 1268 (1936).

9. Section 115 of the 1936 Act.

property, the stock dividend was taxable. The stock dividend provisions remained the same until 1954. There were, however, certain judicial developments during this period.

For instance, in 1937 the Supreme Court decided *Helvering v. Gowran*,[10] which dealt with the stock dividend provision of the Revenue Act of 1928. Like the 1921 Act, the 1928 Act provided for nontaxable treatment upon the receipt of a stock dividend. The taxpayer was a common shareholder and had received a preferred stock dividend in respect of his common. About three months after the dividend, the preferred was redeemed. The taxpayer treated the gain as a capital gain on the theory that the holding period for his common was included in the holding period of his preferred. He also allocated, in accordance with the Commissioner's regulations, a portion of his basis in the common to the preferred. The Commissioner disagreed with the taxpayer's treatment and assessed a deficiency on the grounds that the stock dividend was followed by a redemption and was, therefore, substantially equivalent to a taxable dividend. The Supreme Court held that (1) although the taxpayer received a different interest, such interest was not taxable because of the statutory exclusion for stock dividends, (2) the preferred had a zero basis, and (3) the gain was ordinary income because the holding period of the common did not tack to the preferred, and the redemption, in any event, was substantially equivalent to a taxable dividend.

The result of the decisions in *Koshland* and *Gowran* was that the regulation requiring allocation of basis between dividend stock and the stock on which the dividend was paid was valid only for a stock dividend that did not change the shareholder's proportionate interest and, therefore, was not constitutionally taxable.

In the Revenue Act of 1939, Congress enacted the predecessor of § 307.[11] That section overruled the basis results in *Koshland* and *Gowran* by providing that (1) for stock dividends prior to the Revenue Act of 1936, the basis of the old stock would be allocated between the old stock and dividend stock, and (2) for stock dividends subsequent to the 1936 Act, allocation would be required only if the stock dividend was not constitutionally taxable.

In the 1954 Code, Congress replaced the proportionate interest test for determining whether a stock dividend was taxable with § 305, which is described as follows in the Senate Report to the 1969 Tax Reform Act (1969–3 C.B. 423):

> Present law (sec. 305(a)) provides that if a corporation pays a dividend to its shareholders in its own stock (or in rights to acquire its stock), the shareholders are not required to include the value of the dividend in income. There are two exceptions to this general

---

10. 302 U.S. 238, 58 S.Ct. 154, 82 L.Ed. 224 (1937). *See also Helvering v. Griffiths,* 318 U.S. 371, 63 S.Ct. 636, 87 L.Ed. 843 (1943); *Strassburger v. Commissioner,* 318 U.S. 604, 63 S.Ct. 791, 87 L.Ed. 1029 (1943); and *Helvering v. Sprouse,* 318 U.S. 604, 63 S.Ct. 791, 87 L.Ed. 1029 (1943).

11. Section 113(a)(19) of the 1939 Act.

rule. First, stock dividends paid in discharge of preference dividends for the current or immediately preceding taxable year are taxable. Second, a stock dividend is taxable if any shareholder may elect to receive his dividend in cash or other property instead of stock.

These provisions were enacted as part of the Internal Revenue Code of 1954. Before 1954 the taxability of stock dividends was determined under the "proportionate interest test," which developed out of a series of Supreme Court cases, beginning with *Eisner v. Macomber,* 252 U.S. 189 (1920). In these cases the Court held, in general, that a stock dividend was taxable if it increased any shareholder's proportionate interest in the corporation. The lower courts often had difficulty in applying the test as formulated in these cases, particularly where unusual corporate capital structures were involved.

Also, in 1954, Congress adopted § 306 to deal with the preferred stock bail out situation, and included in § 307 the basis allocation provisions initially enacted in the 1936 Act. The Tax Equity and Fiscal Responsibility Act of 1982 amended § 306 to provide that in certain cases § 306 stock can arise in a § 351 transaction.

In the 1969 Tax Reform Act, Congress revised § 305 by adopting a modified version of the proportionate interest test of pre–1954 law. The following excerpt from the Senate Report to the 1969 Tax Reform Act (1969–3 C.B. 423) explains the reasons for the 1969 amendment:

> Soon after the proportionate interest test was eliminated in the 1954 Code, corporations began to develop methods by which shareholders could, in effect, be given a choice between receiving cash dividends or increasing their proportionate interests in the corporation in much the same way as if they had received cash dividends and reinvested them in the corporation. The earliest of these methods involves dividing the common stock of the corporation into two classes, A and B. The two classes share equally in earnings and profits and in assets on liquidation. The only difference is that the class A stock pays only stock dividends and class B stock pays only cash dividends. The market value of the stock dividends paid on the class A stock is equated annually to the cash dividends paid on the class B stock. Class A stock may be converted into class B stock at any time. The stockholders can choose, either when the classes are established, when they purchase new stock, or through the convertibility option whether to own class A stock or class B stock.

* * *

On January 10, 1969, the Internal Revenue Service issued final regulations (T.D. 6990) under which a number of methods of achieving the effect of a cash dividend to some shareholders and a corresponding increase in the proportionate interest of other shareholders are brought under the exceptions in section 305(b), with the result that shareholders who receive increases in proportionate interest are treated as receiving taxable distributions.

General reasons for change.—The final regulations issued on January 10, 1969, do not cover all of the arrangements by which cash dividends can be paid to some shareholders and other shareholders can be given corresponding increases in proportionate interest. For example, the periodic redemption plan described above is not covered by the regulations, and the committee believes it is not covered by the present statutory language (of sec. 305(b)(2)).

Methods have also been devised to give preferred stockholders the equivalent of dividends on preferred stock which are not taxable as such under present law. For example, a corporation may issue preferred stock for $100 per share which pays no dividends, but which may be redeemed in 20 years for $200. The effect is the same as if the corporation distributed preferred stock equal to 5 percent of the original stock each year during the 20–year period in lieu of cash dividends. The committee believes that dividends paid on preferred stock should be taxed whether they are received in cash or in another form, such as stock, rights to receive stock, or rights to receive an increased amount on redemption. Moreover, the committee believes that dividends on preferred stock should be taxed to the recipients whether they are attributable to the current or immediately preceding taxable year or to earlier taxable years.

Finally, the Revenue Reconciliation Act of 1990 amended § 305(b) to provide that any redemption premium arising on the issuance of preferred stock be treated as distributed to the holder of the stock on an economic accrual basis over the period the stock is outstanding.

§ 6.4 THE OPERATION OF § 305

A. SCOPE OF § 305(a)

1. *In General*

Under § 305(a), stock dividends are not included in gross income, except to the extent otherwise provided in § 305(b) and (c). The term "stock" as used in § 305 includes "rights to acquire stock" and the term "shareholder" includes a "holder of rights or of convertible securities." *See* § 305(d).

Section 307 requires that the basis of the stock (old stock) on which is paid a nontaxable stock dividend under § 305(a) (new stock) be allocated between the old and new stock. A special rule is contained in § 307(b) for stock rights. For an illustration of the operation of § 307, *see* Rev.Rul. 56–653, 1956–2 C.B. 185 (need for proper identification of stock sold after stock dividend), Rev.Rul. 71–350, 1971 C.B. 176 (basis of dividend stock received at various times); and Rev.Rul. 74–501, 1974–2 C.B. 98 (treatment of subscription rights).

2. Distribution by Parent of Subsidiary's Stock Rights

REVENUE RULING 80–292
1980–2 C.B. 104.

ISSUE (1). Whether a direct issuance by a subsidiary corporation (S) of nontransferable [subscription] rights to acquire S stock to the shareholders of its parent corporation (P) should be treated, for federal income tax purposes, as a non-taxable distribution of stock rights by S to P under section 305(a) of the Internal Revenue Code followed by a distribution of property by P to its shareholders under section 301.

ISSUE (2). If the transaction is so viewed, whether the constructive distribution by P to its shareholders is taxable under section 301 of the Code on the date the nontransferable rights to purchase stock are constructively distributed by P, or on the date that the shareholder of P exercises the rights to purchase the subsidiary's stock.

* * *

ANALYSIS

ISSUE (1). The subscription rights issued by S appear to represent merely an offer by S to the P shareholders to purchase S stock that was made because those shareholders are likely purchasers of S stock since they own P stock. However, because of the corporate-shareholder relationship of the parties, a question arises as to whether the form of the transaction should determine its characterization for federal income tax purposes. * * *

* * * The value of the right was evidenced by the fact that the S stock was trading at an average price, during the exercise period, which substantially exceeded the 15 dollar subscription price. If S had distributed rights to purchase its stock to P and P in turn distributed those rights, without consideration, to the P shareholders, the distribution to the P shareholders would be a taxable distribution of property, within the meaning of section 317(a), under section 301. Consequently, considering P's control over S it is appropriate to view the transaction, for federal income tax purposes, as a distribution of stock rights by S to P under section 305(a) of the Code followed by a distribution of property, within the meaning of section 317(a), in the form of stock rights to purchase S stock by P to its shareholders subject to the provisions of section 301, especially since this view is consistent with the economic realities of the transaction.

* * *

ANALYSIS

ISSUE (2). Prior to enactment of the 1954 Code, the Supreme Court of the United States held that a corporation's issuance of rights to purchase stock of another corporation did not constitute a dividend, and instead amounted to an offer that could result in dividend treatment only when the offer was accepted by exercise. *Palmer v. Commissioner,* 302 U.S. 63 (1937), 1937-2 C.B. 251. Following enactment of the 1954 Code, the Supreme Court indicated that it has not been authoritatively settled whether an issue of rights to acquire stock of another corporation at less than fair market value itself constitutes a dividend, or whether the dividend occurs only on the exercise of the right. *Commissioner v. Gordon,* 391 U.S. 83 (1968), 1968-2 C.B. 148.

In Rev.Rul. 70-521, the Service concluded that since under the revised 1954 Code treatment of corporate distributions, rights to acquire stock in a corporation other than the distributing corporation are "property" within the meaning of section 317(a) of the Code, a distribution of such rights is taxable as provided under section 301(c) as of the time of distribution. Thus, the *Palmer* doctrine would not be applied so as to avoid ordinary dividend taxation on the distribution of transferable rights to acquire stock of another corporation on the date of distribution.
* * *

HOLDING

ISSUE (2). The constructive distribution by P to its shareholders of nontransferable rights to purchase S stock is a distribution of property on the date of distribution (January 20, 1978), taxable as provided in section 301(c) of the Code. The amount distributed to an individual [or corporate] shareholder of P upon receipt of each right to purchase a share of S stock is the fair market value of each right on the date of distribution. [*See* § 301(b)(1)].

3. Issuance of Poison Pill

REVENUE RULING 90-11

1990-1 C.B. 10.

ISSUE

What are the federal income tax consequences, if any, of a corporation's adoption of a plan as described below, commonly referred to as a "poison pill" plan, which provides the corporation's shareholders with the right to purchase additional shares of stock upon the occurrence of certain events?

FACTS

X is a publicly held domestic corporation. X's board of directors adopted a plan (the "Plan") that provides the common shareholders of X with "poison pill" rights (the "Rights"). The adoption of the Plan constituted the distribution of a dividend under state law. The principal purpose of the adoption of the Plan was to establish a mechanism by which the corporation could, in the future, provide shareholders with rights to purchase stock at substantially less than fair market value as a means of responding to unsolicited offers to acquire X.

The Rights are rights to purchase a fraction of a share of "preferred stock" for each share of common stock held upon the occurrence of a "triggering event," subject to the restrictions described below. The fractional share of preferred stock has voting, dividend, and liquidation rights that make it the economic equivalent of one common share. Until the issuance of the Rights certificates, as described below, the Rights are not exercisable or separately tradable, nor are they represented by any certificate other than the common stock certificate itself. If no triggering event occurs, the Rights expire a years after their creation.

A triggering event is the earlier of the tender offer for, or actual acquisition of, at least b percent of X's common stock by an investor or investor group. If X does not redeem the Rights, as described below, by the end of the c–day period following a triggering event, it must issue Rights certificates to all persons that held X common stock on the date of the triggering event, including the investor or investor group that caused the triggering event. Once issued, the Rights certificates are tradable separately from the common stock. At any time until d days after the actual acquisition by an investor or investor group of at least b percent of X's common stock, X can redeem the Rights without shareholder approval (whether or not X has at that time issued Rights certificates, as described above) for e cents per Right, which is a nominal amount in relation to the current market value of the share of X common stock.

Upon the issuance of the Rights certificates, the Rights can be exercised but, until a "flip-in" or "flip-over" event, the exercise price is several times the trading price of a share of common stock at the time X adopted the Plan. A flip-in event is either (1) the actual acquisition by an investor or inventor group of f percent of X's common stock, or (2) a business combination in which X is the surviving corporation. A flip-over event is a business combination in which X is not the surviving corporation. The occurrence of a flip-in event gives the holder of each Right other than the investor or investor group the right to buy, for g dollars, stock of X that has a value substantially greater than g dollars. A flip-over event gives the holder of each Right other than the investor or investor group the right to buy, for g dollars, stock of the surviving corporation that has a value substantially greater than g dollars.

At the time X's board of directors adopted the Plan, the likelihood that the Rights would, at any time, be exercised was both remote and speculative.

Holding

The adoption of the Plan by X's board of directors does not constitute the distribution of stock or property by X to its shareholders, an exchange of property or stock (either taxable or nontaxable), or any other event giving rise to the realization of gross income by any taxpayer. This revenue ruling does not address the federal income tax consequences of any redemption of Rights, or of any transaction involving Rights subsequent to a triggering event.

* * *

B. THE EXCEPTIONS IN § 305(b)

See §§ 1.305-3, -6.

1. In General

Section 305(b) sets forth five exceptions to the general rule of nontaxability in § 305(a):

(1) Distributions which, at the election of the taxpayer-shareholder, are payable either in stock or property (*see* § 305(b)(1));

(2) Distributions having the result of the receipt of property by some shareholders and an increase in the proportionate interest of other shareholders in the corporation's assets or earnings (*see* § 305(b)(2));

(3) Distributions having the result of the receipt of preferred by some common stock shareholders and the receipt of common stock by other common stock shareholders (*see* § 305(b)(3));

(4) Distributions on preferred stock other than increases in a conversion ratio to avoid dilution (*see* § 305(b)(4)); and

(5) Distributions of convertible preferred unless it is established that such distribution will not have the effect of a receipt of property by some shareholders and an increase in the proportionate interest of other shareholders (*see* § 305(b)(5)).

In each of the above distributions, the stock dividend or the increase in proportionate interest is treated as a § 301 distribution.

The Senate Report to the 1969 Tax Reform Act (1969-3 C.B. 423) explains these exceptions:

Explanation of provisions.—The bill continues (in sec. 305(b)(1)) the provision of present law that a stock dividend is taxable if it is payable at the election of any shareholder in property instead of stock.

The bill provides (in sec. 305(b)(2)) that if there is a distribution or series of distributions of stock which has the result of the receipt of cash or other property by some shareholders and an increase in the proportionate interests of other shareholders in the assets or earnings and profits of the corporation, the shareholders receiving stock are to be taxable (under sec. 301).

For example, if a corporation has two classes of common stock, one paying regular cash dividends and the other paying corresponding stock dividends (whether in common or preferred stock), the stock dividends are to be taxable.

On the other hand, if a corporation has a single class of common stock and a class of preferred stock which pays cash dividends and is not convertible, and it distributes a pro rata common stock dividend with respect to its common stock, the stock distribution is not taxable because the distribution does not have the result of increasing the proportionate interests of any of the stockholders.

In determining whether there is a disproportionate distribution, any security convertible into stock or any right to acquire stock is to be treated as outstanding stock. For example, if a corporation has common stock and convertible debentures outstanding, and it pays interest on the convertible debentures and stock dividends on the common stock, there is a disproportionate distribution, and the stock dividends are to be taxable (under section 301). In addition, in determining whether there is a disproportionate distribution with respect to a shareholder, each class of stock is to be considered separately.

The committee has added two provisions to the House bill (secs. 305(b)(3) and (4)) which carry out more explicitly the intention of the House with regard to distributions of common and preferred stock on common stock, and stock distributions on preferred stock. The first of these provides that if a distribution or series of distributions has the result of the receipt of preferred stock by some common shareholders and the receipt of common stock by other common shareholders, all of the shareholders are taxable (under sec. 301) on the receipt of the stock.

The second of the provisions added by the committee (sec. 305(b)(4)) provides that distributions of stock with respect to preferred stock are taxable (under sec. 301). This provision applies to all distributions on preferred stock except increases in the conversion ratio of convertible preferred stock made solely to take account of stock dividends or stock splits with respect to the stock into which the convertible stock is convertible.

The bill provides (in section 305(b)(5)) that a distribution of convertible preferred stock is taxable (under sec. 301) unless it is established to the satisfaction of the Secretary or his delegate that it will not have the result of a disproportionate distribution described above. For example, if a corporation makes a pro rata distribution on its common stock of preferred stock convertible into common stock at a price slightly higher than the market price of the common stock on the date of distribution, and the period during which the stock must be converted is 4 months, it is likely that a distribution would have the result of a disproportionate distribution. Those stockholders who wish to increase their interests in the corporation would convert their stock into common stock at the end of the 4-month period, and those stockholders who wish to receive cash would sell their stock or have it redeemed. On the other hand, if the stock were convertible for a period of 20 years from the date of issuance, there would be a likelihood that substantially all of the stock would be converted into common stock, and there would be no change in the proportionate interest of the common shareholders.

2. Illustration of Distribution in Lieu of Money Under § 305(b)(1): Immediately Redeemable Preferred

REVENUE RULING 76-258
1976-2 C.B. 95.

Advice has been requested whether a distribution of preferred stock that is immediately redeemable at the option of a shareholder is an election within the meaning of section 305(b)(1) of the Internal Revenue Code of 1954 and, thus, a distribution of property to which section 301 applies.

X corporation distributed pro rata shares of its preferred stock to the holders of its common stock. The preferred stock is redeemable at any time after the distribution at the option of a shareholder. The preferred stock is redeemable at its par value for money.

* * *

Since the preferred stock is redeemable immediately after the distribution at the option of a shareholder, a shareholder may either hold the preferred stock or have it redeemed for money. Thus, the effect of the immediate redeemability feature of the preferred stock is to give a shareholder an election to receive either stock or property within the meaning of section 305(b)(1)(A) and (B) of the Code.

Accordingly, in the instant case, the distribution is treated as a distribution of property to which section 301 of the Code applies.

Note

See also Rev.Rul. 90-98, 1990-2 C.B. 56 (immediately redeemable preferred of Federal Home Loan Banks); Rev.Rul. 78-375, 1978-2 C.B. 130 (elective dividend reinvestment plans).

3. Illustration of Distribution Under § 305(b)(4): Distribution of Common Stock on Convertible Preferred as Anti–Dilution Device

REVENUE RULING 83-42
1983-1 C.B. 76.

Issue

Is the distribution of common stock on convertible preferred stock, as described below, treated as the distribution of property to which section 301 of the Internal Revenue Code applies by reason of section 305(b)(4)?

Facts

X is a corporation that has both common and convertible preferred stock outstanding. The convertible preferred stock has been issued earlier in connection with the acquisition of an unrelated corporation. The convertible preferred stock is convertible into common stock according to a certain conversion ratio. The terms of the convertible preferred stock do not provide for anti-dilution protection by means of an increase in the conversion ratio made solely to take account of a stock dividend or stock split with respect to the stock into which such convertible stock is convertible.

On June 1, 1981, *X* distributed a 10 percent common stock dividend to the holders of its common stock. In addition, *X* distributed shares of its common stock to holders of its convertible preferred stock in order to offset the dilution of the holder's conversion rights. Dilution of the conversion rights of the holders of convertible preferred would have occurred but for the distribution of common stock to them because of the lack of a full adjustment in the conversion ratio of the preferred stock to reflect the stock dividend on the common stock.

Law and Analysis

* * *

The exception contained in section 305(b)(4) of the Code would permit *X* to adjust the conversion ratio of its preferred stock to eliminate the dilution which resulted from the 10 percent common stock dividend on June 1, but it will not permit an actual distribution of stock to the holders of preferred stock, even if undertaken for the same anti-dilution purposes. The "distribution" referred to in section 1.305–5(a) of the regulations is only the deemed distribution which is considered to result when the conversion ratio is adjusted for the purpose described in section 305(b)(4). All other distributions on preferred stock are taxable, as expressly provided by section 305(b)(4).

Holding

The distribution of *X* common stock to holders of its convertible preferred stock is a distribution to which section 301 of the Code applies by reason of section 305(b)(4).

4. *Impact on Earnings and Profit*

The fair market value of a stock dividend covered by § 305(b) or (c) generates dividend treatment to the extent of the corporation's E & P, and E & P is "reduced by the fair market value of the [taxable dividend]." *See* § 1.312–1(d).

C. CERTAIN TRANSACTIONS TREATED AS DISTRIBUTIONS WITHIN § 305(c)

See § 1.305-7.

1. *Background on the First Sentence of § 305(c)*

The first sentence of § 305(c), which was added to the Code by the Tax Reform Act of 1969, authorizes the Secretary to promulgate regulations that treat as a § 301 dividend certain transactions in which a shareholder's "proportionate interest in the earnings and profits or assets of the corporation is increased." The covered transactions are:

(1) a change in conversion ratio;

(2) a change in redemption price;

(3) a difference between redemption price and issue price;

(4) a redemption that is treated as a § 301 distribution; or

(5) any transaction (including a recapitalization) having a similar effect.

The following excerpt from the Senate Report to the 1969 Tax Reform Act (1969-3 C.B. 423) explains this provision:

> The bill provides (in sec. 305(c)) that under regulations prescribed by the Secretary or his delegate, a change in conversion ratio, a change in redemption price, a difference between redemption price and issue price, a redemption treated as a section 301 distribution, or any transaction (including a recapitalization) having a similar effect on the interest of any shareholder is to be treated as a distribution with respect to each shareholder whose proportionate interest is thereby increased. The purpose of this provision is to give the Secretary authority to deal with transactions that have the effect of distributions, but in which stock is not actually distributed.
>
> The proportionate interest of a shareholder can be increased not only by the payment of a stock dividend not paid to other shareholders, but by such methods as increasing the ratio at which his stock, convertible securities, or rights to stock may be converted into other stock, by decreasing the ratio at which other stock, convertible securities, or rights to stock can be converted into stock of the class he owns, or by the periodic redemption of stock owned by other shareholders. It is not clear under present law to what extent increases of this kind would be considered distributions of stock or rights to stock. In order to eliminate uncertainty, the committee has authorized the Secretary or his delegate to prescribe regulations governing the extent to which such transactions shall be treated as taxable distributions.
>
> For example, if a corporation has a single class of common stock which pays no dividends and a class of preferred stock which pays

regular cash dividends, and which is convertible into the common stock at a conversion ratio that decreases each year to adjust for the payment of the cash dividends on the preferred stock, it is anticipated that the regulations will provide in appropriate circumstances that the holders of the common stock will be treated as receiving stock in a disproportionate distribution (under sec. 305(b)(2)).

It is anticipated that the regulations will establish rules for determining when and to what extent the automatic increase in proportionate interest accruing to stockholders as a result of redemptions under a periodic redemption plan are to be treated as taxable distributions. A periodic redemption plan may exist, for example, where a corporation agrees to redeem a small percentage of each common shareholder's stock annually at the election of the shareholder. The shareholders whose stock is redeemed receive cash, and the shareholders whose stock is not redeemed receive an automatic increase in their proportionate interests. However, the committee does not intend that this regulatory authority is to be used to bring isolated redemptions of stock under the disproportionate distribution rule (of sec. 305(b)(2)). For example, a 30 percent stockholder would not be treated as receiving a constructive dividend because a 70 percent stockholder causes a corporation to redeem 15 percent of its stock from him.

* * *

2. Illustrations of the Operation of the First Sentence of § 305(c).

a. *Periodic Redemption Plan Gives Rise to Stock Dividend to Nonredeemed Shareholders*

REVENUE RULING 78-60
1978–1 C.B. 81.

Advice has been requested whether under section 302(a) of the Internal Revenue Code of 1954 the stock redemptions described below qualified for exchange treatment and whether under section 305(b)(2) and (c) the shareholders who experienced increases in their proportionate interests in the redeeming corporation as a result of the stock redemptions will be treated as having received distributions of property to which section 301 applies.

Corporation Z has only one class of stock outstanding. The Z common stock is held by 24 shareholders, all of whom are descendants, or spouses of descendants, of the founder of Z.

In 1975, when Z had 6,000 shares of common stock outstanding, the board of directors of Z adopted a plan of annual redemption to provide a means for its shareholders to sell their stock. The plan provides that Z will annually redeem up to 40 shares of its outstanding stock at a price established annually by the Z board of directors. Each shareholder of Z is entitled to cause Z to redeem two-thirds of one percent of the shareholder's stock each year. If some shareholders choose not to participate fully in the plan during any year, the other shareholders can cause Z to redeem more than two-thirds of one percent of their stock, up to the maximum of 40 shares.

Pursuant to the plan of annual redemption, Z redeemed 40 shares of its stock in 1976. Eight shareholders participated in the redemptions.

* * *

ISSUE 1

None of the redemptions here qualified under section 302(b)(3) of the Code because all of the shareholders who participated in the redemptions continue to own stock of Z. Moreover, none of the redemptions qualified under section 302(b)(2) because none of the shareholders who participated in the redemptions experienced a reduction in interest of more than 20 percent, as section 302(b)(2)(C) requires. Therefore, the first question is whether the redemptions were "not essentially equivalent to a dividend" within the meaning of section 302(b)(1).

* * *

Several of the shareholders of Z experienced reductions in their proportionate interests in Z (taking into account constructive stock ownership under section 318 of the Code) as a result of the 1976 redemptions. If their reductions were "meaningful," they are entitled to exchange treatment for their redemptions under section 302(a). Whether the reductions in proportionate interests were "meaningful" depends on the facts and circumstances.

In this case, an important fact is that the 1976 redemptions were not isolated occurrences but were undertaken pursuant to an ongoing plan for Z to redeem 40 shares of its stock each year. None of the reductions in proportionate interests experienced by Z shareholders as a result of the 1976 redemptions was "meaningful" because the reductions were small and each shareholder has the power to recover the lost interest by electing not to participate in the redemption plan in later years.

Accordingly, none of the 1976 redemptions qualified for exchange treatment under section 302(a) of the Code. All of the redemptions are to be treated as distributions of property to which section 301 applies.

ISSUE 2

Section 1.305–7(a) of the Income Tax Regulations provides that a redemption treated as a section 301 distribution will generally be treated as a distribution to which sections 305(b)(2) and 301 of the Code apply if the proportionate interest of any shareholder in the earnings and profits or assets of the corporation deemed to have made the stock distribution is increased by the redemption, and the distribution has the result described in section 305(b)(2). The distribution is to be deemed made to any shareholder whose interest in the earnings and profits or assets of the distributing corporation is increased by the redemption.

Section 1.305–3(b)(3) of the regulations provides that for a distribution of property to meet the requirements of section 305(b)(2) of the Code, the distribution must be made to a shareholder in the capacity as a shareholder and must be a distribution to which section 301 [or one of several other specified sections] applies. A distribution of property incident to an isolated redemption will not cause section 305(b)(2) to apply even though the redemption distribution is treated as a section 301 distribution.

Section 305 of the Code does not make the constructive stock ownership rules of section 318(a) applicable to its provisions.

The 16 shareholders of Z who did not tender any stock for redemption in 1976 experienced increases in their proportionate interests of the earnings and profits and assets of Z (without taking into account constructive stock ownership under section 318 of the Code) as a result of the redemptions. * * * The 1976 redemptions were not isolated but were undertaken pursuant to an ongoing plan of annual stock redemptions. Finally, the 1976 redemptions are to be treated as distributions of property to which section 301 of the Code applies.

Accordingly, * * * the 16 shareholders of Z who did not participate in the 1976 redemptions are deemed to have received stock distributions to which sections 305(b)(2) and 301 of the Code apply. See examples (8) and (9) of section 1.305–3(c) of the regulations for a method of computing the amounts of the deemed distributions.

Questions

What is the precise holding of Rev.Rul. 78–60? Would the result have changed if the redemptions had been treated as sales or exchanges under § 302(a)? Articulate precisely the reason the 16 nonredeemed shareholders have a distribution under § 301. What is the amount of the distribution to the nonredeemed shareholders, and how is the amount determined? *See* § 1.305–3(e) (Exp. 8).

b. *Isolated Redemptions from Retired–Shareholder Employees*

REVENUE RULING 77–19
1977–1 C.B. 83.

Advice has been requested whether under the circumstances described below, past redemptions and a current redemption by a corporation constitute a periodic redemption plan the effect of which is to increase the proportionate interests of certain shareholders within the meaning of section 305(b)(2) and (c) of the Internal Revenue Code of 1954.

Corporation X is a publicly held corporation with 450,000 shares of common stock outstanding. Its stock has been traded over-the-counter, but no active market for X stock currently exists.

Although no formal plan or resolution has been adopted calling for X to redeem shares of its stock, X, over the previous 36 months, has redeemed 20,000 shares of its common stock in 20 separate transactions. The redeeming shareholders have consisted principally of retiring employees of X or the estates of deceased shareholders. Eighteen of these transactions were distributions in redemption of stock within the meaning of section 302(a) of the Code. The remaining two were distributions to which section 301 applied.

* * *

In the instant case, all of the redemptions that occurred in the past 36 months were principally from retiring employees of X or the estates of deceased shareholders. Also, the redemptions completely terminated the direct ownership of the redeemed shareholders. * * *

Accordingly, in the instant case the redemptions are not deemed, under section 305(c) of the Code, to result in distributions to which sections 305(b)(2) and 301 apply.

D. TREATMENT OF REDEMPTION PREMIUMS ON PREFERRED STOCK UNDER SECOND SENTENCE OF § 305(c)

HOUSE REPORT TO THE REVENUE RECONCILIATION ACT OF 1990

98–100 (1990).

Prior Law

A stockholder is deemed to receive constructive distributions with respect to preferred stock if the stock may be redeemed after a specified time at a price that exceeds the issue price by more than a reasonable redemption premium. Under the present regulations, a redemption premium is considered to be reasonable if it is in the nature of a penalty for a premature redemption and if such premium is not in excess of the amount the corporation would be required to pay for the right to make such premature redemption under market conditions existing at the time of issuance. In addition, the regulations state that a redemption premium not in excess of 10 percent of the issue price on stock that is not redeemable for 5 years from the date of issue is considered to be reasonable (Treas.Reg. sec. 1.305–5(b)(2)).

If preferred stock is considered to have an unreasonable redemption premium, the portion of the premium that is considered to be unreasonable is deemed to be distributed to the preferred stockholder ratably over the time during which such stock cannot be called for redemption. Thus, if preferred stock that is issued with an unreasonable redemption premium also is callable throughout its term, no part of the premium is included in the holder's income until redemption (even if such call right is never exercised).

Treatment of debt issued with original issue discount

If a debt instrument is issued with a stated redemption price at maturity in excess of its issue price, such instrument is considered to be issued with original issue discount (OID). An instrument is not considered to have OID if the stated redemption price at maturity of the instrument exceeds its issue price by an amount that is less than the product of: (1) one-quarter of one percent of the stated redemption price and (2) the number of complete years to maturity. The holder of an OID instrument includes the amount of OID in gross income over the term of the instrument on an economic accrual basis.

REASONS FOR CHANGE

Income from a financial instrument that is payable on a deferred basis generally is better measured by requiring the accrual of such income on an economic basis over the period during which payment is deferred. Accordingly, the economic accrual rules applicable to debt instruments issued with OID also should generally apply to certain preferred stock issued with a redemption premium if the stock will be redeemed, or if it can reasonably be assumed that the stock will be redeemed, on a fixed date. Also, it is recognized that certain preferred stock issued with a redemption premium resembles debt issued at a discount.

It is appropriate to allow a higher threshold for purposes of determining whether callable preferred stock is subject to these new rules because the decision to redeem the stock rests with the issuer, and not the holder, of the stock.

EXPLANATION OF PROVISION

General rule

The bill generally requires the entire amount of a redemption premium on certain preferred stock to be treated as being distributed to the holders of such preferred stock on an economic accrual basis over the period that the stock is outstanding (the economic accrual rule). An instrument generally will be considered to have a redemption premium for this purpose if the redemption price at maturity exceeds the issue price by an amount that equals or exceeds the product of: (1) one-quarter of one percent of the redemption price and (2) the number of complete years to maturity (the OID de minimis rule).

The economic accrual rule and the OID de minimis rule apply to preferred stock that is subject to a mandatory redemption or that is puttable by the holder. The redemption premium on preferred stock that is subject to a mandatory redemption or that is puttable will not fail to be subject to the economic accrual rule and the OID de minimis rule merely because the stock is also callable at the issuer's option.

It is understood that Treasury regulations will provide special rules consistent with the OID rules in order to determine the maturity date and price of puttable preferred stock.

Special rules for callable preferred stock

In general, the OID de minimis rule will not apply to preferred stock that is callable solely at the option of the issuer (unless such stock is subject to a mandatory redemption or is puttable). Nonetheless, the economic accrual rule will apply to the entire call premium on such stock if such premium is considered to be unreasonable under regulations in effect without regard to this provision. * * *

E. STRIPPED PREFERRED

See § 305(e).

HOUSE REPORT TO THE REVENUE RECONCILIATION ACT OF 1993
202 (1993).

PRESENT LAW

In general, if a bond is issued at a price approximately equal to its redemption price at maturity, the expected return to the holder of the bond is in the form of periodic interest payments. In the case of original issue discount ("OID") bonds, however, the issue price is below the redemption price, and the holder receives part or all of his expected return in the form of price appreciation. The difference between the issue price and the redemption price is the OID, and a portion of the OID is required to be accrued and included in the income of the holder annually. Similarly, for certain preferred stock that is issued at a discount from its redemption price, a portion of the redemption premium must be included in income annually.

A stripped bond (i.e., a bond issued with interest coupons some of which are subsequently "stripped" so that the ownership of the bond is separated from the ownership of the interest coupons) generally is treated as a bond issued with OID equal to (1) the stated redemption price of the bond at maturity minus (2) the amount paid for the stripped bond.

If preferred stock is stripped of some of its dividend rights, however, the stripped stock is not subject to the rules that apply to stripped bonds or to the rules that apply to bonds and certain preferred stock issued at a discount.

REASONS FOR CHANGE

The committee believes that the purchaser of stripped preferred stock may, in effect, be purchasing at a discount the right to a fixed amount payable at a future date. The committee is concerned that taxpayers may purchase stripped preferred stock as a means of converting ordinary income to capital gains. Therefore, under these circumstances, the committee believes that the rules that apply to stripped bonds provide the appropriate tax treatment.

EXPLANATION OF PROVISION [See § 305(e)]

The bill treats the purchaser of stripped preferred stock (and a person who strips preferred stock and disposes of the stripped dividend rights) in generally the same way that the purchaser of a stripped bond would be treated under the OID rules. Thus, stripped stock is treated like a bond issued with OID equal to (1) the stated redemption price of the stock minus (2) the amount paid for the stock. The discount accrued under the provision is treated as ordinary income and not as interest or dividends.

Stripped preferred stock is defined as any preferred stock where the ownership of the stock has been separated from the right to receive any dividend that has not yet become payable. The provision applies to stock that is limited and preferred as to dividends, does not participate in corporate growth to any significant extent, and has a fixed redemption price.

* * *

§ 6.5 OPERATION OF § 306

A. ORDINARY INCOME UNDER § 306(a)

A distribution of preferred stock in respect of common stock is nontaxable under § 305(a), unless it falls within one of the exceptions in § 305(b) or (c). Preferred that is treated as a tax-free distribution under § 305(a) is "section 306 stock," as defined in § 306(c). The definition of § 306 stock is explored below. As a consequence, the amount realized on the disposition of the preferred is treated as ordinary income to the extent of "such stock's ratable share of the amount which would have been a dividend at the time of distribution if (in lieu of § 306 stock) the corporation had distributed money in an amount equal to the fair market value of the stock at the time of distribution." See § 306(a)(1)(A). No loss can be recognized. See § 306(a)(1)(C). Any excess of the amount realized over the sum of the amount treated as ordinary income plus the adjusted basis of the stock is treated as gain from the sale of the stock. This rule does not apply to transactions excepted by § 306(b) or to redemptions. The § 306(b) exceptions are discussed below. If the stock is disposed of in a redemption (other than in a termination of interest under § 302(b)(3)), the full amount realized is treated as a distribution of property under § 301. See § 306(a)(2).

The Senate Report to the 1954 Code explains the operation of these provisions:

> [Section 306(a)] prescribes the general rules as to the tax treatment of the disposition or redemption of section 306 stock. [Section 306(a)(1)] relates to dispositions of such stock other than by redemption. The term disposition includes sales and also includes pledges of the stock under certain circumstances, particularly where the pledgee can look only to the stock itself as his security. If

the section 306 stock is sold the amount realized is treated as gain from the sale of property which is not a capital asset to the extent of the stock's ratable share of earnings and profits of the issuing corporation at the time of its distribution. Thus, assume that a shareholder owns 1,000 shares of the common stock of a corporation and that they are the only shares of its stock outstanding. Assume also that the shareholder acquires 1,000 shares of preferred stock with a fair market value for each share of $100 issued to him as a dividend on his common stock at a time when the corporation has $100,000 in accumulated earnings. There is no tax to the shareholder at the time of receipt of the stock but it is characterized as section 306 stock. If it is sold for $100,000 the shareholder will be taxed on the entire sale proceeds at the rates applicable to ordinary income.

The determination of the section 306 stock's ratable share of earnings at the time of its distribution is to be made in accordance with its fair market value at such time. It should also be noted that it would be immaterial that $100,000 were distributed to the stockholder as a dividend on his common stock subsequent to the distribution of the stock dividend. The stock dividend is nevertheless section 306 stock because of the corporate earnings in existence at the time of its distribution. A shareholder may, in such a case, only dispose of his section 306 stock through redemption by the issuing corporation and thereby avoid its inherent ordinary income characteristics. See discussion of paragraph (2) of subsection (a), below.

[Section 306(a)(1)(B)] provides that if the amount received from the sale of section 306 stock exceeds the amount treated as ordinary income, such excess, shall, to the extent of gain, be accorded capital-gain treatment. Thus, if in the preceding example the stock had been sold for $110,000 (instead of $100,000) the $10,000 would be taxed at the rates applicable to capital gain [, but only to the extent that $110,000 exceeds the sum of (1) the $100,000 included as ordinary income, plus (2) the basis of the stock. If, for instance, the basis under § 307 for the preferred was $4,000, then the shareholder's capital gain would be $6,000.] [Section 306(a)(1)(C)] provides that in no event is any loss to be allowed with respect to the sale of section 306 stock.

[Section 306(a)(2)] provides that if the section 306 stock is redeemed, the amount realized is to be treated as a distribution of property to which section 301 applies. Thus, if the section 306 stock was distributed at a time when there was an amount of corporate earnings attributable to it equal to its full fair market value at that time, but if there are no corporate earnings, accumulated or current, at the time of redemption, the amount received on redemption of section 306 stock would be treated under section 301 as a return of capital. No loss would be allowed in such a case under section 301.

It should be noted that where section 306 stock is redeemed the rules of section 302(a) and (b), relating to cases where amounts received in redemption of stock will be taxed at capital gain rates, are not applicable. Section 306 operates independently of section 302 and contains its own rules concerning instances where your committee does not consider it appropriate to tax proceeds received with respect to section 306 stock at the rates applicable to ordinary income.

B. SECTION 306(b) EXCEPTIONS TO THE ORDINARY INCOME RULES OF § 306(a)

1. *In General*

Section 306(b) provides exceptions to the ordinary income rules of § 306(a) for certain types of dispositions of § 306 stock. Under § 306(b), § 306(a) does not apply where:

(1) The shareholder's interest is terminated in certain sales to third parties or redemptions under § 302(b)(3) (*see* § 306(b)(1));

(2) The shareholder's interest is redeemed in a complete liquidation (*see* § 306(b)(2));

(3) The § 306 stock is disposed of in a nonrecognition transaction (*see* § 306(b)(3)); or

(4) The transaction is not one of tax avoidance (*see* § 306(b)(4)).

2. *Section 306(b)(4) Transaction Not in Avoidance of Tax*

See § 1.306–2(b)(3).

The Senate Report to the 1954 Code explains the operation of and purposes behind § 306(b)(4):

[Section 306(b)(4)] excepts from the general rule of subsection (a) those transactions not in avoidance of this section where it is established to the satisfaction of the Secretary that the transaction was not in pursuance of a plan having as one of its principal purposes the avoidance of Federal Income Tax. [Section 306(b)(4)(A)] applies to cases where the distribution itself, coupled with the disposition or redemption was not in pursuance of such a plan. This subparagraph is intended to apply to the case of dividends and isolated dispositions of section 306 stock by minority shareholders who do not in the aggregate have control of the distributing corporation. In such a case it would seem to your committee to be inappropriate to impute to such shareholders an intention to remove corporate earnings at the tax rates applicable only to capital gains.

[Section 306(b)(4)(B)] applies to a case where the shareholder has made a prior or simultaneous disposition (or redemption) of the underlying stock with respect to which the section 306 stock was issued. Thus if a shareholder received a distribution of 100 shares of section 306 stock on his holdings of 100 shares of voting common stock in a corporation and sells his voting common stock before he disposes of his section 306 stock, the subsequent disposition of his section 306 stock would not ordinarily be considered a tax avoidance disposition since he has previously parted with the stock which allows him to participate in the ownership of the business. However, variations of the above example may give rise to tax avoidance possibilities which are not within the exception of [section 304(b)(4)(B)]. Thus if a corporation has only one class of common stock outstanding and it issues stock under circumstances that characterize it as section 306 stock, a subsequent issue of a different class of common having greater voting rights than the original common will not permit a simultaneous disposition of the section 306 stock together with the original common to escape the rules of subsection (a) of section 306.

C. DEFINITION OF § 306 STOCK IN § 306(c).

See § 1.306-3.

1. *In General*

The starting point for any problem under § 306 is the determination of whether stock is considered "§ 306 stock" under § 306(c). Four types of stock are treated as § 306 stock:

(1) Stock, other than common, that was distributed as a dividend and was excluded from gross income under § 305(a) (*see* § 306(c)(1)(A));

(2) Stock, other than common, (a) received in a reorganization or in a § 355 distribution that has "substantially" the same effect as a stock dividend, or (b) received in a reorganization or § 355 distribution in exchange for § 306 stock (*see* § 306(c)(1)(B));

(3) Stock that has a basis determined by reference to the basis of § 306 stock (*see* § 306(c)(1)(C)); and

(4) Preferred stock issued in § 351 transactions involving formation of holding companies (*see* § 306(c)(3)).

The treatment of § 306 stock issued in reorganizations and § 355 distributions specified in paragraph (2) above is taken up in Chapters 11 and 13, respectively.

Section 306 stock does not include, "any stock no part of the distribution of which would have been a dividend at the time of the distribution if money had been distributed in lieu of the stock." *See* § 306(c)(2). Under § 306(c)(4), the § 318 attribution of ownership rules apply for purposes of determining whether preferred stock issued in a corporate reorganization or in a § 351 transaction is § 306 stock. The scope of this § 351/§ 306 issue is discussed further below.

The Senate Report to the 1954 Code explains the operation of § 306(c):

> Section 306(c) sets forth the definition of section 306 stock. [Section 306(c)(1)(A)] provides that section 306 is any stock (other than common stock issued with respect to common stock) distributed to the seller thereof, if by reason of section 305(a) any part of such distribution was not includible in the gross income of the shareholder. Thus, a stock dividend (other than a dividend in common stock issued with respect to common stock) is considered section 306 stock * * *
>
> [Section 306(c)(1)(B)] provides that stock received in connection with a plan of reorganization within the meaning of section 368(a), or in a disposition or exchange to which section 355 applies, is section 306 stock, if the effect of the transaction was substantially the same as the receipt of a stock dividend. The subparagraph also makes it clear that section 306 stock exchanged for section 306 stock shall retain its characteristics. This subparagraph provides that common stock received as a result of a corporate reorganization or separation shall not be considered section 306 stock in any event. Thus, the shareholder is always permitted an opportunity to downgrade preferred stock characterized as section 306 stock in his hands by causing a recapitalization and exchange of such stock for common stock. [Section 306(c)(1)(B) is examined further in Sec. 11.18.]
>
> [Section 306(c)(1)(C)] provides that section 306 stock includes stock the basis of which in the hands of the shareholder selling or otherwise disposing of such stock is determined by reference to the basis of section 306 stock. [Section 306(c)(1)(C)] however, is limited to cases other than those to which subparagraph (B) is applicable, that is, the reorganization type of case which would otherwise be within this subparagraph. Under this subparagraph common stock could be section 306 stock. Thus, if a person owning section 306 stock transfers it to a corporation controlled by him in exchange for common stock, the common stock received would be section 306 stock in his hands and subject to the rules of subsection (a) on its disposition. Subparagraph (C) also would remove from the category of section 306 stock, stock owned by a decedent at death since such stock takes a new basis under section 1014.
>
> [Section 306(c)(2)] excepts from the definition of section 306 stock any stock no part of the distribution of which would have been a dividend at the time of distribution if money had been distributed in lieu of the stock. Thus, preferred stock received at the time of original incorporation would not be section 306 stock. Also, stock issued at the time an existing corporation had no earnings and profits would not be section 306 stock.

2. Section 306 Stock on Formation of Holding Company Under § 351—Application of § 304 Principles

a. *The General Principle*

CONFERENCE REPORT TO TAX EQUITY AND FISCAL RESPONSIBILITY ACT OF 1982
541–542 (1982).

* * *

Another device to bail out earnings is to cause a corporation to issue preferred stock as a nontaxable stock dividend to its shareholders. A sale of the preferred stock at capital gain rates would not dilute the interests of the selling shareholders in future corporate growth while they would receive an amount representing corporate earnings. Preferred stock issued under these circumstances (described as section 306 stock) is tainted under present law so that its subsequent sale or redemption results in ordinary income to the shareholder. This provision does not taint stock of a newly formed corporation issued in a tax-free transaction in exchange for stock in a corporation with earnings and profits. Thus, creation of a holding company issuing both common and preferred stock offers the same bailout opportunity as a preferred stock dividend but does not result in tainted section 306 stock.

* * *

Under the conference agreement, section 306 is made applicable to preferred stock acquired in a section 351 exchange if, had money in lieu of stock been received, its receipt would have been a dividend to any extent. [*See* § 306(c)(3).] Thus, if the receipt of cash by the shareholder rather than stock would have caused section 304 as amended by the bill, rather than section 351, to apply to such receipt, some or all of the amount received might have been treated as a dividend. [*See* § 304(b)(3) and Sec. 5.12.] In such case, the preferred stock acquired in the exchange will be § 306 stock.

b. *The Dividend Rule*

See § 306(c)(3) (second sentence).

HOUSE WAYS AND MEANS COMMITTEE REPORT TO THE TAX REFORM BILL OF 1983
321–22 (1983).

[The following discussion addresses the issue of how much earnings and profits exist for purposes of determining treatment of preferred stock received on the formation of a holding company.]

PRESENT LAW

If, in lieu of the receipt of cash or other property, shareholders who transfer stock in a controlled corporation to another controlled corporation receive in exchange preferred stock in a transaction in which gain or loss is not recognized, subsequent disposition of the preferred stock may result in ordinary income to the shareholders, if receipt of cash in lieu of stock would have been treated as a dividend. [See § 306(c)(3).] The determination of the character of the hypothetical receipt of cash is made under the rules providing for stock redemption and possible dividend treatment when stock is sold to a commonly controlled corporation. [See § 304.] This extension of the treatment generally applicable to preferred stock dividends to preferred stock received in an exchange with a controlled corporation to which the nonrecognition rules apply was adopted by TEFRA. However, the preferred stock affected by this rule may be disposed of in a stock redemption; whether ordinary income results from such redemption is determined by treating it solely as a distribution by the acquiring corporation. The acquiring corporation may be a corporation newly formed or may have little or no earnings and profits so that the distribution would not constitute a dividend.

EXPLANATION OF PROVISION

The bill provides that the dividend equivalence test applied with respect to a hypothetical distribution of cash will be applicable at the time of redemption or other disposition of the preferred stock (or stock whose basis is determined by reference to the basis of the preferred stock) as well as at the time of its receipt. [See § 306(c)(3) (second sentence).] Under this test, treatment of the redemption of the preferred stock as a dividend to the shareholders will be determined with reference to the earnings and profits of the corporation the stock of which was acquired as well as the acquiring corporation.

3. Determining Whether Stock Is "Other Than Common"

Section 306 stock is stock "other than common stock." Normally such stock is preferred; however, nonpreferred stock may be § 306 stock. In Rev.Rul. 57–132, 1957–1 C.B. 115, the Service held that nonvoting and redeemable common stock was § 306 stock. In Rev.Rul. 76–386, 1976–2 C.B. 95, however, the Service distinguished Rev.Rul. 57–132, holding that voting common subject to the corporation's right of first refusal was not § 306 stock. In Rev.Rul. 76–387, 1976–2 C.B. 96 the Service held that nonvoting common issued in a recapitalization was not § 306 stock. There the Service reasoned:

In determining whether newly issued stock is "common stock" for purposes of section 306 of the Code, the bailout abuse Congress sought to preclude by enactment of that section provides guidance. A bailout occurs if the stockholders can dispose of their stock in question without a loss of voting control and interest in the unrestricted equitable growth of the corporation.

While the class A nonvoting common stock in the instant case can be disposed of without a loss of voting control in *X*, it cannot be disposed of without the shareholder parting irretrievably with an interest in the unrestricted equitable growth of X represented by such stock.

Accordingly, the class A nonvoting common stock in the instant case is "common stock" for purposes of section 306(c)(1)(B) of the Code.

§ 6.6 SUMMARY PROBLEMS ON STOCK DIVIDENDS

1. Corporation X is wholly owned by individual A. At the time of its initial capitalization X issued to A 100 shares of common and 100 shares of preferred. Both the common and preferred have an adjusted basis of $75K and a fair market value of $100K. X has $100K of E & P. What result to A and X under the following circumstances?

(a) X distributes a stock dividend of 50 common shares in respect of the outstanding common?

(b) X distributes a stock dividend of 50 common shares in respect of the outstanding preferred?

(c) X distributes a stock dividend of 50 preferred shares with a fair market value of $20K in respect of the common?

(d) One year after the distribution in (c), A sells the dividend stock for $25K? For $85K? *See* § 1.312–1(d).

2. Corporation Y is owned by 20 unrelated individuals, each of whom owns 5% of the stock. Only common is outstanding. Y has a redemption plan pursuant to which it will redeem a maximum of 1% of its stock each year with any one shareholder being limited to 2% of *his holdings*. Thus, for example, if all shareholders elected to participate in the redemption, each shareholder could have 1% of his stock redeemed, and if the holders of half the shares elected to participate, each could have 2% of his holdings redeemed. What results under the plan if every year all the shareholders elect? What result if every year the same ten shareholders elect and each has 2% of his stock redeemed?

3. Corporation X has 100 shares of common stock outstanding. Shareholders A and B each own 50 shares. X redeems 25 of A's shares. What results to A and B?

4. Individual A owns all of the stock of corporation X which has only common outstanding. A forms a new holding company H and transfers all of his X stock to H in exchange for preferred and common. What result to A?

5. Corporation A issues for $70K preferred stock with a redemption price of $100K. The preferred pays dividends of 3% per year and is redeemable in ten years. In general, what result to the holder of the preferred?

6. Individual A incorporates his sole proprietorship by transferring the assets and liabilities to a newly formed corporation in exchange for all of the corporation's common and preferred shares. What result to A?

Chapter 7

INTRODUCTION TO ACCUMULATED EARNINGS TAX AND PERSONAL HOLDING COMPANY TAX

§ 7.1 SCOPE

This chapter considers the accumulated earnings tax and the personal holding company tax. These two penalty taxes apply to certain C corporations that retain income. Sec. 7.2 introduces these taxes; Sec. 7.3 examines the basic aspects of the accumulated earnings tax; and Sec. 7.4 considers the basic aspects of the personal holding company tax.

The accumulated earnings tax is addressed in greater detail in Chapter 12 of *Federal Taxation of Business Enterprises, supra* Chapter 1, note 1, and the personal holding company tax is covered in Chapter 13. Both of these taxes are examined in Chapter 8 of Bittker and Eustice, *Corporations, supra* Sec. 1.4.

§ 7.2 INTRODUCTORY NOTE ON THE ACCUMULATED EARNINGS TAX AND THE PERSONAL HOLDING COMPANY TAX

The maximum rate of tax on dividends paid to individual shareholders is 36.9%. *See* § 1. The maximum rate of tax on the taxable income of subchapter C corporations is 35%. *See* § 11. The maximum combined corporate and individual rate of tax on distributed corporate earnings is approximately 61%. For example, $100 of taxable income at the corporate level can produce a tax of $35, leaving $65 available for distribution to the shareholders. Upon distribution of the $65, the maximum individual rate of 39.6%, say 40% would produce a tax of $26. Thus, the maximum double tax on the $100 of earnings is $61, leaving only $39 after tax.

In order to avoid the double tax, a shareholder may accumulate earnings in his subchapter C corporation, and then realize on the earnings in a capital gain transaction, such as a liquidation or sale of the stock. Such a transaction would be subject to a maximum rate of 28%. *See* § 1(h). Also, under § 1014, the basis of stock is stepped up to the date of death value, thereby reducing the amount of capital gains on sale or liquidation.

The accumulated earnings tax (§ 531 et seq.) and the personal holding company tax (§ 541 et seq.) are designed to prevent the accumulation of earnings in a corporation for the purpose of tax avoidance. Both taxes are penalty taxes imposed at the corporate level and can be avoided if the corporation distributes its earnings. Neither the accumulated earnings tax nor the personal holding company tax applies to S corporations. *See* § 1363(a).

§ 7.3 THE ACCUMULATED EARNINGS TAX

A. IMPOSITION OF THE TAX

Section 531 imposes an accumulated earnings tax ("AET") for each taxable year on the "accumulated taxable income * * * of every corporation described in § 532 * * *". The tax is equal to 39.6% of the corporation's accumulated taxable income ("ATI"). The tax is in addition to all other taxes imposed by the Code.

1. *Corporations Subject to the Tax*

Section 532(a) specifies those corporations that are subject to the AET. The tax applies to "every corporation (other than those described in [§ 532(b)]) formed or availed of *for the purpose of* avoiding the income tax with respect to its shareholders or the shareholders of any other corporation, by permitting earnings and profits to accumulate instead of being divided or distributed." Thus, the AET does not apply unless "the purpose" of the accumulation is tax avoidance. This purpose requirement is explored below.

Section 532(b) excepts from the AET, personal holding companies, foreign personal holding companies, tax exempt corporations, and passive foreign investment companies. The AET applies to "any domestic or foreign corporation" that is not specifically excepted by § 532(b). *See* § 1.532–1(a)(1). Also, § 1.532–1(a)(2) provides that the tax "may apply if the avoidance is accomplished through the formation or use of one corporation or a chain of corporations." The AET applies to both private and public corporations. *See* § 532(c).

2. *Evidence of a Purpose to Avoid Tax*

Section 533(a) sets out a rule for determining whether a corporation is "formed or availed" of for the proscribed tax avoidance purpose:

[T]he fact that the earnings and profits of a corporation are permitted to accumulate beyond the reasonable needs of the business shall be determinative of the purpose to avoid the income tax with respect to the shareholders, unless the corporation by the preponderance of the evidence shall prove to the contrary.

Section 1.533-1(a)(2) provides that the "existence or nonexistence of the purpose to avoid income tax with respect to the shareholders may be indicated by circumstances other than the conditions specified in section 533." The determination is made by reference to the "particular circumstances of each case." This regulation sets out three factors to be considered in making this determination:

> (i) Dealings between the corporation and its shareholders, such as withdrawals by the shareholders as personal loans or the expenditure of funds by the corporation for the personal benefit of the shareholders,

> (ii) The investment by the corporation of undistributed earnings in assets having no reasonable connection with the business of the corporation (see § 1.537-3), and

> (iii) The extent to which the corporation has distributed its earnings and profits.

Section 533(b) provides that "[t]he fact that a corporation is a mere holding or investment company shall be prima facie evidence of the purpose to avoid the income tax with respect to the shareholders." Section 1.533-1(b) provides guidance for determining whether a corporation is a "mere holding or investment company":

> A corporation having practically no activities except holding property and collecting the income therefrom or investing therein shall be considered a holding company within the meaning of section 533(b). If the activities further include, or consist substantially of, buying and selling stocks, securities, real estate, or other investment property (whether upon an outright or marginal basis) so that the income is derived not only from the investment yield but also from profits upon market fluctuations, the corporation shall be considered an investment company within the meaning of section 533(b).

3. The Interaction Between §§ 532 and 533: "The Purpose" to Avoid Taxes

a. Introduction

Under § 532(a), the AET applies to every corporation "formed or availed of for *the purpose* of avoiding the income tax with respect to its shareholders." Under § 533(a), an accumulation beyond the reasonable needs of the business is determinative of "*the purpose* to avoid the income tax with respect to shareholders." In *United States v. Donruss Co.*, set out immediately below, the Supreme Court addressed the meaning of "the purpose" as used in §§ 532(a) and 533(a).

b. *Meaning of "The Purpose" to Avoid Income Taxes*

UNITED STATES v. DONRUSS CO.
Supreme Court of the United States, 1969.
393 U.S. 297, 89 S.Ct. 501, 21 L.Ed.2d 495.

Mr. Justice Marshall delivered the opinion of the Court.

* * *

The dispute before us is a narrow one. The Government contends that in order to rebut the presumption contained in § 533(a), the taxpayer must establish by the preponderance of the evidence that tax avoidance with respect to shareholders was not "one of the purposes" for the accumulation of earnings beyond the reasonable needs of the business. Respondent argues that it may rebut that presumption by demonstrating that tax avoidance was not the "dominant, controlling, or impelling" reason for the accumulation. * * *

We conclude from an examination of the language, the purpose, and the legislative history of the statute that the Government's construction is the correct one. Accordingly, we reverse the judgment of the court below and remand the case for a new trial on the issue of whether avoidance of shareholder tax was one of the purposes of respondent's accumulations.

* * *

III.

[T]he legislative history of the accumulated earnings tax demonstrates a continuing concern with the use of the corporate form to avoid income tax on a corporation's shareholders. Numerous methods were employed to prevent this practice, all of which proved unsatisfactory in one way or another. Two conclusions can be drawn from Congress' efforts. First, Congress recognized the tremendous difficulty of ascertaining the purpose of corporate accumulations. Second, it saw that accumulation was often necessary for legitimate and reasonable business purposes. It appears clear to us that the congressional response to these facts has been to emphasize unreasonable accumulation as the most significant factor in the incident of the tax. The reasonableness of an accumulation, while subject to honest difference of opinion, is a much more objective inquiry, and is susceptible of more effective scrutiny, than are the vagaries of corporate motive.

Respondent would have us adopt a test that requires that tax avoidance purpose need be dominant, impelling, or controlling. It seems to us that such a test would exacerbate the problems that Congress was trying to avoid. Rarely is there one motive, or even one dominant motive, for corporate decisions. Numerous factors contribute to the action ultimately decided upon. Respondent's test would allow taxpayers to escape the tax when it is proved that at least one other motive was equal to tax avoidance. We doubt that such a determination can be made with any accuracy, and it is certainly one which will depend almost exclusively on the interested testimony of corporate management. Respondent's test would thus go a long way toward destroying the presumption that Congress created to meet this very problem.

* * *

Reversed and remanded.

Questions

A, the sole shareholder of corporation X, purposefully causes X to retain earnings beyond the reasonable needs of the business. What facts could save X from the imposition of an accumulated earnings tax?

4. Burden of Proof

Section 534 provides a mechanism for the corporation involved in an AET proceeding in the Tax Court to shift the burden of proof to the Commissioner. The following case illustrates this burden shifting provision:

J.H. RUTTER REX MANUFACTURING COMPANY v. COMMISSIONER

United States Court of Appeals, Fifth Circuit, 1988.
853 F.2d 1275, 1282–1284.

[The Commissioner asserted an AET liability against the Rutter Rex corporation, and the issue addressed in the part of the opinion set out below is whether Rutter Rex has complied with the requirements of § 534 to shift the burden of proof to the Commissioner.]

Rutter Rex claims the Tax Court erred in not shifting the burden of proof to the Commissioner as to the first five grounds contained in its § 534 statement for accumulating its earnings and profits during 1977 and 1978. * * * Rutter Rex claims the Tax Court applied an incorrect legal standard in determining the burden of proof issue contrary to our holding in Motor Fuel Carriers, Inc. v. Commissioner, 559 F.2d 1348 (5th Cir.1977). Our independent review of Rutter Rex's § 534 statement, and our reading of Motor Fuel Carriers, however, convinces us that the Tax Court did not err in refusing to shift the burden of proof to the Commissioner as to the first five grounds in the § 534 statement.

* * *

* * * Contrary to Rutter Rex's contention, we did not hold in Motor Fuel Carriers that § 534 is satisfied if the taxpayer merely gives notice in general terms to the Commissioner of the grounds asserted to justify the accumulation of earnings. To satisfy its "notice function," the § 534 statement must contain sufficiently detailed factual allegations supporting the grounds. Obviously the statute does not contemplate

shifting the burden of proof when a taxpayer merely tells the Commissioner it is going to challenge the imposition of the accumulated earnings tax. There must be notice of the specific grounds and contentions.

* * *

B. DETERMINATION OF THE REASONABLE NEEDS OF THE BUSINESS

1. In General

Under § 537(a), the term "reasonable needs of the business" includes:

(1) the reasonably anticipated needs of the business,

(2) the section 303 redemption needs of the business, and

(3) the excess business holdings needs of the business.

Also, § 537(b)(4), provides that certain accumulations for product liability reserves are considered reasonable.

The "section 303 redemption needs" as defined in § 537(b)(1) means the amounts needed to redeem the stock of a deceased shareholder where the redemption is governed by § 303. This exception protects only those amounts that are accumulated in the taxable year of the corporation during which the shareholder's death occurs and in later taxable years. Section 537(b)(5) provides that the determination of whether an accumulation for a year prior to the death of the shareholder is unreasonable "shall be made without regard to the fact that distributions in [a § 303] redemption * * * were subsequently made."

Under § 537(b)(3), amounts accumulated to discharge an obligation incurred by the corporation in making a § 303 redemption are considered as having been accumulated for the purpose of making such redemption.

Although not specified in § 537, amounts accumulated to effectuate a redemption that is not within § 303 may satisfy the reasonable needs test. *John B. Lambert & Associates v. United States*, 212 Ct.Cl. 71 (1976), sets out the standard that courts apply in analyzing nonsection 537(b)(1) redemptions:

> [I]n the cases which have upheld a corporation's decision to redeem a shareholder's interest on grounds of reasonable business need, the dispositive factual consideration was always the existence of competing demands among shareholders of a sort that imperiled the very existence of the corporation or, at least, the manner in which up to then it had been successfully conducting its business affairs.

An example is *Mountain State Steel Foundries, Inc. v. Commissioner*, 284 F.2d 737 (4th Cir.1960), a case in which it was held that the application of present and future earnings and profits for the redemption of 50 percent of the corporation's stock served a reasonable business need (rather than as a vehicle for dividend avoidance) in light of the fact that the two families owning all the stock had antagonistic interests which, if left unresolved, would have resulted in the corporation's liquidation.

The regulations under § 537 give further guidance for determining the reasonable needs of the business. As a general proposition, an accumulation is "in excess of the reasonable needs of the business if it exceeds the amount a prudent businessman would consider appropriate for the present business purposes and for the reasonably anticipated future needs of the business." *See* § 1.537–1(a). Thus, there is a "prudent businessman" standard. Also, the accumulation must be "directly connected with the needs of the corporation itself and must be for bona fide business purposes." *See* § 1.537–1(a).

Section 1.537–1(b)(1) gives the following guidance for determining whether an accumulation is for a corporation's "reasonably anticipated needs":

> In order for a corporation to justify an accumulation of earnings and profits for reasonably anticipated future needs, there must be an indication that the future needs of the business require such accumulation, and the corporation must have specific, definite, and feasible plans for the use of such accumulation. Such an accumulation need not be used immediately, nor must the plans for its use be consummated within a short period after the close of the taxable year, provided that such accumulation will be used within a reasonable time depending upon all the facts and circumstances relating to the future needs of the business. Where the future needs of the business are uncertain or vague, where the plans for the future use of an accumulation are not specific, definite, and feasible, or where the execution of such a plan is postponed indefinitely, an accumulation cannot be justified on the grounds of reasonably anticipated needs of the business.

The regulations require that the determination be made "on the basis of the facts at the close of the taxable year" and not on the basis of "subsequent events." However, subsequent events may be "considered to determine whether the taxpayer actually intended to consummate" the plans for which the accumulation was made. *See* § 1.537–1(b)(2).

Section 1.537–2(b) sets out grounds that may be used as "guides under ordinary circumstances" for determining whether an accumulation is reasonable:

> (1) To provide for bona fide expansion of business or replacement of plant:
>
> (2) To acquire a business enterprise through purchasing stock or assets:
>
> (3) To provide for the retirement of bona fide indebtedness created in connection with the trade or business, such as the establishment of a sinking fund for the purpose of retiring bonds

issued by the corporation in accordance with contract obligations incurred on issue:

(4) To provide necessary working capital for the business, such as, for the procurement of inventories; or

(5) To provide for investments or loans to suppliers or customers if necessary in order to maintain the business of the corporation.

(6) To provide for the payment of reasonably anticipated product liability losses

On the other hand, § 1.537–2(c) says that the following transactions may indicate an unreasonable accumulation:

(1) Loans to shareholders, or the expenditure of funds of the corporation for the personal benefit of the shareholders:

(2) Loans having no reasonable relation to the conduct of the business made to relatives or friends of shareholders, or to other persons;

(3) Loans to another corporation, the business of which is not that of the taxpayer corporation, if the capital stock of such other corporation is owned, directly or indirectly, by the shareholder or shareholders of the taxpayer corporation and such shareholder or shareholders are in control of both corporations;

(4) Investments in properties, or securities which are unrelated to the activities of the business of the taxpayer corporation; or

(5) Retention of earnings and profits to provide against unrealistic hazards.

The regulations also give guidance for determining the scope of a corporation's business. A corporation's business includes not only a business it has previously operated but also "any line of commerce which it may undertake." *See* § 1.537–3(a). Also, the business of a subsidiary may be considered the business of its parent, thus allowing a parent to invest its earnings in its subsidiary's business through stock acquisitions. *See* § 1.537–3(b).

2. *An Illustration of the Determination of Reasonable Needs of the Business*

J.H. RUTTER REX MFG. COMPANY, INC. v. COMMISSIONER

United States Court of Appeals, Fifth Circuit, 1988.
853 F.2d 1275.

[The IRS asserted an AET liability against Rutter Rex.]

The accumulated earnings tax applies to corporations "formed or availed of for the purpose of avoiding the income tax with respect to its shareholders or the shareholders of any other corporation, by permitting earnings and profits to accumulate instead of being divided or distributed." [See § 532(a).] A corporation is not subject to the accumulated earnings tax if its accumulations are required for the "reasonable needs of the business." [See § 535(c)(1).] Thus, there are two elements to the imposition of the tax: (1) intent to avoid shareholder taxes, and (2) accumulation of earnings and profits beyond the corporation's reasonable business needs. The parties' primary focus in this case is on the second issue, the question of whether there were unreasonable accumulations by Rutter Rex. * * *

* * *

Several Treasury Regulations have been promulgated under [§ 537] to provide a framework for evaluating the reasonable needs of a business. [See Sec. 7.3.B.1.]

* * *

A. Calculation of Rutter Rex's Operating Cycle

In analyzing the working capital needs of corporations, the courts usually have calculated the corporation's working capital needs for a single, complete "operating cycle." An operating cycle for a manufacturing business like Rutter Rex is the period of time needed to convert cash into raw materials, raw materials into inventory, inventory into accounts receivable, and accounts receivable into cash. In other words, an operating cycle is the time a corporation's working capital is tied up in producing and selling its product. The operating cycle calculation is part of the so-called "Bardahl formula" which is named after the case that originated this approach. Bardahl Manufacturing Corp. v. Commissioner, 24 T.C.M. (CCH) 1030 (1965).

The courts have applied the Bardahl formula in various ways to reflect more accurately the realities of the business operation of each particular taxpayer involved. Although the Bardahl formula is a "well-established tool" that is "routinely applied" by the courts, it is not a precise rule of law but instead merely a rule of thumb, "rising only to the level of administrative convenience." * * *

The "operating cycle" as originally formulated in Bardahl Manufacturing is broken down into two sub-cycles: an inventory cycle and an accounts receivable cycle. These cycles are measured in terms of days. An inventory cycle is the time necessary to convert raw materials into finished goods and to sell those goods. An accounts receivable cycle is the time necessary to convert the accounts receivable created by the sale of finished goods into cash. These two cycles are added together to determine the total number of days in the operating cycle. The number of days in the operating cycle is then divided by 365; the resulting fraction is multiplied by the amount of the corporation's operating expenses for one year, including costs of goods sold, selling expenses, general and administrative expenses, and estimated federal and state income tax payments (but excluding depreciation). The resulting figure is the amount of liquid assets necessary to meet the ordinary operating expenses for a complete operating cycle.

[The court here applies these principles to Rutter Rex's operating cycle.]

B. Determination of Rutter Rex's Other Business Needs

Rutter Rex asserts other justifications for accumulating its earnings beyond its needs for working capital for its day-to-day operating expenses. As explained in the Treasury Regulations, the "reasonable needs of the business" include "the reasonably anticipated future needs of the business." Treas.Reg. § 1.537-1(a). These needs would include future expansion, modernization, or diversification, replacement of equipment or plants, and provisions for adverse business risks and contingencies. The regulations, however, require that "[i]n order for a corporation to justify an accumulation of earnings and profits for reasonably anticipated future needs, there must be an indication that the future needs of the business require such accumulation, and the corporation must have specific, definite, and feasible plans for the use of such accumulation." Treas.Reg. § 1.537-1(b).

With regard to plans for expansion, modernization, diversification, replacement of equipment, and similar business needs, the relevant inquiry is "whether the company's plans appear to have been a real consideration during the tax year in question rather than simply an afterthought to justify the challenged accumulations." * * * In order for such plans to be specific and definite, however, the taxpayer corporation need not have "formal blueprints for action." * * *

The test is whether the taxpayer's intent to undertake the plan is manifested by some "substantial active move toward implementation," such as incurring expenditures to further the plan. * * * If definite plans do exist, the taxpayer "need not necessarily consummate these plans in a relatively short period after the close of the taxable year." The accumulation, however, must be used within a reasonable time after the close of the tax year. Treas.Reg. § 1.537-1(b)(1).

The reasonableness of the accumulation is to be determined based on the facts and conditions existing at the end of the tax year at issue. This is when the decision regarding the accumulation was presumably made. Evidence of subsequent events, however, such as the completion of the project, is relevant if it throws light on the facts as they existed in the challenged years.

Earnings may also be accumulated to provide for potential adverse business risks and contingencies. An accumulation, however, cannot be justified merely for the purpose of protecting the taxpayer corporation from some theoretical contingency that might never transpire. * * * Nor does the actual occurrence of the contingency in subsequent years necessarily justify the accumulation in prior years unless the taxpayer corporation can show that it had planned for this contingency and is not using its occurrence as an after-the-fact justification for the accumulation.

[The court here applies these principles to the facts in *Rutter Rex*.]

C. COMPUTATION OF ACCUMULATED TAXABLE INCOME

The accumulated earnings tax is imposed, under § 531, on the corporation's "accumulated taxable income" ("ATI"). ATI is defined in § 535(a) as the corporation's "taxable income adjusted in the manner provided in (b), minus the sum of the dividends paid deduction * * * and the accumulated earnings credit. * * *"

The starting point for determining ATI is the following list of adjustments to taxable income required by § 535(b):

(1) The regular tax liability is deducted from taxable income;

(2) The charitable deduction is allowed without limitation;

(3) The dividends paid deductions under §§ 243 *et seq.* are not allowed;

(4) The net operating loss is not allowed;

(5) Capital losses are allowed without regard to the limitation in § 1211(a);

(6) The net capital gain, minus the taxes attributable thereto, is allowed as a deduction; and

(7) No allowance is made for the capital loss carryback or carryover provided in § 1212.

Special rules apply for holding companies and foreign corporations.

The resulting figure ("adjusted taxable income") approximates the corporation's current earnings and profits. This figure, however, does not include tax exempt income, such as tax exempt interest, earned by the corporation. Consequently, although an accumulation of tax exempt interest may be beyond the reasonable needs of the business, the interest is not included in the ATI base.

The second step in computing ATI is to subtract from adjusted taxable income the "dividends paid deduction," which § 561 defines as the sum of (1) the dividends paid during the taxable year, and (2) the § 565 consent dividends. Rules for determining the dividends eligible for the dividends paid deduction are set out in §§ 562 and 563.

Section 562(b) provides that amounts distributed in certain liquidations may qualify for the dividends paid deduction. Section 562(c) requires that to qualify for the dividends paid deduction, the dividend must be pro rata and without preference, except for the "rights of preference inherent in any class of stock. * * *" See § 1.562–2(a).

Pursuant to § 563(a), any dividend paid within 2½ months of the close of the corporation's taxable year is considered as paid during such taxable year for purposes of computing the dividends paid deduction.

Under § 565, the shareholders of a corporation may consent to be treated as having received a dividend. A consent dividend is considered as part of the dividends paid deduction under § 561, and the consenting shareholder is deemed to have received a distribution of money on the last day of the corporation's taxable year and to have immediately made a contribution of such money to the corporation, thereby increasing the basis for his stock. Many of the rules of §§ 561 through 565 also apply to personal holding companies.

After subtracting the dividends paid deduction from the adjusted taxable income, the final step in computing ATI is to subtract the "accumulated earnings credit." Under § 535(c), there is a minimum credit of $250,000. *See* § 535(c)(2). A special rule applies for certain service corporations. The minimum credit for any particular year is computed by subtracting from $250,000 "the accumulated earnings and profits of the corporation at the close of the preceding taxable year." Thus, if the accumulated earnings and profits at the close of a preceding taxable year exceeds $250,000 there is no credit for the taxable year.

A "mere holding or investment company" is allowed only the $250,000 minimum credit. However, the credit for other corporations is the greater of (1) the minimum credit, or (2):

> "(A) an amount equal to such part of the earnings and profits for the taxable year as are retained for the reasonable needs of the business, minus (B) the deduction for [net capital gains which is allowed in computing accumulated taxable income.]" *See* § 535(c)(1).

Thus, accumulations that are for the reasonable needs of the business are not subject to the AET.

D. INTERRELATIONSHIP BETWEEN §§ 533 AND 535: IMPACT OF MARKETABLE SECURITIES

The Supreme Court's decision in *Ivan Allen Co.*, set out immediately below, illustrates the interrelationship between the determination under § 533 of whether an accumulation is beyond the reasonable needs of the business and the computation of ATI.

IVAN ALLEN CO. v. UNITED STATES
United States Supreme Court, 1975.
422 U.S. 617, 95 S.Ct. 2501, 45 L.Ed.2d 435.

MR. JUSTICE BLACKMUN delivered the opinion of the Court.

* * *

It is agreed that the taxpayer had reasonable business needs for operating capital amounting to $1,198,309 and $1,455,222 at the close of fiscal 1965 and fiscal 1966, respectively. * * * It is stipulated, in particular, that if the taxpayer's marketable securities are to be taken into account at *cost*, its net liquid assets (current assets less current liabilities), at the end of each of those taxable years, and fully available for use in its business, were then exactly equal to its reasonable business needs for operating capital; that is, the above-stated figures of $1,198,-309 and $1,455,222. It would follow, accordingly, that the earnings and profits of the two taxable years had *not* been permitted to accumulate beyond the taxpayer's reasonable and reasonably anticipated business needs, within the meaning of § 533(a), App. 57, and no accumulated earnings taxes were incurred. It is still further stipulated, however, that if the taxpayer's marketable securities are to be taken into account at *fair market value* (less the cost of converting them into cash), as of the ends of those fiscal years, the taxpayer's net liquid assets would then be $2,235,029 and $3,152,009, respectively. * * * From this it would follow that the earnings and profits of the two taxable years *had* been permitted to accumulate beyond the taxpayer's reasonable and reasonably anticipated business needs. Then, if those accumulations had been for "the purpose of avoiding the income tax with respect to its shareholders," under § 532(a), accumulated earnings taxes would be incurred.

The issue, therefore, is clear and precise: whether, for purposes of applying § 533(a), the taxpayer's readily marketable securities should be taken into account at cost, as the taxpayer contends, or at net liquidation value, as the Government contends.

* * *

II

* * *

It is to be noted that the focus and impositions of the accumulated earnings tax are upon "accumulated taxable income," § 531. This is defined in § 535(a) to mean the corporation's "taxable income," as adjusted. The adjustments consist of the various items described in § 535(b), including federal income tax, the deduction for dividends paid, defined in § 561, and the accumulated earnings credit defined in § 535(c). * * *

* * *

It is important to emphasize that we are concerned here with a tax on "accumulated taxable income," § 531, and that the tax attaches only when a corporation has permitted "earnings and profits to accumulate instead of being divided or distributed," § 532(a). What is essential is that there be "income" and "earnings and profits." This at once eliminates, from the measure of the tax itself, any unrealized appreciation in the value of the taxpayer's portfolio securities over cost, for any such unrealized appreciation does not enter into the computation of the corporation's "income" and "earnings and profits."

The corporation's readily marketable portfolio securities and their unrealized appreciation, nonetheless, are of profound importance in making the entirely discrete determination whether the corporation has permitted what, concededly, are earnings and profits to accumulate beyond its reasonable business needs. If the securities, as here, are readily available as liquid assets, then the recognized earnings and profits that have been accumulated may well have been unnecessarily accumulated, so far as the reasonable needs of the business are concerned. On the other hand, if those portfolio securities are not liquid and are not readily available for the needs of the business, the accumulation of earnings and profits may be viewed in a different light. * * *

We disagree with the taxpayer and conclude that cost is not the stopping point; that the application of the accumulated earnings tax, in a given case, may well depend on whether the corporation has available readily marketable portfolio securities; and that the proper measure of those securities, for purposes of the tax, is their net realizable value. * * *

This taxpayer's securities, being liquid and readily marketable, clearly were available for the business needs of the corporation, and their fair market value, net, was such that, according to the stipulation, the taxpayer's undistributed earnings and profits for the two fiscal years in question were permitted to accumulate beyond the reasonable and reasonably anticipated needs of the business.

* * *

The judgment of the Court of Appeals is affirmed.

It is so ordered.

[Dissenting Opinion deleted.]

E. SUMMARY PROBLEMS ON THE ACCUMULATED EARNINGS TAX

1. The *X* corporation is wholly owned by individual *A*, who is in the top tax bracket. *X* has operated for several years, and has $100K of accumulated earnings and profits. *X* is not a personal holding company. For the current year, *X* has taxable income of $600K and a federal income tax liability of $200K. $100K of *X*'s $600K taxable income is attributable to a net capital gain from the sale of securities, and *X*'s tax on this net capital gain is $40K. *X* distributes a dividend of $30K to *A* on the last day of the year. Assuming that *X* could muster no proof that its accumulated earnings are not beyond the reasonable needs of the business, what is *X*'s exposure to the accumulated earnings tax for the current year?

    (a) What is *X*'s accumulated taxable income? *See* § 535.

    (b) What is *X*'s accumulated earnings tax? *See* § 531.

    (c) In general, what result if *A* held both common and preferred stock of *X* and the $30K dividend was made in respect of the preferred in accordance with its terms? *See* § 562(c) and § 1.562–2.

    (d) In general, what result if *A* held class A common and class B common and the $30K dividend was distributed on the class B at the discretion of the board of directors? *See* § 562(e) and § 1.562–2.

(e) In general, what result if the $30K dividend had been paid on the first day of the third month after the close of *X's* taxable year? The first day of the fourth month? *See* § 563(a) and (c).

(f) Is there any way *X* can avoid the accumulated earnings tax without making an actual distribution to *A*? If so, in general, what result to *A*? *See* § 565.

2. In general, what effect does an accumulation of tax exempt interest have on the computation of accumulated taxable income under § 535?

§ 7.4 THE PERSONAL HOLDING COMPANY TAX

A. INTRODUCTORY NOTE ON THE PERSONAL HOLDING COMPANY TAX

The personal holding company tax is a penalty tax imposed on certain closely held corporations that are engaged in passive investment activities. Under § 541, the tax is equal to 39.6% of the "undistributed personal holding company income." The rules governing personal holding companies are very mechanical. The following discussion focuses on the high points; the summary problems illustrate the operation of the provisions.

B. DEFINITION OF PERSONAL HOLDING COMPANY

1. *In General*

The term personal holding company ("PHC"), defined in § 542(a), contains two elements:

(1) a passive income element, and

(2) a stock ownership element.

The passive income element of § 542(a)(1) is satisfied if "[a]t least 60% of [the corporation's] *adjusted ordinary gross income* * * * for the taxable year is *personal holding company income* * * *." The term "personal holding company income" ("PHCI") is defined in § 543(a), and the term "adjusted ordinary gross income" ("AOGI") is defined in § 543(b)(2). Basically, PHCI includes a corporation's passive income, such as dividends and interest; AOGI is operating income minus operating deductions. These two terms are examined further below.

The stock ownership element of § 542(a)(2) is satisfied if "[a]t any time during the last half of the taxable year, more than 50% in value of [the corporation's] outstanding stock is owned, directly or indirectly, by or for not more than 5 individuals." Section 544 sets forth constructive ownership rules for determining stock ownership. These rules differ in many respects from those of § 318. Whereas, the family attribution rules of § 544(a)(2) apply to a person's spouse, brothers, sisters, ancestors and lineal descendants, a person's family under § 318(a)(1) includes only his spouse, parents, children and grandchildren. Also, under § 544(a)(1), the stock owned directly or indirectly by or for a corporation is considered as owned proportionately by its shareholders. Under § 318(a)(2), however, attribution from a corporation applies only to shareholders who have at least a 50% interest.

Under § 542(c), various types of corporations, such as exempt organizations and life insurance companies, are not treated as PHC's. Section 542(b) provides special rules for determining whether corporations that are members of a consolidated group are PHC's.

In summary, a corporation will be a PHC if (1) more than 50% in value of its stock is owned directly or indirectly by 5 or fewer individuals, and (2) 60% of its AOGI for the taxable year is PHCI.

2. *The Inadvertent Personal Holding Company*

WEISS v. UNITED STATES

United States District Court, Northern District of Ohio, 1975.
1975–2 USTC ¶ 9538.

The claim grows out of the sale of the business and corporate liquidation of the Weiss Noodle Co., an Ohio corporation wholly owned by plaintiff Albert Weiss. Generally the issues are (1) whether the corporation was a personal holding company during the period of liquidation and (2) whether interest income earned from investment of the cash assets during this period and distributed with the assets to the plaintiff Albert Weiss constituted a dividend of the personal holding company taxable at ordinary income rates, or part of the distribution taxable as a capital gain.

I. The Weiss Noodle Co. manufactured and sold noodle products. On August 23, 1968, it adopted a plan to complete liquidation in accordance with [former] section 337 of the Internal Revenue Code. It then sold its business, including its name, on August 29, 1968, and changed its name to Seldoon Corporation.

The proceeds of the sale were $1,916,948; and the basis in those assets was $120,864. Seldoon filed its income tax return for the fiscal year ended September 30, 1968. Because of [former] section 337, it was not required to recognize, or include, its gain of $1,796,084 on the sale of its assets.

During the short tax year from October 1, 1968 to February 14, 1969, when it filed its final income tax return, Seldoon invested the sale proceeds of $1,916,948. Its activities during this period consisted of

> The purchase and distribution of United States Treasury bills and certificates of deposits and the collection and distribution of interest thereon.

Seldoon conducted no other business. On December 13, 1968, Seldoon surrendered its corporate charter to the State of Ohio.

As of February 14, 1969, all of Seldoon's assets were distributed to Albert Weiss in accordance with the plan of complete liquidation. For Seldoon's short tax year from October 1, 1968 to February 14, 1969, the Commissioner determined that Seldoon was a personal holding company, as defined by section 542. The Commission further decided that $22,374.73 earned during the short tax year as interest on the treasury bills and certificates of deposit was personal holding company income.

* * *

The proof shows that Seldoon fits the section 542 definition of a personal holding company for the short tax year under consideration. Seldoon satisfies section 542(a)(1) and section 543(a) (definition of personal holding company income). One hundred percent of Seldoon's adjusted ordinary gross income in that period was interest income. The stock ownership requirement of section 542(a)(2) (more than 50 percent in value of the stock owned by not more than five individuals) is met by Albert Weiss' ownership of all of Seldoon's stock. By the general rule of section 542(a)

> The term "personal holding company" means "*any* corporation (other than a corporation described in subsection (c)). [Emphasis added.]

A literal reading of section 542 appears to sustain the Government's finding that Seldoon was a personal holding company for its last (short) tax year. Nevertheless, the plaintiffs make several arguments against the application of section 542 to Seldoon.

First, it is argued that section 542 applies only to going concerns, not to corporations in liquidation. Treasury Regulation 1.6012-2(a)(2) meets this argument. It provides

> A corporation in existence during any portion of a taxable year is required to make a return.

* * *

> A corporation is not in existence after it ceases business and dissolves, *retaining no assets,* whether or not under State law it may thereafter be treated as continuing as a corporation * * * [Emphasis added.]

Thus, a corporation that ceases business but retains assets is a corporation "in existence" for purposes of the Code and required to file a return. Seldoon recognized this requirement in filing its final return for the period October 1, 1968 to February 14, 1969. Since Seldoon was in existence for tax purposes, it could not disregard some Code provisions and follow others merely because it had ceased to be an operating company.

* * *

C. DEFINITION OF PERSONAL HOLDING COMPANY INCOME (PHCI)

Section 543(a) provides that PHCI consists of the following items:

(1) Dividends, interest, royalties and annuities (*see* § 543(a)(1));

(2) Adjusted income from rents, unless such rents are a substantial part of the corporation's AOGI and a minimum dividend is paid. (This is discussed further below.) (*See* § 543(a)(2));

(3) Certain mineral, oil and gas royalties (*see* § 543(a)(3));

(4) Certain copyright royalties (*see* § 543(a)(4));

(5) Certain produced film rents (*see* § 543(a)(5));

(6) Certain amounts received by the corporation from a 25% or more shareholder as compensation for the use of tangible property of the corporation (*see* § 543(a)(6));

(7) Certain amounts received by the corporation under a contract pursuant to which the corporation is to furnish personal services (*see* § 543(a)(7)); and

(8) Certain amounts received from trusts or estates (*see* § 543(a)(8)).

Section 543(b)(3) defines "adjusted income from rents" ("Rents") as the gross income from rents, minus depreciation, property taxes, and interest allocable thereto. Under § 543(a)(2), Rents are excluded from PHCI if (1) 50% or more of the corporation's AOGI consists of Rents, and (2) the dividends equal or exceed the amount by which the corporation's other items of PHCI exceed 10% of the ordinary gross income ("OGI"). OGI is discussed below. Algebraically, Rents are not included in PHCI if:

1) Rents $\geq$ [50% of AOGI]

and

2) Dividends $\geq$ [other PHCI > 10% of OGI]

Thus, for example, if a corporation's only source of income is rents from real property, the Rents are not PHCI because they constitute more than 50% of the corporation's AOGI and there are no other items of PHCI. This exception permits closely held corporations to engage in the business of holding rental real estate.

D. DEFINITION OF AOGI AND OGI

AOGI is defined in § 543(b)(2) as OGI minus certain allocable expenses. OGI is defined in § 543(b)(1) as gross income minus gains from the sale of capital assets and § 1231(b) property, etc. AOGI, therefore, includes all items of PHCI, plus the corporation's operating income.

E. SIGNIFICANCE OF OGI AND AOGI IN DETERMINING PERSONAL HOLDING COMPANY STATUS

PLEASANT SUMMIT LAND CORPORATION v. COMMISSIONER

United States Court of Appeals, Third Circuit, 1988.
863 F.2d 263.

* * * PSLC challenges the Tax Court's conclusion that it was a "personal holding company" subject to the tax on personal holding companies in its tax year in issue. Resolution of its appeal depends on whether its sale of the Summit House apartments in West Orange, New Jersey, was of a capital asset and thus resulted in a capital gain or whether the Summit House was a property it held primarily for sale to customers in the ordinary course of its trade or business so that its sale resulted in ordinary gross income.

* * *

A. *The Mechanical Test of the Personal Holding Company Tax*

Section 541 of the Internal Revenue Code imposes an additional tax on undistributed personal holding company income, as defined in section 545, for "every personal holding company (as defined in section 542)." Section 542(a) provides that any corporation is a personal holding company if it meets mechanical tests relating to the number of stockholders and to the character of income earned during the tax year. Inasmuch as all PSLC stock was owned by one person, PSLC agrees that the stockholder test was met and thus we do not describe that test in detail.

The character of income requirement is contained in section 542(a)(1), which provides that "[a]t least 60 percent of [the corporation's] adjusted ordinary gross income (as defined in section 543(b)(2)) for the taxable year [must be] personal holding company income (as defined in section 543(a))." This may be expressed as follows: a corporation is a personal holding company if the fraction consisting of personal holding company income as the numerator and adjusted ordinary gross income as the denominator is greater than or equal to sixty percent (60%). Our task in establishing this fraction is simplified by the circumstance that during its applicable tax year PSLC had only two kinds of income, income from interest payments on debts arising from the Summit House transactions and income from the sale of the Summit House property.

Inasmuch as the parties agree that only the interest payments constituted personal holding company income, the numerator of the fraction is not in dispute. They disagree, however, over calculation of the denominator of the fraction. If the gain from the sale of Summit House is included in the denominator then PSLC is not a personal holding company. But if the gain is excluded then only the interest income is included in both the numerator and the denominator, giving the fraction a value of one or 100% and, since 100% is greater than 60%, PSLC is a personal holding company.

B. Calculation of the Denominator

The denominator of the fraction consists of "adjusted ordinary gross income (as defined in section 543(b)(2))." I.R.C. § 542(a)(1). Section 543(b)(2) defines adjusted ordinary gross income as "ordinary gross income" subject to certain reductions not applicable to this case.

"Ordinary gross income" is defined by section 543(b)(1)(A) as gross income less "all gains from the sale or other disposition of capital assets." A "capital asset" is defined by section 1221 to include all property of a taxpayer subject to certain specific exceptions. PSLC argues that the exception for "property held by the taxpayer primarily for sale to customers in the ordinary course of his trade or business" applies to the Summit House. I.R.C. § 1221(1).

C. Whether the Sale was Within the Ordinary Course of Trade or Business

* * * A determination that PSLC's sale of Summit House was not within the ordinary course of its trade or business would result in the exception of section 1221(1) not applying and, inasmuch as PSLC has not argued that any other exception applies, the general rule of section 1221 would govern. Thus, Summit House would be deemed to be a capital asset and the gain on its sale would be excluded from both PSLC's ordinary gross income and adjusted ordinary gross income. Consequently, PSLC's interest income would constitute the only element of both the numerator and denominator giving the fraction a value of one or 100% and PSLC would qualify as a personal holding company.

* * *

* * * We hold that the Tax Court's factual finding that the sale was not within the ordinary course of PSLC's trade or business was not clearly erroneous.

* * *

F. UNDISTRIBUTED PERSONAL HOLDING COMPANY INCOME (UPHCI)

The 39.6% tax under § 541 is imposed on undistributed personal holding company income ("UPHCI"). This term is defined in § 545(a) as the corporation's taxable income with certain adjustments, minus the dividends paid deduction of § 561. The adjustments to taxable income are specified in § 545(b), (c) and (d). The adjustments in (b) are similar to the adjustments to taxable income required by § 535(b) in computing accumulated taxable income for purposes of the accumulated earnings tax. For instance, taxes are deducted, the deduction for dividends received is disallowed, and a deduction is allowed for net capital gain minus the taxes attributable thereto.

After making these adjustments to taxable income, the final step in computing UPHCI is the deduction for dividends paid, defined in § 561 as the sum of:

(1) the dividends paid during the taxable year;

(2) the consent dividends; and

(3) the dividend carryover described in section 564.

Items (1) and (2) also apply in computing accumulated taxable income under § 535, but the dividend carryover only applies to personal holding companies.

Under § 563(b), at the shareholder's election, dividends paid within 2½ months after the close of a taxable year are treated (subject to certain limitations) as having been made in the prior taxable year.

The consent dividend procedure in § 565 permits the shareholders to agree to be treated as having received a dividend distribution and having immediately recontributed the dividend to the corporation. Under § 564, if the amount of the dividends paid deduction for a taxable year exceeds the corporation's taxable income after the adjustments provided in § 545, the corporation may carry over such excess for two years.

If a corporation is determined to be a PHC for a prior year, § 547 allows the corporation to avoid the 39.6% tax under § 541 (but not the interest, additional amounts, and penalties computed with respect to such tax) by making a "deficiency dividend" distribution.

G. SUMMARY PROBLEMS ON THE PERSONAL HOLDING COMPANY TAX

1. The stock of corporation X is owned as follows: 10 percent each by individuals A, B, C, D, E, F, G, H and I and corporation Y. Corporation Y is wholly owned by individual M. Assuming that none of the individual shareholders are related, is the stock ownership requirement of § 542(a)(2) met? See § 541.

(a) Would the ownership test be met if A owned 10 percent of the stock of Y? See § 544.

(b) Would the ownership test be met if A and B were cousins? Brothers? What if A and M were brothers? See § 544.

(c) Would the ownership test be met if individual N was M's sister and A's wife? (Recall that M is the sole shareholder of Y). B's sister and A's wife? See § 544.

2. Corporation X is wholly owned by individual A. For its current year, X has the following items of gross income:

Interest	$100K
Rents	$110K
Capital Gains	$ 90K
Total	$300K

The deductions, all of which were allocable to the rents, are $60K, and, therefore, the taxable income is $240K. The total tax liability is $77K and the tax on the net capital gain of $90K is $27K. No dividends were distributed.

(a) What is the corporation's "adjusted ordinary gross income" and "ordinary gross income"? *See* § 543(b)(2) and (b)(1).

(b) What is the corporation's personal holding company income? *See* § 543(a)(1) and (a)(2).

(c) Is the corporation a personal holding company under § 542?

(d) What is the corporation's undistributed personal holding company income? *See* § 545(a), (b)(1) and (b)(5).

(e) What is the corporation's personal holding company tax liability? *See* § 541.

(f) What would be the impact on the corporation if it took advantage of the deficiency dividend provision? *See* § 547.

3. Same as in (2) except the deductions, all of which are attributable to the rents, are $10K as opposed to $60K and the corporation distributed a cash dividend of $80K.

(a) Same question as in (2)(a)–2(g).

4. In general, what effect does an accumulation of tax-exempt interest have on the computation of undistributed personal holding company taxable income under § 545?

5. Individual A is the sole shareholder of corporation X, an operating concern. A has a low basis for his stock, but X has a high basis for its assets. A desires to sell either the stock or assets of X. How would you evaluate the relative advantage of, on the one hand, having A sell the stock and investing the proceeds in tax exempt bonds and, on the other hand, having X sell its assets, stay in existence and invest the proceeds in tax exempt bonds?

Chapter 8

INTRODUCTION TO CONSOLIDATED RETURNS

§ 8.1 SCOPE

This chapter introduces several of the basic concepts relating to the filing by related corporations of consolidated returns. Sec. 8.2 presents a historical perspective on the investment adjustment issue that can arise with consolidated returns, and Sec. 8.3 provides additional background information. Sec. 8.4 addresses the definition of "affiliated group", which is the predicate for filing consolidated returns. Sec. 8.5 provides a quick overview of the consolidated return regulations, and Sec. 8.6 contains an introduction to the basic steps in computing consolidated tax liability.

Sec. 8.7 examines intercompany transactions, which involve, for example, sales of property between members of a consolidated group. Sec. 8.8 considers the treatment of inter-group dividends, which are dividends paid by a subsidiary of a consolidated group to its parent member. Sec. 8.9 looks at the investment adjustment system in the consolidated return regulations, including adjustments to stock basis and earnings and profits and the treatment of excess loss accounts. Finally Sec. 8.10 provides a set of summary problems dealing with consolidated returns. Other aspects of the consolidated return regulations, such as the disallowance of loss rules, and the SRLY rules, principally arise in the context of taxable stock acquisitions. For that reason, these provisions are covered in *Taxable and Tax-Free Corporate Mergers, Acquisitions and LBOs, supra* Sec. 1.4.

The issues addressed here are covered in greater detail in Chapter 14 of *Federal Taxation of Business Enterprises, supra* Chapter 1, note 1; Chapter 15 of Bittker and Eustice, *Corporations, supra* Sec. 1.4.; and various chapters of Peel, *Consolidated Returns, supra* Sec. 1.4.

§ 8.2 THE HISTORICAL PERSPECTIVE

CHARLES ILFELD CO. v. HERNANDEZ

Supreme Court of the United States, 1934.
292 U.S. 62, 54 S.Ct. 596, 78 L.Ed. 1127.

MR. JUSTICE BUTLER delivered the opinion of the Court.

In 1917 petitioner purchased all the capital stock of the Springer Trading Company for $40,000 and in 1920 all that of the Roy Trading Company for $50,000. It held these shares until late in 1929 when both companies were dissolved. In that period it advanced the Springer Company sums amounting to $69,030.27, and the Roy Company $9,782.22. Nothing having been paid it on account of these advances, petitioner had an investment in the former of $109,030.27 and in the latter of $59,782.22. It made consolidated returns which took into account the gains and losses of each subsidiary. Operations of the Springer Company resulted in losses in all but two of the years and those of the Roy Company in all but four. The losses of the former exceeded its gains by $118,510.53, and those of the latter by $57,127.85. In 1929, before the end of November, the subsidiaries sold all their property to outside interests. After paying debts to others, each had a balance—the Springer Company $22,914.22, and the Roy Company, $15,106.16—which it paid petitioner on December 23. Both subsidiaries were dissolved December 30 in that year.

Petitioner made a consolidated return for 1929 based on the results of operation and the liquidation of each subsidiary but made no deduction of losses resulting to itself from the liquidations. The returns showed a tax of $20,836.20 which was duly paid. In May, 1931, petitioner filed an amended return and claimed a refund of $14,406.43. This return does not take into account profits or losses of subsidiaries in that year but deducts the losses above shown to have resulted to petitioner from its investments in them * * *

The question is whether petitioner is entitled to deduct from its 1929 income any part of the losses resulting from its investment in the subsidiaries.

* * *

The allowance claimed would permit petitioner twice to use the subsidiaries' losses for the reduction of its taxable income. By means of the consolidated returns in earlier years it was enabled to deduct them. And now it claims for 1929 deductions for diminution of assets resulting from the same losses. If allowed, this would be the practical equivalent of double deduction. In the absence of a provision of the Act definitely requiring it, a purpose so opposed to precedent and equality of treatment of taxpayers will not be attributed to lawmakers * * *

There is nothing in the Act that purports to authorize double deduction of losses or in the regulations to suggest that the commissioner construed any of its provisions to empower him to prescribe a regulation that would permit consolidated returns to be made on the basis now claimed by petitioner. [Therefore, we hold for the commissioner.]

* * *

Note and Questions

In *Ilfeld* the taxpayer-parent claimed deductions for the operating losses attributable to its consolidated subsidiaries. Then, upon liquidation of the subsidiaries, the taxpayer claimed a second loss under the predecessor of § 331. Section 331 provides that a liquidation is a taxable exchange to the shareholder. Since the taxpayer-parent was not required by the consolidated return regulations to reduce its basis in the subsidiaries' stock by the amount of the operating losses, its basis for the stock exceeded the proceeds received upon liquidation. This gave rise to a taxable loss on the liquidation. What is the precise holding in *Ilfeld*? Would the issue in *Ilfeld* arise under the current consolidated return regulations?

§ 8.3 IN GENERAL

Section 1501 gives an "affiliated group of corporations the privilege of making a consolidated return * * *." If the privilege is elected, the affiliated group files a single federal income tax return rather than separate returns for each corporation. Section 1501 also requires as a condition for filing a consolidated return "that all corporations which at any time during the taxable year have been members of the affiliated group consent to all the consolidated return regulations prescribed under section 1502 prior to the last day prescribed by law for filing such a return." This section further provides that the "making of a consolidated return shall be considered as such consent."

Section 1502 directs the Secretary of Treasury to

> * * * prescribe such regulations as he may deem necessary in order that the tax liability of any affiliated group of corporations making a consolidated return and of each corporation in the group, both during and after the period of affiliation, may be returned, determined, computed, assessed, collected, and adjusted, in such manner as clearly to reflect the income tax liability and the various factors necessary for the determination of such liability, and in order to prevent avoidance of such tax liability.

Virtually all of the law on consolidated returns is in the regulations, rulings and cases. The statutory provisions merely authorize the filing of a consolidated return (§ 1501), direct the Secretary to promulgate the regulations (§ 1502), provide that the tax is determined in accordance with the regulations (§ 1503), and define an affiliated group of corporations (§ 1504).

§ 8.4 DEFINITION OF AFFILIATED GROUP

A. IN GENERAL

GENERAL EXPLANATION OF DEFICIT REDUCTION TAX ACT OF 1984
170–173 (1984).

* * *

Reasons for Change

* * * The Congress was aware that * * * corporations were filing consolidated returns under circumstances in which a parent corporation's interest in the issuing corporation accounted for less than 80 percent of the real equity value of such corporation. Further, the Congress was aware that this may have permitted certain unwarranted tax benefit transfers. * * *

Explanation of Provisions

Affiliated group [See § 1504(a)(1) and (2).]

Under the Act, the definition of the term "affiliated group" is amended for all purposes of subtitle A. Under the amended definition, 2 corporations do not qualify as an affiliated group (and, among other things, are therefore not eligible to elect to file, or continue to file, a consolidated return) unless 1 owns, directly, stock (1) possessing at least 80 percent of the total voting power of all classes of stock, and (2) having a fair market value equal to at least 80 percent of the total value of all outstanding stock, of such other corporation. For this purpose, as described below, certain preferred stock is to be disregarded. Similar rules apply in determining whether any other corporation is, or continues to be, a member of the group.

Preferred stock and employer securities [See § 1504(a)(4).]

[C]ertain stock is to be disregarded in testing for affiliated group status. The stock to be disregarded is stock which (1) is not entitled to vote, (2) is limited and preferred as to dividends and does not participate in corporate growth to any significant extent, (3) has redemption and liquidation rights that do not exceed the stock's paid-in capital and/or par value (except for a reasonable redemption premium), and (4) is not convertible into any other class of stock. * * *

* * *

Regulations [See § 1504(a)(5).]

* * *

Authority is also provided for the Secretary to prescribe regulations necessary or appropriate to carry out the purposes of the provision including, but not limited to, regulations: (1) which treat warrants, obligations convertible into stock, and other similar interests as stock, and stock (like "puttable" stock) as not stock; and (2) which treat options to acquire or sell stock as having been exercised. * * *

B. THE OPTION REGULATIONS

See § 1.1502–1 to –4.

PREAMBLE TO PROPOSED REGULATIONS UNDER § 1504
CO–152–84 (March 2, 1992).

[These regulations were finalized on December 29, 1992.]

OVERVIEW

The proposed regulations provide guidance regarding circumstances under which options will be treated as exercised for purposes of determining whether the 80 percent voting power and value tests for affiliation under section 1504(a) are satisfied. In general, options will be disregarded in determining whether a corporation is a member of an affiliated group. An option, however, will be treated as exercised for purposes of determining affiliation when a reasonable certainty exists, on a specified measurement date (generally the issuance, modification, or transfer date), that the option will be exercised and the issuance or transfer of the option in lieu of the underlying stock would result (but for these regulations) in the elimination of a substantial amount of federal income tax liability.

* * *

REASONABLE CERTAINTY OF EXERCISE

An option is considered reasonably certain to be exercised only if a strong probability exists that the option will be exercised. The determination of whether an option is reasonably certain to be exercised depends on all the facts and circumstances on a measurement date. [See § 1.1504–4(g).]

The proposed regulations provide objective "safe harbors" which treat qualifying options as not being reasonably certain to be exercised. The first safe harbor applies to an option to acquire stock that must be exercised, if at all, within 24 months of a measurement date and that has an exercise price which is equal to or greater than 90 percent (or, in the case of an option to sell stock, equal to or less than 110 percent) of the fair market value of the underlying stock on the measurement date. [See § 1.1504–4(g)(3).] A second safe harbor applies to an option to acquire stock if the terms of the option provide that the exercise price of the option is equal to or greater than (or, in the case of an option to sell stock, equal to or less than) the fair market value of the underlying stock on the exercise date. [See § 1.1504–4(g)(3).]

§ 8.5 A QUICK WALK THROUGH THE REGULATIONS

The following discussion introduces some of the basic provisions in the consolidated return regulations.

Section 1.1502–1 contains certain definitions, many of which are concerned with transactions in which a corporation either becomes a member of an affiliated group or ceases to be a member. These definitions are important for the study of taxable acquisitions and reorganizations covered in Part VI. There are three terms of general significance: "group," "member," and "subsidiary." *See* § 1.1502–1(a), (b), and (c).

Sections 1.1502–2 through –7 are concerned with the "consolidated tax liability." Section 1.1502–2 requires that a group's tax liability be determined by adding, *inter alia,* the § 11 tax on consolidated taxable income and the personal holding company tax on consolidated undistributed personal holding company income. Section 1.1502–3 sets forth regulations on the consolidated investment tax credit, and –4 deals with the consolidated foreign tax credit. Section 1.1502–5 contains rules for computing the estimated tax. Section 1.1502–6(a) provides that the parent and subsidiaries in the group are "severally" liable for the tax of the group. However, –6(b) imposes a rule of separate liability when a subsidiary ceases to be a member of a group by reason of a sale or exchange of its stock for fair value prior to the assessment of a deficiency, provided that the district director "believes" that the assessment or collection of the balance will not be jeopardized. Section 1.1502–6(c) provides that intercompany agreements shall not have an effect on the group's "several liability."

Section 1.1502–11 specifies rules for computing consolidated taxable income. It is computed by taking into account the "separate taxable income" of each member and the items requiring computation on a consolidated basis, such as the consolidated net operating loss deduction and the consolidated net capital gain. Section 1.1502–11(b) governs the determination of gain or loss and the computation of consolidated taxable income on the disposition of the stock of a subsidiary.

Sections 1.1502–12 through –19 set forth rules concerning the computation of the member's separate taxable income. Section 1.1502–12 provides that separate taxable income is computed in accordance with the rules governing the determination of taxable income of separate corporations, subject to the special rules that govern items such as intercompany transactions (–13), intercompany distributions with respect to stock (–14(a)), intercompany stock redemptions (–14(b)), the determination of basis of the stock of a member (–31 and –32), and the determination of earnings and profits (–33). Also, –12 provides that (1) in computing separate taxable income, no deductions are taken for net operating losses, charitable contributions, or dividends received under section 243, and (2) capital gains and losses and section 1231 gains and losses are not taken into account. Each of these items is computed on a consolidated basis.

The intercompany transactions governed by § 1.1502–13 include sales of property by one member to another. *See also* –13T. Intercompany distributions of dividends are covered by –14(a). *See also* –14T. Section 1.1502–15 contains a limitation on "built-in deductions." These are deductions that have accrued prior to affiliation. This topic is considered in *Taxable and Tax-Free Corporate Mergers, Acquisitions and LBOs, supra* Sec. 1.4. The special rules for mine exploration expenditures (–16), and inventory adjustments (–18) are not examined here. Section 1.1502–17 provides that the rules of § 446 apply to the determination of each member's accounting method. Section 1.1502–19, which deals with the disposition of the stock of a member for which there is an excess loss account, is examined in Sec. 8.9.

Sections 1.1502–21 through –27 pertain to the computation of the consolidated items (*e.g.*, net operating losses (–21), capital gains and losses (–22), § 1231 gains and losses (–23), and charitable deductions (–24)). The consolidated net operating loss deduction (–21) is examined in *Taxable and Tax-Free Corporate Mergers, Acquisitions and LBOs, supra* Sec. 1.4.

Sections 1.1502–31 through –34 contain the "basis, stock ownership, and earnings and profits rules." *See also* –31T, –32T and –33T. In 1992, the Treasury issued proposed regulations that would amend these investment adjustment provisions. These rules are important in the normal operation of a consolidated group and are considered in detail below. Sections 1.1502–41 through –47 are concerned with "special taxes and taxpayers" and are not examined.

Sections 1.1502–75 through –79 contain "administrative provisions and other rules." Section 1.1502–75 sets forth rules governing the election to file a consolidated return. *See also* –75T. Once an election is made, a consolidated return must be filed for future taxable years unless, under –75(c), the group elects, with the permission of the Commissioner, to discontinue filing consolidated returns.

Section 1.1502–76 deals with the taxable year of members and the income included in the consolidated return. Under –76(a), the consolidated return must be filed on the basis of the common parent's taxable year when it becomes a member of a group. Under –76(b), the group's consolidated return "must include the income of the common parent for [it's] entire taxable year * * * and * * * the income of each subsidiary for the portion of such taxable year during which it was a member of the group." The rules for allocating a subsidiary's income between separate and consolidated returns are discussed in *Taxable and Tax-Free Corporate Mergers, Acquisitions and LBOs, supra* Sec. 1.4.

Section 1.1502–77 provides that the common parent is the agent for subsidiaries and –78 deals with the tentative carryback adjustment. Finally, –79 sets forth rules governing the carryover and carryback of consolidated net operating losses to separate return years. These rules are examined in *Taxable and Tax-Free Corporate Mergers, Acquisitions and LBOs, supra* Sec. 1.4.

§ 8.6 THE STEPS IN COMPUTING CONSOLIDATED TAX LIABILITY

Pursuant to § 1.1502–11, "consolidated taxable income" is computed by adding the "separate taxable income" of each member and the group's "consolidated" items. The separate taxable income is computed under –12 in accordance with the provisions governing the determination of the taxable income of separate corporations. Special rules govern such items as intercompany transactions and distributions. Section 1.1502–12(*o*) provides that "separate taxable income shall include a case in which the determination [of separate taxable income] results in an excess of deductions over gross income." Consequently, if a member has a separate operating loss, the loss is technically the member's separate taxable income.

Once the separate taxable income of each member and the consolidated items of the group are computed, the items are aggregated to arrive at the consolidated taxable income. (*See* –11.) For example, assume there is a three corporation group. The common parent, *P*, owns 100% of the stock of each of two subsidiaries, *S* 1 and *S* 2. There are no consolidated items, and the separate taxable income of each member is as follows:

Member	Separate Taxable Income (Loss)
P	$100K
S^1	($50K)
S^2	$ 25K

The consolidated taxable income of the group is, therefore, $75K.

After the consolidated taxable income is computed, the consolidated tax liability is computed under –2. If *P* in the above example is a regular corporation (*i.e.*, not a personal holding company or life insurance company, etc.), the consolidated tax liability is computed under § 11, and the group receives credit against the liability for, *inter alia*, its consolidated foreign tax credit (–4), and its consolidated estimated tax payments (–5).

§ 8.7 INTERCOMPANY TRANSACTIONS UNDER § 1.1502–13

A. INTRODUCTION

Portions of the regulations under § 1.1502–13 are set out in the next section. Study those regulations in connection with your study of this text.

An intercompany transaction is defined in –13(a)(1)(i) as "a transaction during a consolidated return year between corporations which are members of the same group immediately after such transaction." For example, a sale of property from one member to another would be an intercompany transaction.

Intercompany transactions can be either deferred or nondeferred. Deferred intercompany transactions are defined in –13(a)(2) to include intercompany sales. Deferred intercompany transactions include situations where one member (the selling member) would normally take the expenditure into income in the year received, but the other member (the purchasing member) would normally capitalize the expenditure. This results in an accounting asymmetry within the group. For example, in the P–S group, P sells to S for $100K depreciable property for which P has an adjusted basis of $50K. P has gain recognition in the year of sale, but S has an asset with a basis of $100K, depreciable (for example) over a 10–year period. P has a gain recognized of $50K in the first year but S has only a depreciation deduction of, say, $10K. Thus, if the P–S group otherwise broke even, the group would have $40K of taxable income for the year (i.e., P's $50K of income less S's $10K of depreciation).

This asymmetry is avoided by –13(c), which provides that the selling member (i.e., the member who sold the property, performed the services or made the loan) shall defer reporting the gain or loss (the "deferred gain or loss"), and shall take into account the deferred amount in accordance with –13(d), (e) or (f).

Section 1.1502–13(d)(1)(i) deals with the "restoration of deferred gain or loss for property subject to depreciation, amortization or depletion." It provides that in a deferred intercompany transaction where property in the hands of a purchasing member of the group is subject to an allowance for depreciation, amortization or depletion, the selling member takes into account a portion of the deferred intercompany gain or loss in accordance with the provision of –13(d)(1)(ii). The portion of the gain or loss to be taken into account by the selling member is determined by the following formula:

1) [Amount of the Deferred Gain or Loss]
[Multiplied by]

2) [Depreciation, Amortization or Depletion Allowed in the Year to the Purchasing Member]
[Divided by]

3) [Purchasing Member's Depreciable Basis for Property Immediately After the Transaction]

Under –13(d)(3), the amount restored by the selling member reduces the deferred gain or loss. Thus, in the above example where P sells to S property for $100K and realizes a $50K gain, P takes into account $5K of the gain in each of the following ten years:

1)	[The Selling Member's Deferred Gain ($50K)] [Multiplied by]
2)	[The Depreciation Allowed to the Purchasing Member for Each Year ($10K)] [Divided by]
3)	[The Purchasing Member's Depreciable Basis for the Property Immediately After the Transaction ($100K)]

Thus, $\$50K \times \dfrac{10K}{100K} = \$5K$.

Section 1.1502–13(f) provides for the restoration of deferred gain or loss on dispositions. Under –13(c)(4), the character of deferred gain or loss at the time of restoration is generally determined by reference to the character of the gain or loss at the time of the initial transaction. Finally under –13(c)(3), a group may elect not to defer gain or loss.

The regulations under –13T provide special rules regarding the creation and restoration of deferred gain and loss.

B. EXCERPT FROM DEFERRED INTERCOMPANY TRANSACTION REGULATIONS UNDER § 1.1502–13

§ 1.1502–13. **Intercompany transactions.**—(a) *Definitions.*

(1) *"Intercompany transaction."* (i) * * * [T]he term "intercompany transaction" means a transaction during a consolidated return year between corporations which are members of the same group immediately after such transaction. Thus, for example, an intercompany transaction would include a sale of property by one member of a group (hereinafter referred to as the "selling member") to another member of the same group ("purchasing member"), the performance of services by one member of a group ("selling member") for another member of the same group ("purchasing member"), or the payment of interest by one member of a group ("purchasing member") to another member of the same group ("selling member"), during a consolidated return year.

* * *

(2) *"Deferred intercompany transaction".* The term "deferred intercompany transaction" means—

(i) The sale or exchange of property,

(ii) The performance of services in a case where the amount of the expenditure for such services is capitalized (for example, a builder's fee, architect's fee, or other similar cost which is included in the basis of property), or

(iii) Any other expenditure in a case where the amount of the expenditure is capitalized (for example, prepaid rent, or interest which is included in the basis of property),

in an intercompany transaction.

* * *

(c) *Deferral of gain or loss on deferred intercompany transactions*—(1) *General rule.* (i) To the extent gain or loss on a deferred intercompany transaction is recognized under the Code for a consolidated return year, such gain or loss shall be deferred by the selling member (hereinafter referred to as "deferred gain or loss").

* * *

(3) *Election not to defer.* A group may elect with the consent of the Commissioner not to defer gain or loss on any deferred intercompany transactions with respect to all property or any class or classes of property.

* * *

(4) *Character and source of deferred gain or loss.* (i) Except as provided in subdivision (ii) of this subparagraph, the character and source of deferred gain or loss on a deferred intercompany transaction shall be determined at the time of the deferred intercompany transaction as if such transaction had not occurred during a consolidated return year.

* * *

(d) *Restoration of deferred gain or loss for property subject to depreciation, amortization, or depletion*—(1) *General rule.* (i) If property (including a capitalized expenditure for services, or any other capitalized expenditure) acquired in a deferred intercompany transaction is, in the hands of any member of the group, subject to depreciation, amortization, or depletion, then, for each taxable year (whether consolidated or separate) for which a depreciation, amortization, or depletion deduction is allowed to any member of the group with respect to such property, a portion (as determined under subdivision (ii) of this subparagraph) of the deferred gain or loss attributable to such property shall be taken into account by the selling member.

(ii) The portion of the deferred gain or loss attributable to any property which shall be taken into account by the selling member shall be an amount equal to—

(*a*) The amount of gain or loss deferred by the selling member at the time of the deferred intercompany transaction (and if a member has transferred the property to another member of the group, the remaining balance at the time of such transfer), multiplied by

(*b*) A fraction, the numerator of which is the amount of the depreciation, amortization, or depletion deduction with respect to such property allowed to any member of the group for the year (whether consolidated or separate), and the denominator of which is the depreciable basis (*i.e.,* basis reduced by salvage value required to be taken into account, if any) of such property in the hands of such member immediately after such property was transferred to such member.

* * *

(f) *Restoration of deferred gain or loss on dispositions, etc.*—(1) *General rule.* The remaining balance (after taking into account any prior reductions) * * * of the deferred gain or loss attributable to property, services, or other expenditure shall be taken into account by the selling member as of the earliest of the following dates:

(i) The date on which such property is disposed of outside the group * * *;

(iii) Immediately preceding the time when either the selling member or the member which owns the property ceases to be a member of the group;

§ 8.8 INTERGROUP DIVIDENDS UNDER § 1.1502–14

A. DISCUSSION

Portions of the regulations under § 1.1502–14 and –14T dealing with intergroup dividends are set out below. The treatment of intergroup dividends is determined under § 1.1502–14. Section 1.1502–14(a) provides that "[a] dividend distributed by one member to another member shall be eliminated." This means that intergroup dividends are not included in taxable income. Contrast this with the 70% or 80% dividends received deduction under § 243 for non-affiliated group dividends. *See* Sec. 4.4.

The term "dividend" is defined in –14(a)(1) as a distribution described in § 301(c)(1). Under –14T(a) if a subsidiary recognizes gain or loss on the distribution of property to its parent, the gain or loss is deferred and is taken into account under the deferred intercompany transaction rules under –13, discussed in Sec. 13.7. Under –13, the parent takes a fair market value basis for distributed property as provided in § 301(d). The example in –14T(c)(1), set out below, illustrates the treatment of a distribution of appreciated property.

Pursuant to –14(a)(2), if a distribution is not out of earnings and profits of a subsidiary, the distribution reduces the basis of the subsidiary's stock. After the basis is reduced to zero, the distribution creates an excess loss account. *See* Sec. 8.9.

B. EXCERPTS FROM § 1.1502–14 AND –14T REGULATIONS

§ 1.1502–14. **Stock, bonds, and other obligations of members.**—(a) *Intercompany distributions with respect to stock*—(1) *Dividends.* A dividend distributed by one member to another member during a consolidated return year shall be eliminated. For purposes of this paragraph, the term "dividend" means a distribution which is described in section 301(c)(1) * * *

(2) *Nondividend distributions.* No gain shall be recognized to the distributee on a distribution with respect to stock, from one member to another member during a consolidated return year, which is described in section 301(c)(2) or (3). Such distribution shall be applied against and reduce the adjusted basis * * * of such stock in the distributing corporation held by the distributee, and to the extent such distribution exceeds the adjusted basis, the excess shall be (or shall be added to) the excess loss account for such stock in the distributing corporation held by the distributee.

* * *

§ 1.1502–14T. **Treatment of distributing corporation** * * *.— (a) *Deferral of gain or loss.* To the extent gain or loss is recognized to the distributing corporation on a distribution described in § 1.1502–14(a) or (b) (including any amount which is treated as gain under sections 311, 336 * * *), such gain or loss shall be deferred by the distributing corporation. Such deferred gain or loss shall be taken into account at the time and in the manner specified in [the restoration rules in] § 1.1502–13(d), (e), and (f) * * *, as if such distributing corporation were a "selling member," the distributee were a "purchasing member" and the distribution described in § 1.1502–14 were a "deferred intercompany transaction."

* * *

Example (1). (i) Corporation P, S, and T file consolidated returns on a calendar year basis. P owns all 100 shares of the outstanding stock of S. S owns all 200 shares of the outstanding stock of T. The T shares have an adjusted basis of $1,000 and a value of $10,000. S distributes all of its T stock to P. As a result of the distribution, S recognizes $9,000 of gain under section 311(b) and the gain is deferred under paragraph (a) of this section. P receives a $10,000 basis in the T stock under § 1.1502–31(a).

§ 8.9 INVESTMENT ADJUSTMENT SYSTEM: STOCK BASIS, EXCESS LOSS ACCOUNTS AND EARNINGS AND PROFITS

A. INTRODUCTION

Recall that in *Ilfeld, supra* Sec. 8.2, the taxpayer-parent deducted the operating losses attributable to its consolidated subsidiaries in computing its consolidated tax liability. The parent was not required to reduce the basis of the subsidiaries' stock by the amount of the losses. Consequently, upon liquidation of the subsidiaries the parent claimed a second loss under the predecessor of § 331. The Supreme Court, however, disallowed the double deduction.

Under the present consolidated return regulations, a parent generally must reduce the basis of a subsidiary's stock by the amount of the subsidiary's operating losses and must increase the basis by the amount of the subsidiary's income. The basis may be reduced below zero, creating an "excess loss account" for the subsidiary's stock. Conceptually this is similar to a negative basis for the subsidiary's stock. If a subsidiary's stock for which there is an excess loss account is sold, the parent must include in income the amount of the excess loss account. These rules are discussed below.

The rules under § 1.1502–20, which disallow loss on the disposition of the stock of a subsidiary in mirror subsidiary type transactions are discussed in *Taxable and Tax-Free Mergers, Acquisitions, and LBOs, supra* Sec. 1.4.

On November 12, 1992, the Treasury issued Proposed Regulations revising the investment adjustment system of the consolidated returns regulations, including the rules governing earnings and profits and excess loss accounts. *See* Notice of Proposed Rulemaking, CO–30–92, November 12, 1992. The following sections briefly introduce both the current and proposed rules.

B. THE CURRENT INVESTMENT ADJUSTMENT SYSTEM

1. *In General*

The current investment adjustment system is described as follows in the preamble to the proposed regulations:

PREAMBLE TO PROPOSED REGULATIONS ON INVESTMENT ADJUSTMENTS

CO–30–92 (Nov. 12, 1992).

The current investment adjustment system (§§ 1.1502–19, 1.1502–32, and 1.1502–33) combines single entity and separate entity treatment of subsidiaries in consolidated groups. Unlike a single corporation with divisions, a consolidated group must determine gain or loss from the disposition of a subsidiary's stock, and each subsidiary must maintain a separate earnings and profits account. These requirements reflect the group's treatment as a collection of separate entities. The investment adjustment system was developed to modify the separate entity treatment of subsidiaries in favor of single entity treatment.

Under current § 1.1502–32, an owning member (P) must adjust its basis in the stock of a subsidiary (S) to reflect S's earnings and profits, whether positive or negative (E & P). P's basis is also reduced by the amount of any dividends distributed by S to P, if the distributed E & P is deemed to be reflected in P's basis in S's stock (e.g., if S's E & P arose in a prior consolidated return year and is reflected in stock basis through investment adjustments). To the extent reductions exceed P's basis in S's stock, they result in an excess loss account in the stock. P must include its excess loss account in income under current § 1.1502–19, generally when S's stock is sold to a nonmember or becomes worthless. These rules reflect the treatment of P and S as a single entity by causing P's basis (or excess loss account) in S's stock to reflect amounts recognized by S and taken into account in determining consolidated taxable income, and S's distributions to P.

Under current § 1.1502–33, P must adjust its E & P account to reflect the adjustments to its basis in S's stock. As a result, S's E & P is currently "tiered up" to P's E & P through the investment adjustment system. If P is also a subsidiary, P's E & P (which includes S's E & P) is also tiered up through the investment adjustment system and ultimately reflected in the E & P of the common parent. Each member retains its own E & P, however, including its share of the E & P of lower tier members.

P's stock basis and E & P adjustments are generally determined separately for each share of S's stock and are limited to the share's "allocable part" of S's E & P. For example, if the group owns 80 percent of S's only class of stock, only 80 percent of S's E & P tiers up.

The current rules are expressed as a series of complex, mechanical adjustments. The purposes of the investment adjustment system are not articulated in the regulations, and tax policy concerns with respect to stock basis adjustments (e.g., to prevent overstatement of stock basis) often conflict with those for E & P adjustments (e.g., to prevent understatement of E & P). As a result, the current rules do not easily accommodate changes in the tax law, particularly those giving rise to the growing disparity between taxable income and E & P.

2. *The Woods Investment Problem*

Woods Investment Co. v. Commissioner, 85 T.C. 274 (1985), *acq.,* 1986–1 C.B.1, held that the basis of stock of a subsidiary was to be determined by reference to E & P computed on a straight line basis under 312(k), as provided in the current consolidated return regulations. As a result, the basis reductions computed on straight line depreciation were less than the subsidiary's losses which were based on accelerated depreciation, and on the sale of stock of the subsidiary the parent, in essence, realized what amounted to a double loss (one passed through from the subsidiary's operation, and a second on the sale of the stock of the subsidiary). The amount of the double loss is the difference between accelerated and straight line depreciation.

3. *Section 1503(e)(1)(A) Response to Woods Investment*

The preamble to the proposed regulations explains the Congressional reaction to *Woods Investment:*

PREAMBLE TO PROPOSED REGULATIONS ON INVESTMENT ADJUSTMENTS
CO–30–92 (Nov. 12, 1992).

Section 1503(e)(1)(A) was enacted in 1987 to overrule *Woods* and reverse the effects of sections 312(k) and (n) on stock basis adjustments. Under section 1503(e)(1)(A), stock basis adjustments must generally be determined without regard to section 312(k) and (n) for purposes of determining gain or loss on dispositions of subsidiary stock after December 15, 1987. * * *

Because section 1503(e)(1)(A) does not apply for purposes of tiering up S's E & P, adjustments to stock basis and to E & P have been delinked. Thus, two separate systems are currently required—one for determining stock basis and the other for determining E & P.

Congress expected that the principles of section 1503(e)(1) would be incorporated into the investment adjustment system. The legislative history states—

> [T]he committee does not believe that the consequences of a disposition of stock in a member of the group should be more favorable than if the operations of the subsidiary had been conducted (and the assets had been owned) directly by the parent corporation. The amendments made by this provision are intended to prevent this result, and the committee expects that appropriate modifications will be made not only to the basis adjustment rules, but to other provisions of the consolidated return regulations, in furtherance of this objective. H.R.Rep. No. 391 (Part 2), 100th Cong., 1st Sess. 1089 (1987).

C. GENERAL APPROACH OF PROPOSED REGULATIONS

The preamble says the following about the general approach of the Proposed Regulations:

PREAMBLE TO PROPOSED REGULATIONS ON INVESTMENT ADJUSTMENTS
CO–30–92 (Nov. 12, 1992).

The proposed rules represent a comprehensive revision of the investment adjustment system, as well as a revision of the related consolidated return rules for the determination and adjustment of P's basis in S's stock. * * *

In connection with the revision of the investment adjustment system, several methods for adjusting stock basis and E & P were considered, and the policies underlying the present system were reexamined. For example, consideration was given to conforming basis and partial conforming basis regimes. Under a conforming basis regime, the basis of a subsidiary's stock would conform to the net asset basis of the subsidiary (generally, the basis of its assets, minus its liabilities). Under a partial conforming basis regime, changes in stock basis would be measured by changes in the member's net asset basis.

Each system has significant sources of complexity and presents significant policy issues. The Treasury Department and the Service concluded that the greatest simplification would be achieved by adopting, to the extent feasible, the existing principles for adjusting the basis of partnership interests (section 705) and stock in S corporations (section 1367). The adjustments under these other systems are similar to the adjustments under the current investment adjustment system, and groups therefore should be familiar with the approach. Additional modifications have been adopted to simplify operation of the current rules and to correct anomalies. * * *

The proposed rules delink stock basis adjustments from E & P adjustments. Separating these systems prevents policies specific to one system from distorting the other. Stock basis adjustments and E & P continue to tier up, but under separate systems.

In general, P's stock basis adjustments are measured by reference to S's taxable income rather than S's E & P. As in the case of partnerships and S corporations, the rules also take into account tax-exempt income and expenditures that are not deductible or chargeable to capital account.

Because the proposed rules conform the investment adjustment system to recent Code amendments under section 1503(e), the Treasury Department and the Service anticipate that the proposed rules will not materially alter the investment adjustments of most subsidiaries as determined under current law. * * *

D. BASIS ADJUSTMENT RULES UNDER PROP.REG. § 1.1502–32

1. Background

The preamble to the Proposed Regulations explains the general operation of the investment adjustment rules as follows:

PREAMBLE TO PROPOSED REGULATIONS ON INVESTMENT ADJUSTMENTS
CO–30–92 (Nov. 12, 1992).

Under the proposed rules, P's stock basis adjustments with respect to S's stock are determined by reference to S's taxable income or loss, certain tax-exempt and noncapital, nondeductible items, and distributions. As under the current system, a positive adjustment increases, and a negative adjustment decreases, P's basis in S's stock. If a negative adjustment exceeds P's basis, the excess is referred to as P's excess loss account.

Section 1.1502–32(a) describes the basic purposes of the stock basis adjustment rules as reflecting the treatment of P and S as a single entity. Thus, stock basis adjustments prevent items recognized by S from being recognized a second time on P's disposition of S's stock. In addition, even if the adjustments are not necessary to prevent duplication of S's items (e.g., the items are attributable to unrealized loss of S that is reflected in P's cost basis for S's stock), the adjustments have the effect of causing P to recapture the items. (But see § 1.1502–20, disallowing certain stock losses to implement the repeal of the *General Utilities* doctrine.)

1. AMOUNT OF ADJUSTMENT

The adjustment is the net amount (treating income and gain items as increases and losses, deductions, and distributions as decreases) of S's—

(i) Taxable income or tax loss;

(ii) Tax-exempt income;

(iii) Noncapital, nondeductible expenses; and

(iv) Distributions with respect to S's stock.

2. *Stock Basis Under Prop.Reg. § 1.1502–32(b)(2)(i)*

Prop.Reg. § 1.1502–32(b)(2)(i) provides the following rules for determining stock basis:

Stock basis. P's basis in S's stock is increased by positive adjustments and decreased by negative adjustments under paragraph (b)(3) of this section. [*Infra*].

3. *Amount of the Adjustment Under Prop.Reg. § 1.1502–32(b)(3)*

Prop.Reg. § 1.1502–32(b)(3) provides the following rules for determining the amount of the adjustment:

Amount of adjustment. The adjustment, made as of the time of the adjustment, is the net amount (treating income and gain items as increases and losses, deductions, expenses, and distributions as decreases) of S's—

(i) Taxable income or tax loss;

(ii) Tax-exempt income;

(iii) Noncapital, nondeductible expenses; and

(iv) Distributions with respect to S's stock.

4. *Operating Rules Under Prop.Reg. § 1.1502–32(b)(4)(i)*

A variety of operating rules are set forth in Prop.Reg. § 1.1502–32(b)(4)(i), including the following rules regarding a subsidiary's taxable income and tax loss:

Taxable income and tax loss. S's taxable income is consolidated taxable income determined by taking into account only S's items of income, gain, deduction, and loss, and S's deductions and losses are taken into account whether or not they are absorbed by S. If S's deductions and losses exceed its gross income, the excess is referred to as S's tax loss. For this purpose—

(A) To the extent that S's tax loss is absorbed in the year it arises (by a member other than S) or is carried forward and absorbed in a subsequent year (by any member, including S), the loss is treated as a tax loss under paragraph (b)(3)(i) of this section [amount of adjustment, *supra*] in the year in which it is absorbed;

(B) To the extent that S's tax loss is carried back to a prior year (whether consolidated or separate) and absorbed (by any member, including S), the loss is treated as a tax loss under paragraph (b)(3)(i) of this section [amount of adjustment, *supra*] in the year in which it arises and not in the year in which it is absorbed. * * *

5. Determining the Amount of an Excess Loss Account Under Prop.Reg. § 1.1502–32(b)(2)(ii)

Prop.Reg. § 1.1502–32(b)(2)(ii) provides the following rules for determining the amount of an excess loss account:

Excess loss account. If an adjustment under paragraph (b)(3) of this section is negative and exceeds P's basis in S's stock, the excess is referred to as P's excess loss account. Subsequent, positive adjustments first eliminate the excess loss account and any remaining amount increases P's basis in S's stock. See § 1.1502–19 [*infra*] for rules relating to excess loss accounts, including basis determinations and adjustments under other applicable rules of law that may result in an excess loss account.

6. Illustration: Taxable Income

Prop.Reg. § 1.1502–32(b)(5) Example 1 gives the following illustration of the investment adjustment system when a subsidiary has taxable income:

Example 1. Taxable income. (a) During Year 1, the P group has $100 of consolidated taxable income when determined by taking into account only S's items of income, gain, deduction, and loss. Under paragraph (b)(1) [timing of adjustment] of this section, P must adjust its basis in S's stock as of the close of Year 1. Under paragraphs (b)(3) and (b)(4)(i) [taxable income operating rules, *supra*] of this section, P has a $100 positive adjustment [amount of adjustment, *supra*] with respect to S's stock for Year 1. Under paragraph (b)(2) [stock basis, *supra*] of this section, this positive adjustment increases P's basis in S's stock by $100 as of the close of Year 1.

7. *Illustration: Tax Loss*

Prop.Reg. § 1.1502–32(b)(5) Example 2 gives the following illustration of the investment adjustment system when a subsidiary has a tax loss:

Example 2. Tax loss. (a) During Year 2, the P group has a $50 consolidated net operating loss when determined by taking into account only S's items of income, gain, deduction, and loss. S's loss is absorbed by the P group in Year 2, offsetting P's income for that year. Under paragraphs (b)(3) [amount of adjustment, *supra*] and (b)(4)(i)(A) [operating rules, *supra*] of this section because S's loss is absorbed in the year it arises, the loss is treated as a $50 tax loss for Year 2 and P has a $50 negative adjustment with respect to S's stock. Under paragraph (b)(2) [stock basis, *supra*] of this section, this negative adjustment decreases P's basis in S's stock by $50. Under paragraph (b)(2)(ii) of this section [excess loss account, *supra*] if the decrease exceeds P's basis in S's stock, the excess is P's excess loss account in S's stock.

8. *Allocation Among Shares of Stock*

Prop.Reg. § 1.1502–32(*o*) provides special rules for allocating adjustments among shares of stock when a subsidiary is less than wholly owned or has multiple classes of stock. The preamble gives the following general description of the present and proposed allocation process:

PREAMBLE TO PROPOSED REGULATIONS ON INVESTMENT ADJUSTMENTS
CO–30–92 (Nov. 12, 1992).

2. ALLOCATION OF ADJUSTMENTS

The current rules provide that the basis of each share of S's stock must be adjusted to reflect its "allocable part" of S's E & P, but the rules do not specify how the allocable part is determined. Only limited rules are provided for allocations between common and preferred stock; positive adjustments are allocated to preferred stock only to reflect dividends in arrears and negative adjustments only to reflect distributions of dividends.

The Treasury Department and the Service understand that most subsidiaries have only common stock outstanding and are wholly owned within a group, and that the basis of members in a subsidiary's stock is generally uniform. Where subsidiaries have issued preferred stock, the stock is generally described in section 1504(a)(4). Thus, rules for allocating stock basis adjustments among shares in unusual circumstances are generally not necessary. For those cases in which P owns less than all of S's stock or has different bases in different blocks of stock, or in which S has more than one class of stock outstanding, the proposed rules provide additional guidance.

The negative adjustment for distributions is allocated to the shares of S's stock entitled to the distributions. The remainder of the adjustment with respect to S's stock (the portion described in proposed § 1.1502–32(b)(3)(i) to (iii)) is allocated among the shares of S's stock, including shares owned by nonmembers. However, the allocation to nonmembers has no effect on their basis in S's stock. If the adjustment under proposed § 1.1502–32(b)(3) (without taking distributions into account) is positive, it is allocated first to any preferred stock to cover distributions and arrearages, and then to the common stock. If it is negative, it is allocated only to common stock. An allocation is then made among the classes of preferred and common stock and then among the shares within each class. * * *

E. EARNINGS AND PROFITS UNDER PROP.REG. § 1.1502–33

1. *Purpose and Effect of E & P Tiering Rules*

The preamble to the Proposed Regulations gives the following explanation of the purpose and effect of the current and proposed E & P tiering rules:

PREAMBLE TO PROPOSED REGULATIONS ON INVESTMENT ADJUSTMENTS
CO–30–92 (Nov. 12, 1992).

A principal effect of the current investment adjustment system is to consolidate a group's E & P in the E & P account of the common parent. Because of the stock ownership requirements under section 1504, the common parent is typically the only member of a group whose stock is held largely by nonmembers. Therefore, to determine whether distributions to nonmembers should be characterized as dividends, the group's E & P must be consolidated in the common parent.

The proposed rules establish a separate system for adjusting and tiering up E & P. Consequently, anomalies resulting from the interdependence of stock basis adjustments and E & P adjustments are eliminated. For example, if S sustains an E & P deficit and a corresponding tax loss, P's basis in S's stock is not reduced to reflect the E & P deficit under the current rules until the tax loss is absorbed. Because the stock basis adjustment is deferred, the current linked system automatically defers the tiering up of the E & P deficit. The E & P result is incorrect because the group's E & P, determined on a single entity basis, should be reduced to reflect S's E & P deficit when the deficit is sustained.

The proposed rules provide for separately adjusting the basis of S's stock for E & P purposes to determine P's E & P on the disposition of

S's stock. Separate stock basis adjustments for E & P purposes are necessary to avoid duplicating E & P. For example, if S earns $100 of E & P that tiers up and increases P's E & P by $100, P should not have another $100 of E & P if it subsequently sells S's stock for an additional $100 because of S's earnings.

2. *Guiding Principles Under Prop.Reg. § 1.1502-33(a)(1)*

Prop.Reg. § 1.1502-33 sets forth the purpose of the regulations:

(1) *Purpose.* This section provides rules for determining the earnings and profits of a subsidiary (S) and any member (P) owning S's stock. In general, earnings and profits of members are determined under applicable provisions of law, including section 312. This section modifies the general determination to reflect the treatment of P and S as a single entity by causing the earnings and profits of lower tier members to be reflected in the earnings and profits of higher tier members and consolidating the group's earnings and profits in the common parent.

3. *The Tiering Rules Under Prop.Reg. § 1.1502-33(b)(1)*

Prop.Reg. § 1.1502-33(b)(1) sets forth the general rule for tiering up E & P:

(1) *General rule.* P's earnings and profits are adjusted under this section to reflect S's earnings and profits in accordance with the applicable principles of § 1.1502-32(b) [relating to basis adjustment]. For example, the adjustments are determined as of the close of each consolidated return year, and as of any other time if a determination at that time is necessary to determine the earnings and profits of any person, and they are applied in the order of the tiers, from the lowest to the highest. * * *

4. *Illustration of Tiering Rules*

Prop.Reg. § 1.1502-33(b)(3) Example (1) illustrates the tiering rules:

Example 1. Tiering up earnings and profits. (a) P forms S on January 1 of Year 1 with $100 capital contribution. S has $100 of earnings and profits during Year 1, and no earnings and profits during Year 2. During Year 2, S distributes a $50 dividend to P.

(b) Under paragraph (b)(1) of this section and the applicable principles of § 1.1502-32(b), S's $100 of earnings and profits for Year 1 also increase P's earnings and profits for Year 1. P has no additional earnings and profits for Year 2 as a result of the $50 distribution in Year 2, because there is a $50 increase in P's earnings and profits as a result of the receipt of the dividend and a corresponding $50 decrease in S's earnings and profits under section 312(a) that is reflected in P's earnings and profits under paragraph (b)(1) of this section.

* * *

5. Allocation of Tax Liability in Computing Earnings and Profits

a. Introduction

Section 1552 and the regulations thereunder set forth rules for determining the impact of the group's tax liability on the computation of earnings and profits. Section 1552 provides three optional formulas for allocating the tax liability among the members of the group, and also provides for an allocation in accordance with any method selected by the group and approved by the Secretary. Absent an election, the first option applies. This option apportions the tax liability among the members in accordance with the following formula:

$$\frac{\text{Member's Portion of Consolidated Taxable Income}}{\text{Group's Consolidated Taxable Income}} \times \text{Group's Tax Liability}$$

Section 1.1552–1(b), which determines the effect of an allocation, provides that each member's earnings and profits are reduced by the amount of the tax liability allocated to it. If another member has paid the liability, the payment is treated as a "distribution with respect to stock, a contribution to capital, or a combination thereof."

b. Purpose and Effect of Allocations of Tax Liability Under the Proposed Regulations

PREAMBLE TO PROPOSED REGULATIONS ON INVESTMENT ADJUSTMENTS

CO–30–92 (Nov. 12, 1992).

E & P is generally reduced for federal taxes, and each member must adjust its E & P for an allocable part of the tax liability of the group, determined under section 1552. The current E & P rules also permit groups to allocate additional amounts. For example, if P has $100 of income and S has $100 of loss, the group's consolidated taxable income is $0 and nothing is allocated under section 1552. Current § 1.1502–33(d) provides elective methods by which P may be treated as incurring a liability to S in recognition of P's income offsetting S's loss.

The elective allocation methods of current § 1.1502–33(d) are retained under the proposed rules but are rewritten to improve comprehension. Although these rules are the most complex feature of the current E & P rules, they are retained because the Treasury Department and the Service understand that groups rely on them for non-tax purposes, such as ratemaking for public utilities. * * *

c. *General Rules for Allocating Tax Liability Under Prop.Reg. § 1.1502–33(d)(1)*

Prop.Reg. § 1.1502–33(d)(1) sets forth the following general principles for allocating tax liabilities:

PREAMBLE TO PROPOSED REGULATIONS ON INVESTMENT ADJUSTMENTS
CO–30–92 (Nov. 12, 1992).

Section 1552 allocates the tax liability of a consolidated group among its members for purposes of determining the amounts by which their earnings and profits are reduced by taxes. Section 1552 does not accurately reflect the use by one member of another member's deductions and losses. For example, if P's $100 of income is offset by S's $100 of deductions, consolidated tax liability is $0 and no amount may be allocated under section 1552. Nevertheless, members may compensate other members for the absorption of losses or credits. In addition, the group may elect under this paragraph (d) to allocate additional amounts to reflect the compensation of regular tax liability as defined in section 26(b). Permissible methods are set forth in paragraphs (d)(2) through (4), and election procedures are described in paragraph (d)(5) of this section.

* * *

[The Proposed Regulations provide for a wait-and-see method, (*see* Prop.Reg. § 1.1502–33(d)(2)), a percentage method (*see* Prop.Reg. § 1.1502–33(d)(3)) and any other method approved by the Commissioner. *See* Prop.Reg. § 1.1502–33(d)(4).]

d. *The Wait-and-See Method of Prop.Reg. § 1.1502–33(d)(2)*

Prop.Reg. § 1.1502–33(d)(2) sets forth the following general rules regarding the wait-and-see method:

PREAMBLE TO PROPOSED REGULATIONS ON INVESTMENT ADJUSTMENTS
CO–30–92 (Nov. 12, 1992).

The wait-and-see method under this paragraph (d)(2) is derived from Securities and Exchange Commission procedures. In the year that a member's loss or credit is absorbed, the group's consolidated tax liability is allocated in accordance with the group's method under section 1552. When, in effect, the member with the loss or credit could have absorbed the attribute on a separate return basis in a later year, a portion of the group's consolidated tax liability for the later year that is otherwise allocated to members under section 1552 is reallocated.

e. Illustration of the Wait-and-See Method

Prop.Reg. § 1.1502–33(d)(6), Example 1 illustrates the wait-and-see method as follows:

PREAMBLE TO PROPOSED REGULATIONS ON INVESTMENT ADJUSTMENTS
CO–30–92 (Nov. 12, 1992).

Example 1. Wait-and-see method. (a) P owns all of the stock of S1 and S2. The P group elects in accordance with paragraph (d)(5) of this section to use the wait-and-see method of allocation under paragraph (d)(2) of this section in conjunction with § 1.1552–1(a)(1). During Year 1, each member's taxable income, determined as if the member had filed separate returns and under § 1.1552–1(a)(1), is as follows: P $0, S1 $2,000, and S2 ($1,000). Thus, the P group's consolidated tax liability for Year 1 is $340 (assuming a 34 percent tax rate).

(b) Under § 1.1552–1(a)(1)(i), the tax liability of the P group is allocated among the members in accordance with the portion of the consolidated taxable income attributable to each member having taxable income. Thus, all of the P group's $340 consolidated tax liability is allocated to S1 under section 1552. As a result, S1 decreases its earnings and profits by $340 even if S1 does not pay the tax liability. No further allocations are made under paragraph (d)(2) of this section because S2 cannot yet absorb its loss on a separate return basis.

(c) If S1 pays the $340 tax liability there is no further effect on the income, earnings and profits, or stock basis of any member. If P pays the $340 tax liability (and the payment is not a loan from P to S1), P is treated as making a $340 contribution to the capital of S1; if S2 pays the $340 tax liability (and the payment is not a loan from S2 to S1), S2 is treated as making a $340 distribution to P with respect to its stock, and P is treated as making a $340 contribution to the capital of S1. See § 1.1552–1(b)(2).

F. EXCESS LOSS ACCOUNTS UNDER PROP.REG. § 1.1502–19

1. *Purpose and Effect of Excess Loss Accounts*

The preamble to the Proposed Regulations gives the following general description of the purpose and effect of the excess loss account (ELA) rules:

PREAMBLE TO PROPOSED REGULATIONS ON INVESTMENT ADJUSTMENTS
CO–30–92 (Nov. 12, 1992).

The excess loss account (ELA) rules are an extension of the rules for adjusting stock basis. P's basis in S's stock is reduced as the group absorbs S's losses and as S makes distributions to P. The reductions are not limited to the group's basis in S's stock and, to the extent reductions exceed stock basis, they result in an ELA with respect to P's S stock. P's ELA is included in its income when P disposes of the stock, and the income is generally treated as gain from the sale of the stock.

An ELA ordinarily arises with respect to a share of S's stock only if S's losses and distributions are funded with capital not reflected in the basis of the share. The reductions may be funded by creditors or by other shareholders, including other members.

2. *General Description of the Rules*

The preamble to the Proposed Regulations gives the following general description of the operation of the rules:

PREAMBLE TO PROPOSED REGULATIONS ON INVESTMENT ADJUSTMENTS
CO–30–92 (Nov. 12, 1992).

The proposed rules revise and simplify the current rules by applying principles. In general, an ELA is treated as negative basis for computational purposes, to eliminate the need for special ELA rules paralleling the basis rules of the Code. Similarly, the rules of the Code are generally used to determine the timing for inclusion of an ELA in income. For example, if S has an ELA in T's stock and distributes the stock to P in a transaction to which section 355 applies, section 358 eliminates S's ELA (instead, P's basis in T's stock is an allocable part of P's basis in S's stock), and section 355 provides that any gain realized by S from the disposition of T's stock is not recognized. Although P's ELA in S's stock is generally included in income when P or S becomes nonmembers of the group, a special exception is provided if they cease to be members by reason of the acquisition of the entire group. Unlike the current rules, the proposed rules do not provide special investment adjustments to prevent income attributable to preacquisition ELAs from increasing the E & P or the stock basis of members of the acquiring group. An ELA is merely one form of built-in gain to the acquiring group, and built-in gain is more generally addressed by § 1.1502–20.

3. Determining the Amount of an Excess Loss Account

See Sec. 8.9.D.5. above.

4. General Rule of Income Recognition

Prop.Reg. § 1.1502–19(b)(1) provides the general rule of income realization for an ELA:

(1) General rule. If P is treated under this section as disposing of a share of S's stock, P's excess loss account in the share is taken into account as an amount realized by P from the disposition. Except as provided in paragraph (b)(4) of this section **[relating to insolvency],** the disposition is treated as a sale or exchange for purposes of determining the character of the amount realized.

Dispositions of stock are defined broadly in Prop.Reg. § 1.1502–19(c) to include transfers, deconsolidations and worthlessness.

5. Illustration

Prop.Reg. § 1.1502–19(e) Example (1) gives the following illustration of the recognition of an ELA upon the sale of stock of a subsidiary:

Example 1. Sale of stock. (a) On January 1 of Year 1, P has a $150 basis in S's stock, and S has a $100 basis in T's stock. During Year 1, P has $500 of ordinary income, S has no income or loss, and T has a $200 ordinary loss. On December 31 of Year 1, S sells T's stock to a nonmember for $60. Immediately before the sale, under § 1.1502–32(b), S decreases its basis in T's stock to zero and establishes a $100 excess loss account in T's stock.

(b) Under paragraph (c) of this section, S is treated as disposing of T's stock on December 31 of Year 1 (the day of the sale). Under paragraph (b)(1) of this section, the excess loss account is treated as an additional $100 realized by S from the sale. Consequently, S recognizes a $160 gain from the sale which is taken into account in determining the group's consolidated taxable income. Under § 1.1502–32(b), T's $200 loss and S's $160 gain result in a $40 decrease in P's basis in S's stock as of the close of Year 1, from $150 to $110.

6. Modifications of Excess Loss Recapture Rules to Prevent Shifting of ELA to Debt

See § 1503(e)(4).

SENATE FINANCE COMMITTEE REPORT TO THE RECONCILIATION ACT OF 1989
88–89 (1989).

PRESENT LAW

* * *

Under the present consolidated return regulations, a parent corporation that has an excess loss account in the stock of a subsidiary can, on disposition of the subsidiary's stock, elect to apply the excess loss account to reduce the basis of other stock or debt held by the parent in the subsidiary after the disposition.

REASONS FOR CHANGE

The committee believes that when deductions creating an excess loss account have been taken with respect to an equity investment that is disposed of, it is not appropriate to permit deferral of gain recognition by shifting the recapture liability to a debt investment. * * *

EXPLANATION OF PROVISION

[Section 1503(e)(4)] modifies the excess loss account recapture rules to prevent the reallocation of the excess loss account to reduce the basis of debt in the subsidiary held by the parent corporation after a disposition. Thus, on disposition of the stock of a subsidiary corporation, gain attributable to an excess loss account must be recognized rather than deferred through a reduction in the basis of debt held by the parent corporation in the subsidiary.

* * *

7. *The Validity of the § 1.1502–19 Excess Loss Regulations*

See Covil Insulation Co., 65 T.C. 364 (1975).

§ 8.10 SUMMARY PROBLEMS ON CONSOLIDATED RETURNS

1. P and S, both newly organized corporations, file a consolidated return. S has only common stock outstanding, and P owns 90 percent of the common. P's basis for the common is $40K. In the first year of operations, S has a separate taxable loss of $20K and P has separate taxable income of $230K.

    a. What is the group's consolidated taxable income and tax liability (assuming 34 percent rate)? *See* § 1.1502–11, –12 and –2; and Sec. 8.6.

    b. What is P's basis for the S common, and what are P's and S's earnings and profits at the beginning of the second year? *See* discussion of Proposed Regulations in Sec. 8.9.

c. Same questions as in (a) and (b) above, except that instead of $20K loss for the year, S had a $100K loss. *See* discussion of Proposed Regulations in Sec. 8.9.

2. At the beginning of 1990, P sold to its wholly owned subsidiary, S, a machine for which P had an adjusted basis of $50K. The original cost of the machine was $75K. The selling price to S was $100K. One year later S sold the machine to a third party for $125K. Prior to the sale, S took $10K of depreciation on the machine. P and S file a consolidated return. What result from the transactions? *See* Sec. 8.7.

Chapter 9

LIQUIDATION OF C CORPORATIONS

§ 9.1 SCOPE

This chapter examines various aspects involved in the liquidation of C corporations. Sec. 9.2 explores the treatment under § 331 of a shareholder upon receipt of a liquidating distribution, and Sec. 9.3 examines the nonrecognition treatment available under § 332 to a parent corporation upon the liquidation of a subsidiary into the parent. Sec. 9.4 examines §§ 336 and 337 which embody the repeal of the *General Utilities* doctrine. Section 336 provides that a liquidating corporation recognizes gain and, in certain cases, loss on the distribution of its property, and § 337 provides an exception to this rule for liquidating distributions by a subsidiary to its parent corporation. Sec. 9.5 briefly introduces § 338, which provides for an elective step-up in basis after an acquisition of the stock of a target corporation. Sec. 9.6 provides a set of problems dealing with these liquidation issues. Finally, Sec. 9.7 examines the policy issue of whether there should be relief for C corporations from the repeal of the *General Utilities* doctrine.

The issues in this chapter are covered in greater detail in Chapters 29, 30 and 32 of *Federal Taxation of Business Enterprises, supra,* Chapter 1, note 1 and in Chapter 11 of Bittker and Eustice, *Corporations, supra* Sec. 1.4.

§ 9.2 GENERAL RULE OF SHAREHOLDER RECOGNITION OF GAIN OR LOSS ON COMPLETE LIQUIDATION

A. INTRODUCTION TO GENERAL RULE OF SHAREHOLDER RECOGNITION UNDER § 331 AND § 334(a)

Section 331 provides that amounts distributed in either a complete or partial liquidation of a corporation are "treated" as "payment in exchange for the stock." Since these liquidation transactions are treated as exchanges, the rules of § 1001 apply; the shareholder recognizes a gain or loss, depending upon the amount realized and the adjusted basis of his stock. *See* § 1.331–1(b). The gain or loss is separately calculated on a share-by-share basis; consequently, there may be gain on some shares and loss on others. *See* § 1.331–1(e). Any nonrecourse or recourse liabilities transferred to the shareholder reduce the shareholder's gain recognized. A distributee shareholder's basis for the property received in a § 331 liquidation is the fair market value of the property. *See* § 334(a).

Section 331(b) provides that the dividend rules of § 301 do not apply to complete liquidations, except in certain liquidations of personal holding companies. *See* § 316(b)(2)(B). This exception permits a personal holding company to satisfy its dividend distribution requirements during the period in which it is being liquidated.

B. WHEN IS A CORPORATION BEING LIQUIDATED?

CLEVELAND v. COMMISSIONER

Tax Court of the United States, 1963.
39 T.C. 657, *affirmed* 335 F.2d 473 (3d Cir.1964).

OPINION

The sole issue is whether the four distributions by Britton Contracting Co. to the petitioners were liquidating distributions within the meaning of the [predecessor of § 331] or whether they were essentially equivalent to a dividend. * * *

[T]he term "liquidation" is not defined in the 1939 Code. This court defined the term in *T.T. Word Supply Co.*, 41 B.T.A. 965, 980 (1949), as follows:

> The liquidation of a corporation is the process of winding up its affairs by realizing upon its assets, paying its debts, and appropriating the amount of its profit and loss. It differs from normal operation for current profit in that it ordinarily results in the winding up of the corporation's affairs, and *there must be a manifest intention to liquidate, a continuing purpose to terminate its affairs and dissolve the corporation, and its activities must be directed and confined thereto.* A mere declaration is not enough, and the question whether a corporation is in liquidation is one of fact. [Emphasis added.]

The fact that no formal plan of liquidation was adopted has some weight but is not decisive. * * * The real question here is whether, after the petitioners bought their stock, Britton was in liquidation and its activities were confined to the winding up of its affairs. At the time of the distributions to petitioners in the period from November 23, 1953, to February 8, 1954, Britton was actively seeking the very large and lucrative United Fuel contract, which it later obtained. Such activity certainly does not manifest a continuing purpose to terminate all business and confine corporate activities to the winding up of its affairs. The termination of its existing contracts, the discharge of various employees, and the sale of its machinery indicate a business contraction and winding up, but this is illusory in the light of the United Fuel contract. There was no substantial or real contraction of business since it was known that other employees and an even greater amount of machinery and equipment would soon be needed for the United Fuel job, and the size of that contract was such as to manifest an intention to continue actively in its usual business operations, at least until that big job was finished.

The fact that a liquidating corporation engages in some new business does not always preclude a liquidation. In *R.D. Merrill Co.,* 4 T.C. 955 (1945), the corporation acquired additional timberland during the period of liquidation. However, the Court found that this was "a minor transaction * * * and its purchase was incidental to and of assistance in the logging of other timber." Also, in *Rollestone Corporation,* 38 B.T.A. 1093 (1938), the liquidating corporation engaged in some drilling operations which the Court found "insignificant and unimportant." The contract with United Fuel, however, would provide receipts in excess of 50 percent of Britton's total receipts for the year 1953. The size and consequent importance of this contract is patent. It was neither a minor transaction nor, as we have found, was it incidental to the liquidation process.

[We find that] Britton intended to obtain and perform substantial new business and was actively and aggressively seeking to procure the United Fuel contract when the distributions to petitioners were being made.

We hold that Britton was not in the process of liquidation at the time of the distributions and that it remained a going concern until after the United Fuel contract was performed.

Questions

What tax stakes are involved in the determination of whether a distribution is a liquidating distribution? What is the treatment of accumulated E & P upon liquidation?

C. SERIES OF LIQUIDATING DISTRIBUTIONS

REVENUE RULING 85–48
1985–1 C.B. 126.

Issue

What is the proper federal income tax treatment of amounts received by a shareholder pursuant to a series of distributions in complete liquidation of a multiple-shareholder corporation under the circumstances described below?

* * *

LAW AND ANALYSIS

Section 346(a) of the Internal Revenue Code provides that a distribution will be treated as in complete liquidation of a corporation if the distribution is one of a series of distributions in redemption of all the stock of the corporation pursuant to a plan.

Rev.Rul. 68–348, 1968–2 C.B. 141, provides that where a sole shareholder owns more than one block of shares of a corporation and receives a series of distributions in complete liquidation of the corporation, each distribution must be allocated ratably among the several blocks of shares in the proportion that the number of shares in a particularly block bears to the total number of shares outstanding. Where a corporation has multiple shareholders, liquidation distributions must be allocated among blocks of shares held by different shareholders as well as among different blocks of shares owned by a particular shareholder. Rev.Rul. 79–10, 1979–1 C.B. 140, holds that distributions under a plan of complete liquidation made by a corporation having a single class of stock will be treated as pro-rata distributions among all the outstanding shares of the corporation. Consistent with Rev.Rul. 68–348, the liquidation distributions allocated to a particular shareholder must be allocated among the several blocks of shares owned by the shareholder in the proportion that the number of shares in a particular block bears to the total number of shares owned by that shareholder.

* * *

D. OPEN TRANSACTION DOCTRINE

1. *Recognition of Gain*

COMMISSIONER v. CARTER

United States Court of Appeals, Second Circuit, 1948.
170 F.2d 911.

SWAN, CIRCUIT JUDGE.

This appeal presents the question whether income received by the taxpayer in 1943 is taxable as long-term capital gain, as the Tax Court ruled, or as ordinary income as the Commissioner contends. The facts are not in dispute. The taxpayer, Mrs. Carter, had owned for ten years all the stock of a corporation which was dissolved on December 31, 1942. Upon its dissolution all of its assets were distributed to her in kind, subject to all its liabilities which she assumed. In the distribution she received property having a fair market value exceeding by about $20,000 the cost basis of her stock, and she reported such excess as a capital gain in her 1942 return and paid the tax thereon. In the corporate liquidation she also received 32 oil brokerage contracts which the parties stipulated had no ascertainable fair market value when distributed. Each contract provided for payment to the corporation of commissions on future deliveries of oil by a named seller to a named buyer. The contracts required no additional services to be performed by the corporation or its distributee, and the future commissions were conditioned on contingencies which made uncertain the amount and time of payment. In 1943 the taxpayer collected commissions of $34,992.20 under these contracts. She reported this sum as a long-term capital gain; the Commissioner determined it to be ordinary income. The Tax Court held it taxable as capital gain. The correctness of this decision is the sole question presented by the Commissioner's appeal.

[The court here outlined the predecessors of §§ 331 and 1001.] [I]t is obvious that if the oil brokerage contracts distributed to the taxpayer had then had a "fair market value," such value would have increased correspondingly the "amount realized" by her in exchange for her stock and would have been taxable as long-term capital gain, not as ordinary income. * * * The question presented by the present appeal is whether a different result is required when contract obligations having no ascertainable fair market value are distributed in liquidation of a corporation and collections thereunder are made by the distributee in later years.

In answering this question in the negative, the Tax Court relied primarily upon *Burnet v. Logan,* 283 U.S. 404, 51 S.Ct. 550, 75 L.Ed. 1143 (1931) [, which held that a taxpayer who sold property for a contingent payment that could not be valued would first recover basis.]

The Commissioner argues that the *Logan* case is inapplicable because there the taxpayer had not recovered the cost basis of her stock while here she had. The Tax Court thought the distinction immaterial. We agree. The Supreme Court spoke of the annual payments as constituting "profit" after the seller's capital investment should be returned. Until such return it cannot be known whether gain or loss will result from a sale; thereafter it becomes certain that future payments will result in gain. No reason is apparent for taxing them as ordinary income. As this court said in *Commissioner of Internal Revenue v. Hopkinson,* 2 Cir., 126 F.2d 406, 410, "payments received by the seller after his basis had been extinguished would have been taxable to him as capital gains from the sale of the property," citing *Burnet v. Logan* as authority.

The Commissioner also urges that the *Logan* case is distinguishable because it dealt with a sale of stock rather than exchange of stock for assets distributed in a corporate liquidation. * * *

[W]e agree with the Tax Court's ruling that the principle of the *Logan* case is applicable to a corporate liquidation where stock is exchanged in part for contracts having no ascertainable market value, and that future collections under such contracts are taxable as capital gain in the year when received if the distributee has previously recovered the cost basis for the stock.

* * *

For the foregoing reasons we think the decision of the Tax Court correct. It is affirmed.

Questions and Problem

1. How does *Carter* amplify the *Burnet v. Logan* doctrine? What was the taxpayer's basis in *Carter* for the oil brokerage contracts received in the liquidation? What is the treatment of a shareholder who recognizes a capital gain on a liquidation and years later is required to discharge an obligation of the dissolved corporation?

2. What is the impact of the OID provisions on the transaction in *Carter*? *See* Sec. 3.10. What if Mrs. Carter received a contingent payment note from a corporation that purchased the liquidating corporation's assets?

3. Individual A owns all of the stock of corporation X. A's basis for his stock is $50K. X is liquidated and distributes to A cash and tangible assets with a value of $20K and oil brokerage contracts with an unascertainable fair market value. What result to A if he collects $10K per year in each of the next five years from the contracts? $5K per year? Suppose instead that the contracts were valued at $40K upon receipt, and A collects $10K per year in each of the next five years? $5K per year?

2. Recognition of Loss

REVENUE RULING 69-334
1969-1 C.B. 98

In 1966 the assets of a corporation consisted of bonds of another company and cash amounting to less than one percent of the total assets. Pursuant to a plan of complete liquidation, the shareholders in that year surrendered their stock and received from the corporation the bonds of the other company together with participation certificates entitling them to proportionate interest in final distribution. It was determined that the amount of cash would result in a distribution of only a few cents per share. The remaining cash was distributed to the shareholders in 1968.

Held, under these facts, the loss on the liquidation was sustained in 1966 and was deductible for that year.

E. INSTALLMENT SALE TREATMENT UNDER § 453(h)

The receipt by a shareholder of a liquidating distribution of an installment obligation that was received by the liquidating corporation during the 12 month period prior to its liquidation generally is not treated as the receipt of payment by the shareholder. *See* § 453(h)(1)(A). Instead, the shareholder takes gain into account as payments are received on the installment obligation. This is a continuation of the rule that applied under former § 337 prior to the Tax Reform Act of 1986. This special extension of installment sale treatment to shareholders of a liquidating corporation does not apply to obligations received by the liquidating corporation from non bulk sales of inventory. *See* § 453(h)(1)(B). Also, special rules apply to installment obligations of related parties. *See* § 453(h)(1)(C).

F. CORPORATE ASSETS TRANSFERRED TO PARTNERSHIP

REVENUE RULING 69-534
1969-2 C.B. 48.

A corporation was liquidated and its business was thereafter conducted as a partnership by the three individuals who had owned all of the stock of the corporation and who acquired the same relative interests in the partnership that they had previously held in the corporation.

The account of each partner was credited on the books of the partnership with his share of the equity of the corporation, but no amount was actually distributed to the individuals.

Held, the credit given to each shareholder on the books of the partnership that succeeded the corporation was equivalent to a distribution of such assets to the partners since upon the dissolution of the corporation each of its three shareholders became entitled to his proportionate share of its entire net assets. Accordingly, gain or loss is recognized to each shareholder measured by the difference between his aliquot portion of the fair market value of the assets of the corporation distributed in liquidation and the cost or other basis of his stock as provided by section 331 of the Internal Revenue Code of 1954.

* * *

G. NON-PRO RATA DISTRIBUTION

REVENUE RULING 79-10
1979-1 C.B. 140.

Issue

Whether a non pro rata liquidating distribution to shareholders of a corporation having only one class of stock outstanding will be treated for federal income tax purposes as having been made pro rata to each of the shareholders.

Facts

Individual A formed corporation X to engage in a business enterprise. X issued 70,000 shares of no par value common stock to A at a price of $1x$ dollars per share. Shortly thereafter X, through a public offering, sold an additional 30,000 shares of the same class to approximately 1,000 shareholders (minority shareholders) at a price of $5x$ dollars per share.

Several years later, A, possessing the requisite voting power under state law, decided that X should be liquidated.

Under the circumstances at the time, if X had made a pro rata liquidation distribution, the minority shareholders would have suffered losses on their investments while A would have realized a substantial gain as a result of the relatively lower purchase price paid by A for the X stock. For various reasons, A decided to avoid this result by accepting less than the pro rata share of the liquidating distribution to which A was entitled so that the minority shareholders would receive more than the pro rata share of the distribution to which they were entitled, ensuring to the minority stockholders a profit from their investment.

Accordingly, on December 10, 1977, X adopted a plan of complete liquidation and distributed its property to its shareholders, in such non pro rata amounts, in exchange for their stock. In each case, the amount received by the shareholder exceeded the adjusted basis of the X stock surrendered in liquidation. The X stock was a capital asset, as defined in section 1221 of the Internal Revenue Code of 1954, in the hands of each shareholder. X was not a collapsible corporation as defined in section 341(b). X had no other stock outstanding.

LAW AND ANALYSIS

* * *

The legislative background of section 331(a)(1) of the Code indicates that Congress intended to have liquidating distributions treated as if they were proceeds of a sale of stock. In other words, a liquidating distribution is viewed as the proceeds of a purchase of the shareholder's interest by the corporation. Since section 331(a)(1) confers "exchange" status upon the liquidating proceeds, they will generally qualify for capital gain or loss treatment provided the stock of the liquidating corporation is a capital asset in the hands of the shareholder * * *.

The amount realized by the shareholder on the surrender of his stock should be measured by his pro rata share of the assets. If a shareholder receives an amount that is less than his pro rata share, he will be treated for federal income tax purposes as if he had received his pro rata share, and the difference will be treated as if it had been used in a separate transaction to make gifts, to pay compensation, to satisfy obligations of the transferor of any kind, or otherwise depending upon the particular facts and circumstances. Compare section 1.351–1(b)(1) * * *.

HOLDING

The non pro rata liquidating distribution to the shareholders of X is treated for federal income tax purposes as if there had been a pro rata distribution to each shareholder by X in full payment in exchange for each shareholder's X stock, together with a transfer by A to the minority shareholders of an amount equal to the excess of the amount received by the minority over the minority's pro rata share of the liquidating distribution. In substance, the amounts received by the minority shareholders of X represented the total of two separate transactions: the first being the receipt of their pro rata share of the liquidating proceeds, and the second being a payment attributable to A in an amount equal to the excess over their pro rata share. A is deemed to have received his entire pro rata share of the liquidating distribution. The difference between

A's pro rata share and the amount actually received by *A* is treated as having been paid over by *A* to the minority shareholders in a separate transaction. The federal tax consequences of that transaction will depend upon the underlying nature of the payments which in turn depends upon all of the relevant facts and circumstances, which must be determined from all of the extrinsic and intrinsic evidence surrounding the transaction.

Questions

H and *W* are 50–50 shareholders of corporation *X*, which has assets with a value of $100K. *H*'s basis for his shares is $25K and *W*'s basis is $75K. *X* is liquidated with *H* receiving assets worth $25K and *W* receiving assets worth $75K. What result to *H* and *W*? Suppose *W* was *H*'s employee?

H. GIFTS OF STOCK BEFORE RECEIPT OF LIQUIDATING PROCEEDS

JONES v. UNITED STATES

United States Court of Appeals, Sixth Circuit, 1976.
531 F.2d 1343.

McCree, Circuit Judge: * * * The only issue on appeal is whether the taxpayer's donation of shares of corporate stock to a charity, after the corporation had adopted a plan of complete liquidation, constitutes an anticipatory assignment of income that warrants treating the liquidation proceeds as income to the taxpayer. We determine that the transaction should be treated as an anticipatory assignment of income and, accordingly, overrule our decision to the contrary in *Jacobs v. United States,* 390 F.2d 877 (6th Cir.1968), *aff'g per curiam* 280 F.Supp. 437 (S.D.Ohio 1966).

The relevant facts were stipulated and may be briefly stated. Virginia Kelsey Jones owned approximately ten percent of the outstanding stock in the Buckeye Union Casualty Company, a business that owned two subsidiary insurance companies, Mayflower Insurance Company and Buckeye Union Fire Insurance. On January 19, 1965, the directors of the three companies adopted a plan of liquidation. On February 15, 1965, the stockholders of the companies ratified and approved the liquidation plan by a vote of 968,605 to 175. After the ratification, the companies sought and obtained approval from the Department of Insurance of the State of Ohio for the issuance of re-insurance agreements and for the sale of goodwill and fixed assets to another insurance company. On June 15, 1965, the Buckeye Union Casualty Company board of directors approved several liquidation arrangements. At the same time, the directors authorized the sending of a letter to the stockholders informing them that the first liquidating dividends would be exchanged for stock in October 1965.

On June 17, 1965, the taxpayer donated 4,250 shares of Casualty stock to various public charities. As planned, the liquidating distributions began in October and were completed by January 14, 1966, within one year of the adoption of the plan of liquidation as required to qualify for nonrecognition of the gain to the corporation under [former] section 337 of the Internal Revenue Code of 1954. The taxpayer claimed a charitable deduction from her 1965 federal income tax return of $170,-000 for the donated stock. The Internal Revenue Service allowed the charitable deduction, but, viewing the transactions as anticipatory assignments of liquidation proceeds, determined that the taxpayer also received income in the amount of $168,328.29 (the basis of the stock was $1,671.71). Accordingly, the IRS assessed the long-term capital gain tax due as $42,082.07. Taxpayer paid that amount and, on May 24, 1973, filed this tax refund suit in federal district court.

On the stipulated facts, the district court granted summary judgment in favor of the taxpayer. Correctly applying the rationale of *Jacobs v. United States* * * * the district court reasoned that because Casualty shareholders could have abandoned liquidation proceedings after taxpayer had made her gift, the gift should not be viewed as an anticipatory assignment of liquidation proceeds. In *Jacobs,* as in this case, the taxpayer donated corporate stock to a charity after the shareholders had adopted a plan of complete liquidation but before actual distribution of the liquidation proceeds was made. The *Jacobs* court held that the taxpayer was entitled to exclude the corporate liquidation dividend from income because abandonment of the adopted plan, although apparently unlikely, was "entirely possible." 280 F.Supp. at 439.

The Government asks us to overrule our precedent and align ourselves with the views expressed by two other circuits after our decision in *Jacobs*. *Hudspeth v. United States,* 471 F.2d 275 (8th Cir.1972) and *Kinsey v. Commissioner,* 477 F.2d 1058 (2d Cir.1973). In *Hudspeth,* a majority stockholder in a closely held corporation donated part of his holdings to nine tax-exempt charities approximately nine months after the corporation had adopted a plan of liquidation. The Eighth Circuit agreed with the Government's contention that "the realities and substance of the events must govern * * * rather than formalities and remote hypothetical possibilities." 471 F.2d at 277.

The *Hudspeth* court analyzed the facts in the case as follows:

The shareholders' vote is the critical turning point because it provides the necessary evidence of taxpayer's intent to convert his corporation into its essential elements of investment basis and, if it has been successful, the resulting gains. This initial evidence of the taxpayers' intent to liquidate is reinforced by the corporation's contracting to sell its principal assets and the winding-up of its business functions. In the face of this manifest intent, only evidence to the contrary could rebut the presumption that the taxpayer was, in fact, liquidating his corporation. Yet here the record is barren of any evidence that the taxpayer had any intent other than that of following through on the dissolution. The liquidation had proceeded to such a point where we may infer that it was patently never taxpayer's intention that his donees should exercise any ownership in a viable corporation, but merely that they should participate in the proceeds of the liquidation.

471 F.2d at 279.

* * *

Upon consideration, we are persuaded to adopt the rule expressed by the Second and Eighth Circuits that the "realities and substance" of the events and not hypothetical possibilities should govern our determination whether an anticipatory assignment of income has occurred. We conclude that the realities and substance of the events in this case indicate that the taxpayer expected the liquidation proceedings to be completed. * * *

Taxpayer attempts to distinguish *Hudspeth* and *Kinsey* because the taxpayers in those cases were controlling shareholders of the corporation that was to be liquidated. The *Hudspeth* court did emphasize the fact that taxpayer controlled the corporation and that the donees would be "powerless to vitiate taxpayers' manifest intent to liquidate. * * *" 471 F.2d at 279. However, we view a taxpayer's control over the corporation as only one factor in determining whether a liquidation is practically certain to occur, and we determine here that there is sufficient evidence to conclude that the liquidation plan was practically certain to be completed despite the remote and hypothetical possibility of abandonment. Also, we do not regard as significant the four-to-seven month delay from the date of the gift until the time that the liquidating distributions were made to the donees. * * * Accordingly, we overrule *Jacobs v. United States* * * * and reverse the judgment of the district court.

Reversed and remanded.

[Dissenting opinion deleted.]

§ 9.3 NON–TAXABLE LIQUIDATIONS OF SUBSIDIARIES UNDER § 332

A. INTRODUCTION

Section 332 provides an exception to the general recognition rule of § 331 for liquidating distributions. Section 332(a) provides that "[n]o gain or loss shall be recognized on the receipt by a corporation of property distributed in complete liquidation of another corporation." This very broad rule is limited, however, by § 332(b) which provides that a distribution is considered to be in complete liquidation only if the following two requirements are satisfied.

First, under § 332(b)(1), the parent corporation must own stock of the subsidiary meeting the 80% requirement of § 1504(a)(2). Section 1504(a)(2) is satisfied if the parent owns stock of the subsidiary which possesses at least 80% of the total voting power of the stock of the corporation and at least 80% of the total value of the stock of the corporation. Certain nonvoting, limited, preferred stock is not included as stock for purposes of § 1504(a)(2). Section 1504(a)(2) is examined in Chapter 8. This 80% stock ownership requirement must be satisfied "on the date of the adoption of the plan of liquidation and at all times until receipt of the property." See § 332(b)(1).

Second, the distribution of the property must be either (1) completed within the taxable year (see § 332(b)(2)), or (2) one of a series of distributions pursuant to a plan of liquidation that is to be completed within three years after the close of the taxable year during which the first of the series of distributions is made. See § 332(b)(3). The Secretary may require a bond or waiver of the statute of limitations in the case of a series of distributions spanning two or more taxable years. See § 332(b) (first sentence of flush language).

A liquidation satisfying the conditions of § 332 is treated as a liquidation even though the transaction may be characterized differently (e.g., as a merger) under local law. See § 332(b) (second sentence of flush language). Also, § 332 applies to a transaction in which a less than wholly owned but more than 80% subsidiary is merged into the parent in a nontaxable reorganization where the parent receives all of the subsidiary's assets and the minority shareholders receive the parent's stock. See § 332(b) (second sentence of flush language) and § 1.332–2(d) and (e).

As discussed in Sec. 9.4.D.3.c., under § 337, the liquidating subsidiary generally does not have gain or loss on the liquidation. Under § 334(b)(1), the parent corporation takes a carryover basis for property received in a § 332 liquidation.

If a subsidiary is owned both by a parent corporation that satisfies the 80% stock ownership requirement and also by a minority shareholder or shareholders who own up to 20% of the stock of the subsidiary, then the liquidation of the subsidiary falls within §§ 332 and 334(b) for the parent and within §§ 331 and 334(a) for the minority shareholders.

B. THE SUBSIDIARY CANNOT RETAIN ANY ASSETS

REVENUE RULING 76–525

1976–2 C.B. 98.

The retention by a subsidiary corporation of any property, no matter how small in amount, for the purpose of continuing the operation of its present business or for the purpose of engaging in a new business, will prevent the distribution of the property that is actually distributed to its parent from qualifying as a distribution in complete liquidation within the meaning of section 332 of the Internal Revenue Code of 1954.

Note

The transfer of a nominal amount of cash to a new subsidiary in order to preserve the corporate name does not prevent a liquidation from qualifying under § 332. See Rev.Rul. 84-2, 1984-1 C.B. 92.

C. ELECTIVITY OF § 332 NONRECOGNITION TREATMENT

See Granite Trust discussed in *Riggs.*

GEORGE L. RIGGS v. COMMISSIONER
Tax Court of the United States, 1975.
64 T.C. 474.

OPINION

The only question for decision is whether petitioner owned at least 80 per cent of the outstanding stock of its subsidiary, Riggs–Young Corp., at the time Riggs–Young Corp. adopted a plan of liquidation within the meaning of section 332, I.R.C. 1954, so that the gain realized by petitioner on the liquidation of Riggs–Young is not to be recognized by virtue of that section. The vital question is when did Riggs–Young adopt a plan of liquidation within the meaning of section 332.

* * * [P]etitioner contends that the plan of liquidation of Riggs–Young was first adopted when it was formally adopted by vote of the stockholders on June 20, 1968, or at the earliest when counsel for petitioner recommended to petitioner in the early days of June 1968 that it liquidate Riggs–Young. Petitioner also contends that section 332 is an elective section and a taxpayer, by taking appropriate steps, can render that section applicable or inapplicable.

The parties are in agreement that by May 9, 1968, petitioner was the owner of at least 80 percent of the outstanding stock of Riggs–Young.

The * * * respondent's contention is that there was a general intent on the part of petitioner's advisers * * * prior to May 9, 1968, to liquidate Riggs–Young when and if petitioner achieved 80–percent ownership of Riggs–Young stock as a result of the tender offer. However, the formation of a conditional general intention to liquidate in the future is not the adoption of a plan of liquidation. *City Bank of Washington, supra.*

A mere intent by a taxpayer-corporation to liquidate a subsidiary prior to meeting the 80–percent requirement of section 332 should not be tantamount to the adoption of a plan of liquidation for the subsidiary at the point in time when that intent is formulated or manifested. Such a result would thwart the congressional intent of section 332 and prior judicial interpretations of this section and its predecessor.

The predecessor of section 332, I.R.C. 1954, was section 112(b)(6), first enacted in 1935. The purpose of section 112(b)(6) was to encourage the simplification of corporation structures and allow the tax-free liquidation of a subsidiary. * * *

Under section 112(b)(6), the parent corporation not only was required to own at least 80 percent of the stock of the subsidiary from the date of adoption of the plan of liquidation until the property was received (as still required by section 332), but also was forbidden to dispose of any stock between the date of adoption and the time of the receipt of the property. The courts in interpreting section 112(b)(6) determined that a taxpayer could remove itself from the provision of that section by taking the appropriate steps of either intentionally reducing its stock ownership below 80 percent prior to the actual adoption of a liquidation plan or disposing of a small amount of stock between the date of adoption and the time the distributed property was received. *Granite Trust Co. v. United States*, 238 F.2d 670 (1st Cir.1956). * * *

In *Granite Trust Co. v. United States, supra,* the circuit court concluded that section 112(b)(6) was inapplicable and based this decision on the fact that the corporation disposed of stock in violation of the second requirement of section 112(b)(6) (subsequently deleted from section 332, I.R.C. 1954). The court reached this decision even though the corporation had made the dispositions in an attempt to avoid the application of this section. The court then traced this section into the 1954 Code stating at pages 676–677:

> Now, what did the Congress do in 1954 in view of *Commissioner of Internal Revenue v. Day & Zimmermann, Inc.,* holding that a parent corporation contemplating the liquidation of a wholly owned subsidiary might elect, by making a transfer of an appropriate portion of the stock in the subsidiary, to avoid the conditions precedent to the nonrecognition of gain or loss prescribed in § 112(b)(6)? In reenacting that section in 1954, the Congress struck out the second condition, but left in the first condition which the taxpayer had successfully utilized in the *Day & Zimmermann* case in order to avoid a nonrecognition of a realized loss. This is what the Report of the Senate Finance Committee said at the time:
>
> "Section 332. Complete Liquidations of Subsidiaries.
>
> "Except for subsection (c) section 332 corresponds to and in general restates section 112(b)(6) of the 1939 Code and provides for the liquidation of a subsidiary corporation by its parent without the recognition of gain or loss to the parent corporation. Your committee has, however, deleted a provision which now appears in section 112(b)(6)(A) which removes a liquidation from the application of that section if the parent corporation at some time on or after the time of the adoption of the plan of liquidation and until the receipt of the property owns more stock than that owned at the time of the receipt of the property. Your committee has removed this provision with the view to limiting the elective features of the section." (Sen. Finance Committee Report, H.R. 8300, 83d Cong., 2d Sess. 255 (1954).)

The above reference to the "elective features" of the subsection seems inescapably to reflect a legislative understanding (admittedly not contemporaneous with enactment, however) that taxpayers can, by taking appropriate steps, render the subsection applicable or inapplicable as they choose, rather than be at the mercy of the Commissioner on an "end-result" theory. Nowhere in the subsection is there any express reference to an "election" or an "option," and the use of the word "elective" in the committee report therefore strongly indicates, as the taxpayer argues, that the committee believed that corporations could avoid the nonrecognition provisions by transfers designed to eliminate the specific conditions contained in the subsection.

Based on legislative history of this section and prior judicial decisions, we conclude that section 332 is elective in the sense that with advance planning and properly structured transactions, a corporation should be able to render section 332 applicable or inapplicable * * *

Decision will be entered for the petitioner.

Reviewed by the Court.

Questions

Parent corporation (*P*) owns 80% of the stock of a subsidiary (*S*). It has owned the stock for five years. *P*'s basis for the *S* stock is $175K. *S*'s assets have a basis of $25K and a value of $200K. What result to *P* upon the liquidation of *S* and the transfer of 80% of its assets to *P*? What result if *P* sold 1% of *S*'s stock after the date of adoption of the plan to liquidate *S* but before the receipt of the liquidating distribution?

D. WORTHLESS STOCK AND SECURITIES UNDER § 165(g)(3) OR § 332 LIQUIDATION

1. Is Debt Treated as Debt or as Equity: Is Distribution Within § 332?

WATERMAN STEAMSHIP CORP. v. UNITED STATES

United States District Court, Southern District of Alabama, 1962.
203 F.Supp. 915, *reversed on other grounds* 330 F.2d 128 (5th Cir.1964),
cert. denied 401 U.S. 939, 91 S.Ct. 936, 28 L.Ed.2d 219 (1971).

DANIEL HOLCOMBE THOMAS, DISTRICT JUDGE.

* * *

I.

WATERMAN BUILDING

This issue raises the questions (A) whether advances to a wholly owned subsidiary resulted in loans to or investments in the subsidiary by the parent and, if it were a loan or an indebtedness, whether or not it became worthless during the taxable year in question; and (B) whether certain stock in the subsidiary owned by plaintiff became worthless during the taxable year in question.

* * *

In May of 1946, plaintiff filed an application with the Civilian Production Administration for authority to construct a sixteen-story office building and adjacent restaurant at an estimated cost of $2,600,000, exclusive of the land and architect's and engineer's fees. Shortly thereafter, plaintiff entered into a cost-plus contract with J.P. Ewin, Inc., for construction of the buildings. An architect was also employed to design the buildings.

Plaintiff determined to establish a subsidiary company to construct, own, and operate the office building. * * * On July 19, 1946, Waterman Building Corporation (hereinafter referred to as Building Corporation) was organized as a wholly owned subsidiary of plaintiff with authorized capital stock of $1,500,000 and paid-in capital stock of $375,000. Immediately thereafter, plaintiff assigned to Building Corporation its agreements with the architects and with the contractors for the construction of the building in question. By virtue of this assignment plaintiff was released and Building Corporation assumed all of the plaintiff's duties under the two contracts.

Construction on the new buildings commenced in 1946, with an estimated completion time of eighteen months. However, due to labor difficulties and the failure of materialmen or suppliers to meet schedules, the building was in construction for two years. The ultimate costs of the buildings, without furniture, fixtures, and equipment, came to approximately $4,250,000—greatly in excess of the estimated costs of $2,600,000.

* * *

Upon completion of the building and the long-term financing, plaintiff had made loans to Building Corporation in the total amount of $3,125,000. With the loan of $1,000,000 from Massachusetts, $400,000 of this amount was repaid by Building Corporation. However, during operations in 1949, plaintiff had to make further advances to its subsidiary, so that as of September 30, 1949, Building Corporation owed plaintiff, on open account, $3,110,000. Due to the greatly increased cost of the construction of the building and partially to the failure to have a lease on the restaurant building which would return some income to Building Corporation, the latter was not able, from the income derived from the lease with plaintiff, to repay the indebtedness to plaintiff after making its payments to Massachusetts Mutual. After nine months of operation, it was apparent to the officers of plaintiff that not only was the building corporation failing to show a profit, but it was not generating sufficient cash to reduce the indebtedness to plaintiff within any reasonable period, after meeting its fixed obligations and operating costs. The directors of plaintiff then determined that it would be in the best interest of and would result in material savings to plaintiff, to transfer all of the assets of Building Corporation to plaintiff, with plaintiff assuming all the obligations of Building Corporation, in reduction of the indebtedness of Building Corporation to plaintiff by the market value of those assets less the amount of its obligations assumed. This action was approved by the directors and stockholders of Building Corporation and by the Executive Committee and Directors of the plaintiff, subject to appraisal of building and land by independent real estate appraisers. An agreement between plaintiff and Building Corporation dated September 30, 1949, effectuated this plan.

A.

The first question raised is whether the advances made by plaintiff to its wholly owned subsidiary constitute loans or capital contributions. Different tax consequences attend each such classification. If those advances constitute "debts" as that term is used in Title 26 U.S.C. Sec. 23(k) [now § 166(a)] plaintiff is entitled to a bad debt loss deduction. On the other hand, if those advances constitute capital contributions, reference must be made to those sections of the code concerning liquidation. * * * The answer depends on the intent of the parties, which is to be ascertained from all relevant facts and circumstances.

When making the advances to the Building Corporation, plaintiff never requested or received any notes or other evidence of indebtedness or a mortgage as security. Nor did it request or receive any interest for the use of the funds advanced, nor was a payment date discussed or agreed upon. The government contends that such factors indicate an intention to contribute to the capital of the subsidiary. Such contention, however, fails to recognize what the testimony of plaintiff's witness clearly sets forth. Waterman Corporation dealt with all of its subsidiaries on similar open accounts without interest. Absence of these arrangements is not fatal to the creation of a creditor-debtor relationship. Moreover, the testimony shows that Building Corporation intended to repay the advances through renting to the parent and from income from the restaurant.

* * *

The court is of the opinion that the advances in question were intended to, and did in fact, constitute loans to the subsidiary, for which the taxpayer may deduct a bad debt loss as provided for in section 23(k) [now § 166(a)]. It is therefore unnecessary to discuss the tax aspects of the inadequately capitalized corporation, an issue raised by the government's view of the facts.

Having decided the advances made by plaintiff to Building Corporation were loans, there remains to be determined whether such indebtedness became worthless in the taxable year 1949 and, if so, the amount of such worthless debt.

There is no doubt that on September 30, 1949, Building Corporation transferred all of its assets to plaintiff, with the exception of certain cash and deferred charges in an amount less than $15,000, in return for plaintiff's assuming all the obligations of Building Corporation. As of December 31, 1949, the only assets which Building Corporation owned were certain cash and deferred charges amounting to approximately $12,500. At that time, there was no way possible for Building Corporation to repay the indebtedness due plaintiff. Building Corporation had no marketable assets or any means to raise capital. It was, for practical purposes, finished. The Court finds as a matter of fact that the debt due plaintiff from its subsidiary was worthless, which was determined and fixed in 1949 when all of the assets of the subsidiary were transferred to plaintiff.

The value to be attributed to the Waterman Building, restaurant, and land, for purposes of computing the amount of the bad debt loss deduction, is the fair market value of those properties as of September 30, 1949, which the court finds to be $2,067,600. The determination is one of fact.

B.

Plaintiff is also seeking a deduction from its gross income for a loss occasioned by the Building Corporation stock owned by it becoming worthless (Section 23(g)(2)) [now § 165(g)(3)]. It is the position of the Government that the stock was exchanged, within the meaning of Sections 115(c) and 112(b)(6), [now § 332] for the property received on September 30, 1949, and hence is not subject to recognition as a capital loss.

The applicable code provisions are explicit in their terms. "For the purposes of this paragraph a distribution shall be considered to be in complete liquidation only if * * * (C) the distribution is by such other corporation in complete cancellation or redemption of all its stock * * * (Section 112(b)(6)) [now § 332].

In the instant case, the property transferred by Building Corporation was in consideration of reducing the debt owed by it to the plaintiff. The evidence conclusively establishes that fact. The Tax Court has had opportunity to speak on this point on at least three occasions: *Iron Fireman Manufacturing Co.,* 5 T.C. 452; *Spaulding Bakeries, Inc. v. Commissioner,* 27 T.C. 684; *affirmed on appeal,* 2nd Cir., 1958, 252 F.2d 693; *Northern Coal & Dock Co.,* 12 T.C. 42. See also, *H.G. Hill Stores, Inc.,* 44 B.T.A. 1182. In the *Spaulding* case the Tax Court made these comments:

> "The principle set forth in a number of our decisions where the sole stockholder parent is also the creditor of the subsidiary is applicable here. In those cases we held, in what would otherwise be a Section 112(b)(6) [now § 332] liquidation but for the fact that the distribution to the parent is insufficient to satisfy more than a part of the debt, the parent has both a deductible bad debt and a deductible stock loss." (27 T.C. p. 688)

In view of the foregoing, it is clear that plaintiff is entitled to deduct the sum of $375,000.00 as the amount of worthless stock held by it.

Question

Was it crucial to Waterman Steamship's case that the court find that the open account indebtedness was bona fide debt and not equity? What guidance does *Waterman Steamship* give for structuring a subsidiary's capital?

2. Worthless Common Stock But Not Preferred: Is Distribution Within § 332?

H.K. PORTER COMPANY, INC. v. COMMISSIONER

Tax Court of the United States, 1986.
87 T.C. 689.

OPINION

CLAPP, JUDGE: Respondent determined deficiencies in petitioner's 1978 and 1979 Federal income tax in the amounts of $105,281.00 and $745,161.00, respectively. After concessions, the issue for decision is whether section 332 applies to bar the recognition of gain or loss on the liquidation of H.K. Porter Australia, Pty., Ltd., petitioner's subsidiary.

* * *

Petitioner, H.K. Porter Company, Inc., and Subsidiaries, is a Delaware business corporation. At the time it filed its petition in this case, petitioner's principal place of business was Pittsburgh, Pennsylvania.

* * *

In 1962, petitioner paid $219,336.00 for all of the outstanding stock of an Australian business corporation which manufactured saws, brake linings and clutch facings. Petitioner changed the name of the corporation to H.K. Porter Australia, Pty., Ltd. (Porter Australia) and loaned Porter Australia the funds it needed to operate. At all relevant times, petitioner owned all of Porter Australia's outstanding stock.

In 1966, Porter Australia authorized 400,000 shares of $1.00 par common stock and 1,000,000 shares of $1.00 par preferred stock. In 1968, it authorized 2,000,000 additional shares of preferred stock.

The preferred stock only had voting rights at meetings convened to wind up the business, reduce its capital, sanction the sale of a business, or consider any question affecting the rights and privileges of the preferred stock. It had a five percent, non-cumulative dividend, was redeemable and had a $2,452,000 liquidation preference over the common stock.

In September 1966, and again in December 1968, Porter Australia capitalized loans from petitioner of $1,000,000 and issued to petitioner 896,861 shares of preferred stock on each occasion. In November 1969, it capitalized loans from petitioner totalling $452,000 and issued petitioner 405,380 shares of preferred stock. Porter Australia capitalized the loans because it was unable to "satisfy" the loans in the short term and it wanted to avoid any further claim by respondent that income should be allocated to petitioner by reason of those loans.

In October 1978, petitioner's board of directors voted to terminate Porter Australia's operations, because they were unprofitable, and dispose of all its assets. In May 1979, pursuant to Australian law, a certified liquidator was appointed to liquidate Porter Australia. In December 1979, petitioner surrendered all of its common and preferred stock in Porter Australia in exchange for a $477,876 liquidating distribution which included $10,288 to satisfy an intercompany receivable. Said distribution was not enough to cover the $2,452,000 liquidation preference of the preferred stock.

As of December 31, 1978, petitioner's adjusted basis in its 182,664 shares of Porter Australia's common stock was $249,981. As of January 1, 1979, petitioner's adjusted basis in its 2,199,102 shares of Porter Australia's preferred stock was $2,425,358.

On its 1978 and 1979 Federal income tax returns, petitioner claimed losses with respect to its Porter Australia stock. In his notice of deficiency, respondent disallowed said losses because "under I.R.C. Sec. 332, no gain or loss is recognized on the receipt of property distributed in complete liquidation of a subsidiary corporation."

* * *

Respondent contends that section 332 bars the recognition of petitioner's losses. Petitioner contends that section 332 is inapplicable and cites *Spaulding Bakeries, Inc. v. Commissioner,* 27 T.C. 684 (1957), affd. 252 F.2d 693 (2d Cir.1958).

In *Spaulding Bakeries,* the taxpayer purchased all the outstanding common and preferred stock of Hazleton Bakeries, Inc. between 1930 and 1946. In 1950, Hazleton Bakeries was liquidated and the taxpayer received the assets distributed in the liquidation. The distributed assets failed to cover the preferred stock's liquidation preference. No assets were distributed with respect to the common stock. On its 1950 Federal income tax return, the taxpayer claimed a worthless stock deduction with respect to the common stock. Respondent disallowed the deduction because of section 112(b)(6), the predecessor of section 332. The sole issue for decision was whether section 112(b)(6) barred the recognition of the taxpayer's claimed losses. Specifically, the issue focused on whether Hazleton Bakeries distributed its assets in complete cancellation or redemption of "all its stock."

In a court reviewed opinion, we held that the phrase "all its stock" did not include "nonvoting stock which is limited and preferred as to dividends." 27 T.C. at 688. Thus, Hazleton Bakeries' distribution, which was in respect of only the nonvoting preferred stock, was not a distribution in complete cancellation or redemption of all its stock.

The Second Circuit, in affirming this Court, states:

The [taxpayer], it seems to us, argues with convincing force that the two classes of stock of Hazleton cannot be treated as though they were but one class, nor can the distribution in respect to the preferred stock be treated as though it were a distribution by Hazleton in respect to *all* its stock, all classes. It is convincingly argued as a matter of law, that there could be no distribution in respect to the common stock until the prior claim of the preferred stock had been satisfied. [252 F.2d at 697; Emphasis in original.]

Respondent, in essence, advances two arguments: 1) *Spaulding Bakeries* was erroneously decided and the decision should be reconsidered; and 2) even under the rationale of *Spaulding Bakeries,* section 332 applies.

Spaulding Bakeries Reconsidered

Respondent contends that *Spaulding Bakeries* was erroneously decided because: 1) the phrase "all its stock" was misread as referring to only voting or common stock and not to nonvoting preferred stock; 2) an inappropriate analogy was constructed between preferred stock and indebtedness; and 3) the legislative history suggests that section 332 applies when a liquidating distribution is made on preferred stock only.

"All Its Stock"

In *Spaulding Bakeries* we stated:

The statute is specific in that there must be a "distribution" in liquidation and the distribution must be "in complete cancellation or redemption of *all its [parent's] stock.*" What does the phrase "all its stock" mean? Clearly it means at least 80 per cent of the common or voting stock. Does it also mean to include nonvoting stock which is limited and preferred as to dividends? We think not. The statute specifically excepts such preferred stock from the classes of stock which the parent should own—it could be owned by the parent or outsiders. * * * This means the payment in liquidation, in satisfaction of the preferred stock claim, whether to the parent or outsiders, will be immaterial. * * * Here there was no payment or distribution to the parent after the payment of the preferred stock claim in liquidation. The preferred stock claim captured all of the assets. There was nothing left to distribute to the parent as a common stockholder in the subsidiary. We hold the parent received no distribution in liquidation on its common stock within the intendment of the statute. Petitioner merely received in liquidation, payment of a part of its preferred stock claim—a fact which the statute, in effect, states will be immaterial. [27 T.C. at 688; Emphasis added.]

In summary, we held that "its" referred to the parent's stock, *i.e.,* the distribution had to be in complete cancellation or redemption of all the stock the parent owned in the subsidiary. Furthermore, because the parent had to own only 80 percent of each class of stock except nonvoting stock which was limited and preferred as to dividends, any distribution with respect to only the nonvoting preferred stock was "immaterial," *i.e.*, not with respect to all the stock.

We agree with respondent that the phrase "all its stock" might be better interpreted as all *the subsidiary's* stock. Our decision, however, was not based on this analysis alone, and, as discussed below, we are not required to reach a different result.

Analogy Between Preferred Stock and Indebtedness

In *Spaulding Bakeries*, we cited cases which set forth the proposition that where the parent was the sole stockholder and also a creditor of the subsidiary, and the liquidating distribution to the parent was insufficient to satisfy the debt, the parent has both a deductible bad debt and a deductible stock loss. We analogized those cases to the facts in *Spaulding Bakeries*. We concluded that those cases were "authority for the conclusion that nothing was or could be 'distributed' on dissolution to the common stockholders until the full liquidation preference of the preferred stockholders was satisfied." 27 T.C. at 689.

Respondent contends that it was illogical to analogize preferred stock to indebtedness rather than to common stock. We disagree. We previously thought the analogy appropriate; the Second Circuit cited our analogy with approval; and we again find said analogy logical.

* * *

Respondent gives us no new reason as to why the unitary theory, a theory implicitly rejected or accorded little weight by the Second Circuit and our majority opinion, should control the disposition of this case. He simply points to the dissenting opinion in *Spaulding Bakeries*. Suffice it to say that we are not persuaded. See *Commissioner v. Spaulding Bakeries, supra.*

* * *

Notwithstanding Spaulding Bakeries, Does Section 332 Apply?

Respondent alternatively argues that section 332 applies, even under the rationale of *Spaulding Bakeries*, because: 1) Porter Australia's preferred stock had voting rights and, therefore, the distribution in the present case cannot be considered "immaterial;" and 2) substance prevails over form and, here, petitioner in substance held only one class of stock. [The court rejects these arguments.]

§ 9.4 TREATMENT OF THE CORPORATION: REPEAL OF THE GENERAL UTILITIES DOCTRINE

See §§ 336 and 337.

A. THE GENERAL UTILITIES DOCTRINE

Review *General Utilities,* Sec. 1.3.D., *Court Holding,* Sec. 1.3.G.3.a and *Cumberland Service,* Sec. 1.3.G.3.b.

B. IMPACT OF REPEAL OF GENERAL UTILITIES ON NONLIQUIDATING DISTRIBUTIONS

Review the discussion of the repeal of the *General Utilities* doctrine in the General Explanation of the Tax Reform Act of 1986, Sec. 4.3.B.

C. THE REPEAL OF THE GENERAL UTILITIES DOCTRINE BY THE TAX REFORM ACT OF 1986

See §§ 336 and 337.

The repeal of the *General Utilities* doctrine by the Tax Reform Act of 1986 is embodied in §§ 311, 336 and 337. Section 311, which requires that a corporation recognize gain on the non-liquidating distribution of appreciated property, is examined in Chapter 4. *See* Sec. 4.3. Section 336 provides that a corporation recognizes gain and in certain cases loss on the liquidating distribution of property. Section 337 provides an exception to this recognition rule for liquidating distributions by subsidiary corporations to parent corporations in § 332 tax-free liquidations. The legislative history of §§ 336 and 337 is set out in the next section.

D. LEGISLATIVE HISTORY OF §§ 336 AND 337

EXCERPTS FROM (1) GENERAL EXPLANATION OF THE TAX REFORM ACT OF 1986, 328–346 (1987), (2) CONFERENCE REPORT TO THE REVENUE RECONCILIATION ACT OF 1987, 966–969 (1987), AND (3) SENATE FINANCE COMMITTEE REPORT TO THE TECHNICAL AND MISCELLANEOUS REVENUE ACT OF 1988, 67–73 (1988) (TAMRA).

[1.] Prior Law

[a. The General Utilities Rule]

Although the *General Utilities* [*See* Sec. 1.3.D.] case involved a dividend distribution of appreciated property by an ongoing business, the term "*General Utilities* rule" was often used in a broader sense to refer to the nonrecognition treatment accorded in certain situations to liquidating as well as nonliquidating distributions to shareholders and to liquidating sales. The rule was reflected in Code sections 311, 336, and 337 of prior law: Section 311 governed the treatment of nonliquidating distributions of property (dividends and redemptions), while section 336 governed the treatment of liquidating distributions in kind. Section 337 provided nonrecognition treatment for certain sales of property pursuant to a plan of complete liquidation.

Numerous limitations on the *General Utilities* rule, both statutory and judicial, developed over the years following its codification. Some directly limited the statutory provisions embodying the rule, while others, including the collapsible corporation provisions, the recapture provisions, and the tax benefit doctrine, did so indirectly.

* * *

Five years after the decision in *General Utilities*, in a case in which the corporation played a substantial role in the sale of distributed property by its shareholders, the Commissioner successfully advanced the imputed sale argument the Court had rejected earlier on procedural grounds. In *Commissioner v. Court Holding Co.,* [See Sec. 1.3.G.3.a.] the Court upheld the Commissioner's determination that, in substance, the corporation rather than the shareholders had executed the sale and, accordingly, was required to recognize gain.

In *United States v. Cumberland Public Service Co.,* [See Sec. 1.3.G.3.b.] the Supreme Court reached a contrary result where the facts showed the shareholders had in fact negotiated a sale on their own behalf. The Court stated that Congress had imposed no tax on liquidating distributions in kind or on dissolution, and that a corporation could liquidate without subjecting itself to corporate gains tax notwithstanding the primary motive is to avoid the corporate tax.

In its 1954 revision of the Internal Revenue Code, Congress reviewed *General Utilities* and its progeny and decided to address the corporate-level consequences of distributions statutorily. It essentially codified the result in *General Utilities* by enacting section 311(a) of prior law, which provided that a corporation recognized no gain or loss on a nonliquidating distribution of property with respect to its stock. Congress also enacted section 336, which in its original form provided for nonrecognition of gain or loss to a corporation on distributions of property in partial or complete liquidation. Although distributions in partial liquidations were eventually removed from the jurisdiction of section 336, in certain limited circumstances a distribution in partial liquidation could, prior to the Act, still qualify for nonrecognition at the corporate level.

Finally, Congress in the 1954 Act provided that a corporation did not recognize gain or loss on a sale of property if it adopted a plan of complete liquidation and distributed all of its assets to its shareholders within twelve months of the date of adoption of the plan (sec. 337). Thus, the distinction drawn in *Court Holding Co.* and *Cumberland Public Service Co.,* between a sale of assets followed by liquidating distribution of the proceeds and a liquidating distribution in kind followed by a shareholder sale, was in large part eliminated. Regulations subsequently issued under section 311 acknowledged that a distribution in redemption of stock constituted a "distribution with respect to * * * stock" within the meaning of the statute. The 1954 Code in its original form, therefore, generally exempted all forms of nonliquidating as well as liquidating distributions to shareholders from the corporate-level tax.

* * *

[b.] Liquidating Distributions and Sales: Sections 336 and 337

The rules regarding nonrecognition of gain on distributions in liquidation of a corporation were less restrictive than those applicable to nonliquidating distributions under prior law. Section 336 of prior law generally provided for nonrecognition of gain or loss by a corporation on the distribution of property in complete liquidation of the corporation. Gain was recognized, however, on a distribution of an installment obligation, unless the obligation was acquired in a liquidating sale that would have been tax-free under section 337, or the distribution was by a controlled subsidiary in a section 332 liquidation where the parent took a carryover basis under section 334(b)(1). Section 336 also required recognition of the LIFO recapture amount in liquidating distributions.

Section 337 of prior law provided that if a corporation adopted a plan of complete liquidation and within twelve months distributed all of its assets in complete liquidation, gain or loss on any sales by the corporation during that period generally was not recognized. Section 337 did not apply, and recognition was required, on sales of inventory (other than inventory sold in bulk), stock in trade, and property held primarily for sale to customers in the ordinary course of business. If the corporation accounted for inventory on a LIFO basis, section 337 required that the LIFO recapture amount be included in income.

* * *

[c.] Recapture Rules

The nonrecognition provisions of sections 311, 336, and 337 were subject to several additional limitations beyond those expressly set forth in those sections. These limitations included the statutory "recapture" rules for depreciation deductions, investment tax credits, and certain other items that might have produced a tax benefit for the transferor-taxpayer in prior years.

* * *

[d.] Collapsible Corporation Rules

Under prior law (as under present law), section 341 modified the tax treatment of transactions involving stock in or property held by "collapsible" corporations. In general, a collapsible corporation was one the purpose of which was to convert ordinary income into capital gain through the sale of stock by its shareholders, or through liquidation of the corporation, before substantial income had been realized.

* * *

[Although § 341 is still part of the Code, it has little, if any, significance, and it is not studied here.]

[e.] *Judicially Created Doctrines*

Under prior law, the courts applied nonstatutory doctrines from other areas of the tax law to in-kind distributions to shareholders. * * *

* * *

The courts also applied the assignment of income doctrine to require a corporation to recognize income on liquidating and nonliquidating distributions of its property.

[2.] REASONS FOR CHANGE

Congress believed that the *General Utilities* rule, even in its more limited form, produced many incongruities and inequities in the tax system. First, the rule could create significant distortions in business behavior. Economically, a liquidating distribution is indistinguishable from a nonliquidating distribution; yet the Code provided a substantial preference for the former. A corporation acquiring the assets of a liquidating corporation was able to obtain a basis in assets equal to their fair market value, although the transferor recognized no gain (other than possibly recapture amounts) on the sale. The tax benefits made the assets potentially more valuable in the hands of a transferee than in the hands of the current owner. This might induce corporations with substantial appreciated assets to liquidate and transfer their assets to other corporations for tax reasons, when economic considerations might indicate a different course of action. Accordingly, Congress reasoned, the *General Utilities* rule could be at least partly responsible for the dramatic increase in corporate mergers and acquisitions in recent years. Congress believed that the Code should not artificially encourage corporate liquidations and acquisitions, and that repeal of the *General Utilities* rule was a major step towards that goal.

Second, the *General Utilities* rule tended to undermine the corporate income tax. Under normally applicable tax principles, nonrecognition of gain is available only if the transferee takes a carryover basis in the transferred property, thus assuring that a tax will eventually be collected on the appreciation. Where the *General Utilities* rule applied, assets generally were permitted to leave corporate solution and to take a stepped-up basis in the hands of the transferee without the imposition of a corporate-level tax. Thus, the effect of the rule was to grant a permanent exemption from the corporate income tax.

* * *

[3.] EXPLANATION OF PROVISIONS
[a.] *Overview*

The Act provides that gain or loss generally is recognized by a corporation on liquidating distributions of its property as if the property had been sold at fair market value to the distributee. [See § 336.] Gain or loss is also recognized by a corporation on liquidating sales of its property. Exceptions are provided for distributions in which an 80–percent corporate shareholder receives property with a carryover basis in a liquidation under section 332, and certain distributions and exchanges involving property that may be received tax-free by the shareholder under subchapter C of the Code. * * * [See § 337.]

[b.] Distributions in Complete Liquidation [Under Section 336]

[(1)] General Rule [See § 336(a) and (b).]

The Act provides that, in general, gain or loss is recognized to a corporation on a distribution of its property in complete liquidation. The distributing corporation is treated as if it had sold the property at fair market value to the distributee-shareholders. [See § 336(a).]

If the distributed property is subject to a liability, the fair market value of the property for this purpose is deemed to be no less than the amount of the liability. [See § 336(b).] Thus, for example, if the amount of the liability exceeds the value of the property that secures it, the selling corporation will recognize gain in an amount equal to the excess of the liability over the adjusted basis of the property. [See also § 7701(g).] Likewise, if the shareholders of the liquidating corporation assume liabilities of the corporation and the amount of liabilities assumed exceeds the fair market value of the distributed property, the corporation will recognize gain to the extent the assumed liabilities exceed the adjusted basis of the property. However, the provision does not affect, and no inference was intended regarding, the amount realized by or basis of property received by the distributee-shareholders in these circumstances.

* * *

[A liquidating corporation recognizes gain on a distribution of § 453 installment note obligations. See § 453B(a).]

[(2)] Tax–Free Reorganizations and Distributions [See § 336(c).]

The general rule requiring gain or loss recognition on liquidating distributions of property is inapplicable to [distributions in pursuance of a plan of reorganization. See § 361(c)(4).]

[(3)] Limitations on Recognition of Losses [See § 336(d).]

The Act includes two provisions designed to prevent inappropriate corporate-level recognition of losses on liquidating dispositions of property. In enacting these provisions, Congress did not intend to create any inference regarding the deductibility of such losses under other statutory provisions or judicially created doctrines, or to preclude the application of such provisions or doctrines where appropriate.

[(4)] Distributions to Related Persons [See § 336(d)(1).]

Under the first loss limitation rule, a liquidating corporation may not recognize loss with respect to a distribution of property to a related person within the meaning of section 267, unless (i) the property is distributed to all shareholders on a pro rata basis *and* (ii) the property was not acquired by the liquidating corporation in a section 351 transaction or as a contribution to capital during the five years preceding the distribution.

Thus, for example, a liquidating corporation may not recognize loss on a distribution of recently acquired property to a shareholder who, directly or indirectly, owns more than 50 percent in value of the stock of the corporation. Similarly, a liquidating corporation may not recognize a loss on any property, regardless of when or how acquired, that is distributed to such a shareholder on a non-pro rata basis.

[(5)] *Dispositions of Certain Carryover Basis Property Acquired for Tax–Avoidance Purpose [See § 336(d)(3).]*

Under the second loss limitation rule, recognition of loss may be limited if property whose adjusted basis exceeds its value is contributed to a liquidating corporation, in a carryover basis transaction, with a principal purpose of recognizing the loss upon the sale or distribution of the property (and thus eliminating or otherwise limiting corporate level gain). In these circumstances, the basis of the property for purposes of determining loss is reduced, but not below zero, by the excess of the adjusted basis of the property on the date of contribution over its fair market value on such date.

If the adoption of a plan of complete liquidation occurs in a taxable year following the date on which the tax return including the loss disallowed by this provision is filed, except as provided in regulations, the liquidating corporation will recapture the disallowed loss on the tax return for the taxable year in which such plan of liquidation is adopted. In the alternative, regulations may provide for the corporation to file an amended return for the taxable year in which the loss was reported.

* * *

[(6)] *Presumption of Tax–Avoidance Purpose in Case of Contributions Within Two Years of Liquidation [See § 336(d)(2)(B)(iii).]*

For purposes of the loss limitation rule, there is a statutory presumption that the tax-avoidance purpose is present with respect to any section 351 transfer or contribution to capital of built-in loss property [after the date two years before] the adoption of the plan of liquidation. [*See* § 336(d)(2)(B)(ii).] Although Congress recognized that a contribution more than two years before the adoption of a plan of liquidation might have been made for such a tax-avoidance purpose, Congress also recognized that the determination that such purpose existed in such circumstances might be difficult for the Internal Revenue Service to establish and therefore as a practical matter might occur infrequently or in relatively unusual cases.

Congress intended that the Treasury Department will issue regulations generally providing that the presumed prohibited purpose for contributions of property within two years of the adoption of a plan of liquidation will be disregarded *unless* there is no clear and substantial relationship between the contributed property and the conduct of the corporation's current or future business enterprises. * * *

* * *

[(7)] Election to Treat Sale or Distribution of Subsidiary Stock as Disposition of Subsidiary's Assets [See § 336(e).]

The Act generally conforms the treatment of liquidating sales and distributions of subsidiary stock to the prior-law treatment of nonliquidating sales or distributions of such stock; thus, such liquidating sales or distributions are generally taxable at the corporate level. Congress believed it was appropriate to conform the treatment of liquidating and nonliquidating sales or distributions and to require recognition when appreciated property, including stock of a subsidiary, is transferred to a corporate or individual recipient outside the economic unit of the selling or distributing corporation.

However, Congress believed it was appropriate to provide relief from a potential multiple taxation at the corporate level of the same economic gain, which may result when a transfer of appreciated corporate stock is taxed without providing a corresponding step-up in basis of the assets of the corporation. In addition to retaining the election available under section 338(h)(10) of prior law, the Act permits the expansion of the concept of that provision, [(which permits a parent corporation to treat the sale of the stock of a subsidiary as a sale of the subsidiary's assets) *see* Sec. 9.5.], to the extent provided in regulations, to dispositions of a controlling interest in a corporation for which this election is currently unavailable. For example, the election could be made available where the selling corporation owns 80 percent of the value and voting power of the subsidiary but does not file a consolidated return with the subsidiary. Moreover, the Act provides that, under regulations, principles similar to those of section 338(h)(10) may be applied to taxable distributions of controlled corporation stock.

* * *

[c. Liquidations of Subsidiaries Under §§ 332 and 337]
[(1) General Rules]

An exception to the recognition rule is provided for certain distributions in connection with the liquidation of a controlled subsidiary into its parent corporation. Under new section 337 of the Code, no gain or loss is generally recognized with respect to property distributed to a corporate shareholder (an "80–percent distributee") in a liquidation to which section 332 applies. If a minority shareholder receives property in such a liquidation, the distribution to the minority shareholder is treated in the same manner as a distribution in a nonliquidating redemption. Accordingly, gain (but not loss) is recognized to the distributing corporation.

The exception for 80–percent corporate shareholders does not apply where the shareholder is a tax-exempt organization unless the property received in the distribution is used by the organization in an activity, the income from which is subject to tax as unrelated business taxable income (UBTI), immediately after the distribution. * * *

If gain is recognized on a distribution of property in a liquidation described in section 332(a), a corresponding increase in the distributee's basis in the property will be permitted. [See § 334(b)(1).]

The Act relocates the provisions of section 332(c) to section 337(b) of the Code. Distributions of property to the controlling parent corporation in liquidations to which section 332 applies in exchange for debt obligations of the subsidiary are treated in the same manner as distributions in exchange for stock of the subsidiary, as under prior law section 332(c).

[Gain is not recognized on the distribution by a subsidiary of § 453 installment-sale obligations in a § 337 liquidation. See § 453B(d).]

[(2) The 80% Distributee and Introduction to Mirror Subsidiaries]

[Section 337 was amended by the Revenue Reconciliation Act of 1987 to address the mirror subsidiary and related issues. Mirror subsidiary transactions involved attempts to avoid the repeal of *General Utilities* by causing a subsidiary to liquidate into two (or more) intermediate parent corporations (mirror subsidiaries) that were members of the same affiliated group as the subsidiary and which in the aggregate (but not individually) owned 80% of the subsidiary's stock. The stock of the mirror subsidiaries was owned by the ultimate parent corporation. Wanted assets would be distributed to one of the mirror subsidiaries and unwanted assets would go to the other. Under Reg. § 1.1502–34 of the consolidated return regulations, this type of liquidation is within § 332, and prior to the Revenue Reconciliation Act of 1987, the liquidation arguably was within § 337. Consequently, neither the mirror subsidiaries nor the liquidating subsidiary would recognize gain on the liquidation. The ultimate parent could then dispose of the mirror subsidiary that held unwanted assets. The issues involving mirror subsidiaries arise in stock acquisitions and are addressed in detail in *Taxable and Tax-Free Corporate Mergers, Acquisitions and LBOs*, supra Sec. 1.4. The following excerpt from the Conference Report to the Revenue Reconciliation Act of 1987 elaborates on the definition of an "80 percent distributee" in § 337(c).]

As under present law, gain will not be recognized by a corporation on liquidating distributions to a corporate shareholder directly owning 80 percent (by vote and value) of the stock of the distributing corporation. However, under the conference agreement, gain is recognized on any distribution to a corporation that does not meet the 80–percent test by direct ownership. Thus, for example, the distributing corporation recognizes gain on any distribution to a corporation within an affiliated group filing a consolidated tax return if the distributee would be treated as an 80–percent owner for purposes of section 332 solely by reason of the aggregation rules of section 1.1502–34 of the Treasury Regulations.

Treasury Regulations may provide that gain on a distribution to a less than 80–percent owner within an affiliated group filing a consolidated return may be deferred until a recognition event other than the

liquidation itself occurs. (Compare Treas.Reg. sec. 1.1502–14(c)(2)).
* * *

* * *

[(3)] Regulatory Authority to Prevent Circumvention of General Utilities Repeal [See § 337(d)]

The repeal of the *General Utilities* rule is designed to require the corporate level recognition of gain on a corporation's sale or distribution of appreciated property, irrespective of whether it occurs in a liquidating or nonliquidating context. Congress expected the Treasury Department to issue, or to amend, regulations to ensure that the purpose of the new provisions (including the new subchapter S built-in gain provisions) is not circumvented through the use of any other provision, including the consolidated return regulations or the tax-free reorganization provisions of the Code (part III of subchapter C) or through the use of other pass-through entities such as regulated investment companies (RICs) or real estate investment trusts (REITs). For example, this would include rules to require the recognition of gain if appreciated property of a C corporation is transferred to a RIC or a REIT in a carryover basis transaction that would otherwise eliminate corporate-level tax on the built-in appreciation.

[(4)] Application of Other Statutory Rules and Judicial Doctrines

In providing for recognition of gain on liquidating distributions, Congress did not intend to supersede other existing statutory rules and judicial doctrines, including (but not limited to) sections 1245 and 1250 recapture, the tax benefit doctrine, and the assignment of income doctrine. Accordingly, these rules will continue to apply to determine the character of gain recognized on liquidating distributions where they are otherwise applicable.

* * *

§ 9.5 INTRODUCTION TO § 338

1. *In General* *

Section 338, generally, provides that, if the stock of a corporation ("Target") (*see* § 338(d)(2)) is acquired by another corporation ("Purchasing Corporation") (*see* § 338(d)(1)) in a Qualified Stock Purchase, *see* § 338(d)(3), the Purchasing Corporation may elect (or may be deemed to elect under certain consistency rules) to have the Target treated as if it had sold all of its assets (as "Old Target") and then purchased those assets (as "New Target"). *See* § 338(a). Thus, as a result of a § 338 election, the Target recognizes gain or loss with respect to the deemed sale of its assets and takes a fair market value basis for those assets.

---

* This section is based on § 33:02 of *Federal Taxation of Business Enterprises*, *supra*, Chapter 1, note 1, with permission.

The deemed sale of assets by Old Target takes place at the close of the day on which the purchase occurred ("Acquisition Date"). See § 338(a)(1) and (h)(2). New Target is deemed to purchase those assets ("Acquisition Date Assets") at the beginning of the day after the Acquisition Date. See § 338(a)(2).

Section 338(b) sets forth the framework for determining the aggregate amount of New Target's deemed purchase price of Old Target's assets ("adjusted grossed-up basis") and allocating this amount among New Target's acquisition date assets. A Purchasing Corporation is a corporation that makes a qualified stock purchase (Qualified Stock Purchase) of another corporation. See § 338(d)(1). A Target is a corporation the stock of which is acquired by purchase in a Qualified Stock Purchase by the Purchasing Corporation. See § 338(d)(2).

A Qualified Stock Purchase is defined as any transaction or series of transactions in which a Purchasing Corporation acquires, by purchase, at least 80% of the total combined voting power of all classes entitled to vote and at least 80% of the total number of all other classes of stock (except nonvoting stock which is limited and preferred as to dividends) of the Target during the Acquisition Period. See § 338(d)(3). Members of the same affiliated group are treated as one corporation and shares purchased by different members of the group are aggregated in determining if a Qualified Stock Purchase has occurred. See § 338(h)(8).

The term "Acquisition Period" is defined as the period of 12 months beginning the first day on which a stock purchase that is part of a Qualified Stock Purchase is made. See § 338(h)(1).

The term "Acquisition Date" is defined as the first date on which the Purchaser acquires all of the stock necessary for a Qualified Stock Purchase. See § 338(h)(2).

After a Qualifying Stock Purchase, the Purchasing Corporation may elect (or may be deemed to have elected) the application of § 338 with respect to the transaction. Pursuant to § 338(a)(1), the Target is deemed to have sold all its assets on the Acquisition Date for their fair market value in a single taxable transaction. See § 338(g).

The above concepts are illustrated as follows: Assume that corporation P purchases 5% of the stock of corporation T on February 1, 1993 and that P purchases another 30% of T's stock on June 1, 1993. Assume further that P purchases another 50% of T's stock on March 15, 1994. P makes a Qualified Stock Purchase of T as of March 15, 1994. The acquisition period commences on June 1, 1993 despite the earlier purchase. The Acquisition Date is March 15, 1994, the first date on which P is considered to have made a Qualified Stock Purchase. P may elect under § 338(g) to treat T as if it sold and then reacquired its assets on the Acquisition Date. Any gain or loss the Target recognizes is reported on the Target's final return filed for the taxable year that ends on the Acquisition Date. See Prop.Reg. § 1.338–1(e)(1).

As a result of the repeal of the former § 337 by the Tax Reform Act of 1986 (*i.e.*, General Utilities repeal), the Target has full gain or loss on the deemed sale of its assets resulting from a § 338 election. Consequently, it is rarely beneficial for the Purchasing Corporation to make a § 338 election. There are two major exceptions to this general rule. First, if a stand-alone Target has net operating losses or other capital losses that can offset the § 338 gain, then it might be beneficial for the Purchasing Corporation to make a § 338 election. The utilization of a Target's net operating and net capital losses in a § 338 deemed sale is not limited under § 382. *See* § 382(h)(1)(C).

The second exception involves the acquisition of the stock of a subsidiary corporation. This transaction can qualify under § 338(h)(10), which permits a parent corporation that is selling the stock of a subsidiary to elect with the purchasing corporation to treat the transaction as if the subsidiary is selling assets. The parent may agree to such treatment if the basis for the parent's stock in the subsidiary is not significantly higher than the basis of the subsidiary's assets.

Section 338 is examined in greater detail in *Taxable and Tax–Free Corporate Mergers, Acquisitions, and LBOs., supra* Sec. 1.4.

2. *Taxable Reverse Subsidiary Merger Treated as Qualified Stock Acquisition*

REVENUE RULING 90–95
1990–2 C.B. 67.

Issues

(1) If a corporation organizes a subsidiary solely for the purpose of acquiring the stock of a target corporation in a reverse subsidiary cash merger, is the corporation treated on the occurrence of a merger as having acquired the stock of the target in a qualified stock purchase under section 338 of the Internal Revenue Code?

(2) If the corporation makes a qualified stock purchase of the target stock and immediately liquidates the target as part of a plan to acquire the assets of the target, is the corporation treated as having made an asset acquisition pursuant to the *Kimbell–Diamond* doctrine or a section 338 qualified stock purchase followed by a liquidation of the target?

Facts

Situation 1. P, a domestic corporation, formed a wholly owned domestic subsidiary corporation, S, for the sole purpose of acquiring all of the stock of an unrelated domestic target corporation, T, by means of a reverse subsidiary cash merger. Prior to the merger, S conducted no activities other than those required for the merger.

Pursuant to the plan of merger, S merged into T with T surviving. The shareholders of T exchanged all of their T stock for cash from S. Part of the cash used to carry out the acquisition was received by S from

P; the remaining cash was borrowed by *S*. Following the merger, *P* owned all of the outstanding *T* stock.

Situation 2. The facts are the same as in *Situation 1,* except that *P* planned to acquire *T*'s assets through a prompt liquidation of *T*. State law prohibited *P* from owning the stock of *T*. Pursuant to the plan, *T* merged into *P* immediately following the merger of *S* into *T*. The merger of *T* into *P* satisfied the requirements for a tax-free liquidation under section 332 of the Code. The liquidation was not motivated by the evasion or avoidance of federal income tax.

Law and Analysis

In *Kimbell–Diamond Milling Co. v. Commissioner* [see Sec. 1.3.G.4.] * * * the court held that the purchase of the stock of a target corporation for the purpose of obtaining its assets through a prompt liquidation should be treated by the purchaser as one transaction, namely, a purchase of the target's assets with the purchaser receiving a cost basis in the assets. Old section 334(b)(2) of the Code was added in 1954 to codify the principles of *Kimbell–Diamond.* * * *

In 1982, Congress repealed old section 334(b)(2) of the Code and enacted section 338. Section 338 was "intended to replace any nonstatutory treatment of a stock purchase as an asset purchase under the *Kimbell–Diamond* doctrine." * * * [S]tock purchase or asset purchase treatment generally results whether or not the target is liquidated, merged into another corporation, or otherwise disposed of by the purchasing corporation. *See* section 1.338–4T(d) *Question and Answer 1.* [T]emporary Income Tax Regulations.

* * *

Question and Answer 3 of section 1.338–4T(d) of the temporary regulations provides that the parent of the subsidiary corporation in a reverse subsidiary cash merger is considered to have made a qualified stock purchase of the target if the subsidiary's existence is properly disregarded under the step-transaction doctrine and the requirements of a qualified stock purchase are satisfied. A subsidiary used to acquire target stock in a reverse subsidiary cash merger is ordinarily disregarded for federal income tax purposes if it was formed solely for the purpose of acquiring the stock and did not conduct any activities other than those required for the merger. *See* Rev.Rul. 73–427, 1973–2 C.B. 301.

* * *

In *Situations 1 and 2,* the step-transaction doctrine is properly applied to disregard the existence of *S* for federal income tax purposes. *S* had no significance apart from *P*'s acquisition of the *T* stock. *S* was formed for the sole purpose of enabling *P* to acquire the *T* stock, and *S* did not conduct any activities that were not related to that acquisition. Accordingly, the transaction is treated as a qualified stock purchase of *T* stock by *P*.

In *Situation 2,* the step-transaction doctrine does not apply to treat the stock acquisition and liquidation as an asset purchase. Section 338 of the Code replaced the *Kimbell–Diamond* doctrine and governs whether a corporation's acquisition of stock is treated as an asset purchase. Under section 338, asset purchase treatment turns on whether a section 338 election is made (or is deemed made) following a qualified stock purchase of target stock and not on whether the target's stock is acquired to obtain the assets through a prompt liquidation of the target. The acquiring corporation may receive stock purchase treatment or asset purchase treatment whether or not the target is subsequently liquidated. A qualified stock purchase of target stock is accorded independent significance from a subsequent liquidation of the target regardless of whether a section 338 election is made or deemed made. This treatment results even if the liquidation occurs to comply with state law. Accordingly, in *Situation 2,* the acquisition is treated as a qualified stock purchase by P of T stock followed by a tax-free liquidation of T into P.

HOLDINGS

(1) In *Situations 1 and 2,* P is treated as having acquired stock of T in a qualified stock purchase under section 338 of the Code.

(2) In *Situation 2,* P is treated as having acquired stock of T in a qualified stock purchase under section 338 followed by a liquidation of T into P, rather than having made an acquisition of assets pursuant to the *Kimbell–Diamond* doctrine.

§ 9.6 SUMMARY PROBLEMS ON LIQUIDATIONS UNDER §§ 331, 332, 334, 336, AND 337

1. All of the stock of corporation X is owned by individual A. X has cash of $100K and a plot of raw land with a value of $100K and a basis of $10K. X has earning and profits of $50K. X has no items of income or loss for the year other than as specified below. A's basis for his shares in X is $70K. X's tax rate is 33⅓%. A's tax rate is 28% on capital gains and 33⅓% on ordinary income.

    a. What result to A and X, if X sells its raw land for $100K and then liquidates, distributing all of its assets to A?

    b. What result to A and X, if X sells the land for an installment note that qualifies under § 453 and distributes the note to A in the liquidation?

    c. What result to A and X, if X distributes the land and cash to A in a liquidating distribution?

    d. In general, what result in Questions a and c above, if one year before the transactions, A transferred to X in a § 351 exchange a building with a basis of $100K and a value of $10K. The building is sold for $10K in the transaction in Question a and is distributed to A in the transaction in Question c?

e. In general, what result in Questions a and c above if the building is subject to a liability of $50K? In Question a the building is sold subject to the liability for $50K in cash.

f. Assume further that acquiring corporation (AC) is considering the possible acquisition either of all of the stock of X or of X's raw land. If AC acquires X's land, X will be liquidated after the sale of the land. How much should X pay in an asset acquisition? What are the results to X, A, and AC? How much should X pay in a stock acquisition? What are the results to X, A, and AC? What would be the consequences if, after a stock acquisition, AC made a § 338 election? Should AC make a § 338 election?

2. Corporation P owns all of the stock of corporation S, and P has a basis of $50K for its S stock. P has no other assets or liabilities. S owns raw land with a value of $100K and a basis of $10K. All of P's stock is owned by individual A, who has a $10K basis for her stock.

a. What results to S and P, if S liquidates into P? Is this a case of disappearing basis?

b. Assume that P's basis for S's stock is $10K. What result to S, P, and A, if P liquidates distributing the stock of S to A? *See* § 336(e). What result if after the liquidation of P, S then liquidates, distributing the property to A? What result to S, P, and A, if S first liquidates into P and then P liquidates, distributing the raw land to A?

§ 9.7 POLICY PERSPECTIVE: POTENTIAL RELIEF FROM THE REPEAL OF THE *GENERAL UTILITIES DOCTRINE*

GENERAL EXPLANATION OF THE SUBCHAPTER C REVISION BILL OF 1985

Committee Print S PRT 99-47, 62–67 (1985).

[The following discussion was published before the repeal of the *General Utilities* doctrine by the Tax Reform Act of 1986. The issues discussed have particular significance in view of the repeal of the doctrine.]

C. RELIEF FROM REPEAL OF GENERAL UTILITIES DOCTRINE

Many people who testified at the October, 1983 hearing advocated some form of relief from the repeal of *General Utilities*. * * *

* * *

1. Eligible transactions

Almost all who testified in favor of some form of permanent relief confined their remarks to the need for relief in a complete liquidation or liquidating sale. No one testified as to the need for relief in a non-liquidating setting. Indeed, even as to liquidating transactions, most individuals indicated that any permanent relief should be appropriately limited to the potential "double tax" on long-held capital assets.

However, one of the reasons described above in favor of the repeal of *General Utilities* was the concern that current law creates a bias in favor of certain types of transactions over others, providing much complexity and abuse potential. If any *General Utilities* relief were limited as suggested by those who testified, there was the possibility that the same problems as under current law would be revived.

Providing across-the-board relief in all transactions, liquidating and non-liquidating, seemed out of the question because of revenue considerations. It seemed advisable, therefore, that any permanent relief should be targeted as closely as possible to the specific need for the relief.

In the large majority of cases, opposition to the repeal of *General Utilities,* and support for some form of relief, was based upon the concern that a "double tax" on long-held assets of small businesses was too harsh. The view was expressed that a small businessman whose incorporated business holds appreciating capital assets for an extended period of time should not be required to pay both a corporate level and a shareholder level tax upon the liquidation or acquisition of the business. According to this view, this was particularly true because the gains might be largely inflationary. However sympathetic the preceding case might be, the case of a speculator who owns stock of a large publicly-held corporation just prior to the liquidation or acquisition of such corporation appeared clearly less appealing as to the need for "double tax" relief. Thus, it seemed appropriate to consider limiting any relief to long-held gains of small businesses.

Moreover, there was testimony that the impact of the repeal of *General Utilities* (and the consequent need for some form of relief) would fall almost exclusively upon small, closely-held businesses, and that large, publicly-held corporations would rarely be affected. Finally, to the extent the form of the relief (described below) was criticized at the hearing as being too complex, many of those concerns would be eliminated if the relief were limited to a tightly circumscribed number of cases involving smaller corporations.

Accordingly, the bill provides permanent *General Utilities* relief in the case of a small business which incurs gains on long-held assets in a liquidation or liquidating sale. In those circumstances, the "double tax" is effectively eliminated.

Five years was chosen as the appropriate dividing line for "long-held" capital assets because, to the extent the proposal is an attempt to mitigate the effects of inflation, it was believed that some significant holding period should be required. Other proposals have suggested three years as the appropriate test.

The $1 million fair market value test for "small" businesses was chosen because of similar standards used in other sections of the Code.

In addition, to avoid a cliff effect, the bill proposes to provide relief, in decreasing amounts, for corporations up to $2 million in value.

2. *Form of the relief*

The two principal forms of relief that were considered were a shareholder credit and corporate-level exemption. Testimony was almost evenly divided between the two types of relief. The American Law Institute had recommended a shareholder credit in its proposal. The special ABA Task Force recommended a corporate-level exemption.

The corporate-level exemption was rejected for the same reasons that a complete repeal of *General Utilities* was considered essential. A corporate-level exemption is no more than a partial repeal of *General Utilities*. * * *

* * *

Thus, the bill provides for a shareholder credit type of relief from the repeal of *General Utilities*. Each shareholder of a small corporation is provided a basis adjustment in his stock in the liquidating or acquired corporation to reflect the corporate-level tax on long-held capital assets. The basis adjustment approach rather than a shareholder credit was selected to increase administrative simplicity, in order to harmonize the treatment of shareholders in different tax situations and to reconcile the difference between the corporate and shareholder capital gains rates. The basis adjustment would operate to eliminate the "double tax" on long-held capital assets. Only those shareholders holding the stock for six months or more would be entitled to relief.

* * *

Chapter 10

REORGANIZATIONS: INTRODUCTION AND HISTORICAL PERSPECTIVE

§ 10.1 SCOPE

This chapter introduces the corporate reorganization provisions. Reorganizations can be divided into three broad categories: (1) adjustments in the capital structure of a single corporation (*i.e.*, a "recapitalization" or a "mere change in form"); (2) divisive transactions (*i.e.*, the split-up of a single corporation into two or more corporations); and (3) acquisitive transactions (*i.e.*, a merger, or an acquisition of a target's stock or of its assets). A characteristic common to virtually all reorganizations is the issuance of stock in exchange for either stock or assets. In an acquisitive reorganization, a subsidiary may acquire the target by issuing stock of the subsidiary's parent. Such transactions are known as triangular or subsidiary reorganizations.

A shareholder who participates in a reorganization generally receives nonrecognition treatment upon the exchange of her stock for new stock and takes a substituted basis for her new stock. The acquiring corporation has nonrecognition treatment upon the issuance of its stock and takes a carryover basis for any property or stock received. The target corporation in a merger or asset acquisition receives nonrecognition treatment upon the exchange of its assets for stock of the acquiring corporation.

This chapter provides an introduction and historical perspective, and Chapter 11 examines certain fundamental reorganization concepts, such as the continuity of interest and continuity of business enterprise doctrines. Chapter 12 deals with the recapitalization and the mere change in form reorganizations. Chapter 13 considers the divisive (D) reorganization and § 355 spin-off type transactions. Chapter 14 examines the nondivisive (D) reorganization and the liquidation reincorporation doctrine. Chapter 15 looks at acquisitive stock and asset reorganizations, and Chapter 16 examines some policy aspects of reorganizations.

Sec. 10.2 of this chapter provides a historical perspective of the reorganization provisions, and Sec. 10.3 provides a discussion of the legislative history of the reorganization provisions. An introductory note on the provisions is provided in Sec. 10.4, and Sec. 10.5 sets forth introductory problems designed to help develop a basic understanding of the broad sweep of the reorganization provisions.

These issues are addressed in greater detail in Chapter 41 of *Federal Taxation of Business Enterprises, supra* Chapter 1, note 1 and in Chapter 14 of Bittker and Eustice, *Corporations, supra* Sec. 1.4.

§ 10.2 HISTORICAL PERSPECTIVE: THE CASE LAW UNDER THE PRE-1918 STATUTE

MARR v. UNITED STATES

Supreme Court of the United States, 1925.
268 U.S. 536, 45 S.Ct. 575, 69 L.Ed. 1079.

MR. JUSTICE BRANDEIS delivered the opinion of the Court.

Prior to March 1, 1913, Marr and wife purchased 339 shares of the preferred and 425 shares of the common stock of the General Motors Company of New Jersey [GM, N.J.] for $76,400. In 1916, [GM, NJ was reincorporated in Delaware and] they received in exchange for this stock 451 shares of the preferred and 2,125 shares of the common stock of the General Motors Corporation of Delaware which (including a small cash payment) had the aggregate market value of $400,866.57. The difference between the cost of their stock in the New Jersey corporation and the value of the stock in the Delaware corporation was $324,466.57. The Treasury Department ruled that this difference was gain or income under the Act of September 8, 1916. * * *

* * *

* * * Marr contends that, since the new corporation was organized to take over the assets and continue the business of the old, and his capital remained invested in the same business enterprise, the additional securities distributed were in legal effect a stock dividend; and that under the rule of *Eisner v. Macomber,* 252 U.S. 189, 40 S.Ct. 189, 189 L.Ed. 521, 9 A.L.R. 1570, applied in *Weiss v. Stearn,* 265 U.S. 242, 44 S.Ct. 490, 68 L.Ed. 1001, 33 A.L.R. 520, he was not taxable thereon as income, because he still held the whole investment. The government insists that identity of the business enterprise is not conclusive; that gain in value resulting from profits is taxable as income, not only when it is represented by an interest in a different business enterprise or property, but also when it is represented by an essentially different interest in the same business enterprise or property; that, in the case at bar, the gain actually made is represented by securities with essentially different characteristics in an essentially different corporation; and that, consequently, the additional value of the new securities, although they are still held by the Marrs, is income under the rule applied in *United States v. Phellis,* 257 U.S. 156, 42 S.Ct. 63, 66 L.Ed. 180; *Rockefeller v. United States,* 257 U.S. 176, 42 S.Ct. 68, 66 L.Ed. 186; and *Cullinan v. Walker,* 262 U.S. 134, 43 S.Ct. 495, 67 L.Ed. 906. In our opinion the government is right.

In each of the five cases named, as in the case at bar, the business enterprise actually conducted remained exactly the same. In *United States v. Phellis,* in *Rockefeller v. United States* and in *Cullinan v. Walker,* where the additional value in new securities distributed was held to be taxable as income, there had been changes of corporate identity. That is, the corporate property, or a part thereof, was no longer held and operated by the same corporation; and, after the distribution, the stockholders no longer owned merely the same proportional interest of the same character in the same corporation. In *Eisner v. Macomber* and in *Weiss v. Stearn,* where the additional value in new securities was held not to be taxable, the identity was deemed to have been preserved. In *Eisner v. Macomber* the identity was literally maintained. There was no new corporate entity. The same interest in the same corporation was represented after the distribution by more shares of precisely the same character. It was as if the par value of the stock had been reduced, and three shares of reduced par value stock had been issued in place of every two old shares. That is, there was an exchange of certificates but not of interests. In *Weiss v. Stearn* a new corporation had, in fact, been organized to take over the assets and business of the old. Technically there was a new entity; but the corporate identity was deemed to have been substantially maintained because the new corporation was organized under the laws of the same state, with presumably the same powers as the old. There was also no change in the character of securities issued. By reason of these facts, the proportional interest of the stockholder after the distribution of the new securities was deemed to be exactly the same as if the par value of the stock in the old corporation had been reduced, and five shares of reduced par value stock had been issued in place of every two shares of the old stock. Thus, in *Weiss v. Stearn,* as in *Eisner v. Macomber,* the transaction was considered, in essence, an exchange of certificates representing the same interest, not an exchange of interests.

In the case at bar, the new corporation is essentially different from the old. A corporation organized under the laws of Delaware does not have the same rights and powers as one organized under the laws of New Jersey. Because of these inherent differences in rights and powers, both the preferred and the common stock of the old corporation is an essentially different thing from stock of the same general kind in the new. But there are also adventitious differences, substantial in character. A 6 per cent nonvoting preferred stock is an essentially different thing from a 7 per cent voting preferred stock. A common stock subject to the priority of $20,000,000 preferred and a $1,200,000 annual dividend charge is an essentially different thing from a common stock subject only to $15,000,000 preferred and a $1,050,000 annual dividend charge. The case at bar is not one in which after the distribution the stockholders have the same proportional interest of the same kind in essentially the same corporation.

Affirmed.

§ 10.3 PURPOSE AND LEGISLATIVE HISTORY OF THE REORGANIZATION PROVISIONS

Excerpt from CHAPMAN v. COMMISSIONER

United States Court of Appeals, First Circuit, 1980.
618 F.2d 856.

I.

One exception to [the general rule of recognition in § 1001(c)] appears in Section 354(a)(1), which provides that gain or loss shall not be recognized if stock or securities in a corporation are, in pursuance of the plan of reorganization, exchanged solely for stock or securities in another corporation which is a party to the reorganization. This exception does not grant a complete tax exemption for reorganizations, but rather defers the recognition of gain or loss until some later event such as a sale of stock acquired in the exchange. [See § 358] Section 354(a)(1) does not apply to an exchange unless the exchange falls within one of the six categories of "reorganization" defined in Section 368(a)(1).[11] * * *

[The initial predecessor of the reorganization provisions was enacted in 1918 and was comprehensively revised in 1924.]

B.

The 1924 Code defined reorganization, in part, as "a merger or consolidation (including the acquisition by one corporation of at least a majority of the voting stock and at least a majority of the total number of shares of all other classes of stock of another corporation, or substantially all the properties of another corporation)." Although the statute did not specifically limit the consideration that could be given in exchange for stock or assets, courts eventually developed the so-called "continuity of interest" doctrine, which held that exchanges that did not include some quantum of stock as consideration were ineligible for reorganization treatment for lack of a continuing property interest on the part of the acquiree's shareholders. [See Chapter 11.]

Despite this judicial development, sentiment was widespread in Congress that the reorganization provisions lent themselves to abuse,

---

11. In the tax practice, these six categories are referred to by their alphabetic designations in the 1954 Code: hence, an (A) reorganization is a statutory merger or consolidation, a (B) reorganization is a stock-for-stock acquisition, a (C) reorganization is a stock-for-assets acquisition, a (D) reorganization is a corporate transfer of assets to a controlled corporation, an (E) reorganization is a recapitalization, and an (F) reorganization is a mere change in identity, form, or place of organization.

* * *

particularly in the form of so-called "disguised sales." In 1934, the House Ways and Means Committee proposed abolition of the stock-acquisition and asset-acquisition reorganizations which had appeared in the parenthetical section of the 1924 Act quoted above. The Senate Finance Committee countered with a proposal to retain these provisions, but with "restrictions designed to prevent tax avoidance." One of these restrictions was the requirement that the acquiring corporation obtain at least 80 percent, rather than a bare majority, of the stock of the acquiree. The second requirement was stated in the Senate Report as follows: "the acquisition, whether of stock or of substantially all the properties, must be in exchange solely for the voting stock of the acquiring corporation." The Senate amendments were enacted as Section 112(g)(1) of the Revenue Act of 1934, 48 Stat. 680, which provided in pertinent part:

> "(1) The term 'reorganization' means (A) a statutory merger or consolidation, or (B) the acquisition by one corporation in exchange solely for all or a part of its voting stock: of at least 80 per centum of the voting stock and at least 80 per centum of the total number of shares of all other classes of stock of another corporation; or of substantially all the properties of another corporation * * *."

Congress revised this definition in 1939 in response to the Supreme Court's decision in *United States v. Hendler,* 303 U.S. 564, 58 S.Ct. 655, 82 L.Ed. 1018 (1938), which held that an acquiring corporation's assumption of the acquiree's liabilities in an asset-acquisition was equivalent to the receipt of "boot" by the acquiree. Since virtually all asset-acquisition reorganizations necessarily involve the assumption of the acquiree's liabilities, a literal application of the "solely for * * * voting stock" requirement would have effectively abolished this form of tax-free reorganization. In the Revenue Act of 1939, Congress separated the stock-acquisition and asset-acquisition provisions in order to exempt the assumption of liabilities in the latter category of cases from the "solely for * * * voting stock" requirement. Section 112(g)(1) of the revised statute then read, in pertinent part, as follows:

> "(1) the term 'reorganization' means (A) a statutory merger or consolidation, or (B) the acquisition by one corporation, in exchange solely for all or a part of its voting stock, of at least 80 per centum of the voting stock and at least 80 per centum of the total number of shares of all other classes of stock of another corporation, or (C) the acquisition by one corporation, in exchange solely for all or a part of its voting stock, of substantially all the properties of another corporation, but in determining whether the exchange is solely for voting stock the assumption by the acquiring corporation of a liability of the other, or the fact that property acquired is subject to liability, shall be disregarded * * *."

The next major change in this provision occurred in 1954. In that year, the House Bill, H.R. 8300, would have drastically altered the corporate reorganization sections of the Tax Code, permitting, for example, both stock and "boot" as consideration in a corporate acquisition, with gain recognized only to the extent of the "boot." The Senate Finance Committee, in order to preserve the familiar terminology and structure of the 1939 Code, proposed a new version of Section 112(g)(1), which would retain the "solely for * * * voting stock" requirement, but alter the existing control requirement to permit so-called "creeping acquisitions." Under the Senate Bill, [in a (B) reorganization] it would no longer be necessary for the acquiring corporation to obtain 80 percent or more of the acquiree's stock in one "reorganization." The Senate's proposal permitted an acquisition to occur in stages; a bloc of shares representing less than 80 percent could be added to earlier acquisitions, regardless of the consideration given earlier, to meet the control requirement. * * *

* * *

At the same time the Senate was revising the (B) provision, (while leaving intact the "solely for * * * voting stock" requirement), it was also rewriting the (C) provision to explicitly permit up to 20 percent of the consideration in an asset acquisition to take the form of money or other nonstock property. The Senate revisions of subsections (B) and (C) were ultimately passed, and have remained largely unchanged since 1954. Proposals for altering the (B) provision to allow "boot" as consideration have been made, but none has been enacted.

[In 1954 Congress also added the triangular (C) and the over-and-down under § 368(a)(2)(C). The triangular (B) was added in 1964; the forward subsidiary merger under § 368(a)(2)(D) was added in 1968; and the reverse subsidiary merger under § 368(a)(2)(E) was added in 1970.]

As this history shows, Congress has had conflicting aims in this complex and difficult area. On the one hand, the 1934 Act evidences a strong intention to limit the reorganization provisions to prevent forms of tax avoidance that had proliferated under the earlier revenue acts. This intention arguably has been carried forward in the current versions through retention of the "solely for * * * voting stock" requirement in (B), even while the (C) provision was being loosened. On the other hand, both the 1939 and 1954 revisions represented attempts to make the reorganization procedures more accessible and practical in both the (B) and (C) areas. * * *

§ 10.4 INTRODUCTORY NOTE ON THE CURRENT REORGANIZATION PROVISIONS

A. INTRODUCTION

This section is designed to introduce the broad sweep of the reorganization provisions. Each of the forms of reorganization is introduced, and the treatment of the parties to a reorganization is discussed. Each topic is explored in greater detail in later chapters. The problems in

Sec. 10.5 are designed to assist in an understanding of the basic principles.

B. IN GENERAL

The term "reorganization" is defined in § 368(a)(1) as:

(1) a statutory merger or consolidation (the "(A)") (*see* § 368(a)(1)(A));

(2) a stock for stock acquisition (the "(B)") (*see* § 368(a)(1)(B));

(3) a stock for asset acquisition (the "(C)") (*see* § 368(a)(1)(C));

(4) a transfer of property by one corporation to another, including a split-up of a single corporation into two or more corporations (the "(D)") (*see* § 368(a)(1)(D));

(5) a recapitalization (the "(E)") (*see* § 368(a)(1)(E));

(6) a mere change in form (the "(F)") (*see* § 368(a)(1)(F)); and

(7) certain transfers by corporations in connection with bankruptcy reorganizations (the "G") (*see* § 386(a)(1)(G)).

Section 368(a)(2) provides special rules relating to the reorganizations defined in § 368(a)(1). Section 368 says nothing about the treatment of the taxpayers involved in a reorganization; it merely describes those transactions that are reorganizations. The tax treatment to the various taxpayers is governed by §§ 354 through 362 and 381 to 383. The (G) bankruptcy reorganization and mergers between investment companies are not discussed here. *See* § 386(a)(2)(F).

Basically, reorganization transactions are shifts in corporate ownership in which the exchanging stockholder or security holder has a continuing interest in the corporation and has not merely been cashed out. For example, an acquiring corporation may acquire the stock of a target corporation by issuing its own stock to the target's shareholders. The target's former shareholders then have a continuing interest in the target's assets, even though the direct ownership of the target has passed to the acquiring corporation. Such a transaction might qualify as a stock for stock (B) reorganization. In a (B), the target's shareholders receive nonrecognition under § 354 and take a substituted basis (*i.e.,* an exchanged basis under § 7701(a)(42)) for the stock received under § 358. On the other hand, the acquiring corporation has non-recognition treatment under § 1032 upon the issuance of its stock and takes a carryover basis under § 362(b) for the target's stock (*i.e.,* a transferred basis under § 7701(a)(42)). The reorganization provisions thus provide an exception to the recognition rule of § 1001 and the cost basis rule of § 1012.

In the discussion below, the tax treatment to the various taxpayers involved in a reorganization is outlined, and this is followed by an examination of the types of reorganizations.

C. TAX TREATMENT TO THE TAXPAYERS INVOLVED IN A REORGANIZATION

Section 354(a)(1) gives shareholders and security holders nonrecognition treatment upon an exchange, pursuant to a "plan of reorganization," of stock or securities in a corporation that is a "party to a reorganization," provided the exchange is "solely" for stock or securities in such corporation or in another corporation that is a party to a reorganization. The term "plan of reorganization" is not defined in the statute; the regulations say, however, that the plan must be "adopted" by each of the corporate parties thereto. See § 1.368–3(a). The term "party to a reorganization" is defined in § 368(b) to include all of the corporations involved in a reorganization under § 368(a).

Section 354(a)(2) limits the nonrecognition treatment for security holders to cases in which the principal amount of the securities received is equal to the principal amount surrendered. In the event cash or other property (boot) is received or the principal amount of the securities received exceeds the principal amount of the securities surrendered, then under § 356 the exchanging shareholder or security holder recognizes the gain realized to the extent of the boot and the fair market value of the excess principal amount of the securities received. See §§ 356(a)(1) and 356(d)(1) and (2)(A) and (B). Under § 356(a)(2), any gain recognized with respect to stock may be treated as a dividend, to the extent of the shareholder's pro rata share of the accumulated earnings and profits, if the exchange "has the effect of the distribution of a dividend." The issue of whether gain is treated as a dividend is examined in Chapter 11. No loss is recognized. See § 356(c).

Under § 358, the exchanging shareholder or security holder who receives nonrecognition treatment under § 354 or partial nonrecognition treatment under § 356 takes the stock or securities received at a substituted basis, decreased by the amount of any boot received and increased by any gain recognized. The basis of the boot, other than money, is the fair market value thereof. See § 358(a)(2).

For example, assume that individual *S* owns all the stock of target corporation (*TC*). The stock has a value of $1 million, and *S*'s basis is $500K. *TC* merges into acquiring corporation (*AC*) in a transaction that qualifies as an (A) reorganization under § 368(a)(1)(A). *S* surrenders his *TC* stock and receives *AC* stock with a value of $1 million. Under § 354, *S* has nonrecognition treatment, and under § 358, *S* takes a substituted basis of $500K for the *AC* stock. Assume, on the other hand, that *S* receives $900K of *AC* stock and $100K of cash (boot). The transaction still constitutes an (A) reorganization; however, *S* has a recognized gain of $100K under § 356(a)(1), and the gain might be treated as a dividend under § 356(a)(2). See Chapter 11. *S*'s basis under § 358(a) for his *AC* stock is $500K (*i.e.,* the basis of his *TC* stock ($500K), minus the cash received ($100K), plus the gain recognized

($100K)). Since the value of his *AC* stock is $900K, *S* has deferred $400K of his gain.

On the corporate side of the ledger, § 1032 provides for nonrecognition treatment upon the issuance of stock by a corporation. Also, no gain is recognized by a corporation upon the issuance of its securities. *See* § 1.61–12(c)(1). Under § 362(b), the acquiring corporation's basis for stock or assets received is a carryover basis, increased by the amount of any gain recognized by the transferor.

If a corporation (the target) that is a "party to a reorganization" exchanges its property solely for stock of another corporation (the acquiring corporation) that is a party to the reorganization, then under § 361(a), the target corporation does not recognize any gain or loss. Under § 358, the basis to the target corporation of the stock or securities it receives from the acquiring corporation is a substituted basis, decreased by the boot received and increased by the gain recognized.

Under § 361(b), if the target corporation receives both stock and boot, the target recognizes the gain realized to the extent of the boot, unless the boot is distributed pursuant to the plan of reorganization. Under § 361(c), the target does not recognize gain or loss on the distribution of stock of the acquiring corporation. Section 361 is explored in detail in Chapter 11.

Pursuant to § 357(a), liabilities transferred from a target to an acquiring corporation generally do not constitute boot. *See* § 357(b) and (c).

For example, where *TC* merges into *AC* with *TC*'s shareholder, *S*, receiving *AC* stock, *TC* has nonrecognition treatment under § 361(a). *AC* has nonrecognition under § 1032 upon the issuance of its stock, and takes a carryover basis under § 362(b) for *TC*'s assets (*i.e.*, if *TC*'s basis for its assets was $200K, *AC*'s basis would be $200K).

Section 381 provides that in reorganizations in which the target's assets are transferred to the acquiring corporation, the target corporation's tax attributes (*e.g.*, earnings and profits and net operating losses) carry over to the acquiring corporation after the reorganization. This same rule applies for subsidiary liquidations under § 332 in which the parent takes a carryover basis under § 334(b)(1) for the assets received. Section 381 is examined in Chapter 15.

Section 382 limits the amount of a target's net operating losses that can be deducted after a reorganization. Also, § 382 limits the carryover of capital losses and certain credits. Section 382 is discussed in Chapter 15 and in *Taxable and Tax-Free Corporate Mergers, Acquisitions and LBOs, supra* Sec. 1.4.

The reorganizations under § 368 can be broadly categorized into acquisitive reorganizations and non-acquisitive reorganizations. Acquisitive reorganizations can be subdivided into asset reorganizations, which are transactions in which an acquiring corporation acquires the assets of a target corporation and stock reorganizations, which are transactions in which an acquiring corporation acquires the stock of a target corporation. The following sections give a brief introduction to acquisitive and non-acquisitive reorganizations. Acquisitive reorganizations are examined in greater detail in *Taxable and Tax-Free Corporate Mergers, Acquisitions and LBOs, supra* Sec. 1.4.

D. THE ACQUISITIVE REORGANIZATIONS

1. The (A) Merger

Section 1.368–2(b)(1) provides that in order to qualify as an (A) reorganization the "merger or consolidation must be effected pursuant to the corporate laws of the United States, a State or Territory or the District of Columbia." In a merger the target's assets and liabilities are by operation of law transferred to the acquiring corporation, and the shareholders of the target by operation of law swap their stock in the target for the merger consideration issued by the acquiring corporation. *See* Delaware Business Corporation Law § 251.

Although the statute does not refer to the type of consideration the target's shareholders must receive, courts have held that the shareholders must receive a "continuity of interest" in the acquiring corporation (*i.e.*, a substantial stock interest). This continuity of interest requirement, which also applies to the other forms of acquisitive reorganizations, is examined in detail in Chapter 11.

In an (A) reorganization in which only stock of the acquiring corporation is used, the target receives nonrecognition under § 361. The target's shareholders receive nonrecognition under § 354 and take a substituted basis for the stock of the acquiring corporation received under § 358. The acquiror has nonrecognition under § 1032 upon the issuance of its stock, and under § 362(b), the acquiror takes a carryover basis (*i.e.*, the target's basis) for the assets acquired. Also, under § 381 the target's other tax attributes pass over to the acquiring corporation. The (A) reorganization is considered in Chapter 15.

2. The Straight and Triangular (B), Stock for Stock

In a (B) reorganization, the acquiring corporation issues "solely" *its* voting stock or "solely" the voting stock of its parent for stock of the target corporation amounting to "control" thereof. "Control" is defined in § 368(c) as, in essence, 80 percent stock ownership. Transactions in which the consideration paid by the acquiring corporation is the voting stock of its parent corporation are generally known as triangular reorganizations. There are a variety of triangular reorganizations. In the following discussion, the term "Acquiring Subsidiary" refers to a subsidiary corporation that uses its parent's stock in making an acquisition. The parent is referred to as the "Acquiring Parent."

In a straight (B) (*i.e.*, nontriangular), the target's shareholders receive nonrecognition treatment under § 354 and take a substituted basis under § 358. The acquiror receives nonrecognition under § 1032 and takes a carryover basis under § 362 for the stock of the target. If the acquiror liquidates the target, the liquidation is a nonrecognition transaction under § 332, and the acquiror takes a carryover basis under § 334(b)(1) for the target's assets. Similar rules apply in the triangular (B). The (B) reorganization is examined in Chapter 15.

3. *The Straight and Triangular (C), Stock for Assets*

In a (C) reorganization, the acquiring corporation exchanges "solely" its voting stock or "solely" the voting stock of its parent for "substantially all of the properties" of the target corporation. Under § 368(a)(2)(G), the target must distribute the stock and securities received together with its other properties in pursuance of the plan of reorganization.

The target corporation's liabilities are ignored in determining whether the transaction is "solely" for voting stock. The solely for voting stock requirement in a stock for asset (C) reorganization may be "relaxed" by § 368(a)(2)(B), which provides that in certain cases 20 percent of the consideration paid by the acquiring corporation can be cash or other property (boot). In determining the amount of boot that can be utilized, liabilities of the target taken over by the acquiring corporation must be counted as boot. The rule of § 368(a)(2)(B) is known in tax parlance as the "boot relaxation rule."

In a nontriangular (C) in which only voting stock of the acquiror is used, the target receives nonrecognition treatment under § 361(a) and takes a substituted basis for the acquiror's stock under § 358. The target has no gain or loss upon the distribution of the stock in pursuance of the plan of reorganization. *See* § 362(c). The target's shareholders receive nonrecognition under § 354 and take a substituted basis under § 358. Under § 362(b), the acquiror takes a carryover basis (*i.e.*, the target's basis) for the assets acquired, and under § 381 the acquiror takes over the target's other tax attributes. The (C) reorganization is examined in Chapter 15.

4. *The Over and Down (a)(2)(C)*

Section 368(a)(2)(C) provides that in (A), (B) and (C) reorganizations, the stock or assets acquired by the acquiring corporation may be dropped down into a subsidiary of the acquiring corporation without disqualifying the transaction as a reorganization on the grounds that the continuity of interest has become too remote. These types of transactions are sometimes referred to as "over and down" reorganizations. The "over" portion of the transaction is taxed in accordance with the principles discussed above; the "down" portion is a § 351 transaction.

5. *Forward Subsidiary Merger Under (a)(2)(D)*

Section 368(a)(2)(D) provides that a merger of a target corporation into an Acquiring Subsidiary may qualify as an (A) reorganization provided (1) the Acquiring Subsidiary acquires in exchange for stock of the Acquiring Parent "substantially all" of the properties of the target, (2) the transaction would have been a merger if it had been directly between the Acquiring Parent and the target, and (3) no stock of the Acquiring Subsidiary is used in the transaction. In providing for triangular mergers, § 368(a)(2)(D) expands the (A) reorganization in the same way the parenthetical clauses in both the (B) and (C) expand those reorganizations to include triangular acquisitions. A transaction that comes within § 368(a)(2)(D) is sometimes referred to as a "forward subsidiary merger." The forward subsidiary merger is explored in detail in Chapter 15.

6. *Reverse Subsidiary Merger Under (a)(2)(E)*

Section 368(a)(2)(E) provides that a merger of an Acquiring Subsidiary into a target corporation may qualify as an (A) reorganization if (1) after the merger the target corporation holds "substantially all of its properties and [substantially all] of the properties of the merged [Acquiring Subsidiary] corporation, (other than stock of the [Acquiring Parent] distributed in the transaction)," and (2) the former shareholders of the target exchange stock of the target amounting to control for voting stock of the Acquiring Parent. This transaction, which is sometimes known as a "reverse subsidiary merger," is examined in detail in Chapter 15.

7. *Summary of Acquisitive Reorganizations*

Each of the above types of transaction is acquisitive in nature; one corporation acquires either the stock or assets of another corporation. In summary, there are seven basic types of acquisitive reorganizations:

(1) A straight merger between a target and an acquiror (*see* § 368(a)(1)(A));

(2) A forward subsidiary merger of a target into an Acquiring Subsidiary (*see* § 368(a)(2)(D));

(3) A reverse subsidiary merger of an Acquiring Subsidiary into a target (*see* § 368(a)(2)(E));

(4) A straight stock for stock acquisition (*see* § 368(a)(1)(B));

(5) A triangular stock for stock acquisition (*see* § 368(a)(1)(B));

(6) A straight stock for asset acquisition (*see* § 368(a)(1)(C)); and

(7) A triangular stock for asset acquisition (*see* § 368(a)(1)(C)).

Also, after each of these reorganizations, the assets or stock may be pushed down to a subsidiary of the acquiring corporation.

These seven forms of acquisitive reorganizations can be subdivided into four asset reorganizations and three stock reorganizations:

- *Asset Reorganizations:* The (A) merger reorganization, the straight and triangular (C) stock for asset reorganizations, and the forward subsidiary merger reorganization under § 368(a)(2)(D). Each of these asset reorganizations is explored in Chapter 15.

- *Stock Reorganizations:* The straight and triangular (B) stock for stock reorganization and the reverse subsidiary merger under § 368(a)(2)(E). Each of these stock reorganizations is explored in Chapter 15.

E. THE NON-ACQUISITIVE REORGANIZATIONS

1. *The (D) Reorganization*

In a (D) reorganization, a corporation (the "distributing corporation") transfers all or part of its assets to another corporation (the "controlled corporation"), and immediately after the transfer, the distributing corporation or its shareholders or a combination thereof are in control of the controlled corporation. The distribution by the distributing corporation to its shareholders of stock or securities of the controlled corporation must qualify under §§ 354, 355 or 356.

The (D) reorganization contemplated by § 354 is a transaction in which the distributing corporation (1) transfers "substantially all" of its assets to the controlled corporation, and (2) distributes pursuant to the plan of reorganization the stock or securities and other property received as well as its other properties. Thus, the distributing corporation is stripped of its assets and liquidated. *See* § 354(b). This type of transaction is known as a nondivisive (D). The distributing corporation receives nonrecognition under §§ 351 and 361 on the transfer of the assets to the controlled corporation and receives nonrecognition under § 361 on the distribution of the stock and securities of the controlled corporation. The controlled corporation receives nonrecognition under § 1032 on the issuance of its stock and takes a carryover basis for the assets under § 362. The shareholders of the distributing corporation receive nonrecognition treatment under § 354 and take a carryover basis under § 358. The nondivisive (D) reorganization is examined in Chapter 14.

Section 355 encompasses divisive (D) reorganizations in which there is a breakup of a corporation into two or more corporations. Divisive (D) reorganizations generally fall into three broad categories: spin-offs, split-offs and split-ups. In a spin-off, a distributing corporation transfers part of its assets to a controlled corporation and then distributes to its shareholders the stock of the controlled corporation in a pro rata distribution. Thus, the shareholders continue their same pro rata interest but in two corporations rather than one. In a split-off, stock of the distributing corporation is redeemed in exchange for stock of the controlled corporation. In the split-up, the distributing corporation distributes its assets to two or more controlled corporations and then liquidates, distributing the stock to its shareholders. Section 355 applies not only to (D) reorganizations; it also applies to distributions of the stock of existing subsidiaries. In order for a transaction to fit within § 355, the following requirements must be satisfied:

> (A) The distributing corporation must distribute to its shareholders or security holders "solely" stock or securities of the controlled corporation (*see* §§ 355(a)(1)(A) and 355(a)(2)); the distribution need not be pro rata. If boot is distributed, § 356 will apply (*see* § 356(a) and (b));

> (B) The transaction must not be a "device" for the distribution of E & P (*see* § 355(a)(1)(B));

> (C) A separate active trade or business that has been conducted for at least five years must continue to be conducted after the distribution by each of the distributing and controlled corporations (*see* §§ 355(a)(1)(C) and 355(b));

> (D) The distributing corporation must distribute all of the stock or securities of the controlled corporation or an amount of stock of the controlled corporation amounting to control, provided that in the latter case it is established that the retention of stock or securities of the controlled corporation is not for tax avoidance purposes (*see* § 355(a)(1)(D)).

For transactions that fall within § 355, the shareholders or security holders of the distributing corporation receive nonrecognition treatment on receipt of the stock or securities of the controlled corporation. *See* § 355(a). Thus, § 355 is analogous to § 354, which gives nonrecognition treatment for reorganizations other than the divisive (D). In the event boot is distributed in a § 355 transaction, gain is recognized to the extent of the boot. *See* § 356(a)(1). The gain recognized is generally treated as a dividend. *See* §§ 356(a)(2) and 356(b). The divisive (D) and § 355 are explored in Chapter 13.

2. *The (E) Recapitalization*

The (E) reorganization is a recapitalization of a corporation; that is, a restructuring of the capital of a single corporation. For example, if the shareholders of a corporation exchange their common stock for new common stock, the transaction may constitute a recapitalization. The shareholders receive non-recognition treatment under § 354 and take a substituted basis under § 358. The corporation has nonrecognition treatment under § 1032 upon the issuance of its stock. The recapitalization is examined in Chapter 12.

3. *The (F) Mere Change in Form*

The (F) reorganization is a "mere change in identity, form, or place of organization." For instance, a New York corporation reincorporates in Virginia. Under § 381(b)(3), post reorganization net operating losses can be carried back to a former corporation only in an (F). The (F) reorganization is explored in Chapter 12.

§ 10.5 INTRODUCTORY PROBLEMS

The following problems are designed to illustrate the basic operation of the reorganization provisions.

Individuals A and B each own 50 percent of the outstanding stock of target corporation (TC). A's basis for his stock is $50K, and B's basis is $150K. The value of TC's stock is $200K, and, consequently, A's and B's shares are each worth $100K. The fair market value of TC's assets is $220K, and the adjusted basis thereof is $100K. TC has liabilities of $20K and E & P of $100K. Acquiring corporation (AC) is interested in acquiring TC in a nontaxable reorganization.

(a) What result to A, B, TC and AC if TC merges into AC in a transaction in which A and B each receive voting stock of AC with a fair market value of $100K? See §§ 368(a)(1)(A), 368(b), 354, 356, 357, 358, 361, 362, and 1032.

(b) What if AC forms a subsidiary (AC–S) by transferring AC voting stock to it, and TC merges into AC–S with A and B receiving the AC stock? Focus only on the treatment of A and B and AC–S's basis for the TC assets. What if AC–S merges into TC? Focus only on the treatment of A and B. See §§ 368(a)(1)(A), (a)(2)(D), (a)(2)(E), 368(b), 368(c), 354, 357, 358, 361, 362, and 1032.

(c) What result to A, B, TC and AC if AC acquires the stock of TC from A and B in exchange for $200K of voting stock of AC? What result if AC–S makes the acquisition using AC voting stock? Focus only on the treatment of A and B and AC–S's basis for the TC stock. See §§ 368(a)(1)(B), 368(b), 368(c), 354, 357, 358, 361, 362, and 1032.

(d) What results to A, B, TC and AC if AC acquires the assets and liabilities of TC in exchange for $200K of voting stock of AC, and TC is then liquidated? Suppose AC–S makes the acquisition using $200K of AC voting stock? See §§ 368(a)(1)(C), (a)(2)(B), 368(b), 354, 356, 357, 358, 361, 362, and 1032.

(e) In general, what result if after the transactions described in (a) through (d) above, the acquiring corporation contributes the stock or assets acquired to a subsidiary of the acquiring corporation? See §§ 368(a)(2)(C), 368(b), 351, 354, 357, 358, 361, 362, and 1032.

(f) Assume A and B disagree on selling out to AC, and they decide to split up and go their separate ways. In general, is there any way TC can be divided down the middle into two corporations in a nontaxable division? See §§ 368(a)(1)(D), 368(b), 351, 355, 357, 358, 361, 362, and 1032.

(g) Assume that A is quite old and would like very much to pull out of the business and that B is young and wants to continue. In general, what result if *A* turns in his common stock for a new issue of preferred stock that pays a 12% dividend, and *B* thereby becomes the only common shareholder? *See* §§ 368(a)(1)(E), 368(b), 354, 357, 358, and 1032. Is the preferred § 306 stock? *See* §§ 305(a) and 306(c).

(h) In general, what result if *TC* changes its state of incorporation? *See* §§ 368(a)(1)(F), 354, 357, 358, 361, 362, and 1032.

(i) How would the transaction in *Marr* (*see* Sec. 10.2) be taxed under the current statute? What if in *Marr* G.M.N.J. had issued new common and preferred for its old common and preferred? What if in *Marr* G.M.N.J. had merged into Ford and the shareholders of G.M.N.J. exchanged their shares for Ford shares?

Chapter 11

FUNDAMENTAL REORGANIZATION CONCEPTS

§ 11.1 SCOPE

This chapter which is divided into six parts, addresses several fundamental concepts concerning reorganizations. Part A, which deals with concepts relating to the reorganization definition in § 368, looks at (1) the continuity of interest doctrine in Sec. 11.2; (2) the continuity of business enterprise doctrine in Sec. 11.3; (3) the meaning of solely for voting stock in Sec. 11.4; (4) the definition of control in Sec. 11.5; (5) the meaning of the "plan of reorganization" in Sec. 11.6; and (6) the ever-present business purposes doctrine in Sec. 11.7.

Part B, which deals with concepts relating to the exchanging stockholders and security holders, examines (1) the meaning of "securities exchange" in Sec. 11.8; (2) the treatment of warrants in Sec. 11.9; (3) the treatment of a swap of securities for securities in Sec. 11.10; and (4) the determination of the shareholder's basis in Sec. 11.11.

Part C, which deals with concepts relating to treatment of boot under § 356, examines (1) the requirement of a reorganization as a condition for § 356 treatment in Sec. 11.12, and (2) the impact of the *Clark* case in determining whether a distribution has the effect of the distribution of the dividend in Sec. 11.13.

Part D, which deals with concepts relating to the treatment of the target corporation, examines (1) the treatment of the target corporation upon the receipt and distribution of stock, securities, and boot in Sec. 11.14, and (2) the impact of the treatment of liabilities in Sec. 11.15.

Part E, which deals with concepts relating to acquiror, examines the carryover basis rule in Sec. 11.16.

Part F, which focuses on the impact of stock dividends and § 306 stock, examines the impact of § 305 in Sec. 11.17 and the impact of § 306 in Sec. 11.18.

Finally, Part G, surveys various overlap issues between § 351 and the reorganization provisions. *See* Sec. 11.19.

These issues are covered in greater detail in Chapter 42 of *Federal Taxation of Business Enterprises, supra* Chapter 1, note 1; Chapter 14 of Bittker and Eustice, *Corporations, supra* Sec. 1.4; and Chapters 6 and 9 of Ginsburg and Levin, *Mergers, supra* Sec. 1.4. *See also* the most recent edition of ALI, *Tax Strategies, supra* Sec. 1.4.

PART A. CONCEPTS RELATING TO REORGANIZATION DEFINITION: § 368

§ 11.2 THE CONCEPT OF CONTINUITY OF INTEREST

A. INTRODUCTION

The regulations under § 1.368–1 and –2 refer in several places to the requirement that the transferor in a reorganization or its shareholders must have a continuity of interest in the assets transferred. This means that the target corporation or its shareholders must have as a result of the reorganization an ownership interest in the acquiring corporation. There is no reference in § 368 to continuity of interest; the concept was judicially developed. The stock for stock (B) reorganization, the stock for asset (C) reorganization, and the reverse subsidiary merger under § 368(a)(2)(E), have their own continuity of interest requirements, in that the acquiring corporation must use its own or its parent's voting stock in making the acquisition. None of the other forms of reorganization have this voting stock requirement, and, consequently, the cases that have developed the concept are still important.

B. WHAT TYPE OF INTEREST SATISFIES THE CONTINUITY OF INTEREST REQUIREMENT

1. Short–Term Notes Do Not Provide Continuity of Interest: The (C) Before the Solely for Voting Stock Requirement

PINELLAS ICE & COLD STORAGE CO. v. COMMISSIONER

Supreme Court of the United States, 1933.
287 U.S. 462, 53 S.Ct. 257, 77 L.Ed. 428.

Mr. Justice McReynolds delivered the opinion of the Court.

Petitioner, a Florida corporation, made and sold ice at St. Petersburg. Substantially the same stockholders owned the Citizens' Ice & Cold Storage Company, engaged in like business at the same place. In February, 1926, Lewis, general manager of both companies, began negotiations for the sale of their properties to the National Public Service Corporation. Their directors and stockholders were anxious to sell, distribute the assets, and dissolve the corporations. The prospective vendee desired to acquire the properties of both companies, but not of one without the other.

In October, 1926, agreement was reached and the vendor's directors again approved the plan for distribution and dissolution. In November, 1926, petitioner and the National Corporation entered into a formal written contract conditioned upon a like one by the Citizens' Company. This referred to petitioner as "vendor" and the National Corporation as "purchaser." [The consideration was $400,000 in cash and $1,000,000 in short-term notes due within six months.]

* * *

The Commissioner of Internal Revenue determined that the petitioner derived taxable gain exceeding $500,000 and assessed it accordingly under the Revenue Act of 1926. The Board of Tax Appeals and the Circuit Court of Appeals approved this action.

The facts are not in controversy. The gain is admitted; but it is said this was definitely exempted from taxation by section 203, [now § 361(b)(2)] Revenue Act of 1926.

Counsel for the petitioner maintain—

The record discloses a "reorganization" to which petitioner was party and a preliminary plan strictly pursued. The Florida West Coast Ice Company acquired substantially all of petitioner's property in exchange for cash and securities which were promptly distributed to the latter's stockholders. Consequently, under section 203, the admitted gain was not taxable.

The Board of Tax Appeals held that the transaction in question amounted to a sale of petitioner's property for money and not an exchange for securities within the true meaning of the statute. It, accordingly and as we think properly, upheld the Commissioner's action.

The "vendor" agreed "to sell," and the "purchaser" agreed "to purchase," certain described property for a definite sum of money. Part of this sum was paid in cash; for the balance the purchaser executed three promissory notes, secured by the deposit of mortgage bonds, payable, with interest, in about forty-five, seventy-five, and one hundred and five days, respectively. These notes—mere evidence of obligation to pay the purchase price—were not securities within the intendment of the act and were properly regarded as the equivalent of cash. It would require clear language to lead us to conclude that Congress intended to grant exemption to one who sells property and for the purchase price accepts well secured, short-term notes (all payable within four months), when another who makes a like sale and receives cash certainly would be taxed. We can discover no good basis in reason for the contrary view and its acceptance would make evasion of taxation very easy. In substance the petitioner sold for the equivalent of cash; the gain must be recognized.

The court below held that the facts disclosed failed to show a "reorganization" within the statutory definition. And, in the circumstances, we approve that conclusion. But the construction which the court seems to have placed upon clause A, paragraph (h)(1), section 203

(26 USCA § 934(h)(1), cls. (A, B), [now § 368(a)(1)] we think is too narrow. It conflicts with established practice of the tax officers and, if passed without comment, may produce perplexity.

The court said: "It must be assumed that in adopting paragraph (h) [now § 368(a)(1)] Congress intended to use the words 'merger' and 'consolidation' in their ordinary and accepted meanings. Giving the matter in parenthesis the most liberal construction, it is only when there is an acquisition of substantially all the property of another corporation in connection with a merger or consolidation that a reorganization takes place. Clause (B) of the paragraph removes any doubts as to the intention of Congress on this point."

The paragraph in question directs: "The term 'reorganization' means (A) a merger or consolidation (including the acquisition by one corporation of at least a majority of the voting stock and at least a majority of the total number of shares of all other classes of stock of another corporation, or substantially all the properties of another corporation)." The words within the parenthesis may not be disregarded. They expand the meaning of "merger" or "consolidation" so as to include some things which partake of the nature of a merger or consolidation but are beyond the ordinary and commonly accepted meaning of those words—so as to embrace circumstances difficult to delimit but which in strictness cannot be designated as either merger or consolidation. But the mere purchase for money of the assets of one company by another is beyond the evident purpose of the provision, and has no real semblance to a merger or consolidation. Certainly, we think that to be within the exemption the seller must acquire an interest in the affairs of the purchasing company more definite than that incident to ownership of its short-term purchase-money notes. This general view is adopted and well sustained in *Cortland Specialty Co. v. Commissioner of Internal Revenue* (C.C.A.) 60 F.(2d) 937, 939, 940. It harmonizes with the underlying purpose of the provisions in respect of exemptions and gives some effect to all the words employed.

The judgment of the court below is affirmed.

Questions

Who is the taxpayer in *Pinellas*? What was the lower court's narrower reading of the statute which the Supreme Court in *Pinellas* rejects? The Court said the "seller must acquire an interest in the affairs of the purchasing company more definite than that incident to ownership of its short-term purchase-money notes." What type of interest would meet such a requirement? What result in *Pinellas* under the current statute? Does *Pinellas* have any continuing vitality with respect to the (C) reorganization? The (A) reorganization? The forward subsidiary merger under § 368(a)(2)(D)? The reverse subsidiary merger under § 368(a)(2)(E)?

2. Interest Must Be "Definite and Material" and "Substantial Part of Value of the Thing Transferred": Cash and Common Received in a (C) Before the Solely for Voting Stock Requirement

HELVERING v. MINNESOTA TEA CO.
Supreme Court of the United States, 1935.
296 U.S. 378, 56 S.Ct. 269, 80 L.Ed. 284 (Minnesota Tea I).

MR. JUSTICE MCREYNOLDS delivered the opinion of the Court.

Respondent, a Minnesota corporation with three stockholders, assailed a deficiency assessment for 1928 income tax, and prevailed below. The Commissioner seeks reversal. He claims the transaction out of which the assessment arose was not a reorganization within section 112, par. (i)(1)(A), Revenue Act, 1928. [Now § 368(a)(1).]

* * *

July 14, 1928, respondent caused Peterson Investment Company to be organized, and transferred to the latter real estate, investments, and miscellaneous assets in exchange for the transferee's entire capital stock. The shares thus obtained were immediately distributed among the three stockholders. August 23, 1928, it transferred all remaining assets to Grand Union Company in exchange for voting trust certificates, representing 18,000 shares of the transferee's common stock, and $426,842.52 cash. It retained the certificates; but immediately distributed the money among the stockholders, who agreed to pay $106,471.73 of its outstanding debts. Although of opinion that there had been reorganization, the Commissioner treated as taxable gain the amount of the assumed debts upon the view that this amount of the cash received by the company was really appropriated to the payment of its debts.

The matter went before the Board of Tax Appeals upon the question whether the Commissioner ruled rightly in respect of this taxable gain. Both parties proceeded upon the view that there had been reorganization. Of its own motion, the Board questioned and denied the existence of one. It then ruled that the corporation had realized taxable gain amounting to the difference between cost of the property transferred and the cash received, plus the value of the 18,000 shares; $712,195.90.

The Circuit Court of Appeals found there was reorganization within the statute, and reversed the Board. It concluded that the words, "the acquisition by one corporation of * * * substantially all the properties of another corporation," plainly include the transaction under consideration. Also, that clause (B), § 112(i)(1) [now § 368(a)(1)], first introduced by Revenue Act of 1924, and continued in later statutes, did not narrow the scope of clause (A). Further, that reorganization was not dependent upon dissolution by the conveying corporation. And, finally, that its conclusions find support in treasury regulations long in force.

* * *

[In *Pinellas* we said that] "we think that to be within the exemption the seller must acquire an interest in the affairs of the purchasing company more definite than that incident to ownership of its short-term purchase-money notes." And we now add that this interest must be definite and material; it must represent a substantial part of the value of the thing transferred. This much is necessary in order that the result accomplished may genuinely partake of the nature of merger or consolidation.

Gregory v. Helvering, 293 U.S. 465, 55 S.Ct. 266, 79 L.Ed. 596, 97 A.L.R. 1355, revealed a sham; a mere device intended to obscure the character of the transaction. We, of course, disregarded the mask and dealt with realities. The present record discloses no such situation; nothing suggests other than a bona fide business move.

The transaction here was no sale, but partook of the nature of a reorganization, in that the seller acquired a definite and substantial interest in the purchaser.

True it is that the relationship of the taxpayer to the assets conveyed was substantially changed, but this is not inhibited by the statute. Also, a large part of the consideration was cash. This, we think, is permissible so long as the taxpayer received an interest in the affairs of the transferee which represented a material part of the value of the transferred assets.

Finally, it is said the transferor was not dissolved, and therefore the transaction does not adequately resemble consolidation. But dissolution is not prescribed, and we are unable to see that such action is essential to the end in view.

* * *

We think the court below rightly decided there was a reorganization. It reversed the Board of Tax Appeals, and remanded the cause for further proceedings, and its judgment must be affirmed.

Questions

Who is the taxpayer here? Following its decision in *Pinellas,* the Court here again rejects the narrower reading of § 203(h)(1)(A) of the 1924 and 1926 Acts as encompassing only mergers or consolidations. Thus, the Court sanctions the asset acquisition reorganization. The Court goes on to add to what it said in *Pinellas,* that in order to constitute a reorganization the interest acquired must be "definite and material; it must represent a substantial part of the value of the thing transferred." What is a "definite and material" interest? What is a "substantial part" of the thing transferred? How much cash (boot) could be paid before breaking a reorganization? Does *Minnesota Tea I* have any continuing vitality for the (C) reorganization? The (A) reorganization? The (B) reorganization? The forward subsidiary merger under § 368(a)(2)(D)? The reverse subsidiary merger under § 368(a)(2)(E)? How would the transaction be treated under the current statute?

3. Nonvoting Preferred Carries Continuity of Interest in a (C) Before the Solely for Voting Stock Requirement

JOHN A. NELSON CO. v. HELVERING

Supreme Court of the United States, 1935.
296 U.S. 374, 56 S.Ct. 273, 80 L.Ed. 281.

MR. JUSTICE MCREYNOLDS delivered the opinion of the Court.

The petitioner contests a deficiency income assessment made on account of alleged gains during 1926. It claims that the transaction out of which the assessment arose was reorganization within the statute. Section 203, Revenue Act, 1926, [now § 361(b)(2)] * * * relied upon. * * *

In 1926, under an agreement with petitioner, the Elliott–Fisher Corporation organized a new corporation with 12,500 shares non-voting preferred stock and 30,000 shares of common stock. It purchased the latter for $2,000,000 cash. This new corporation then acquired substantially all of petitioner's property, except $100,000, in return for $2,000,000 cash and the entire issue of preferred stock. Part of this cash was used to retire petitioner's own preferred shares, and the remainder and the preferred stock of the new company went to its stockholders. It retained its franchise and $100,000, and continued to be liable for certain obligations. The preferred stock so distributed, except in case of default, had no voice in the control of the issuing corporation.

The Commissioner, Board of Tax Appeals, and the court all concluded there was no reorganization. This, we think, was error.

The court below thought the facts showed "that the transaction essentially constituted a sale of the greater part of petitioner's assets for cash and the preferred stock in the new corporation, leaving the Elliott–Fisher Company in entire control of the new corporation by virtue of its ownership of the common stock."

True, the mere acquisition of the assets of one corporation by another does not amount to reorganization within the statutory definition. *Pinellas, Ice & Cold Storage Co. v. Commissioner of Internal Revenue,* 287 U.S. 462, 53 S.Ct. 257, 77 L.Ed. 428, so affirmed. But where, as here, the seller acquires a definite and substantial interest in the affairs of the purchasing corporation, a wholly different situation arises. The owner of preferred stock is not without substantial interest in the affairs of the issuing corporation, although denied voting rights. The statute does not require participation in the management of the purchaser; nor does it demand that the conveying corporation be dissolved. A controlling interest in the transferee corporation is not made a requisite by section 203(h)(1)(A) [now § 368(a)(1)] (26 U.S.C.A. § 112 note) * * *.

Finally, as has been pointed out in the *Minnesota Tea Case,* paragraph (h)(1)(B) was not intended to modify the provisions of paragraph (h)(1)(A). It describes a class. Whether some overlapping is possible is not presently important.

The judgment below must be reversed.

Questions

Who is the taxpayer here? The Supreme Court here holds that nonvoting preferred constitutes a "definite and substantial interest in the affairs of the purchasing corporation." The preferred amounted to only 38% of the total consideration. Is the nonvoting preferred in *John A. Nelson* that much different from the notes in *Pinellas?* Suppose the preferred had been redeemable at the option of the corporation? Does *John A. Nelson* have any continuing vitality with respect to the (C) reorganization? The (A) reorganization? The (B)? The forward subsidiary merger under § 368(a)(2)(D)? The reverse subsidiary merger under § 368(a)(2)(E)?

4. Receipt of Stock and Bonds in a (B) Before the Solely for Voting Stock Requirement: Bonds Are Securities

HELVERING v. WATTS

Supreme Court of the United States, 1935.
96 U.S. 387, 56 S.Ct. 275, 80 L.Ed. 289.

MR. JUSTICE MCREYNOLDS delivered the opinion of the Court.

These causes involved deficiency assessments for income tax against the three respondents for the year 1924.

They were the sole stockholders of United States Ferro Alloys Corporation, herein Ferro Alloys, and the causes, alike in all essential particulars, were dealt with below in one opinion.

The respondents maintain that they exchanged all stock of Ferro Alloys for shares of Vanadium Corporation of America and bonds of Ferro Alloys guaranteed by Vanadium; that these two corporations were parties to a reorganization, and that under section 203(b)(2), [now § 354] Revenue Act 1924, 43 Stat. 256 (26 U.S.C.A. § 112 note), no taxable gain resulted. The Commissioner insists that the transaction was a sale of all the stock of the Ferro Alloys, and therefore taxable gain resulted.

* * *

In December, 1924, respondents owned all the stock of Ferro Alloys Corporation. They exchanged this with the Vanadium Corporation for stock of the latter valued at $30 per share and for $1,161,184.50 mortgage bonds of Ferro Alloys guaranteed by Vanadium. Ferro Alloys continued to conduct business until its dissolution in 1928. Article 1574 of Treasury Regulations 65 provided that under the Act of 1924 no gain or loss shall be recognized to the shareholders from the exchange of stock made in connection with the reorganization, if two or more corporations reorganize; for example, by either the sale of the stock of B to A, or the acquisition by A of a majority of the total number of shares of all other classes of stock of B.

The transaction here involved is within the description of reorganization recognized by the Treasury Regulation above quoted. And if the regulation can be taken as properly interpreting the statute, the challenged judgment must be affirmed.

The court below recites the history of the Treasury Regulation above quoted, and concludes that, in view of the re-enactment of the paragraph to which it refers without change, Congress intended to approve the regulation as written.

The Commissioner here maintains that the definition of reorganization found in section 203(h)(1)(A), Revenue Act 1924, [now § 362(a)(1)] * * * should be limited to transactions which partake of the nature of mergers or consolidations, and that here the Vanadium merely made an investment in Ferro Alloys stock and obtained only the rights of a stockholder therein. It is also urged that an exchange of stocks for bonds results in a substantial change of position and that such bonds are "other property" within the meaning of the statute, and, as such, subject to tax. Much of the argument presented is the same as the one considered in the *Minnesota Tea Company Case,* and it need not be again followed in detail. The bonds, we think, were securities within the definition, and cannot be regarded as cash, as were the short-term notes referred to in *Pinellas*.

* * *

The judgment of the court below must be affirmed.

Questions

What result if the transaction had been structured as an (A) reorganization? What was the mix of consideration here? How would the transaction be treated under the current statute?

5. *Acquiring Corporation Acquires Stock of Target in Exchange For 25% Stock and 75% Cash Consideration in (B) Reorganization Prior to Enactment of Solely for Voting Stock Requirement*

MILLER v. COMMISSIONER OF INTERNAL REVENUE

United States Court of Appeals, Sixth Circuit, 1936.
84 F.2d 415.

SIMONS, CIRCUIT JUDGE.

The review here sought is of orders of the Board of Tax Appeals sustaining deficiencies determined by the respondent in the taxes of the petitioners for the year 1928. In that year the petitioner A.L. Miller and Mrs. Hawk's decedent, Henry C. Hawk, then the majority stockholders of the Enquirer–News Company, a newspaper publishing corporation of Battle Creek, Mich., transferred all of their stock in that corporation to Federated Publications, Inc., for a consideration partly in cash and partly in stock of the purchasing company, which at the same time acquired all of the minority stock of the Enquirer–News Company. [Only 25% of the consideration paid by the acquiring corporation was stock of the acquiring corporation.] Concededly gain was derived by the petitioners through the transaction. Whether gain is to be recognized upon the stock exchanged as well as on that sold for cash is the question to be decided, and this in turn depends upon whether the transaction was a sale, or, within the applicable statute, a merger or reorganization.

The taxes here involved are governed by section 112 of the Revenue Act of 1928 [now § 1001]. Subsection (a) declares the general rule that upon the sale or exchange of property the entire amount of the gain or loss shall be recognized except as thereinafter provided. By subsection (b)(3) [now § 354] no gain or loss is recognized if stock or securities in a corporation which is a party to a reorganization are, in pursuance of the plan of reorganization, exchanged solely for stock or securities in another corporation which is a party to the reorganization. Subsection (i)(1) [now § 368(a)(1)], in so far as here applicable, defines the term "reorganization" to mean: "(A) a merger or consolidation (including the acquisition by one corporation of at least a majority of the voting stock and at least a majority of the total number of shares of all other classes of stock of another corporation, or substantially all the properties of another corporation), or * * *."

It is not disputed that Federated Publications, Inc., acquired all of the stock of the Enquirer–News Company, so that the transaction is within the literal wording of the parenthetical clause of subsection (i)(1). But this, says the respondent, is not enough, for every acquisition of a majority of stock of one corporation by another does not constitute reorganization within the purview of the statute. Only those acquisitions satisfy the statute which partake of the nature of a merger or consolidation, but for some reason do not come entirely within the precise definition of those terms. * * *

* * *

The Supreme Court has of course, neither in the Minnesota Tea Company nor in companion cases, defined what is meant by a "definite and material interest," or "a substantial part of the value of the thing transferred," which it considers necessary in order that the result accomplished may genuinely partake of the nature of merger or consolidation. Manifestly, it could not be precise, for in the final analysis each case must rest upon its own peculiar facts. However, a controlling interest in the transferee corporation is not requisite. Nelson Company v. Helvering, supra. It was there held also that the owner of preferred stock is not without substantial interest in the affairs of the issuing corporation, although denied voting rights, for the statute does not require participation in the management of the purchaser. In the present case we find that the petitioners acquired an interest in the transferee of the value of $125,000. * * * It will therefore be seen that the petitioners acquired an interest in the new corporation almost equal to 50 per cent. of the interest they had in the old company, and exactly equal to 25 per cent. of the value of the total number of shares transferred. It is idle to say that this is not a substantial part of the value of the thing transferred, or does not constitute a definite and material interest in the affairs of the purchasing company. In the commonly accepted legal sense, a substantial interest is something more than a merely nominal interest, and, in respect to corporations, a definite and material interest is an interest beyond what is usually referred to as represented by "qualifying shares."

We attach no importance to the fact that some of the stockholders in the transferring corporation acquired no interest in the transferee. This is certainly not a test by which the effectuation of a merger or consolidation is to be determined, for it will rarely result when reorganizations, even in their strict literal sense, are undertaken that all stockholders will approve. It is almost universal experience that some nonassenting stock must be acquired otherwise than through the mechanics of the consolidation plan. * * * The transaction between the two corporations was a merger or consolidation within the statute.

The orders of the Board of Tax Appeals are set aside.

Questions

What is the treatment of the transaction in *Miller* under the current statute? Does the holding in *Miller* have any continuing significance for the (B) reorganization? The (C)? The (A)? The forward subsidiary merger under § 368(a)(2)(D)? The reverse subsidiary merger under § 368(a)(2)(E)?

6. Receipt of Cash and Bonds in a (C) Before the Solely for Voting Stock Requirement

LE TULLE v. SCOFIELD

United States Supreme Court, 1940.
308 U.S. 415, 60 S.Ct. 313, 84 L.Ed. 355.

MR. JUSTICE ROBERTS delivered the opinion of the Court.

* * *

The Gulf Coast Irrigation Company was the owner of irrigation properties. Petitioner was its sole stockholder. He personally owned certain lands and other irrigation properties. November 4, 1931, the Irrigation Company, the Gulf Coast Water Company, and the petitioner, entered into an agreement which recited that the petitioner owned all of the stock of the Irrigation Company; described the company's properties, and stated that, prior to conveyance to be made pursuant to the contract, the Irrigation Company would be the owner of certain other lands and irrigation properties. These other lands and properties were those which the petitioner individually owned. The contract called for a conveyance of all the properties owned, and to be owned, by the Irrigation Company for $50,000 in cash and $750,000 in bonds of the Water Company, payable serially over the period January 1, 1933, to January 1, 1944. The petitioner joined in this agreement as a guarantor of the title of the Irrigation Company and for the purpose of covenanting that he would not personally enter into the irrigation business within a fixed area during a specified period after the execution of the contract. Three days later, at a special meeting of stockholders of the Irrigation Company, the proposed reorganization was approved, the minutes stating that the taxpayer, "desiring also to reorganize his interest in the properties," had consented to be a party to the reorganization. The capital stock of the Irrigation Company was increased and thereupon the taxpayer subscribed for the new stock and paid for it by conveyance of his individual properties.

The contract between the two corporations was carried out November 18, with the result that the Water Company became owner of all the properties then owned by the Irrigation Company including the property theretofore owned by the petitioner individually. Subsequently all of its assets, including the bonds received from the Water Company, were distributed to the petitioner. The company was then dissolved. The petitioner and his wife filed a tax return as members of a community in which they reported no gain as a result of the receipt of the liquidating dividend from the Irrigation Company. The latter reported no gain for the taxable year in virtue of its receipt of bonds and cash from the Water Company. The Commissioner of Internal Revenue assessed additional taxes against the community, as individual taxpayers, by reason of the receipt of the liquidating dividend, and against the petitioner as transferee of the Irrigation Company's assets in virtue of the gain realized by the company on the sale of its property. The tax was paid and claims for refund were filed. [Petitioner] alleged that the transaction constituted a tax-exempt reorganization as defined by the Revenue Act. * * *

The respondent's contention that the transaction amounted merely to a sale of assets by the petitioner and the Irrigation Company and did not fall within the statutory definition of a tax-free reorganization was overruled by the District Court and judgment was entered for the petitioner.

The respondent appealed. * * *

The Circuit Court of Appeals [reversed].

* * *

[W]e are of opinion that the transaction did not amount to a reorganization and that, therefore, the petitioner cannot complain, as the judgment must be affirmed on the ground that no tax-free reorganization was effected within the meaning of the statute.

Section 112(i) [now § 368(a)(1)] provides, so far as material: "(1) The term 'reorganization' means (A) a merger or consolidation (including the acquisition by one corporation of at least a majority of the voting stock and at least a majority of the total number of shares of all other classes of stock of another corporation, or substantially all the properties of another corporation) * * *.

As the court below properly stated, the section is not to be read literally, as denominating the transfer of all the assets of one company for what amounts to a cash consideration given by the other a reorganization. We have held that where the consideration consists of cash and short term notes the transfer does not amount to a reorganization within the true meaning of the statute, but is a sale upon which gain or loss must be reckoned. We have said that the statute was not satisfied unless the transferor retained a substantial stake in the enterprise and such a stake was thought to be retained where a large proportion of the consideration was in common stock of the transferee, or where the transferor took cash and the entire issue of preferred stock of the transferee corporation. And, where the consideration is represented by a substantial proportion of stock, and the balance in bonds, the total consideration received is exempt from tax under Sec. 112(b)(4) and 112(g).

In applying our decision in the *Pinellas* case, supra, the courts have generally held that receipt of long term bonds as distinguished from short term notes constitutes the retention of an interest in the purchasing corporation. There has naturally been some difficulty in classifying the securities involved in various cases.

We are of opinion that the term of the obligations is not material. Where the consideration is wholly in the transferee's bonds, or part cash and part such bonds, we think it cannot be said that the transferor retains any proprietary interest in the enterprise.

* * *

Questions

Who are the taxpayers here? What is the difference between the bonds in *Le Tulle* and the nonvoting preferred in *John A. Nelson?* In which of the following situations is the interest more definite and material: (1) target corporation sells its assets for $1 million of long-term bonds of the acquiring corporation, and (2) target sells its assets for $500K of cash and $500K of nonvoting preferred of the acquiring corporation? Does *Le Tulle* have any continuing vitality for the (C) reorganization? The (A) reorganization?

7. Bankrupt Corporation: Noteholders Exchange Notes for Stock

HELVERING v. ALABAMA ASPHALTIC LIMESTONE CO.

Supreme Court of the United States, 1942.
315 U.S. 179, 62 S.Ct. 540, 86 L.Ed. 775.

MR. JUSTICE DOUGLAS delivered the opinion of the Court.

Respondent in 1931 acquired all the assets of Alabama Rock Asphalt, Inc., pursuant to a reorganization plan consummated with the aid of the bankruptcy court. In computing its depreciation and depletion allowances for the year 1934, respondent treated its assets as having the same basis which they had in the hands of the old corporation. The Commissioner determined a deficiency, computed on the price paid at the bankruptcy sale. The Board of Tax Appeals rejected the position of the Commissioner. 41 B.T.A. 324. The Circuit Court of Appeals affirmed. 5 Cir., 119 F.2d 819. We granted the petition for certiorari.
* * *

The answer to the question turns on the meaning of that part of § 112(i)(1) of the Revenue Act of 1928 [now § 368(a)(1)], which provides: "The term 'reorganization' means (A) a merger or consolidation (including the acquisition by one corporation of * * * substantially all the properties of another corporation) * * *."

The essential facts can be stated briefly. The old corporation was a subsidiary of a corporation which was in receivership in 1929. Stockholders of the parent had financed the old corporation taking unsecured notes for their advances. Maturity of the notes was approaching and not all of the noteholders would agree to take stock for their claims. Accordingly a creditors' committee was formed late in 1929 and a plan of reorganization was proposed to which all the noteholders, except two, assented. The plan provided that a new corporation would be formed which would acquire all the assets of the old corporation. The stock of the new corporation, preferred and common, would be issued to the creditors in satisfaction of their claims. Pursuant to the plan involuntary bankruptcy proceedings were instituted in 1930. The appraised value of the bankrupt corporation's assets was about $155,000. Its obligations were about $838,000, the unsecured notes with accrued interest aggregating somewhat over $793,000. The bankruptcy trustee offered the assets for sale at public auction. They were bid in by the creditors' committee for $150,000. The price was paid by $15,000 in cash, by agreements of creditors to accept stock of a new corporation in full discharge of their claims, and by an offer of the committee to meet the various costs of administration, etc. Thereafter respondent was formed and acquired all the assets of the bankrupt corporation. It does not appear whether the acquisition was directly from the old corporation on assignment of the bid or from the committee. Pursuant to the plan respondent issued its stock to the creditors of the old corporation—over 95% to the noteholders and the balance to small creditors. Nonassenting creditors were paid in cash. Operations were not interrupted by the reorganization and were carried on subsequently by substantially the same persons as before.

* * * On the basis of the continuity of interest theory as explained in the *Le Tulle* case it is now earnestly contended that a substantial ownership interest in the transferee company must be retained by the holders of the ownership interest in the transferor. * * *

We conclude, however, that it is immaterial that the transfer shifted the ownership of the equity in the property from the stockholders to the creditors of the old corporation. Plainly the old continuity of interest was broken. Technically that did not occur in this proceeding until the judicial sale took place. For practical purposes, however, it took place not later than the time when the creditors took steps to enforce their demands against their insolvent debtor. In this case, that was the date of the institution of bankruptcy proceedings. From that time on they had effective command over the disposition of the property. * * *

That conclusion involves no conflict with the principle of the *Le Tulle* case. A bondholder interest in a solvent company plainly is not the equivalent of a proprietary interest, even though upon default the bondholders could retake the property transferred. The mere possibility of a proprietary interest is of course not its equivalent. But the determinative and controlling factors of the debtor's insolvency and an effective command by the creditors over the property were absent in the *Le Tulle* case.

Nor are there any other considerations which prevent this transaction from qualifying as a "reorganization" within the meaning of the Act. The *Pinellas* case makes plain that "merger" and "consolidation" as used in the Act includes transactions which "are beyond the ordinary and commonly accepted meaning of those words". 287 U.S. page 470, 53 S.Ct. page 260, 77 L.Ed. 428. Insolvency reorganizations are within the family of financial readjustments embraced in those terms as used in this particular statute.

Questions

What were the tax stakes in *Alabama Asphaltic?* What side of the reorganization transaction is *Alabama Asphaltic* concerned with? If a holder of short-term notes of a target corporation exchanges his notes for stock of an acquiring corporation in a transaction in which the acquiring corporation acquires the stock or assets of the target in a bona fide reorganization, will the exchanging noteholder receive nonrecognition treatment? Suppose the target is on the verge of bankruptcy?

8. Receipt of Bonds in an (A)

ROEBLING v. COMMISSIONER
United States Court of Appeals, Third Circuit, 1944.
143 F.2d 810.

KALODNER, DISTRICT JUDGE.

This appeal presents three questions: (1) Whether the transaction hereafter stated between a lessor corporation and a lessee corporation constituted a "statutory merger", within the meaning of Sec. 112(g)(1)(A) of the Revenue Act of 1938, [now § 368(a)(1)]; (2) whether the doctrine of "continuity of interest" as enunciated in *Le Tulle v. Scofield,* applies to a "statutory merger", and (3) whether under the facts a "continuity of interest" actually existed.

On May 10, 1937, the directors of South Jersey and of Public Service Electric and Gas Company adopted a "Plan of Reorganization" under which it was proposed that the former company be merged into the latter in accordance with the statutes of New Jersey. This plan provided that the stockholders of South Jersey (other than Public Service Electric and Gas Company) should exchange, dollar for dollar, their stock in South Jersey for 8% one hundred years first mortgage bonds of Public Service Electric and Gas Company. These bonds were to be issued under a prior mortgage of Public Service Electric and Gas Company dated August 1, 1924, and under a supplemental indenture later to be executed. It was expressly provided in the "Agreement of Merger" executed on the same day: "The capital stock of the Public Service Electric and Gas Company * * * will not be changed by reason of this agreement." Also, the stock of South Jersey held by Public Service Electric and Gas Company was not to participate in the exchange but was to be delivered up and cancelled.

* * *

The "Agreement of Merger" was consummated pursuant to its provisions. In accordance therewith the taxpayer received in exchange for his 166 shares of stock in South Jersey, $16,600, principal amount of 8% bonds which on November 25, 1938, had a fair market value of $34,777.

The Commissioner determined that the difference between the basis of the taxpayer's stock in South Jersey and the fair market value of the bonds received in exchange therefor must be recognized as taxable income in 1938 and he asserted a deficiency which the Tax Court sustained, so far as it was based upon this item.

The issues presented here arise by reason of taxpayer's contention (1) that the merger of South Jersey into Public Service Electric and Gas Co. was a "true statutory merger" under the laws of the state of New Jersey and therefore the exchange of stock for bonds was not a taxable event under Sec. 112 of the Revenue Act of 1938; [now § 368(a)(1)]; (2)

that since there was a "true statutory merger" the "continuity of interest" doctrine in the *Le Tulle v. Scofield* case is inapplicable and (3) that in any event a "continuity of interest" actually existed in the instant case.

As to the taxpayer's first two contentions, which may be considered together: The admitted fact that the merger of the two corporations was a "true statutory merger" under the New Jersey law is not dispositive of the question as to whether there was a "statutory merger" here within the meaning of Sec. 112(g)(1)(A) [now § 368(a)(1).] It is well-settled that a State law cannot alter the essential characteristics required to enable a taxpayer to obtain exemption under the provisions of a Federal Revenue Act.

* * * [W]e cannot subscribe to the taxpayer's contention that under Sec. 112(g)(1)(A) [now § 368(a)(1)] of the Revenue Act of 1938 the requirements of New Jersey law supersede the "continuity of interest" test as applied in *Le Tulle v. Scofield* and the numerous other decisions.

The taxpayer's remaining contention that the requisite "continuity of interest" is present under the peculiar facts in this case is premised on a rather novel theory. He urges that "prior to the merger, the stockholders of South Jersey had *no proprietary interest* in its properties in any real sense", and that in sanctioning the merger "the decision of the New Jersey courts recognized that the stock in the lessor companies was substantially equivalent to a perpetual 8% bond."

* * *

In view of the incontrovertible facts the taxpayer's argument that the stockholders in South Jersey had *no* proprietary interest is without basis.

Finally, it is equally clear that when the stockholders of South Jersey exchanged their stock in that corporation for the long-term bonds of Public Service Electric and Gas Company, they surrendered their proprietary interest and simply became creditors of Public Service. They no longer owned any of the former property of South Jersey and they had no proprietary interest in the property of Public Service.

* * *

For the reasons stated the decision of the Tax Court of the United States is affirmed.

Questions

Roebling specifically holds that the continuity of interest requirement enunciated in *Le Tulle v. Scofield* and its predecessors, which dealt principally with asset acquisitions, is applicable to mergers under the (A) reorganization. What is the practical effect of this holding? How would this transaction be treated under today's statute?

9. Determination of Whether Stock Represents a Substantial Part of Assets Transferred in an (A)

SOUTHWEST NATURAL GAS CO. v. COMMISSIONER

United States Court of Appeals, Fifth Circuit, 1951.
189 F.2d 332, *cert. denied* 342 U.S. 860, 72 S.Ct. 88, 96 L.Ed. 647 (1951).

RUSSELL, CIRCUIT JUDGE.

* * * [The question is] whether a merger of Peoples Gas & Fuel Corporation with the taxpayer, effected in accordance with the laws of Delaware, was a sale, as asserted by the Commissioner, or a "reorganization" within the terms of Section 112(g) of the Internal Revenue Code, [now § 368(a)(1)] as contended by the taxpayer * * *.

* * * [The Tax] Court held that literal compliance with the provisions of a state law authorizing a merger would not in itself effect a "reorganization" within the terms applicable under Internal Revenue Statutes; that the test of continuity of interest was nevertheless applicable; and that the transaction in question did not meet this test.

* * *

* * * [W]e think, that the accomplishment of a statutory merger does not *ipso facto* constitute a "reorganization" within the terms of the statute here involved. This has been expressly held by the Court of Appeals for the Third Circuit in a well considered opinion, supported by numerous authorities cited. *Roebling v. Commissioner*, 143 F.2d 810.

* * *

It is thus clear that the test of "continuity of interest" announced and applied by these cited authorities, supra, must be met before a statutory merger may properly be held a reorganization within the terms of Section 112(g)(1)(A) [now § 368(a)(1)(A).] Each case must in its final analysis be controlled by its own peculiar facts. While no precise formula has been expressed for determining whether there has been retention of the requisite interest, it seems clear that the requirement of continuity of interest consistent with the statutory intent is not fulfilled in the absence of a showing: (1) that the transferor corporation or its shareholders retained a substantial proprietary stake in the enterprise represented by a material interest in the affairs of the transferee corporation, and, (2) that such retained interest represents a substantial part of the value of the property transferred.

Among other facts, the Tax Court found that under the merger all of Peoples' assets were acquired by the petitioner in exchange for specified amounts of stock, bonds, cash and the assumption of debts. There was a total of 18,875 shares common stock of Peoples' entitled to participate under the agreement of merger. The stockholders were offered Option A and Option B. The holders of 7,690 of such shares exercised Option B of that agreement and received $30.00 in cash for each share, or a total of $230,700.00. In respect to the stock now involved, the stockholders who exercised Option A, the holders of 59.2 per cent of the common stock received in exchange 16.4 per cent of petitioner's outstanding common stock plus $340,350.00 principal amount of six per cent mortgage bonds (of the market value of 90 per cent of principal), which had been assumed by petitioner in a prior merger, and $17,779.59 cash. The 16.4 per cent of the common stock referred to was represented by 111,850 shares having a market value of $5,592.50, or five cents per share, and represented the continuing proprietary interest of the participating stockholders in the enterprise. This was less than one per cent of the consideration paid by the taxpayers.

We think it clear that these and other facts found by the Tax Court find substantial support in the evidence, and the conclusion of the Tax Court that they failed to evidence sufficient continuity of interest to bring the transaction within the requirements of the applicable statute is correct.

The decision of the Tax Court is

Affirmed.

[Dissenting opinion deleted.]

Questions

What was the mix of consideration paid by the acquiring corporation in *Southwest Natural Gas Co.?* How much stock of the acquiring corporation is needed to constitute a "substantial part of the value of the property transferred"?

10. Receipt of Pass Book Savings Accounts on Merger of Savings and Loan Association

PAULSEN v. COMMISSIONER

United States Supreme Court, 1985.
469 U.S. 131, 105 S.Ct. 627, 83 L.Ed.2d 540.

JUSTICE REHNQUIST delivered the opinion of the Court.

Commerce Savings and Loan Association of Tacoma, Wash., merged into Citizens Federal Savings and Loan Association of Seattle in July 1976. Petitioners Harold and Marie Paulsen sought to treat their exchange of stock in Commerce for [passbook savings accounts and time certificates of deposit] in Citizens as a tax-free reorganization under 26 U.S.C. §§ 354(a)(1) and 368(a)(1)(A). The Court of Appeals for the Ninth Circuit, disagreeing with the Court of Claims and other Courts of Appeals, reversed a decision of the Tax Court in favor of petitioners. We granted certiorari, to resolve these conflicting interpretations of an important provision of the Internal Revenue Code.

* * *

* * * These shares are the association's only means of raising capital. Here they are divided into passbook accounts and certificates of deposit. In reality, these shares are hybrid instruments having both equity and debt characteristics. They combine in one instrument the separate characteristics of the guaranty stock and the savings accounts of stock associations like Commerce.

The Citizens shares have several equity characteristics. The most important is the fact that they are the only ownership instrument of the association. Each share carries in addition to its deposit value a part ownership interest in the bricks and mortar, the goodwill, and all the other assets of Citizens. Another equity characteristic is the right to vote on matters for which the association's management must obtain shareholder approval. The shareholders also receive dividends rather than interest on their accounts; the dividends are paid out of net earnings, and the shareholders have no legal right to have a dividend declared or to have a fixed return on their investment. The shareholders further have a right to a pro rata distribution of any remaining assets after a solvent dissolution.

These equity characteristics, however, are not as substantial as they appear on the surface. * * *

* * *

In our view, the debt characteristics of Citizens' shares greatly outweigh the equity characteristics. The face value of petitioners' passbook accounts and certificates of deposit was $210,000. Petitioners have stipulated that they had a right to withdraw the face amount of the deposits in cash, on demand after one year or at stated intervals thereafter. Their investment was virtually risk free and the dividends received were equivalent to prevailing interest rates for savings accounts in other types of savings institutions. The debt value of the shares was the same as the face value, $210,000; because no one would pay more than this for the shares, the incremental value attributable to the equity features was, practically, zero. Accordingly, we hold that petitioners' passbook accounts and certificates of deposit were cash equivalents.

Petitioners have failed to satisfy the continuity-of-interest requirement to qualify for a tax-free reorganization. In exchange for their guaranty stock in Commerce, they received essentially cash with an insubstantial equity interest. Under *Minnesota Tea Co.*, their equity interest in Citizens would have to be "a substantial part of the value of the thing transferred." Assuming an arm's-length transaction in which what petitioners gave up and what they received were of equivalent worth, their Commerce stock was worth $210,000 in withdrawable deposits and an unquantifiably small incremental equity interest. This retained equity interest in the reorganized enterprise, therefore, is not a "substantial" part of the value of the Commerce stock which was given up. We agree with the Commissioner that the equity interests attached to the Citizens shares are too insubstantial to satisfy *Minnesota Tea Co.* The Citizens shares are not significantly different from the notes that this Court found to be the mere "equivalent of cash" in *Pinellas & Cold Storage Ice Co.* The ownership interest of the Citizens shareholders is closer to that of the secured bondholders in *Le Tulle v. Scofield*, than to that of the preferred stockholders in *John A. Nelson Co. v. Helvering.* The latter case involved a classic ownership instrument—preferred stock carrying voting rights only in the event of a dividend default—which we held to represent "a definite and substantial interest in the affairs of the purchasing corporation."

* * *

C. THE SERVICE'S RULING POLICY REQUIREMENT ON CONTINUITY OF INTEREST

REVENUE PROCEDURE 77-37
1977-2 C.B. 568. § 3.02.

.02 The "continuity of interest" requirement of section 1.368-1(b) of the Income Tax Regulations is satisfied if there is continuing interest through stock ownership in the acquiring or transferee corporation (or a corporation in "control" thereof within the meaning of section 368(c) of the Code) on the part of the former shareholders of the acquired or transferor corporation which is equal in value, as of the effective date of the reorganization, to at least 50 percent of the value of all of the formerly outstanding stock of the acquired or transferor corporation as of the same date. It is not necessary that each shareholder of the acquired or transferor corporation receive in the exchange stock of the acquiring or transferee corporation, or a corporation in "control" thereof, which is equal in value to at least 50 percent of the value of his former stock interest in the acquired or transferor corporation, so long as one or more of the shareholders of the acquired or transferor corporation have a continuing interest through stock ownership in the acquiring or transferee corporation (or a corporation in "control" thereof) which is, in the aggregate, equal in value to at least 50 percent of the value of all of the formerly outstanding stock of the acquired or transferor corporation. Sales, redemptions, and other dispositions of stock occurring prior or subsequent to the plan of reorganization will be considered in determining whether there is a 50 percent continuing interest through stock ownership as of the effective date of the reorganization.

Questions

1. What types of reorganizations are covered by the above rule? Does the 50% continuity rule affect the (A), the (B), the (C), the forward subsidiary merger under § 368(a)(2)(D), and the reverse subsidiary merger under § 368(a)(2)(E)? In 1934 Congress added the "solely for voting stock" requirement for the (B) and the (C), and when Congress adopted the reverse subsidiary merger under § 368(a)(2)(E) in 1970 it included an 80% voting stock requirement. Thus, the (B), the (C), and the (a)(2)(E) have their own

statutory continuity of interest rules. Is it sensible to have (1) a 50% continuity requirement for the (A) and the (a)(2)(D), (2) a solely for voting stock requirement for a (B), (3) a solely for voting stock requirement, subject to the 20% boot relaxation rule, for a (C), and (4) an 80% voting stock requirement for the (a)(2)(E)?

2. The 100 outstanding shares of target corporation (TC) are held one share each by 100 individuals. Acquiring corporation (AC) wants to acquire all of target's stock or assets and is indifferent between paying cash or issuing its common stock. TC's charter requires a vote of 85% of the outstanding shares for either a merger or sale of substantially all of its assets. 84% of TC's shareholders are willing to sell out to AC in either a stock for stock acquisition, a merger or a sale of substantially all of TC's properties, so long as they receive AC stock and have nonrecognition treatment. The remaining 16% of TC's shareholders are willing to sell but insist upon receiving cash. AC will not do the deal unless it receives 100% of TC's stock or assets. Can the transaction be structured as a tax-free exchange to the 84% shareholders and as a taxable transaction to the 16%?

3. Individual S is the sole shareholder of target corporation (TC). The shares of TC have a value of $1 million. S sells 60% of his TC stock to acquiring corporation (AC) for $600K. Shortly thereafter, TC merges into AC with S receiving $200K of AC common stock and $200K of cash. Does the transaction satisfy the continuity of interest requirement? Suppose instead that TC merged into AC with S receiving $1 million in common stock of AC. Shortly thereafter, AC redeemed $600K of S's stock. Does the merger satisfy the continuity of interest requirement? *See* Rev.Rul. 78–142 under E.3 below.

D. AN ILLUSTRATION OF THE 50% CONTINUITY REQUIREMENT

REVENUE RULING 66–224
1966–2 C.B. 114.

Corporation X was merged under state law into corporation Y. Corporation X had four stockholders (A, B, C, D), each of whom owned 25 percent of its stock. Corporation Y paid A and B each $50,000 in cash for their stock of corporation X, and C and D each received corporation Y stock with a value of $50,000 in exchange for their stock of corporation X. There are no other facts present that should be taken into account in determining whether the continuity of interest requirement of section 1.368–1(b) of the Income Tax Regulations has been satisfied, such as sales, redemptions or other dispositions of stock prior to or subsequent to the exchange which were part of the plan of reorganization.

Held, the continuity of interest requirement of section 1.368–1(b) of the regulations has been satisfied. It would also be satisfied if the facts were the same except corporation Y paid each stockholder $25,000 in cash and each stockholder received corporation Y stock with a value of $25,000.

E. PERIOD FOR WHICH CONTINUITY OF INTEREST MUST CONTINUE

1. *Court Order to Divest Within Seven Years*

REVENUE RULING 66–23
1966–1 C.B. 67.

Advice has been requested whether a statutory merger pursuant to applicable State law constitutes a reorganization as defined in section 368(a)(1)(A) of the Internal Revenue Code of 1954 when a shareholder (X) who owns 60 percent of the outstanding stock of the transferor corporation (Z) is subject to a court order to divest itself within 7 years of all of the stock of the transferee corporation received in the merger.

* * *

It is the position of the Internal Revenue Service that the continuity of interest requirements of a reorganization can be satisfied where the shareholder of the transferor corporation receives stock of the transferee corporation without any preconceived plan or arrangement for disposing of any of the stock and with unrestricted rights of ownership for a period of time sufficient to warrant the conclusion that such ownership is definite and substantial, notwithstanding that at the time of the reorganization the shareholder is required by a court decree to dispose of the stock before the end of such period. Ordinarily, the Service will treat 5 years of unrestricted rights of ownership as a sufficient period for the purpose of satisfying the continuity of interest requirements of a reorganization.

Further, if in fact X does sell some or all of the Z shares within 5 years of the date of the reorganization, the status of the reorganization will not be affected, since at the time of the reorganization X had no preconceived plan or arrangement for such sales.

Accordingly, since X has 7 years of complete discretion as to whether it will retain or dispose of the Z shares received in the reorganization, the shares received by X are held to represent a continuing interest in the enterprise.

Question

Is the Service's five-year holding period rule sound?

2. *Redeemable, Preferred Capital Certificates*

REVENUE RULING 68–22
1968–1 C.B. 142.

Y is a farmers' cooperative association which markets and processes agricultural products for its members. Its member-patrons possess membership certificates evidencing their proprietary interests in the association. Only such members are entitled to vote.

Y proposes to acquire all the assets of X corporation in a statutory merger. X is engaged in the business of buying, warehousing and selling agricultural products similar to those handled by Y.

In exchange for their common stock in X, the shareholders of X will receive five percent cumulative preferred capital certificates of interest in Y. The certificates are entitled to five percent cumulative dividends and are transferable on the books of Y when properly endorsed by the registered owners thereof. In the event of the liquidation of Y, the certificates are subordinate to the claims of noteholders and open account creditors but are preferred over any distribution to members in respect of membership certificates. The certificates received by the shareholders of X are redeemable solely in the discretion of Y's board of directors to the extent of ten percent of their face value annually beginning one year after issuance. Y has no present intention to redeem any of the certificates.

Under the facts the five percent cumulative preferred capital certificates of interest to be issued by Y represents an equity interest in the association.

Accordingly, the exchange of X's common stock for Y's certificates will qualify as an exchange of stock in a reorganization described in section 368(a)(1)(A) of the Code and no gain or loss will be recognized to the shareholders of X on the exchange as provided in section 354(a)(1) of the Code.

Questions

1. What result in the ruling if the association had been obligated to redeem 10% of the certificates each year beginning one year after issuance? *See* Rev.Proc. 77–37 under C. above and Rev.Rul. 66–23 under E.1. above. Assuming the transaction qualifies as a reorganization, what is the treatment to the holders upon redemption? *See* § 302.

2. What result if the consideration the association had paid was 50% in cash and 50% in certificates, and the association was obligated to redeem 20% of the certificates each year beginning six years after issuance? Suppose instead that the certificates had been redeemable 10% per year beginning one year after issuance?

3. Could the tax treatment in questions 1 and 2 be duplicated by structuring the transactions as a § 453 sale?

3. *Periodic Redemptions and Rescission Rights*

REVENUE RULING 78–142
1978–1 C.B. 111.

Advice has been requested as to the Federal income tax consequences of a statutory merger intended to qualify as a reorganization under section 368(a)(1)(A) of the Internal Revenue Code of 1954 by reason of section 368(a)(2)(D) under the circumstances described below.

§ 11.2   THE CONCEPT OF CONTINUITY   409

Corporation S, a wholly owned newly formed subsidiary of corporation P whose stock is widely held, acquired, pursuant to a statutory merger, the assets of corporation T, an unrelated corporation, in exchange for 50x shares of P preferred stock and the assumption by S of the liabilities of T.

The preferred stock of P issued in the statutory merger was callable after 5 years following the effective date of this merger and was subject to mandatory serial redemption requirements after 5 years following the effective date of the merger. Such redemptions of the shares of preferred stock would not be made at more than 110 percent of the issue price of the preferred stock which is defined as the fair market value of the T stock exchanged for the P preferred stock. The obligation to redeem the preferred stock could be satisfied only out of the surplus of P. Each share of the P preferred stock was entitled to 1 vote per share, as was P's common stock. The P preferred stock was convertible into P common stock. Dividends payable on the P preferred stock were cumulative. Dividends were payable solely from earnings and were dependent solely upon declaration in the discretion of the board of directors, subject to typical shareholder remedies in case of nonpayment.

The terms of the P preferred stock included the following covenants that remained in effect as long as not less than 10x shares of P preferred stock remained outstanding: performance by P of its obligations with respect to the mandatory serial redemption of the P preferred stock; maintenance by P of its shareholders equity by maintaining the consolidated net current assets in P and S at certain specified levels; [etc.].

The terms of the P preferred stock also provided that in the event of a default by P with respect to any of the above covenants, the holders of the preferred stock of P have the option, exercisable through the representative, to require P to redeem all of the preferred stock of P for a redemption price payable in (a) all of the outstanding stock of S plus (b) an amount of P common stock determined by a formula. The formula is in the nature of a penalty payable to the former T shareholders for the expense and inconvenience of the default and subsequent exercise of the option. The number of shares of P common stock to be issued under the formula is decreased as the shares of P preferred stock are converted or redeemed.

In order to facilitate the distribution of S's stock in the event of a default with respect to any covenant and a subsequent exercise of the option, all of S's stock was placed in escrow. The provisions of the escrow agreement provided that until S's stock became distributable to the former T shareholders because of a default by P with respect to any covenant, P was to receive all cash dividends paid on S's stock. Prior to the occurrence of a default, P had the right to vote S's stock on all matters other than amendments to the certificate of incorporation or the by-laws of S, or on a disposition of the assets or business of S. In the event of default, the escrow agent had the immediate right to vote S's stock, in accordance with the representative's instructions, on all matters including the right to remove the directors elected by P and to elect new directors of S. Until the occurrence of a default, P had the right to elect all directors of S (with the exception of the two designated by the representative) and P also had the right to designate the total number of directors to serve on S's board of directors.

A default on any covenant gave the former T shareholders the option to rescind the transaction, but this was not a commitment on their part to do so. The terms of the escrow agreement did not grant to the former T shareholders any rights with respect to S's stock beyond those necessary to preserve their rights under the option.

The specific issues in the instant case are whether the merger meets the continuity of interest requirement necessary for qualification as a reorganization under sections 368(a)(1)(A) and 368(a)(2)(D) of the Code, and whether the rescission provisions contained in the stock constitutes "other property" under section 356.

* * *

In the instant case, the rescission provision does not violate the continuity of interest requirement of section 1.368–1(b) of the regulations since the former T shareholders retained a continuity equity interest in the enterprise through the ownership of the P preferred stock. Rescission was contingent and beyond the control of the former T shareholders. Furthermore, the mandatory serial redemption feature does not violate the continuity of interest requirement because such redemptions cannot commence until after five years from the consummation of the reorganization. Rev.Rul. 66–23, 1966–1 C.B. 67.

The rescission provision contained in the terms of the preferred stock of P does not constitute "other property" within the meaning of section 356 because of the qualified and contingent nature of this provision and because this provision is inherent in the P preferred stock and is not personal to the former T shareholders. See Rev.Rul. 75–33, 1975–1 C.B. 115.

Accordingly, since the merger of T into S meets the requirements of sections 368(a)(1)(A) and 368(a)(2)(D) of the Code and since the continuity of interest requirement of section 1.368–1(b) of the regulations is met, the merger qualifies as a reorganization under these Code sections and under section 354(a)(1) no gain or loss is recognized to the former T shareholders upon the exchange of their T stock for P preferred stock.

Questions

What result in the ruling if the mandatory serial redemption was to begin a year after the reorganization and 10% of the preferred was to be redeemed each year? Would the result in the ruling change if 50% of the consideration paid had been cash and the rescission rights had related only to the preferred stock received?

4. Obligation of Target Shareholders to Sell Back to Acquiror

UNITED STATES v. ADKINS–PHELPS, INC.
United States Court of Appeals, Eighth Circuit, 1968.
400 F.2d 737.

Van Oosterhout, Chief Judge.

* * *

Adkins–Phelps, Incorporated, an Arkansas corporation, acquired the assets of J.F. Weinmann Milling Company (Weinmann), also an Arkansas corporation, through corporate reorganization procedures effected on November 11, 1959, which were admittedly in conformity with Arkansas law.

[Taxpayer, the Acquiring Corporation, contends that the transaction in question was a valid reorganization under § 368(a)(1)(A) and that, consequently, it was entitled to deduct the target corporation's unused net operating loss carryover (by virtue of the provision for perpetuation of the target corporation's tax attributes in § 381(c)). The trial court found that Mrs. Weinmann, who held 99% of the Weinmann stock and owned approximately one-sixth of the outstanding stock of Adkins–Phelps after the merger, "maintained a substantial equity interest in Adkins–Phelps."]

The Government does not seriously contend that a one-sixth stock interest would not be sufficient to establish continuity of interest. Principal reliance is placed upon a portion of the merger agreement reciting that the par value of Adkins–Phelps stock is $1.00 per share and the provision granting a stock option, which reads: "that for and as part of the consideration of the merger that the stockholders of the consolidated corporation, continuing under the name of Adkins–Phelps, Inc., bind themselves and agree that each stockholder will not transfer his, her or its capital stock in the Adkins–Phelps, Inc., corporation without first offering said stock to Adkins–Phelps, Inc., for par value."

The Government contends that by reason of the foregoing agreement all attributes of stock ownership are absent in the 997 shares of stock acquired by Mrs. Weinmann in the merger and that Mrs. Weinmann's stock interest would never be worth more than its $997 aggregate par value.

Such argument lacks validity for the reasons hereinafter set out:

1. Mrs. Weinmann, except for the sale restriction if valid, possessed all rights of a stockholder, including the right to vote the stock, the right to receive distribution of profits realized in the form of cash or stock dividends, preemptive rights to a proportionate share of any new stock issued, and a right to pledge the stock as security. Such rights are substantial attributes of stock ownership.

2. The agreement placed Mrs. Weinmann under no obligation to sell the stock to the other shareholders. She had a complete right to continue to hold the stock.

* * *

3. The purchase option agreement applied alike to all then existing stockholders.

* * *

[Affirmed.]

Questions

Of what relevance is it that Mrs. Weinmann received 16% of the stock of the acquiring corporation, Adkins–Phelps, Inc., in exchange for her stock of the target, J.F. Weinmann Milling Company? Would the result in the case change if she had received only 1% of the stock of Adkins–Phelps? Why would Mrs. Weinmann agree to the right of first refusal to be exercisable at par? Would the result change if she had been obligated to sell to Adkins–Phelps 20% of her stock in each of the first five years after the reorganization?

5. Planned Sales at the Time of the Transaction

a. Step Transaction Doctrine Applies: No Reorganization

McDONALD'S RESTAURANTS OF ILLINOIS v. COMMISSIONER

United States Court of Appeals, Seventh Circuit, 1982.
688 F.2d 520.

CUMMINGS, CHIEF JUDGE.

* * * [T]axpayers were 27 wholly-owned subsidiaries of McDonald's Corporation (McDonald's), the Delaware corporation that franchises and operates fast-food restaurants. * * *

On the opposite end of the transaction at issue here were Melvin Garb, Harold Stern and Lewis Imerman (known collectively as the Garb–Stern group). The group had begun with a single McDonald's franchise in Saginaw, Michigan, in the late 1950's and expanded its holdings to include McDonald's restaurants elsewhere in Michigan and in Oklahoma, Wisconsin, Nevada and California. After 1968 relations between the Garb–Stern group and McDonald's deteriorated. In 1971 McDonald's considered buying some of the group's restaurants in Oklahoma, but abandoned the idea when it became clear that the acquisition could not be treated as a "pooling of interests" for accounting purposes [2]

---

[2]. The Tax Court's opinion describes "pooling of interests" as follows:

The pooling of interests method accounts for a business combination as the uniting of the ownership interests of two or more companies by exchange of equity securities. No acquisition is recognized because the combination is accomplished without disbursing resources of the constituents. Ownership interests continue unless all of the Garb–Stern group's restaurants were acquired simultaneously. In November 1972, however, negotiations resumed, McDonald's having decided that total acquisition was necessary to eliminate the Garb–Stern group's friction.

The sticking point in the negotiations was that the Garb–Stern group wanted cash for its operations, while McDonald's wanted to acquire the Garb–Stern group's holdings for stock, consistent with its earlier expressed preference for treating the transaction as a "pooling of interests" for accounting purposes. McDonald's proposed a plan to satisfy both sides: it would acquire the Garb–Stern companies for McDonald's common stock, but it would include the common stock in a planned June 1973 registration so that the Garb–Stern group could sell it promptly.

Final agreement was not reached until March 1973. Negotiations then were hectic; for a variety of accounting and securities-law reasons, the acquisition had to be consummated not before and not after April 1, 1973. The final deal was substantially what had been proposed earlier. The Garb–Stern companies would be merged in stages into McDonald's, which would in turn transfer the restaurant assets to the 27 subsidiaries that are the taxpayers here. In return the Garb–Stern group would receive 361,235 shares of unregistered common stock. The agreement provided that the Garb–Stern group could participate in McDonald's planned June 1973 registration and underwriting or in any other registration and underwriting McDonald's might undertake within six years (Art. 7.4); the group also had a one-time right to demand registration in the event that McDonald's did not seek registration within the first year (Art. 7.5). The Garb–Stern group was not obligated by contract to sell its McDonald's stock but fully intended to do so.

After the April 1 closing, both parties proceeded on the assumption that the Garb–Stern group's shares would be included in the June 1973 "piggyback" registration. In mid-June a widely publicized negative report about McDonald's stock caused the price to drop from $60 to $52 a share in two weeks, and McDonald's therefore decided to postpone the registration and sale of additional stock. The Garb–Stern group acquiesced, although it had made no effort to withdraw from the registration before McDonald's decided to cancel it.

Through the rest of the summer, the price of McDonald's stock staged a recovery. In late August McDonald's decided to proceed with the registration, and the Garb–Stern group asked to have its shares included. The registration was announced on September 17 and completed on October 3, 1973. The Garb–Stern group thereupon sold

and the former bases of accounting are retained. The recorded assets and liabilities of the constituents are carried forward to the combined corporation at their recorded amounts. Income of the combined corporation includes income of the constituents for the entire fiscal period in which the combination occurs. The reported income of the constituents for prior periods is combined and restated as income of the combined corporation.

* * *

414 FUNDAMENTAL REORGANIZATION CONCEPTS Ch. 11

virtually all of the stock it had acquired in the transaction at a price of more than $71 per share.

In its financial statements McDonald's treated the transaction as a "pooling of interests". In its tax returns for 1973, however, it treated it as a purchase. Consistent with that characterization, McDonald's gave itself a stepped-up basis in the assets acquired from the Garb–Stern group to reflect their cost ($29,029,000, representing the value of the common stock transferred and a $1–2 million "nuisance premium" paid to eliminate the Garb–Stern group from the McDonald's organization). It allocated that basis among various Garb–Stern assets, then dropped the restaurant assets to the 27 taxpayer subsidiaries pursuant to Section 351 of the Internal Revenue Code governing transfers to corporations controlled by the transferor. The subsidiaries used the stepped-up basis allocable to them to compute depreciation and amortization deductions in their own 1973 tax returns.

It is those deductions by the subsidiary taxpayers that the Commissioner reduced. He ruled that the transfer of the Garb–Stern group's assets to McDonald's was not a taxable acquisition but a statutory merger or consolidation under Section 368(a)(1)(A) of the Code, and that under Section 362(b) McDonald's was required to assume the Garb–Stern group's basis in the assets acquired. In turn, the subsidiaries were required to compute depreciation and amortization deductions on this lower, carryover basis. With properly computed deductions, the subsidiary taxpayers owed an additional $566,403 in 1973 income taxes. The Tax Court upheld the Commissioner's deficiency assessments, and this appeal is the result.

* * *

The taxpayers, the Commissioner, and the Tax Court all agree that the Garb–Stern group holdings were acquired by statutory merger. They also all agree that the "continuity of interest" test is determinative of the tax treatment of the transaction of which the statutory merger was a part. But the taxpayers on the one hand, and the Commissioner and the Tax Court on the other, part company over how the test is to be applied, and what result it should have produced. In affirming the Commissioner, the Tax Court recognized that the Garb–Stern group had a settled and firm determination to sell their McDonald's shares at the first possible opportunity rather than continue as investors. It nonetheless concluded that because the Garb–Stern group was not contractually bound to sell, the merger and the sale could be treated as entirely separate transactions and the continuity-of-interest test applied in the narrow time-frame of the April transaction only. Thus tested, the transaction was in Judge Hall's view a nontaxable reorganization, and the taxpayer subsidiaries were therefore saddled with the Garb–Stern group's basis in taking depreciation and amortization deductions. The taxpayers by contrast argue that the step-transaction doctrine should have been applied to treat the April merger and stock transfer and the October sale as one taxable transaction. They also argue that the Tax

Court's extremely narrow view of both the step-transaction doctrine and the continuity-of-interest test in this case is not consonant with appellate court case law, the Tax Court's own precedents, or the Service's practices hitherto. We agree with the taxpayers.

THE STEP-TRANSACTION DOCTRINE

The step-transaction doctrine is a particular manifestation of the more general tax law principle that purely formal distinctions cannot obscure the substance of a transaction. * * *

* * *

Nonetheless, under any of the tests devised—including the intermediate one nominally adopted by the Tax Court and the most restrictive one actually applied in its decision—the transactions here would be stepped together. For example, under the "end result test," "purportedly separate transactions will be amalgamated with a single transaction when it appears that they were really component parts of a single transaction intended from the outset to be taken for the purpose of reaching the ultimate result." Here there can be little doubt that all the steps were taken to cash out the Garb–Stern group, although McDonald's sought to do so in a way that would enable it to use certain accounting procedures. Admittedly, not every transaction would be as pellucid as this one, but here the history of the parties' relationships, the abortive attempt to buy some of the group's holdings, the final comprehensive deal, and the Garb–Stern group's determination to sell out even in the face of falling prices in the stock all are consistent and probative.

A second test is the "interdependence" test, which focuses on whether "the steps are so interdependent that the legal relations created by one transaction would have been fruitless without a completion of the series." This is the test the Tax Court purported to apply, although its version of the test is indistinguishable from yet another formulation, the "binding commitment" test. That is, the Tax Court would have found interdependence only if the Garb–Stern group had itself been legally bound to sell its stock. In fact, the "interdependence" test is more practical and less legalistic than that. It concentrates on the relationship between the steps, rather than on the "end result". Here it would ask whether the merger would have taken place without the guarantees of saleability, and the answer is certainly no. The Garb–Stern group's insistence on this point is demonstrated both by its historic stance in these negotiations and by the hammered-out terms of the agreement. Although the Tax Court emphasized the permissive terms about "piggyback" registration, it glossed over the Garb–Stern group's one-time right to force registration—and hence sale—under the agreement. The very detail of the provisions about how McDonald's would ensure free transferability of the Garb–Stern group's McDonald's stock shows that they were the *quid pro quo* of the merger agreement.

Finally the "binding commitment" test most restricts the application of the step-transaction doctrine, and is the test the Tax Court actually applied, despite its statements otherwise. The "binding commitment" test forbids use of the step-transaction doctrine unless "if one transaction is to be characterized as a 'first step' there [is] a binding commitment to take the later steps." The Tax Court found the test unsatisfied because the Garb–Stern group was not legally obliged to sell its McDonald's stock. We think it misconceived the purpose of the test and misapplied it to the facts of this case.

In the first place, the "binding commitment" test is the most rigorous limitation on the step-transaction doctrine because it was formulated to deal with the characterization of a transaction that in fact spanned several tax years and could have remained "not only indeterminable but unfixed for an indefinite and unlimited period in the future, awaiting events that might or might not happen." By contrast this transaction was complete in six months and fell entirely within a single tax year. * * *

* * *

Under any of the three applicable criteria, then, the merger and subsequent sale should have been stepped together. Substance over form is the key. Had the Tax Court taken a pragmatic view of the actions of the Garb–Stern group, it would have found that they clearly failed to satisfy the continuity-of-interest requirement that has been engrafted onto the Code provisions governing nonrecognition treatment for acquisitive reorganizations.

Statutory Merger Precedents

Quite apart from the proper application of the step-transaction doctrine, the available precedents dealing with statutory mergers and the effect of post-merger sales by acquired shareholders—though scanty—strongly support the taxpayers. No case supports the myopic position adopted below that although "the crux of the continuity-of-interest test lies in the *continuation* of the acquired shareholders' proprietary interest" (76 T.C. at 997), the test "by itself does not require *any length* of postmerger retention," (*id.*) (emphasis supplied).

* * *

Additional Considerations

Part of the reason that there is so little litigation about statutory mergers and the effect of post-merger events on tax treatment is that people involved in nontaxable reorganizations usually seek advice in the form of private letter rulings beforehand.

The Commissioner's usual position in this context is not the one adopted by the Tax Court, namely, that the intent of the acquired shareholders is irrelevant and no period of post-merger retention is required. 76 T.C. at 990, 992, 997. See, for example, Rev.Proc. 77–37, [Sec. 11.2.C.]

Moreover, the Commissioner usually does not limit his scrutiny to explicit, contemporaneous commitments to sell out. In fact, taxpayers who seek a ruling in advance of a reorganization must represent that there is "no plan or intention on the part of the Acquired shareholders to [reduce their new holdings] to a number of shares having, in the aggregate, a value of less than 50 percent of the total value of the Acquired stock outstanding immediately prior to the proposed transaction."

Against this background, the Commissioner's treatment of the McDonald's transaction—as affirmed by the Tax Court—seems opportunistic. The agency's practice, described above, suggests that if McDonald's had laid its plan before the Internal Revenue Service ahead of time, it would not have been deemed a nontaxable reorganization. * * *

* * *

The decisions appealed from are reversed, with instructions to enter fresh decisions in the taxpayers' favor.

b. *Step Transaction Doctrine Not Applicable: Reorganization*

PENROD v. COMMISSIONER

Tax Court of the United States, 1987.
88 T.C. 1415.

Opinion

The first issue for decision in this case is whether the exchange of stock owned by the petitioners for stock in McDonald's qualifies as a reorganization under section 368. The parties agree that the transaction constituted a statutory merger that was in form eligible for reorganization treatment under section 368(a)(1)(A). However, the Commissioner determined that such exchange of stock did not qualify as a reorganization because the petitioners failed to maintain a sufficient equity interest in McDonald's after the exchange. [The petitioners sold their stock pursuant to a post reorganization public offering.]

It is well settled that, in addition to meeting specific statutory requirements, a reorganization under section 368(a)(1)(A) must also satisfy the continuity of interest doctrine. * * *

The entire consideration received by the Penrods pursuant to the May 15, 1975, merger consisted of McDonald's common stock. Thus, the parties agree that, in form, the nature and amount of such consideration satisfied the continuity of interest test. However, they do not agree on the effect of the Penrods' subsequent actions.

The Commissioner argues that the acquisition and the subsequent sale of McDonald's stock by the Penrods was part of an overall plan to "cash out" their investment in the acquired corporations and that, therefore, the two events should be considered to be, in substance, one transaction. The consequence of his position would be to treat the petitioners as having received all cash on the date of the acquisition, and therefore, the acquisition would fail the continuity of interest test. On the other hand, the petitioners argue that their decision to sell their McDonald's stock was based only upon events which occurred after the acquisition and that the acquisition and subsequent sale should therefore be treated as separate transactions.

The resolution of this issue turns on the application of the so-called step transaction doctrine. * * * [The court discussed the three-step transaction tests: (1) binding commitment, (2) end result, and (3) interdependence. Also, the court discussed the *McDonald's* case, *supra*.]

In the present case, there was no binding commitment by the Penrods at the time of the acquisition to sell their stock. However, we need not decide whether the absence of a binding commitment, standing alone, is sufficient to prevent the application of the step transaction doctrine; after carefully examining and evaluating all the circumstances surrounding the acquisition and subsequent sale of the McDonald's stock received by the Penrods, we have concluded that, at the time of the acquisition, the Penrods did not intend to sell their McDonald's stock and that therefore the step transaction doctrine is not applicable under either the interdependence test or the end result test.

* * *

In August 1975, the Penrods could have demanded registration of their McDonald's stock, but they did not. * * *

We do not know why the Penrods did not demand registration of their McDonald's stock at the earliest opportunity; we do know that the value of the stock was depressed in August 1975 (approximately $44 a share) and that the value had risen to $58 a share on November 11, 1975. On that day, the Penrods took the first public action to sell their McDonald's stock. At the outset, they planned to sell 60,000 shares, but by December 1975, they increased the number to 96,554. In December, the value of the stock had dropped slightly, but the general trend was upward. They received $60 a share for the stock when it was sold in January 1976. It may be that by the fall of 1975, Jack decided to sell his McDonald's stock in part because he wanted the funds to open the Wuv's restaurants and in part because the market for the stock was favorable. Yet, a review of the record of events that occurred in 1975 supports Jack's testimony that he did not intend to sell his McDonald's stock when he acquired it and that he expected to be able to continue to hold that stock and to operate the Wuv's restaurants simultaneously.

* * *

For these reasons, we have concluded that Jack and the other Penrods intended to continue to hold the McDonald's stock acquired by them in the acquisition. Accordingly, in our judgment, the acquisition of the stock and its subsequent sale were not interdependent steps, nor were they steps in a plan the end result of which was to cash out their interests in the restaurants. Under such circumstances, we hold that such transactions should not be stepped together, that the Penrods' ownership of the McDonald's stock satisfied the continuity of interest requirement, and that the acquisition of such stock constituted a reorganization within the meaning of section 368(a)(1)(A). Thus, we hold here (as did this Court in *McDonald's,* but on a different factual record) that there was a continuity of interest. In addition, since we have found as a fact that the acquired shareholders intended to continue to hold the stock acquired by them, and since the record fully supports that factual conclusion, we believe that our opinion here is factually distinguishable from that of the Seventh Circuit in the *McDonald's* case.

* * *

c. *Illustration of Differences Between McDonald's and Penrod*

ESTATE OF ELIZABETH CHRISTIAN v. COMMISSIONER

Tax Court of the United States, 1989.
57 T.C.M. 1231.

OPINION

The issue for decision in this case is whether the exchange of stock owned by petitioners for stock in McDonald's qualifies as a reorganization under section 368. We observe that the transaction constituted a statutory merger that was in form eligible for reorganization treatment under section 368(a)(1)(A). However, respondent determined that such exchange of stock did not qualify as a reorganization because petitioners failed to maintain a sufficient equity interest in McDonald's after the exchange. [The petitioners sold their shares pursuant to a registered offering.]

The entire consideration received by petitioners pursuant to the February 28, 1973, merger consisted of McDonald's common stock. Thus, in form, the nature and amount of such consideration satisfied the continuity of interest test. However, the parties to this litigation do not agree on the effect of petitioners' subsequent actions.

Respondent argues that the acquisition and the subsequent sale of McDonald's stock by petitioners was part of an overall plan to "cash out" their investment and, therefore, that the two events should be considered to be in substance one transaction. The consequence of his position would be to treat petitioners as having received all cash on the date of the acquisition, and, therefore, the acquisition would fail the continuity of interest test. On the other hand, petitioners argue that their decision to sell all their McDonald's stock was based only upon events which occurred after the acquisition and that the acquisition and subsequent sale should therefore be treated as separate transactions.

The resolution of this issue turns on the application of the step transaction doctrine. * * *

* * *

Following the lead of the Seventh Circuit, the circuit to which this case is appealable, in its decision in *McDonald's Restaurants of Illinois,* we likewise consider the merger and subsequent stock sale before us in light of the three alternative tests of the step-transaction doctrine. Prior to doing so, we initially address whether, at the time of the merger, petitioners intended to sell the McDonald's stock they were to receive. In ascertaining this intent, we must necessarily rely rather heavily on objective facts under the theory that one's actions generally reflect one's intentions. * * *

In our view, the weight of the evidence indicates that, from the outset and at the time of the acquisition, petitioners did not intend to sell enough shares of their McDonald's stock to destroy their continued interest or proprietary stake in the ongoing enterprise. We reach this conclusion based on the cumulative effect of the following facts: First, through the course of the negotiations leading to the execution of the merger's documents, McDonald's never offered nor did the Fein–Christian Companies request that the consideration for the merger include cash.

Second, the relationship between McDonald's and the principals of the Fein–Christian Companies was at all times positive. * * *

Third, as noted by Baer [the petitioner's attorney] in contemporaneous notes prepared in February of 1973, the month of the Fein–Christian Companies' merger into McDonald's his clients gave no consideration to the possibility of selling their soon-to-be-acquired McDonald's shares.

Fourth, the exigencies of timing in the instant merger were dictated by McDonald's wants. * * *

Fifth, though in the course of negotiating the final deal Baer suggested changes in the Agreement and Plan of Merger, we find that his actions as petitioners' attorney do not support the inference that petitioners had a preconceived intention or commitment to sell the McDonald's stock they were to receive. In asking for demand registration rights, Baer was acting on his own initiative, hoping to secure for petitioners a benefit, which his experience in handling the sale of privately held companies to larger, publicly traded concerns had taught him was a necessity. Moreover, Baer's insistence that the merger hinge on an approved listing of the shares on the NYSE represents nothing more than a tough bargaining position from which a future compromise, in the form of indemnification rights running to petitioners, was forthcoming. * * *

Sixth, the evidence in this record is noticeably void of the changes in structure and contract language which led to our finding in McDonald's of Zion that the Garb–Stern group "intended from the outset to sell their McDonald's stock at the earliest possible moment." * * *

* * *

In our judgment the acquisition of the stock and subsequent sale were not steps in a plan the end result of which was to cash out petitioners' interests, were not interdependent steps, and were not linked by a binding commitment. Under these circumstances, we hold that the instant merger and stock sale should not be stepped together, that petitioners' ownership of the McDonald's stock satisfied the continuity of interest requirement, and that the acquisition of stock constituted a reorganization within the meaning of section 368(a)(1)(A). We have found as fact that, at the time of the instant merger, the acquired shareholders did not intend to sell the stock acquired by them. We respectfully submit that the instant case is factually distinguishable from the case considered by the Seventh Circuit in *McDonald's Restaurants of Illinois*.

* * *

F. IMPACT OF PRIOR PURCHASE TO TARGET STOCK

1. Acquiror Purchases 85% of Target's Stock After Which Target's Assets Acquired by Acquiror's Subsidiary in Exchange for Subsidiary's Stock and Cash

YOC HEATING CORP. v. COMMISSIONER

Tax Court of the United States, 1973.
61 T.C. 168.

[On September 14, 1961, Reliance purchased approximately 85% of the stock of Old Nassau. Reliance later purchased a small number of the shares of Old Nassau. Reliance formed a subsidiary, New Nassau, and New Nassau offered to purchase the assets of Old Nassau under terms pursuant to which the shareholders of Old Nassau (including Reliance) would receive either cash or stock of New Nassau. All of the minority shareholders of Old Nassau elected to receive cash and Reliance elected to receive stock of New Nassau. The purchase of assets of Old Nassau was completed on July 3, 1962, nine months after the first purchase by Reliance of Old Nassau's shares. Old Nassau was later liquidated. New Nassau incurred an operating loss during its first six months of operation.]

* * *

Reliance's purpose in purchasing the stock of Old Nassau was to acquire the underlying assets of that corporation through the vehicle of New Nassau. The organization of New Nassau, the transfer of all the assets of Old Nassau to New Nassau, and the accompanying transfer to Reliance of the stock of New Nassau in exchange for the stock of Old Nassau and the payments by New Nassau to minority shareholders of Old Nassau were each steps in a single plan to accomplish that purpose.

The resolution of the issues presented in this case will depend upon the proper characterization of the following transactions:

(1) The purchase by Reliance from unrelated sellers of more than 85 percent of the common stock of Old Nassau.

(2) The organization of New Nassau.

(3) The transfer to New Nassau by Old Nassau of all its assets and the assumption by New Nassau of all of Old Nassau's liabilities against the issuance of common stock of New Nassau or the payment of cash to the shareholders of Old Nassau.

The first question raised by this series of transactions is the basis to New Nassau of the assets it acquired from Old Nassau. Respondent contends that the transaction whereby New Nassau acquired all the assets of Old Nassau constituted a reorganization within the meaning of section 368(a)(1)(F) or, alternatively, section 368(a)(1)(D). The acquired assets would then retain the same basis in the hands of New Nassau as they had in the hands of Old Nassau. Sec. 362(b). Petitioner (New Nassau) claims a higher basis in those assets equal to the cost of the Old Nassau stock purchased during the series of transactions summarized above, either under section 334(b)(2), the *Kimbell–Diamond* doctrine, or the broader principle sometimes referred to as the "integrated transaction" doctrine.

* * *

For the purpose of determining petitioner's basis in the assets acquired from Old Nassau, it is immaterial whether the transaction herein qualifies as a reorganization under clause (D) or clause (F) of section 368(a)(1). * * *

In view of the foregoing, we hold that a comparison of the stock ownership of Old Nassau immediately prior to the inception of the series of transactions involved herein with the situation which obtained immediately after the transfer by Old Nassau of its assets and liabilities to New Nassau clearly reveals that the control requirements of a (D) reorganization were not satisfied.

By a parity of reasoning rooted in the judicial "continuity of interest" principle applicable to reorganizations rather than in the specific statutory definition of "control" contained in section 368(c), there was likewise no (F) reorganization. *Helvering v. Southwest Corp.*, 315 U.S. 194 (1942); *Hyman H. Berghash*, 43 T.C. 743 (1965), affd. 361 F.2d 257 (C.A. 2, 1966). Compare *May B. Kass*, 60 T.C. 218 (1973), on appeal (C.A. 3, July 16, 1973). Compare also *Casco Products Corp.*, 49 T.C. 32 (1967), where the intention was from the outset to acquire stock and not assets.

Since there was no (D) or (F) reorganization, there can be no carryover of Old Nassau's basis under section 362(b). Likewise, in the absence of an (F) reorganization, the carryback of petitioner's net operating loss to the prior taxable years of Old Nassau is not permitted. Sec. 381(b)(3).

Having concluded that the assets and liabilities of Old Nassau were acquired by New Nassau other than by way of a reorganization or a liquidation of Old Nassau, it remains for us to determine how that acquisition should be characterized. Under all the circumstances, we conclude that such acquisition was by way of purchase with an accompanying step up in basis to petitioner and we so hold. We posit our holding on the "integrated transaction" doctrine in terms of the application of that principle generally and not in terms of the narrower *Kimbell–Diamond* doctrine. * * *

2. *Shareholder of Acquiror Purchases Target's Stock Followed by Merger of Target Into Acquiror*

SUPERIOR COACH OF FLORIDA, INC. v. COMMISSIONER

Tax Court of the United States, 1983.
80 T.C. 895.

[The Zaffrans owned the stock of the acquiror, SCF. The Zaffrans purchased all the stock of the target, Byerly, and the next day merged Byerly into SCF in a transition in which the Zaffrans received additional Byerly stock.]

The first issue for decision is whether SCF is entitled to carry over the Byerly net operating loss to its 1974 taxable year. The resolution of such issue requires us to consider certain provisions of sections 381 and [former] 382. [Read § 381(a).]

Section 381(c) provides that a net operating loss carryover is one of the items referred to in section 381(a). However, [former] section 382(b) [limits the deduction of net operating loss carryovers in reorganization].

The Commissioner takes the position that SCF is not entitled to carry over the Byerly net operating loss because the merger of Byerly into SCF did not qualify as a reorganization within the meaning of section 368(a)(1)(A). He contends that for the merger to qualify as such a reorganization, the continuity-of-interest requirement must be satisfied, that in applying such requirement, the step-transaction doctrine must be considered, that we must apply the continuity-of-interest requirement by looking to whether there was a continuity of interest of the historic shareholders of Byerly, and that when so applied, the continuity-of-interest requirement was not satisfied. Thus, he maintains that we need not reach the question of the applicability of section 382(b) since the merger did not meet the requirements of section 368(a)(1)(A). On the other hand, SCF argues that since the Zaffrans owned all the stock of Byerly before the merger and virtually all the stock of SCF after the merger, the continuity-of-interest requirement was satisfied. * * *

It is well settled that for a corporate reorganization to qualify as nontaxable, there must be a continuity of proprietary interest. * * *

* * *

The requirement that the "historic" owners retain a continuing interest in the reorganized corporation was born of a judicial effort to confine the tax-free reorganization provisions to their proper function. * * *

* * * The step-transaction doctrine is a particular manifestation of the more general tax law principle that purely formal distinctions cannot obscure the substance of a transaction. * * * Where a step transaction is involved in a reorganization, it is necessary to look at the makeup or identity of the stockholders *before* the initial step in the series of steps and those after the final step to ascertain whether the requisite continuity of interest has been maintained by the historic shareholders.

It is clear that the merger of Byerly and SCF was effected by the Zaffrans as part of an overall plan to acquire the business of Byerly. Prior to effecting such merger, Mr. Zaffran learned of Byerly's weak financial position. He discussed with Mr. Byerly the possibility of "merging" their operations and thereafter secured the approval of Superior. In addition, Mr. Zaffran reviewed the contents of Byerly's interim financial statements and consulted with his attorney before proceeding with the plan to acquire the Byerly stock. On the day after such stock was acquired, the Zaffrans merged Byerly into SCF. A review of such record shows beyond a doubt that the ultimate objective of Mr. Zaffran was to acquire the assets of Byerly and that the purchase of the Byerly stock and its subsequent liquidation were merely steps in the accomplishment of that objective. "A given result at the end of a straight path is not made a different result because reached by following a devious path." *Minnesota Tea Co. v. Helvering,* 302 U.S. 609, 613 (1938).

The facts of the present case are very similar to those of *Estate of McWhorter v. Commissioner,* 69 T.C. 650 (1978), affd. in an unpublished opinion 590 F.2d 340 (8th Cir.1978). In *McWhorter,* a corporation (Ozark) entered into an agreement with the shareholders of a second corporation (Benton) to purchase all of Benton's stock. Benton had a large net operating loss. Pursuant to the purchase agreement, Ozark became the sole shareholder in Benton. Eighteen days later, Ozark and Benton adopted a plan of merger, and after the merger was effected, Ozark was the surviving corporation. [The Court disallowed] Ozark's use of Benton's net operating loss * * *.

* * *

In *McWhorter,* the corporation acquired the stock and liquidated the acquired corporation, whereas in the present case, it was the Zaffrans, the shareholders of the acquiring corporation, who acquired the stock and liquidated the acquired corporation; but in both cases, the acquisition of the stock and the liquidation were merely steps in the acquisition of the assets of the acquired corporation. Thus, the Byerly shares could hardly be considered "old and cold" in the hands of the Zaffrans for purposes of characterizing them as the historic shareholders. *Estate of McWhorter v. Commissioner,* 69 T.C. at 664; *Yoc Heating Corp.* [*see* Sec. 11.2.F.2.] In our view, the Zaffrans' acquisition of the Byerly shares was inextricably interwoven with their intent to effect a merger of Byerly and SCF, and since the historic shareholders of Byerly retained no proprietary interest in SCF, the requisite test of continuity was not

§ 11.2   THE CONCEPT OF CONTINUITY   425

satisfied. Accordingly, we conclude that the merger did not qualify as a reorganization under section 368(a)(1)(A), and since the carryover of tax attributes under section 381(a)(2) is conditioned on the existence of a reorganization qualifying under section 368(a)(1), we hold that SCF has not satisfied the requirement of section 381(a)(2).

* * *

G. REMOTE CONTINUITY

1. *Party to the Reorganization; Remote Continuity; The Groman and Bashford Doctrines*

One of the conditions for nonrecognition treatment for the exchanging shareholder or security holder under § 354(a) and for the target corporation under § 361(a) is that each corporation involved in the transaction be a "party to the reorganization," as defined in § 368(b).

In *Groman v. Commissioner,* 302 U.S. 82, 58 S.Ct. 108, 82 L.Ed. 63 (1937), Sec. G.2. *supra,* and *Helvering v. Bashford,* 302 U.S. 454, 58 S.Ct. 307, 82 L.Ed. 367 (1938), Sec. 11.2.G.3. *supra,* the Supreme Court held that in a transaction in which a subsidiary used its parent's stock in the acquisition of a target corporation, the parent's stock did not count for continuity of interest purposes because the parent was not a "party to the reorganization." The *Groman* and *Bashford* doctrines have been overruled for certain triangular reorganizations by amendments to the definition of "party to the reorganization" in § 368(b). The amendments include, for instance, the parent in a triangular (C) as a party to the reorganization. These amendments are explored in connection with the examination of acquisitive reorganizations in Chapter 15. The **Groman** and **Bashford** doctrines are of continuing validity where not overridden by statute.

2. *The Early Anti–Triangular Reorganization Cases*

a. *Acquisition of Stock of Target in Exchange for (1) Stock of Acquiring Parent, (2) Stock of Acquiring Sub, and (3) Cash*

GROMAN v. COMMISSIONER
Supreme Court of the United States, 1937.
302 U.S. 82, 58 S.Ct. 108, 82 L.Ed. 63.

MR. JUSTICE ROBERTS delivered the opinion of the Court.

Glidden [the acquiring parent] organized Ohio [the acquiring sub] and became the owner of all its common stock but none of its preferred stock.

[T]he shareholders of Indiana [the target corporation] transferred their stock to Ohio and received therefor a total consideration of $1,207,016 consisting of Glidden prior preference stock valued at $533,980, shares of the preferred stock of Ohio valued at $500,000, and $153,036 in cash. Indiana then transferred its assets to Ohio and was dissolved.

As a result of the reorganization petitioner received shares of Glidden stock, shares of Ohio stock, and $17,293 in cash. In his return for 1929 he included the $17,293 as income received but ignored the shares of Glidden and of Ohio as stock received in exchange in a reorganization. The respondent ruled that Glidden was not a party to a reorganization within the meaning of the Revenue Act, treated the transaction as a taxable exchange to the extent of the cash and shares of Glidden, and determined a deficiency of $7,420. * * *

* * *

The question is whether that portion of the consideration consisting of prior preference shares of Glidden should be recognized in determining petitioner's taxable gain. The decision of this question depends upon whether Glidden's stock was that of a party to the reorganization for, if so, the statute declares gain or loss due to its receipt shall not be included in the taxpayer's computation of income for the year in which the exchange was made.

If section 112(i)(2) [now § 368(b)] is a definition of a party to a reorganization and excludes corporations not therein described, Glidden was not a party since its relation to the transaction is not within the terms of the definition. It was not a corporation resulting from the reorganization; and it did not acquire a majority of the shares of voting stock and a majority of the shares of all other classes of stock of any other corporation in the reorganization. The Circuit Court of Appeals thought the section was intended as a definition of the term party as used in the act and excluded all corporations not specifically described. It therefore held Glidden could not be considered a party to the reorganization.

* * *

It is argued, however, that Ohio was the alter ego of Glidden; that in truth Glidden was the principal and Ohio its agent; that we should look at the realities of the situation, disregard the corporate entity of Ohio, and treat it as Glidden. But to do so would be to ignore the purpose of the reorganization sections of the statute, which, as we have said, is that where, pursuant to a plan, the interest of the stockholders of a corporation continues to be definitely represented in substantial measure in a new or different one, then to the extent, but only to the extent, of that continuity of interest, the exchange is to be treated as one not giving rise to present gain or loss. If cash or "other property," that is, property other than stock or securities of the reorganized corporations, is received, present gain or loss must be recognized. Was not Glidden's prior preference stock "other property" in the sense that its ownership represented a participation in assets in which Ohio, and its shareholders through it, had no proprietorship? Was it not "other property" in the sense that qua that stock the shareholders of Indiana assumed a relation toward the conveyed assets not measured by a continued substantial interest in those assets in the ownership of Ohio, but an interest in the assets of Glidden a part of which was the common stock of Ohio? These questions we think must be answered in the affirmative. To reject the plain meaning of the term "party," and to attribute that relation to Glidden, would be not only to disregard the letter but also to violate the spirit of the Revenue Act.

We hold that Glidden was not a party to the reorganization and the receipt of its stock by Indiana's shareholders in exchange, in part, for their stock was the basis for computation of taxable gain to them in the year 1929.

The judgment is affirmed.

Mr. Justice Black took no part in the consideration or decision of this case.

b. *Acquisition of Three Targets by Consolidation with Target's Shareholders Receiving (1) Stock of Acquiring Parent, (2) Stock of Acquiring Sub, and (3) Cash*

HELVERING v. BASHFORD

Supreme Court of the United States, 1938.
302 U.S. 454, 58 S.Ct. 307, 82 L.Ed. 367.

Mr. Justice Brandeis delivered the opinion of the Court.

Atlas Powder Company [the acquiring parent] desired to eliminate the competition of three concerns—Peerless Explosives Company, Union Explosives Company, and Black Diamond Powder Company. Deeming it unwise to do so by buying either their stock or their assets, Atlas conceived and consummated a plan for consolidating the three competitors into a new corporation [the acquiring sub], with Atlas to get a majority of its stock. To this end holders of the stock of the three companies were duly approached by individuals who represented Atlas; their agreements to carry out the plan were obtained; the new corporation was formed and became the owner practically of all the stock, and all the assets of the three competitors; Atlas became the owner of all the preferred stock and 57 per cent of the common stock of the new corporation; and in exchange for the stock in the three companies each of the former stockholders received some common stock in the new company, some Atlas stock, and some cash which Atlas supplied.

Bashford, one of the stockholders in Peerless, received in exchange for his stock 2,720.08 shares of the common stock of the new corporation, $25,306.67 in cash, 625 shares of Atlas preferred, and 1,344 shares of Atlas common. In his income tax return for the year 1930 he included all the cash, but did not include the gain on stock of either the new corporation or Atlas. The Commissioner concedes that gain on the stock in the new corporation was properly omitted, since the new company was a "reorganization" of Peerless. He insists that the Atlas stock should have been included, as it was "other property" on which gain was taxable under section 112(c)(1) of the Revenue Act of 1928, [now § 354] since Atlas was not "a party to the reorganization." The Board of Tax Appeals (33 B.T.A. 10) held that Atlas was "a party to the reorganization," and hence that gain on its stock was properly omitted by Bashford. * * *

Applying the rule here, we hold likewise that the [Atlas] stock was "other property" and Bashford, therefore, liable on the deficiency assessment; because the Atlas Powder Company was not "a party to the reorganization."

* * *

Any direct ownership by Atlas of Peerless, Black Diamond, and Union was transitory and without real substance; it was part of a plan which contemplated the immediate transfer of the stock or the assets or both of the three reorganized companies to the new Atlas subsidiary. Hence, under the rule stated, the [factual] distinctions are not of legal significance. The difference in the degree of stock control by the parent company of its subsidiary and the difference in the method or means by which that control was secured are not material. The participation of Atlas in the reorganization of its competitors into a new company which became a subsidiary did not make Atlas "a party to the reorganization." The continuity of interest required by the rule is lacking.

Reversed.

Questions

In both *Groman* and *Bashford* the Board of Tax Appeals held that the parent corporation (Glidden in *Groman* and Atlas in *Bashford*) was a party to a reorganization and that, consequently, its stock was not boot in the reorganization. What result under the current statute if S, a wholly owned subsidiary of P, acquires T in a merger in which the consideration paid by S is 50% S stock and 50% P stock? In *Bashford*, Atlas only owned 57% of the new corporation. Would it be possible under the current statute for the parent in a triangular reorganization to own only 57% of the stock of the subsidiary?

3. *Distribution of Acquiring Corporation's Stock to Target's Parent Corporation*

REVENUE RULING 84–30
1984–1 C.B. 114.

Issue

Whether the continuity of proprietary interest requirement of section 1.368–1(b) of the Income Tax Regulations is satisfied in the following situation.

Facts

Corporation X owns all the stock of the corporation Y and Z. Z in turn, owns all the stock of corporation N. This relationship has existed for many years, during which each corporation has been engaged in the active conduct of a separate trade or business.

Pursuant to an integrated plan of acquisition adopted for good business reasons, Y acquired substantially all of the assets of N solely in exchange for shares of Y voting stock and the assumption by Y of the liabilities of N. N was liquidated and the Y stock received by N was distributed to Z and then immediately by Z to X.

* * *

[T]he distribution by Z of the Y stock to X does not result in a change in X's aggregate interests, because X was the 100 percent parent of Z, which, in turn, owned all of N. Accordingly, the distribution of Y stock by Z to X did not violate the continuity of proprietary interest requirement because X was an indirect owner of N within the meaning of such phrase in section 1.368–1(b) of the regulations.

Holding

The continuity of proprietary interest requirement of section 1.368–1(b) of the regulations is satisfied when the stock of the acquiring corporation given in exchange for the acquired corporation is distributed through its 100 percent parent corporation to such corporation's 100 percent parent.

4. *Drop Down of Acquiring Stock to Partnership*

GENERAL COUNSEL MEMORANDUM
39150, October 1, 1982.

* * *

Issue: Is the status of a purported reorganization under I.R.C. § 368(a)(1)(C) affected by the transferor's exchange with a partnership, immediately before the purported reorganization, of one-third of the transferor's assets for a ninety-nine percent interest in that partnership, which interest was transferred with the transferor's other assets in the purported reorganization?

Conclusion: You concluded that the drop down into the partnership did not affect the status of the reorganization. We agree.

* * *

Analysis: Requisite to a reorganization are (a) continuity of business enterprise and (b) continuity of interest. Treas.Reg. § 1.368–1(b). We conclude both of these requirements are satisfied here.

A. Continuity of Business Enterprise

* * *

B. Continuity of Proprietary Interest

Treas.Reg. § 1.368–1(b) provides that requisite to a reorganization is a continuity of interest in the modified corporate form on the part of those persons who, directly or indirectly, were the owners of the enterprise prior to the reorganization.

In * * * G.C.M. 35117, I–4763 (Nov. 15, 1972), this office considered a transaction in which, as part of the plan, a merger was followed by a drop-down of all the assets of the acquired corporation into a partnership, of which the acquiring corporation was the sole general partner with a capital interest of 63.75%. We found no reorganization under the rule of *Groman v. Commissioner,* 302 U.S. 82 (1937), and *Helvering v. Bashford,* 302 U.S. 454 (1938), because continuity of interest was "remote" rather than direct. * * *

* * *

Here, section 368(a)(2)(C) overrules in part the "remote continuity" problem of *Groman* and *Bashford* * * * There is, however, no statutory provision sanctioning the drop down of assets into the partnership. This raises the question whether the continuity of interest requirement is satisfied when some but not all the transferred assets are transferred in turn outside the provisions of section 368(a)(2)(C).

Taxpayers asserted in G.C.M. 35117 that because partnerships are treated as conduits under Subchapter K, a drop down into a partnership should not raise a remote continuity problem. We continue to disagree. A partnership's nature as a conduit is irrelevant; to discover whether continuity of interest is remote requires examining how the transferred assets are held. In this respect, a partnership differs fundamentally from a corporation. For example, a stockholder's control of a corporation is directly proportional to the amount of stock owned. No such proportionate relationship exists for partners and their partnerships. * * *

* * *

[W]e agree with your conclusion that G.C.M. 35117 is distinguishable, and conclude that the continuity of interest requirement is met here. The focus here and in G.C.M. 35117 is on the remoteness portion of the qualitative aspect of continuity of interest. That is, did each share of stock represent a sufficiently direct continuing interest in the former assets of the transferor corporation? We are aware of no precedent in which the issue was the amount of the acquired assets that must be retained, as compared with those dropped down to remote entities, in order to satisfy the continuity of interest requirement. We believe that issue is best resolved by analogy to the continuity of business enterprise requirement and, to some extent, the quantitative aspect of the continuity of interest requirement.

* * *

Regarding the quantitative aspect of the continuity of interest requirement, the Service, for rulings purposes, states in section 3.02 of Rev.Proc. 77–37 [*see* Sec. 11.2.c.]

[Rev.Proc. 77-37] recognizes that it is necessary only for the shareholders of the transferor corporation, in the aggregate, to keep a percentage of their investment in the transferor corporation invested in the transferee corporation; one-half of their aggregate investment may be cashed out. At least arguably, the allowance of a sale of some of the transferor stock suggests that a sale of some of the transferor's assets (the equivalent under *Groman* and *Bashford* of a transfer to a subsidiary) would also not violate continuity of interest because in both situations the investment in the transferor has been diluted.

* * *

H. USE OF CONTINGENT OR ESCROW STOCK IN A REORGANIZATION

1. *General Principles*

REVENUE RULING 84-42
1984-1 C.B. 194.

SEC. 2. PROCEDURE

.01 Section 3.03 of Rev.Proc. 77-37 is amplified to read as follows:

In transactions under sections 368(a)(1)(A), 368(a)(1)(B), 368(a)(1)(C), 368(a)(1)(D), 368(a)(1)(E), and 351 of the Code, it is not necessary that all the stock which is to be issued in exchange for the requisite stock or property, be issued immediately provided (1) that all the stock will be issued within 5 years from the date of transfer of assets or stock for reorganizations under sections 368(a)(1)(A), 368(a)(1)(C), 368(a)(1)(D), and 368(a)(1)(E), or within 5 years from the date of the initial distribution in the case of transactions under sections 368(a)(1)(B), and 351; (2) there is a valid business reason for not issuing all the stock immediately, such as difficulty in determining the value of one or both of the corporations involved in the transaction; (3) the maximum number of shares which may be issued in the exchange is stated; (4) at least 50 percent of the maximum number of shares of each class of stock which may be issued is issued in the initial distribution; (5) the agreement evidencing the right to receive stock in the future prohibits assignment (except by operation of law) or if the agreement does not prohibit assignment, the right must not be evidenced by negotiable certificates of any kind and must not be readily marketable; (6) such right can give rise to the receipt only of additional stock of the corporation making the underlying distribution; (7) such stock issuance will not be triggered by an event the occurrence or nonoccurrence of which is within the control of shareholders; (8) such stock issuance will not be triggered by the payment of additional tax or reduction in tax paid as a result of a Service audit of the shareholders or the corporation either (a) with respect to the reorganization or section 351 transaction in which the contingent stock will be issued, or (b) when the reorganization or section 351 transaction in which the contingent stock will be issued, or (c) when the reorganization or section 351 transaction in which the escrowed stock will be issued involves persons related within the meaning of section 267(c)(4) of the Code; and (9) the mechanism for the calculation of the additional stock to be issued is objective and readily ascertainable. Stock issued as compensation, royalties or any other consideration other than in exchange for stock or assets will not be considered to have been received in the exchange. Until the final distribution of the total number of shares of stock to be issued in the exchange is made, the interim basis of the stock of the issuing corporation received in the exchange by the shareholders (not including that portion of each share representing interest) will be determined, pursuant to section 358(a), as though the maximum number of shares to be issued (not including that portion of each share representing interest) has been received by the shareholders.

In connection with item 3.03(8) above, the Service reserves the right to refuse to rule if, based on all the facts and circumstances of a case, it is determined that the principal purpose of the triggering mechanism is the reduction in federal income taxes (see section 3.02(1) of Rev.Proc. 84–22, 1984–13 I.R.B. 18).

.02 Section 3.06 of Rev.Proc. 77–37 is amplified to read as follows:

In transactions under section 368(a)(1)(A), 368(a)(1)(B), 368(a)(1)(C), 368(a)(1)(D), 368(a)(1)(E), and 351 of the Code, a portion of the stock issued in exchange for the requisite stock or property may be placed in escrow by the exchanging shareholders, or may be made subject to a condition pursuant to the agreement, or plan of reorganization or of the transaction, for possible return to the issuing corporation under specified conditions provided (1) there is a valid business reason for establishing the arrangement; (2) the stock subject to such arrangement appears as issued and outstanding on the balance sheet of the issuing corporation and such stock is legally outstanding under applicable state law; (3) all dividends paid on such stock will be distributed currently to the exchanging shareholders; (4) all voting rights of such stock (if any) are exercisable by or on behalf of the shareholders or their authorized agent; (5) no shares of such stock are subject to restrictions requiring their return to the issuing corporation because of death, failure to continue employment, or similar restrictions; (6) all such stock is released from the arrangement within 5 years from the date of consummation of the transaction (except where there is a bona fide dispute as to whom the stock should be released); (7) at least 50 percent of the number of shares of each class of stock issued initially to the shareholders (exclusive of shares of stock to be issued at a later date as described in .01 above) is not subject to the arrangement; (8) the return of stock will not be triggered by an event the occurrence or nonoccurrence of which is within the control of shareholders; (9) the return of stock will not be triggered by the payment of additional tax or reduction in tax paid as a result of a Service audit of the shareholders or the corporation either (a) with respect to the reorganization or section 351 transaction in which the escrowed stock will be issued, or (b) when the reorganization or section 351 transaction in which the escrowed stock will be issued involves persons related within the meaning of section 267(c)(4) of the Code; and (10) the mechanism for the calculation of the number of shares of stock to be returned is objective and readily ascertainable.

In connection with item 3.06(9) above, the Service reserves the right to refuse to rule if, based on all the facts and circumstances of a case, it is determined that the principal purpose of the triggering mechanism is the reduction in federal income taxes (see section 3.02(1) of the Rev. Proc. 84–22, 1984–13 I.R.B. 18).

2. *Applicability of Imputed Interest Rules to Contingent Payouts*

SOLOMON v. COMMISSIONER

United States Circuit Court of Appeals, Second Circuit, 1977.
570 F.2d 28

MANSFIELD, CIRCUIT JUDGE: * * * The only question before us is whether [former] § 483 of the Internal Revenue Code, which requires that a portion of deferred payments received on account of the sale or exchange of property must be treated as interest rather than capital, applies to a "non-taxable corporate reorganization," see §§ 354(a)(1), 368(a)(1)(B), so as to render part of those shares interest income [, where shares of the acquiring corporation (Whittaker) are received after the date of acquisition pursuant to a contingent payout arrangement]. [This type of transaction is now subject to the contingent interest rules of §§ 1274 and 1275. *See* Sec. 3.10.]

The Tax Court held that § 483 was applicable. We affirm.

DISCUSSION

[Former §] 483 provides in pertinent part that in the case of any contract for the sale or exchange of property under which any payment constituting part or all of the sales price is deferred for more than one year after the sale or exchange without providing for payment of any interest or of adequate interest on the deferred payment or payments, a portion of each payment received by the seller more than six months after the date of the sale or exchange shall be treated as unstated interest. * * *

* * *

* * * [W]e agree with the Commissioner that the purpose of § 483 [and presumably the purpose of §§ 1274 and 1275 do] not conflict with the purpose underlying the Code's corporate reorganization provisions. * * * The purpose of § 483 * * * is to end an abuse whereby ordinary interest income was being converted into capital gain; the legislative history indicates that Congress intended its solution to encompass all transactions with certain objective characteristics, whether or not they were consciously designed to avoid taxes. The transaction before us may be taxed so as to give effect to both of these purposes and without any

eventual tax overlap. A finding that this transaction constituted only "a readjustment of continuing interest in property under modified corporate forms" does not foreclose implementation of Congress' prophylactic solution to the problem of unstated interest. Taxation of the interest portion does not conflict with maintenance of the tax-free status of the portion received in an exchange of capital assets.

* * *

§ 11.3 THE CONTINUITY OF BUSINESS ENTERPRISE DOCTRINE

A. INTRODUCTION TO THE CURRENT REGULATIONS

See § 1.368–1(d).

PREAMBLE REGULATIONS UNDER § 1.368–1(d)
Treasury Decision 7745 (December 29, 1980).

Summary: This document contains final regulations clarifying the continuity of business enterprise requirement for corporate reorganizations. The continuity of business enterprise requirement is fundamental to the notion that tax-free reorganizations merely readjust continuing interests in property. Recent developments involving the availability of tax-free reorganization treatment for certain mutual fund transactions require clarification, in general, of the continuity of business enterprise requirement.

* * *

GENERAL DESCRIPTION OF REGULATION

The regulation sets forth certain basic concepts underlying the continuity of business enterprise requirement. Continuity of business enterprise requires that the transferee (P) either continue the transferor's (T's) historic business or use a significant portion of T's historic business assets. P is not required to continue T's business. However, there must be significant use of T's historic business assets in P's business.

The facts of the examples in the regulation are based, in large part, upon administrative rulings and judicial opinions. Example (1), which is based on *Lewis v. Commissioner,* 176 F.2d 646 (1st Cir.1949), shows that continuity of business enterprise requires only that P continue one of the significant lines of T's business. Example (2), which is based on *Atlas Tool Co. v. Commissioner,* 70 T.C. 86 (1978), *aff'd* 614 F.2d 860 (3d Cir.1980), *cert. denied,* ___ U.S. ___ (1980), shows that continuity of business enterprise may exist even if P's use of T's assets differs from T's use of those assets.

Example (3) shows that stocks and bonds acquired following the sale of T's historic business as part of a plan of reorganization are not T's historic business assets. Compare *Lester J. Workman,* T.C.Memo 1977–378.

The facts in example (4) are a variation of those in Rev.Rul. 63–29, 1963–1 C.B. 77, although the example reaches a different result. This transaction is not a mere purchase by T of P stock because T receives third party notes which are not cash equivalents. Example (5) shows that a disposition of T's assets by P does not differ in result from a disposition of those assets by T.

* * *

OVERALL POLICY CONSIDERATIONS

* * *

The courts have long recognized that a tax-free reorganization presupposes that T's shareholders retain a material proprietary interest in P (continuity of interest). A necessary corollary to this continuity of interest requirement is that the interest retained represents a link to T's business or its business assets. The continuity of business enterprise requirement ensures that tax-free reorganizations effect only a readjustment of the T shareholders' continuing interest in T's property under a modified corporate form. See, § 1.368–1(b). Absent such a link between T's shareholders and T's business or assets there would be no reason to require T's shareholders to retain a continuing stock interest in P. If the shareholders' link to T's business or its assets is broken by, for example, a sale of T's business to an unrelated party as part of the overall plan of reorganization, the interest received in P is no different than an interest in any corporation. An exchange of stock without a link to the underlying business or business assets resembles any stock for stock exchange and, as such, is a taxable event. * * *

* * *

E. *"Historic" concept based on step transaction principles*

The regulation requires a continuing link between T's shareholders and T's business or assets. The examples in the regulation illustrate that the transfer of sale proceeds is not sufficient. It follows that it is not sufficient to transfer assets acquired with the sale proceeds as part of a plan of reorganization. * * *

B. SALE OF ASSETS IN ANTICIPATION OF REORGANIZATION

1. *Sale by Target Before a (C) Reorganization*

REVENUE RULING 79–434

1979–2 C.B. 155.

ISSUE

Does the transfer by a corporation, previously engaged in a manufacturing business, of its assets (cash and short-term Treasury notes) for stock of a regulated investment company qualify as a reorganization under section 368(a)(1) of the Internal Revenue Code?

FACTS

Corporation X, a corporation engaged in manufacturing, sold all of its assets to unrelated corporation Z for $1,000x$ cash. This sale was made in anticipation of X's acquisition by corporation Y, an open-end diversified investment company that qualifies as a regulated investment company as that term is defined in section 851 of the Code. Pursuant to an agreement between X and Y, X transferred all of its assets (cash and short-term Treasury notes that X had purchased with the proceeds from the sale of its assets) to Y in return for 1,000 shares of Y. As provided in the agreement, X dissolved after the transfer and distributed the stock of Y to its shareholders, individuals A and B, in exchange for their X stock.

LAW AND ANALYSIS

A tax-free reorganization assumes that "the new enterprise, the new corporate structure, and the new property are substantially continuations of the old [ones] still unliquidated." Section 1.1002–1(c). [A] transaction that in substance is a mere purchase by one corporation of stock in another corporation is not a reorganization.

HOLDING

The transfer of cash or short-term Treasury notes for stock does not qualify as a reorganization under section 368(a)(1) of the Code because in substance it represents a purchase by X of the shares of Y prior to X's liquidation.

The fair market value of the Y stock distributed by X to its shareholders in complete liquidation will be treated as in full payment in exchange for their X stock under section 331 of the Code. Gain or loss is recognized to the shareholders of X under section 1001.

2. Sale by Target Before a (B) Reorganization

REVENUE RULING 81–92
1981–1 C.B. 133.

ISSUE

Does the acquisition by one corporation of all of the stock of another corporation solely in exchange for voting stock of the acquiring corporation qualify as a tax-free reorganization under section 368(a)(1)(B) if the acquired corporation's assets consist solely of cash that it realized from the sale of assets it previously used in its manufacturing business?

FACTS

T, a corporation engaged in manufacturing, sold all of its assets for cash to Z, an unrelated corporation. The sale was made as part of a plan of reorganization in which P, a corporation engaged in the manufacture of products different than those previously manufactured by T, acquired all of the outstanding stock in T from T's shareholders, in exchange solely for P voting stock. T, as a wholly owned subsidiary of P, then used the cash realized on the sale of its manufacturing assets to engage in a business entirely unrelated to its previous manufacturing business.

LAW AND ANALYSIS

* * *

Section 1.368–1(d) of the regulations provides, in general, that the continuity of business enterprise requirement of section 1.368–1(b) is satisfied if the transferee in a corporate reorganization either (i) continues the transferor's historic business or (ii) uses a significant portion of the transferor's historic business assets in a business. Because the continuity of business enterprise requirement must be met for a transaction to qualify as a reorganization, section 1.368–1(d) is applicable to a transaction intended to qualify as a tax free reorganization under section 368(a)(1)(B) of the Code. See section 1.368–1(d)(1)(iii). Therefore, the transferee corporation must continue the transferor's historic business, or continue to use a significant portion of the transferor's historic business assets, in modified corporate form as a subsidiary of the transferee corporation for the transaction to qualify under section 368(a)(1)(B).

HOLDING

In the instant transaction, the acquisition by P of the T stock solely for P's voting stock does not qualify as a tax-free reorganization under section 368(a)(1)(B) since P did not continue T's historic (the manufacturing) business or use a significant portion of T's historic business assets (those used in the manufacturing business) in a business conducted as a subsidiary of P after the transaction.

Accordingly, gain or loss is realized and recognized to the former shareholders of T upon the receipt by them from P of the P voting stock in exchange for their T stock under section 1001 of the Code.

3. Acquisition of Investment Company in a (C) Reorganization

REVENUE RULING 87–76
1987–2 C.B. 84.

ISSUE

Are the requirements of section 1.368–1(d) of the Income Tax Regulations, relating to continuity of business enterprise, satisfied under the circumstances described below?

FACTS

T is a corporation engaged in the investment business since 1975. From its inception, T's investment practice has been to maintain approximately one-third of the value of its investment portfolio in diversified corporate stock purchased primarily for equity growth, one-third in corporate stock purchased with a view to maximizing current income, and the remaining one-third in general corporate bonds purchased with a view to producing steady, predictable returns of income. T has no other significant assets, tangible or intangible.

P is a diversified open-end management investment company whose investment policy since it was organized in 1978 has been to attract investors who wish to participate in a managed portfolio consisting exclusively of high grade municipal bonds, the income from which is exempt from federal income tax.

In 1982, P acquired substantially all of T's assets in exchange solely for shares of P voting common stock in a transaction intended to qualify as a reorganization described in section 368(a)(1)(C) of the Internal Revenue Code. Pursuant to the plan of reorganization, T was required, prior to the reorganization, to sell its entire portfolio of corporate stock and bonds, and reinvest the proceeds therefrom in municipal bonds that were subject to P's approval.

* * *

LAW AND ANALYSIS

* * *

In the present situation, the transaction does not meet the asset continuity test since all of T's historic assets, the portfolio of corporate stocks and bonds, were, as part of the plan of reorganization, sold before the transaction was consummated, and the proceeds were reinvested in municipal bonds. Consequently, the issue is whether P will continue T's historic business.

Section 1.368–1(d)(3)(i) of the regulations provides that the fact that the acquiring corporation is in the same line of business as the acquired corporation tends to establish the requisite continuity, but is not alone sufficient. * * *

HOLDING

The continuity of business enterprise requirement of section 1.368–1(d) of the regulations is not met upon the transfer to P of all of T's assets consisting of municipal bonds T purchased with the proceeds from the sale of its historic business assets. Accordingly, the transaction does not qualify as a reorganization under section 368(a)(1)(C) of the Code.

C. CONTINUITY OF BUSINESS ENTERPRISE IN AN OVER AND DOWN TRIANGULAR REORGANIZATION

REVENUE RULING 81-247
1981-2 C.B. 87.

ISSUE

Will the application of the continuity of business enterprise rules of section 1.368-1(d) of the Income Tax Regulations to *Situations 1, 2,* and *3* prevent the transactions between X and Y in each of the situations from qualifying as tax free reorganizations under sections 368(a)(1)(A) and (a)(2)(C) of the Internal Revenue Code?

FACTS

Situation 1:

In a transaction meant to qualify as a tax free reorganization under sections 368(a)(1)(A) and (a)(2)(C) of the Code, corporation X, a holding company, acquired, under the applicable merger laws of State M, a significant portion of the historic business assets of corporation Y, a manufacturing business. Immediately thereafter, X transferred all assets received from Y to corporation Z, its wholly-owned subsidiary engaged in a manufacturing business. Z then used the assets in its manufacturing business.

Situation 2:

The facts are the same as in *Situation 1* except that X was also engaged in a manufacturing business, and X transferred less than a significant portion of Y's assets to Z and retained less than a significant part of Y's assets. Both X and Z used their respective parts of Y's assets (which together totaled more than a significant portion of the historic business assets of Y) in their separate manufacturing businesses.

Situation 3:

The facts are the same as in *Situation 1*, except that X transferred a part of the assets received from Y to each of three wholly owned manufacturing subsidiaries. The separate parts of the assets transferred to the three wholly owned subsidiaries each represented less than a significant portion of the historic business assets X received from Y. However, the total of all of the assets X transferred to the three subsidiaries represented all the assets X received from Y which, as stated above, was a significant portion of Y's historic business assets.

In none of the situations described above did X, Z or any of X's other subsidiaries, continue an historic trade or business of Y.

LAW AND ANALYSIS

* * *

In Rev.Rul. 68–261, 1968–1 C.B. 147, a parent corporation acquired all the assets of a target corporation. The target had conducted its business through six divisions. Immediately after the merger of the parent and the target corporation, the parent transferred the assets of each of the six divisions of the target to six wholly owned subsidiaries of the parent. The revenue ruling concludes that the transaction is a reorganization within the meaning of sections 368(a)(1)(A) and 368(a)(2)(C) of the Code.

In Rev.Rul. 64–73, 1964–1 (Part I) C.B. 142, a parent corporation acquired the assets of a target corporation in a reorganization under sections 368(a)(1)(C) and 368(a)(2)(C) of the Code. Some of the target assets were transferred to the parent and some of the assets were transferred to a second tier subsidiary of the parent, wholly owned by a wholly owned subsidiary of the parent. The revenue ruling states that neither the assets transferred to the subsidiary nor to the parent constituted separately substantially all of the target assets, but together constituted all of the target's assets. The revenue ruling concludes that the transaction qualifies as a reorganization as defined in section 368(a)(1)(C).

Both Rev.Rul. 68–261 and Rev.Rul. 64–73 are consistent with the legislative intent of section 368(a)(2)(C) of the Code, which permits transactions to continue to qualify as reorganizations within the meaning of section 368(a)(1)(A) and 368(a)(1)(C) whether any of the assets received by the acquiring corporation are transferred to corporations it controls.

Holding

The application of the continuity of business enterprise rules of section 1.368–1(d) of the regulations to *Situations 1, 2,* and *3* will not prevent the transactions between X and Y, in each of the situations, from qualifying as tax free reorganizations under sections 368(a)(1)(A) and (a)(2)(C) of the Code, because the significant portion of Y's historical business assets received by X remained with X or corporations directly controlled by X. Therefore, in *Situations 1, 2,* and *3* the mergers of Y into X, followed by the specific transfers described in each situation, are statutory mergers within the meaning of sections 368(a)(1)(A) and 368(a)(2)(C).

The above holdings regarding *Situations 1, 2,* and *3* would also apply in situations that meet the qualifications of an asset acquisition under section 368(a)(1)(C) and (a)(2)(C) or a stock acquisition within the meaning of section 368(a)(1)(B) and (a)(2)(C) of the Code.

D. NO CONTINUITY OF BUSINESS ENTERPRISE REQUIREMENTS IN A RECAPITALIZATION

REVENUE RULING 82-34
1982-1 C.B. 59.

Issue

Advice has been requested regarding whether continuity of business enterprise is a requirement for a recapitalization to qualify as a reorganization under section 368(a)(1)(E) of the Internal Revenue Code.

Law, Analysis and Holding

[T]he Code provides that a "recapitalization" is a reorganization. A recapitalization has been defined as a "reshuffling of a capital structure within the framework of an existing corporation." * * *

* * *

The "continuity of business enterprise" requirement is closely related to the "continuity of shareholder interest" requirement in section 1.368-1(b) of the regulations in that both are concerned with determining whether a transaction involves an otherwise taxable transfer of stock or assets of one corporation to another corporation, as distinguished from a tax-free reorganization, which assumes only a readjustment of continuing interests under modified corporate form. The consideration of whether a transaction involves an otherwise taxable transfer of stock or assets of one corporation to another corporation is not present in a recapitalization because a recapitalization involves only a single corporation. Therefore, Rev.Rul. 77-415, 1977-2 C.B. 311, consistent with several court decisions, concludes that continuity of shareholder interest is not a requirement for a recapitalization to qualify as a reorganization under section 368(a)(1)(E) of the Code. Similarly, continuity of business enterprise is not a requirement for a recapitalization to qualify as a reorganization under section 368(a)(1)(E).

§ 11.4 THE MEANING OF SOLELY FOR VOTING STOCK: AN INTRODUCTION

HELVERING v. SOUTHWEST CONSOLIDATED CORPORATION

Supreme Court of the United States, 1942.
315 U.S. 194, 62 S.Ct. 546, 86 L.Ed. 789.

Mr. Justice Douglas delivered the opinion of the Court.

[The assets of a financially troubled corporation were acquired in exchange for cash, the acquiring corporation's voting stock and Class A and B warrants. The issue was whether the transaction qualified as a reorganization under clause (B) of § 112(g)(1) of the 1934 Act, which is a predecessor of the current (C) reorganization. The 1934 Act amended the reorganization definition to require that "solely voting stock" be used in a stock for stock and a stock for asset acquisition.]

[C]lause (B) of § 112(g)(1) of the 1934 Act effects an important change as respects transactions whereby one corporation acquires substantially all of the assets of another. The continuity of interest test is made much stricter. Congress has provided that the assets of the transferor corporation must be acquired in exchange "solely" for "voting stock" of the transferee. "Solely" leaves no leeway. Voting stock plus some other consideration does not meet the statutory requirement. Congress, however, in 1939 amended clause (B) of § 112(g)(1) by adding, "but in determining whether the exchange is solely for voting stock the assumption by the acquiring corporation of a liability of the other, or the fact that property acquired is subject to a liability, shall be disregarded." That amendment was made to avoid the consequences of *United States v. Hendler,* [*see* Sec. 3.15.A.] * * * But with that exception, the requirements of § 112(g)(1)(B) are not met if properties are acquired in exchange for a consideration other than, or in addition to, voting stock. Under that test this transaction fails to qualify as a "reorganization" under clause (B).

In the first place, security holders of the old company owning $440,000 face amount of obligations were paid off in cash.

* * *

In the second place, the warrants which were issued were not "voting stock". Whatever rights a warrant holder may have "to require the obligor corporation to maintain the integrity of the shares" covered by the warrants, he is not a shareholder.

* * * Accordingly, the acquisition in this case was not made "solely" for voting stock. And it makes no difference that in the long run the unexercised warrants expired and nothing but voting stock was outstanding. The critical time is the date of the exchange. In that posture of the case it is no different than if other convertible securities had been issued, all of which had been converted within the conversion period.

Reversed.

Questions and Notes

In general, what impact does *Southwest Consolidated* have on the interpretation of the phrase "solely for voting stock"? In a (B) reorganization, can the acquiring corporation pay cash in lieu of fractional shares? *See* Rev.Rul. 66–365, Chapter 15. What about paying the shareholders reorganization expenses? *See* Rev.Rul. 73–54, Chapter 15. As a general proposition in planning a (B) or (C), the cautious tax advisor should be doubly sure that there is no hidden boot. The solely for voting stock issue is examined further in Chapter 15.

§ 11.5 DEFINITION OF CONTROL IN § 368(c)

REVENUE RULING 76-223
1976-1 C.B.

Advice has been requested whether the transaction described below satisfies the "control" requirements of section 368(c) of the Internal Revenue Code of 1954.

For valid business reasons corporation X desired to acquire the stock of corporation Y in a transaction within the meaning of section 368(a)(1)(B) of the Code. Y had 81 shares of voting common stock and 19 shares of non-voting preferred stock outstanding. X did not want to acquire any of the outstanding preferred stock of Y in the proposed transaction. Therefore, as a part of the overall plan and prior to the consummation of the acquisition, the charter of Y was amended to permanently give voting rights to holders of the preferred stock of Y, on a one vote per share basis, the same right attributable to the voting common stock. Subsequently, X acquired 81 shares of Y voting common stock solely in exchange for shares of X voting stock. There was no plan to later amend Y's charter and thereby revoke the voting rights of holders of Y preferred stock.

Immediately after the transaction by which X acquired 81 shares of the voting common stock of Y in exchange for voting stock of X, X owned 81 percent of the total combined voting power of all classes of the stock of Y entitled to vote. The exchange of non-voting preferred for voting preferred resulted in a permanent change in the rights of preferred shareholders prior to the acquisition of the voting common stock. Thus, there were no classes of nonvoting stock of Y outstanding at the time of the acquisition.

Accordingly, in the instant case, the control requirements of section 368(c) of the Code have been satisfied and the transaction qualifies as a reorganization within the meaning of section 368(a)(1)(B). Furthermore, no gain or loss is recognized under section 1036 upon the exchange of the Y nonvoting preferred stock for Y voting preferred stock pursuant to the amendment of Y's charter.

§ 11.6 PLAN OF REORGANIZATION

A "plan of reorganization" is one of the conditions for nonrecognition treatment both for the exchanging stockholder or security holder under § 354(a) and for the target corporation under § 361(a). Although the term is not defined in the Code, § 1.368-2(g) says that a plan of reorganization "has reference to a consummated transaction specifically defined as a reorganization under § 368(a)(1)." This regulation goes on to say that the term is "not to be construed as broadening the definition of reorganization * * * but is to be taken as limiting the nonrecognition of gain or loss to such exchanges or distributions and is directly a part of the [reorganization] transaction * * *." Reflecting the business purpose doctrine of *Gregory v. Helvering, see* Sec. 1.3.G.2., the regulation further provides that "the transaction or series of transactions, embraced in a plan of reorganization must not only come within the specific language of section 368(a), but * * * must be undertaken for reasons germane to the continuance of the business of the corporation * * *." Although it is possible that a plan of reorganization need not be in any particular form and need not be in writing, *see C.T. Investment Co. v. Commissioner,* 88 F.2d 582 (8th Cir.1937), it is advisable to have the "plan of reorganization" reflected in the corporate records. Indeed, § 1.368–3, which specifies the records to be kept with respect to a reorganization, says that "the plan of reorganization must be adopted by each of the corporation's parties thereto and the adoption must be shown by the acts of its duly constituted responsible officers, and appear upon the official records of the corporation."

§ 11.7 THE BUSINESS PURPOSE DOCTRINE

A. IN GENERAL

The regulations under § 368 make it clear that in order to constitute a reorganization a transaction must have a business purpose. Specifically, the regulations say that to be a reorganization a transaction (1) must be required by the "business exigencies" (*see* § 1.368–1(b)), (2) must satisfy "both the terms of the specifications [of the reorganization provisions] and their underlying assumptions and purposes" (*id.*), (3) must be an "ordinary and necessary incident of the conduct of the enterprise" (*see* § 1.368–1(c)); (4) must not be a "mere device that puts on the form of a reorganization" but that has "no business or corporate purpose" (*id.*), and (5) must be "undertaken for reasons germane to the continuance of the business of the corporation" (*see* § 1.368–1(g)).

B. BUSINESS PURPOSE IN THE (D) BEFORE § 355

Review *Gregory v. Helvering,* 293 U.S. 465, 55 S.Ct. 266, 79 L.Ed. 596 (1935), *supra* Sec. 1.3.G.2.

C. BUSINESS PURPOSE IN A RECAPITALIZATION

BAZLEY v. COMMISSIONER
Supreme Court of the United States, 1947.
331 U.S. 737, 67 S.Ct. 1489, 91 L.Ed. 1782.

Mr. Justice Frankfurter delivered the opinion of the Court.

* * *

In *Bazley* the Commissioner of Internal Revenue assessed an income tax deficiency against the taxpayer for the year 1939. Its validity depends on the legal significance of the recapitalization in that year of a

§ 11.7 THE BUSINESS PURPOSE DOCTRINE

family corporation in which the taxpayer and his wife owned all but one of the Company's one thousand shares. These had a par value of $100. Under the plan of reorganization the taxpayer, his wife, and the holder of the additional share were to turn in their old shares and receive in exchange for each old share five new shares of no par value, but of a stated value of $60, and new debenture bonds, having a total face value of $400,000, payable in ten years but callable at any time. Accordingly, the taxpayer received 3,990 shares of the new stock for the 798 shares of his old holding and debentures in the amount of $319,200. At the time of these transactions the earned surplus of the corporation was $855,-783.82.

* * *

The Commissioner charged to the taxpayer as income the full value of the debentures. The Tax Court affirmed the Commissioner's determination, against the taxpayer's contention that as a "recapitalization" the transaction was a tax-free "reorganization" and that the debentures were "securities in a corporation a party to a reorganization," "exchanged solely for stock or securities in such corporation" "in pursuance of a plan of reorganization," and as such no gain is recognized for income tax purposes. Internal Revenue Code, §§ 112(g)(1)(E) * * * The Tax Court found that the recapitalization had "no legitimate corporate business purpose" and was therefore not a "reorganization" within the statute. The distribution of debentures, it concluded, was a disguised dividend, taxable as earned income under §§ 22(a) and 115(a) and (g) [now § 301]. The Circuit Court of Appeals for the Third Circuit, sitting en banc, affirmed, two judges dissenting.

* * *

It was not the purpose of the reorganization provision to exempt from payment of a tax what as a practical matter is realized gain. Normally, a distribution by a corporation, whatever form it takes, is a definite and rather unambiguous event. It furnishes the proper occasion for the determination and taxation of gain. But there are circumstances where a formal distribution, directly or through exchange of securities, represents merely a new form of the previous participation in an enterprise, involving no change of substance in the rights and relations of the interested parties one to another or to the corporate assets. As to these, Congress has said that they are not to be deemed significant occasions for determining taxable gain.

* * *

No doubt there was a recapitalization of the Bazley corporation in the sense that the symbols that represented its capital were changed, so that the fiscal basis of its operations would appear very differently on its books. But the form of a transaction as reflected by correct corporate accounting opens questions as to the proper application of a taxing statute; it does not close them. * * *

What have we here? No doubt, if the Bazley corporation had issued the debentures to Bazley and his wife without any recapitalization, it would have made a taxable distribution. [See § 301.]

The Commissioner, the Tax Court and the Circuit Court of Appeals agree that nothing was accomplished that would not have been accomplished by an outright debenture dividend. * * * A "reorganization" which is merely a vehicle, however elaborate or elegant, for conveying earnings from accumulations to the stockholders is not a reorganization under § 112 [now § 368]. This disposes of the case as a matter of law, since the facts as found by the Tax Court bring them within it. * * *

* * *

Questions

1. *Bazley* was decided prior to the adoption of §§ 354(a)(2) and 356(d)(2)(B) in 1954. What result under the current statute if a Court were to find that the transaction in *Bazley* constituted a reorganization?

2. Individual *A* is the sole shareholder of corporation *X*. *X* has substantial E & P. *A* exchanges half of his stock for newly issued debentures of *X* in a transaction that purports to qualify as a recapitalization. *A* realizes no gain or loss on the transaction because the adjusted basis of his stock equals the fair market value of the debentures. Does *A* have a dividend? See § 356 and § 1.301–1(*l*).

PART B. CONCEPTS RELATING TO EXCHANGING STOCKHOLDERS AND SECURITY HOLDERS UNDER §§ 354 AND 358

§ 11.8 MEANING OF "SECURITIES EXCHANGED" UNDER § 354

A. EXCHANGE OF SHORT–TERM NOTES FOR DEBENTURES

NEVILLE COKE & CHEMICAL CO. v. COMMISSIONER

United States Court of Appeals, Third Circuit, 1945.
148 F.2d 599, *cert. denied* 326 U.S. 726, 66 S.Ct. 32, 90 L.Ed. 431 (1945).

GOODRICH, CIRCUIT JUDGE.

[Upon the recapitalization of a financially troubled corporation, the holder of short-term notes received debentures and stock in exchange therefor. The issue was whether the noteholder received nonrecognition treatment under a predecessor of § 354(a)(1).]

There is no gain or loss recognized if "stock or securities in a corporation * * * are * * * exchanged solely for stock or securities in such corporation * * *." Were the notes of Davison, which the taxpayer had in its possession, and which it exchanged for debentures and shares of stock issued by the reorganized debtor, "securities" within the wording of the statute? No question has been raised as to the sufficiency of the evidence of obligations issued by the reorganized debtor to qualify under the description of "stock or securities", and the problem is limited to the consideration of what the taxpayer turned in, that is, the notes above mentioned.

What then are "securities" within the meaning of the section? The taxpayer makes a tentative argument that the word ought to be taken in its common, accepted interpretation and that interpretation includes evidence of indebtedness, but he goes on to admit that the Supreme Court has read into the term a meaning differing radically from common interpretation.

It is to be noted that the phrase "stock or securities" appears twice in § 112(b)(3) [now § 354(a)]. Once it refers to what a party turns into a corporation being reorganized. The second appearance of the phrase relates to what a recipient takes from the reorganized company as a result of the transaction. We have no reason for thinking that the phrase has a different meaning in either of the two instances and the argument by the taxpayer that it does differ fails to convince us * * *.

[The court went on to hold that the notes surrendered were not securities.]

Questions

What is the significance of *Neville Coke?* Could an open account trade creditor get nonrecognition treatment upon the extinguishment of the obligations in exchange for the debtor's common stock?

B. EXCHANGE OF BONDS FOR STOCK: ARE BONDS SECURITIES?

REVENUE RULING 59–98
1959–1 C.B. 76.

Advice has been requested whether the exchange of bonds and accrued interest thereon for stock of the corporation which issued such bonds is a recapitalization under the terms of section 368(a)(1)(E) of the Internal Revenue Code of 1954 and whether such bonds constitute "securities" within the meaning of section 354(a)(1) of the Code.

In 1957, the corporation here involved, which had been in serious financial difficulties for several years, exchanged newly issued common stock for all its outstanding first mortgage bonds and the accrued unpaid interest thereon, so that after the exchange the former bondholders owned 40 percent of the common stock outstanding. The bonds surrendered had been issued in 1946 and had originally been payable in from three to ten years, the average time to maturity at issuance being six and one-half years. The corporation had not deducted any of the unpaid interest, either in its computation of income or in its computation of earnings and profits. Before the bonds were surrendered none of the bondholders owned any of the common stock. The exchange of stock for bonds was arranged in order to bring the corporation out of the financial difficulties which had made it unable to pay the principal and interest of the bonds when due. The fair market value of the stock issued for each bond was substantially less than the principal amount of the bond. All of the bonds were purchased at issuance by various individuals as investments.

Section 354(a)(1) of the Code states, in part, that no gain or loss shall be recognized if *securities* in a corporation a party to a reorganization are, in pursuance of a plan of reorganization, exchanged solely for stock in such corporation. Section 368(a)(1)(E) states that a "reorganization" includes a *recapitalization*.

[S]ince in the instant case the bonds were secured by a mortgage on the corporate property, since they had an average life of six and one-half years when issued, and since they were purchased for investment purposes by persons other than the stockholders, it is held that these bonds constitute securities for purposes of subchapter C, chapter 1, of the Code. Thus the change in the capital structure of the corporation constitutes a recapitalization and, therefore, a reorganization as defined in section 368(a)(1)(E) of the Code. Accordingly, under section 354(a) of the Code, no gain or loss is recognized to the bondholders from the exchange of the mortgage bonds, together with the unpaid accrued interest thereon, for capital stock of the corporation.

Note

As indicated in the ruling, "securities" are long term debt instruments. Although there are no hard and fast rules, in attempting to structure a security it would be prudent to provide for an average life of at least six and one half years as set forth in the ruling.

§ 11.9 WARRANTS ARE NOT STOCK WITHIN § 354

WILLIAM H. BATEMAN v. COMMISSIONER
Tax Court of the United States, 1963.
40 T.C. 408 (First Issue).

OPINION

SCOTT, JUDGE: * * *

The issues for decision are:

(1) Should gain to petitioners be recognized under the provisions of section 356(a)(1) of the Internal Revenue Code of 1954 to the extent of the fair market value of common stock purchase warrants of the Symington Wayne Corp. which were received by William H. Bateman in addition to common stock of that corporation in exchange for common stock of the Wayne Pump Co. upon its merger into Symington Wayne Corp.?

* * *

Respondent contends the stock purchase warrants are neither stock nor securities within the meaning of section 354(a)(1), but rather constitute other property within the meaning of section 356. Respondent asserts the distribution of the warrants has the effect of a dividend within the meaning of section 356(a)(2) and that the amount of the fair market value of the warrants on March 12, 1958, should be taxed to petitioner as a dividend.

* * *

Respondent, in his regulations, [says] that section 354(a)(1) applies only where stock is surrendered for stock, securities are surrendered for securities, or securities are surrendered for stock and securities * * *. We think that respondent's regulations correctly interpret section 354(a)(2)(B) as making section 354(a)(1) inapplicable if only stock is surrendered and stock and securities are received * * *. We will therefore confine our consideration to whether the warrants constitute stock within the meaning of section 354(a)(1).

In *Helvering v. Southwest Corp.,* 315 U.S. 194 (1942), warrants to purchase voting stock were held not to be voting stock. In *E.P. Raymond,* 37 B.T.A. 423 (1938), we held stock purchase warrants to be securities and in so doing apparently accepted as a fact that these securities were not stock * * *. In the instant case a payment was required before the warrant holder would be entitled to receive stock and the warrants did not entitle the holder to any dividends or other rights of stockholders until exercised with the required payments to receive the stock. The provisions of the warrants here involved are not distinguishable in any material respect from those involved in *Helvering v. Southwest Corp., supra.* We, therefore, hold that the stock purchase warrants did not constitute stock. If they were securities, section 354(a)(1) is made inapplicable to this exchange by the provisions of section 354(a)(2)(B) and the fair market value of the warrants is recognized as gain to the extent provided in section 356 just as it would be if the warrants were not securities but were "other property."

* * *

Questions

Could the receipt of stock warrants in a reorganization give rise to boot dividend treatment under § 356? *See* § 317(a). Are warrants securities for purposes of § 354?

§ 11.10 SUBSTITUTION OF ACQUIROR'S CONVERTIBLE SECURITIES FOR TARGET'S CONVERTIBLE SECURITIES: TREATMENT UNDER § 354(a)(2)

REVENUE RULING 79-155
1979-1 C.B. 153.

Issues

(1) Will changes, negotiated as part of a plan of reorganization, in terms of the securities of T, the acquired corporation in a reorganization under section 368(a)(1)(A) and (a)(2)(D) of the Internal Revenue Code of 1954, constitute a taxable exchange to the T security holders?

* * *

Facts

Corporation T, incorporated in state A, had outstanding one class of common stock and 8 percent convertible securities in the principal amount of 50,000x dollars with a maturity date of July 1, 1995. The terms of the securities contained a provision that they were convertible into T common stock, but did not impart to the holders thereof any rights or liabilities as shareholders of T. The security holders owned no T stock.

In order to have the stock of T owned by a holding company, and to enable joint sharing of the liability for the convertible securities, corporation P and its wholly-owned subsidiary, S, were incorporated in state A to effect a merger of T into S.

Pursuant to the laws of state A, T merged into S in exchange for the stock of P, and S received all of the assets of T and assumed all of T's liabilities. The shareholders of T exchanged their T stock for P common stock. If T had merged into P the merger would have been a reorganization under section 368(a)(1)(A) of the Code.

As part of the plan of reorganization, negotiations were entered into with the T security holders, whose consent was a precondition to the merger. An agreement was reached pursuant to which P and S became jointly and severally liable for the convertible securities; the securities became convertible into P common stock; the security holders obtained the right to convert the securities into S common stock if P disposed of its S stock, although there was no plan on the part of P to do so; the interest rate on the securities was increased to 9 percent; the maturity date was changed to July 1, 1990; and the T security holders consented to the merger. The principal amount of the outstanding securities remained unchanged.

* * *

Law and Analysis

Issue (1). Under section 368(a)(2)(D) of the Code the acquisition by S in exchange for stock of P, of substantially all of the properties of T, which in the transaction is merged into S, will not be disqualified under section 368(a)(1)(A) provided the transaction would qualify under section 368(a)(1)(A) if the merger had been into P and no stock of S is used in the transaction.

The transaction in the instant case is a reorganization as defined in section 368(a)(2)(D) of the Code. The convertible debentures of T do not confer upon the holders thereof rights or liabilities as shareholders of S unless and until P divests itself of its S stock and subsequently the security holders elect to convert their securities into S stock. Moreover, there was no intention on the part of P to divest itself of its S stock at the time of the merger. Thus, S stock is not deemed to have been issued upon the merger of T into S. See Rev.Rul. 69–91, 1969–1 C.B. 106. Further, no gain or loss is recognized to T upon the assumption by P and S of the liability for the convertible securities. See section 357 and section 1.368–2(b)(2) of the Income Tax Regulations. See also Rev.Rul. 73–257, 1973–1 C.B. 189.

Under section 1001 of the Code and section 1.1001–1(a) of the regulations, unless otherwise provided in subtitle A of the Code, the gain or loss realized from the exchange of property for other property differing materially either in kind or in extent is treated as income or as loss sustained.

Under section 354(a)(1) and (a)(2) of the Code no gain or loss shall be recognized if securities in a corporation a party to a reorganization are, in pursuance of the plan of reorganization, exchanged solely for securities in such corporation or in another corporation a party to the reorganization if the principal amount of any securities received does not exceed the principal amount of any such securities surrendered.

When the changes in the terms of outstanding securities are so material as to amount virtually to the issuance of a new security, the income tax consequences will follow as if the new security were actually issued. See Rev.Rul. 73–160, 1973–1 C.B. 365.

In this instant case, the convertible securities of T, an operating company, became the joint and several obligations of P and S, a holding company and an operating company, respectively, and became accompanied by a right of conversion into stock of P. The addition of P as an obligor, the change in conversion rights from the right to convert into the stock of an operating company, T, to the right to convert into the stock of a holding company, P, the increase in the interest rate, and the earlier maturity date, are, taken together, material changes that would otherwise constitute an exchange subject to recognition of gain or loss under section 1001 of the Code. However, section 354(a)(1) and (a)(2) applies to the transaction since it qualified as a reorganization under section 368(a)(1)(A) and (a)(2)(D) and since the securities deemed to be exchanged were of the same principal amount.

* * *

§ 11.11 SECTION 358 SUBSTITUTED BASIS FOR TARGET SHAREHOLDERS AND SECURITY HOLDERS

See 358.

Review Revenue Ruling 85–164, Sec. 2.2.D.

PART C. CONCEPTS RELATING TO TREATMENT OF BOOT UNDER § 356

§ 11.12 REORGANIZATION, A CONDITION TO § 356 TREATMENT

TURNBOW v. COMMISSIONER

Supreme Court of the United States, 1961.
368 U.S. 337, 82 S.Ct. 353, 7 L.Ed.2d 326.

Mr. Justice Whittaker delivered the opinion of the Court.

* * * Specifically the question presented is whether, in the absence of a "reorganization," as that term is defined in [§ 368(a)(1)(B)] and used in § [354], the gain on an exchange of stock for stock *plus cash* is to be recognized in full, or, because of the provisions of § [356(a)(1)], is to be recognized only to the extent of the cash.

The facts are simple and undisputed. Petitioner owned all of the 5,000 shares of outstanding stock of International Dairy Supply Company ("International"), a Nevada corporation. In 1952, petitioner transferred all of the International stock to Foremost Dairies, Inc. ("Foremost"), a New York corporation, in exchange for 82,375 shares (a minor percentage) of Foremost's common (voting) stock of the fair market value of $15 per share or $1,235,625 *plus cash* in the amount of $3,000,000. Petitioner's basis in the International stock was $50,000, and his expenses in connection with the transfer were $21,933.06. Petitioner therefore received for his International stock property and money of a value exceeding his basis and expenses by $4,163,691.94.

In his income tax return for 1952, petitioner treated his gain as recognizable only to the extent of the cash he received. The Commissioner concluded that the whole of the gain was recognizable and accordingly proposed a deficiency.

* * *

There is no dispute between the parties about the fact that the transaction involved was not a "reorganization," as defined in § [368(a)(1)(B)], because "the acquisition by" Foremost was not "in exchange *solely* for * * * its voting stock," but was partly for such stock and partly for cash * * *.

But petitioner contends that § [356(a)(1)] authorizes the indulging of assumptions, contrary to the actual facts, hypothetically to supply the missing elements that are necessary to make the exchange a "reorganization." * * * To the contrary, we think that an actual "reorganization," as defined in § [368] and used in § [354] must exist before § [356(a)(1)] can apply thereto.

Affirmed.

Mr. Justice Harlan concurs in the result.

Questions

What result in the transaction if the taxpayer had received 90% voting stock and 10% cash? Suppose he sold 10% of his stock for cash, and six months later exchanged the balance for the acquiror's voting stock?

§ 11.13 DETERMINATION OF WHETHER A DISTRIBUTION HAS THE "EFFECT" OF THE DISTRIBUTION OF A DIVIDEND

See § 368(a)(2).

A. THE SUPREME COURT DECISION

COMMISSIONER v. CLARK

Supreme Court of the United States, 1989.
489 U.S. 726, 109 S.Ct. 1455, 103 L.Ed.2d 753.

Justice Stevens delivered the opinion of the Court.

This is the third case in which the Government has asked us to decide that a shareholder's receipt of a cash payment in exchange for a portion of his stock was taxable as a dividend. In the two earlier cases, *Commissioner v. Estate of Bedford,* 325 U.S. 283, 65 S.Ct. 1157, 89 L.Ed. 1611 (1945), and *United States v. Davis,* 397 U.S. 301, 90 S.Ct. 1041, 25 L.Ed.2d 323 (1970), we agreed with the Government largely because the transactions involved redemptions of stock by single corporations that did not "result in a meaningful reduction of the shareholder's proportionate interest in the corporation." In the case we decide today, however, the taxpayer in an arm's-length transaction exchanged his interest in the acquired corporation for less than 1% of the stock of the acquiring corporation and a substantial cash payment. The taxpayer held no interest in the acquiring corporation prior to the reorganization. Viewing the exchange as a whole, we conclude that the cash payment is not appropriately characterized as a dividend. We accordingly agree with the Tax Court and with the Court of Appeals that the taxpayer is entitled to capital gains treatment of the cash payment.

I

In determining tax liability under the Internal Revenue Code of 1954, gain resulting from the sale or exchange of property is generally treated as capital gain, whereas the receipt of cash dividends is treated as ordinary income. The Code, however, imposes no current tax on certain stock-for-stock exchanges. In particular, § 354(a)(1) provides, subject to various limitations, for nonrecognition of gain resulting from the exchange of stock or securities solely for other stock or securities, provided that the exchange is pursuant to a plan of corporate reorganization and that the stock or securities are those of a party to the reorganization. 26 U.S.C. § 354(a)(1).

Under § 356(a)(1) of the Code, if such a stock-for-stock exchange is accompanied by additional consideration in the form of a cash payment or other property—something that tax practitioners refer to as "boot"—"then the gain, if any, to the recipient shall be recognized, but in an amount not in excess of the sum of such money and the fair market value of such other property." 26 U.S.C. § 356(a)(1). That is, if the shareholder receives boot, he or she must recognize the gain on the exchange up to the value of the boot. Boot is accordingly generally treated as a gain from the sale or exchange of property and is recognized in the current tax year.

Section 356(a)(2), which controls the decision in this case, creates an exception to that general rule. It provided in 1979:

> "If an exchange is described in paragraph (1) but has the effect of the distribution of a dividend, then there shall be treated as a dividend to each distributee such an amount of the gain recognized under paragraph (1) as is not in excess of his ratable share of the undistributed earnings and profits of the corporation accumulated after February 28, 1913. The remainder, if any, of the gain recognized under paragraph (1) shall be treated as gain from the exchange of property." 26 U.S.C. § 356(a)(2) (1976 ed.).

Thus, if the "exchange * * * has the effect of the distribution of a dividend," the boot must be treated as a dividend and is therefore appropriately taxed as ordinary income to the extent that gain is realized. In contrast, if the exchange does not have "the effect of the distribution of a dividend," the boot must be treated as a payment in exchange for property and, insofar as gain is realized, accorded capital gains treatment. The question in this case is thus whether the exchange between the taxpayer and the acquiring corporation had "the effect of the distribution of a dividend" within the meaning of § 356(a)(2).

The relevant facts are easily summarized. For approximately 15 years prior to April 1979, the taxpayer was the president of Basin Surveys, Inc. (Basin). In January 1978, he became sole shareholder in Basin, a company in which he had invested approximately $85,000. The corporation operated a successful business providing various technical services to the petroleum industry. In 1978, N.L. Industries, Inc. (NL), a publicly owned corporation engaged in the manufacture and supply of

§ 11.13 "EFFECT" OF DISTRIBUTION OF A DIVIDEND 455

petroleum equipment and services, initiated negotiations with the taxpayer regarding the possible acquisition of Basin. On April 3, 1979, after months of negotiations, the taxpayer and NL entered into a contract.

The agreement provided for a "triangular merger," whereby Basin was merged into a wholly owned subsidiary of NL. In exchange for transferring all of the outstanding shares in Basin to NL's subsidiary, the taxpayer elected to receive 300,000 shares of NL common stock and cash boot of $3,250,000, passing up an alternative offer of 425,000 shares of NL common stock. The 300,000 shares of NL issued to the taxpayer amounted to approximately 0.92% of the outstanding common shares of NL. If the taxpayer had instead accepted the pure stock-for-stock offer, he would have held approximately 1.3% of the outstanding common shares. The Commissioner and the taxpayer agree that the merger at issue qualifies as a reorganization under §§ 368(a)(1)(A) and (a)(2)(D).

Respondents filed a joint federal income tax return for 1979. As required by § 356(a)(1), they reported the cash boot as taxable gain. In calculating the tax owed, respondents characterized the payment as long-term capital gain. The Commissioner on audit disagreed with this characterization. In his view, the payment had "the effect of the distribution of a dividend" and was thus taxable as ordinary income up to $2,319,611, the amount of Basin's accumulated earnings and profits at the time of the merger. The Commissioner assessed a deficiency of $972,504.74.

Respondents petitioned for review in the Tax Court, which, in a reviewed decision, held in their favor. 86 T.C. 138 (1986). The court started from the premise that the question whether the boot payment had "the effect of the distribution of a dividend" turns on the choice between "two judicially articulated tests." *Id.*, at 140. Under the test advocated by the Commissioner and given voice in *Shimberg v. United States*, 577 F.2d 283 (CA5 1978), cert. denied, 439 U.S. 1115, 99 S.Ct. 1019, 59 L.Ed.2d 73 (1979), the boot payment is treated as though it were made in a hypothetical redemption by the acquired corporation (Basin) immediately *prior* to the reorganization. Under this test, the cash payment received by the taxpayer indisputably would have been treated as a dividend. [See § 302 and Chapter 5.] The second test, urged by the taxpayer and finding support in *Wright v. United States*, 482 F.2d 600 (CA8 1973), proposes an alternative hypothetical redemption. Rather than concentrating on the taxpayer's prereorganization interest in the acquired corporation, this test requires that one imagine a pure stock-for-stock exchange, followed immediately by a *post*-reorganization redemption of a portion of the taxpayer's shares in the acquiring corporation (NL) in return for a payment in an amount equal to the boot. Under § 302 of the Code, which defines when a redemption of stock should be treated as a distribution of dividend, NL's redemption of 125,000 shares of its stock from the taxpayer in exchange for the $3,250,000 boot payment would have been treated as capital gain. [See § 302(b)(2) and Chapter 5.]

The Tax Court rejected the prereorganization test favored by the Commissioner because it considered it improper "to view the cash payment as an isolated event totally separate from the reorganization." 86 T.C., at 151. Indeed, it suggested that this test requires that courts make the "determination of dividend equivalency fantasizing that the reorganization does not exist." The court then acknowledged that a similar criticism could be made of the taxpayer's contention that the cash payment should be viewed as a postreorganization redemption. It concluded, however, that since it was perfectly clear that the cash payment would not have taken place without the reorganization, it was better to treat the boot "as the equivalent of a redemption *in the course of implementing the reorganization*," than "as having occurred *prior to and separate from the reorganization*." Id., at 152 (emphasis in original).

The Court of Appeals for the Fourth Circuit affirmed. 828 F.2d 221 (1987). Like the Tax Court, it concluded that although "[s]ection 302 does not explicitly apply in the reorganization context," id., at 223, and although § 302 differs from § 356 in important respects, id., at 224, it nonetheless provides "the appropriate test for determining whether boot is ordinary income or a capital gain," id., at 223. Thus, as explicated in § 302(b)(2), if the taxpayer relinquished more than 20% of his corporate control and retained less than 50% of the voting shares after the distribution, the boot would be treated as capital gain. However, as the Court of Appeals recognized, "[b]ecause § 302 was designed to deal with a stock redemption by a single corporation, rather than a reorganization involving two companies, the section does not indicate which corporation [the taxpayer] lost interest in." Thus, like the Tax Court, the Court of Appeals was left to consider whether the hypothetical redemption should be treated as a prereorganization distribution coming from the acquired corporation or as a postreorganization distribution coming from the acquiring corporation. It concluded:

> "Based on the language and legislative history of § 356, the change-in-ownership principle of § 302, and the need to review the reorganization as an integrated transaction, we conclude that the boot should be characterized as a post-reorganization stock redemption by N.L. that affected [the taxpayer's] interest in the new corporation. Because this redemption reduced [the taxpayer's] N.L. holdings by more than 20%, the boot should be taxed as a capital gain." Id., at 224–225.

This decision by the Court of Appeals for the Fourth Circuit is in conflict with the decision of the Fifth Circuit in *Shimberg v. United States,* 577 F.2d 283 (1978), in two important respects. In *Shimberg,* the court concluded that it was inappropriate to apply stock redemption principles in reorganization cases "on a wholesale basis." In addition, the court adopted the prereorganization test, holding that "§ 356(a)(2) requires a determination of whether the distribution would have been taxed as a dividend if made prior to the reorganization or if no reorganization had occurred."

To resolve this conflict on a question of importance to the administration of the federal tax laws, we granted certiorari.

II

We agree with the Tax Court and the Court of Appeals for the Fourth Circuit that the question under § 356(a)(2) whether an "exchange * * * has the effect of the distribution of a dividend" should be answered by examining the effect of the exchange as a whole. We think the language and history of the statute, as well as a commonsense understanding of the economic substance of the transaction at issue, support this approach.

The language of § 356(a) strongly supports our understanding that the transaction should be treated as an integrated whole. Section 356(a)(2) asks whether "*an exchange* is described in paragraph (1)" that "has the effect of the distribution of a dividend." (Emphasis supplied.) The statute does not provide that boot shall be treated as a dividend if its payment has the effect of the distribution of a dividend. Rather, the inquiry turns on whether the "exchange" has that effect. Moreover, paragraph (1), in turn, looks to whether "the property received in *the exchange* consists not only of property permitted by section 354 or 355 to be received without the recognition of gain but also of other property or money." (Emphasis supplied.) Again, the statute plainly refers to one integrated transaction and, again, makes clear that we are to look to the character of the exchange as a whole and not simply its component parts. Finally, it is significant that § 356 expressly limits the extent to which boot may be taxed to the amount of gain realized in the reorganization. This limitation suggests that Congress intended that boot not be treated in isolation from the overall reorganization.

Our reading of the statute as requiring that the transaction be treated as a unified whole is reinforced by the well-established "step-transaction" doctrine, a doctrine that the Government has applied in related contexts. * * *

Viewing the exchange in this case as an integrated whole, we are unable to accept the Commissioner's prereorganization analogy. The analogy severs the payment of boot from the context of the reorganization. Indeed, only by straining to abstract the payment of boot from the context of the overall exchange, and thus imagining that Basin made a distribution to the taxpayer independently of NL's planned acquisition, can we reach the rather counterintuitive conclusion urged by the Commissioner—that the taxpayer suffered no meaningful reduction in his ownership interest as a result of the cash payment. We conclude that such a limited view of the transaction is plainly inconsistent with the statute's direction that we look to the effect of the entire exchange.

* * *

The postreorganization approach adopted by the Tax Court and the Court of Appeals is, in our view, preferable to the Commissioner's approach. Most significantly, this approach does a far better job of treating the payment of boot as a component of the overall exchange. Unlike the pre-reorganization view, this approach acknowledges that there would have been no cash payment absent the exchange and also that, by accepting the cash payment, the taxpayer experienced a meaningful reduction in his potential ownership interest.

Once the postreorganization approach is adopted, the result in this case is pellucidly clear. Section 302(a) of the Code provides that if a redemption fits within any one of the four categories set out in § 302(b), the redemption "shall be treated as a distribution in part or full payment in exchange for the stock," and thus not regarded as a dividend. As the Tax Court and the Court of Appeals correctly determined, the hypothetical postreorganization redemption by NL of a portion of the taxpayer's shares satisfies at least one of the subsections of § 302(b). In particular, the safe harbor provisions of subsection (b)(2) provide that redemptions in which the taxpayer relinquishes more than 20% of his or her share of the corporation's voting stock and retains less than 50% of the voting stock after the redemption shall not be treated as distributions of a dividend. Here, we treat the transaction as though NL redeemed 125,000 shares of its common stock (*i.e.*, the number of shares of NL common stock forgone in favor of the boot) in return for a cash payment to the taxpayer of $3,250,000 (*i.e.*, the amount of the boot). As a result of this redemption, the taxpayer's interest in NL was reduced from 1.3% of the outstanding common stock to 0.9%. Thus, the taxpayer relinquished approximately 29% of his interest in NL and retained less than a 1% voting interest in the corporation after the transaction, easily satisfying the "substantially disproportionate" standards of § 302(b)(2). We accordingly conclude that the boot payment did not have the effect of a dividend and that the payment was properly treated as capital gain.

* * *

Note and Questions

1. In Rev.Rul. 74–515, 1974–2 C.B. 118, which was issued before the *Clark* decision, the Service said that it would apply § 302 principles in making the dividend determination under § 356(a)(2). *Clark* confirms this approach and sets forth the methodology for applying § 302 principles. State precisely the holding in *Clark*.

2. Individuals A and B each own 50% of the stock of target corporation (TC). Both have a basis of $10K for their stock. Acquiring corporation (AC) acquires TC in a merger by issuing $100K of AC stock and paying $100K in cash. The $100K of AC stock amounts to 1% of the outstanding AC stock after the merger. What is the treatment of the $100K boot in each of the following cases?

    a. A and B each receive $50K of the stock and $50K of cash?

    b. A receives $100K of AC stock, and B receives $100K of cash?

    c. A receives $75K of cash and $25K of AC stock, and B receives $75K of AC stock and $25K of cash?

3. The facts are the same as in Question 2, except the $100K of AC stock amounts to 50% of the outstanding stock of AC after the merger. Same questions as in 2a–2c.

B. THE SERVICE'S POSITION

REVENUE RULING 93–61, IRB 1993–36
10 (Oct. 4, 1993)

This revenue ruling revokes Rev.Rul. 75–83, 1975–1 C.B. 112.

LAW AND ANALYSIS

Section 354(a) of the Internal Revenue Code provides that no gain or loss shall be recognized if stock or securities in a corporation a party to a reorganization are exchanged solely for stock or securities in such corporation or in another corporation a party to the reorganization. If section 354 would apply to the exchange except for the receipt of money or property other than stock or securities in a corporate party to the reorganization, referred to as boot, section 356(a)(1) provides that the recipient shall recognize gain, but in an amount not in excess of the sum of the money and the fair market value of the other property. Under section 356(a)(2), if an exchange described in section 356(a)(1) has the effect of the distribution of a dividend, the shareholder must treat the gain recognized on the exchange as a dividend to the extent of the distributee's ratable share of the undistributed earnings and profits of the corporation accumulated after February 28, 1913.

In Rev.Rul. 75–83, X corporation merged into Y corporation in a reorganization under section 368(a)(1)(A) of the Code. The sole shareholder of X corporation received shares of Y corporation stock and a note, which was treated as boot under section 356(a)(1). To determine whether the exchange had the effect of the distribution of a dividend under section 356(a)(2), the Service treated the distribution as though it were made by the acquired corporation (X) and not the acquiring corporation (Y). Therefore, the Service concluded that the exchange had the effect of a dividend under section 356(a)(2).

In *Commissioner v. Clark*, 489 U.S. 726 (1989), 1989–2 C.B. 68, the sole shareholder of a target corporation exchanged his target stock for stock of an acquiring corporation and cash. The Supreme Court applied the dividend equivalency rules for redemptions contained in section 302 of the Code to determine whether the boot payment had the effect of a dividend distribution under section 356(a)(2). At issue was whether the boot payment should be treated as if it were made (i) by the target corporation in a hypothetical section 302 redemption of a portion of the shareholder's target stock prior to and separate from the reorganization exchange, or (ii) by the acquiring corporation in a hypothetical section 302 redemption of the acquiring stock that the shareholder would have received in the reorganization exchange if there had been no boot distribution. The Court concluded that the treatment of a boot distribution is determined "by examining the effect of the exchange as a whole,"

489 U.S. 726, 737, and held that the second approach better tested the effect of the payment of boot as a component in the overall exchange.

HOLDING

In an acquisitive reorganization, the determination of whether boot is treated as a dividend distribution under section 356(a)(2) of the Code is made by comparing the interest the shareholder actually received in the acquiring corporation in the reorganization exchange with the interest the shareholder would have received in the acquiring corporation if solely stock had been received.

EFFECT ON OTHER RULINGS

Rev.Rul. 75–83 is revoked.

* * *

C. APPLICATION OF § 318 ATTRIBUTION RULES UNDER § 356(a)(2)

HOUSE CONFERENCE REPORT, TO THE TAX EQUITY AND FISCAL RESPONSIBILITY ACT OF 1982

544 (1982).

PRESENT LAW

To determine whether a shareholder is entitled to sale or exchange treatment on a stock redemption, stock held by related parties is attributed to the shareholder in determining whether the shareholder's interest in the corporation was terminated or significantly reduced. [*See* §§ 302(c) and 318.] The attribution rules do not apply to some transactions that are economically equivalent to straight stock redemptions and that offer an equivalent opportunity to bail out earnings. For example, * * * a shareholder exchanging stock in a reorganization for property other than stock or securities may have dividend consequences if the transaction has the effect of the distribution of a dividend. For this purpose, attribution rules do not apply.

* * *

The conference agreement extends the ownership attribution rules * * * in determining whether the receipt of property in a reorganization has the effect of a dividend. * * * [*See* § 356(a)(2).]

D. CASH FOR FRACTIONAL SHARES

REVENUE PROCEDURE 77–41

1977–2 C.B. 574.

Rev.Rul. 77–37, 1977–2 C.B. 568, contains operating rules for the issuance of advance rulings as to matters within the jurisdiction of the Reorganization Branch of the Internal Revenue Service. Rev.Proc. 77–37 is amplified to include the following:

A ruling will usually be issued under section 302(a) of the Code that cash to be distributed to shareholders in lieu of fractional share interests arising in corporate reorganizations, stock splits, stock dividends, conversion of convertible stocks, and other similar transactions will be treated as having been received in part or full payment in exchange for the stock redeemed if the cash distribution is undertaken solely for the purpose of saving the corporation the expense and inconvenience of issuing and transferring fractional shares, and is not separately bargained-for consideration. The purpose of the transaction giving rise to the fractional share interests, the maximum amount of cash that may be received by any one shareholder, and the percentage of the total consideration that will be cash are among the factors that will be considered in determining whether a ruling is to be issued.

Rev.Proc. 73–35, 1973–2 C.B. 490, calls for the submission of certain information with requests for rulings under section 302 of the Code. This information need not be supplied with requests for rulings with respect to redemptions of fractional share interests. However, Rev.Proc. 72–3, 1972–1 C.B. 698, and section 601.201 of the Statement of Procedural Rules (26 CFR 601.201 (1977)), which contain the procedures to be followed for the issuance of ruling letters, should be complied with.

Rev.Proc. 77–37 is amplified and Rev.Proc. 73–35 is modified.

E. NO DIVIDEND WHERE BOOT PAID IN RESPECT OF SECURITIES

REVENUE RULING 71–427

1971–2 C.B. 183.

The shareholders of X, a solvent corporation, approved a plan of reorganization in order to eliminate outstanding debt in the form of debentures, which qualified as securities under section 354(a)(1) of the Code. Pursuant to the plan, the debenture holders exchanged their securities for common stock of X and cash in a transaction which qualified as a reorganization (recapitalization) under section 368(a)(1)(E) of the Code.

* * * [T]he receipt of the cash payment in addition to the stock of X results in the recognition of gain under section 356(a) of the Code to the former holders of the debentures who realized a gain, but in an amount not in excess of the cash received. Section 356(a)(2) of the Code providing for dividend treatment is not applicable to the recognized gain since the distributees received the cash payment as creditors, and not as shareholders of X. Thus, any recognized gain will be treated as a gain from the exchange of property under section 356 of the Code. However, losses, if any, from the exchange described above, will not be recognized pursuant to section 356(c) of the Code.

F. DETERMINATION OF E & P UNDER § 356(a)(2)

Which corporation's E & P is counted for purposes of § 356(a)(2)? Is it the target's? The acquiror's? Or both? Suppose there is a (D) reorganization with boot? The Tax Court's position is that only the transferor's E & P is considered. *See American Manufacturing Co. v. Commissioner,* 55 T.C. 204 (1970) and *Atlas Tool Co. v. Commissioner,* 70 T.C. 86 (1978) (both of which dealt with (D) reorganizations). The Fifth Circuit has held that in a (D) reorganization the E & P of both the distributing and the controlled corporations are counted for purposes of § 356(a)(2). *See Davant* in Chapter 14.

PART D. CONCEPTS RELATING TO TREATMENT OF TARGET UNDER §§ 361 AND 357

§ 11.14 TREATMENT OF TARGET CORPORATION UPON RECEIPT AND DISTRIBUTION OF STOCK, SECURITIES, AND BOOT

See § 351.

TECHNICAL CORRECTIONS PROVISIONS OF HOUSE MISCELLANEOUS REVENUE BILL OF 1988

371–373 (1988).

Present Law

The Tax Reform Act of 1984 generally required that all property received by a corporation in a "C" reorganization be distributed. In addition, that Act provided that a corporation must recognize gain on the distribution of appreciated property to its shareholders in a nonliquidating distribution. The 1986 Act made a series of amendments to the reorganization provisions attempting to conform those provisions with changes made by the 1984 Act. However, numerous technical problems with the 1986 amendments have arisen. The bill responds to these technical problems with a complete revision of the 1986 amendments.

Explanation of Provision

Treatment of reorganization exchange.—The bill restores the provisions of section 361, relating to the nonrecognition treatment of an exchange pursuant to a plan of reorganization, as in effect prior to the amendments made by the 1986 Act. Thus, as under prior law, gain or loss will generally not be recognized to a corporation which exchanges property, in pursuance of the plan of reorganization, for stock and securities in another corporation a party to the reorganization. [*See* § 361(a).] However, as under prior law, gain will be recognized to the extent the corporation receives property other than such stock or securities and does not distribute the other property pursuant to the plan of reorganization.[96] [See § 361(b).]

The bill amends prior law by providing that transfers of property to creditors in satisfaction of the corporation's indebtedness in connection with the reorganization are treated as distributions pursuant to the plan of reorganization for this purpose.[97] [See § 361(b)(3).] The Secretary of the Treasury may prescribe regulations necessary to prevent tax avoidance by reason of this provision. This amendment is not intended to change in any way the definition of a reorganization within the meaning of section 368.

Treatment of distributions in reorganizations.—The bill also conforms the treatment of distributions of property by a corporation to its shareholders in pursuance of a plan of reorganization to the treatment of nonliquidating distributions (under section 311). Under the bill, the distributing corporation generally will recognize gain, but not loss, on the distribution of property in pursuance of the plan of reorganization. [See § 361(c).] However, no gain will be recognized on the distribution of "qualified property". [See § 361(c)(2)(B).] For this purpose, "qualified property" means (1) stock (or rights to acquire stock) in, or the obligation of, the distributing corporation and (2) stock (or rights to acquire stock) in, or the obligation of, another corporation which is a party to the reorganization and which were received by the distributing corporation in the exchange.[98] [See § 361(c)(2)(B).] The bill also provides that the transfer of qualified property by a corporation to its creditors in satisfaction of indebtedness is treated as a distribution pursuant to the plan of reorganization.[99] [See § 361(c)(3).]

Basis.—The bill clarifies that the basis of property received in an exchange to which section 361 applies, other than stock or securities in another corporation a party to the reorganization, is the fair market value of the property at the time of the transaction (pursuant to section 358(a)(2)). [See § 358(f).] Thus the distributing corporation will recognize only post-acquisition gain on any taxable disposition of such property received pursuant to the plan of reorganization. Of course, the other corporation will recognize gain or loss on the transfer of its property under the usual tax principles governing the recognition of gain or loss.

§ 11.15 TREATMENT OF LIABILITIES

A. INTRODUCTION

In response to the *Hendler* case, [see Sec. 2.3.A.] Congress (1) provided in § 357(a) that liabilities are to be disregarded in a § 361

---

96. This could occur, for example, where liabilities are assumed in a transaction to which section 357(b) or (c) applies.

97. This overrules the holding in *Minnesota Tea Company v. Helvering*, 302 U.S. 609 (1938).

98. For analysis that acquiring corporation voting stock held by the acquired corporation in a Type C reorganization is transferred to the acquiring corporation in exchange for the same stock, see Rev.Rul. 78-47, 1978-1 C.B. 113.

99. These amendments are not intended to affect the treatment of any income from the discharge of indebtedness arising in connection with a corporate reorganization.

transaction, and (2) provided in the definition of the (C) reorganization that the transfer of the target's liabilities to the acquiror is to be disregarded in determining whether the acquisition is "solely for voting stock." Section 357(a) does not apply, however, if the transfer of the liabilities is for tax avoidance purposes (*see* § 357(b)) or if the liabilities exceed basis in a (D) reorganization to which § 361 applies (*see* § 357(c)(1)(B)). Section 1.368–2(d)(1) says that, although an assumption of a target's liabilities will not prevent the transaction from qualifying as a (C), an assumption may in some cases "so alter the character of the transaction as to place the transaction outside the purposes and assumptions of the reorganization provisions." *See Wortham Machinery Co., infra.*

B. DISCHARGE OF INTERCORPORATE DEBT IN AN (A) REORGANIZATION

REVENUE RULING 72–464
1972–2 C.B. 214.

Advice has been requested whether, under the circumstances described below, the acquisition of assets in exchange for stock and assumption of liabilities pursuant to a plan of reorganization under section 368(a)(1)(A) of the Internal Revenue Code of 1954 results in the recognition of gain to either the acquired or the acquiring corporation.

In a prior transaction, unrelated to the present statutory merger, X corporation purchased from certain banks, at a cost of $20,000, outstanding notes of Y corporation in the unpaid face amount of $25,000. Y subsequently merged with and into X in a transaction qualifying as a reorganization under section 368(a)(1)(A) of the Code. In the merger, X transferred solely its stock. X received all of Y's assets and assumed all of Y's liabilities. The liabilities assumed included Y's obligation to pay X the $25,000 for the Y notes, which was also their fair market value.

* * *

The statutory merger of Y into X is a reorganization within the meaning of section 368(a)(1)(A) of the Code. X and Y are each a party to this reorganization within the meaning of section 368(b) of the Code.

The question presented is whether Y should be viewed as transferring a portion of its assets to X in satisfaction of its indebtedness on the notes. And, if so viewed, whether any gain or loss realized by X or Y on the transaction would fall outside of the nonrecognition provisions of sections 361(a) and 1032(a) of the Code.

* * *

[T]he extinguishment of the debt in the instant case is incident to the statutory merger because the termination of the debtor-creditor relationship was merely a consequence of X and Y achieving a readjustment of their corporate structures. Accordingly, sections 357(a) and

361(a) of the Code prevent Y from recognizing any gain or loss on the satisfaction of its indebtedness. * * *

However, X, the acquiring corporation, will recognize gain on the satisfaction of the indebtedness of Y purchased at market discount. Such gain will be $5,000, the difference between the adjusted basis of the notes in the hands of X and the face amount of the notes. * * *

In addition, the basis of the assets received in satisfaction of the indebtedness will be determined under section 362(b) of the Code so that such property takes a carryover basis equal to the transferor's basis. * * *

PART E. CONCEPTS RELATING TO TREATMENT OF ACQUIROR

§ 11.16 INCREASE BASIS BY AMOUNT OF TRANSFEROR'S GAIN RECOGNIZED, NOT ITS SHAREHOLDERS' GAIN RECOGNIZED

SCHWEITZER & CONRAD, INC. v. COMMISSIONER

Tax Court of the United States, 1940.
41 B.T.A. 533.

Mellott: [The petitioner, the acquiring corporation, acquired the assets of Illinois, the target, in a (C) reorganization in which Illinois shareholders recognized gain. The issue was whether the petitioner could, under the predecessor of § 362(b), increase the basis of Illinois' assets by the amount of such gain.]

Section 113(a)(7) [now § 362(b)] of the Revenue Act of 1932, *supra*, provides that the basis of the transferee corporation "shall be the same as it would be in the hands of the transferor, increased in the amount of gain or decreased in the amount of loss recognized to the transferor * * *." Petitioner urges that the word "transferor" should be construed to mean "transferor *or its stockholders*", and has attempted to show by reference to the legislative history of the section that Congress intended, when it used the word "transferor", to cover both the transferor corporation and its stockholders.

* * *

* * * Nonrecognition of gain to the transferor corporation and nonrecognition of gain to both the transferor or transferee corporations are two different things. When the reorganization provisions of the statute provide for the nonrecognition of gain to the transferor, they usually provide a method by which the Government will realize a tax from the transferee. In other words, these provisions merely result in a postponement or deferment of the tax, and not its forfeiture by the Government. Provisions relating to the basis of the transferee, such as section 113(a)(7) [now § 362(b)], must be read in this light; and in providing that the basis of the transferee is to be the basis in the hands

of the transferor it is apparent that Congress intended that the transferee should take the assets subject to the income tax which might properly have been assessed to the transferor corporation but for the provisions of section 112(d)(1) [now § 361].

* * *

Problems

Target corporation, *TC*, has assets with a basis of $10K and a fair market value of $100K. *TC*'s shareholder, *A*, has a basis of $50K for the stock of *TC*. Pursuant to the merger of *TC* into *AC*, *A* receives $75K of *AC* stock and $25K of cash. What is the tax treatment to the parties, and, specifically, what is *AC*'s basis for *TC*'s assets?

PART F. CONCEPTS RELATING TO IMPACT OF STOCK DIVIDENDS AND § 306 PREFERRED STOCK IN REORGANIZATIONS

§ 11.17 IMPACT OF § 305 IN THE CONTEXT OF REORGANIZATIONS

A. IN GENERAL

Under § 305, which is examined generally in Chapter 6, a distribution of a stock dividend in certain circumstances gives rise to dividend treatment. This dividend treatment may arise in the context of reorganizations, particularly if preferred stock is issued with a redemption premium. The rulings in the following section illustrate this issue in the context of acquisitive reorganizations. The same principles apply to each form of acquisitive reorganization. *See* Chapter 15. The issue is also addressed for recapitalizations in Chapter 12.

B. ILLUSTRATION OF IMPACT OF § 305 IN ACQUISITIVE REORGANIZATIONS

1. Is Issuance of Acquiring Corporation Preferred: A § 305 Distribution?

REVENUE RULING 82–158
1982–2 C.B. 77.

Issue

Whether the exchange of *T* common stock for *P* preferred stock incident to the acquisition of *T* will be treated as a distribution of property to which section 301 of the Internal Revenue Code applies by reason of the application of section 305(b) or (c).

FACTS

T is a publicly held corporation that had a single class of common stock outstanding. In a transaction intended to qualify as a reorganization under sections 368(a)(1)(A) and (a)(2)(D), P, an unrelated holding company, acquired the assets of T by having T merge into S, a wholly owned subsidiary of P. The shareholders of T received shares of a new class of P preferred stock in exchange for their shares of T common stock. Shareholders of T who elected to receive cash for their stock, or who dissented to the merger, received from P a cash payment equal to the fair market value of their shares. The merger was contingent upon no more than 20 percent of the T stock being surrendered for cash.

LAW AND ANALYSIS

Section 305(a) of the Code and the exceptions under sections 305(b) and (c) apply only to distributions made by a corporation to its shareholders with respect to its stock. Therefore, any distribution by a corporation, either actual or constructive, that is not made with respect to its stock will not be within the purview of section 305. The issuance of P preferred stock to the shareholders of T cannot be viewed as a distribution with respect to its (P's) stock.

* * *

2. Redeemable Preferred Issued in a (B) Reorganization

The following ruling deals with the treatment of redemption premiums on preferred stock under § 305(c). Although § 305(c) has been amended to make it parallel to the original issue discount provisions, the principles discussed in the ruling should still apply. However, under the amended § 305(c), a premium is reasonable only if it does not exceed the de minimis rule of § 1273(a)(3). *See* § 305(c)(1) and Chapter 6.

REVENUE RULING 81-190
1981-2 C.B. 84.

ISSUE

Is the redemption premium reasonable, for purposes of section 305(b)(4) and (c) of the Internal Revenue Code, when a class of stock created for issuance in a reorganization between two widely held corporations is intended to have a 10 percent [now a de minimis], redemption premium, but as a result of an unanticipated market fluctuation it actually has a redemption premium in excess of 10 percent of the issue price?

* * *

In this situation, there was a redemption premium of only 10 percent at the time the terms of reorganization were agreed to by the managements of X and Y and at the time the prospectus was submitted to the S.E.C. Moreover, it was reasonably anticipated by an independent advisor possessing relevant expertise that the redemption premium at the time of issue would not exceed 10 percent of the issue price of the preferred stock. The increase in the redemption premium to 21 percent arose from an event that was found not to have been reasonably foreseeable. This event caused the fair market value of the X preferred stock to be less on the date of exchange than it was on the date the terms for the transaction were agreed to.

* * * The essential facts are that here: (i) when the agreement was made, a redemption premium in excess of 10 percent was not bargained for, it was not intended that the redemption premium exceed the amount of a typical call premium, and it was not reasonably foreseeable that it would exceed such amount; and (ii) subsequently, when the size of the redemption premium was foreseeable, business constraints made it no longer possible for the terms of the stock to be renegotiated.

HOLDING

The difference between the redemption price and issue price of the X preferred stock is a reasonable redemption premium. Therefore, the redemption premium will not be treated as a distribution of property to which section 301 of the Code applies by virtue of the application of section 305(b)(4) and (c).

§ 11.18 IMPACT OF § 306 IN THE CONTEXT OF REORGANIZATIONS

A. IN GENERAL

Under § 306, which is discussed in Chapter 6, preferred stock that does not give rise to dividend treatment under § 305, may produce ordinary income upon sale. Section 306(c), which defines § 306 stock, provides in § 306(c)(1)(B) that in certain cases preferred stock issued in a reorganization may be treated as § 306 stock. The materials in this section introduce this topic and illustrate the application of the rules in acquisitive reorganizations. The principles are the same for each form of acquisitive reorganization. *See* Chapter 15. This issue is also addressed in the context of recapitalizations and mere changes in form in Chapter 12 and divisive (D) reorganizations under § 355 in Chapter 13.

B. INTRODUCTION TO § 306(c)(1)(B)

Section 306(c)(1)(B) provides that § 306 stock includes stock that is not common stock that is received tax free in a reorganization or a § 355 distribution, "but only to the extent that either the effect of the transaction was substantially the same as the receipt of a stock dividend, or the stock was received in exchange for section 306 stock." The attribution rules of § 318 apply in determining whether the effect of the transaction is substantially the same as the receipt of a stock dividend. *See* § 306(c)(4).

Section 1.306–3(d) sets out a cash substitution test for determining whether preferred stock issued in a reorganization or § 355 distribution is § 306 stock. Section 306 stock arises "if cash received in lieu of [the preferred] would have been a dividend under section 356(a)(2) or would have been treated as a distribution to which section 301 applies by virtue of section 356(b) or section 302(d)." The regulations give the following examples of this provision:

Example (1). Corporation A, having only common stock outstanding, is merged in a statutory merger (qualifying as a reorganization under section 368(a)) with Corporation B. Pursuant to such merger, the shareholders of Corporation A received both common and preferred stock in Corporation B. The preferred stock received by such shareholders is section 306 stock.

Example (2). X and Y each own one-half of the 2,000 outstanding shares of preferred stock and one-half of the 2,000 outstanding shares of common stock of Corporation C. Pursuant to a reorganization within the meaning of section 368(a)(1)(E) (recapitalization) each shareholder exchanges his preferred stock for preferred stock of a new issue which is not substantially different from the preferred stock previously held. Unless the preferred stock exchanged was itself section 306 stock the preferred stock received is not section 306 stock.

The first example does not give any reasons for its conclusion that the preferred received in the merger is § 306 stock. This regulation may be based on the automatic dividend rule of the *Bedford* case and Rev.Rul. 56–220, both of which have been rejected by *Clark*.

C. ILLUSTRATION OF IMPACT OF § 306(c)(1)(B) IN AN ACQUISITIVE REORGANIZATION

1. ISSUANCE OF ACQUIRING CORPORATION'S PREFERRED FOR SUBSTANTIALLY SIMILAR TARGET PREFERRED

REVENUE RULING 88–100
1988–2 C.B. 46.

ISSUE

If preferred stock of an acquired corporation that is not "section 306 stock" is exchanged in an acquisitive reorganization for an acquiring corporation's preferred stock of equal value and with terms not substantially different, is the preferred stock issued "section 306 stock" within the meaning of section 306(c)(1)(B) of the Internal Revenue Code?

FACTS

X, a publicly held corporation, had outstanding a single class of common stock. Y, also a publicly held corporation, had outstanding for many years one class of common stock and one class of preferred stock. None of the Y preferred stock was "section 306 stock" within the meaning of section 306(c) of the Code. A, an individual, owned ten shares of Y common stock and ten shares of Y preferred stock, which A had held for at least ten years. A owned no X stock.

Y merged into X in a transaction qualifying as a reorganization under section 368(a)(1)(A) of the Code. Each share of Y common stock was exchanged for one share of X common stock of equal value. Each share of Y preferred stock was exchanged for one share of newly issued X preferred stock of equal value. The terms of the new X preferred stock were not substantially different from those of the Y preferred stock. X had no plan to redeem its newly issued preferred stock. A realized gain on the exchange. Y had sufficient earnings and profits so that if Y had distributed an amount of cash equal to the value of the X preferred stock actually exchanged in the transaction, the cash distribution would have been taxed as a dividend.

LAW AND ANALYSIS

Section 306(c)(1)(B) of the Code provides that the term "section 306 stock" includes stock which is not common stock and which was received pursuant to a tax-free reorganization, but only to the extent that either the effect of the transaction was substantially the same as the receipt of a stock dividend, or the stock was received in exchange for "section 306 stock."

Section 1.306–3(d) of the Income Tax Regulations provides that, ordinarily, "section 306 stock" includes stock which is not common stock received in pursuance of a plan of reorganization if cash received in lieu of such stock would have been treated as a dividend under section 356(a)(2) of the Code or would have been treated as a distribution to which section 301 applies by virtue of section 356(b) or section 302(d).

An exception to the application of the "cash in lieu of" test is provided by Example (2) of section 1.306–3(d) of the regulations ("Example (2)"). Example (2) deals with a recapitalization under section 368(a)(1)(E) of the Code in which preferred stock was exchanged for preferred stock of a new issue. The new stock was not substantially different from the preferred stock previously held. Example (2) states that unless the preferred stock exchange was itself "section 306 stock" the preferred stock received is not "section 306 stock."

* * *

In the instant situation, the issuance of the X preferred stock in exchange for Y preferred stock of equal value and with terms not substantially different does not have the effect of the distribution of the earnings and profits of X or Y. The receipt of X preferred stock left the former Y preferred shareholders in no better position to convert corporate earnings into capital gains on a disposition of the stock than they had been in before. As the Y preferred stock was not "section 306 stock," the X preferred stock is not "section 306 stock," pursuant to the exception to the "cash in lieu of" test provided by Example (2).

* * *

2. Impact of § 306(b)(4) on § 306(c)(1)(B) Determination: Widely Held Target

REVENUE RULING 89-63
1989-1 C.B. 90.

* * *

LAW AND ANALYSIS

Section 306(a) of the Code concerns the treatment of the amount realized on the disposition or redemption of section 306 stock (as defined in section 306(c)). Section 306(b)(4) provides in part that section 306(a) shall not apply if it is established to the satisfaction of the Secretary that the distribution and the disposition or redemption of the section 306 stock was not in pursuance of a plan having as one of its principal purposes the avoidance of federal income tax.

In Rev.Rul. 56-116, two widely held corporations, X and Y, were merged in a reorganization qualifying under section 368(a)(1)(A) of the Code. In the merger, both preferred and common stock of X were issued in exchange for the common stock of Y. There was a business reason for issuing both preferred and common stock of X in exchange for the Y common stock. The management of X had no intention of redeeming any of the preferred stock issued in connection with the merger, except as required under the provisions of purchase fund and sinking fund agreements.

That ruling holds that the X preferred stock issued in connection with the merger is section 306 stock, but it concludes without full explanation that section 306(a)(1) of the Code does not apply to the proceeds of the disposition of such stock, unless the disposition is in anticipation of redemption.

* * *

Rev.Rul. 57-212 reasons that Rev.Rul. 56-116 stands for the proposition that section 306(b)(4) of the Code provides relief from section 306(a)(1) on the disposition of section 306 stock issued by a widely held corporation unless the disposition was in anticipation of redemption.
* * *

Upon reconsideration, the Service has concluded that the fact that the section 306 stock is issued by a corporation whose stock is widely held is not sufficient grounds for the application of section 306(b)(4) of the Code. Thus, in such circumstances, relief from the provisions of section 306(a) should not be automatic. * * *

* * *

PART G. CONCEPTS RELATING TO OVERLAP BETWEEN § 351 AND REORGANIZATIONAL PROVISIONS

§ 11.19 SURVEY OF OVERLAP ISSUE

A. INCORPORATION IN ANTICIPATION OF REORGANIZATION

Review Rev.Rul. 70–140, Sec. 2.7.A.

B. IMPACT OF §§ 357(c) AND 381(a) IN A TRANSACTION QUALIFYING AS BOTH A § 351 EXCHANGE AND A (C) REORGANIZATION

REVENUE RULING 76–188
1976–1 C.B. 99.

Advice has been requested whether, under the circumstances described below, the provisions of sections 357(c)(1)(A) and 381(a) of the Internal Revenue Code of 1954 apply to a transaction that meets the requirements of both sections 351 and 368(a)(1)(C).

P corporation transferred all of the assets used in its business to newly formed S corporation solely in exchange for all the stock (voting common) of S and the assumption by S of the liabilities of P. The liabilities assumed by S exceeded the total of the adjusted basis of the property transferred by P to S. After the transfer, P remained in existence and did not distribute or intend to distribute the stock of S received in the transfer. The transaction qualified as a reorganization as defined in section 368(a)(1)(C) of the Code and it also qualified as a transfer of property to a controlled corporation within the meaning of section 351.

* * *

Section 357(a) of the Code provides, in part, that an assumption of a liability in a transaction to which either section 351 or 361 applies will not be treated as money or other property received in the exchange. However, section 357(c)(1)(A) and (B) provides, in part, that in an exchange to which section 351 or 368(a)(1)(D) applies, respectively, the amount by which the liabilities assumed exceeds the total of the adjusted basis of the property transferred will be considered as gain from the sale or exchange of a capital asset or of property that is not a capital asset, as the case may be.

* * *

The questions presented in the instant case are (1) whether section 357(c)(1)(A) of the Code is inapplicable to the transaction because of the fact that the transaction also qualifies as a reorganization under section

368(a)(1)(C) to which the provisions of section 357(c)(1)(A), by its terms, are not applicable, and (2) whether section 381(a) is inapplicable to the transaction because of the fact that the transaction also qualifies under section 351 to which the provisions of section 381, by its terms, are not applicable.

Section 368(a)(2)(A) of the Code provides that if a transaction is "described in" both section 368(a)(1)(C) and section 368(a)(1)(D), it will be treated as described only in section 368(a)(1)(D). As explained in Rev.Rul. 74–545, 1974–2 C.B. 122, the fact that a transaction does not qualify as a reorganization under section 368(a)(1)(D) does not necessarily mean that it is not "described in" that section within the meaning of section 368(a)(2)(A). A transaction is considered to be "described in" section 368(a)(1)(D) if it involves a transfer of assets to a controlled corporation and a distribution of the stock of the transferee corporation to the shareholders of the transferor corporation, regardless of whether such distribution actually qualifies under section 354, 355, or 356. In the instant case, although the assets are transferred to a controlled corporation, the transaction is not "described in" section 368(a)(1)(D) since the transferor corporation, *P,* did not distribute the stock of the transferee corporation to the shareholders of the transferor.

While section 368(a)(2)(A) of the Code deals with the concurrent application of section 368(a)(1)(C) and (D) to a reorganization transaction, there is no comparable provision in the Code or regulations that deals with the concurrent application of section 351 and section 368(a)(1)(C) to a transaction.

* * *

Rev.Rul. 75–161, 1975–1 C.B. 114, states that section 357(c)(1)(B) of the Code contains no exception for its application where a reorganization qualifies under section 368(a)(1)(A) as well as under section 368(a)(1)(D). Therefore, since the transaction in Rev.Rul. 75–161 qualified both as a reorganization within the meaning of section 368(a)(1)(D) and as an exchange pursuant to section 361, section 357(c)(1)(B) was found to be applicable even though the transaction also qualified as a reorganization under section 368(a)(1)(A).

Likewise, section 357(c)(1)(A) of the Code contains no exception for its application where a transaction qualifies as a reorganization under section 368(a)(1)(C) as well as an exchange to which section 351 applies. Thus, in the instant case, since section 351 is applicable, section 357(c)(1)(A) applies notwithstanding that the transaction also qualifies as a reorganization under section 368(a)(1)(C).

Moreover, section 381 of the Code does not contain an exception for its application where a transaction qualifies as an exchange under section 351 as well as a reorganization under section 368(a)(1)(C). Hence, in the instant case, because section 361 applies by virtue of the exchange qualifying as a reorganization under section 368(a)(1)(C), section 381(a) applies, despite qualification of the exchange under section 351.

Accordingly, under the provisions of section 357(c)(1)(A) of the Code, to the extent that the amount of the liabilities assumed exceeds the total of the adjusted basis of the property transferred, gain is recognized to P on the transfer. Furthermore, pursuant to section 381(a), S will succeed to and take into account the items of P described in section 381(c).

C. COMBINATION TRIANGULAR REORGANIZATION AND PURPORTED § 351. DETERMINATION OF CONTROL

REVENUE RULING 84-44
1984-1 C.B. 105.

Issue

Under the facts described below, does section 351 of the Internal Revenue Code apply to the transfer of assets from Y to P in exchange for P stock?

Facts

X, Y and P were unrelated corporations. In a transaction qualifying as a reorganization under sections 368(a)(1)(A) and (a)(2)(D) of the Code, X was merged into S, a wholly owned subsidiary of P. In the transaction, the shareholders of X received shares of P stock in exchange for their shares of X stock. At the same time, as part of an overall plan, Y transferred part (but less than substantially all) of its assets to P in exchange for P stock. While Y did not have the requisite control of P to qualify its transfer of assets within the provisions of section 351, Y together with the former shareholders of X were in control of P within the meaning of section 368(c) of the Code.

Law and Analysis

Section 368(a)(2)(D) of the Code provides that the acquisition by one corporation, in exchange for stock of a corporation which is in control of the acquiring corporation, of substantially all of the properties of another corporation shall not disqualify the transaction under section 368(a)(1)(A) if no stock of the acquiring corporation is used in the transaction and the transaction would have qualified as a reorganization under section 368(a)(1)(A) had the merger been into the controlling corporation.

Section 351(a) of the Code provides that no gain or loss will be recognized if property is transferred to a corporation solely in exchange for its stock and immediately after the exchange the transferors are in control of the corporation (as defined in section 368(c)).

Although P stock was used as the consideration in the merger of X into S, the shareholders of X did not transfer any property to P. Therefore, since P is not the transferee of the stock of X, the P stock received by the shareholders of X is not taken into account with the P

stock received by Y in determining whether the requirements of section 351 of the Code have been met. The only assets received by P were transferred by Y, and since Y was not in control of P immediately after the transfer, the transaction does not qualify under section 351. Additionally, since P is not the transferee of the X assets, the receipt of P stock by X upon the transfer of its assets to S cannot be aggregated with the P stock received by Y in determining whether the 80 percent control requirement of section 351 could be met by X and Y.

The instant case should be compared with Rev.Rul. 68–357, 1968–2 C.B. 144, and Rev.Rul. 76–123, 1976–1 C.B. 94. In those rulings, stock received by individual transferors was aggregated with stock received in reorganizations for purposes of the control requirement of section 351 of the Code when the transfers were to the same corporation.

HOLDING

Since the control requirement of section 351 of the Code was not met by Y, any gain or loss realized by Y on the exchange will be recognized as provided by section 1001 of the Code. No gain or loss is recognized to P under section 1032(a) upon the exchange with Y of P stock for assets of Y.

EFFECT ON OTHER REVENUE RULING

Rev.Rul. 68–357 and Rev.Rul. 76–123 are distinguished.

D. USE OF § 351 TO AVOID CONTINUITY OF INTEREST REQUIREMENT

REVENUE RULING 84–71
1984–2 C.B. 106.

The Internal Revenue Service has reconsidered Rev.Rul. 80–284, 1980–2 C.B. 117, and Rev.Rul. 80–285, 1980–2 C.B. 119, in which transfers that satisfied the technical requirements of section 351(a) of the Internal Revenue Code were nevertheless held to constitute taxable exchanges because they were part of larger acquisitive transactions that did not meet the continuity of interest test generally applicable to acquisitive reorganizations.

In Rev.Rul. 80–284, fourteen percent of T corporation's stock was held by A, president and chairman of the board, and eighty-six percent by the public. P, an unrelated, publicly held corporation wished to purchase the stock of T. All the T stockholders except A were willing to sell the T stock for cash. A wished to avoid recognition of gain.

In order to accommodate these wishes, the following transactions were carried out as part of an overall plan. *First, P* and A formed a new corporation, *S.P.* transferred cash and other property to S in exchange solely for all of S's common stock; A transferred T stock to S solely in exchange for all S's preferred stock. These transfers were intended to be tax-free under section 351 of the Code. Second, S organized a new corporation, D, and transferred to D the cash it had received from P in exchange for all the D common stock. Third, D was merged into T under state law. As a result of the merger, each share of T stock, except those shares held by S, were surrendered for cash equal to the stock's fair market value and each share of D stock was converted into T stock.

Rev.Rul. 80–284 concluded that if a purported section 351 exchange is an integral part of a larger transaction that fits a pattern common to acquisitive reorganizations, and if the continuity of shareholder interest requirement of section 1.368–1(b) of the Income Tax Regulations is not satisfied with respect to the larger transaction, then the transaction as a whole resembles a sale and the exchange cannot qualify under section 351 because that section is not intended to apply to sales. Rev.Rul. 80–285 reached a similar conclusion with respect to an asset, rather than stock, acquisition in which a purported section 351 exchange was also part of a larger acquisitive transaction.

Upon reconsideration, the Service has concluded that the fact that "larger acquisitive transactions," such as those described in Rev.Rul. 80–284 and Rev.Rul. 80–285, fail to meet the requirements for tax-free treatment under the reorganization provisions of the Code does not preclude the applicability of section 351(a) to transfers that may be described as part of such larger transactions, but also, either alone or in conjunction with other transfers, meet the requirements of section 351(a).

Effect on Other Revenue Rulings

Rev.Rul. 80–284 and Rev.Rul. 80–285 are revoked.

* * *

Chapter 12

RECAPITALIZATIONS AND MERE CHANGES IN FORM

§ 12.1 SCOPE

This chapter focuses on the recapitalization reorganization under § 368(a)(1)(E), and the mere change in form reorganization under § 368(a)(1)(F). Sec. 12.2 introduces the recapitalization, and Sec. 12.3 considers a recapitalization in which preferred stock is issued in exchange for a retiring shareholder's common stock. Sec. 12.4 considers the issuance of new debentures for old debentures in a recapitalization. Sec. 12.5 examines the sale of stock after a recapitalization, and Sec. 12.6 looks at the exercise of a conversion privilege in stock and debentures. Sec. 12.7 examines the impact of the continuity of business enterprises doctrine, and Secs. 12.8 and 12.9 examine, respectively, the impact of §§ 305 and 306 in recapitalizations. Sec. 12.10 presents summary problems on recapitalization. Sec. 12.11 introduces the F reorganization.

For a more detailed discussion of the issues covered in this chapter, see Chapter 43 of *Federal Taxation of Business Enterprises, supra* Chapter 1, note 1, and Chapter 14 of Bittker and Eustice, *Corporations, supra* Sec. 1.4.

§ 12.2 INTRODUCTORY NOTE ON RECAPITALIZATIONS

Recapitalizations can go "upstream," "downstream" or merely "tread water." In an upstream recapitalization, the exchanging shareholder exchanges his interest for a more secure interest, such as an exchange of common stock for preferred, or an exchange of preferred for securities. In a downstream recapitalization, the exchanging shareholder or security holder exchanges his interest for a more equity-flavored interest. For example, a security holder exchanges his securities for preferred or common stock, or a holder of preferred exchanges his preferred for common. In a recapitalization that merely treads water, there is no difference in the nature of the interest exchanged; *e.g.,* common is exchanged for common, or preferred is exchanged for preferred.

Section 1.368–2(e) gives five examples of a recapitalization. In the first example, bonds are exchanged for new common, and in the second and fourth examples, preferred is exchanged for new common. *See* § 1.368–2(e)(1), (2) and (4). These are downstream recapitalizations. In the third example, old common is exchanged for new preferred, an upstream recapitalization. *See* § 1.368–2(e)(3). The fifth example illustrates how a recapitalization can give rise to a taxable stock dividend. *See* § 1.368–2(e)(5).

These examples do not cover a case where a preferred or common shareholder exchanges his stock for securities. *See Bazley, supra* Sec. 11.7.C. Although such a transaction may constitute a recapitalization (*see* Rev.Rul. 77–415, *infra*), Sec. 23.4.B, the exchanging shareholder would have gain recognition under §§ 354(a)(2) and 356(d)(2)(B). Moreover, under § 1.301–1(*l*) and *Bazley* if the bonds are distributed pro rata, the shareholder would have a dividend in the full amount of the fair market value of the bonds, assuming the corporation had adequate E & P. Section 1.301–1(*l*) treats recapitalizations in which the shareholders receive a pro rata distribution of bonds as the equivalent of a mere dividend distribution of bonds. *See* § 317. If § 1.301–1(*l*) were not applicable the shareholder might nonetheless have a boot dividend under § 356(a)(2).

The exchanging shareholder or security holder in a recapitalization receives nonrecognition treatment under § 354, subject, of course, to the boot gain and dividend rules of § 356. The issuing corporation is a "party to the reorganization." *See* Rev.Rul. 77–206, 1972–1 C.B. 104. The shareholder takes a substituted basis, with adjustments, under § 358. The corporation has nonrecognition upon the issuance of its stock or debt instruments. *See* § 1032 and § 1.61–12(c).

§ 12.3 ISSUANCE OF PREFERRED IN EXCHANGE FOR RETIRING SHAREHOLDER'S COMMON

REVENUE RULING 74–269
1974–1 C.B. 87.

Advice has been requested whether the situation described below constitutes a recapitalization and, therefore, a reorganization under section 368(a)(1)(E) of the Internal Revenue Code of 1954.

A, the founder of *X* corporation, owns 50 of *X*'s outstanding 100 shares of common stock. *B* and *C, A*'s sons, each owns 25 shares. In anticipation of *A*'s retirement and pursuant to a plan of recapitalization, *X* proposes to exchange shares of newly issued $100 par value six percent cumulative nonvoting preferred stock for all of *A*'s common stock. *B* and C will not participate in the exchange. The terms of the preferred stock provides that on liquidation, the preferred shareholder will receive the par value of his shares plus accrued dividends. The book value per share of X common stock was calculated to be $10x, or a total book value of $500x for the 50 shares held by A.

Pursuant to the plan, A will exchange all of his X common stock with a book value of $500x for five shares of new X preferred stock with a par value of $500x.

In the exchange of stock described above, the parties contend that the fair market value of the preferred stock is equal to the fair market value of the common stock exchanged therefor. As support for this contention, the parties use the book value of the common stock and par value of the preferred stock.

The fair market value of stock is a factual determination and is not necessarily the book value or par value of the stock. However, to the extent that the fair market value of the preferred stock received in the instant case is found, in fact, to be equal to the fair market value of the common stock exchanged therefor, the transaction will constitute an exchange pursuant to a reorganization within the meaning of section 368(a)(1)(E) of the Code.

Accordingly, the exchange of stock described above will constitute a reorganization within the meaning of section 368(a)(1)(E) of the Code and no gain or loss will be recognized to A under section 354 on the exchange of those shares of his common stock which are equal in value to the value of the shares of the preferred stock which are received in exchange therefor. Under section 358 the basis of the preferred stock received by A in the exchange will be the same as the basis of those shares of the common stock which are considered exchanged under section 354. However, if A receives shares of preferred stock having a fair market value in excess of the fair market value of the common stock surrendered, or surrenders shares of common stock having a fair market value in excess of the fair market value of the preferred stock received, the amount representing such excess will be treated as having been used to make gifts, pay compensation, satisfy obligations of any kind, or for whatever purpose the facts indicate. The reorganization will not diminish the accumulated earnings and profits of X corporation available for the subsequent distribution of dividends within the meaning of section 316.

Note and Questions

1. One collateral benefit of this type of recapitalization is that the preferred may be more easily valued for estate tax purposes than the common. This type of recapitalization is sometimes referred to as "an estate freezing recap."

2. Why is the Service concerned that the fair market value of the preferred equal the fair market value of the common? *See* § 356(f).

§ 12.4 ISSUANCE OF DEBENTURES IN A RECAPITALIZATION

A. DEBENTURE DISTRIBUTION EQUALS DIVIDEND

See § 1.301–1(l).

REVIEW BAZLEY v. COMMISSIONER
Supreme Court of the United States, 1947.
331 U.S. 737, 67 S.Ct. 1489, 91 L.Ed. 1782.

Supra, Sec. 11.7.C.

B. NO REQUIREMENT OF CONTINUITY OF INTEREST IN A RECAPITALIZATION

REVENUE RULING 77–415
1977–2 C.B. 311.

In order to improve its financial condition M, a solvent domestic corporation, undertook to rearrange its capital structure. M had outstanding voting common stock, nonvoting preferred stock, and subordinated debentures, all of which were widely held and actively traded on an established securities market. Pursuant to a plan, M offered to exchange its new 10–year 10–percent subordinated debentures maturing July 1985, for a like principal amount of its outstanding 20–year 8–percent debentures on the date of their maturity, July 6, 1975. Under the plan, M also offered to exchange its new debentures in the principal amount of $500,000x$ dollars for shares of its preferred stock outstanding in the ratio of $20x$ dollars principal amount of the new debentures for each share of outstanding preferred stock. The preferred stock had been issued for cash and there were no dividend arrearages.

On July 6, 1975, M acquired 25,000 shares of its preferred stock in exchange for a total amount of $500,000x$ dollars of its $20x$ dollars principal amount debentures. The mean of the high and low selling price of the preferred stock on the day after the exchange was $18x$ dollars. On the day of the exchange M also acquired all of its outstanding debentures in the principal amount of $1,000,000x$ dollars in exchange for its new debentures of the same amount. The debentures represent a bona fide indebtedness of the corporation and are "securities" within the meaning of that term as used in sections 354 and 356 of the Code. A, who owned 100 shares of M preferred stock, exchanged such stock for $2,000x$ dollars principal amount of debentures. B, who owned debentures in the principal amount of $5,000x$ dollars, exchanged them for new M debentures of the same principal amount. Neither A nor B owned any stock of M constructively under the rules set forth in section 318.

The specific issues presented are * * * (2) whether the provisions of section 354 or 356 apply to the exchanges by A and B.

* * *

Section 368(a)(1)(E) of the Code provides that a "recapitalization" is a "reorganization". For this purpose a recapitalization has been defined as a "reshuffling of a capital structure within the framework of an existing corporation". *Helvering v. Southwest Consolidated Corp.*, 315 U.S. 194 (1942), 1942–1 C.B. 218.

Section 1.368–1(b) of the Income Tax Regulations provides, in part, that requisite to a reorganization is a continuity of interest in the business enterprise on the part of those persons who were the owners of the enterprise prior to the reorganization.

In the instant case, the creation by the corporation of securities in the form of the debentures and its issuance of the debentures in exchange for outstanding debentures and stock is a reshuffling of the corporation's capital structure and, therefore, a recapitalization. *See Commissioner v. Neustadt's Trust*, 131 F.2d 528 (2d Cir.1942), *aff'g* 43 B.T.A. 848 (1941), *nonacq.*, 1941–1 C.B. 17, *nonacq. withdrawn, acq.*, 1951–1 C.B. 2. The courts have held that the continuity-of-interest principle need not be applied to recapitalizations under section 368(a)(1)(E) of the Code. The considerations that make the continuity-of-interest requirement necessary in acquisitive reorganizations are not present in recapitalizations involving a single corporation. Thus, the recapitalization is a reorganization * * *, though *A* did not maintain a continuity of proprietary interest in *M*.

* * *

Accordingly, in the instant case, since the principal amount of securities received does not exceed the principal amount of securities surrendered by *B*, no gain or loss is recognized to *B* on the exchange of the *M* debentures for new debentures under section 354(a)(1) of the Code. The nonrecognition provisions of section 354(a)(1) do not apply, however, to the exchange by *A* of *M* stock for the new debentures because of section 354(a)(2)(B). Therefore, since *A*'s exchange of stock for debentures does not qualify under section 354(a)(1), section 356 is not applicable to the exchange.

However, since *M* acquired its stock from *A* in exchange for property within the meaning of section 317(a) of the Code, the exchange with *A* is a redemption as defined in section 317(b).

Thus, the distribution of the debentures to *A* is a distribution in complete redemption of *A*'s stock interest in the corporation within the meaning of section 302(b)(3) of the Code and, therefore, is treated as a distribution in full payment in exchange for the stock under section 302(a).

§ 12.5 SALE OF STOCK AFTER A RECAPITALIZATION

REVENUE RULING 77-479
1977-2 C.B. 119.

Advice has been requested whether the recapitalization described below qualifies as a reorganization under section 368(a)(1)(E) of the Internal Revenue Code of 1954 when part of the stock received in the recapitalization is sold pursuant to a prearranged plan.

Individuals A and B each owned one half of each class of the outstanding stock of Z corporation, which consisted of 50,000 shares of voting common stock and 50,000 shares of nonvoting preferred stock. Under a plan to offer some of the Z stock to the public, A and B made arrangements with an investment broker for a secondary offering of 80 percent of their stock. To facilitate the sale by making the stock a more attractive investment, the broker suggested that the existing common and preferred stock be converted into one new class of common stock. Thus, Z effected a recapitalization in which all of its outstanding shares of common and preferred stock were exchanged by A and B for shares of one new class of voting common stock of Z on a share-for-share basis. A and B each then sold 40,000 shares of the new voting common stock to the public through the broker.

Section 368(a)(1)(E) of the Code provides that a "recapitalization" is a "reorganization". For this purpose a recapitalization has been defined as a "reshuffling of a capital structure within the framework of an existing corporation". *Helvering v. Southwest Consolidated Corp.*, 315 U.S. 194 (1942), 1942-1 C.B. 218.

* * *

The exchange by A and B of their common and preferred stock for new common stock meets the definition of a reorganization under section 368(a)(1)(E) of the Code. However, when a shareholder receives stock in a reorganization described in section 368(a)(1) and any of the stock received is disposed of pursuant to a prearranged plan, a question arises whether the continuity of interest requirement for a reorganization is satisfied. See Rev.Rul. 66-23, 1966-1 C.B. 67.

In Rev.Rul. 77-415, 1977-2 C.B. 311, a shareholder who owned only preferred stock in a corporation exchanged all of this stock for bonds of the corporation pursuant to a plan of recapitalization. Rev.Rul. 77-415, states, consistent with several court decisions, that the continuity of interest requirement need not be applied to a recapitalization under section 368(a)(1)(E) of the Code because the considerations that make the continuity of interest requirement necessary in acquisitive reorganizations are not present in recapitalizations involving a single corporation. Thus, Rev.Rul. 77-415 concludes that the transaction was a recapitalization under section 368(a)(1)(E) even though the shareholder did not retain a proprietary interest in the corporation.

Accordingly, since continuity of interest is not required for the recapitalization of Z to qualify as a reorganization described in section 368(a)(1)(E) of the Code, the subsequent sale by A and B of the stock received by them as a result of the recapitalization does not affect the qualification of the transaction as a reorganization under section 368(a)(1)(E). Therefore, no gain or loss is recognized to A or B on the exchange of their common and preferred Z stock for new Z common stock pursuant to section 354(a). The basis to A and B of the new common stock is the same as the basis of the Z common and preferred stock exchanged therefor pursuant to section 358(a). Any gain realized or loss sustained by A or B upon the sale of the new Z stock to the public is recognized to them pursuant to section 1001.

§ 12.6 EXERCISE OF CONVERSION PRIVILEGE

A. CONVERSION OF DEBENTURES INTO STOCK

REVENUE RULING 72-265
1972-1 C.B. 222.

Advice has been requested concerning the Federal income tax consequences to the owner of a corporate debenture of his exercise of the right, provided for in the debenture, to surrender it and to receive in exchange common stock of the corporation.

A purchased on the open market in 1967 for $500x$ dollars a debenture of Y corporation with a principal amount of $500x$ dollars. The terms of the offering of this issue of debentures in 1965 had included a provision that, at any time before January 1, 1970, the holder of any debenture could surrender all or part (in multiples of $100x$ dollars of principal amount) of his holdings of this issue of debentures and would receive 20 shares of Y common stock for each $100x$ dollars of principal amount of the debentures surrendered. In 1969 A exercised the right to surrender the debenture and received therefor 100 shares of Y common stock with a total fair market value of $1000x$ dollars.

* * *

The conclusion that no gain or loss is realized upon the conversion of a corporate debenture into stock of the obligor corporation was initially stated in Article 1563 of Treasury Regulations 45 (1920 edition) under the Revenue Act of 1918. This rule remains applicable except where provisions of the Code specifically require that gain be recognized. See Revenue Ruling 72-264. * * * No gain is therefore realized by A upon his exercise of the right to surrender the debenture for common stock. Similarly, the unadjusted basis of the 100 shares of Y common stock is $500x$ dollars, the cost of the debenture. The conversion of a debenture into stock of a different corporation, however, is a taxable event. See Revenue Ruling 69-135, C.B. 1969-1, 198.

* * *

B. CONVERSION OF COMMON INTO PREFERRED AND CONVERSION OF PREFERRED INTO COMMON: REQUIREMENT OF BUSINESS PURPOSE

REVENUE RULING 77-238
1977-2 C.B. 115.

Advice has been requested concerning the Federal income tax consequences, in the situations described below, upon the conversion of common stock of a corporation into preferred stock of the same corporation and upon the conversion of preferred stock of a corporation into common stock of the same corporation.

SITUATION 1.

Corporation X is engaged in a manufacturing business and has shares of voting common stock and shares of nonvoting preferred stock outstanding. All the common stock is owned by employees of X. The certificate of incorporation requires that the shareholders of X convert their common stock into preferred stock at a specified exchange rate upon their retirement from X, or have the stock redeemed for cash. The taxpayer, a retiring employee of X, exchanged the X common stock for X preferred stock of equal value pursuant to the conversion privilege. The purpose of the conversion privilege is to eliminate common stock ownership by retiring employees and to reduce the cash expenditures by X that would otherwise result if the common stock of retiring employees were redeemed for cash.

SITUATION 2.

Corporation Y is engaged in a manufacturing business and has shares of voting common stock and shares of nonvoting preferred stock outstanding. The certificate of incorporation gives the shareholders of Y the right to convert their preferred stock into common stock at a specified exchange rate. The taxpayer, pursuant to the conversion privilege, exchanged preferred stock for Y common stock of equal value. The purpose of the conversion privilege is to encourage the conversion of preferred stock into common stock in order to simplify the capital structure of the corporation by eliminating the preferred stock.

* * *

Section 1.368-2(e) of the Income Tax Regulations provides, in part, that a transaction involving the exchange of common stock for preferred stock of the same corporation and a transaction involving the exchange of preferred stock for common stock are recapitalizations within the meaning of section 368(a)(1)(E) of the Code.

* * *

Section 1.368–1(c) of the regulations provides that the nonrecognition provisions of the Code relating to exchanges pursuant to reorganizations defined in section 368(a)(1) of the Code are not applicable unless the exchanges are in pursuance of a plan of reorganization.

Section 1.368–2(g) of the regulations provides that the transaction embraced in a plan of reorganization must not only come within the specific language of section 368(a) of the Code, but the readjustments involved in the exchange or distributions effected in the consummation thereof must be undertaken for reasons germane to the continuance of the business of a corporation a party to the reorganization.

The conversions of stock in *Situation 1* were in furtherance of a corporate business purpose to encourage the conversion of common stock into preferred stock thereby permitting the corporation to use the cash that would otherwise be expended to redeem the common stock for other business purposes, and were pursuant to a continuing plan of reorganization represented by the conversion privilege embodied in the certificate of incorporation. Likewise, the conversions of stock in *Situation 2* were in furtherance of a corporate business purpose to simplify the capital structure, and were in pursuance of a plan of reorganization. See Rev.Rul. 56–179, 1956–1 C.B. 187.

Accordingly, the exchanges of stock in *Situation 1* and *Situation 2* pursuant to the conversion privileges involved are reorganizations within the meaning of section 368(a)(1)(E) of the Code. Under section 354(a)(1), no gain or loss is recognized to the taxpayers involved upon the exchanges of stock pursuant to the conversion privileges.

Compare Rev.Rul. 72–265, 1972–1 C.B. 222, regarding the exercise of the conversion privilege provided for in a corporate debenture.

Note and Question

See Rev.Rul. 56–179, 1956–1 C.B. 187. What is the impact of § 1036 on the above transactions?

§ 12.7 NO CONTINUITY OF BUSINESS ENTERPRISE REQUIREMENT

See Revenue Ruling 82–34 in Sec. 11.3.D.

§ 12.8 ILLUSTRATION OF IMPACT OF § 305 IN A RECAPITALIZATION: ISOLATED TRANSACTION THAT INCREASES SHAREHOLDER'S PROPORTIONATE INTEREST

REVENUE RULING 75–93
1975–1 C.B. 101.

* * *

X had outstanding $700x$ shares of $2.00 par value class A common stock, $2,100x$ shares of $0.20 par value class B common stock, and $62x$

shares of no-par-value convertible preferred stock. All of the class B common stock was held by officers and directors of X who owned no class A common stock. The class A common stock was widely held and traded in the over-the-counter market. Regular cash dividends are paid on the preferred stock.

The class A common stock and class B common stock, both subordinated to the preferred stock, shared in dividends and liquidating distributions in relation to their par values, that is 10 to 1. The class A common stock and class B common stock each carried one vote per share. Therefore, as a class, the class A common stock represented 25 percent of the voting power of X, and the class B common stock represented 75 percent. The preferred stock is convertible into class A common stock of X at a fixed conversion price and is fully protected against dilution in the event of a stock dividend or stock split.

X recapitalized for valid business reasons in a transaction satisfying the definition of a reorganization described in section 368(a)(1)(E) of the Code and exchanged shares of unissued class A common stock for all of the outstanding shares of class B common stock. Since each share of class B common stock shared in dividends and liquidating distributions to the extent of one-tenth of the class A common stock, ten shares of class B common stock should have been exchanged for one share of class A common stock, for an aggregate of $210x$ shares of class A common stock. Since it had more voting power as a class, however, the class B common stock was more valuable than the class A common stock. Therefore, seven shares of class B common stock were exchanged for one share of class A common stock, for an aggregate of $300x$ shares of class A common stock.

As a result of the recapitalization, the former class B shareholders increased their proportionate interests in the assets and earnings and profits of X by receiving $90x$ shares of class A common stock in the exchange attributable to the surrender of their concerted voting power in X. The recapitalization was an isolated transaction and was not part of a plan to periodically increase a shareholder's proportionate interest in the assets or earnings and profits of X.

* * *

Section 1.305–7(a) of the regulations provides, in part, that a transaction, including a recapitalization, described in section 305(c) of the Code will be treated as a distribution to which sections 305(b) and 301 apply if (1) the proportionate interest of any shareholder in the earnings and profits or assets of the corporation deemed to have made such distribution is increased by such transaction, and (2) such distribution has the result described in paragraph (2), (3), (4) or (5) of section 305(b). Section 1.305–7(c)(1) provides that a recapitalization, whether or not an isolated transaction, will be deemed to result in a distribution to which section 305(c) applies if it is pursuant to a plan to periodically increase a shareholder's proportionate interest in the assets or earnings and profits of the corporation.

Section 305(b)(2) of the Code is applicable to a transaction only if there is an actual distribution or a deemed distribution within the meaning of section 305(c). There was no actual distribution in this case. Since the recapitalization was not part of a plan to periodically increase a shareholder's proportionate interest, there was no deemed distribution within the meaning of section 305(c). Thus, the transaction was not a distribution to which section 305(b)(2) applies. This is so notwithstanding the fact that the recapitalization had the effect of a transaction described in that section since the former class B shareholders increased their proportionate interests in the assets and earnings and profits of X by receiving additional shares of class A common stock in exchange for the surrender of their concerted voting power in X while other shareholders (the preferred shareholders) received money in the form of regular cash dividends paid on the preferred stock.

This is consistent with the conclusions reached in Examples (10), (11), and (13) in section 1.305–3(e) of the regulations where isolated redemptions do not cause section 305(b)(2) to apply even though there are increased proportionate interests in the assets and earnings and profits of the corporations by some shareholders and receipts of property by other shareholders.

Accordingly, the recapitalization in the instant case is not deemed, under section 305(c) of the Code, to result in a distribution to which sections 305(b)(2) and 301 apply.

§ 12.9 ILLUSTRATION OF § 306 STOCK IN A RECAPITALIZATION

REVENUE RULING 82–191

1982–2 C.B. 78.

Issue

Is the voting preferred stock received by A "section 306 stock" within the meaning of section 306(c) of the Internal Revenue Code?

Facts

X corporation had outstanding 100 shares of no par value voting common stock. Shareholder A owned 20 of these shares. X had accumulated earnings and profits. For valid business reasons X entered into a plan of recapitalization under which all the X shareholders surrendered their outstanding shares of voting common stock (old common) to X in exchange for shares of a class of newly created voting preferred stock. A received 15 of these shares, while the remaining shareholders received 80. The preferred stock was nonredeemable, limited and preferred as to dividends, and had a fixed liquidation preference. A holder thereof was not entitled to any further participation in X beyond these payments. The transaction was claimed to qualify as a reorganization (recapitalization) under section 368(a)(1)(E) of the Code and no gain or loss was claimed to be recognized to the exchanging shareholders under section 354. Shortly thereafter, and as an integral part of the overall transaction, A purchased from X for an amount equal to approximately one-half its value all the outstanding shares (10) of a newly created class of nonvoting common stock (new common) of X. This gave A an unrestricted interest in the future equity growth of X and an unrestricted right, after liquidation of the preferred stock, to share in the assets or earnings and profits of X upon its liquidation.

LAW AND ANALYSIS

Section 306(c)(1)(B) of the Code provides that "section 306 stock" is any stock, except common stock, that is received by a shareholder pursuant to a plan of reorganization under section 368 with respect to the receipt of which gain or loss to the shareholder was to any extent not recognized by reason of section 354, but only to the extent that the effect of the transaction is substantially the same as the receipt of a stock dividend.

Section 306 of the Code was enacted in 1954 to prevent what is known as a "preferred stock bailout". *S.Rep.No. 1622*, 83rd Cong., 2d Sess. 46 (1954). The object of such a bailout is to allow the shareholders to receive corporate earnings and profits, which otherwise might be taxed as ordinary income, at favorable capital gains rates by way of the sale of other than common stock received as a distribution on their common stock. The shareholders would then retain their unrestricted right to share in the equity growth of the corporation through the ownership of their common stock. This bailout can be achieved by the shareholders of the common stock through the disposition of any stock which is other than common stock and which is received in a transaction described in section 306(c). * * *

* * *

The classic bailout situation generally involves the issuance of preferred stock to those shareholders who already own the common stock of the corporation or who receive the common stock as part of a plan. The instant case differs in form from the classic bailout situation since the former shareholders of X old common apparently own no X common stock, old or new, immediately after the recapitalization exchange. The substance of the transaction, however, is that the right to share in the future unrestricted equitable growth of X is represented by the new common (which A purchased pursuant to the plan of reorganization) and much of the earnings and profits up to the date of the recapitalization are represented by the X preferred stock. If the form of the transaction was followed in this case, A could later dispose of his or her preferred stock without the loss of his or her right to participate in the future equity growth of X and section 306 of the Code apparently would not be applicable because no shareholder owned any common stock of X immediately after the exchange.

In the instant transaction, it is not reasonable to assume that at the time of the exchange it was intended that no old shareholder be entitled to participate in X beyond the preferred stock preferences. Therefore, the transaction in the instant case will be treated, for federal income tax purposes, as though A exchanged 15 shares of his or her X old common for 15 shares of the X preferred stock. A also exchanged 5 shares of his or her X old common plus cash for the X new common, and the new common will be treated as the old common for purposes of making the section 306 determination.

HOLDING

The X preferred stock received by A is "section 306 stock" within the meaning of section 306(c)(1)(B) of the Code.

§ 12.10 SUMMARY PROBLEMS ON RECAPITALIZATIONS

Corporation X is solely owned by individual A, who has a $100K basis for his X common stock. No other class of stock is outstanding. The value of X's common is estimated to be $1 million. A also owns a $100K long-term debenture issued by X. A's basis for the debenture is $90K. X has substantial accumulated E & P. There is no OID on the debenture. A is elderly and would like to step back from the business and bring his son S into the management. He also would like to give S a financial stake in the business. What are the income tax results for each of the following transactions. In addition to the reorganization provisions, be sure to consider the stock dividend and § 306 stock provisions.

First Plan: X is recapitalized by issuing its preferred stock, with both a par value and fair market value of $900K, in exchange for 90% of A's common stock. A then gives to his son his remaining common and pays the appropriate gift tax? Suppose the preferred is redeemable after 5 years at an amount equal to 115% of par? Suppose that instead of issuing preferred, X issued its debentures with a face and value of $900K in exchange for A's common?

Second Plan: A gives S 10% of the common stock. X is then recapitalized with X issuing its preferred with a par and fair market value of $900K to A in exchange for all of his stock? Suppose that as part of the above transaction, X redeems the debenture held by A by transferring to A $100K in cash? Suppose instead that X issues in exchange for A's debenture its new debenture with a face of $120K, but a value of $100K? Assume that there is no OID on this new debenture. What if instead of exchanging a debenture for a debenture, A exchanges a 1-year note owed to him by X for a 20-year X debenture of an equal value?

§ 12.11 THE (F) REORGANIZATION

A. THE CURRENT STATUTE

CONFERENCE COMMITTEE REPORT TO TAX EQUITY AND FISCAL RESPONSIBILITY ACT

540–541 (1982).

D. REORGANIZATIONS CONSTITUTING CHANGES IN FORM

Present law

A reorganization includes "a mere change in identity, form, or place of organization" (an F reorganization). Generally, present law requires a transferor corporation's taxable year to be closed on the date of a reorganization transfer [*see* § 381(b)(1)], and precludes a post-reorganization loss from being carried back to a taxable year of the transferor. [*See* § 381(b)(3).] However, F reorganizations are excluded from these limitations in recognition of the intended scope of such reorganizations as embracing only formal changes in a single operating corporation. [*See* § 381(b).]

* * *

Conference agreement

The conference agreement limits the F reorganization definition to a change in identity, form, or place of organization of a single operating corporation.

This limitation does not preclude the use of more than one entity to consummate the transaction provided only one operating company is involved. The reincorporation of an operating company in a different State, for example, is an F reorganization that requires that more than one corporation be involved.

* * *

Note

The Service has ruled that in order to qualify as an (F) reorganization, there must be "complete identity of shareholders and their proprietary interest in the transferor corporation and acquiring corporations." Rev.Rul. 75–561, 1975–2 C.B. 129.

B. ILLUSTRATION OF § 306 ISSUE IN AN (F) REORGANIZATION

REVENUE RULING 79–287

1979–2 C.B. 130.

Issue

Will preferred stock received in a reorganization defined in section 368(a)(1)(F) of the Internal Revenue Code, involving a change of place of organization, be "section 306 stock" if received in exchange for the same number of shares of preferred stock with identical terms that was not previously "section 306 stock" in the hands of the exchanging shareholders?

Facts

X corporation organized in M state has outstanding common stock and preferred stock. The preferred stock is not section 306 stock.

Because of state income tax considerations X intends to change its place of organization from M to N state. To accomplish this, X formed Y, a new corporation, in N. In a transaction that will qualify as a reorganization within the meaning of section 368(a)(1)(F) of the Code, X will merge into Y. Y will acquire all of the assets and assume all of the liabilities of X. The exchanging shareholders will receive on a share-for-share basis both common and preferred stock of Y in exchange for their common and preferred stock of X. Some exchanging shareholders own both common and preferred X stock and therefore they will receive both common and preferred Y stock in the transaction. The stock received by the exchanging shareholders will be identical in terms with the corresponding stock exchanged therefor.

Law and Analysis

Section 306(c)(1)(B) of the Code provides that the term "section 306 stock" means stock which is not common stock and which was received pursuant to a tax-free reorganization, but only to the extent that either the effect of the transaction was substantially the same as the receipt of a stock dividend, or the stock was received in exchange for section 306 stock.

* * *

Although the instant transaction does not involve a recapitalization under section 368(a)(1)(E) of the Code (that is, it is not a reshuffling of a capital structure within the framework of an existing corporation), it is in fact merely a change in the state of incorporation. The instant situation is only a reorganization of a single business enterprise resulting from a reincorporation of a corporation in another state achieved by the creation of a new corporate shell. This leaves the shareholders and the surviving corporation exactly as they were before the transaction, except for the technical change of the state of incorporation. Furthermore, for the same reasons *Example (2)* of section 1.306–3(d) of the regulations is an exception to the "cash in lieu of" test, the preferred stock received in the exchange in the present revenue ruling was not substantially the same as the receipt of a stock dividend within the meaning of section 306(c)(1)(B). Therefore, the principle of *Example (2)* of section 1.306–3(d) is also applicable to a single entity section 368(a)(1)(F) reorganization as described above.

HOLDING

The preferred stock received in the single entity reorganization under section 368(a)(1)(F) of the Code, as described above, is not section 306 stock.

Chapter 13

THE DIVISIVE (D) REORGANIZATION AND SECTION 355

§ 13.1 SCOPE

This chapter examines divisive (D) reorganizations and § 355 spin-off transactions. Sec. 13.2 introduces § 355 and the (D) reorganization, and Sec. 13.3 provides the legislative background of these provisions. Sec. 13.4 introduces the regulations, rulings and cases under § 355, including the treatment of (1) the business purpose requirement, (2) the device clause, (3) the continuity of business requirement, and (4) the active conduct of a trade or business requirement. Sec. 13.5 illustrates the impact of § 306 in a (D) reorganization under § 355, and Sec. 13.6 addresses the issue of whether boot distributed in a § 355 transaction is treated as a dividend. Finally Sec. 13.7 presents summary problems.

For more detailed discussion on the issues covered here, see Chapter 44 of *Federal Taxation of Business Enterprises, supra* Chapter 1, note 1; Chapter 13 of Bittker and Eustice, *Corporations, supra* Sec. 1.4; and Chapter 10 of Ginsburg and Levin, *Mergers, supra* Sec. 1.4. *See also* the most recent edition of *Tax Strategies, supra* Sec. 1.4.

§ 13.2 INTRODUCTION TO § 355 DISTRIBUTIONS AND (D) REORGANIZATIONS

Section 355 deals with divisive (D) reorganizations in which one corporation is broken up into two or more corporations. For instance, the distributing corporation transfers "a part" of its assets to the controlled corporation in exchange for the stock therein and distributes the stock of the controlled corporation to the shareholders of the distributing corporation. Section 355 also encompasses the distribution of a preexisting controlled corporation that is not organized in a (D) transaction.

There are three types of § 355 transactions: spin-offs, split-offs and split-ups. In a spin-off, the stock of the controlled corporation is distributed to the shareholders of the distributing corporation. If the transaction does not qualify under § 355, the distribution is a dividend. In a split-off, the shareholders of the distributing corporation surrender a portion of their stock in exchange for stock of the controlled corporation. If the transaction does not qualify under § 355, the shareholder receives either sale or exchange treatment or dividend treatment. The shareholder has sale or exchange treatment if the transaction satisfies any of the paragraphs in § 302(b). In a split-up, the distributing corporation makes a liquidating distribution of the stock of two or more controlled corporations. If the transaction does not qualify under § 355, the shareholders have a taxable exchange under § 331, unless the transaction is treated as a liquidation-reincorporation. *See* Chapter 14.

In order for a transaction to fit within § 355 and thereby qualify the shareholder for nonrecognition treatment under § 355(a), the following four basic statutory requirements must be satisfied:

(1) The distributing corporation must distribute (either pro rata or non-pro rata) to its shareholders or security holders "solely" stock or securities of the controlled corporation (*see* § 355(a)(1)(A), (a)(2) and (a)(3)). If boot is distributed, § 356 will apply (*see* § 356(a) and (b)). Boot includes (1) an excess principal amount of securities, and (2) stock of a controlled corporation acquired by the distributing corporation in a wholly or partially taxable transaction within five years of the distribution (*see* § 355(a)(3));

(2) The transaction must not be a "device" for the distribution of E & P (*see* § 355(a)(1)(B) and Sec. 13.4.C);

(3) A separate active trade or business that has been conducted for at least five years must continue to be conducted after the distribution by both the distributing and the controlled corporations (*see* § 355(a)(1)(C) and (b) and 13.4.F);

(4) The distributing corporation must distribute all of the stock or securities of the controlled corporation or an amount of stock of the controlled corporation amounting to control, provided that in the latter case it is established that the retention of stock or securities of the controlled corporation is not for tax avoidance purposes (*see* § 355(a)(1)(D)).

The tax treatment to the parties in a (D) reorganization that qualifies under § 355 is as follows. Under § 361, the distributing corporation receives nonrecognition on the transfer of its assets in exchange for stock and securities of the controlled corporation. Therefore, the distributing corporation takes a § 358 substituted basis for the stock or securities received. The controlled corporation has nonrecognition under § 1032 and § 1.61–12(c) upon the issuance of its stock and securities and takes a carryover basis under 362. Unless the disqualified distribution rule of § 355(d) applies, the distributing corporation has nonrecognition under § 355(c) upon the distribution of the stock and securities of the controlled corporation. The shareholders of the distributing corporation have nonrecognition treatment under § 355(a)(1) if they receive solely stock and no boot. See § 355(a)(3). If the shareholders exchange stock in the distributing corporation for stock in the controlled corporation plus boot, the boot gain and boot dividend rules of § 356(a) apply. If, however, they receive a distribution of stock of the controlled corporation plus boot, without exchanging stock of the distributing corporation, the boot is treated as a § 301 dividend. See § 356(b).

§ 13.3 LEGISLATIVE BACKGROUND ON THE (D) REORGANIZATION UNDER §§ 355 AND 354(b)

A. LEGISLATIVE DEVELOPMENTS THROUGH 1954

To qualify as a § 368(a)(1)(D) reorganization, a transaction must satisfy three requirements. First, one corporation (the "distributing corporation") must transfer all or a part of its assets to another corporation (the "controlled corporation"). Second, immediately after the transfer, the distributing corporation, or one or more of its shareholders, or any combination thereof, must control, within the meaning of § 368(c), the controlled corporation. Finally, the stock or securities of the controlled corporation must be distributed in a transaction that qualifies under §§ 354, 355, or 356.

If a (D) satisfies the conditions in § 354(b), then § 354(a)(1) provides for nonrecognition treatment for a shareholder of a distributing corporation who exchanges his stock or securities in the distributing corporation for stock or securities (of no more than an equal principal amount) in the controlled corporation. If a (D) satisfies the conditions of § 355, then § 355(a) provides for nonrecognition treatment for the shareholder who exchanges stock or securities in the distributing corporation for stock or securities (of no more than an equal principal amount) in the controlled corporation. If the shareholder receives boot, including an excess principal amount of securities, in a transaction that otherwise qualifies under § 354(b) or § 355, then the tax treatment to the shareholder is governed by § 356. A transaction can qualify under § 355 without also constituting a (D); that is, the distribution of stock or securities of a preexisting subsidiary may qualify under § 355. If a transaction fails to qualify under § 354(b) or § 355, the shareholders are taxed under the general rules of subchapter C, *i.e.*, the dividend, redemption and liquidation rules.

The (D) was first added to the tax law by the Revenue Act of 1924. The provision was used by Mrs. Gregory in her attempt to receive capital gains rather than ordinary dividends and to avoid the corporate tax upon the disposition of Monitor securities held by her wholly owned corporation, United Mortgage. Mrs. Gregory caused United Mortgage to form Averill corporation and to transfer the Monitor securities to Averill. Averill was then spun off to Mrs. Gregory, who promptly liquidated it, receiving and then selling the Monitor shares. She argued that the transaction was a tax-free spin-off, followed by a taxable liquidation that produced capital gain to her and a fair market value basis for the Monitor shares. The Supreme Court held that, because the transaction was devoid of a business purpose, it was not a reorganization. *See Gregory v. Helvering,* Sec. 1.3.G.2.

The provision Mrs. Gregory relied on in claiming tax-free treatment upon the receipt of the Averill securities in the "distribution" from Monitor was repealed in the 1934 Act. The (D) transaction remained a part of the law, but only for exchange transactions in which stock or securities of the distributing corporation were exchanged for stock or securities of the controlled corporation.

In 1951, Congress added to the 1939 Code § 112(b)(11), the initial predecessor to § 355. This provision permitted the traditional *Gregory* spin-off so long as it did not "appear" that (1) any of the corporations would fail to continue the active conduct of a trade or business, and (2) the transaction was used principally as a "device" for the distribution of E & P.

In 1954 Congress carried over from the 1939 Code the basic definition of the (D) reorganization. The Senate Report to the 1954 Code (273–274) explains:

> Subparagraph (D) of [§ 368(a)(1)] restates the definition of existing law appearing in section 112(g)(1)(D) of the Internal Revenue Code of 1939. Under this definition the term "reorganization" includes a transfer by a corporation of all or a part of its assets to another corporation if immediately after such transfer the transferor corporation, or its shareholders, or both, are in control of the transferee. Your committee's bill has altered the definition to provide that if the control of the transferee corporation is in the transferor corporation or in persons who were shareholders of the transferor, or any combination thereof, the transfer will, nevertheless, qualify as a reorganization under section 368(a)(1)(D), the control owned by these persons need not be in the same proportion as it was before the transfer. For example, corporation A owns only properties connected with a drug store and a hardware store. Corporation A transfers the drug store properties to corporation D in exchange for all the stock of D and transfers the hardware store properties to corporation H in exchange for all the stock of H. Immediately thereafter, corporation A distributes all the stock in corporation D to X, one of the two shareholders in A, in exchange for all of X's stock and distributes all the stock in corporation H to Y, the other shareholder in A, in exchange for all his stock. The distributions qualify under section 355. The transfer of the properties by A is a reorganization under subparagraph (D). It should be noted, however, that in the event that the values of the properties transferred to corporations D and H are disproportionate to the value of the stock in A held by shareholders X and Y, the transaction at the shareholder level may have the effect of a gift or a compensation. See section 355.

Subparagraph (D) also explicitly states that a transaction of the type described is only to be considered a reorganization when the stock and securities of the transferee corporation or corporations are distributed to the shareholders and security holders under the terms of section 354, 355, or 356. However, where there is no such distribution, the transaction may, nevertheless, result in nonrecognition of gain or loss to the transferor corporation under the terms of section 351.

Paragraph (2) of [§ 368(a)] lists three special rules which modify existing law. It is provided that if a transaction meets the description, both of an acquisition of assets for stock (subsec. (a)(1)(C)) and also meets the description of a transfer to a controlled corporation (subsec. (a)(1)(D)) it shall be treated as described only in subsection (a)(1)(D).

Your committee intends by this rule to insure that the tax consequences of the distribution of stocks or securities to shareholders or security holders in connection with divisive reorganizations will be governed by the requirements of section 355 relating to distribution of stock of a controlled corporation.

B. LEGISLATIVE DEVELOPMENTS SINCE 1954

1. *Prevention of Use of § 355 as Surrogate for a Mirror Transaction*

See § 355(b)(2)(D).

HOUSE REPORT TO THE REVENUE ACT OF 1987
1080–1084 (1987).

PRESENT LAW

Gains on certain distributions to a controlling U.S. corporate shareholder (an 80–percent distributee) are not taxed to the distributing corporation in a liquidation (sec. 337). [*See* § 337(a).] * * *

Certain divisive distributions of corporate stock are also tax-free to the distributing corporation, provided that certain statutory and other constraints are met, including a condition that the transaction not be a device for the distribution of earnings and profits and certain other requirements (sec. 355). * * *

REASONS FOR CHANGE

The Tax Reform Act of 1986 changed the prior-law rules for the treatment of the distributing corporation on liquidating distributions. Such distributions are generally treated in the same manner as nonliquidating distributions, that is, as if the distributing corporation had sold the distributed property to the recipient at fair market value. * * *

The committee understands that some taxpayers take the position that an appreciated subsidiary may be sold or distributed outside the affiliated group without the current recognition of gain on the appreciation by the selling or distributing corporation.

Some of such taxpayers apparently take the position that the so-called "mirror" subsidiary transaction was not curtailed by the 1986 Act. * * * [Mirror transactions are examined in *Taxable and Tax-Free Corporate Mergers, Acquisitions, and LBOs, supra* Sec. 1.4.]

The committee is also aware that some taxpayers take the position that certain other provisions of the Code may permit the creation of structures said to allow the sale or distribution of an appreciated corporate subsidiary without the recognition of current corporate level tax on the appreciation, or structures that have the effect of permitting one or more acquirors to acquire or resell corporate subsidiaries or other assets with more favorable tax results than the original owners could obtain. Such provisions include * * * the provisions of section 355 of the Code that, together with section 358 of the Code, permit a substituted basis when stock of one corporation is distributed by another corporation. Such provisions might be used to claim a stepped-up, fair market value basis when a subsidiary of an acquired corporation is distributed to the acquiring corporation. The committee believes that the requirements of section 355 of the Code should generally prevent the use of that section to accomplish a sale of a recently distributed subsidiary (or its recently acquired parent) without corporate level tax, or effectively to accomplish a sale of a subsidiary to any significant shareholder by a distribution with respect to recently purchased stock. * * *

Explanation of Provision

* * *

The bill provides that a distribution of stock will not qualify for nonrecognition under section 355 of the Code if control of a corporation which was conducting such business was acquired in a taxable transaction within the 5 year period ending on the date of the distribution through one or more corporations, including the distributing corporation. [*See* § 355(b)(2)(D).]

2. Amendment to § 355(c) Relating to Treatment of Distributing Corporation

HOUSE REPORT TO MISCELLANEOUS REVENUE ACT OF 1988

371–373 (1988).

Present Law

* * * The 1986 Act made a series of amendments to the reorganization provisions attempting to conform those provisions with changes made by the 1984 Act. However, numerous technical problems with the 1986 amendments have arisen. The bill responds to these technical problems with a complete revision of the 1986 amendments.

EXPLANATION OF PROVISION

* * *

Treatment of section 355 distributions, etc. * * * [G]ain (but not loss) will be recognized on the distribution of property other than the stock or securities in the controlled corporation in a transfer to which section 355 (or so much of section 356 as relates to section 355) applies. [*See* § 355(c).]

* * *

3. Potential Recognition of Gain in Certain Disqualified Distributions

See § 355(d).

CONFERENCE REPORT TO REVENUE RECONCILIATION ACT OF 1990
82–92 (1990).

PRESENT LAW

A corporation generally must recognize gain on the sale or distribution of appreciated property, including stock of a subsidiary. However, corporate distributions of subsidiary stock that meet the requirements of section 355 of the Code are tax-free both to the distributing corporation and to the distributee shareholders.

Present law imposes a 5-year holding period requirement for any corporate distributee that has acquired 80 percent of the stock of a corporation ("target"), unless the stock was acquired solely in nontaxable transactions. If the 5-year holding period is not met, distributions of subsidiaries by the target corporation are not tax-free under section 355. [*See* § 355(b)(2)(D).]

* * *

CONFERENCE AGREEMENT

* * *

In general

The conference agreement generally requires recognition of corporate-level gain (but does not require recognition by the distributee shareholders) on a distribution of subsidiary stock or securities qualifying under section 355 (whether or not part of a reorganization otherwise described in section 361(c)(2)) if, immediately after the distribution, a shareholder holds a 50-percent or greater interest in the distributing corporation or a distributed subsidiary that is attributable to stock or securities that were acquired by purchase (as defined in the provision) within the preceding 5-year period. [*See* § 355(d)(1) and (2).] Thus, for example, under the provision, the distributing corporation will recognize gain on the distribution of subsidiary stock and securities if a person purchases distributing corporation stock or securities, and within 5 years, 50 percent or more of the subsidiary stock is distributed to that person in exchange for the purchased stock or securities. The distributing corporation will recognize gain as if it had sold the distributed subsidiary stock and securities to the distributee at fair market value.

* * *

Disqualified distribution

A disqualified distribution is any section 355 distribution if, immediately after the distribution, any person holds disqualified stock in either the distributing corporation or any distributed controlled corporation constituting a 50-percent or greater interest in such corporation. [See § 355(d)(2).]

Disqualified stock

The conference agreement defines disqualified stock to include any stock in the distributing corporation or any controlled corporation acquired by purchase (as defined) after October 9, 1990 and during the 5-year period ending on the date of the distribution. * * *

* * *

Assume that after the effective date individual A acquires by purchase a 20-percent interest in corporation P and P redeems stock of other shareholders so that A's interest in P increases to a 30 percent interest. Within 5 years of A's purchase, P distributes 50 percent of the stock of its subsidiary, S, to A in exchange for his 30 percent interest in P (the remainder of the stock of S distributed in the section 355 transaction is distributed to other shareholders). P recognizes gain on the distribution of the stock of S because all 50 percent of the stock of S held by A is disqualified stock.

Fifty percent or greater interest

The conference agreement provides that a 50-percent or greater interest means stock possessing at least 50 percent of the total combined voting power of all classes of stock entitled to vote or at least 50 percent of the total value of all shares of all classes of stock. [See § 355(d)(4).]
* * *

Acquisition by purchase

Stock or securities are generally considered acquired by purchase for purposes of the provision if they are acquired in any transaction in which the acquiror's basis of the stock or securities is not determined in whole or in part by reference to the adjusted basis of such stock or securities in the hands of the person from whom acquired and is not determined under section 1014(a). [See § 355(d)(5).]

* * *

Five-year period

Gain is recognized under the provision in the case of a section 355 distribution within 5 years after a shareholder acquires stock or securities by purchase (if the shareholder meets the 50–percent or more ownership test immediately after the distribution). [See § 335(d)(2) and (3).]

* * *

Regulatory authority

The Treasury Department has general regulatory authority (1) to prevent the avoidance of the purposes of the provision through any means, including through the use of related persons, intermediaries, pass-through entities, options, or other arrangements; and (2) to exclude from the provision transactions that do not violate the purposes of this provision. [See § 355(d)(9).]

* * *

§ 13.4 INTRODUCTION TO THE REGULATIONS, RULINGS AND CASES

A. INTRODUCTION TO THE REGULATIONS

PREAMBLE TO THE § 355 REGULATIONS

Treasury Decision 8238 (January 4, 1989).

* * *

Section 355 provides that, under certain conditions, a corporation may distribute stock, or stock and securities, of a subsidiary without recognition of gain or loss to its shareholders or security holders. The proposed regulations made two major changes to the existing regulations under section 355. First, the regulations under section 355(a)(1)(B) (requiring that the transaction not be used principally as a device for the distribution of earnings and profits) were revised to specify factors to be taken into account in determining whether a transaction was used principally as such a device. Second, the regulations under section 355(b) (relating to active businesses) were revised to permit the separation of a single business, thereby conforming them to the holdings of *Commissioner v. Coady*, 289 F.2d 490 (6th Cir.1961), *aff'g* 33 T.C. 771 (1960), and *United States v. Marett*, 325 F.2d 28 (5th Cir.1963). The proposed regulations also proposed to clarify the business purpose requirement under section 355. * * *

B. THE BUSINESS PURPOSE REQUIREMENT

1. *The Regulations*

See § 1.355–2(b).

PREAMBLE TO THE § 355 REGULATIONS
Treasury Decision 8238 (January 4, 1989).

Comments On, And Changes To, Proposed Regulations

Business Purpose

(1) *Independent requirement.* Section 1.355–2(b)(1) of the proposed regulations expressed the business purpose requirement as an independent requirement under section 355. Commenters objected to the treatment of the business purpose requirement as a separate requirement and suggested that the existence of a corporate business purpose should be considered only in determining whether a transaction was used principally as a device for the distribution of earnings and profits within the meaning of section 355(a)(1)(B).

Treasury and the Internal Revenue Service acknowledge that there is a very close relationship between the business purpose requirement and the requirement that the transaction not be used principally as a device for the distribution of earnings and profits. Accordingly, the final regulations clarify that the corporate business purpose is evidence that the transaction was not used principally as such a device. See § 1.355–2(d)(3)(ii) in this document. This new provision is discussed below under the heading "Evidence of Nondevice."

However, Treasury and the Internal Revenue Service believe that, as held in *Commissioner v. Wilson*, 353 F.2d 184 (9th Cir.1965), a transaction that is not carried out for a corporate business purpose should not qualify under section 355, even if it was not used principally as a device for the distribution of earnings and profits. Accordingly, the final regulations retain the independent business purpose requirement. See § 1.355–2(b)(1) in this document.

(2) *Corporate business purpose.* Section 1.355–2(b)(1) of the proposed regulations provided that a distribution qualifies under section 355 only if it is carried out for one or more corporate business purposes. Corporate business purposes were identified as "real and substantial nontax reasons germane to the business of the corporations."

Commenters objected to the "real and substantial" standard on the grounds that it is not useful and is confusing. However, Treasury and the Internal Revenue Service continue to believe that the "real and substantial" standard provides a useful description of the type of corporate business purpose required under section 355. Accordingly, the final regulations retain that standard. See § 1.355–2(b)(2) in this document.

Commenters requested reconsideration of the "nontax" standard. The Internal Revenue Service has ruled that reduction of state and local capital taxes is a corporate business purpose. Rev.Rul. 76–187, 1976–1 C.B. 97. That rule will remain in effect. However, Treasury and the Internal Revenue Service continue to believe that reduction of Federal taxes should not be regarded as a corporate business purpose. Accordingly, the final regulations replace the "nontax" standard with a "non Federal tax" standard.

Commenters wondered whether the potential reduction of Federal taxes will offset or negate the existence of a non-Federal tax business purpose. In response, the final regulations clarify that only a transaction motivated in whole or in substantial part by a corporate business purpose will satisfy the corporate business purpose requirement. Further, the final regulations clarify that the potential reduction of Federal taxes by the distributing or controlled corporations (or a corporation controlled by either) is relevant in determining whether a corporate business purpose motivated the distribution. The final regulations also provide that a purpose of reducing non Federal taxes is not a corporate business purpose if (i) the transaction will effect a reduction in both Federal and non Federal taxes because of similarities between Federal tax law and the tax law of the other jurisdiction and (ii) the reduction of Federal taxes is greater than or substantially coextensive with the reduction of non Federal taxes. See § 1.355-2(b)(1) and (2) in this document. Three examples are also added in § 1.355-2(b)(5). The first illustrates that a distribution which is made to enable the distributing and/or controlled corporation to make an election to be an S corporation does not meet the corporate business purpose requirement. The second example illustrates that the result is the same if the distribution is made to enable the distributing and/or controlled corporation to elect to become an S corporation both for Federal tax purposes and for purposes of a state that has tax law provisions similar to Subchapter S of the Internal Revenue Code of 1986. The third example illustrates that the magnitude of the potential reduction of Federal taxes is relevant to the determination of whether the distribution is motivated by a corporate business purpose.

(3) *Shareholder purpose.* Section 1.355-2(b)(1) of the proposed regulations provided that a distribution qualifies under section 355 only if it is carried out for purposes "germane to the business of the corporations." It further provided that "a shareholder purpose for a transaction may be so nearly coextensive with a corporate business purpose as to preclude any distinction between them. In such a case, the transaction is carried out for purposes germane to the business of the corporations." Some commenters complained that the proposed regulations did not adequately acknowledge that, in a closely held corporation, the purposes of the shareholders cannot be distinguished from those of the corporation. Other commenters complained that the proposed regulations addressed cases in which the shareholder purposes are totally coextensive with the corporate business purposes, but failed to address the more common cases in which there is only partial overlap.

In response, the final regulations revise example (2) of § 1.355-2(b)(2) of the proposed regulations to present a disproportionate distribution that satisfies the business purpose requirement without a shareholder disagreement. See example (2) of § 1.355–2(b)(5) in this document. * * *

* * *

(4) *Business purposes for distribution.* The final regulations provide that the distribution of the stock, or stock and securities, of the controlled corporation to the shareholders must be carried out for one or more corporate business purposes. In example (3) of § 1.355–2(b)(2) of the proposed regulations, the distribution is not carried out for a corporate business purpose. The alleged corporate business purpose for the transaction is protection of a business from the risks of another business. Because that purpose is satisfied as soon as the risky business is dropped down to a subsidiary, the distribution of the stock of the subsidiary is not carried out for that purpose. * * *

(5) *Availability of alternative arrangement.* Example (4) of § 1.355–2(b)(2) of the proposed regulations involves a transfer by the distributing corporation of one of its two businesses to a new controlled corporation and a distribution of the stock of the controlled corporation where the transfer and the distribution are required by a lender as a condition on additional loans. The example concludes that the distribution was carried out for one or more corporate business purposes. Commenters asked whether the distribution in example (4) would be carried out for one or more corporate business purposes if the lender would have been satisfied to have the distributing corporation transfer its two businesses to two new controlled corporations and continue as a holding company.

* * *

Treasury and the Internal Revenue Service believe that a distribution satisfies the business purpose requirement only if the distributing corporation cannot achieve its corporate business purpose through a nontaxable transaction that does not involve a distribution of the stock of a subsidiary and that is neither impractical nor unduly expensive. Thus, if such an alternative transaction is available, the distribution is not carried out for a corporate business purpose. Accordingly, example (4) is replaced by new examples illustrating this aspect of the business purpose requirement. See examples (4) and (5) of § 1.355–2(b)(5) in this document.

2. Illustration: Combination of Business Purpose and Estate Planning Purpose

REVENUE RULING 75–337
1975–2 C.B. 124.

Advice has been requested whether the "business purpose" requirement of section 1.355–2(c) of the Income Tax Regulations is satisfied in the following transaction, which is otherwise qualified under section 355 of the Internal Revenue Code of 1954 and the regulations thereunder.

X corporation operated an automobile dealership. Its franchise for the sale and service of automobiles was in the name of individual A who managed X and owned 53 percent of its stock. A was 70 years old and this stock constituted the bulk of his estate. The balance of the stock was held by A's five daughters in equal proportions. Three of the daughters were also actively employed in the X business. The other two daughters were not actively employed by X.

Y corporation, a wholly owned subsidiary of X, was engaged in the business of renting automobiles.

The franchise policy of the automobile manufacturer did not favor granting or continuing a franchise where there were inactive shareholders unless the manager holding the franchise owned a majority of the stock. As an alternative, the manufacturer's policy permitted the granting or continuing of a franchise where there was no majority shareholder, provided the shareholders were few in number and all were active in the business. The manufacturer does not grant franchises to corporations, only to individuals or partnerships. The franchise was renewable periodically and was not transferable by inheritance or otherwise.

As the first step in a plan to insure that X's shareholders would be able to renew the franchise upon the death or retirement of A, who was then 70 years old, X distributed three-fourths of the Y stock to the two inactive-daughter shareholders in exchange, value for value, for all of their X stock. The remaining one-fourth of the Y stock was distributed to A in exchange for shares of his X stock of equal value. A intended that upon his death the inactive-daughter shareholders would receive their inheritance in Y stock and assets other than stock of X.

The distribution of the Y stock to A furthered the objective of enabling X's shareholders to retain the automobile franchise by increasing the percentage of ownership in X on the part of the active shareholders (other than A) and by providing A with Y stock which he could bequeath or gift to the inactive-daughter shareholders, leaving his remaining X stock available for bequests or gifts to the active shareholders.

* * *

Upon the death or retirement of A, the present stock ownership of X with proportionate bequests or gifts to A's daughters (because A's X stock represented the bulk of his estate) would preclude the existence of a majority active shareholder of X or all active shareholders in X for the purpose of renewing the X shareholders' franchise under the manufacturer's dealership policy. In order to insure qualification under the alternate conditions of the franchise policy, it was necessary to set the stage for X shareholders to retain the franchise at A's death or retirement, without chancing a potential interruption in the continuity of, or even the loss of, the franchise which might occur if nothing was done until after A's death or retirement. This was accomplished by first causing the Y stock to be distributed and then having A provide in his will or by gift for only the active shareholders to receive his shares of X stock.

Thus, the distribution of Y stock is germane to the continuation of the X business in the reasonably foreseeable future. Execution of the plan will forestall an impending disruption to the X business by reason of the current active family group being unable to renew X's franchise upon A's death or retirement.

In *Rafferty v. Commissioner,* 452 F.2d 767 (1st Cir.1971), it was held, under a plan to avoid any remote possibility of interference in a business by future sons-in-law, that the spin-off had no immediate business reason, involved a personal motive and had as its primary purpose a desire to make bequests in accordance with an estate plan. The difficulties anticipated were so remote that they might never come to pass. The daughters might never marry—thus eliminating completely any cause to worry about business interference by future sons-in-law. There was, at best, "only an envisaged possibility of future debilitating nepotism," and the effect on the business was conjectural.

In the instant case, the problem was immediate due to the advanced age of A and was directly related to the retention of a franchise vital to the business of the distributing corporation. Accordingly, the distribution by X of the Y stock to the inactive-daughter shareholders and to A in exchange for X stock is supported by a valid business purpose within the contemplation of section 1.355–2(c) of the regulations.

C. DEVICE FOR DISTRIBUTION OF EARNINGS AND PROFITS

1. *The Regulations*

See § 1.355–2(b).

PREAMBLE TO THE § 355 REGULATIONS
Treasury Decision 8238 (January 4, 1989).

DEVICE FOR DISTRIBUTION OF EARNINGS AND PROFITS

In General

Section 1.355–2(c) of the proposed regulations interpreted the requirement of section 355(a)(1)(B) that the transaction not be used principally as a device for the distribution of earnings and profits of the distributing corporation, the controlled corporation, or both (a "device"). That interpretation consisted of a description of the tax avoidance that could be achieved through the use of a device, a specification of factors ("device factors") whose presence is evidence that the transaction was used principally as a device ("evidence of device"), and a specification of certain transactions that ordinarily would not be considered to be a device for the distribution of earnings and profits. The final regulations generally retain these provisions. At the request of commenters, they also specify factors ("nondevice factors") whose presence is evidence that the transaction was not used principally as a device ("evidence of nondevice"). See § 1.355-2(d) in this document.

Section 1.355-2(c)(1) of the proposed regulations explained that a corporate separation can present potential for the avoidance of the dividend provisions of the Code. The final regulations make clear that avoidance potential is presented by the substitution of stock interests in two or more corporations for a stock interest in a single corporation. In particular, avoidance potential can be presented by distributions in which the distributing corporation liquidates as well as by distributions in which the distributing corporation does not liquidate. The final regulations also replace the reference to sales or liquidations with a reference to sales, exchanges, or transactions that are treated as exchanges under the Code, thus making clear that redemptions as well as liquidations are covered by the rules. They also limit the rules to transactions involving stock on the grounds that sections 355(a)(3) and 356(d)(2)(C) generally render transactions involving securities incapable of use to avoid the dividend provisions of the Code. At the request of commenters, the final regulations clarify that the determination whether a transaction was used principally as a device depends on all of the facts and circumstances, and that the presence of the device factors specified in § 1.355-2(d)(2) is not alone controlling. See § 1.355-2(d)(1) in this document. The final regulations also make clear that a device can include a transaction that effects a recovery of basis.

The provision in § 1.355-2(c)(1) of the proposed regulations regarding pro rata distributions is clarified and made a separate provision in the final regulations. See § 1.355-2(d)(2)(ii) in this document. Certain transactions that are ordinarily considered not to have been used principally as a device are specified in a separate provision in the final regulations. As suggested by commenters, that provision clarifies that these transactions are ordinarily considered not to have been used principally as a device, notwithstanding the presence of any of the device factors specified in § 1.355-2(d)(2). See § 1.355-2(d)(5) in this document.

Nature And Use Of Assets

(1) Assets not used in a qualifying trade or business.

Section 1.355-2(c)(3)(iii) of the proposed regulations provided that the transfer or retention of cash or liquid assets in excess of the reasonable needs of the post-distribution business of the transferee or the retaining corporation ("excess liquid assets") is evidence of device. Some commenters agreed that the transfer of excess liquid assets should be evidence of device, but asserted that the retention of excess liquid assets should be a neutral factor. Other commenters noted that, because liquid assets must either be transferred or retained, the proposed regulations appeared to find evidence of device whenever excess liquid assets are present.

Section 1.355–2(c)(3)(ii) of the proposed regulations provided that, if a substantial portion of the post-distribution assets of the distributing or the controlled corporation consists of a trade or business acquired during the five-year period preceding the distribution in a transaction in which the basis of the assets was not determined in whole or in part by reference to the transferor's basis, this fact is evidence of device (the "new trade or business device factor"). Some commenters objected to this device factor on the grounds that the acquisition of a trade or business should be treated under the active business requirements of section 355(b) instead of the device clause of section 355(a)(1)(B). They pointed out that section 355(b)(2)(C) denies qualification under section 355 to a distribution after which the only trade or business of the distributing or the controlled corporation is a trade or business that was acquired during the five-year period preceding the distribution in a transaction in which the basis of the assets was not determined in whole or in part by reference to the transferor's basis. Other commenters objected to this device factor on the grounds that the presence of operating assets, even if newly acquired, should not be evidence of device. They argued that operating assets are not suitable for use in a device.

Treasury and the Internal Revenue Service believe that the presence of excess liquid assets permits avoidance of the dividend provisions of the Code, regardless of the corporation that holds them. Treasury and the Internal Revenue Service also believe that the active business requirements of section 355(b) do not render unnecessary the principle of the new trade or business device factor of § 1.355–2(c)(3)(ii) of the proposed regulations. * * *

* * *

Accordingly, the final regulations provide that the existence of assets that are not used in a trade or business that satisfies the requirements of section 355(b) is evidence of device. * * *

(2) *Related function.* Section 1.355–2(c)(3)(iv) of the proposed regulations provided that the continued integration of a function with the business from which it has been separated is evidence of device. Commenters objected to this device factor on the grounds that the specified conditions present no compelling evidence of device.

Treasury and the Internal Revenue Service believe that the continued integration of a function with the business from which it has been separated should be evidence of device. This belief is based on the interpretation of section 355(a)(1)(B) expressed in § 1.355–2(c)(1) of the proposed regulations. Under certain circumstances, continued integration indicates a likelihood of avoidance of the dividend provisions of the Code.

* * *

Evidence Of Nondevice

Section 1.355–2(c)(1), (2), and (3) of the proposed regulations specified device factors whose presence is evidence of device. At the request of commenters, the final regulations specify several nondevice factors whose presence is evidence of nondevice. See § 1.355–2(d)(3) in this document.

* * *

The final regulations provide that the corporate business purposes for a transaction present evidence of nondevice. In accordance with the facts and circumstances standard of § 1.355–2(c)(1) of the proposed regulations, the strength of this evidence depends on all of the facts and circumstances. The final regulations adopt a sliding scale approach. Thus, the greater the evidence of device, the stronger the corporate business purpose necessary to outweigh that evidence. Evidence of device presented by a disproportionate allocation of assets not used in a trade or business that satisfies the requirements of section 355(b) can be outweighed by the presence of a strong corporate business purpose for that allocation. The final regulations also specify nonexclusive factors to be taken into account in assessing the strength of a corporate business purpose. See § 1.355–2(d)(3)(ii) in this document.

The final regulations specify other nondevice factors. One of these nondevice factors is that the distributing corporation is publicly traded and has no shareholders who hold large blocks of stock. See § 1.355–2(d)(3)(iii) in this document. Another nondevice factor is that all of the distributees are domestic corporations that would be entitled to the deduction under section 243(a)(1) available to corporations meeting the stock ownership requirements of section 243(c), 243(a)(2), 243(a)(3), or 245(b) if the distribution were taxable as a dividend. See § 1.355–2(d)(3)(iv) in this document.

Examples

In light of the changes made to the device rules in the final regulations, the examples in § 1.355–2(c)(4) of the proposed regulations are replaced by new examples. The examples illustrate the application of the facts and circumstances device standard of § 1.355–2(d)(1) and the balancing of the evidence of device presented by the device factors specified in § 1.355(d)(2) against the evidence of nondevice presented by the corporate business purpose nondevice factor specified in § 1.355–2(d)(3)(ii). See § 1.355–2(d)(4) in this document.

Example (1) illustrates that the transaction will be considered to have been used principally as a device if there is a subsequent sale of stock by a shareholder to a key employee that is negotiated or agreed upon before the distribution, even though the employee could have acquired an equivalent amount of stock directly from the corporation.

* * *

Transactions Ordinarily Not A Device

Section 1.355–2(c)(1) of the proposed regulations specified two transactions that are ordinarily not considered to be a device for the distribution of earnings and profits. The final regulations specify those transactions in a separate provision. As suggested by commenters, that provision clarifies that such a transaction is ordinarily considered not to have been used principally as a device, notwithstanding the presence of any of the device factors specified in § 1.355–2(d)(2). See § 1.355–2(d)(5)(i) in this document.

Section 1.355–2(c)(1) of the proposed regulations accorded a presumption against device to a distribution if, in the absence of section 355, no part of a distribution of money by the distributing corporation, the controlled corporation, or any corporation controlled, directly or indirectly, by either of those corporations would be taxable as a dividend because of the absence of earnings and profits.

Commenters questioned the relevance of the earnings and profits of the corporations other than the distributing corporation. They argued that the dividend avoidance interpretation of section 355(a)(1)(B) expressed in § 1.355–2(c)(1) of the proposed regulations made only the earnings and profits of the distributing corporation relevant. Treasury and the Internal Revenue Service, however, believe that the earnings and profits of both the distributing and controlled corporations must be taken into account, and the final regulations so provide. See § 1.355–2(d)(5)(ii) in this document. Also, the application of the presumption must take into account the possibility that a distribution by the distributing corporation would create earnings and profits if section 355 did not apply.

* * *

The final regulations also clarify that a transaction to which section 302(a) or 303(a) would apply if section 355 did not is not accorded the presumption against device if it involves the distribution of the stock of more than one controlled corporation and facilitates the avoidance of the dividend provisions of the Code through the subsequent sale or exchange of the stock of one corporation and the retention of the stock of another. The final regulations also add an example of a transaction that is not accorded the presumption because it presents such tax avoidance potential. See example (2) of § 1.355–2(d)(5)(v) in this document.

2. Illustration: Non-pro Rata Split Off

REVENUE RULING 71–383
1971–2 C.B. 180.

Advice has been requested as to the Federal income tax consequences of a non-pro rata distribution by a corporation of stock of a controlled corporation to certain of its shareholders in exchange for 85 percent of their stock in the distributing corporation, under the circumstances described below.

In 1968, *X*, a widely held corporation, acquired all of the outstanding stock of *Y* corporation, which was owned by two shareholders (*A* and *B*), in a transaction qualifying as a reorganization within the meaning of section 368(a)(1)(B) of the Internal Revenue Code of 1954. No gain or loss was recognized in whole or in part in that transaction. Both corporations had been engaged in the active conduct of their respective business for more than five years. *X* corporation was engaged in the business of developing and manufacturing custom components for high technology industries. *Y* was engaged in the business of designing and manufacturing of microwave instrumentation.

In 1970, for valid business reasons, *X* distributed all of the stock of *Y* to *A* and *B* in exchange for 85 percent of the *X* stock of each which was equal in fair market value to the *Y* stock received. Immediately prior to the exchange a substantial capital contribution was made by *X* to *Y* in order to reduce the disparity in the market values of the respective stocks. The capital contribution did not cause a change in the character of *Y's* business. The *X* stock owned by *A* and *B*, was less than five percent of the outstanding *X* stock and consisted solely of the stock received pursuant to the reorganization in 1968. *A* and *B* were completely unrelated to the other shareholders of *X*. * * *

* * *

A substantial capital contribution made to a subsidiary by its parent prior to a distribution of the subsidiary's stock to the parent's shareholders may be considered evidence of a device under section 355(a)(1)(B) of the Code. However, in the instant case, if the distribution were considered taxable, it would not result in dividend income to the two shareholders receiving *Y* stock because the exchange of their *X* stock as to each would have been a substantially disproportionate redemption under section 302(b)(2) of the Code and thus would have been treated as a distribution in part or full payment in exchange for such stock under section 302(a) of the Code. Consequently, the transaction is not a device to distribute earnings and profits (that is, to convert dividend income into capital gains) * * *.

Accordingly, no gain or loss is recognized to *A* and *B* upon the receipt of the *Y* stock in exchange for their *X* stock under section 355(a) of the Code.

D. SUBSEQUENT SALE OR EXCHANGE OF STOCK: IMPACT ON THE DEVICE CLAUSE

1. Background

a. *Spin–Off of Controlled Corporation Followed by Sale of Distributing Corporation*

REVENUE RULING 55–103
1955–1 C.B. 31.

The X Corporation is engaged in the manufacture of paper products. It also owns 80 percent of the stock of Y, a foreign corporation, which operates a lumber business. The Y Corporation's stock has greatly appreciated in value and constitutes a large proportion of the total asset value of X Corporation. The X Corporation has common stock of 120x dollars and an earned surplus of 100x dollars. For the past several years, the X Corporation has suffered severe operating losses and its stockholders have received no dividends. For that reason the stockholders of X have voted to liquidate and start dissolution proceedings on a specified date, unless negotiations to sell their stock have been completed on or before such date.

The Z Corporation is interested in buying all of the outstanding common stock of X Corporation and has made an offer to purchase such stock which has not yet been acted upon by X or its stockholders. However, the Z Corporation's offer does not contemplate payment for the value of the Y Corporation's stock as an asset of X Corporation.

Since the Z Corporation has no interest in Y stock held by X Corporation, the latter corporation proposes to distribute this stock to its shareholders, prior to the completion of the sale negotiations.

* * *

In the instant case, subsequent to the proposed distribution of Y stock by X, the stock of X Corporation may be sold by the present stockholders pursuant to an arrangement negotiated immediately prior to the distribution. The sale of stock of the distributing corporation immediately subsequent to a distribution of stock of a controlled corporation, when negotiations for such a sale are already in process, is generally considered sufficient evidence that the distribution of stock was used principally as a device for the distribution of earnings and profits of the distributing corporation. The purpose of the requirement that the transaction not be used principally as a device for the distribution of earnings and profits is to limit the application of section 355 of such Code to those cases in which the distribution of stock of the controlled corporation effects only a readjustment of continuing interests in property under modified corporate forms.

In the instant case, the purpose in distributing the Y stock is to facilitate the sale of stock of X Corporation. No continuing interest in X on the part of any of the present stockholders is contemplated. The distribution of the Y stock is merely a device to give to the X stockholders certain assets for which the prospective purchaser of their stock is unwilling to pay. Therefore, it is an arrangement for distributing the earnings and profits of X Corporation and section 355 of the Code is not applicable to such a transaction.

Accordingly, it is held that the amount and taxability of the distribution of the stock of Y Corporation to the stockholders of X Corporation will be determined in accordance with the provisions of section 301(c)(1) of the Internal Revenue Code of 1954. The portion of the distribution constituting a dividend will be determined under the provisions of section 316 of such Code.

b. *Spin–Off of Controlled Corporation Followed by Merger of Distributing Corporation into Acquiring Corporation*

COMMISSIONER v. MORRIS TRUST

United States Court of Appeals, Fourth Circuit, 1966.
367 F.2d 794.

HAYNSWORTH, CHIEF JUDGE:

Its nubility impaired by the existence of an insurance department it had operated for many years, a state bank divested itself of that business before merging with a national bank. The divestiture was in the form of a traditional "spin-off," but, because it was a preliminary step to the merger of the banks, the Commissioner treated their receipt of stock of the insurance company as ordinary income to the stockholders of the state bank. We agree with the Tax Court, that gain to the stockholders of the state bank was not recognizable under § 355 of the 1954 Code.

In 1960, a merger agreement was negotiated by the directors of American Commercial Bank, a North Carolina corporation with its principal office in Charlotte, and Security National Bank of Greensboro, a national bank. * * *

For many years, American had operated an insurance department. This was a substantial impediment to the accomplishment of the merger, for a national bank is prohibited from operating an insurance department except in towns having a population of not more than 5000 inhabitants. To avoid a violation of the national banking laws, therefore, and to accomplish the merger under Security's national charter, it was prerequisite that American rid itself of its insurance business.

The required step to make it nubile was accomplished by American's organization of a new corporation, American Commercial Agency, Inc., to which American transferred its insurance business assets in exchange for Agency's stock which was immediately distributed to American's stockholders. At the same time, American paid a cash dividend fully taxable to its stockholders. The merger of the two banks was then accomplished.

Though American's spin-off of its insurance business was a "D" reorganization, as defined in § 368(a)(1), provided the distribution of Agency's stock qualified for non-recognition of gain under § 355, the Commissioner contended that the active business requirements of § 355(b)(1)(A) were not met, since American's banking business was not continued in unaltered corporate form. He also finds an inherent incompatibility in substantially simultaneous divisive and amalgamating reorganizations.

Section 355(b)(1)(A) requires that both the distributing corporation and the controlled corporation be "engaged immediately after the distribution in the active conduct of a trade or business." There was literal compliance with that requirement, for the spin-off, including the distribution of Agency's stock to American's stockholders, preceded the merger. The Commissioner asks that we look at both steps together, contending that North Carolina National Bank was not the distributing corporation and that its subsequent conduct of American's banking business does not satisfy the requirement.

* * *

The Commissioner, indeed, concedes that American's stockholders would have realized no gain had American not been merged into Security after, but substantially contemporaneously with, Agency's spin-off. Insofar as it is contended that § 355(b)(1)(A) requires the distributing corporation to continue the conduct of an active business, recognition of gain to American's stockholders on their receipt of Agency's stock would depend upon the economically irrelevant technicality of the identity of the surviving corporation in the merger. Had American been the survivor, it would in every literal and substantive sense have continued the conduct of its banking business.

* * *

There is no distinction in the statute between subsequent amalgamating reorganizations in which the stockholders of the spin-off transferor would own 80% or more of the relevant classes of stock of the reorganized transferor, and those in which they would not. The statute draws no line between major and minor amalgamations in prospect at the time of the spin-off. Nothing of the sort is suggested by the detailed control-active business requirements in the five-year pre-distribution period, for there the distinction is between taxable and nontaxable acquisitions, and a tax free exchange within the five-year period does not violate the active business-control requirement whether it was a major or a minor acquisition. Reorganizations in which no gain or loss is recognized, sanctioned by the statute's control provision when occurring in the five years preceding the spin-off, are not prohibited in the post-distribution period.

As we have noticed above, the merger cannot by any stretch of imagination be said to have affected the continuity of interest of American's stockholders or to have constituted a violation of the principle underlying the statutory control requirement. The view is the same whether it be directed to each of the successive steps severally or to the whole.

Nor can we find elsewhere in the Code any support for the Commissioner's suggestion of incompatibility between substantially contemporaneous devisive and amalgamating reorganizations. The 1954 Code contains no inkling of it; nor does its immediate legislative history. The difficulties encountered under the 1924 Code and its successors, in dealing with formalistic distortions of taxable transactions into the spin-off shape, contain no implication of any such incompatibility. Section 317 of the Revenue Act of 1951 and the Senate Committee Report, to which we have referred, did require an intention that the distributing corporation continue the conduct of its active business, but that transitory requirement is of slight relevance to an interpretation of the very different provisions of the 1954 Code and is devoid of any implication of incompatibility. If that provision, during the years it was in effect, would have resulted in recognition of gain in a spin-off if the distributing corporation later, but substantially simultaneously, was a party to a merger in which it lost its identity, a question we do not decide, it would not inhibit successive reorganizations if the merger preceded the spin-off.

The Congress intended to encourage six types of reorganizations. * * * The "D" reorganization has no lesser standing. It is on the same plane as the others and, provided all of the "D" requirements are met, is as available as the others in successive reorganizations.

* * *

Our conclusion that gain was not recognizable to American's stockholders as a result of the spin-off, therefore, is uninfluenced by the fact that the subsequent merger was under the National Banking Act. It would have been the same if the merger had been accomplished under state laws. * * *

* * *

While we reject the technical provision of the National Banking Act as a basis for decision, therefore, it is important to the result that, as in every merger, there was substantive continuity of each constituent and its business. In framing the 1954 Code, the Congress was concerned with substance, not formalisms. Its approach was that of the courts in the *Gregory v. Helvering* series of cases. Ours must be the same. The technicalities of corporate structure cannot obscure the continuity of American's business, its employees, its customers, its locations or the substantive fact that North Carolina National Bank was both American and Security.

A decision of the Sixth Circuit [16] appears to be at odds with our conclusion. In *Curtis,* it appears that one corporation was merged into another after spinning-off a warehouse building which was an unwanted

---

16. *Curtis v. United States,* 6 Cir., 336 F.2d 714 [16 AFTR 2d 5685].

asset because the negotiators could not agree upon its value. The Court of Appeals for the Sixth Circuit affirmed a District Court judgment holding that the value of the warehouse company shares was taxable as ordinary income to the stockholders of the first corporation.

A possible distinction may lie between the spin-off of an asset unwanted by the acquiring corporation in an "A" reorganization solely because of disagreement as to its value and the preliminary spin-off of an active business which the acquiring corporation is prohibited by law from operating. We cannot stand upon so nebulous a distinction, however. We simply take a different view. The reliance in *Curtis* upon the Report of the Senate Committee explaining § 317 of the Revenue Act of 1951, quite dissimilar to the 1954 Code, reinforces our appraisal of the relevant materials.

* * *

For the reasons which we have canvassed, we think the Tax Court, which had before it the opinion of the District Court in *Curtis,* though not that of the affirming Court of Appeals, correctly decided that American's stockholders realized no recognizable taxable gain upon their receipt in the "D" reorganization of the stock of Agency.

Affirmed.

c. *The Service Accepts Morris Trust*

REVENUE RULING 68–603
1968–2 C.B. 148.

The Internal Revenue Service will follow the decision of the United States Court of Appeals for the Fourth Circuit in the case of *Commissioner v. Mary Archer W. Morris Trust,* 367 F.2d 794 (1966), to the extent it holds that (1) the active business requirements of section 355(b)(1)(A) of the Internal Revenue Code of 1954 were satisfied even though the distributing corporation immediately after the spin-off merged into another corporation, (2) the control requirement of section 368(a)(1)(D) of the Code implies no limitation upon a reorganization of the transferor corporation after the distribution of stock of the transferee corporation, and (3) there was a business purpose for the spin-off and the merger.

2. *The Regulations*

See § 1.355–2(d)(2)(iii).

PREAMBLE TO THE § 355 REGULATIONS
Treasury Decision 8238 (January 4, 1989).

SUBSEQUENT SALE OR EXCHANGE OF STOCK

(1) *Per se rule.* Section 1.355–2(c)(2) of the proposed regulations provided that a subsequent sale or exchange of 20 percent or more of the

stock of either the distributing or the controlled corporation, negotiated or agreed upon before the distribution, is conclusive evidence of device. Commenters objected to this rule on the grounds that it is arbitrary, that it has no case law support, and that it is inconsistent with the facts and circumstances standard mandated by the Code and expressed in § 1.355-1(c)(1) of the proposed regulations.

Upon reconsideration, Treasury and the Internal Revenue Service continue to believe that a subsequent sale or exchange of stock of either the distributing or the controlled corporation, negotiated or agreed upon before the distribution, is substantial evidence of device. However, they agree with the commenters that section 355(a)(1)(B) does not require that this evidence be treated as conclusive, and that taxpayers should not be denied the opportunity to prove that, despite the sale or exchange, the transaction was not used principally as a device. Accordingly, the *per se* rule is eliminated in the final regulations.

The final regulations provide that a subsequent sale or exchange of stock of either the distributing or the controlled corporation, negotiated or agreed upon before the distribution, is substantial evidence of device. Generally, the greater the percentage of stock sold or exchanged, the stronger the evidence of device. See § 1.355-2(d)(2)(iii)(A) in this document. In addition, the shorter the period of time between the distribution and the sale or exchange, the stronger the evidence of device.

(2) *Negotiated or agreed upon before the distribution.* The final regulations retain the rules of the proposed regulations concerning whether a sale or exchange is considered to be negotiated or agreed upon before the distribution. See § 1.355-2(d)(2)(iii)(D) in this document.

(3) *Subsequent reorganizations.* The final regulations retain the provision in § 1.355-2(c)(2) of the proposed regulations that an exchange of stock pursuant to a plan of reorganization in which either no gain or loss or only an insubstantial amount of gain is recognized is not evidence of device. The final regulations provide that for this purpose, gain treated as a dividend pursuant to sections 356(a)(2) and 316 shall be disregarded. They also add a provision that any stock received in a reorganization exchange excepted from the subsequent sale rules will be treated, for purposes of those subsequent sale rules, as the stock surrendered. Thus, any sale or exchange of the stock received will be subject to the subsequent sale rules. See § 1.355-2(d)(2)(iii)(E) in this document.

E. CONTINUITY OF INTEREST REQUIREMENT: THE REGULATIONS

See § 1.355-2(c).

PREAMBLE TO THE § 355 REGULATIONS
Treasury Decision 8238 (January 4, 1989).

CONTINUITY OF INTEREST

Section 1.355–2(b)(1) of the proposed regulations provided that section 355 contemplates a continuity of interest in all or part of the business enterprise on the part of those persons who, directly or indirectly, were the owners of the enterprise prior to the distribution or exchange. There was concern it could be argued that the phrase "all or part" meant a transaction could qualify even if none of the owners of the enterprise before the separation had, after the distribution, an interest in the business enterprise of one of the separated corporations. The final regulations make clear that the separation must effect only a readjustment of continuing interests in the property of the distributing and controlled corporations. In this regard, section 355 requires that one or more persons who, directly or indirectly, were the owners of the enterprise prior to the distribution or exchange own, in the aggregate, an amount of stock establishing a continuity of interest in each of the modified corporate forms in which the enterprise is conducted after the separation. These rules have been relocated in a new § 1.355–2(c). Four examples illustrating the continuity of interest requirement are added, the principles of which are based on previously published revenue rulings. See Rev.Rul. 69–293, 1969–1 C.B. 102 and Rev.Rul. 79–293, 1979–2 C.B. 125.

F. ACTIVE CONDUCT OF A TRADE OR BUSINESS

1. *The Regulations*

See § 1.355–3.

PREAMBLE TO THE § 355 REGULATIONS
Treasury Decision 8238 (January 4, 1989).

ACTIVE CONDUCT OF A TRADE OR BUSINESS

(1) *In general.* Section 1.355–3 of the proposed regulations interpreted the active business requirements of section 355(b). The final regulations retain those provisions and make clarifying revisions to § 1.355–3(b)(2)(iii) (the "active conduct" requirement of section 355(b)(2)(A)) and § 1.355–3(b)(3) (the "five-year active conduct" requirement of section 355(b)(2)(B)).

Section 1.355–3(b)(2)(iii) of the proposed regulations provided that the active conduct of a trade or business requires the performance of active and substantial management and operational functions. Commenters inquired whether a corporation may satisfy that requirement if some or all of its activities are performed by independent contractors. In response, the final regulations clarify that, in determining whether a corporation is actively conducting a trade or business, the activities performed by persons outside the corporation, including independent contractors, generally will not be taken into account. However, a corporation may satisfy that requirement through the activities that it performs directly, even though other activities are performed by independent contractors. See § 1.355–3(b)(2)(iii) in this document.

The final regulations slightly revise examples (1), (2), and (3) of § 1.355–3(c) of the proposed regulations to explain why the described activities do not satisfy the active business requirements. Example (1) illustrates that the holding of investment securities is not the active conduct of a trade or business. See § 1.355–3(b)(2)(iv)(A) in this document. This example is consistent with Rev.Rul. 66–204, 1966 C.B. 113, which holds that activity generated by trading in stock and securities held for one's own account is an investment function and is not the active conduct of a trade or business within the meaning of section 355. Examples (2) and (3) illustrate that the activities relied upon to satisfy the active business requirements must have been actively conducted throughout the five-year period preceding the distribution. See § 1.355–3(b)(3) in this document.

(2) *Separation of a single business.* The proposed regulations provided for the separation of a single business in § 1.355–1(a). They interpreted the five-year active conduct requirement accordingly in § 1.355–3(b)(3). The final regulations retain these provisions. They redesignate example (10) of § 1.355–3(c) of the proposed regulations, which was based on *Commissioner v. Coady,* 289 F.2d 490 (6th Cir.1961), *aff'g* 33 T.C. 771 (1960), as example (4). They redesignate example (11) of § 1.355–3(c) of the proposed regulations, which was based on *United States v. Marett,* 325 F.2d 28 (5th Cir.1963), as example (5) and revise it to conform more closely to the facts of that case. See examples (4) and (5) of § 1.355–3(c) in this document.

(3) *Single or multiple businesses.* In reexamining the active business requirements, Treasury and the Internal Revenue Service recognized that it is often difficult to determine whether a corporation is conducting a single business, which may be separated under section 355 if it has been actively conducted for five years, or multiple businesses, which may be separated from each other under section 355 only if each has been actively conducted for five years. Correlatively, they recognized that it is difficult to determine whether a corporate expenditure for a new activity constitutes the acquisition or creation of a new business or the expansion of an existing business. Accordingly, it is considered to be appropriate to simplify these determinations.

As in *Estate of Lockwood v. Commissioner,* 350 F.2d 712 (8th Cir.1965), the final regulations provide that, for purposes of the five-year active conduct requirement, a new activity in the same line of business as an activity that has been actively conducted by the distributing corporation for the five-year period preceding the distribution ordinarily will not be considered a separate business. As a result, the distribution of a new activity will more easily satisfy the five-year active conduct requirement. See § 1.355–3(b)(3)(ii) in this document.

In example (12) of § 1.355–3(c) of the proposed regulations, a department store that was constructed within the preceding five years is separated from a department store business that has been actively conducted for nine years. The separation satisfies the five-year active conduct requirement because the newly constructed department store became part of the existing business. The final regulations revise example (12) and redesignate it as example (7). Example (7) illustrates that the five-year active conduct requirement is met, whether or not the new and old stores are operated as a single unit prior to the separation. The final regulations also add a new example (8) to illustrate that the same result obtains, whether the new activity results from internal corporate expansion or is purchased as a going concern. See examples (7) and (8) of § 1.355–3(c) in this document.

(4) *Functional separations.* The proposed regulations provided for the separation of a single business in § 1.355–1(a). They interpreted the five-year active conduct requirement accordingly in § 1.355–3(b)(3). Examples (8), (9), and (14) of § 1.355–3(c) of the proposed regulations presented separations of businesses along functional lines satisfying the active business requirements. These examples are grouped together as examples (9), (10), and (11) in the final regulations. Example (14) of the proposed regulations presented the separation of a research department from a business engaged in the manufacture and sale of household products. The final regulations redesignate example (14) as example (9) and revise it to illustrate that the separation satisfies the active business requirements, whether the research department subsequently provides services only to the business from which it was separated or also to others. See examples (9), (10), and (11) of § 1.355–3(c) in this document. It should be noted that functional separations may present evidence of device under § 1.355–2(d)(2)(iv)(C).

(5) *Owner-occupied real estate.* The proposed regulations interpreted the active business requirements to permit functional separations. Commenters noted that, in appropriate cases, the separation of real estate occupied by its owner prior to the distribution ("owner-occupied real estate") should satisfy those requirements. Treasury and the Internal Revenue Service recognize that the separation of owner-occupied real estate may satisfy the active business requirements, but they also recognize that such a separation presents significant tax avoidance opportunities. Accordingly, the final regulations revise § 1.355–3(b)(2)(iv)(B) of the proposed regulations to provide that the separation of owner-occupied real estate will be subject to careful scrutiny under the active business requirements. Also, such a separation may be subject to close examination under the related function device factor of § 1.355–2(d)(2)(iv)(C).

* * *

2. Illustration: Non-operator Owner of Working Interest in Oil and Gas Property

REVENUE RULING 89-27
1989-1 C.B. 106.

Issue

Can a corporation that is a nonoperator owner of working interests in oil and gas properties satisfy the active conduct of a trade or business requirement of section 355(b) of the Internal Revenue Code?

Facts

For more than 5 years, X, a domestic corporation, has been engaged directly and through its subsidiaries in the exploration, development, production and marketing of petroleum products.

Y is a domestic corporation engaged, as discussed below, in the oil and gas business in state Z. All of the stock of Y has been owned by X for more than 5 years. The activities of Y are performed by its employees. Y employs, on a full time basis, geologists, petroleum engineers, accountants and other employees necessary to conduct its business.

Y is in constant search for properties that may yield commercial quantities of oil and gas and has, in previous years, acquired nonoperator working interests in such properties.

As an owner of a working interest, Y participates in deciding whether to develop the property. This requires extensive gathering and analyzing of technical data by Y. Once a decision is made to develop any property, Y enters into a standard form operating agreement with other owners of working interests in the property.

Under the agreement, one working interest owner (other than Y) is designated as operator and generally supervises the daily activities involved in development and production. Y pays its pro rata share of costs of development and expenses of operations involving the property. In addition, Y meaningfully participates in management decisions, inspects the drilling site to determine if the drilling operations conform to the agreement, and analyzes data obtained from drillsite activities. Y also participates in deciding the location and depth of the wells to be drilled and whether to drill a new well, deepen an old well, and to abandon a well. Although the operating agreement reserves the right to Y to take the production in kind, Y typically authorizes an agent to market the production. Y has derived substantial revenue from its oil and gas operations during the last 5 years.

For valid business reasons, X proposes to distribute pro-rata to its shareholders all of the shares of Y. Thereafter, Y will continue its present operations, including the acquisition of additional working interests in new properties.

Except for the question here at issue concerning the active conduct of a trade or business requirement of section 355(b) of the Code, the distribution by X of the Y shares meets all of the other requirements of section 355 and the regulations thereunder.

LAW AND ANALYSIS

* * *

Section 1.355–3(b)(2)(ii) of the Income Tax Regulations, in defining "trade or business" for section 355 purposes, provides that a trade or business consists of a specific existing group of activities being carried on for the purpose of earning income or profit from such group of activities, and the activities included in such group must include every operation which forms a part of, or a step in, the process of earning income or profit. Such group of activities ordinarily must include the collection of income and the payment of expenses.

In defining "active conduct" of a trade or business the regulations indicate that in order for a trade or business to be actively conducted, substantial management and operational activities generally must be directly carried on by the corporation itself and such activities generally do not include the activities of others outside the corporation, including independent contractors. However, the fact that a portion of a corporation's business activities is performed by others will not preclude the corporation from being engaged in the active conduct of a trade or business if the corporation itself directly performs active and substantial management and operational functions. Section 1.355–3(b)(2)(iii) of the regulations.

* * *

A determination whether a trade or business is actively conducted for purposes of section 355(b) is based on all the facts and circumstances. In the instant case, Y's business activities include its direct performance of active and substantial management and operational functions, apart from those activities performed by others.

HOLDING

Under the facts of this case, Y, a non-operator owner of working interests in oil and gas properties, is engaged in the active conduct of a trade or business within the meaning of section 355(b) of the Code. Accordingly, the distribution by X to its shareholders of the Y stock qualifies as a tax-free distribution under section 355(a)(1) of the Code.

G. IS RETENTION BY DISTRIBUTING CORPORATION OF STOCK OR SECURITIES OF CONTROLLED CORPORATION NOT FOR TAX AVOIDANCE WITHIN § 355(a)(1)(D)(ii)?

REVENUE RULING 75-321

1975-2 C.B. 123.

For valid business purposes, X intends to distribute to its shareholders, with respect to their stock, 95 percent of the stock of Y corporation, one of its wholly owned subsidiaries. Y is engaged in the business of banking and is X's only subsidiary so engaged. Y, as well as each of the other subsidiary corporations of X, has been actively engaged in business for more than 5 years. The business purpose behind the proposed distribution is involuntary in nature in that the applicable Federal banking laws require X to qualify as a bank holding company or to limit its stock ownership in any bank to no more than a 5 per cent interest. X could not readily qualify as a bank holding company because under banking laws X would be required to divest itself of all of its subsidiaries other than Y. Therefore, X was required to divest itself of 95 percent of its stock interest in its wholly owned subsidiary, Y. The proposed distribution will accomplish that result. The business purpose behind the retention of 5 percent of the Y stock by X is to enable X to have assets of sufficient value (the Y stock) to serve as collateral so as to enable X to obtain needed short-term financing for its remaining business enterprise.

* * *

In the instant case the facts show that (1) a genuine separation of the corporate entities will be effected since the distributing corporation will distribute 95 percent of the stock of the controlled corporation; (2) retention of a 5 percent stock interest will not enable the distributing corporation to maintain practical control since several shareholders of the controlled corporation, following the distribution, will each own nearly as much stock in the controlled corporation as will be owned by the distributing corporation; and (3) a sufficient business purpose for the retention of the 5 percent interest is shown to exist. Therefore, the facts establish, in the instant case, that the retention by X of 5 percent of the Y stock was not in pursuance of a plan having as one of its principal purposes the avoidance of Federal income tax. The facts also establish that the transaction is not a device for the distribution of earnings and profits within the meaning of section 355(a)(1)(B) of the Code.

Accordingly, in the instant case, since all of the requirements of section 355(a) of the Code will be satisfied, no gain or loss will be recognized to (and no amount will be includible in the income of) the shareholders of X on the receipt of 95 percent of the Y stock.

Note

For a similar result dealing with the retention of debentures, *see* Rev.Rul. 75-469, 1975-2 C.B. 126.

H. CARRYOVER OF TAX ATTRIBUTES IN A DIVISIVE § 355

Section 381, which provides for the carryover of certain assets, such as NOLS, in certain asset reorganizations, is not applicable to § 355 divisive transactions. However, § 1.312–10 sets forth the rules for allocating E & P between the controlled corporation and the distributing corporation. In general, in the case of a newly formed controlled corporation, the E & P is allocated in accordance with the relative fair market values of the business retained by the distributing corporation and that contributed to the controlled corporation.

§ 13.5 ILLUSTRATION OF § 306 STOCK IN A (D) REORGANIZATION UNDER § 355

REVENUE RULING 77–335
1977–2 C.B. 95.

* * *

X corporation owned all of the outstanding stock of Y corporation for over 5 years. The Y stock consisted solely of preferred and common stock. X and Y were each engaged in a separate manufacturing business for more than 5 years. The preferred stock of Y was not section 306 stock in the hands of X.

For valid business reasons X distributed to its shareholders on a pro rata basis all its common and preferred stock of Y in a transaction qualifying under section 355 of the Code. At the time of the distribution X had earnings and profits greater than the fair market value of the Y preferred stock while Y had no earnings and profits.

* * *

The test outlined by section 1.306–3(d) of the regulations provides that ordinarily section 306 stock includes stock that is not common stock and that is received in a distribution to which section 355 of the Code applies if cash received in lieu of such stock would have been treated as a dividend under section 356(a)(2) or would have been treated as a distribution to which section 301 applies by virtue of section 356(b) or section 302(d).

In the instant case the shareholders of X received the preferred stock of Y in a distribution to which section 355 of the Code applied. Had cash been distributed by X in lieu of the preferred stock of Y, such amounts would have been treated as a distribution to which section 301 applies by virtue of section 356(b), making such a distribution taxable to the shareholders as a dividend since X had sufficient earnings and profits at the time of the distribution. Thus, the preferred stock distributed by X to its shareholders meets the definitional terms of section 306(c)(1)(B) and none of the exceptions in section 306(b) applies.

§ 13.6 DETERMINATION OF WHETHER BOOT IS TREATED AS A DIVIDEND

REVENUE RULING 93–62, IRB 1993–30
11 (Oct. 4, 1993.)

ISSUE

Whether gain recognized on the receipt of cash in an exchange of stock that otherwise qualifies under section 355 of the Internal Revenue Code is treated as a dividend distribution under section 356(a)(2).

FACTS

Distributing is a corporation with 1,000 shares of a single class of stock outstanding. Each share has a fair market value of $1x. A, one of five unrelated individual shareholders, owns 400 shares of Distributing stock. Distributing owns all of the outstanding stock of a subsidiary corporation, Controlled. The Controlled stock has a fair market value of $200x.

Distributing distributes all the stock of Controlled plus $200x cash to A in exchange for all of A's Distributing stock. The exchange satisfies the requirements of section 355 but for the receipt of the cash.

LAW AND ANALYSIS

Section 355(a)(1) of the Code provides, in general, that the shareholders of a distributing corporation will not recognize gain or loss on the exchange of the distributing corporation's stock or securities solely for stock or securities of a controlled subsidiary if the requirements of section 355 are satisfied.

Section 356(a)(1) of the Code provides for recognition of gain on exchanges in which gain would otherwise not be recognized under section 354 (relating to tax-free acquisitive reorganizations) or section 355 if the property received in the exchange consists of property permitted to be received without gain recognition and other property or money ("boot"). The amount of gain recognized is limited to the sum of the money and the fair market value of the other property.

Under section 356(a)(2) of the Code, gain recognized in an exchange described in section 356(a)(1) that "has the effect of the distribution of a dividend" is treated as a dividend to the extent of the distributee's ratable share of the undistributed earnings and profits accumulated after February 28, 1913. Any remaining gain is treated as gain from the exchange of property.

Determinations of whether the receipt of boot has the effect of a dividend are made by applying the principles of section 302 of the Code. *Commissioner v. Clark,* 489 U.S. 726 (1989), 1989-2 C.B. 68. Section 302 contains rules for determining whether payments in redemption of stock are treated as payments in exchange for the stock or as distributions to which section 301 applies.

Under section 302(a) of the Code, a redemption will be treated as an exchange if it satisfies one of the tests of section 302(b). Section 302(b)(2) provides exchange treatment for substantially disproportionate redemptions of stock. A distribution is substantially disproportionate if (1) the shareholder's voting stock interest and common stock interest in the corporation immediately after the redemption are each less than 80 percent of those interests immediately before the redemption, and (2) the shareholder owns less than 50 percent of the voting power of all classes of stock immediately after the redemption.

In *Clark,* the Supreme Court determined whether gain recognized under section 356 of the Code on the receipt of boot in an acquisitive reorganization under section 368(a)(1)(A) and (a)(2)(D) should be treated as a dividend distribution. In that case, the sole shareholder of the target corporation exchanged his target stock for stock of the acquiring corporation and cash. In applying section 302 to determine whether the boot payment had the effect of a dividend distribution, the Court considered whether section 302 should be applied to the boot payment as if it were made (i) by the target corporation in a pre-reorganization hypothetical redemption of a portion of the shareholder's target stock, or (ii) by the acquiring corporation in a post-reorganization hypothetical redemption of the acquiring corporation stock that the shareholder would have received in the reorganization exchange if there had been no boot distribution.

The Supreme Court stated that the treatment of boot under section 356(a)(2) of the Code should be determined "by examining the effect of the exchange as a whole," and concluded that treating the boot as received in a redemption of target stock would improperly isolate the boot payment from the overall reorganization by disregarding the effect of the subsequent merger. Consequently, the Court tested whether the boot payment had the effect of a dividend distribution by comparing the interest the taxpayer actually received in the acquiring corporation with the interest the taxpayer would have had if solely stock in the acquiring corporation had been received in the reorganization exchange.

Prior to the decision in *Clark,* the Service considered the facts and issue presented in this revenue ruling in Rev.Rul. 74-516, 1974-2 C.B. 121. The determination of whether the exchange of Distributing stock for Controlled stock and boot under section 355 of the Code had the effect of a dividend distribution under section 356(a)(2) was made by comparing A's interest in Distributing prior to the exchange with the interest A would have retained if A had not received Controlled stock and had only surrendered the Distributing stock equal in value to the boot. The Court's decision in *Clark* does not change the conclusion in Rev.Rul. 74–516, because, like *Clark*, the ruling determined whether the exchange in question had the effect of a dividend distribution based on an analysis of the overall transaction.

The exchange of A's Distributing stock for stock of Controlled qualifies for non-recognition treatment under section 355 of the Code in part because the overall effect of the exchange is an adjustment of A's continuing interest in Distributing in a modified corporate form. *See* section 1.355–2(c) of the Income Tax Regulations. The Controlled stock received by A represents a continuing interest in a portion of Distributing's assets that were formerly held by A as an indirect equity interest. The boot payment has reduced A's proportionate interest in the overall corporate enterprise that includes both Distributing and Controlled. Thus, the boot is treated as received in redemption of *A*'s Distributing stock, and *A*'s interest in Distributing immediately before the exchange is compared to the interest *A* would have retained if *A* had surrendered only the Distributing shares equal in value to the boot.

Under the facts presented here, before the exchange, A owned 400 of the 1,000 shares, or 40 percent, of the outstanding Distributing stock. If A had surrendered only the 200 shares for which A received boot, A would still hold 200 of the 800 shares, or 25 percent, of the Distributing stock outstanding after the exchange. This 25 percent stock interest would represent 62.5 percent of *A*'s pre-exchange stock interest in Distributing. Therefore, the deemed redemption would be treated as an exchange because it qualifies as substantially disproportionate under section 302(b)(2) of the Code.

Holding

In an exchange of stock that otherwise qualifies under section 355 of the Code, whether the payment of boot is treated as a dividend distribution under section 356(a)(2) is determined prior to the exchange. This determination is made by treating the recipient shareholder as if the shareholder had retained the distributing corporation stock actually exchanged for controlled corporation stock and received the boot in exchange for distributing corporation stock equal in value to the boot.

Effect on Other Rulings

Rev.Rul. 74–516 is superseded.

* * *

§ 13.7 SUMMARY PROBLEM ON (D) REORGANIZATIONS AND § 355

1. Individuals *A* and *B* are equal shareholders of *X* corporation. *A* has an adjusted basis of $25K for his stock, and *B* has a basis of $75K. *X* is engaged in two separate businesses: (1) manufacturing widgets, and (2) manufacturing wodgets. The fair market value of each business is

$50K, and the adjusted basis of each is $25K. *X* has been engaged in these two businesses since it was organized in 1950. *X* has $25K of accumulated E & P all of which was produced by the widget business. The wodget business has always operated on a break even basis, but it now looks as though it will become profitable. *A* and *B* are not able to get along very well, and they have decided to go their separate ways with *A* taking the widget business and *B* taking the wodget business. *B* is thinking of abandoning business altogether and he may cash out his interest. What result to each of the parties (including corporations) in each of the following plans?

    a. *X* is liquidated, distributing the widget business to *A* and the wodget business to *B*?

    b. *X* distributes the wodget business to *B* in redemption of his stock. *A* is then the sole shareholder of *X*? Suppose *B* immediately sells the business to corporation *Y* that had been negotiating with *X* over the purchase of the wodget business?

    c. *X* sells the wodget business and distributes the proceeds to *B* in redemption of his stock. *A* is then the sole shareholder?

    d. *X* transfers the widget business to a new subsidiary, *S–1*, and the wodget business to a new subsidiary, *S–2*, and then distributes the stock of *S–1* to *A* and the stock of *S–2* to *B*. Both *S–1* and *S–2* are capitalized with both common and preferred. *X* is liquidated after the distributions?

    (1) Suppose that after the above transaction *B* sells his stock of *S–2* to corporation *Y*? *B* had always planned to make the sale. Suppose that instead of a sale, *B* disposes of his *S–2* stock in a (B) reorganization?

    (2) Suppose the facts are the same as in d, but instead of a wodget business, *X*'s second business is holding rental real estate, and it transfers the real estate to *S–2*? What if, instead, there was just one business (widgets) and *X* transferred one half the business to *S–1* and one half to *S–2*?

    (3) Suppose the facts are the same as in d, except that the wodget business had been purchased by *X* three years ago? Suppose *X* had acquired it three years ago in an (A) merger?

2. Target Corporation (*TC*) is engaged in two lines of business: manufacturing wodgets and manufacturing widgets. Both businesses have been conducted by *TC* for over 10 years, and the assets of both are substantially appreciated. The widget business has a value of $10 million and the wodget business has a value of $5 million. *TC* has substantial earnings and profits. Acquiring Corporation (*AC*) purchases all of the stock of *TC* for $15 million. Two years after the acquisition, *AC* causes *TC* to transfer the assets and liabilities of the wodget business to a new subsidiary and then to distribute the stock of the new subsidiary to *AC*. At the time of the distribution, the widget and wodget

businesses have the same values they had at the time of the acquisition of *TC*'s stock by *AC*.

 a. What result to the parties in the above transaction?

 b. What result if three years after the distributions, *AC* sells the stock of the subsidiary that holds the wodget business?

 c. What result if instead of purchasing all of *TC*'s stock, *AC* had purchased one-third of *TC*'s stock and two years after the acquisition *TC* distributed the stock of the wodget subsidiary to *AC* in exchange for *AC*'s one-third stock interest in *TC*?

Chapter 14

NONDIVISIVE (D) REORGANIZATION AND THE LIQUIDATION REINCORPORATION DOCTRINE

§ 14.1 SCOPE

This chapter addresses the nondivisive (D) reorganization under § 354(b) and the liquidation-reincorporation doctrine. Sec. 14.2 introduces the nondivisive (D), and Sec. 14.3 introduces the liquidation reincorporation doctrine. Sec. 14.4 presents the *Davant* case, which dealt with an attempt to avoid the liquidation-reincorporation doctrine by the use of a straw man.

For a more detailed discussion of the issues addressed in this chapter, *see* Chapter 45 of *Federal Taxation of Business Enterprises,* *supra* Chapter 1, note 1 and Chapter 14 of Bittker and Eustice, *Corporations, supra* Sec. 1.4.

§ 14.2 THE § 354(b) NONDIVISIVE (D)

A. IN GENERAL

In order for a § 368(a)(1)(D) distribution to qualify under § 354(b), the distributing corporation must (1) transfer "substantially all" of its assets to a controlled corporation, and (2) distribute, pursuant to a plan of reorganization, the stock, securities, and other property received by the distributing corporation together with its retained properties. The control test is satisfied if one or more of the shareholders of the distributing corporation own 50% of the stock of the controlled corporation. *See* § 368(a)(2)(H). The regulations say that the transfer must be to a single corporation. The regulations also say that the distributing corporation may use its retained property or property received from the controlled corporation to discharge its "existing liabilities." *See*

§ 1.354–1(a). Although there is no explicit requirement that the distributing corporation be liquidated, as a practical matter it will be liquidated. This is a nondivisive (D) reorganization.

The tax treatment to the parties in a § 354(b) nondivisive (D) is as follows. The transfer of the assets to the controlled corporation is a § 351 transfer, as well as a (D). Therefore, the distributing corporation receives nonrecognition treatment on the transfer under both §§ 351 and 361 and takes a § 358 substituted basis for the stock received. If the distributing corporation receives boot from the controlled corporation, the tax treatment of the distributing corporation would vary depending on whether § 351 or § 361 applies to the transaction. If § 351 applies, the distributing corporation has gain recognition to the extent of the boot. If § 361(b) applies, gain is recognized only if the boot is not distributed. There does not appear to be any official Service position on this point, but § 361(b) should control.

The controlled corporation receives nonrecognition treatment under § 1032 and § 1.61–12(c) upon the issuance of its stock and securities and takes a carryover basis for the properties under § 362. The carryover basis would come under § 362(a) if § 351 controls and under § 362(b) if § 361 controls. The distribution of the stock and securities of the controlled corporation is a nonrecognition distribution to the distributing corporation under § 361. The shareholders of the distributing corporation receive nonrecognition treatment under § 354(a) if they exchange stock in the distributing corporation solely for stock in the controlled corporation. They also receive nonrecognition treatment if they exchange securities in the distributing corporation for securities of an equal principal amount in the controlled corporation. If they receive an excess principal amount of securities or other boot, the shareholders have gain or dividend treatment under § 356. If the transaction fails to qualify as a (D) reorganization, the shareholders have a capital gain or loss under § 331, and the distributing corporation has gain or loss under § 336.

B. 1984 AMENDMENT TO THE CONTROL REQUIREMENT IN THE NONDIVISIVE (D)

See § 368(a)(2)(H).

THE SENATE FINANCE COMMITTEE'S REPORT ON THE DEFICIT REDUCTION TAX BILL OF 1984
207–209 (1984).

PRESENT LAW

D reorganizations

Under section 368(a)(1)(D), a transfer by a corporation of all or a part of its assets to a corporation controlled immediately after the transfer by the transferor or one or more of its shareholders is generally treated as a D reorganization if, among among other things, stock or securities of the controlled corporation are distributed pursuant to the plan of reorganization in a transaction qualifying under sections 354, 355, or 356. A D reorganization may involve the acquisition of substantially all of the assets of a corporation (an acquisitive or nondivisive transaction) or the division of an existing corporation (a divisive transaction). For purposes of a D reorganization, the term "control" is defined as the ownership of stock possessing at least 80 percent of the total combined voting power of all classes of stock entitled to vote and at least 80 percent of the total number of shares of all other classes of stock of the corporation. No attribution rules are explicitly made applicable.

If a nondivisive transaction qualifies as a D reorganization, generally no gain or loss is recognized by the transferor corporation or its shareholders. The acquiring corporation's basis in the assets acquired from the transferor corporation is generally the same as it was in the hands of the transferor corporation. If boot (i.e., money or other property other than stock or securities of the transferee corporation) is distributed to the shareholders of the transferor corporation, then any gain realized by such shareholders is recognized, but in an amount not in excess of the sum of such money and the fair market value of such other property. If the distribution of the boot has the effect of a dividend, it is treated by the shareholder as a dividend to the extent of his or her pro rata share of the corporation's undistributed earnings and profits.[1]

Liquidation and contribution to a related corporation

In general, under section 331, amounts distributed to a shareholder in complete liquidation of a corporation are treated as full payment in exchange for the shareholder's stock. If the stock is a capital asset in the hands of the shareholder, a complete liquidation will result in capital gain or loss, the shareholder's basis in the property received in the taxable liquidation is the fair market value of the property at the time of the distribution. With several exceptions, no gain or loss is recognized to the distributing corporation on a distribution in complete liquidation of such corporation or a liquidating sale by the corporation.

The Internal Revenue Service has taken the position, and a number of cases have held, that a liquidation followed by a contribution of a substantial part of the distributed properties to a corporation controlled by the shareholders of the liquidating corporation can constitute a D reorganization. In such cases, the transferee corporation's basis in acquired assets is the same as the basis in the transferor corporation's hands prior to the transfer. Further, the transferee corporation inherits tax attributes of the transferor corporation, which would generally disappear in the case of a liquidation. If money or property (other than stock or securities in the transferee corporation) is distributed to the

---

1. The IRS takes the position that for purposes of determining dividend equivalency, a boot distribution is treated as having been made by the acquired corporation (i.e., the transferor) rather than by the acquiring corporation. Rev.Rul. 75–83, 1975–1, C.B. 112. See also *Shimberg v. United States*, 577 F.2d 283 (5th Cir.1978). But see *Wright v. United States*, 482 F.2d 600 (8th Cir.1973).

shareholders of the transferor corporation, the shareholders may be treated as having received a dividend rather than a payment in exchange for stock.[2]

Sale of stock to commonly controlled corporation

Under present law, a sale of stock in one corporation by a shareholder to a commonly controlled corporation is generally treated under section 304 as a redemption rather than as a sale to an independent third party. A distribution in redemption of stock is generally treated by the shareholders as in part or full payment in exchange for the stock if (1) it is not essentially equivalent to a dividend, (2) it is substantially disproportionate with respect to the shareholder, (3) it is in complete termination of the shareholder's interest, or (4) certain other requirements are satisfied. Distributions in redemption of a shareholder's stock that are not treated as in part or full payment in exchange for the stock are treated as dividends to the extent of undistributed earnings of profits.

For purposes of section 304, the term control means the ownership of stock possessing at least 50 percent of the total combined voting power of all classes of stock entitled to vote, or at least 50 percent of the total value of shares of all classes of stock. Attribution rules apply for purposes of determining ownership of stock.

REASONS FOR CHANGE

Liquidation-reincorporation transactions (i.e., transactions involving the liquidation of a corporation coupled with a transfer of its operating assets to a new corporation in which the shareholders of the transferor corporation have a substantial stock interest) that are not treated as reorganizations can be used to accomplish a bail-out of earnings and profits at capital gains rates. Further, these transactions can be used by a shareholder (or group of shareholders) to obtain a step-up in the basis of assets that are held in corporate solution largely at the cost of a shareholder-level capital gains tax without a significant change in ownership.

The D reorganization provisions generally envision the continuation of the transferor corporation's business in a corporation in which the transferor corporation or its shareholders have a substantial interest. In many transactions, the liquidating corporation's business is being continued by a related corporation. However, the control requirement that applies in the case of a D reorganization has in some instances prevented the Service from successfully asserting that these transactions constitute D reorganizations.

Also, the D reorganization provisions and section 304 both operate to prevent the bail-out of earnings and profits at capital gains rates. Further, both apply to transactions in which property is transferred from one corporation to another corporation in a transaction in which money or other property is received by common shareholders. Nonethe-

---

2. See, e.g., *James Armour, Inc.*, 43 IC 295 (1965).

less, the control requirement under section 304 is a 50–percent requirement. Further, attribution rules apply for purposes of determining stock ownership under section 304. The committee believes that the control test in the case of the D reorganization provisions should more closely conform to that of section 304.

The absence of explicit attribution rules to determine ownership of stock for purposes of the control requirement may enable taxpayers to bail-out earnings and profits at capital gains rates by transferring assets to a corporation controlled by a related person rather than to a corporation controlled by them.

EXPLANATION OF PROVISION

Under the bill, in the case of a transaction otherwise qualifying as a nondivisive D reorganization, the transferor corporation or its shareholders are treated as having control of the transferee corporation if the transferor corporation or its shareholders own stock possessing at least 50 percent of the total combined voting power of all classes of stock entitled to vote and at least 50 percent of the total number of shares of all other classes of stock of the corporation. [See § 368(a)(2)(H).] Further, the constructive ownership of stock rules contained in section 318(a), modified, are applicable for purposes of determining whether the transferor corporation or its shareholders are in control of the transferee corporation.

* * *

[The Conference adopted the above provision except that control is defined as the ownership, directly or indirectly, of stock possessing at least 50 percent of the total combined voting power of all classes of stock entitled to vote, or at least 50 percent of the total value of all shares of all classes of stock. The Conference Report says that the conferees do not intend that "recharacterization as a D reorganization * * * be the exclusive means for the Service to challenge liquidation-reincorporation and similar transactions. For example, it is not intended that this provision supersede or otherwise replace the various doctrines that have been developed by the Service and the courts to deal with such transactions. *See, e.g.,* Rev.Rul. 61–156 * * * *Telephone Answering Service* * * * and *Smothers.*"]

C. TRANSFER OF "SUBSTANTIALLY ALL" THE ASSETS

1. *Illustration*

MOFFATT v. COMMISSIONER

United States Court of Appeals, Ninth Circuit, 1966.
363 F.2d 262, *cert. denied* 386 U.S. 1016, 87 S.Ct. 1370, 18 L.Ed.2d 453 (1967).

BARNES, CIRCUIT JUDGE:

* * * We must determine whether distributions by the corporation, Moffatt & Nichol, Inc., to its shareholders (petitioners) were liquidating distributions under Sections 331(a) and therefore taxable as capital gains, or were distributions incident to a plan of reorganization under Sections 354 and 368, and therefore taxable as dividends under Section 356. Taxpayers challenge the decision of the Tax Court on the grounds (1) that the steps taken to liquidate Moffatt & Nichol, Inc. were not part of an integrated plan of reorganization, and (2) that the steps taken, even if viewed as interrelated, did not satisfy the statutory reorganization requirements of Sections 354 and 368.

From the date of its incorporation in 1947 until approximately October 1957, Moffatt & Nichol, ["Inc"] was primarily engaged in consulting engineering. * * * The company's stock was owned by taxpayers John G. Moffatt (45%), Frank E. Nichol (45%) and George G. Murray (10%). * * *

On April 12, 1957, Henry E. Howard, a certified public accountant, was engaged by Inc. to review the company's tax problems. Howard attended a conference with Inc.'s counsel on April 30, 1957, and afterwards prepared a memorandum concerning those tax matters discussed.

* * * Moffatt and Nichol had each suffered substantial nonbusiness bad debt losses in 1954, 1956 and 1957, and both anticipated future bad debt losses on outstanding loans to one Powers. [Howard's] proposal sought primarily to provide ample capital gains against which the capital losses could be offset.

In substance, [Howard's plan] was adopted by Inc.'s management. A new entity, Moffatt & Nichol, Engineers (hereinafter referred to as Engineers), was incorporated on July 22, 1957, with the same principal place of business as Inc. On October 10, 1957, the stock was authorized to be issued to Moffatt (40%), Nichol (40%), Murray (10%), and 10% to Bobisch, a structural engineer, who for some time had been negotiating to purchase a proprietary interest in the consulting engineering operation. [Pursuant to the plan, Engineers purchased the operating assets of Inc., and Inc. was liquidated.]

As a result of this series of transactions, Moffatt and Nichol each reported long-term capital gain in respect of liquidating dividends of Inc. totaling $88,162.89 for the taxable years 1958 and 1959. Substantial capital losses were offset by each taxpayer against these reported gains. The Tax Court, however, held that the distributions in liquidation by Inc. were "boot" incident to a corporate reorganization (§ 368(a)(1)(D)), and as such were taxable as ordinary income under Section 356 of the Internal Revenue Code of 1954.

* * *

The findings alluded to above clearly disclose that the transactions in question were pursuant to an integrated plan and did involve an exchange of stock for stock. [*See Davant,* Sec. 14.4, on this issue.] This leaves as the only Section 354 requirement that must be met for the transaction to qualify as a type "D" reorganization under Section 368 that the new corporation acquired "substantially all" of the assets of the old corporation.

The taxpayers in the present case strenuously contend that not substantially all of Inc.'s assets were transferred to Engineers, and a 368(a)(1)(D) reorganization therefore did not occur. The taxpayers rely primarily on the fact that a large portion of the book assets of Inc. (35.48%) was in the form of land investment and building plans (held for a proposed building construction) which never came into the ownership of Engineers. We find substance to taxpayers' contention when we apply a straight percentage of book assets test to determine what constitutes "substantially all." * * *

We are of the opinion, however, that a sounder view is espoused by Rev.Rul. 57–518, 1957–2 C.B. 253, to the effect that no particular or specific percentage should be controlling. Rather, the ruling advises that "the nature of the properties retained by the transferor, the purpose of retention, and the amount thereof" are all to be considered. * * *

* * *

In the setting of a service organization such as a consulting engineering operation, the retention of physical nonoperating assets such as land should not cloud the fact that the essential tangible and intangible assets of one corporation have been transferred to another corporation. That is what occurred here. * * *

* * *

[W]e find, in accordance with the position taken by the Tax Court, that Inc. transferred *substantially* all of its assets to Engineers. We therefore find that the transactions in question did constitute a type "D" reorganization.

The decisions of the Tax Court are affirmed.

[Dissenting Opinion deleted.]

2. Service's Position on Determining Whether "Substantially All" the Distributing Corporation's Assets Are Contributed to the Controlled Corporation

The Service's ruling policy is that "substantially all," for purposes of, *inter alia,* § 354(b), means 90% of the net assets and 70% of the gross assets. See § 3.01 of Rev.Proc. 77–37, 1977–2 C.B. 568.

D. CARRYOVER OF TAX ATTRIBUTES

The nondivisive (D) reorganization under § 354(b) is subject to the carryover of attribute rules in § 381. The rules of § 381 do not apply to divisive reorganizations under § 355.

§ 14.3 THE LIQUIDATION-REINCORPORATION DOCTRINE

A. AN ILLUSTRATION

REVENUE RULING 61-156
1961-2 C.B. 62.

Advice has been requested whether the transaction described below should be treated, for Federal income tax purposes, as a sale of corporate assets to a newly organized corporation followed by the liquidation of the "selling" corporation under sections 337 and 331 of the Internal Revenue Code of 1954, or whether the transaction should be treated as a reorganization within the meaning of section 368 of the Code.

Within a 12-month period following the adoption of a plan of complete liquidation, a corporation sold substantially all of its assets to a new corporation formed by the management of the selling corporation. The "purchasing" corporation paid $18,000x$ dollars for the assets as follows:

(a) $2,025x$ dollars in shares of its stock equal to 45 percent of all the shares to be issued,

(b) $4,975x$ dollars in long-term notes, and

(c) $11,000x$ dollars in cash obtained through a first mortgage borrowing on the assets acquired.

Immediately thereafter, the new corporation sold shares of its stock, equal to 55 percent of all the shares to be issued, to the public through underwriters.

The "selling" corporation was then completely liquidated, paying off its funded and unfunded liabilities and distributing the balance of its assets, including the 45 percent stock interest in the purchasing corporation, the long-term notes, and cash to its shareholders. As a result of the transaction, the business enterprise continued without interruption in the corporate form with a substantial continuing stock interest on the part of those persons who were shareholders in the selling corporation.

Section 1.331-1(c) of the Income Tax Regulations provides as follows:

> A liquidation which is followed by a transfer to another corporation of all or part of the assets of the liquidating corporation or which is preceded by such a transfer may, however, have the effect of the distribution of a dividend or of a transaction in which no loss is recognized and gain is recognized only to the extent of "other property." See sections 301 and 356.

In this case, if the issuance of stock to the new investors is disregarded, there is clearly a mere recapitalization and reincorporation coupled with a withdrawal of funds. The withdrawal would be treated either under section 356(a) of the Code as "money or other property" received in connection with a reorganization exchange of stock for stock, or under section 301 of the Code as an unrelated distribution to the shareholders.

The issuance of stock to new investors can be disregarded as being a separate transaction, since even without it the dominant purpose—to withdraw corporate earnings while continuing the equity interest in substantial part in a business enterprise conducted in corporate form—was fully achieved. The issuance of stock to new investors was not needed to implement the dominant purpose and, therefore, the rest of the transaction was not fruitless without it and so dependent on it.

The transaction was shaped so as to make it essentially "a device whereby it has been attempted to withdraw corporate earnings at capital gains rates by distributing all the assets of a corporation in complete liquidation and promptly reincorporating" them. See Conference Report No. 2543, 83d Cong., to accompany H.R. 8300 (Internal Revenue Code of 1954), page 41.

It was not intended by Congress that such a device should obtain the benefits of section 337 and avoid dividend taxation. In substance there was no reality to the "sale" of corporate assets or to the "liquidation" of the selling corporation, since each was only a formal step in a reorganization of the existing corporation. The entire transaction was consummated pursuant to a plan of reorganization which readjusted interests in property continuing in a modified corporate form. Sections 1.368–1(b) and 1.368–2(g) of the regulations.

The newly formed "purchasing" corporation was utilized to effect, in substance, a recapitalization and a change in identity, form, or place of organization of the "selling" corporation and, at the same time, to withdraw accumulated earnings from the corporate enterprise for the benefit of the shareholders, while they nevertheless continued a substantial equity interest in the enterprise.

The fact that the shareholders of the "selling" corporation own only 45 percent of the stock of the "purchasing" corporation because of the public stock offering does not dispose of the reorganization question. A surrender of voting control, or ownership of less than 50 percent of the stock of a newly-formed corporation, does not in itself mark a discontinuity of interest. In *John A. Nelson Co. v. Helvering,* 296 U.S. 374, Ct.D. 1062, C.B. XV–1, 274 (1936), the Supreme Court of the United States held that there was a "reorganization" even though the shareholders of the acquired corporation received less than half of the stock of the acquiring corporation and received only nonvoting preferred stock therein. It is necessary only that the shareholders continue to have a definite and substantial equity interest in the assets of the acquiring corporation.

In view of the foregoing, it is held that the transaction here described constitutes a reorganization within the meaning of section 368(a)(1)(E) and (F) of the Code. No gain or loss is recognized to the "selling" corporation on the exchange of property, as provided by section 361 of the Code. The basis of the assets in the hands of the "purchasing" corporation will be the same as in the hands of the "selling" corporation, as provided in section 362(b) of the Code. No gain or loss is recognized under section 354 of the Code on the exchange of the stock of the "selling" corporation for stock of the "purchasing" corporation pursuant to the plan of reorganization.

With regard to the stockholders' withdrawal of money and other property from the corporate solution, it is necessary to determine whether such withdrawal is to be treated as "boot" received as part of the consideration for their stock in the "selling" corporation in accordance with section 356(a) of the Code or as a separate dividend distribution taxable in accordance with the provisions of section 301 of the Code. See sections 1.301–1(1) and 1.331–1(c) of the regulations and *J. Robert Bazley v. Commissioner*. [Sec. 11.7.]

* * *

[I]t is concluded that the distribution to stockholders of the "selling" corporation of the cash, long-term notes, and other assets should be treated as a distribution under section 301 of the Code.

* * *

B. CONTINUING THE BUSINESS OF A SUBSIDIARY AFTER THE LIQUIDATION

TELEPHONE ANSWERING SERVICE CO. v. COMMISSIONER

Tax Court of the United States, 1974.
63 T.C. 423, affirmed unpublished decision (4th Cir.1976), *cert. denied*
431 U.S. 914, 97 S.Ct. 2174, 53 L.Ed.2d 224 (1977).

* * *

Petitioner (TASCO) was a corporation engaged, directly and through its wholly owned subsidiaries (Houston and North American), in the operation of telephone-answering services in various parts of the country. * * * TASCO was approached by an unrelated party desiring to purchase the Houston operation. Willing to part with its subsidiary, but unwilling to be taxed on the gain it would realize thereby, TASCO planned and executed within a 12–month period this series of transactions: It adopted a "Plan of Complete Liquidation and Dissolution," then sold the Houston stock for cash. Next, it transferred all of its directly owned business assets to a recently organized subsidiary (New TASCO) in exchange for that corporation's stock. Finally, TASCO dissolved, distributing pro rata among its shareholders the cash it received from the sale of Houston plus the North American and New TASCO stock.

Petitioner claims that following these steps it was completely liquidated, and therefore [former] section 337 requires nonrecognition of the gain realized on its sale of Houston. We disagree, and hold that the requirements of that section have not been satisfied. Our decision is founded on both the history and the purpose of the statute.

* * *

The Internal Revenue Code does not define a complete liquidation. Clearly, the term conveys more than the formal dissolution of a corporation under State law. * * *

* * * While a complete liquidation is a prerequisite to the application of former section 337, the mere adoption of a plan denominated as one of "complete liquidation" and purported compliance therewith does not preclude further inquiry on our part. It is the reality and substance of the liquidation that counts.

* * *

The businesses which petitioner directly operated were continued without interruption by New TASCO, with substantial continuity of shareholder interest. The only result of the transaction was to place the North American stock and a sizable amount of cash in the shareholders' hands. New TASCO was merely the alter ego of petitioner with respect to all of its directly owned business assets; its formation and utilization served no purpose other than masking a distribution as one in complete liquidation. * * * The transitory coexistence of TASCO and New TASCO does not support the conclusion that the subsequent but prearranged liquidation of the former effected a sufficient transmutation of the assets of petitioner out of corporate solution to satisfy the requirement of [former] section 337 that "all of the assets of the corporation" be distributed. To hold for the petitioner in the instant case would frustrate the congressional purpose to deny [former] section 337 treatment in connection with distributions of ongoing corporations. * * *

* * *

Here, immediately after the dissolution of TASCO both of its directly owned businesses were continued by New TASCO, and * * * there remains a degree of shareholder continuity in excess of 84 percent. In short, petitioner has not satisfied the requirements of [former] section 337.

Questions

What is the precise holding of *Telephone Answering Service?* Corporation X conducts a trade or business and owns all the stock of S. X sells all of the assets used in its trade or business and then liquidates, distributing to its shareholders the cash received and the S stock. What result to X and its shareholders? *See* Rev.Rul. 74–544, 1974–2 C.B. 108.

§ 14.4 LIQUIDATION REINCORPORATION WITH THE USE OF A STRAW MAN: SCOPE OF § 368(a)(1)(D): NO REQUIREMENT OF ISSUANCE OF STOCK; POSSIBLY LOOK TO BOTH CORPORATIONS IN DETERMINING E & P

DAVANT v. COMMISSIONER
United States Court of Appeals, Fifth Circuit, 1966.
366 F.2d 874, *cert. denied* 386 U.S. 1022, 87 S.Ct. 1370, 18 L.Ed.2d 460 (1967).

RIVES, CIRCUIT JUDGE:

The petitioners are persons who claim that the income from the sale of their stock in the South Texas Rice Warehouse Company should be taxed solely as a capital gain. The Tax Court found that a corporate reorganization had taken place and held that at least part of petitioners' income should be taxed as a dividend constituting ordinary income. The government took a cross appeal contending that the Tax Court should have held that a greater portion of petitioners' income was ordinary income. Since we agree with the government, we affirm in part and reverse in part.

South Texas Rice Warehouse Co. was incorporated under the laws of the State of Texas in 1936. The principal business of Warehouse consisted of drying, cleaning, and storing rice. Warehouse's principal source of rice was land owned by a brother corporation, South Texas Water Co.

Water was incorporated under the laws of the State of Texas in 1934. Water had two principal businesses. It owned land which it rented to a partnership, South Texas Rice Farms, and it owned and operated an irrigation canal system used to irrigate the ricelands that it leased to Farms.

* * *

Warehouse and Water were each owned in equal proportions by four families. * * *

In 1960 a number of the stockholders consulted an attorney, Homer L. Bruce, Esq., about the possibility of transferring Warehouse's operating assets to Water for $700,000 and then liquidating Warehouse. * * *

In the attorney's opinion, former section 337 would allow the individuals to obtain capital gains treatment for any income they might receive in the transaction they contemplated. However, Mr. Bruce advised against such a course of conduct. He told them that in a situation where such a sale and distribution was made when the stockholders of the two corporations were identical it was probable that the Internal Revenue Service would take the position that the stockholders had received a dividend taxable at ordinary rates and not a capital gain.

Mr. Bruce then suggested an alternate course of conduct which he believed would have the desired effect of having any gains taxed at the capital rather than the ordinary rate. The suggestion was that if the stockholders made a sale of their stock to a person not connected with them or their corporations at a fair price which would allow that person to make a reasonable profit, then that person could sell Warehouse's operating assets to Water and liquidate Warehouse without endangering the original stockholders' capital gains treatment.

Homer L. Bruce, Jr., a practicing attorney and the son of petitioners' attorney, was suggested by one of the stockholders as an appropriate person to buy their stock. Both Water and Warehouse had a corporate account with the Bank of the Southwest and the Bank had for many years been represented by Mr. Bruce's law firm.

Mr. Bruce contacted A.M. Ball, a vice-president of the Bank. He told Mr. Ball that his son wished to buy Warehouse for $914,200 and wished to borrow the necessary funds from the Bank. The stock of Warehouse was to be the collateral for the $914,200 note of Bruce, Jr. It was understood that Water would then buy the assets of Warehouse for $700,000, and that this money plus part of the approximately $230,000 which Warehouse had in its bank account would be used, after Warehouse was liquidated, to repay the loan. This procedure allowed Bruce, Jr. to receive $15,583.30 for his part in the transaction, and allowed the Bank to receive what the parties designated as one day's interest on its $914,200 loan or $152.37.

* * *

Petitioners take the position that the sale of their stock in Warehouse to Bruce, Jr. was a *bona fide* sale and that they properly reported their profits as the gain from the sale of a capital asset held over six months. The Commissioner argues that the transaction involved in this case is a corporate reorganization and that to the extent of the earnings and profits of both Warehouse and Water the gain reported here must be considered as a dividend taxable as ordinary income. The Tax Court held that the instant transaction constituted a corporate reorganization coming under section 368(a)(1)(D) of the Internal Revenue Code of 1954. However, the Tax Court also held that the gain was taxable as a dividend only to the extent of Warehouse's earnings and profits.

* * *

All of the steps taken by taxpayer in this case with regard to the $200,000 worth of earnings and profits generated by Warehouse and the $700,000 worth of earnings and profits generated by Water were for the sole purpose of turning what otherwise would be a dividend taxed at the ordinary income rate into a gain made on the sale or exchange of a capital asset taxed at the much lower capital gains rate.

* * *

It would appear at first blush that petitioners have carefully fitted themselves directly within the statutory wording. But in the landmark case of *Gregory v. Helvering* [see Sec. 1.3.G.2.], the Supreme Court refused to give effect to a corporate transaction which complied precisely with the formal requirements for a nontaxable corporate reorganization, on the ground that the transaction had served no function other than that of a contrivance to bail out corporate earnings at capital gains tax rates. That is precisely the charge made here. Let us examine what legitimate purposes might be served by the transactions here under consideration. Three distinct and separate things occurred.

First, $700,000 in earnings and profits possessed by Water were passed through Warehouse to petitioners. Second, $200,000 in earnings and profits from Warehouse were distributed to petitioners. Third, the operating assets of Warehouse were combined with Water and were from that point on owned and controlled through Water. Only one business nontax-avoidance purpose can be found to support any of these events: petitioners wished to eliminate one of the corporate shells and thereafter control all of the properties under one roof. This motive legitimately explains why petitioners transferred the operating assets of Warehouse to Water. But it does not explain either of the first two steps. Under the reorganization provisions of the Code petitioners could have transferred all of Warehouse's assets, including its earnings and profits, to Water without paying any tax. Thus, the payment of $200,000 from Warehouse to petitioners cannot be explained as necessary in order to place both businesses under the same roof. Likewise, there was no need for petitioners to cast the transfer of Warehouse's operating assets in the form of a sale. The businesses could be combined under one roof without the $700,000 from Water ever coming over to Warehouse. * * *

Clearly, this liquidation cannot come within the intention of Congress in enacting the complete liquidation provisions. * * *

* * *

Since this interchange of events cannot be viewed as a complete liquidation, we must now decide, for the purposes of the federal tax code, what it is. In the Tax Court the Government contended that this was a § 368(a)(1)(D) or (F) reorganization.

* * *

* * * At least where there is a complete identity of shareholders and their proprietary interests, as here, we hold that the type of transaction involved is a type (F) reorganization.

In the alternative, we also hold that the Tax Court correctly held that these events constituted a § 368(a)(1)(D) reorganization. * * * In this case, it is clear that the petitioners have satisfied part one of the type (D) definition. Warehouse is a "corporation" and it transferred "a part of its assets to another corporation," Water. Since both corporations were owned identically by petitioners the "control" requisite was fulfilled.

Petitioners argue that the provision cannot apply to them because in part two Congress specifically required that "stock or securities" of the transferee corporation be passed to petitioners. They, of course, point out that they received no new stock in Water as a part of their transaction. We cannot agree that this statutory requirement must be taken literally, especially where it would prevent the effectuation of the tax policies of Congress.

The (D) reorganization provisions have never been confined to a strictly literal application. It will be noted that section 368(a)(1)(D) requires that the transferor be "a corporation." But it has been consistently held that a proper interpretation and application does not prevent from coming under the aegis of 368(a)(1)(D) a transfer made by "persons" who have received assets from a corporation with the intention of transferring them to another corporation.

* * *

Moreover, since the operative sections [*i.e.* §§ 354, 355, and 356] were cast in terms of stock transfers, it was only normal that in referring to those sections in 368(a)(1)(D) that Congress referred to "stock or securities" "distributed in a transaction which qualifies under section 354, 355, or 356." Congress thus did not intend to place any special emphasis on the idea that stock *must* be transferred, rather Congress only intended to use this convenient terminology in referring to the operating provisions of the Code.

* * *

We come now to the last leg of our journey; the question of whether the earnings and profits of Warehouse and Water should be combined in determining whether the full $900,000 cash received by petitioners should be treated as a dividend. We hold that the $700,000 coming indirectly from Water and the $200,000 coming from Warehouse must be tested against their combined earnings and profits. Whether we reach this result by means of calling this transaction a type (D) or type (F) reorganization, or a dividend declared simultaneously with a reorganization, makes no difference. * * *

* * *

Questions

1. Would this type of transaction qualify as an (F) under the statute today? *See* Sec. 12.11. What result if Bruce, Jr. had operated Warehouse for a respectable period before selling the assets to Water? Is the court correct in holding that it is appropriate to look to the earnings and profits of both corporations? Is the court correct in holding that there is no necessity for an issuance of additional stock on a (D) where both corporations are controlled by the same persons?

2. The Tax Court has continued to hold that the earnings and profits of only the one corporation are to be taken into account. *See American Manufacturing Co.*, 55 T.C. 204 (1970) and *Atlas Tool Co.*, 70 T.C. 86 (1978).

Chapter 15

ACQUISITIVE REORGANIZATIONS AND SECTION 382

§ 15.1 SCOPE

This chapter deals with the seven forms of acquisitive reorganizations. Sec. 15.2 addresses the straight (A) reorganization under § 368(a)(1)(A) in which the target merges directly into the acquiring corporation. Section 15.3 deals with the straight (C) reorganization under § 368(a)(1)(C) in which the acquiring corporation acquires the assets of the target in exchange for voting stock of the acquiring corporation. Sec. 15.4 examines the triangular (C) under § 368(a)(1)(C) in which a subsidiary of the acquiring corporation acquires the assets of a target corporation in exchange for stock of the acquiring corporation. Sec. 15.5 deals with the forward subsidiary merger under § 368(a)(2)(D) in which a target corporation merges into a subsidiary of the acquiring corporation. In each of these four forms of asset reorganizations, the acquiring corporation or a subsidiary of the acquiring corporation acquires either directly or by merger the assets of the target corporation in exchange for stock of the acquiring corporation.

Sec. 15.6 deals with the carryover rules under § 381 which apply in each of these forms of reorganizations, and Sec. 15.7 presents summary problems on these forms of asset reorganizations.

The stock reorganizations under § 368(a)(1)(B) and the reverse subsidiary merger under § 368(a)(2)(E) are taken up in Secs. 15.8 to 15.11. Sec. 15.8 deals with the straight (B) in which the acquiring corporation acquires the stock of the target corporation in return for the acquiring corporation's voting stock. Sec. 15.9 deals with the triangular (B) reorganization in which a subsidiary of the acquiring corporation acquires the stock of the target in exchange for voting stock of the acquiring corporation. Sec. 15.10 deals with the reverse subsidiary merger under § 368(a)(2)(E). This transaction has the effect of a stock acquisition and, therefore, is considered together with the (B) reorganization. Sec. 15.11 presents summary problems on these forms of acquisitive stock reorganizations.

Sec. 15.12 deals with the impact of § 382 on the utilization of the target's net operating losses after a taxable or tax-free acquisition.

These and other issues relating to acquisitions are examined in greater detail in the companion volume, *Taxable and Tax–Free Corporate Mergers, Acquisitions, and LBO's, supra* Sec. 1.4. For a more detailed discussion of these issues, see Chapters 46, 47, 48, 51, 52 and 53 of *Federal Taxation of Business Enterprises, supra* Chapter 1, note 1; Chapters 7, 8 and 12 of Ginsburg and Levin, *Mergers, supra* Sec. 1.4; and Chapters 14 and 16 of Bittker and Eustice, *Corporations, supra* Sec. 1.4. *See also* the most recent edition of PLI, *Tax Strategies, supra* Sec. 1.4.

§ 15.2 THE STRAIGHT (A) REORGANIZATION: STATUTORY MERGER OR CONSOLIDATION

A. INTRODUCTION

The (A) reorganization has been a part of the tax law since the adoption of the first reorganization statute in 1918. Section 368(a)(1)(A) does not say much about the (A); it merely states that a "statutory merger or consolidation" is a reorganization. There is no solely for voting stock requirement as in the (B), the (C) and the (a)(2)(E), nor is there a "substantially all" requirement as in the (C), the (a)(2)(D), and (a)(2)(E). The regulations, however, make it clear that the statutory merger or consolidation must be "effected pursuant to the corporation laws of the United States or a State or Territory or the District of Columbia." Although a merger under foreign law does not constitute an (A), such a merger might qualify, for instance, as a (C) or a § 354(b) nondivisive (D) reorganization. *See, e.g.,* Rev.Rul. 67–326, 1967–2 C.B. 143, holding that prior to the enactment of § 368(a)(2)(D), a forward subsidiary merger of the target into the acquiring subsidiary in exchange for voting stock of the acquiring parent was a triangular (C).

Notwithstanding the absence of a formal voting stock or a similar requirement, the Supreme Court has made it clear that in order to qualify as an (A), there must be a "continuity of interest." The leading cases dealing with the continuity of interest doctrine, beginning with the Supreme Court's decision in *Pinellas,* are collected in Sec. 11.2. These cases have a continuing impact on reorganizations, particularly on the (A) since it has no statutorily imposed voting stock requirement. The forward subsidiary merger under § 368(a)(2)(D) is the only other acquisitive reorganization that does not have a statutorily mandated voting stock requirement.

The regulations under § 368 reflect in several places the continuity of interest requirement, and the Service's current ruling policy on continuity of interest is set out in Sec. 11.2.C. Before proceeding with the study of the (A), the reader should master the materials on continuity of interest in Sec. 11.2. In addition to satisfying the continuity of interest requirement, the continuity of business enterprise doctrine, examined in Sec. 11.3, must also be satisfied.

By way of summary, the tax treatment to the parties in an (A) is as follows:

(1) The target has nonrecognition treatment under § 361. Under § 357(a), liabilities assumed by the acquiror are not boot to the target.

(2) The acquiror has nonrecognition treatment upon the issuance of its stock or securities under § 1032 and § 1.61–12.

(3) The acquiror takes a carryover basis for the target's assets under § 362(b).

(4) The target's tax attributes, other than basis, carry over to the acquiror in accordance with the principles in §§ 381, 382, and 383. *See* Sec. 15.6 and 15.12.

(5) The target's shareholders receive nonrecognition treatment under § 354 and boot gain treatment under § 356. The fair market value of any excess principal amount of securities received is treated as boot under §§ 354(a)(2) and 356(d). Under § 356(a)(2), the shareholders' gain is treated as a dividend to the extent of their pro rata share of the accumulated E & P if the boot has the effect of a distribution of a dividend. *See* Sec. 11.13. for a full exploration of § 356(a)(2) and the Supreme Court's decision in *Clark*.

(6) The target's shareholders take a substituted basis under § 358 for the stock or securities received.

B. THE CONTINUITY OF INTEREST REQUIREMENT

See generally Sec. 11.2.

See § 3.02 Revenue Procedure 77–37 in Sec. 11.2.C.

C. PURCHASE OF A PORTION OF TARGET'S STOCK FOLLOWED BY UPSTREAM MERGER WITH MINORITY SHAREHOLDERS RECEIVING PARENT'S STOCK

KASS v. COMMISSIONER
Tax Court of the United States, 1973.
60 T.C. 218.

OPINION

DAWSON, JUDGE: * * *

The only issue for decision is whether petitioner, a minority shareholder of an 84-percent-owned subsidiary, must recognize gain upon the receipt of the parent's stock pursuant to a statutory merger of the subsidiary into the parent.

* * *

For a period greater than 6 months prior to 1965, petitioner had owned 2,000 shares of common stock of Atlantic City Racing Association (herein called ACRA). Her basis in the stock was $1,000. The stock in her hands was a capital asset.

ACRA was a New Jersey corporation which was * * * engaged in the business of operating a racetrack. * * *

Track Associates, Inc. (herein called TRACK), is a New Jersey corporation which was formed on November 19, 1965. The total authorized capital stock of TRACK consisted of 500,000 shares of common stock. Its original capitalization consisted of 202,577 shares. Over 50 percent of the original issue was acquired by the Levy family and 8 percent was acquired by the Casey family. The remaining stock went to 18 other individuals. The Levys and the Caseys were also minority shareholders (whether computed separately or as a group) in ACRA. Their purpose in forming TRACK was to gain control over ACRA's racetrack business. They wanted to do away with ACRA's cumbersome capital structure and institute a new corporate policy with regard to capital improvements and higher purses for the races. Control was to be gained by establishing TRACK and then by (1) having TRACK purchase at least 80 percent of the stock of ACRA and (2) subsequently merging ACRA into TRACK.

The Levys acquired 48,300 shares of TRACK stock (out of the total original capitalization of 202,577 shares) in exchange for stock of ACRA. The Caseys acquired 3,450 shares in exchange for their ACRA stock. Together the Levys and Caseys purchased an additional 70,823 shares of TRACK stock as part of the original capitalization.

On December 1, 1965, TRACK offered to purchase the stock of ACRA at $22 per share, subject to the condition that at least 405,000 shares (slightly more than 80 percent of ACRA's outstanding shares) be tendered. As a result of this tender offer, which terminated on February 11, 1966, 424,764 shares of ACRA stock were received and paid for by TRACK. A total of 29,486 shares of ACRA stock were not tendered.[1]

The board of directors of TRACK approved a plan of liquidation providing for the liquidation of ACRA by way of merger into TRACK. * * *

The merger having taken place, the remaining shares of ACRA that were not sold pursuant to the tender offer or the dissenting shareholder provisions were exchanged for TRACK stock, 1 for 1. The petitioner exchanged 2,000 shares of ACRA stock, with a fair market value at the time of $22 per share, for 2,000 shares of TRACK stock. She did not report any capital gain in connection with this transaction.

---

1. All 506,000 shares of ACRA stock can be accounted for as follows: 51,750 (10.23 percent) were transferred to TRACK upon formation; 424,764 (83.95 percent) were purchased by TRACK following the tender offer; 29,486 (5.82 percent) remained in the hands of minority shareholders such as the petitioner.

Petitioner contends that the merger of ACRA into TRACK, although treated at least in part as a liquidation at the corporate level, is at her level, the shareholder level, (1) a true statutory merger and (2) a section 368(a)(1)(A) reorganization, occasioning no recognition of gain on the ensuing exchange. In support of this she cites *Madison Square Garden Corp.*, 58 T.C. 619 (1972). Respondent, on the other hand, argues that the purchase of stock by TRACK and the liquidation of ACRA into TRACK, which took the form of a merger, must be viewed at all levels as an integrated transaction; that the statutory merger does not qualify as a reorganization because it fails the continuity-of-interest test; and that, as a consequence, petitioner falls outside of section 354(a)(1) and must recognize gain pursuant to section [1001].

The problems presented by these facts are somewhat complex. * * * Put another way, does the merger of ACRA into TRACK fall under section 368(a)(1)(A), thus placing the exchange of petitioner's ACRA stock for TRACK stock within the applicable non-recognition provision?

Respondent does not take the position that a statutory merger, such as the one we have here, can never qualify for reorganization-nonrecognition status. He admits that "Theoretically, it is possible for TRACK to get a stepped-up basis in 83.95 percent of the assets of ACRA per [former] section 334(b)(2), IRC [the predecessor of § 338] upon a section 332, IRC liquidation of ACRA into TRACK and at the same time allow nonrecognition reorganization treatment to minority shareholders." Rather, his position is simply that the merger in question fails to meet the time-honored continuity-of-interest test. We agree with this and so hold.

[Former] section 334(b)(2) and the reorganization provisions might apply to the same transaction only in certain cases where the continuity-of-interest test is met. See Sec. 332 (last sentence, last independent clause); sec. 1.332–2(d) and (e), Income Tax Regs. Reorganization treatment is appropriate when the parent's stock ownership in the subsidiary was not acquired as a step in a plan to acquire assets of the subsidiary: the parent's stockholding can be counted as contributing to continuity-of-interest, so that since such holding represented more than 80 percent of the stock of the subsidiary, the continuity-of-interest test would be met. Reorganization treatment is inappropriate when the parent's stock ownership in the subsidiary was purchased as the first step in a plan to acquire the subsidiary's assets in conformance with the provisions of [former] section 334(b)(2). The parent's stockholding could not be counted towards continuity-of-interest, so in the last example there would be a continuity-of-interest of less than 20 percent. (Less than 20–percent continuity would be significantly less continuity-of-interest than that allowed in *John A. Nelson Co. v. Helvering*, 296 U.S. 374 (1935).) In short, where the parent's stock interest is "old and cold," it may contribute to continuity-of-interest. Where the parent's interest is not "old and cold," the sale of shares by the majority of shareholders actually detracts from continuity-of-interest.

* * *

[Petitioner argues that] assuming that the continuity-of-interest test is applied, it is met where all 16 percent of the stockholders of ACRA exchanged their stock for a total of 35 percent of the stock of TRACK. The 16–percent figure (really 16.04 percent) is the sum of the percentage of ACRA stock transferred to TRACK at the time of TRACK's formation (10.22 percent) plus the percentage of ACRA stock exchanged for TRACK stock following the statutory merger (5.82 percent). Fortunately, we need not engage in a game of percentages since the continuity figure argued for by petitioner, 16 percent, is not "tantalizingly" high. The plain fact that more than 80 percent of the shareholders of ACRA sold out for cash is sufficient to prevent this merger from meeting the quantitative test expressed in the *Southwest Natural Gas Co. v. Commissioner,* 189 F.2d 332, 334 (C.A.5, 1951), affirming 14 T.C. 81 (1950):

> While no precise formula has been expressed for determining whether there has been retention of the requisite interest, it seems clear that the requirement of continuity of interest consistent with the statutory intent is not fulfilled in the absence of a showing: (1) that the transferor corporation or its shareholders retained a substantial proprietary stake in the enterprise represented by a material interest in the affairs of the transferee corporation, and, (2) *that such retained interest represents a substantial part of the value of the property transferred.* [Emphasis added.]

The two Supreme Court cases on point are *John A. Nelson Co. v. Helvering, supra,* and *Helvering v. Minnesota Tea Co.,* 296 U.S. 378 (1935).

Finally, we emphasize that the petitioner is not any worse off than her fellow shareholders who sold their stock. She could have also received money instead of stock had she chosen to sell or to dissent from the merger. The nonrecognition of a realized gain is always an important matter. We hold that petitioner is not entitled to such favorable treatment in this case.

Reviewed by the Court.

Decision will be entered for the respondent.

Questions

1. What result to the taxpayer if she had participated with the Caseys and Levys in organizing TRACK? Should the ACRA stock that the Levys and Caseys contributed to TRACK have been included in determining the continuity of interest?

2. What is the significance of (1) the last sentence of § 332(b), and (2) § 1.332–2(d) and (e)? Suppose *P* has always owned 90% of the stock of *S*, and individual *A* owns the 10% balance. *S* has assets with a value of $100K and a basis of $50K. *S* merges upstream into *P*, with *A* receiving *P* stock.

What result to *P, S* and *A*? What result to *P, S* and *A* if, pursuant to the merger, *P* transfers $10K of cash to *A* in cancellation of his shares?

3. Acquiring corporation, *AC*, purchases 85% of the stock of target, *TC*, *AC* then forms a new subsidiary, *AC–S*, and *TC* merges into *AC–S*. In the merger, *AC* receives additional stock of *AC–S* in exchange for its stock of *TC* and the minority shareholders of *TC* receive cash for their stock. What result to each of the parties? *See Yoc Heating Corp. v. Commissioner* in Sec. 11.2.F.1.

§ 15.3 THE STRAIGHT (C) REORGANIZATION

A. INTRODUCTORY NOTE

The stock-for-asset (C) reorganization has been a part of the tax law since the 1921 Act. Many of the cases that developed the parameters of the continuity of interest doctrine were (C) transactions. *See* Sec. 11.2. There are three basic requirements to qualify as a straight (C). First, the acquiring corporation must acquire "substantially all of the properties" of the target. The "substantially all" requirement has been in the statute since the 1921 Act. Second, the consideration paid by the acquiring corporation must be "solely" its voting stock. The voting stock requirement was added by the 1934 Act. Third, the target must distribute to the acquiring corporations stock or securities pursuant to the plan of reorganization. *See* § 368(a)(2)(G). This requirement was added by the Deficit Reduction Act of 1984. In determining whether the transaction is solely for voting stock, "the assumption by the acquiring corporation of a liability of the [target], or the fact that property acquired is subject to a liability, shall be disregarded." *See* § 357(a). This qualification was added in 1939 to devitalize the Supreme Court's decision in *Hendler*. *See* Sec. 2.3.A.

The regulations say that although an assumption of liabilities does "not prevent an exchange from being solely for voting stock * * *, it may, however, in some cases, so alter the character of the transaction as to place the transaction outside the purposes and assumptions of the reorganization provisions." *See* § 1.368–2(d). This regulation further says:

> Section 368(a)(1)(C) does not prevent consideration of the effect of an assumption of liabilities on the general character of the transaction but merely provides that the requirement that the exchange be solely for voting stock is satisfied if the only additional consideration is an assumption of liabilities.

* * *

The solely for voting stock requirement in a (C) is relaxed by § 368(a)(2)(B), the "boot relaxation" provision. This provision was added in 1954, and the Senate Report to the 1954 Code explains:

> Paragraph (2)(B) provides that where one corporation acquires substantially all the property of another (subsection (a)(1)(C)) if at

least 80 percent of the fair market value of all the property of the other corporation is acquired solely for voting stock, the remainder of the property acquired may be acquired for cash or other property without disqualifying the transaction as a reorganization. For this purpose only, a liability assumed or to which the property is subject, is considered other property. For example, corporation A has assets worth $100,000 and $10,000 in liabilities. Corporation Y acquires $98,000 worth of assets subject to a liability of $10,000. In exchange for these assets, corporation Y transfers its own voting stock, assumes the $10,000 liability, and pays $8,000 cash. This transaction is a reorganization even though a part of the assets of corporation A is acquired for cash. On the other hand, if the assets of corporation A, worth $100,000, were subject to $50,000 in liabilities, an acquisition of all of the assets subject to the liabilities could only be in exchange for voting stock because the liabilities alone are in excess of 20 percent of the fair market value of the property. Thus, only the rule of subsection (a)(1)(C) could be applicable.

The boot relaxation rule is illustrated in § 1.368–2(d)(3).

If a transaction meets the definition of both a (C) and a (D), § 368(a)(2)(A) provides that the transaction is considered a (D). This provision was added by the 1954 Code. The Senate Report explains:

> Paragraph (2) of subsection (a) lists three special rules which modify existing law. It is provided that if a transaction meets the description, both of an acquisition of assets for stock (subsec. (a)(1)(C)) and also meets the description of a transfer to a controlled corporation (subsec. (a)(1)(D)) it shall be treated as described only in subsection (a)(1)(D).
>
> Your committee intends by this rule to insure that the tax consequences of the distribution of stocks or securities to shareholders or security holders in connection with divisive reorganizations will be governed by the requirements of section 355 relating to distribution of stock of a controlled corporation.

The Senate Finance Committee Report to the Deficit Reduction Act of 1984 gives the following explanation of the distribution requirement:

Reasons for Change

Prior to 1934, Federal statutes provided for reorganization treatment only in the case of a transaction qualifying as a merger or consolidation under state law. The C reorganization provisions were added to the Code because uniform merger or consolidation statutes had not been enacted in all states, and the Congress believed that for Federal tax purposes substantially similar transactions should be treated consistently without regard to state law. Thus, the provisions were intended to apply to transactions that are acquisitive in nature and resemble statutory mergers or consolidations.

Different provisions are intended to apply to divisive transactions. The committee is concerned that since a distribution by the transferor corporation of all its assets is not required in connection with a C reorganization, and after such a reorganization the transferor may be able to engage in an active trade or business and not merely serve as a holding company for its shareholders' interests in the acquiring corporation, transactions that are somewhat divisive in nature can qualify as reorganization without qualifying under the provisions generally applicable to divisive transactions.

* * *

Explanation of Provision

Except as otherwise provided by regulations, an acquisition by one corporation, in exchange solely for all or a part of its voting stock (or in exchange solely for all or a part of the voting stock of a corporation which is in control of the acquiring corporation), of substantially all of the properties of another corporation, is treated as a C reorganization only if the transferor corporation distributes all of its assets (less those retained to meet claims), including consideration received from the acquiring corporation and any retained assets, within 12 months of the acquisition. [See § 368(a)(2)(G).]

Under the bill, the Secretary may prescribe regulations providing exceptions to the distribution requirement. The committee intends that the regulations will provide that a distribution will not be required if substantial hardship, such as the loss of a valuable nontransferable charter, will result. The committee anticipates that any such regulations will impose appropriate conditions so that the abuses intended to be corrected by the bill will not be present.

The Secretary is also directed to prescribe regulations under section 312 providing, among other things, for the allocation of earnings and profits between the acquiring corporation and the transferor corporation in situations in which one corporation owns 80 percent or more of the stock of the transferor corporation before the transaction.

* * *

[The Conference follows the above principles except that the distribution must be pursuant to the plan of reorganization (rather than within 12 months of the acquisition).]

The basic tax treatment to the parties in a (C) is as follows:

(1) The acquiring corporation receives nonrecognition treatment, under § 1032 and § 1.61-12(c), upon the issuance of its stock and securities.

(2) Under § 362(b), the acquiring corporation takes a carryover basis for the target's assets. The carryover basis is increased by any gain recognized by the target but not by the gain recognized by the target's shareholders. *See Sweitzer,* Sec. 11.16.

(3) The target has nonrecognition treatment under § 361(a) for any stock or securities of the acquiring corporation it receives. There is no

analogue in § 361 to the excess principal amount of securities rule in § 354(a)(2). Under § 361(b), the target generally must distribute any boot it receives in order to qualify for nonrecognition. The treatment of the target under § 361 is explored in Sec. 11.14. The boot dividend rule of § 356(a)(2) does not apply to the target. Liabilities transferred to the acquiring corporation are not treated as boot. See § 357(a).

(4) The target takes a substituted basis under § 358 for the stock or securities received.

(5) The target has nonrecognition under § 361(c) upon the distribution of the stock or securities received.

(6) The target's shareholders receive nonrecognition treatment under § 354 and have boot gain or boot dividend treatment under § 356. See Sec. 11.13.

(7) The target's shareholders take a substituted basis under § 358.

B. WHAT CONSTITUTES SUBSTANTIALLY ALL?

EXCERPT FROM REVENUE PROCEDURE 77–37
1977–2 C.B. 568.

SEC. 3. OPERATING RULES FOR ISSUING RULING LETTERS

.01 The "substantially all" requirement of sections 354(b)(1)(A), 368(a)(1)(C), 368(a)(2)(B)(i), 368(a)(2)(D), and 368(a)(2)(E)(i) of the Code is satisfied if there is a transfer (and in the case of a surviving corporation under section 368(a)(2)(E)(i), the retention) of assets representing at least 90 percent of the fair market value of the net assets and at least 70 percent of the fair market value of the gross assets held by the corporation immediately prior to the transfer. All payments to dissenters and all redemptions and distributions (except for regular, normal distributions) made by the corporation immediately preceding the transfer and which are part of the plan of reorganization will be considered as assets held by the corporation immediately prior to the transfer.

Problems

1. Target (*TC*) has $100K of assets and $40K of liabilities. Acquiror (*AC*) proposes to acquire $60K of *TC*'s assets and none of its liabilities solely in exchange for *AC* voting stock. *TC* will use the $40K of retained assets to discharge its $40K of liabilities and will then liquidate, distributing the *AC* voting stock. Will this transaction qualify as a (C) reorganization under the Service's ruling policy? If not, what amount of *TC*'s assets would *AC* have to acquire, assuming *AC* refuses to take over any of the liabilities? In such case what result to *TC*?

2. Assume that three separate target corporations (*TC*) have the following assets and liabilities:

TC	Assets	Liabilities
TC #1	$100K	-0-
TC #2	$100K	$10K
TC #3	$100K	$50K

What is the minimum amount of assets of each *TC* that can be acquired by an acquiring corporation in exchange for its voting stock and still have the transaction qualify as a (C) reorganization under the Service's ruling policy? Assuming all the assets and liabilities of each *TC* are acquired, what is the maximum amount of cash that can be paid under the boot relaxation rule of § 368(a)(2)(B)?

C. THE CREEPING (C)

BAUSCH & LOMB OPTICAL CO. v. COMMISSIONER

United States Court of Appeals, Second Circuit, 1959.
267 F.2d 75, *cert. denied* 361 U.S. 835, 80 S.Ct. 88, 4 L.Ed.2d 76 (1959).

MEDINA, CIRCUIT JUDGE.

Petitioner Bausch & Lomb Optical Company, a New York corporation engaged in the manufacture and sale of ophthalmic products, on March 1, 1950 owned 9923¼ shares of the stock of its subsidiary Riggs Optical Company, or 79.9488% of the 12,412 outstanding shares of Riggs. In order to effectuate certain operating economies, Bausch & Lomb decided to amalgamate Riggs with itself. To this end on April 22, 1950 Bausch & Lomb exchanged 105,508 shares of its unissued voting stock for all of the Riggs assets. An additional 433 shares of Bausch & Lomb stock went to 12 Riggs' employees.

On May 2, 1950, according to a prearranged plan, Riggs dissolved itself, distributing its only asset, Bausch & Lomb stock, pro rata to its shareholders. Bausch & Lomb thus received back 84,347 of its own shares which became treasury stock, while 21,161 shares went to the Riggs minority shareholders.

The Commissioner determined that the substance of these transactions was that Bausch & Lomb received the Riggs assets partly in exchange for its Riggs stock and partly for its own stock, and that the gain which Bausch & Lomb realized upon the Riggs "liquidation" was subject to tax. In other words, that Bausch & Lomb parted with 21,161 shares of its own voting stock, plus 9923¼ shares of its Riggs stock, for the transfer to it of all of the Riggs assets. Bausch & Lomb contends, however, that a "reorganization" was effected under Section 112(g)(1)(C) of the 1939 Internal Revenue Code [now § 368(a)(1)(C)], and that it is therefore entitled to tax-free treatment. The Tax Court sustained the Commissioner's position and held that the acquisition of the Riggs assets and the dissolution of Riggs must be viewed together, and that the surrender by Bausch & Lomb of its Riggs stock was additional consideration. The Tax Court accordingly held that the Riggs assets were not obtained "solely for all or a part of its voting stock." We agree.

Bausch & Lomb concedes that to qualify as a "C" reorganization, it could not furnish any additional consideration over and above its own stock. * * * Moreover, Bausch & Lomb admits, as the correspondence and minutes of pertinent meetings plainly show, that the acquisition of the Riggs assets and the dissolution of Riggs were both part of the same plan. Nevertheless, Bausch & Lomb asserts that the exchange of the Riggs assets for its stock should be treated as separate and distinct from the dissolution. The argument runs to the effect that, if the two steps are viewed apart from one another, a "C" reorganization is effected.

Petitioner contends that, even if a qualification according to the literal terms of Section 112(g)(1)(C) is not found, the amalgamation was in substance a "reorganization" because it has the attributes of one, including "continuity of interest" and business purpose. This is factually not quite true for, while the amalgamation may have been for genuine business reasons, the division into two steps served only to facilitate the liquidation of Riggs. It was considered easier to distribute Bausch & Lomb stock than distribute the Riggs assets. Hence the "business purpose" of dividing the liquidation into two steps lends no support to Bausch & Lomb's contention that in substance and actuality a reorganization was achieved. Moreover, the Congress has defined in Section 112(g)(1)(C) how a reorganization thereunder may be effected, and the only question for us to decide, on this phase of the case, is whether the necessary requirements have been truly fulfilled. It is for the Congress and not for us to say whether some other alleged equivalent set of facts should receive the same tax free status.

Nor does the fact that Bausch & Lomb may well have desired to hold the 84,347 shares of its own voting shares as treasury stock change our opinion of the transaction as a whole.

Bausch & Lomb suggests that under our present holding even if it had but a 1% interest in Riggs, the requirement that the acquisition be "solely for * * * its voting stock" could defeat Section 112(g)(1)(C) reorganization treatment. This hypothesis is a far cry from the facts disclosed in this record, and the lack of controlling interest surrounds it with a mist of unreality. In any event, it will be time to consider such a situation in all its aspects when, as and if it comes before us. We merely hold that the attempt to thwart taxation in this case by carrying out the liquidation process in two steps instead of one fell short of meeting the requirements of a "C" reorganization.

* * *

Of course, the fact that Bausch & Lomb "could have" merged with Riggs and hence qualified the transaction as a reorganization under [section 112(g)(1)(A)] is beside the point. For reasons of its own it chose not to do so. This is clearly not an "A" reorganization.

* * *

Affirmed.

§ 15.4 THE TRIANGULAR (C) REORGANIZATION

A. LEGISLATIVE HISTORY OF THE TRIANGULAR (C) AND § 368(a)(2)(C)

The first legislative override of the *Groman* and *Bashford* doctrines (*see* Sec. 11.2.G.2.) came in the 1954 Code, with the addition of the parenthetical clause to § 368(a)(1)(C), allowing triangular (C) reorganizations, and the addition of § 368(a)(2)(C), allowing the assets acquired in an (A) or (C) reorganization to be dropped into a subsidiary of the acquiring corporation. The term "party to the reorganization" in § 368(b) was amended to include the parent of an acquiring corporation as a party to the reorganization. These amendments were discussed as follows in the Senate Report to the 1954 Code:

> Subparagraph (C) of subsection (a)(1) corresponds to section 112(g)(1)(C) of the 1939 Code relating to the acquisition by one corporation, without the recognition of gain or loss, of substantially all of the properties of another corporation in exchange for part or all of the voting stock of the acquiring corporation. The rule of this subparagraph is intended to modify the rule of *Groman v. Commissioner* (302 U.S. 82) and *Helvering v. Bashford* (302 U.S. 454). Under subparagraph (C) a corporation may acquire substantially all the properties of another corporation solely in exchange of the voting stock of a corporation which is in control of the acquiring corporation. For example, corporation P owns all the stock of corporation A. All the assets of corporation W are transferred to corporation A solely in exchange for the voting stock of corporation P. Such a transaction constitutes a reorganization under subparagraph C.

* * *

> Subparagraph (C) of paragraph (2) provides that if one corporation acquires all, or substantially all, of the assets of another corporation in a reorganization qualifying under section 368(a)(1)(A) or (C), the acquisition will not fail to be a reorganization merely because the acquiring corporation transfers some or all of these assets to a corporation controlled by it. This subparagraph is intended to give further clarification in the area treated in the *Groman* and *Bashford* cases, supra.
>
> Subsection (b) of section 368 defines a "party to a reorganization." It reinstates existing law as now appearing in section 112(g)(2), and in addition provides (with respect to the area of the *Groman* and *Bashford* cases, supra) that the corporation controlling the acquiring corporation is also a party to the reorganization when the stock of such controlling corporation is used to acquire assets.

It also provides that a corporation remains a party to the reorganization although it transfers all or part of the assets acquired to a controlled subsidiary.

B. INTRODUCTION

The basic issues presented in a straight (C) are also present in a triangular (C). *See* Sec. 15.3. Certain additional problems are presented below. Section 1.368–2(d) says that the subsidiary cannot use any of its stock in the acquisition. Thus, the boot relaxation rule does not extend to stock of the subsidiary. Query: what is the reason for this rule?

C. USE OF ACQUIRING SUBSIDIARY TO AVOID *BAUSCH & LOMB* PROBLEM

REVENUE RULING 57–278
1957–1 C.B. 124.

Advice has been requested whether the reorganization plan herein described qualifies for tax-free treatment under section 368(a)(1)(C) of the Internal Revenue Code of 1954 in view of the principle set forth in Revenue Ruling 54–396, C.B. 1954–2, 147.

In the instant case, two existing corporations and a newly formed corporation were involved in the plan of reorganization. Originally, the parent corporation owned 72 percent of the outstanding capital stock of corporation *M*. The remaining 28 percent of *M*'s outstanding stock was widely held by the public. For valid business reasons, the parent desired to eliminate the minority interest of corporation *M* and operate it as a wholly-owned subsidiary.

In order to achieve the desired result, the parent organized a new corporation in a different state and issued to the new corporation a block of its voting stock in exchange for all the stock of the new corporation. In turn, and pursuant to an agreement with the principal minority stockholders of corporation *M*, the new corporation acquired all of the assets of corporation *M* in exchange for the stock of the parent corporation. Following this transaction, corporation *M* distributed to its shareholders the stock of the parent corporation on the basis of one share of the parent corporation's stock for each two shares of *M* corporation's stock.

Corporation *M* exchanged with the parent 72 percent of that portion of the stock of the parent corporation issued to the new corporation upon organization, the total of which was received by it in exchange for all of its assets, for 72 percent of its own capital stock held by the parent corporation. Corporation *M* exchanged the remaining 28 percent of the parent company stock held by it with its minority stockholders for the 28 percent of its stock held by them. As a result of all these transactions, the new corporation became a wholly owned subsidiary and corporation *M* was dissolved.

Section 368(a)(1)(C) of the Internal Revenue Code of 1954, relating to corporate reorganizations, defines a reorganization as "* * * the acquisition by one corporation, in exchange solely for all or part of its voting stock (or in exchange solely for all or a part of the voting stock of a corporation which is in control of the acquiring corporation), of substantially all of the properties of another corporation * * *."

Revenue Ruling 54–396, *supra,* holds that a transaction between two corporations, wherein one, the majority stockholder (but owning less than 80 percent) of the second, acquires all of the assets of the second in exchange for its common stock, is not a nontaxable reorganization within the purview of section 112(g)(1)(C) of the Internal Revenue Code of 1939 (now embodied in section 368(a)(1)(C) of the 1954 Code, since the first corporation, which already owned 79 percent of the second corporation's stock, acquired only 21 percent of the assets of the second corporation through the exchange of stock. The remaining 79 percent of the assets were acquired by the first corporation as a liquidating dividend in exchange for the stock of the second corporation.

The question here involved is whether the principle of Revenue Ruling 54–396 should be extended to the new forms of "C" reorganizations allowed under the Internal Revenue Code of 1954, *i.e.,* where a subsidiary acquires substantially all of the properties of another corporation solely in exchange for its parent's voting stock.

It will be noted that in the instant case the same result would have been achieved if the parent corporation had acquired all of the stock of corporation *M* solely for its own voting stock in a "B" reorganization (meaning reorganizations under section 368(a)(1)(B) of the 1954 Code) and then caused corporation *M* to be reincorporated in another state. Under the 1954 Code, a "B" reorganization may occur even though the acquiring corporation already owns a large block of stock of the other corporation. It, therefore, seems that the new form of "C" reorganization acquisition is tax free in a case in which a "B" reorganization acquisition, in a slightly different form, but having almost the same ultimate effect, would be tax free under the statute. Accordingly, Revenue Ruling 54–396, *supra,* will be restricted to those cases in which the ultimate transferee acquires some of the assets through a liquidation. The transitory ownership of assets by a corporation in a "C" reorganization is in effect to be disregarded. See *Helvering v. Raymond I. Bashford,* 302 U.S. 454, Ct.D. 1299, C.B. 1938–1, 286; *Anheuser-Busch, Inc. et al. v. Helvering,* 115 Fed. (2d) 662, cert. denied 312 U.S. 699. In each of these cases, it was held that a transaction was not a tax-free reorganization despite a transitory ownership which would have qualified it as such under the then existing law.

In view of the foregoing, the Internal Revenue Service holds that the acquisition by the new corporation of all the assets of corporation *M* in exchange solely for stock of the parent corporation constitutes a reorganization within the meaning of section 368(a)(1)(C) of the Internal Revenue Code of 1954. No gain or loss is recognized to the parent, the liquidating corporation, or the new corporation as a result of the exchanges made pursuant to the plan of reorganization. As provided by section 354(a)(1) of the Code, no gain or loss is recognized to the shareholders of corporation *M* upon the exchange of their stock for stock of the parent corporation. Under section 358, the basis of the parent corporation's stock in the hands of corporation *M*'s shareholders is the same as the basis of corporation *M*'s stock exchanged therefor and, under section 362(b), the basis of the properties of corporation *M* acquired by the new corporation is the same as that of *M* corporation. In accordance with section 381(c)(2) of the Code, the earnings and profits of corporation *M* for the taxable year involved are deemed to have been received by the new corporation as of the closing date of the transfer of the properties of the *M* corporation.

Question

What is the basis in this ruling for the holding that the new corporation has no gain or loss?

D. DEALING WITH THE ZERO BASIS PROBLEM

Although the issue is not addressed in the Code, as indicated in Rev.Rul. 57–278, *supra* Sec. 15.4.C., neither the parent nor the acquiring subsidiary have gain recognition in the transaction. *See* Prop.Reg. § 1.1032–2 and Prop.Reg. § 1.358–6. This issue is addressed in detail in *Taxable and Tax–Free Corporate Mergers, Acquisitions, and LBOs, supra* Sec. 1.4.

§ 15.5 FORWARD SUBSIDIARY MERGER UNDER § 368(A)(2)(D)

See Reg. § 1.382–2(b)(2).

A. LEGISLATIVE HISTORY OF THE FORWARD SUBSIDIARY MERGER

In 1968, § 368(a)(2)(D), which allows a forward triangular merger, was added. Also, § 358(e) was amended to change the word "issuance" to "exchange" and to add a parenthetical clause dealing with triangular reorganizations. The operation of these provisions was discussed as follows in the Senate Report:

Explanation of provision.—The bill (sec. 1) permits a corporation which is a controlled subsidiary of another corporation (*i.e.*, the parent holds 80 percent of the voting shares and 80 percent of the total number of shares of all other classes of stock of the subsidiary) to acquire tax free all the assets of a third corporation in a statutory merger in which stock of the *parent* corporation is exchanged for the stock of the transferor corporation. The amendment (new subparagraph (D) in sec. 368(a)(2)) provides that if a parent corporation controls a subsidiary corporation (*i.e.*, has the 80-percent control referred to above), then the acquisition of substantially all the properties of a corporation merged (in a statutory merger) into the subsidiary in exchange for the stock of the parent corporation is not to be disqualified as a type A reorganization if two conditions are met: (1) the merger insofar as the tax laws are concerned would have qualified as a type A reorganization had the merger been made into the parent instead of into the subsidiary, and (2) no stock of the subsidiary is used in the transaction. In addition, the definition of "a party to a reorganization" is modified to include a parent corporation in the case described (by adding a new sentence to sec. 368(b)).

The amendment does not alter or modify the present requirements of "business purpose" or "continuity of enterprise." It modifies the present "continuity of interest" requirement but only in that it permits the use of the stock of the parent in making the acquisition, instead of the stock of the subsidiary.

The amendment applies whether or not the parent corporation is formed immediately before the merger, in anticipation of the merger, or after preliminary steps were taken to merge directly.

B. INTRODUCTORY NOTE

In order to qualify as (a)(2)(D), the following basic conditions must be satisfied:

(1) The acquiring subsidiary must acquire "substantially all" of the target's properties.

(2) The consideration paid by the acquiring subsidiary must be stock of the acquiring parent, and cannot be stock of the acquiring subsidiary.

(3) The target must be merged into the acquiring subsidiary.

(4) The transaction must be such that it would have qualified as an (A) merger if the target had merged into the acquiring parent.

The "substantially all" test is the same as the one that applies in the (C). *See* § 1.368–2(b)(2) and Sec. 15.3.B. The regulations say that the test of whether the transaction would have qualified as an (A) if the target had merged into the acquiring parent "means that the general requirements of a reorganization under § 368(a)(1)(A) (such as a business purpose, continuity of business enterprise and continuity of interest) must be met in addition to the special requirements under § 368(a)(2)(D)." *See* § 1.368–2(b)(2). *See* Chapter 11 for an exploration of business purpose, continuity of business enterprise and continuity of interest. This regulation further says that it is "not relevant whether the merger * * * could have been effected pursuant to State or Federal corporation law."

Although the acquiring subsidiary cannot issue its own stock, it may issue other boot, as long as the continuity of interest test is satisfied. See § 1.368–2(b)(2). The acquiring parent may assume all or a part of the target's liabilities. Id. Finally, § 368(a)(2)(D) applies without respect to the time the acquiring subsidiary is formed. Id.

* * *

C. CREATION OF HOLDING COMPANY

REVENUE RULING 77–428
1977–2 C.B. 117.

Advice has been requested whether the transactions described in *Situation 1* and *Situation 2*, below, qualify as reorganizations under section 368(a)(1)(A) of the Internal Revenue Code of 1954 by reason of section 368(a)(2)(D) and section 368(a)(2)(E), respectively.

SITUATION 1.

P is a corporation chartered under state law that has been engaged in the commercial banking business for a number of years. *P,* for good business reasons, decided that its business activities could be expanded if its banking business were conducted by a corporation whose stock was owned by another corporation. The other corporation could then engage in related nonbanking activities, such as selling insurance to borrowers, and leasing personal property, activities that could not be engaged in directly by *P* under state law. To accomplish this, *P* caused corporation *S1* to be organized as a wholly owned subsidiary. *S1* then caused corporation *S2* to be organized as a wholly owned subsidiary. Other than the cash received from *P* to satisfy capitalization requirements, the only asset of *S1* was the stock of *S2,* and the only asset of *S2* was the cash received from *S1* to satisfy capitalization requirements.

Pursuant to a plan of merger, *P* merged with and into *S2* under the applicable state laws with *S2* being the surviving corporation. On the effective date of the merger, each share of *P* stock held by the *P* shareholders was exchanged for a share of newly issued *S1* stock. Thus, as a result of the merger, all of the assets and business of *P* became the assets and business of *S2,* the *P* shareholders became the shareholders of *S1,* and *S1* then engaged in the nonbanking activities described above. * * * Section 1.368–2(b)(2) of the Income Tax Regulations provides that [section 368(a)(2)(D)] applies whether or not the controlling corporation (or the acquiring corporation) is formed immediately before the merger, in anticipation of the merger, or after preliminary steps have been taken to merge directly into the controlling corporation.

While section 1.368–2(b)(2) of the regulations does not specifically provide for the formation of *both* the controlling and acquiring corporation, or for the acquiring of a related corporation, there is nothing in the legislative history of the enactment of section 368(a)(2)(D) of the Code to indicate that section was not intended to apply where such was the case.

Accordingly, the merger of *P* with and into *S2* qualifies as a reorganization under section 368(a)(1)(A) of the Code by reason of section 368(a)(2)(D) even though *S1* and *S2* were newly organized corporations and even though a related corporation was acquired in the transaction. See Rev.Rul. 72–274, 1972–1 C.B. 97, in which a similar transaction was treated as a reorganization under section 368(a)(1)(A) by reason of section 368(a)(2)(D).

SITUATION 2.

The facts are the same as in *Situation 1* except that *S2* merged with and into *P* under the applicable state laws with *P* being the surviving corporation. On the effective date of the merger the *S2* stock held by *S1* was converted, pursuant to state law, into stock of *P* and each outstanding share of *P* stock not held by *S1* exchanged for a share of *S1* stock. Thus, as a result of the merger *P* became a wholly owned subsidiary of *S1* and the former *P* shareholders became the shareholders of *S1*. After the merger, *P* held all of its assets and all the assets of *S2*.

* * *

The committee reports, *H.R.Rep. No. 91–1778,* 91st Cong., 2nd Sess. (1970), and *S.Rep. No. 91–1533,* 91st Cong., 2nd Sess. (1970), 1971–1 C.B. 622, indicate that section 368(a)(2)(E) of the Code was enacted to allow as a tax-free reorganization a transaction identical to a transaction described in section 368(a)(2)(D) except that the surviving corporation was the acquired rather than the acquiring corporation. Since, as concluded in *Situation 1,* a corporation may form first- and second-tier subsidiaries and then merge into the second-tier subsidiary under section 368(a)(2)(D), a reverse merger of the second-tier subsidiary into the "grandparent" is permissible under section 368(a)(2)(E).

Accordingly, the merger of *S2* with and into *P* qualifies as a reorganization within the meaning of section 368(a)(1)(A) of the Code by reason of section 368(a)(2)(E) even though *S1* and *S2* were newly organized corporations and a related corporation was acquired in the transaction.

D. DEALING WITH THE ZERO BASIS PROBLEM

See Prop.Reg. §§ 1.1032–2 and 1.358–6(a).

See Sec. 15.4.D.

§ 15.6 THE § 381 CARRYOVER RULES: INTRODUCTION

Section 381(a) provides that in the types of transactions specified below the acquiring corporation shall succeed to and take into account, as of the close of the date of distribution or transfer, the items of the distributor or transferor corporation specified in § 381(c), subject to the conditions and limitations specified in § 381(b) and (c). One of these items is the net operating loss carryovers of the distributor of transferor corporation.

Thus, in the transactions described below the acquiring corporation succeeds to the target's net operating losses and other attributes specified in Section 381(c). The carryover of net operating losses is, however, subject to limitation in Section 382, which is addressed in Sec. 26.12.

Section 381(a) covers certain nontaxable liquidations and reorganizations. It covers the liquidation of a subsidiary into its parent in a liquidation governed by § 332 in which the parent takes a carryover basis for the subsidiary's assets under Section 334(b)(1). *See* § 381(a)(1).

The reorganizations which are covered by § 381(a) are (1) mergers under § 368(a)(1)(A); (2) forward triangular mergers under § 368(a)(2)(D); (3) the direct and triangular acquisition of assets for voting stock under § 368(a)(1)(C); (4) the nondivisive (D) under § 368(a)(1)(D) and § 354(b); and (5) mere changes in form under § 368(a)(1)(F). *See* § 381(a)(2). Thus § 381 applies to the acquisitive asset reorganizations discussed in this chapter.

Section 381 is explored in greater detail in *Taxable and Tax–Free Corporate Mergers, Acquisitions, and LBOs, supra* Sec. 1.4.

§ 15.7 SUMMARY PROBLEMS ON STRAIGHT AND TRIANGULAR ACQUISITIVE ASSET REORGANIZATIONS

Target corporation (*TC*) has 100 common shares outstanding (its only stock), which is owned as follows:

	No. of Shares	*Adjusted Basis*
Individual *A*	40	20
Corporation *X*	40	20
Individual *B*	20	10

TC has assets with a value of $130K and a basis of $75K and liabilities of $30K, represented by outstanding debentures. Thus, *TC*'s assets have a net value of $100K. The value of *TC*'s stock is also $100K. *TC* has accumulated E & P of $50K.

Acquiring corporation (*AC*) is a large conglomerate whose stock is traded on the New York Stock Exchange. *AC* wants to acquire *TC*. *AC* wants *A*, who is also an employee of *TC*, to enter into a long-term employment agreement.

What are the tax consequences to each of the parties under each of the following basic asset transactions and the modifications thereof?

TC merges into AC with the shareholders of TC receiving in exchange for their TC stock on a pro rata basis (1) $50K of AC nonvoting common, (2) $25K of cash, and (3) AC debentures with a face and value of $25K. Also, AC issues its debentures with a face and value of $30K in exchange for the TC debentures held by A and Y? There is no OID on AC's or TC's debentures.

Consider each of the following modifications separately.

    a. Suppose the AC debentures issued in exchange for the TC debentures have a face of $36K and a value of $30K?

    b. Suppose that instead of the AC debentures issued in exchange for the TC stock, AC issues its nonvoting preferred?

    c. Suppose that instead of receiving the consideration on a pro rata basis it was received by the shareholders as follows:

Shareholders	AC Stock	AC Debentures	Cash	Total
A	$10K	$20K	$10K	$ 40K
B	$ 5K	$ 5K	$10K	$ 20K
X	$35K	–0–	$ 5K	$ 40K
	$50K	$25K	$25K	$100K

    d. Suppose that instead of a direct merger of TC into AC, AC forms a new subsidiary (AC–S) and transfers to AC–S the consideration specified in the basic transaction. TC then merges into AC–S?

    e. Suppose AC purchases the TC stock held by X for cash of $40K and immediately thereafter merges TC upstream with A receiving $40K of AC voting common and B receiving $20K in AC debentures?

    f. Suppose that prior to the merger of TC into AC, TC redeems B's stock for $20K in cash and then TC merges into AC with A receiving $40K of AC nonvoting preferred and X receiving $40K of AC voting common stock?

    g. Suppose that instead of a merger of TC into AC, AC acquires all of TC's assets and assumes TC's liability to its debenture holders in exchange for the consideration specified in the basic transaction, and TC immediately liquidates, transferring the consideration to its shareholders? Suppose a newly formed subsidiary of AC (AC–S) makes the acquisition for the same consideration? Any suggestions for modifying these transactions?

§ 15.8 THE STRAIGHT (B) REORGANIZATION

A. INTRODUCTION

There are two basic requirements for a straight (B) reorganization under § 368(a)(1)(B). First, an acquiring corporation must acquire a target's stock in exchange "solely for all or a part of the [acquiring corporation's] voting stock." Second, the acquiring corporation must, immediately after the acquisition, have control (within the meaning of § 368(c)) of the target. In determining whether control exists "immediately after," it does not matter "(whether or not [the] acquiring corporation had control immediately before the acquisition)." This parenthetical, which allows a creeping (B), was added to the definition of the (B) by the 1954 Code. The Senate Report to the 1954 Code explains:

> Under section 112(g)(1)(B), of existing law, one corporation can acquire enough stock of another to get control of the second corporation solely for its own voting stock tax free. However, there is doubt as to whether the existing statute permits such an acquisition tax free when the acquiring corporation already owns some of the voting stock of the other corporation. This doubt is removed by your committee's bill and paragraph (B) of subsection (a)(1) permits such an acquisition tax free (in a single transaction or in a series of transactions taking place over a relatively short period of time such as 12 months). For example, corporation A purchased 30 percent of the common stock of corporation W (the only class of stock outstanding) for cash in 1939. On March 1, 1955, corporation A offers to exchange its own voting stock, for all of the stock of corporation W tendered within 6 months from the date of the offer. Within the 6 months period corporation A acquires an additional 60 percent of the stock of W for its own voting stock. As a result of the 1955 transactions, corporation A will own 90 percent of all of corporation W's stock. No gain or loss is recognized with respect to the exchanges of the A stock for the W stock. For this purpose it is immaterial whether such exchanges occurred before corporation A acquired control of W (80 percent) or after such control was acquired. If corporation A had acquired 80 percent of corporation W's stock for cash in 1939, it could likewise acquire some or all of the remainder of such stock solely in exchange for its own voting stock without recognition of gain or loss.

Section 1.368–2(c) repeats almost verbatim the above language.

The following is a summary of the basic tax treatment to the parties in a (B).

> (1) The acquiring corporation has nonrecognition treatment under § 1032 upon the issuance of its stock.

> (2) The acquiring corporation takes a carryover basis under § 362(b) for the stock of the target. If the target is publicly held, statistical sampling may be used to determine the bases of the target shareholder's shares. *See* Rev.Rul. 81–70, 1981–1 C.B. 389.

> (3) The target's shareholders have nonrecognition treatment under § 354(a) upon the exchange of their target stock for the stock of the acquiring corporation. Since the acquiror cannot pay any boot, § 356 does not come into play.

> (4) The target's shareholders take a substituted basis under § 358 for the stock received.

The (B) has been in the tax law in various forms since the Revenue Act of 1921. The "solely for voting stock" requirement was added by the 1934 Act. Thus, unlike the (A), the (B) has a statutorily mandated continuity of interest requirement.

The leading case dealing with the meaning of "solely for voting stock" is *Southwest Consolidated,* which is set out in Sec. 11.4. The determination of whether the consideration paid consists solely of voting stock is one of the most important issues in a (B). Most of the topics covered in this section relate in some respect to the solely for voting stock requirement.

B. CAN THERE BE BOOT IN A (B) REORGANIZATION? THE FIRST CIRCUIT'S VIEW OF ITT–HARTFORD

CHAPMAN v. COMMISSIONER
United States Court of Appeals, First Circuit, 1980.
618 F.2d 856.

LEVIN H. CAMPBELL, CIRCUIT JUDGE.

* * * We must decide whether the requirement of Section 368(a)(1)(B) that the acquisition of stock in one corporation by another be solely in exchange for voting stock of the acquiring corporation is met where, in related transactions, the acquiring corporation first acquires 8 percent of the acquiree's stock for cash and then acquires more than 80 percent of the acquiree in an exchange of stock for voting stock. The Tax Court agreed with the taxpayers that the latter exchange constituted a valid tax-free reorganization. *Reeves v. Commissioner,* 71 T.C. 727 (1979).

[ITT purchased for cash 8% of the stock of Hartford. ITT then proposed to acquire the balance of the stock of Hartford in a (B) reorganization. In order to get a ruling from the IRS to the effect that the stock-for-stock acquisition would qualify as a (B), ITT was required to sell the 8% of the stock that it had purchased to an independent third party before beginning a stock-for-stock exchange. Otherwise the IRS would have viewed the cash purchase as integrated with the stock-for-stock exchange, thereby violating the solely for stock requirement. ITT sold the stock to an Italian bank, Mediobanca, and the IRS ruled that the prior purchase would not be integrated with the stock-for-stock exchange. ITT then completed the stock-for-stock exchange.

After completion of the transaction, the IRS later revoked its ruling on the grounds that ITT and Mediobanca had an understanding that Mediobanca would tender its Hartford shares in the stock-for-stock exchange. The IRS, therefore, treated the stock-for-stock exchange as a taxable transaction on grounds that ITT had acquired Hartford's stock partially for cash and partially for stock.]

* * * For purposes of this motion, the taxpayers conceded that questions of the merits of the revocation of the IRS rulings were not to be considered; the facts were to be viewed as though ITT had not sold the shares previously acquired for cash to Mediobanca. The taxpayers also conceded, solely for purposes of their motion for summary judgment, that the initial cash purchases of Hartford stock had been made for the purpose of furthering ITT's efforts to acquire Hartford.

The Issue

* * *

The single issue raised on this appeal is whether "the acquisition" in this case complied with the requirement that it be "solely for * * * voting stock." It is well settled that the "solely" requirement is mandatory; if any part of "the acquisition" includes a form of consideration other than voting stock, the transaction will not qualify as a (B) reorganization. *See Helvering v. Southwest Consolidated Corp.,* 315 U.S. 194, 198, 62 S.Ct. 546, 550, 86 L.Ed. 789 (1942) ("'Solely' leaves no leeway. Voting stock plus some other consideration does not meet the statutory requirement"). The precise issue before us is thus how broadly to read the term "acquisition." The Internal Revenue Service argues that "the acquisition * * * of stock of another corporation" must be understood to encompass the 1968–69 cash purchases as well as the 1970 exchange offer. If the IRS is correct, "the acquisition" here fails as a (B) reorganization. The taxpayers, on the other hand, would limit "the acquisition" to the part of a sequential transaction of this nature which meets the requirements of subsection (B). They argue that the 1970 exchange of stock for stock was itself an "acquisition" by ITT of stock in Hartford solely in exchange for ITT's voting stock, such that after the exchange took place ITT controlled Hartford. Taxpayers contend that the earlier cash purchases of 8 percent, even if conceded to be part of the same acquisitive plan, are essentially irrelevant to the tax-free reorganization otherwise effected.

The Tax Court accepted the taxpayers' reading of the statute, effectively overruling its own prior decision in *Howard v. Commissioner,* 24 T.C. 792 (1955), *rev'd on other grounds,* 238 F.2d 943 (7th Cir.1956). The plurality opinion stated its "narrow" holding as follows:

> "We hold that where, as is the case herein, 80 percent or more of the stock of a corporation is acquired in one transaction,[18] in exchange for which only voting stock is furnished as consideration, the 'solely for voting stock' requirement of section 368(a)(1)(B) is satisfied."

18. In determining what constitutes 'one transaction,' we include all the acquisitions from shareholders which were clearly part of the same transaction.

71 T.C. at 741. The plurality treated as "irrelevant" the 8 percent of Hartford's stock purchased for cash, although the opinion left somewhat ambiguous the question whether the 8 percent was irrelevant because of the 14–month time interval separating the transactions or because the statute was not concerned with transactions over and above those

mathematically necessary to the acquiring corporation's attainment of control.

II.

For reasons set forth extensively in section III of this opinion, we do not accept the position adopted by the Tax Court. Instead we side with the Commissioner on the narrow issue presented in this appeal, that is, the correctness of taxpayers' so-called "second" argument premised on an assumed relationship between the cash and stock transactions. As explained below, we find a strong implication in the language of the statute, in the legislative history, in the regulations, and in the decisions of other courts that cash purchases which are concededly "parts of" a stock-for-stock exchange must be considered constituent elements of the "acquisition" for purposes of applying the "solely for * * * voting stock" requirement of Section 368(a)(1)(B). We believe the presence of non-stock consideration in such an acquisition, regardless of whether such consideration is necessary to the gaining of control, is inconsistent with treatment of the acquisition as a nontaxable reorganization. It follows for purposes of taxpayers' second argument—which was premised on the assumption that the cash transactions were part of the 1970 exchange offer reorganization—that the stock transfers in question would not qualify for nonrecognition of gain or loss.

* * *

III.

A.

Having summarized in advance our holding, and its intended scope, we shall now revert to the beginning of our analysis, and, in the remainder of this opinion, describe the thinking by which we reached the result just announced. We begin with the words of the statute itself. The reorganization definitions contained in Section 368(a)(1) are precise, technical, and comprehensive. They were intended to define the exclusive means by which nontaxable corporate reorganizations could be effected. In examining the language of the (B) provision, we discern two possible meanings. On the one hand, the statute could be read to say that a successful reorganization occurs whenever Corporation X exchanges its own voting stock for stock in Corporation Y, and, immediately after the transaction, Corporation X controls more than 80 percent of Y's stock. On this reading, purchases of shares for which any part of the consideration takes the form of "boot" should be ignored, since the definition is only concerned with transactions which meet the statutory requirements as to consideration and control. To take an example, if Corporation X bought 50 percent of the shares of Y, and then almost immediately exchanged part of its voting stock for the remaining 50 percent of Y's stock, the question would arise whether the second transaction was a (B) reorganization. Arguably, the statute can be read to support such a finding. In the second transaction, X exchanged only stock for stock (meeting the "solely" requirement), and after the transaction was completed X owned Y (meeting the "control" requirement).

The alternative reading of the statute—the one which we are persuaded to adopt—treats the (B) definition as prescriptive, rather than merely descriptive. We read the statute to mean that the entire transaction which constitutes "the acquisition" must not contain any nonstock consideration if the transaction is to qualify as a (B) reorganization. In the example given above, where X acquired 100 percent of Y's stock, half for cash and half for voting stock, we would interpret "the acquisition" as referring to the entire transaction, so that the "solely for * * * voting stock" requirement would not be met. We believe if Congress had intended the statute to be read as merely descriptive, this intent would have been more clearly spelled out in the statutory language.

We recognize that the Tax Court adopted neither of these two readings. [T]he Tax Court purported to limit its holding to cases, such as this one, where more than 80 percent of the stock of Corporation Y passes to Corporation X in exchange solely for voting stock. The Tax Court presumably would assert that the 50/50 hypothetical posited above can be distinguished from this case, and that its holding implies no view as to the hypothetical. The plurality opinion recognized that the position it adopted creates no small problem with respect to the proper reading of "the acquisition" in the statutory definition. In order to distinguish the 80 percent case from the 50 percent case, it is necessary to read "the acquisition" as referring to at least the amount of stock constituting "control" (80 percent) where related cash purchases are present. Yet the Tax Court recognized that "the acquisition" cannot always refer to the conveyance of an 80 percent bloc of stock in one transaction, since to do so would frustrate the intent of the 1954 amendments to permit so-called "creeping acquisitions."

[The court then reviewed the legislative history of the (B). This portion of the opinion is set out in Sec. 10.3.]

C.

Besides finding support for the IRS position both in the design of the statute and in the legislative history, we find support in the regulations adopted by the Treasury Department construing these statutory provisions.

* * *

D.

Finally, we turn to the body of case law that has developed concerning (B) reorganizations to determine how previous courts have dealt with this question. Of the seven prior cases in this area, all to a greater or lesser degree support the result we have reached, and none supports the result reached by the Tax Court. We recognize that the Tax Court purported to distinguish these precedents from the case before it, and that reasonable persons may differ on the extent to which some of these cases directly control the question raised here. Nevertheless, after carefully reviewing the precedents, we are satisfied that the decision of the Tax Court represents a sharp break with the previous judicial constructions of this statute, and a departure from the usual rule of stare decisis, which applies with special force in the tax field where uncertainty and variety are ordinarily to be avoided.

* * *

IV.

We have stated our ruling, and the reasons that support it. In conclusion, we would like to respond briefly to the arguments raised by the Tax Court, the District Court of Delaware, and the taxpayers in this case against the rule we have reaffirmed today. The principal argument, repeated again and again, concerns the supposed lack of policy behind the rule forbidding cash in a (B) reorganization where the control requirement is met solely for voting stock. It is true that the Service has not pointed to tax loopholes that would be opened were the rule to be relaxed as appellees request. * * *

* * *

Possibly, Congress' insertion of the "solely for * * * voting stock" requirement into the 1934 Act was, as one commentator has suggested, an overreaction to a problem which could have been dealt with through more precise and discriminating measures. But we do not think it appropriate for a court to tell Congress how to do its job in an area such as this. * * *

* * *

Finally, we see no merit at all in the suggestion that we should permit "boot" in a (B) reorganization simply because "boot" is permitted in some instances in (A) and (C) reorganizations. Congress has never indicated that these three distinct categories of transactions are to be interpreted in *pari materia*. In fact, striking differences in the treatment of the three subsections have been evident in the history of the reorganization statutes. We see no reason to believe a difference in the treatment of "boot" in these transactions is impermissible or irrational.

* * *

Notes

1. In May 1981 the IRS and ITT settled this litigation with ITT paying $28.5 million and the IRS agreeing not to pursue claims against the Hartford shareholders. *See* Daily Tax Report, 5/8/81, p. G–5.

2. In Rev.Rul. 72–354, 1972–2 C.B. 216, the Service ruled that a prior purchase by an acquiring corporation of the shares of a target will not violate the "solely for voting stock" requirement of the (B) if, prior to the offer to the target's shareholders in the (B), the acquiring corporation "unconditionally sells such shares to a third party." The ruling reasons:

> Under the facts presented the unconditional sale of the Y shares to X is accorded independent significance for tax purposes since it was neither transitory nor illusory and in no way dependent or conditional upon the subsequent reorganization.

C. BOOT FLOWING DIRECTLY FROM ACQUIROR TO TARGET'S SHAREHOLDERS

1. Purchase of Fractional Shares

REVENUE RULING 66–365
1966–2 C.B. 116.

In *Mills, et al. v. Commissioner*, 331 F.2d 321 (1964), reversing 39 T.C. 393 (1962), the United States Court of Appeals for the Fifth Circuit held that the "solely for voting stock" requirement of section 368(a)(1)(B) of the Code was satisfied where the acquiring corporation received all of the stock of several corporations and distributed in return for such stock, shares of its voting common stock and a small amount of cash in lieu of fractional shares. After finding that the cash given in lieu of fractional shares was simply a mathematical rounding-off for the purpose of simplifying the corporate and accounting problems which would have been caused by the actual issuance of fractional shares, the Court concluded that the receipt of the stock of the acquired corporations was for all practical purposes "solely in exchange for voting stock".

The Internal Revenue Service will follow the decision of the Court of Appeals in *Mills, et al. v. Commissioner* in similar factual situations. Accordingly, the "solely for voting stock" requirement of section 368(a)(1)(B) and (C) of the Code will not be violated where the cash paid by the acquiring corporation is in lieu of fractional share interests to which the shareholders are entitled, representing merely a mechanical rounding-off of the fractions in the exchange, and is not a separately bargained-for consideration. * * *

* * *

[W]here the cash payment made by the acquiring corporation is not bargained for, but is in lieu of fractional share interests to which the shareholders are entitled, such cash payment will be treated under section 302 of the Code as in redemption of the fractional share interests.

* * *

2. Stock for Services

REVENUE RULING 77-271
1977-2 C.B. 116.

A owned all of the outstanding stock of X corporation. X was engaged in the home construction business. A was the president of X and was actively involved in the business. Pursuant to a plan of reorganization, Y corporation, whose stock is widely held, acquired all of the X stock from A in exchange solely for shares of Y voting stock in an amount equal to the fair market value of the X stock received from A in exchange therefor. As part of the agreement between A and Y, A entered into an employment contract under which A was to continue as president of X for a specified period of time and at a specified salary. As consideration for A entering into the employment contract, Y issued additional shares of its voting stock to A.

* * *

[T]he exchange of X stock for Y voting stock of equal value was a reorganization within the meaning of section 368(a)(1)(B) of the Code and, under section 354, no gain or loss was recognized to A. The Y voting stock received by A as consideration for the employment contract was includible in A's gross income as ordinary income in the amount of its fair market value on the date of issuance.

D. REVERSE SUBSIDIARY MERGER MAY CONSTITUTE A (B) REORGANIZATION

REVENUE RULING 67-448
1967-2 C.B. 144.

Corporation P and Corporation Y, incorporated in the same state, are publicly owned corporations. Corporation P wanted to acquire the business of Corporation Y but could do so with an effective result only if the corporate entity of Y were continued intact due to the necessity of preserving its status as a regulated public utility. P also desired to eliminate the possibility of minority shareholders in the event less than all of the shareholders of Y agreed to the transaction. Since an outright acquisition of stock pursuant to a reorganization as defined in section 368(a)(1)(B) of the Code would not achieve this result, the plan of reorganization was consummated as follows:

(a) P transferred shares of its voting stock to its newly formed subsidiary, S, in exchange for shares of S stock.

(b) S (whose only asset consisted of a block of the voting stock of P) merged into Y in a transaction which qualified as a statutory merger under the applicable state law.

(c) Pursuant to the plan of reorganization and by operation of state law, the S stock owned by P was converted into Y stock. At the same time the Y stock held by its shareholders was exchanged for the P stock received by Y on the merger of S into Y. The end result of these actions was that P acquired from the shareholders of Y in exchange for its own voting stock more than 95 percent of the stock of Y.

(d) Y shareholders owning less than five percent of the stock of Y dissented to the merger and had the right to receive the appraised value of their shares paid solely from the assets of Y. No funds, or other property, have been or will be provided by P for this purpose.

Thus, upon the consummation of the plan of reorganization Y became a wholly owned subsidiary of P.

At the time of the transaction P had no plan or intention to liquidate Y or to merge it into any other corporation.

The transaction described above does not constitute a reorganization within the meaning of either section 368(a)(1)(A) or section 368(a)(1)(C) of the Code because no assets of Y were transferred to nor acquired by another corporation in the transaction but rather all assets (except for amounts paid to dissenting shareholders) were retained in the same corporate entity.

* * *

It is evident that the shortest route to the end result described above would have been achieved by a transfer of P voting stock directly to the shareholders of Y in exchange for their stock. This result is not negated because the transaction was cast in the form of a series of interrelated steps. The transitory existence of the new subsidiary, S, will be disregarded. The effect of all the steps taken in the series is that Y became a wholly owned subsidiary of P, and P transferred solely its voting stock to the former shareholders of Y.

Accordingly, the transaction will be treated as an acquisition by P, in exchange solely for part of its voting stock, of stock of Y in an amount constituting control (as defined in section 368(c) of the Code) of Y, which qualifies as a reorganization within the meaning of section 368(a)(1)(B) of the Code.

Questions

Does Rev.Rul. 67–448 make § 368(a)(2)(E) superfluous? Would the result change at all if the acquiring corporation provided the cash to pay the dissenting shareholders? What would the treatment have been in Rev.Rul. 67–448 if prior to the reverse subsidiary merger, P had purchased 10% of the stock of Y for cash?

§ 15.9 THE TRIANGULAR (B) REORGANIZATION

A. LEGISLATIVE HISTORY OF THE TRIANGULAR B

In 1964, the parenthetical clause was added to § 368(a)(1)(B), allowing the triangular (B) reorganization. Also, § 368(a)(2)(C) was amended to allow the stock of a target acquired in a triangular (B) to be dropped into a subsidiary of the acquiring subsidiary. Conforming amendments were made to the definition of party to a reorganization in § 368(b). The following discussion from the Senate Report explains the operation of these amendments:

> [T]he 1954 code permits tax-free reorganizations in the case of the exchange of the parent's stock for the assets of a corporation acquired by the subsidiary. However, a similar result is denied where the subsidiary acquires the stock of the other corporation in exchange for the stock of its parent corporation. Since Congress has considered the "continuity of interest" rule satisfied in the case of asset acquisitions, there seems to be no reason for not applying the same rule to stock acquisitions, since there is little in substance to distinguish an asset acquisition from a stock acquisition.
>
> As a result, your committee has concluded that it is desirable to treat these two types of acquisitions in the same manner. For that reason, it has provided tax-free status for the stock-for-stock reorganization in the same manner that present law provides a tax-free status for stock-for-assets reorganizations.
>
> *(c) General explanation of provision.*—This provision amends the definition of a stock-for-stock reorganization (known as a (B) reorganization) to qualify as a tax-free reorganization a transaction in which a subsidiary corporation acquires the stock of another corporation (and after that is in control of the corporation) in exchange solely for the voting stock of its parent corporation. Present law is also amended to permit the subsidiary corporation acquiring the stock of another corporation in the "(B) reorganization" to transfer all or part of this stock to another corporation which it controls. In addition, conforming changes have been made to the definition of the term "party to the reorganization".

B. INTRODUCTORY NOTE

The issues that arise in a triangular (B) under the parenthetical clause of § 368(a)(1)(B) are essentially the same as those that arise in a straight (B). *See* Sec. 15.8. The principal concern is ensuring that the solely for voting stock requirement is not violated. If the stock the subsidiary uses in making the acquisition was contributed to it by the parent, there is a potential zero basis problem. Also there is a potential recognition problem for the subsidiary.

C. ZERO BASIS PROBLEM

See Prop.Reg. § 1.1032–2 and 1.358–6(b).

See Sec. 15.4.D.

§ 15.10 SECTION 368(a)(2)(E) REVERSE SUBSIDIARY MERGERS

A. LEGISLATIVE HISTORY OF THE REVERSE SUBSIDIARY MERGER

The reverse triangular merger provision, § 368(a)(2)(E), was added in 1970. The operation of this provision was discussed as follows in the Senate Report:

I. Summary

This bill amends the tax law to permit a tax-free statutory merger when stock of a parent corporation is used in a merger between a controlled subsidiary of the parent and another corporation, and the other corporation survives—here called a "reverse merger."

The Treasury Department has indicated that it has no objection to the enactment of this bill.

II. Reasons for the Bill

* * *

[U]nder existing law, corporation X (an unrelated corporation) may be merged into corporation S (a subsidiary) in exchange for the stock in corporation P (the parent of S) in a tax-free statutory merger. [See § 368(a)(2)(D).] However, if for business and legal reasons (wholly unrelated to Federal income taxation) it is considered more desirable to merge S into X (rather than merging X into S), so that X is the surviving corporation—a "reverse merger"—the transaction is not a tax-free statutory merger.

* * *

The committee agrees with the House, that there is no reason why a merger in one direction (S into X in the above example) should be taxable, when the merger in the other direction (X into S), under identical circumstances, is tax-free. Moreover, it sees no reason why in cases of this type the acquisition needs to be made solely for stock. For these reasons the amendment makes statutory mergers tax-free in the circumstances described above.

III. Explanation of the Bill

* * * Under the new provision (sec. 368(a)(2)(E)) * * * a statutory merger may be a tax-free reorganization if it meets several conditions.

First, the corporation surviving the merger must hold substantially all of its own properties and substantially all of the properties of the merged corporation (except stock of the controlling corporation distributed in the transaction).

Second, in the transaction, former shareholders of the surviving corporation must receive voting stock of the controlling corporation in exchange for an amount of stock representing control in the surviving corporation. Control for this purpose (defined in sec. 368(c)) means that the amount of stock in the surviving corporation surrendered for voting stock of the controlling corporation must represent stock possessing at least 80 percent of the total combined voting power (in the surviving corporation), and also stock amounting to at least 80 percent of the total number of shares of all other classes of stock (in the surviving corporation). If voting stock of the controlling corporation is used in the exchange to the extent described, additional stock in the surviving corporation may be acquired for cash or other property (whether or not from the shareholders who received voting stock). Of course, this additional stock in the surviving corporation need not be acquired by the controlling corporation.

The amendment applies not only when the only assets of the merged corporation are the nominal capital required to organize it and the stock of its parent which is to be used in the merger exchange but also when the corporation has substantial properties.

B. INTRODUCTORY NOTE

In order to qualify as a reverse subsidiary merger, the transaction must satisfy the following requirements:

(1) The acquiring subsidiary must merge into the target corporation in a transaction that would otherwise qualify as an (A).

(2) After the merger, the target must hold "substantially all" of its properties and substantially all of the acquiring subsidiary's properties, other than stock of the acquiring parent distributed in the transaction.

(3) The former shareholders of the target must exchange for an amount of voting stock of the acquiring parent, an amount of stock in the target that constitutes control of the target.

The "substantially all" requirement is the same as the one that applies to the (C). *See* Sec. 15.3.B. The (a)(2)(E) has a voting stock requirement, whereas the (a)(2)(D) does not. The (a)(2)(E) is similar to a (B); however, up to 20% of the consideration paid in an (a)(2)(E) can be boot. If the target's shareholders receive solely voting stock of the acquiring corporation, the transaction may also constitute a (B). *See* Rev.Rul. 67–448, *supra* Sec. 15.8.D.

C. EXCERPT FROM PREAMBLE TO FINAL REGULATIONS (T.D. 8059)

PREAMBLE TO FINAL REGULATIONS UNDER § 368(a)(2)(E)

Treasury Decision 8059 (October 21, 1985).

SUMMARY OF PUBLIC COMMENTS AND CHANGES TO PROPOSED REGULATIONS

Control requirement

Section 368(a)(2)(E)(ii) of the Code requires that, in the transaction, former shareholders of the surviving corporation (hereinafter "T") exchange, for voting stock of the controlling corporation (hereinafter "P"), an amount of stock which constitutes control of T (as defined in section 368(c) of the Code). Section 1.368–2(j)(3)(i) of the proposed regulations provides that the amount of T stock surrendered in the transaction by T shareholders in exchange for P voting stock must itself constitute control. Accordingly, if P owns more than 20 percent of T, the transaction does not qualify under section 368(a)(2)(E). Example (3) of proposed § 1.368–2(j)(7) illustrates that result. Numerous commenters suggested that, instead, the regulations provide that the requirement of section 368(a)(2)(E)(ii) is satisfied if, in the transaction, T shareholders surrender in exchange for P voting stock an amount of T stock which, when added to P's prior stock ownership in T, constitutes control.

After careful consideration, it is concluded that the statute does not permit the interpretation advanced by the commenters. Section 1.368–2(j)(3)(i) and example (4) of § 1.368–2(j)(7) of the final regulations retain the rule set forth in the proposed regulations. Examples (6) and (7) of § 1.368–2(j)(7) of the final regulations clarify, however, that the control requirement of section 368(a)(2)(E)(ii) may be satisfied despite the fact that, in the transaction, P contributes money or other property to T in exchange for additional T stock, or P receives T stock in exchange for its prior interest in the merged corporation (hereinafter "S"). However, as illustrated in example (9) of § 1.368–2(j)(7) of the final regulations, the receipt of such T stock will not contribute to satisfaction of that control requirement.

Section 1.368–2(j)(3)(i) of the proposed regulations also provides that, for purposes of the control requirement, T's outstanding stock is measured immediately before the transaction. Further, as illustrated in examples (2) and (4) of proposed § 1.368–2(j)(7), payments to T's shareholders other than P voting stock (such as cash payments to dissenters or payments in redemption of T stock), as part of the transaction, could prevent satisfaction of that requirement. Several commenters suggested that, similar to reorganizations under section 368(a)(1)(B), payments to T's shareholders could be disregarded for purposes of the control requirement, provided the consideration was furnished by T and not by P. In response, § 1.368–2(j)(3)(i) of the final regulations, reflecting an interpretation of the statute which looks to the consideration furnished by P rather than that received by the T shareholders, provides that such payments by T and not by P may be disregarded for purposes of section 368(a)(2)(E)(ii). As with reorganizations under section 368(a)(1)(B), the facts and circumstances of each case will determine whether the payments came from T or P. Examples (2) and (3) of § 1.368–2(j)(7) of the final regulations illustrate that result. However, § 1.368–2(j)(3)(i) and (iii) also clarify that those payments are treated as a reduction of T's properties for purposes of section 368(a)(2)(E)(i), which requires that, after the transaction, T hold substantially all of its properties. In addition, receipt of consideration other than P stock by T shareholders in the transaction could prevent satisfaction of the continuity of interest requirement.

Section 1.368–2(j)(3)(i) of the proposed regulations defines control under section 368(c). Since current law is sufficiently clear as to the definition of control under section 368(c), the final regulations do not contain such a definition.

Section 1.368–2(j)(3)(ii) of the proposed regulations provides that P must acquire control of T in the transaction. Section 1.368–2(j)(3)(ii) of the final regulations clarifies this rule to provide that P must be in control of T immediately after the transaction. Thus, any disposition by P of the T stock acquired (other than a transfer described in section 368(a)(2)(C)), or any new issuance of stock by T to persons other than P, as part of the transaction, which causes P not to be in control of T will prevent the transaction from qualifying under section 368(a)(2)(E). Example (8) of § 1.368–2(j)(7) of the final regulations illustrates this rule.

"Substantially all" requirement

Section 368(a)(2)(E)(i) of the Code requires generally that, after the transaction, T hold substantially all of its properties and substantially all of the properties of S. Section 1.368–2(j)(4) of the proposed regulations indicates that this requirement will not be satisfied where, as part of the transaction, T transfers assets to a corporation controlled by T, notwithstanding section 368(a)(2)(C) of the Code. Several commenters suggested that section 368(a)(2)(C) permits assets of T to be transferred to a controlled corporation without violating the "substantially all" requirement. In response, § 1.368–2(j)(4) of the final regulations provides that such transfers do not violate the "substantially all" requirement.

Section 1.368–2(j)(3)(iii)(E) of the final regulations clarifies that money transferred from P to S to satisfy minimum state capitalization requirements, which eventually is returned to P as part of the transaction, is not taken into account in applying the "substantially all" test to the assets of S.

Assumption of liabilities; exchange of securities

Section 1.368–2(j)(5) of the proposed regulations provides that P may assume liabilities of T without disqualifying the transaction under section 368(a)(2)(E). Commenters requested that the regulations clarify the treatment of such liability assumption by P. Accordingly, § 1.368-2(j)(5) of the final regulations clarifies that liability assumption is a contribution to the capital of T by its shareholder P. In addition, § 1.368-2(j)(5) of the final regulations clarifies that where, pursuant to the plan of reorganization, securities of T are exchanged for securities of P, or for other securities of T which, for example, are convertible into P stock, that exchange is subject to the otherwise applicable provisions of sections 354 and 356.

Relation to section 368(a)(1)(B)

A few commenters suggested that the regulations confirm that a transaction which fails to qualify under section 368(a)(2)(E) may, under appropriate circumstances, qualify as a reorganization described in section 368(a)(1)(B), as in Rev.Rul. 67–448, 1967–2 C.B. 144. Examples (4) and (5) of § 1.368–2(j)(7) of the final regulations confirm this result.

Merged corporation

Finally, in response to comments, § 1.368–2(j)(6) of the final regulations clarifies that S can be an existing corporation as well as a corporation formed for purposes of the section 368(a)(2)(E) transaction.

D. CREATION OF A HOLDING COMPANY

See Revenue Ruling 77–428, Sec. 15.5.C.

E. ZERO BASIS PROBLEM

See Prop.Reg. §§ 1.1032–2 and 1.358–6.

See Sec. 15.4.D.

§ 15.11 SUMMARY PROBLEMS ON STRAIGHT AND TRIANGULAR ACQUISITIVE STOCK REORGANIZATIONS

The facts for the following questions are set out in Sec. 15.7.

What are the tax consequences to each of the parties under each of the following basic stock transactions and the modifications thereof?

AC issues $100K of its voting preferred to *A*, *B* and *X* in exchange for all of their *TC* stock? Also, *AC* issues its debentures with a face amount and value of $30K to *A* and *Y* in exchange for *TC*'s debentures? There is no OID on *AC*'s or *TC*'s debentures.

Consider each of the following modifications separately.

    a. Suppose *B* insists upon being paid in cash, and *AC* pays him $20K for his stock?

    b. Suppose *B* refuses to go along, and *AC* acquires only *A*'s and *X*'s stock?

c. Suppose that prior to the acquisition, *TC* redeems *B*'s stock for $20K in cash?

d. Suppose *AC* forms a new subsidiary (*AC–S*) and contributes to *AC–S* (1) $80K of *AC* voting preferred, (2) $20K of cash, and (3) $30K of *AC* debentures. *AC–S* then acquires (1) *A*'s and *X*'s stock in exchange for *AC* stock, (2) *B*'s stock in exchange for the cash and (3) the *TC* debentures in exchange for the *AC* debentures? Suppose, instead, that *AC–S* merges into *TC* with the parties receiving the same consideration? Suppose, instead, that *TC* merges into *AC–S*?

e. Suppose that in the basic transaction above, *AC* agrees to pay all the expenses of registering the *AC* stock, and *AC* also agrees to pay to *A* an additional $10K of *AC* nonvoting stock as an inducement for *A* to enter into a long-term employment agreement?

f. Suppose that (1) on January 1 of 1993, *AC* acquires *X*'s *TC* stock for *AC* voting preferred, (2) on October 1, 1993, *AC* acquires *B*'s *TC* stock for *AC* voting common stock, and (3) on January 31, 1994, *AC* acquires *A*'s *TC* stock in exchange for *AC* voting preferred?

§ 15.12 THE IMPACT OF § 382 ON THE CARRYOVER OF A TARGET'S NOL AFTER AN ACQUISITION

A. INTRODUCTION TO THE SCOPE AND PURPOSE OF § 382

THE GENERAL EXPLANATION OF THE
TAX REFORM ACT OF 1986.

288–325 (1986).

* * *

PRIOR LAW

Overview

In general, a corporate taxpayer is allowed to carry a net operating loss ("NOL(s)") forward for deduction in a future taxable year, as long as the corporation's legal identity is maintained. After certain nontaxable asset acquisitions in which the acquired corporation goes out of existence, the acquired corporation's NOL carryforwards are inherited by the acquiring corporation. [*See* § 381.] Similar rules apply to tax attributes other than NOLs, such as net capital losses and unused tax credits. [*See* § 381.] Historically, the use of NOL and other carryforwards has been subject to special limitations after specified transactions involving the corporation in which the carryforwards arose (referred to as the "loss corporation"). [*See* former § 382.] Prior law also provided other rules that were intended to limit tax-motivated acquisitions of loss corporations. [*See* e.g. § 269.]

The operation of the special limitations on the use of carryforwards turned on whether the transaction that caused the limitations to apply took the form of a taxable sale or exchange of stock in the loss corporation or one of certain specified tax-free reorganizations in which the loss corporation's tax attributes carried over to a corporate successor. [*See* former § 382.] After a purchase (or other taxable acquisition) of a controlling stock interest in a loss corporation, NOL and other carryforwards were disallowed unless the loss corporation continued to conduct its historical trade or business. [*See* former § 382.] In the case of a tax-free reorganization, NOL and other carryforwards were generally allowed in full if the loss corporation's shareholders received stock representing at least 20 percent of the value of the acquiring corporation. [*See* former § 382.]

* * *

REASONS FOR CHANGE

* * *

Preservation of the averaging function of carryovers

The primary purpose of the special limitations is the preservation of the integrity of the carryover provisions. The carryover provisions perform a needed averaging function by reducing the distortions caused by the annual accounting system. If, on the other hand, carryovers can be transferred in a way that permits a loss to offset unrelated income, no legitimate averaging function is performed. With completely free transferability of tax losses, the carryover provisions become a mechanism for partial recoupment of losses through the tax system. Under such a system, the Federal Government would effectively be required to reimburse a portion of all corporate tax losses. Regardless of the merits of such a reimbursement program, the carryover rules appear to be an inappropriate and inefficient mechanism for delivery of the reimbursement.

* * *

General approach

After reviewing various options for identifying events that present the opportunity for a tax benefit transfer (*e.g.*, changes in a loss corporation's business), it was concluded that changes in a loss corporation's stock ownership continue to be the best indicator of a potentially abusive transaction. Under the Act, the special limitations generally apply when shareholders who bore the economic burden of a corporation's NOLs no longer hold a controlling interest in the corporation. In such a case, the possibility arises that new shareholders will contribute income-producing assets (or divert income opportunities) to the loss corporation, and the corporation will obtain greater utilization of carryforwards than it could have had there been no change in ownership.

To address the concerns described above, the Act adopts the following approach: After a substantial ownership change, rather than reducing the NOL carryforward itself, the earnings against which an NOL carryforward can be deducted are limited. [See § 382.] This general approach has received wide acceptance among tax scholars and practitioners. This "limitation on earnings" approach is intended to permit the survival of NOL carryforwards after an acquisition, while limiting the ability to utilize the carryforwards against unrelated income.

* * *

For purposes of determining the income attributable to a loss corporation's assets, the Act prescribes an objective rate of return on the value of the corporation's equity. * * *

Annual limitation

The annual limitation on the use of pre-acquisition NOL carryforwards is the product of the prescribed rate and the value of the loss corporation's equity immediately before a proscribed ownership change. The average yield for long-term marketable obligations of the U.S. government was selected as the measure of a loss corporation's expected return on its assets.

The rate prescribed by the Act [that is, the long term tax exempt rate] is higher than the average rate at which loss corporations actually absorb NOL carryforwards. * * *

* * *

B. OUTLINE OF SECTION 382 AND THE REGULATIONS

PREAMBLE TO TEMPORARY REGULATIONS UNDER § 382

Treasury Decision 8149 (Aug. 5, 1987).

* * *

After an ownership change occurs with respect to a loss corporation, section 382 limits the amount of taxable income against which NOL carryforwards and certain unrealized built-in losses of the corporation may be applied. The limitation is applied annually and is equal to a prescribed percentage rate, multiplied by the value of the stock of the loss corporation immediately before the ownership change.

* * *

In general, an ownership change occurs if the percentage of stock of a loss corporation owned by one or more "5–percent shareholders" has increased by more than 50 percentage points over the lowest percentage of such stock that was owned by those persons at any time during the testing period. The determination whether an ownership change has occurred is made by adding together the separate increases in percentage ownership of each 5–percent shareholder whose percentage ownership interest in the loss corporation has increased over such shareholder's lowest percentage ownership interest at any time during the testing period. The testing period (described below) generally is the three-year period that precedes any date on which the loss corporation is required to make the determination of whether an ownership change has occurred.

Under the temporary regulations, the determination whether an ownership change has occurred is generally made as of the close of any date (a "testing date") on which there is an owner shift (described below), an equity structure shift (described below), or a transaction in which an option (or other similar interest) is acquired by a 5-percent shareholder (or a person who would be a 5-percent shareholder if the option were exercised). * * *

In general, in determining whether an ownership change has occurred, all transactions (whether related or unrelated) occurring during the testing period that affect the stock ownership of any 5-percent shareholder whose percentage of stock ownership has increased as of the close of the testing date are taken into account. * * *

The determination of the percentage ownership interest of any shareholder is made on the basis of the relative fair market value of the loss corporation stock owned by the shareholder to the total fair market value of the outstanding stock of the loss corporation. In general, all stock of the loss corporation, except certain preferred stock described in section 1504(a)(4), is taken into account. * * *

* * *

C. EXAMPLE OF OWNERSHIP CHANGE IN A STOCK ACQUISITION

The following example of an ownership change from the Conference Report to the TRA 1986 illustrates both the aggregation rule and the attribution out rule:

> Example 15.—L corporation is publicly traded; no shareholder owns as much as five percent. P corporation is publicly traded; no shareholder owns as much as five percent. On January 1, 1988, P corporation purchases 100 percent of L corporation stock on the open market. The L stock owned by P is attributed to the shareholders of P, all of whom are less-than-5-percent shareholders who are treated as a single, separate 5-percent shareholder. Accordingly, there has been an ownership change of L, because the percentage of stock owned by the P shareholders after the purchase (100 percent) has increased by more than 50 percentage points over the lowest percentage of L stock owned by that group at any time during the testing period * * *.

D. EXAMPLE OF OWNERSHIP CHANGE IN AN EQUITY STRUCTURE SHIFT

An *Equity Structure Shift* means any reorganization under section 368, except that the term does not include (1) any 368(a)(1)(D) (split-up) or (G) (bankruptcy) reorganization unless the requirements of section 354(b)(1) (relating to transfer of substantially all the assets) are met, and (2) any section 368(a)(1)(F) (mere change in form) reorganization. *See* § 382(g)(3)(A). The term encompasses both acquisitive asset reorganizations, acquisitive stock reorganizations and also recapitalizations. The term also means, to the extent provided in regulations, any taxable reorganization-type transactions, public offerings and similar transactions. *See* § 382(g)(3)(B).

The Conference Report to the Tax Reform Act of 1986 (p. 177) gives the following example of an *Ownership Change* that results from a tax-free merger of a *Loss Corporation* into a profitable corporation:

> *Example 8.*—On January 1, 1988, L corporation (a loss corporation) is merged (in a transaction described in section 368(a)(1)(A)) into P corporation (not a loss corporation), with P surviving. Both L and P are publicly traded corporations with no shareholder owning five percent or more of either corporation or the surviving corporation. In the merger, L shareholders receive 30 percent of the stock of P. There has been an ownership change of L, because the percentage of P stock owned by the former P shareholders (all of whom are less–than–5–percent shareholders who are treated as a separate, single 5–percent shareholder) after the equity structure shift (70 percent) has increased by more than 50 percentage points over the lowest percentage of L stock owned by such shareholders at any time during the testing period (0 percent prior to the merger). If, however, the former shareholders of L had received at least 50 percent of the stock of P in the merger, there would not have been an ownership change of L.

E. ILLUSTRATION OF COMPUTATION OF SECTION 382 LIMITATION

The computation of the *Section 382 Limitation* is illustrated as follows:

> If there has been an *Ownership Change* with respect to an *Old Loss Corporation* that has (1) a *Pre-Change Loss* of $10 million dollars, and (2) a *Value* (*i.e.* fair market value of the stock immediately before the *Ownership Change*) of $25M, and (3) the *Long Term Tax Exempt Rate* is 10%, then the *Section 382 Limitation* for any *Post–Change Year* is $2.5 million (*i.e.*, $25 million *Value* multiplied by the *Long Term Tax-Exempt Rate*). Thus, under the general limitation rule of § 382(a), the amount of the taxable income of the *New Loss Corporation* for any *Post–Change Year* that can be offset by *Pre-Change Losses* (*i.e.*, $10 million) cannot exceed $2.5 million.

Section 382 and related provisions are examined in greater detail in *Taxable and Tax–Free Corporate Mergers, Acquisitions, and LBOs, supra* Sec. 1.3.

Chapter 16

TAX POLICY ASPECTS OF REORGANIZATIONS

§ 16.1 SCOPE

This chapter deals with the policy aspects of reorganizations. Sec. 16.2 discusses the proposed repeal of the acquisitive reorganization provisions, and Sec. 16.3 presents a proposal for the rationalization of the reorganization provisions.

In addition to the materials included in this chapter, see *ALI 1980 Subchapter C Study, supra* Sec. 1.4; *ALI 1989 Subchapter C Study, supra* Sec. 1.4; *ALI 1993 Integration Study, supra* Sec. 1.4; *Treasury Integration Study, supra* Sec. 1.4; and the articles and other sources cited in Chapter 1 of Thompson, *Reform of the Taxation of Mergers, Acquisitions and LBOs, supra* Sec. 1.4.

§ 16.2 PROPOSAL FOR REPEAL OF REORGANIZATION PROVISIONS

REPORT OF STAFF OF SENATE FINANCE COMMITTEE ON SUBCHAPTER C REVISION BILL OF 1985

37–54 (1985).

[The proposals set out below are based on and are substantially the same as proposals made by The American Law Institute. *See ALI 1980 Subchapter C Study, supra* Sec. 1.4.]

III. REASONS FOR CHANGE

A. General reasons for change

* * * The current law of Subchapter C is seriously flawed. The "law" consists of a series of rules, some statutory and others of judicial origin, which, when taken together, lack consistency, are unnecessarily complex, and are often subject to manipulation. By providing uncertain and often capricious tax consequences to business transactions, the law inadequately addresses the needs of businessmen, their corporations, and their investors. Moreover, by being inconsistent and subject to manipulation, the law is biased, at times encouraging tax-motivated transactions, and at times discouraging or making less efficient legitimate business dealings. * * *

The inadequacy of current law presents three interrelated principal reasons for change. First, current law needs to be made more rational and consistent, thereby providing greater certainty and less complexity in the area. For example, under current law, an "A" reorganization (statutory merger or consolidation) may involve a significant amount of cash consideration, a "B" reorganization (stock-for-stock acquisition) cannot have any cash consideration, and a "C" reorganization (stock-for-assets acquisition) may involve a small amount of cash consideration. No policy justification can be found for these and other distinctions. The bill would propose to eliminate artificial distinctions of that sort.

* * *

B. Detailed reasons for change
1. Problems relating to the definition of "reorganization"

As outlined below, the different definitional requirements for a "reorganization" create much of the complexity in current law. Some of these requirements are based on statutory rules, and others are of judicial origin. There are persuasive arguments for standardizing and making uniform these rules, as well as the rules prescribing the various forms of taxable acquisitions.

a. Boot as consideration.—No consideration other than voting stock is permitted in a B reorganization. A C reorganization permits a limited amount of boot (up to 20 percent of the total consideration). No specific statutory rule limits the amount of boot in an A reorganization, although the continuity of interest doctrine imposes some limitation. In certain cases, the assumption of liabilities may be treated as boot and in certain other cases, it may not be. No policy justification can be found for maintaining these disparate rules in what are essentially economically equivalent transactions.

b. Voting stock as consideration.—The qualifying consideration in a B or C reorganization, or a reverse triangular merger, must be *voting* stock. No such limitation applies in an A reorganization or a forward triangular merger.

c. Stock of corporation in control of acquiring corporation as consideration.—If structured correctly, as many as three tiers of acquiring corporations may be involved in an acquisitive transaction without affecting reorganization status. It is unclear from the statute whether reorganization status can be preserved if the structuring is not proper and, for example, the acquiring corporation is in the third tier of corporations, although the IRS has ruled favorably on the question. It is also questionable whether stock of a corporation involving more remote ownership may be used. This introduces unnecessary rigidity when a target corporation is acquired by one or more members of an affiliated group.

d. Subsidiary mergers.—Different rules apply depending upon the direction of a subsidiary merger under section 368(a)(2)(D) or 368(a)(2)(E). Further, the "substantially all" limitation (discussed below) applies to subsidiary mergers even though they are nominally classified as A reorganizations. Thus, the requirements for a subsidiary merger are closer to C reorganizations than A reorganizations. The different, inconsistent, and complex requirements applicable to an acquisition through a subsidiary have been described as impossible to justify.

e. "Substantially all" requirement.—As noted, C reorganizations and subsidiary mergers impose a "substantially all" limitation. Certain D reorganizations have the same requirement. No such limitation is contained in an A reorganization. Thus, for example, a predisposition of assets prior to an acquisition may cause the transaction to fail as a C reorganization.

Furthermore, the exact meaning of "substantially all" is unclear. Ruling guidelines applicable to C reorganizations and subsidiary mergers establish a 70 percent of gross assets and 90 percent of net assets standard. Case law in the D reorganization area has permitted a much smaller percentage of assets to qualify as "substantially all."

f. Predisposition of assets.—As described above, a predisposition of assets prior to an acquisition may affect qualification as a C reorganization or a subsidiary merger. No such problem generally occurs in an A or B reorganization.

g. Overlap issues.—With the exception of a transaction qualifying as both a C and D reorganization where D reorganization status is mandated, the statute does not provide rules settling overlap questions between and among reorganization provisions. This creates substantial uncertainty where the tax consequences of the transaction depend upon the specific category of reorganization that is satisfied.

h. Continuity of interest requirement.—This judicial doctrine is of uncertain application. The portion of total consideration consisting of an equity interest must be a "material part" of the consideration for the transferred assets. [See *Minnesota Tea, supra* Sec. 11.2.B.2] However, where 38 percent of the consideration consisted of callable preferred stock, this requirement has been considered satisfied. [See *John A. Nelson, supra* Sec. 11.2.B.3.]

Moreover, the assumption underlying the limitation is that preferred treatment should be provided to consideration in the form of stock because stock represents a continuing commitment by the shareholders of the target corporation in the risks of the target business after the acquisition. This policy goal may not be effectively implemented where, for example, preferred stock subject to early redemption is provided tax-free treatment whereas a long-term creditor interest is not. In that case, the preferred stock may represent much less of a continuing commitment in the business risks of the target corporation than the long-term creditor interest.

Further, the IRS has indicated for ruling purposes that continuity of interest is important both before and after an acquisition. As noted, at least one case has held that continuity of interest is not present if the target corporation shareholders dispose of the stock received in the transaction pursuant to a prearranged plan. [See McDonalds, supra Sec. 11.2.E.5.] It is unclear whether significant preacquisition arbitrage activity will preclude tax-free treatment of the subsequent acquisition.

Finally, the existence of continuity of interest may depend upon the nature of the interest in the target corporation surrendered by the target investor. For example, in a merger of a stock savings and loan association into a mutual savings and loan association, where the former shareholders of the target corporation received passbook savings accounts and certificates of deposit of the acquiring entity (the only form of "equity" available in the acquiring entity), the Supreme Court held that the continuity of interest requirement was not satisfied. [See Paulsen, supra Sec. 11.2.B.10.] In contrast, where interests in a mutual savings and loan association were exchanged for interests in an acquiring mutual savings and loan association, the IRS held that continuity of interest was satisfied.

i. Continuity of business enterprise and business purpose doctrines.—Two other non-statutory requirements for a corporate reorganization are the business purpose and continuity of business enterprise doctrines. The regulations were recently amended to provide that the trade or business of the target corporation must be continued, or a "significant portion" of the target company's historic business assets must be used in a trade or business following the acquisition, in order to satisfy the continuity of business enterprise requirement. Some uncertainty surrounds the exact parameters of these tests.

j. Linking of shareholder level consequences to corporate level consequences and to tax treatment of other shareholders.—Current law links the shareholder level consequences of a reorganization to the corporate level consequences and to the tax treatment of other shareholders in the transaction. This produces a number of anomalous results.

For example, a transaction that fails reorganization status at the corporate level (*e.g.*, because a predisposition of assets causes failure of the "substantially all" requirement) will therefore be fully taxable at the shareholder level, even though the shareholders of the target corporation all receive stock in the acquiring corporation. This is contrary to the policy decision that stock in an acquiring corporation should entitle a target shareholder to tax-free treatment.

As another example, failure to satisfy a shareholder level requirement (*e.g.*, continuity of interest) will make a transaction completely taxable at the corporate level. This recently occurred in the case of *Paulsen v. Commissioner* [see Sec. 11.2.B.10.] where, because of failure of continuity of interest, a merger of a stock savings and loan association into a mutual savings and loan association was a taxable transaction. A more rational system would permit the corporate merger to be tax-free so long as the acquiring entity obtained only a carryover basis in the assets transferred.

A final example is illustrated by *May B. Kass v. Commissioner.* [See Sec. 15.2.C.] In that case, a single minority target shareholder who received solely stock in the acquiring corporation in an acquisition, was required to treat the exchange as a taxable one because of failure of the overall transaction to satisfy continuity of interest. No apparent policy reason can be found to justify linking the tax consequences for one shareholder of a target corporation to the tax treatment of other such shareholders. Furthermore, as described earlier, the well-advised may, in any event, be able to obtain nonrecognition treatment for the minority shareholder through the formation of a holding company. [See Rev.Rul. 84–71, *supra* Sec. 11.19.D.]

* * *

IV. Summary of Proposals

The principal proposals contained in the bill are described below. A more detailed description of the proposals is set forth in the Technical Explanation accompanying the bill.

A. *Definition of qualified acquisition (new section 364 of the Code)*

In general, the bill consolidates, simplifies, and makes uniform the rules classifying corporate mergers and acquisitions, whether treated under current law as a "reorganization", a liquidating sale * * * or a section 338 stock acquisition.

New section 364 defines "qualified acquisition" as meaning any "qualified stock acquisition" or any "qualified asset acquisition." A qualified stock acquisition is defined as any transaction or series of transactions during the 12–month acquisition period in which one corporation acquires stock representing control of another corporation. A qualified asset acquisition means (1) any statutory merger or consolidation, or (2) any other transaction in which one corporation acquires at least 70 percent of the gross fair market value and at least 90 percent of the net fair market value of the assets of another corporation held immediately before the acquisition, and the transferor corporation distributes, within 12 months of the acquisition date, all of its assets (other than assets retained to meet claims) to its shareholders or creditors.

For these purposes, the definition of "control" is conformed to that contained in section 1504(a)(2) of the Code.

* * *

The common-law doctrines of continuity of interest, continuity of business enterprise, and business purpose would have no applicability in determining whether a transaction qualifies as a qualified acquisition.

§ 16.2   **PROPOSAL FOR REPEAL**   591

The bill repeals section 368. Acquisitive reorganizations ("A", "B" and "C" reorganizations and subsidiary mergers) under current law would be replaced by the rules for qualified acquisitions. The "D" reorganization rules would be replaced by special rules (described below) relating to qualified acquisitions between related parties. Transactions qualifying under current law as an "E" reorganization (a recapitalization) and an "F" reorganization (a mere change in identity, form, or place of organization of one corporation) are conformed to the definition of qualified acquisitions. Finally, the "G" reorganization rules (bankruptcy reorganizations), developed largely in response to continuity of interest problems in those types of transactions, are no longer needed and therefore are repealed.

B. *Elective tax treatment of qualified acquisitions (new section 365 of the Code)*

The corporate level tax consequences of a qualified acquisition are explicitly made elective. Under new section 365, all qualified acquisitions are treated as "carryover basis acquisitions" unless an election to be treated as a "cost basis acquisition" is made.

In general, elections may be made on a corporation-by-corporation basis. Thus, for example, if an acquiring corporation makes a qualified stock acquisition of both a target corporation and a target subsidiary, a cost basis election may be made for the target corporation but, if desired, no such election need be made for the target subsidiary.

* * *

C. *Corporate level tax consequences of qualified acquisitions (sections 361, 362 and 381 of the Code)*

The corporate level tax consequences of a qualified acquisition result directly from the election made at the corporate level. For example, in the case of a carryover basis acquisition, no gain or loss is recognized by the target corporation and the acquiring corporation obtains a carryover basis in any assets acquired. Attributes carry over under section 381.

In the case of a cost basis acquisition, the target corporation recognizes gain or loss and the acquiring corporation obtains a basis in any assets acquired determined under section 1012. Attributes do not carry over. Where the cost basis acquisition is a qualified stock acquisition, the target corporation is deemed to have sold all of its assets for fair market value at the close of the acquisition date in a transaction in which gain or loss is recognized, and then is treated as a new corporation which purchased all of such assets as of the beginning of the day after the acquisition date.

* * *

D. *Shareholder level tax consequences of qualified acquisitions (sections 354, 356, and 358 of the Code)*

In general, shareholder level tax consequences of a qualified acquisition are determined independent of the corporate level tax consequences and independent of the election made at the corporate level. Thus, even if a transaction is treated as a cost basis acquisition at the corporate level, it may be wholly or partly taxfree at the shareholder level. In addition, shareholder level consequences are generally determined shareholder-by-shareholder, and the consequences to one shareholder do not affect the tax treatment of other shareholders or investors of the target corporation.

As a general rule, nonrecognition treatment is provided to shareholders or security holders of the target corporation upon receipt of "qualifying consideration," *i.e.,* stock or securities of the acquiring corporation and, where the acquiring corporation is a member of an affiliated group, of the common parent of such group and any other member of such group specified in regulations. [*See* § 354(a).] The nonrecognition rule applies to the receipt of securities only to the extent the issue price of any securities received does not exceed the adjusted basis of any securities surrendered. [*See* § 354(a)(2).]

* * *

Receipt of "nonqualifying consideration" (*i.e.,* any consideration other than qualifying consideration) generally results in recognition of gain to the shareholder or security holder. Such gain is treated as gain from the sale or exchange of property unless the receipt of nonqualifying consideration has the effect of a distribution of a dividend. [*See* § 356(a)(2).] The determination of dividend effect is made by treating the shareholder as having received only qualifying consideration in the exchange, and then as being redeemed of all or a portion of such qualifying consideration (to the extent of the non-qualifying consideration received). [This is consistent with the Supreme Court's decision in *Clark,* see Sec. 11.13.A.] For these purposes, earnings and profits of both the target and acquiring corporations are generally taken into account.

* * *

§ 16.3 PROPOSAL FOR RATIONALIZATION OF THE REORGANIZATION PROVISIONS

SAMUEL C. THOMPSON, JR., REFORM OF THE TAXATION OF MERGERS, ACQUISITIONS AND LBOs

12–21 (Carolina Academic Press 1993).

* * *

This book rejects the ALI's suggestion that the reorganization concept be repealed and replaced with what is, in essence, a "like kind exchange" approach at the shareholder level and an express codification of the mirror transaction at the corporate level. Part 2 accepts, although in a more limited form, the ALI's suggestion for elective carryover basis treatment of the target's assets in certain asset acquisitions. Under this carryover basis regime, a target does not have taxable gain on the disposition of its assets, *and the acquiring* corporation takes as its basis for those assets the target's old basis for the assets (*i.e.*, takes a carryover basis). Thus, the price of tax-free treatment to the target is a carryover basis for the assets in the hands of the acquiring corporation.

Five basic tax policy questions are addressed in part 2. First, should Congress adopt the ALI's suggestion that the shareholder level consequences in a corporate acquisition be separated from the corporate level consequences? That is, should (as the ALI has proposed) the acquisitive reorganization concept be eliminated? In this connection, should the continuity of interest doctrine be eliminated, retained, or strengthened? Also, should the "substantially all" concept apply uniformly to all forms of acquisitive reorganizations? Under the "substantially all" concept, which applies to four of the seven forms of acquisitive reorganizations, the acquiring corporation must acquire "substantially all" of the target's assets to qualify the acquisition as a reorganization. With uniformity, tax-free treatment would be available only in an acquisitive transaction in which substantially all of the target's assets are either acquired in an asset reorganization, or held by the target after the acquisition of the target in a stock reorganization.

* * *

Chapter 4 sets out proposals regarding reorganizations, which encompass various types of tax-free acquisitions. These proposals are premised on the judgment that the central themes of the reorganization provisions reflect correct tax policy:

An exception to the general recognition (*i.e.*, taxation) rule of Section 1001 should apply at the corporate and shareholder levels for corporate acquisitions in which for a good business purpose the acquiring corporation acquires the target's historic assets and a significant portion of the consideration received by the target's historic shareholders is stock of the acquiring corporation.

Thus, the position taken in chapter 4 is that the business purpose, continuity of business enterprise, and continuity of interest doctrines of present law are consistent with proper tax policy. If the spirit of these doctrines is satisfied in a corporate acquisition, the transaction is not analogous to a sale or taxable exchange because the target's shareholders have a continuing interest in the historic assets of the target through their ownership of stock of the acquiring corporation. Consequently, it is appropriate in such cases to provide nonrecognition treatment for both the target corporation and its shareholders. This position is directly contrary to that taken in the ALI 1989 Study.

If the reorganization concept is reformed as proposed here, there would be uniformity in the application of both (1) the continuity of interest requirement, and (2) the substantially all requirement. Under present law, the continuity of interest requirement differs for the various types of reorganizations, and the substantially all requirement applies only in the stock for asset reorganization [see § 368(a)(1)(C)] and in the forward and reverse subsidiary merger reorganizations. [See § 368(a)(1)(D) and (E).] Consequently, under the proposals here there would be consistency in the treatment of acquisitive reorganizations, manipulation would be prevented, and the operation of these provisions would be reflective of the underlying policy rationale.

In striving for consistency, chapter 4 attempts to eliminate many of the needless traps in the reorganization provisions, such as the *Bausch & Lomb* doctrine, [see Sec. 15.3.C.] and to codify those principles in the case law and rulings that are consistent with the fundamental concept of a reorganization, such as the *McDonalds* decision. [See Sec. 11.2.E.5.]

No significant changes are suggested here to Sections 354 to 362, which govern the tax treatment of the parties to a reorganization. * * *

* * *

Index

References are to sections of the book.

Accumulated earnings tax, Ch. 7.
  accumulated taxable income, 7.3.C.
  corporations subject to the tax, 7.3.A.1.
  evidence of purpose to avoid tax, 7.3.A.2.
  imposition of the tax, 7.3.A.
  introduction, 7.2.
  marketable securities, 7.3.D.
  reasonable needs of the business, 7.3.B.
  relationship to the personal holding company tax, 7.2.
Adjusted basis, 1.3.A.
Affiliated corporations
  see also consolidated returns
Amount realized, 1.3.A.
Attribution of stock ownership, 5.3.
  personal holding companies, 7.4.B.
  redemptions of stock, 5.3.
  section 318, 5.3.
Basis, 1.3.A.
Business purpose doctrine, 1.3.G.2.
  see also step transaction doctrine
Capital gains, 1.3.F.
Capital structure of the corporation
  see debt-equity issues
Carryover of corporate tax attributes
  consolidated returns
    see consolidated returns
  section 381 carryover rules, 15.6.
  section 382 limitation on net operating loss carryovers, 15.12.
Consolidated returns
  affiliated group, 8.4.
  basis adjustment rules, 8.9.D.
  consolidated tax liability, 8.6.
  earnings and profits, 8.9.E.
  excess loss account, 8.9.F.
  historical perspective, 8.2.
  intercompany transactions, 8.7.
  intergroup dividends, 8.8.
  investment adjustment system, 8.9.
Corporate acquisitions and liquidations
  This title is divided into the following subtitles:
    1. corporation, treatment of
    2. shareholders, treatment of
    3. subsidiaries, liquidation under sections 332 and 337
    4. section 338 step-up in basis
Corporate distributions
  see also dividends, and earnings and profits

Corporate distributions—Cont'd
  current distributions of cash and property, 4.2.
    to corporate shareholders, 4.4.
    to noncorporate shareholders, 4.3.
  impact on distributing corporation, 4.3.B.
Corporate entity doctrine, 1.3.H.
Corporate organizations, Ch. 2
  accommodation transferors, 2.5.B.
  accounts receivable, 2.3.F. and 2.4.B.
  allocation of boot among assets transferred, 2.2.E.3.
  allocation of corporation's basis, 2.2.F.
  allocation of shareholder's basis, 2.2.D.
  assignment of tax detriment or benefit, 2.2.C.
  basis, substituted and carryover, 2.2.A.
  basic elements, 2.2.A.
  boot, 2.2.E.
  business purpose, 2.7.
  capitalization, Ch. 3.
    see also debt-equity issues
  contribution to capital, 2.9.
  contributions of:
    accounts payable, 2.3.F.
    accounts receivable, 2.3.F., 2.4.B.
    cash, 2.4.C.
    intangibles, 2.4.D.
    know-how, 2.4.D.2.
    license, 2.4.D.4 and 5.
    services, 2.4.A.
  control, 2.5.
    immediately after, 2.5.C.
  deduction upon issuance of stock for services, 2.2.H.2.
  formation of a subsidiary, 2.7.C.
  incorporation of existing business, 2.4.B.
  installment obligations, 2.2.E.2.
  intangibles, 2.4.D.
  know-how, 2.4.D.2.
  liabilities, 2.3.
  midstream incorporations, 2.4.B.
  policy aspects.
    see tax policy
  property, 2.4.
  section 482, 2.6.
  section 1032, 2.2.H.
  services, 2.4.A.
  step transaction, 2.7.
  warrants, issuance of, 2.2.H.

INDEX

References are to sections of the book.

Corporate redemptions
  attribution rules, 5.3.
  boot strap sales, 5.10.
  buy sale agreements, 5.11.
  family disharmony, 5.6.C.
  impact on corporation, 5.14.
  introduction, 5.2.
  meaningful reduction, 5.6.
  not essentially equivalent to a dividend, 5.6.
  partial liquidations, 5.7.
  redemptions to pay death taxes, 5.13.
  related corporations § 304, 5.12.
  substantially disproportionate, 5.5.
  suggested methodology, 5.8.
  termination of interest, 5.4.

Corporate reorganizations
  (A) merger reorganization, 15.2.
    continuity of interest, 11.2., 15.2.B.
    introduction, 15.2.A.
    spin-off followed by merger, 13.4.D.
    triangular mergers
      see triangular reorganizations
  (B) voting stock for voting stock reorganization, 15.8.
    boot, 15.8.B., C.
    introduction, 15.8.A.
    reverse subsidiary mergers, 15.8.D.
    the meaning of solely for voting stock, 15.8.B.
    triangular (B)'s
      see triangular reorganizations
  (C) stock for asset reorganization, 15.3.
    assumption of liabilities, 15.3.A.
    boot relaxation rule, 15.3.A.
    creeping (C), 15.3.C.
    introduction, 15.3.A.
    liabilities, 15.3.A.
    "substantially all" the assets, 15.3.B.
    triangular (C)'s
      see triangular reorganizations
  (D) divisive and nondivisive reorganizations, ch. 13
    see also divisive reorganizations and section 355, within corporate reorganizations and liquidation-reincorporation
  (E) recapitalizations, ch. 12.
    continuity of business enterprise, 12.7.
    continuity of interest, 12.5.
    conversion privileges, 12.6
    issuance of
      debentures, 12.4.
      preferred, 12.3.
    section 305, 12.8.
    section 306, 12.9.
  (F) mere change in form reorganization, 12.11.
    basis, 11.11, 11.16.
    business purpose doctrine, 1.3.G.2., 11.7.
    carryover basis, 11.16.
    carryover of tax attributes

Corporate reorganizations—Cont'd
  (F) mere change in form reorganization—Cont'd
    carryover of tax attributes—Cont'd
    see carryover of corporate tax attributes
    contingent consideration in reorganizations, 11.2.H.
    escrow arrangements, 11.2.H.
    imputed interest, 11.2.H.2.
    service's ruling policy, 11.2.H.1.
    continuity of business enterprise, 11.3
    current regulations, 11.3.A.
    over and down under § 368(a)(2)(C), 11.3.C.
    recapitalization, 11.3.D.
    sale of assets, 11.3.B.
  continuity of interest, 11.2.
    contingent consideration, 22.2.H.2.
    period held, 11.2.E.
    prior purchase of target stock, 11.2.F.
    remote continuity, 11.2.G.
    service's ruling policy, 11.2.C.
    type of interest, 11.2.B.
  control, 11.5.
  distribution having the effect of a dividend, 11.13.
  distributions by target corporation, 11.14.
  divisive reorganizations and section 355, ch. 13.
    active conduct of a trade or business, 13.4.F.
    business purpose, 13.4.B.
    carryover of tax attributes, 13.4.H.
    continuity of interest 13.4.E.
    device clause, 13.4.C.
    legislative background, 13.3.
    section 306, 13.5.
    spin-off before acquisitive reorganization, 13.4.D.
  historical perspective, 10.2.
  introduction to current statute, 10.4.
  legislative history, 10.3.
  liabilities, treatment of, 11.15.
  liquidation-reincorporation, ch. 14.
    Davant, 14.4.
    (E) and (F) reorganizations, 14.3.A.
    section 354(b), 14.2.C.
    service's ruling policy, 14.2.C.2.
    substantially all assets, 14.2.C.
  merger
    see (A) merger reorganization within this title
  non-divisive (D), ch. 14
    see liquidation reincorporation
  party to the reorganization, 11.2.G.1.
  plan of reorganization, 11.6.

INDEX

References are to sections of the book.

Corporate reorganizations—Cont'd
  (F) mere change in form reorganization—Cont'd
    recapitalizations, *see* (E) recapitalizations
    relationship with section 351, 11.19.
    section 305 stock, 11.17.
    section 306 stock, 11.18.
    section 351,
      overlap with, 11.19.
    securities, 11.8.A., 11.10.
    solely for voting stock, 11.4, 15.8.B, and C.
    step transaction doctrine, 1.3.G.4.
    stock for assets
      see (C) stock for asset reorganization within this title
    stock for stock
      see (B) voting stock for voting stock reorganization within this title
    subsidiary reorganizations
      see triangular reorganization within this title
    substituted basis, 11.11.
    treatment of liabilities, 11.15.
    triangular reorganizations
      forward subsidiary mergers, section 368(a)(2)(D), 15.5.
      introduction, 10.4.C.
      legislative history, 15.4.A., 15.5.A., 15.9.A.
      reverse subsidiary mergers, section 368(a)(2)(E), 15.10.
      over and downs, section 368(a)(2)(C), 10.4.C.
      triangular (B) reorganizations, 15.9.
      triangular (C) reorganizations, 15.4.
      zero basis problem, 15.4.D., 15.5.D., 15.9.C.
    warrants, 11.9.
Corporation, treatment of
  Court Holding doctrine, 1.3.G.
  General Utilities doctrine, 1.3.D.
  General Utilities, repeal of, 9.4.
  Section 336, 9.4.D.3.b.
  shareholders, treatment of
    gift of stock before receipt of liquidation proceeds, 9.2.H.
    installment sales, 9.2.E.
    liquidation-reincorporation doctrine, 14.3.
    non-pro rata distribution of assets, 9.2.G.
    open transaction, 9.2.D.
    series of liquidating distributions, 9.2.C.
    shareholders gain or loss on liquidation, section 331, 9.2.A.
    tax policy aspects
      see tax policy

Corporation—Cont'd
  shareholders—Cont'd
    transfer of assets to partnership, 9.2.F.
    when is corporation being liquidated, 9.2.B.
  subsidiaries, liquidations under sections 332 and 337.
    elective treatment, 9.3.C.
    Kimbell-Diamond, 1.G.4.
    retention of assets, 9.3.B.
    section 338 step-up in basis, 9.5.
    worthless stock and securities, 9.3.D.
Court Holding doctrine, 1.3.G.
Debt-equity issues, Ch. 3.
  ARCNs, 3.9.
  debt or preferred stock, 3.6.
  dividend or interest, 3.5.
  financing decision 3.2.
  generally, 3.3.
  high yield discount obligations, 3.10.C.
  original issue discount, 3.10.
  policy aspects
    see tax policy
  preferred stock, 3.6.
  section 351 context, 3.4.
  section 385 regulations, 3.8.
  section 1244 stock, 3.12.
  subordinated debt, 3.7.
  tax stakes generally, 3.3.
  worthless stock or securities, 3.11.
Dividends
  see also corporate distributions, earnings and profits
  constructive dividends, 4.7.
  definition of, 4.2.
  dividend before sale and after gift, 4.7 and 4.8.
  general principles, 4.5.
Divisive reorganizations
  see divisive reorganizations and section 355 within corporate reorganizations
Earnings and profits
  see also corporate distributions and dividends
  computation of, 4.6.
  consolidated returns, 8.9.E.
  redemption, effect of, 5.14.B.
Ethical considerations, 1.3.J.
Formation of corporation
  see corporate organizations
Forms of business enterprise, 1.2.
General Utilities doctrine, 1.3.D.
Imputed interest,
  OID, 3.10.
Incorporations
  see corporate organizations
Installment sales, section 453, 1.3.C.
Liabilities
  corporate organizations, 2.3.
  generally, 1.3.E.
  reorganizations, 11.15.
Like kind exchanges, 1.3.I.

References are to sections of the book.

Liquidation-reincorporation
   see corporate reorganizations
Original issue discount, 3.10.
Personal holding companies, 7.4.
   adjusted ordinary gross income, 7.4.D.
   definition of personal holding company, 7.4.B.
   introduction, 7.4.A.
   ordinary gross income, 7.4.D.
   personal holding company income, 7.4.C.
   relationship to the accumulated earnings tax, 7.2.
   undistributed personal holding company income, 7.4.F.
Policy aspects
   see tax policy
Realization and recognition, 1.3.A.
Recapitalizations, ch. 12.
   see also corporate reorganizations
Redemptions of stock
   see corporate redemptions
Sales of stock or corporations assets
   see corporate acquisitions and liquidations
Section 306 stock
   see stock dividends and section 306 stock
Section 332 liquidations, 9.3.

Section 332 liquidations—Cont'd
   see also corporate acquisitions and liquidations
Section 355, Ch. 13.
Section 453, installment sales, 1.3.C.
   see also partnership operations
Step transaction, 1.3.G.2.
   see also business purpose doctrine
Stock dividends and section 306 stock
   definition of section 306 stock, 6.5.C.
   historical perspective, 6.3.
   introduction, 6.2.
   operation of section 305, 6.4.
   operation of section 306, 6.5.
   section 306 stock in reorganizations, 11.18.
Stock redemptions
   see corporate redemptions
Substance over form, 1.3.G.
Tax policy issues
   control, 2.10.
      General Utilities, repeal of, 9.7.
      integration, 4.10
   control requirement, 2.10
   reorganizations
      corporate acquisitions, ch. 16.
      corporate mergers, ch. 16.
      elective cost or carryover basis, 16.2.
      proposed repeal, 16.2
      proposed rationalization, 16.3.

†

0-314-03585-0

9 780314 035851

90000